*Political Culture
and Political Development*

STUDIES IN
POLITICAL DEVELOPMENT

1. *Communications and Political Development*
Edited by Lucian W. Pye

2. *Bureaucracy and Political Development*
Edited by Joseph LaPalombara

3. *Political Modernization in Japan and Turkey*
Edited by Robert E. Ward and Dankwart A. Rustow

4. *Education and Political Development*
Edited by James S. Coleman

5. *Political Culture and Political Development*
Edited by Lucian W. Pye and Sidney Verba

6. *Political Parties and Political Development*
Edited by Joseph LaPalombara and Myron Weiner

7. *Crises in Political Development*
Edited by Leonard Binder, James S. Coleman,
Joseph LaPalombara, Lucian W. Pye, Myron Weiner,
and Sidney Verba

❖

Sponsored by the Committee on
Comparative Politics of the Social
Science Research Council

Lucian W. Pye, *Chairman*

Gabriel A. Almond
Leonard Binder
R. Taylor Cole
James S. Coleman
Herbert Hyman
Joseph LaPalombara
Sidney Verba
Robert E. Ward
Myron Weiner

Bryce Wood, *staff*

Political Culture and Political Development

Edited by Lucian W. Pye
& Sidney Verba

CONTRIBUTORS

LUCIAN W. PYE	DONALD N. LEVINE
ROBERT E. WARD	JOSEPH LAPALOMBARA
RICHARD ROSE	ROBERT E. SCOTT
SIDNEY VERBA	LEONARD BINDER
DANKWART A. RUSTOW	FREDERICK C. BARGHOORN
	MYRON WEINER

PRINCETON, NEW JERSEY
PRINCETON UNIVERSITY PRESS

Copyright © 1965 by Princeton University Press
ALL RIGHTS RESERVED
L.C. Card: 65-10840

◆

Printed in the United States
of America by Princeton University Press
Princeton, New Jersey

First Princeton Paperback Printing, 1969

This book is sold subject to the condition that it shall not, by way of trade, be lent, resold, hired out, or otherwise disposed of without the publisher's consent, in any form of binding or cover other than that in which it is published.

TO *Gabriel A. Almond*

WHOSE INTEREST AND FRIENDSHIP

GUIDED THIS ENTERPRISE

PREFACE

A PRIME objective of the Committee on Comparative Politics of the Social Science Research Council in sponsoring this series of "Studies in Political Development" has been to stimulate a multi-disciplined attack upon the political problems of nation building in the newly emerging countries. In producing the first four volumes of the series our approach was to organize conferences and to invite distinguished scholars to prepare papers which eventually became the chapters of the respective books. More often than not the authors were asked to apply methods and concepts they had developed in other contexts to the problems of political development, with the hope that out of this effort might come not only further refinements of their intellectual contributions but also new insight into the processes of social and political development.

In this fifth volume in the series we have followed a different way and asked competent and knowledgeable authorities on a wide variety of countries to apply a common approach—that of political culture—in reviewing the problems of modernization and development in the countries of their specialization. The authors were given a memorandum, suggestive but not prescriptive, which outlined subjects that might be generally relevant for the analysis of a political culture. They were asked to provide some historical perspective on both the political culture and the processes of political development in their countries and to analyze as far as appropriate the role of the most important agents of political socialization. It was hoped that the first common theme would contribute to our appreciation of the variety of patterns of historical development, while the second emphasis would yield more understanding about the possibilities and limitations for consciously changing a political culture in order to facilitate national development.

The plan for this study did not call for a meeting of all the authors, and at no stage in the enterprise would such a gathering have been feasible. Indeed, the schedules of the various authors meant that some of the chapters were finished in the spring of 1962 while others were completed only by the late fall of 1963. The chapters completed first were reviewed by the Committee during the 1962 summer institute at the Center for Advanced Study in the Behavioral Sciences in

PREFACE

Palo Alto, California. At this time the project benefited from lengthy consultations with Alex Inkeles of Harvard University and Daniel Lerner of the Massachusetts Institute of Technology. At a later stage we received further helpful advice from Christian Bay of Stanford University.

This volume in a uniquely personal fashion reflects the imaginative leadership of Gabriel A. Almond who has been a pioneer in the intellectual history of the concept of political culture and, as a steady guide to the members of the Committee on Comparative Politics, led us to an appreciation of the advantages of studying the problems of political development in terms of political culture. It was he who conceived the plans for this volume, drafted the first memorandum of instructions to the authors, and then constantly encouraged and sustained the editors through to the completion of the enterprise. It is with great pleasure that the editors now welcome this opportunity to acknowledge their deep debt to Gabriel A. Almond.

All the members of the Committee on Comparative Politics have contributed in some fashion to making this study possible. The project also benefited constantly from the strong administrative support of Dr. Bryce Wood. Richard Hatch of the M.I.T. Center for International Studies provided thoughtful editorial suggestions for all authors and prepared the entire manuscript for publication. Finally, the editors are happy to acknowledge their indebtedness to the Center for Advanced Study in the Behavioral Sciences—its always helpful staff and its considerate director, Dr. Ralph Tyler—for providing the perfect environment for completing this study.

LUCIAN W. PYE
SIDNEY VERBA

CONTENTS

Preface and Acknowledgments — vii

1. Introduction: Political Culture and Political Development — 3
   by Lucian W. Pye

2. Japan: The Continuity of Modernization — 27
   by Robert E. Ward

3. England: The Traditionally Modern Political Culture — 83
   by Richard Rose

4. Germany: The Remaking of Political Culture — 130
   by Sidney Verba

5. Turkey: The Modernity of Tradition — 171
   by Dankwart A. Rustow

6. India: Two Political Cultures — 199
   by Myron Weiner

7. Ethiopia: Identity, Authority, and Realism — 245
   by Donald N. Levine

8. Italy: Fragmentation, Isolation, and Alienation — 282
   by Joseph LaPalombara

9. Mexico: The Established Revolution — 330
   by Robert E. Scott

10. Egypt: The Integrative Revolution — 396
    by Leonard Binder

11. Soviet Russia: Orthodoxy and Adaptiveness — 450
    by Frederick C. Barghoorn

CONTENTS

12. Conclusion: Comparative Political Culture 512
    by Sidney Verba

    Contributors 561

    Index 565

*Political Culture
and Political Development*

CHAPTER 1

Introduction:
Political Culture and Political Development

LUCIAN W. PYE

POLITICS defies classification. It reflects at one and the same moment the full splendor and the pettiest meanness of man. The blends of emotion and reasoning that activate politics are invariably mixtures of such powerful but workaday ingredients as prestige, honor, loyalty, hatred, aggression, duty, conscience, material advantage, self-interest, and the search for security in all its forms. There is politics of vision and aspiration; and equally politics of desperation and despair. How to classify a phenomenon that encompasses so much of human experience? Just as we sense that it may embrace the greatness of poetry, we are reminded that at times politics can be as trite and as trivial as the most banal of academic studies of it.

The elusive boundaries of politics seem ever to be shifting. Politics is always more than the mere words and actions of the professed politicians; yet at moments it seems to shrink to the antics of little, scheming, power-thirsty men. At times the spirit of a polity seems to produce a reality that is far more than just the sum of all the people and institutions of the moment; yet politics can only be the acts of specific individuals of whom the few can so readily overshadow the many. Some would say that politics may be found everywhere—in the club room and the business office, among schoolmen and churchmen, and even in the household—but surely politics assumes its great dimensions only when its stage is the state and its powers can shape the law of the land. Yet, even when the limits are set at the politics of nation-states, does not each national community create its own unique pattern of order so that even the skilled politician is at home only in his native setting and becomes an awkward stranger in all foreign polities? How is it possible to classify and differentiate politics when every community and national society seems so spontaneously capable of producing its own distinctive and persisting style, manner, and substantive forms of politics? Politics is so deeply rooted in the native genius of each nation that the continuity of separate political traditions constantly resists the leveling forces at work in the social and economic spheres of modern life.

While it is possible to distinguish different forms of government—monarchies, republics, dictatorships, and the like—such differences do not necessarily govern the manner of politics. The need is for some other basis of classification, but to discover it is so difficult that thinkers and scholars have generally abandoned the search. Some have sought to reduce all of politics to the universal and the generalizable, by speaking in terms of such abstractions as the "state," "sovereignty," "power," and "political man," as though these shadows of politics are the same from place to place and from day to day. Others have given up, at least for the moment, any hope for dealing with the universal properties of politics and have thrown themselves into the study of politics in the particular, the politics of a specific time and place.

The problem of classifying politics could once be left to the curiosities of isolated scholars, but today it has suddenly become one of the great issues of public affairs and international relations. For the dramatic emergence of a host of new sovereign states has abruptly confronted statesmen with baffling questions about the nature of differences in the conduct of politics. What is the meaning of "political development," and what characterizes "modernization" in the realm of politics? In politics is there the same distinction as in economics between "developed" and "underdeveloped"? Are there certain forms and conditions of politics that are necessary to support, or at least not inhibit, other forms of social and economic development? What is the significance of the contention between old and new, between traditional values and modern practices for the stability and maintenance of the political order? Above all, to what extent is it possible to accelerate and direct political change, and how can traditional societies be best transformed into democratic polities? These are the kinds of questions that plague the leaders of the new states as they contemplate the differences between contemporary politics in their societies and their visions of the kind of polities they would build. These are the questions that must be answered by all who would help the new states in realizing their aspirations.

These are also the kinds of questions that students, largely because of the frustrating difficulties in classifying politics, have tended to neglect. Thus scholars are now confronted by the fact that they lack the knowledge necessary to give firm answers to such questions as how democratic values and modern political institutions can be most readily transferred to new environments. Since the scholar's world has never been so isolated from the world of affairs as many laymen and academics would like to pretend, his security has been violently shaken by the realization of how little is known about the dynamics of political development and the significance of political differences.

In the light of these considerations about the pressure of national and international problems upon the direction of academic interests, we may be forgiven for dwelling briefly on developments in the field of comparative politics. The subject involves far more than just the private concerns of professional students, for this is the field which should assume a lead in analyzing, distinguishing, and classifying various types of politics so that we may be able to arrive at better answers to the questions that trouble those seeking political development.

Until recently the student of comparative politics has been concerned more with the study of foreign governments than with comparative analysis. Specialists have generally been experts on particular countries and regions; and advancement in knowledge in the field has encouraged ever-increasing specialization, because the elevation of standards of study of particular countries has lowered the possibility of being respectably knowledgeable about all countries. Consequently the field of comparative politics has become increasingly compartmentalized. This process has led to studies of the various areas, and even of particular countries, developing their distinctive approaches and focuses, and becoming almost sub-fields with the characteristics of separate disciplines.

Without any agreed-upon general criteria of what might be most profitably analyzed and compared in all political systems, the practice has been to stress some factors in the study of certain countries and others with different countries. There has thus been a variety of traditions within comparative politics. For the study of European systems the emphasis has been largely upon legally constituted structures and formally developed ideologies. The study of the British, French, German, and Russian systems has tended to accentuate different themes and issues, to rely upon different kinds of data, and to seek answers to different questions. Even in the study of the new countries there have been a variety of approaches. Far Eastern area studies have been strongly historical, concentrating on the impact of ancient religions, great traditions of civilization, and the development of formal schools of thought. African studies have been closer to the anthropological tradition; while South and Southeast Asian studies have emphasized political movements and nationalism and, when not concentrating on the contemporary scene, they have stressed the analysis of colonialism. These separate traditions and approaches have brought richness and subtlety to comparative politics, and it is proper that we should value highly the scholarship and knowledge that have come from them.

Indeed in the light of their vigorous persistence possibly what is called for if we are to strengthen comparative analysis are approaches that can exploit the richness of the separate traditions in building more general theories. Just as the good theorist welcomes the detailed case study, so the student of comparative analysis should be able to benefit from the strength of the separate traditions of area studies. The situation thus calls for concepts and approaches equally sensitive to both the universal and the unique in both the individual personality and in the ordering of human society. Questions about the limits of variety and the consequences of differences in the attitudes and sentiments that shape politics can be answered only by an approach which combines individual psychology and collective sociology. Only with such an intellectual focus can we hope to get answers to such questions as: Do similar historical processes tend to produce the same distribution of attitudes and feelings about politics? What effect do particular dimensions of traditional cultures have on the capacity of people to engage in the various functions of modern political life? How can the changing feelings and outlooks of individuals affect the politics of the community and, conversely, how can the structural needs in maintaining a nation-state affect the political sentiments of individuals? In short, if we are going to compare polities in order to understand better the dynamics of political development we must make our analyses in terms of the ways in which people develop, maintain, and change the fundamental basis of political behavior, and in terms of the collective stability and instability of different constellations of attitudes and sentiments.

These considerations suggest that analysis which focuses on the phenomenon of culture may be peculiarly well adapted for comparing and classifying political systems in terms that are relevant for understanding the character of political development and change. The result may be an approach which can exploit the richness of the separate traditions of country and area studies while keeping attention focused on universal problems and processes basic to the human condition. The notion of political culture assumes that the attitudes, sentiments, and cognitions that inform and govern political behavior in any society are not just random congeries but represent coherent patterns which fit together and are mutually reinforcing. In spite of the great potentialities for diversity in political orientations, in any particular community there is a limited and distinct political culture which gives meaning, predictability, and form to the political process. The concept of political culture assumes that each individual must, in his own historical context, learn and incorporate into his own personality the knowledge and feelings about the politics of his people and his community. This means in turn that the political culture of a society is limited but given firm structure by the factors basic to dynamic psychology. Each generation must receive its politics from the previous one, each must react against that process to find its own politics, and the total process must follow the laws that govern the development of the individual personality and the general culture of a society.

The concept of political culture as used in this volume comes from Gabriel A. Almond's observation that "every political system is embedded in a particular pattern of orientation to political actions."[1] This is to say that in any operating political system there is an ordered subjective realm of politics which gives meaning to the polity, discipline to institutions, and social relevance to individual acts. The concept of political culture thus suggests that the traditions of a society, the spirit of its public institutions, the passions and the collective reasoning of its citizenry, and the style and operating codes of its leaders are not just random products of historical experience but fit together as a part of a meaningful whole and constitute an intelligible web of relations. For the individual the political culture provides controlling guidelines for effective political behavior, and for the collectivity it gives a systematic structure of values and rational considerations which ensures coherence in the performance of institutions and organizations. In essence, thus, the political culture, as Verba indicates in the concluding chapter of this volume, "consists of the system of empirical beliefs, expressive symbols, and values which de-

---

[1] Almond, "Comparative Political Systems," *Journal of Politics*, 18, 1956, and reprinted in *Political Behavior, a Reader in Theory and Research*, Heinz Eulau, Samuel J. Eldersveld, and Morris Janowitz, eds., Glencoe, Ill., Free Press, 1956, pp. 34-42.

fines the situation in which political action takes place." It encompasses both the political ideals and the operating norms of a polity.

A political culture is the product of both the collective history of a political system and the life histories of the individuals who currently make up the system; and thus it is rooted equally in public events and private experiences. The theory of political culture was developed in response to the need to bridge a growing gap in the behavioral approach in political science between the level of microanalysis based on psychological interpretations of the individual's political behavior and the level of macroanalysis based on the variables common to political sociology. In this sense the theory constitutes an attempt to integrate psychology and sociology in order to be able to apply to dynamic political analysis both the revolutionary findings of modern depth psychology and recent advances in the sociological techniques for measuring attitudes in mass societies. Within the discipline of political science the theory signals an effort to apply an essentially behavioral form of analysis to the study of such classic concepts as "political ideology," "legitimacy," "sovereignty," "nationhood," and the "rule of law."

Indeed, political culture is a recent term which seeks to make more explicit and systematic much of the understanding associated with such long-standing concepts as political ideology, national ethos and spirit, national political psychology, and the fundamental values of a people. Political culture, by embracing the political orientations of both leaders and citizens, is more inclusive than such terms as political style or operational code which focus on elite behavior. On the other hand, the term is more explicitly political and hence more restrictive than such concepts as public opinion and national character.

Not all the political attitudes and sentiments of a people are necessarily relevant in defining their political culture, for many are too ephemeral and lightly held to affect fundamental development. On the other hand, many apparently non-political beliefs—such as feelings of basic trust in human relations, orientations toward time and the possibilities of progress, and the like—can be of overriding importance. This is so because the political culture consists of only those critical but widely shared beliefs and sentiments that form the "particular patterns of orientation" that give order and form to the political process. In sum, the political culture provides structure and meaning to the political sphere in the same manner as culture in general gives coherence and integration to social life.

As with culture in general, political culture touches at several levels of human awareness and sensitivity. Much of political culture stems from explicit citizenship training and conscious learning about the workings of the political system, and it is thus largely shaped by rational understanding and articulated concepts. A political culture, however, has deep emotional dimensions involving the passions of loyalty and community identity, the sentiments of human and geographical attachment. In relating emotions, rational considerations, and ethical values, political culture colors a people's expectations about the realities of politics and instills in them shared ideals as to what their public life might be.

Concern with the phenomenon of political culture represents a significant development in contemporary political analysis for it signals an effort to return to the study of the total political system without losing the benefits of individual psychology. During recent decades, as political science has sought to sort out and absorb relevant developments in all the related social science disciplines, the tendency has been increasingly to focus on the behavior of the individual. In particular as political scientists have sought to capitalize upon the revolutionary discoveries and insights of psychology, the unit of political analysis has tended to become the single act or decision and the principal actors to become the individual decision makers, whether leader, voter, or mere opinion holder. There has, however, been a danger that in the process of uncovering the human underpinnings of public actions all sight would be lost of the equally important reality of the political community as a dynamic, collective entity. There has been a need to discover a method for working back from the complex subtleties of individual psychology to the level of the social aggregate which is the traditional plateau of political science. It is this problem of aggregation—which involves the adding up of the discoveries of individual psychology in such a manner as to make community-wide behavior understandable in the light of individual actions—that is now the great challenge to political science and for which the concept of political culture holds such great promise.

In studying national development in terms of the political cultures of individual countries it is thus possible to bring together in a common focus the approaches of macroanalysis and microanalysis, the study of the behavior and dynamics of both the total system and the individuals who make up the system. In exploring the origins of a political culture it is necessary, for example, to treat both the historical development of the system as a whole and the life experiences of the individuals who currently embody the culture. From the historical approach we can trace the evolution of the institutions and value patterns which give substance to the contemporary political cultures; and in viewing the political socialization patterns by which individuals are inducted into the culture we can note how these institutions impinge on the lives of individuals. This relationship between the private socialization processes and the operations of public institutions provides much of the dynamics of continuity and change in political systems.

The concept of political culture also provides a useful basis for examining the links between social and economic factors and political performance. Through the socialization process which sustains and shapes the political culture of each generation we can observe the impact of not only the explicitly political but also all the relevant non-political dimensions of life in the conditioning and determining of political behavior. In so investigating the social and economic parameters of the political culture we can come to grips with the historically significant issues about the relationship between economic development and the prospects for stable political change.

In analyzing political behavior the concept of political culture helps to present a balanced picture of the relative importance of rational choice and consciously learned values and the more latent, non-rational determinants of human behavior. The political socialization process involves not only the deeply instilled attitudes and sentiments of early childhood and family life but also the later experiences of explicit instruction in politics at schools, through exposure to the mass media, and in contacts with other politically socializing agents. In the past the concept of national character, in becoming a residual category used to "explain" all the differences that could not otherwise be accounted for by objective analysis, tended to be biased toward emphasizing the importance of the unconscious to the point of discounting almost entirely the place of reason in human affairs. Political socialization involves both the early and later stages of personality formation and learning and thus must treat in equal measure the explicit and the tacit, the manifest and the latent in the relationship between individual psychology and social order.

In applying the analysis of political culture to the question of political development it is possible to throw light on the various combinations and constellations of values which may govern different patterns of development and which may be the prime causes of frustration and disappointment over the prospects of national development. In some societies the traditional political culture appears to have provided a ready basis for democratic evolution, while in others the tendencies have been more consistent with authoritarian ways. Hopefully, the analysis of different political cultures will provide us with a better understanding of the policies and necessary investments in various socializing agents which can best produce desired changes in a nation's politics.

It must be acknowledged that the term "political development" is relatively novel to political science. Many people may argue that politics is a universal phenomena, unaffected in essence by time or place, and therefore it is inappropriate to categorize it as being either more or less "developed" as may be done with respect to economic systems and social structures. Another understandable objection to the term is that it seems to imply certain value judgments which open up the danger that objective analysis will become confused with advocacy and idealistic preferences. Much of the strength of contemporary political science is traceable to the acceptance of cultural relativism, to efforts at understanding the realities of actual political operations, and to a moratorium on debates about the ideal state of government. However, in spite of these and other legitimate concerns about the concept, the blunt fact is that leaders in the new states are intensely concerned about the problems of not just economic but also—and in many cases more importantly—political development. And increasingly in recent years there has been a growing and broadening understanding of what constitutes political development. Different people using the term do, however, tend to give it slightly different meanings.

For some people political development means primarily the prerequisite political environment essential for economic and industrial development. Thus political development becomes merely the creation of the political and governmental conditions necessary for realizing higher economic performance. A second and related concept of political development places the emphasis upon governmental performance, and thus development involves an increase in administrative performance and a greater capacity for carrying out public policies. This is the concept of development which was often most congenial to colonial administrations interested primarily in rational, bureaucratic development.

A third way of defining political development has been that of following the lead of social theorists and associating the degree of development with the extent to which patterns of behavior identified as "modern" tend to prevail over those considered to be "traditional." Thus development takes place when achievement considerations replace ascriptive standards, and when functional specificity replaces functional diffuseness in social relations, and when universalistic norms supersede particularistic ones.

A fourth concept of political development involves the test of general performance of the entire system and the capacity of both the administration of government and the polity as a whole to meet increasingly heavy demands and exacting challenges. Development is thus measured by the "load" that the system seems capable of bearing. A coherent, integrated society thus is more "developed" than a fragile and fragmented polity.

In a similar vein is a fifth view which directly relates political development to the creation of a viable nation-state capable of performing effectively in the modern world. Development thus becomes nation building in the contemporary historical context, and there is no need to suggest the existence of inevitable historical processes or the existence of any ultimate or ideal goal of development. The test is the reality of performance in a competitive, modern world. This nation-building view of development is closely related but different from a sixth view which simply relates development to national power. Development then becomes the ability to make the most of a society's inherent resource base.

There is finally the position that development can properly mean democratic development, and hence the greater the state of development the greater the advance of liberty, popular sovereignty, and free institutions. Consistent with this approach is the position that there can be other lines of "development" according to other ideological visions of the ideal political community, and hence there can be more or less "developed" communist or other totalitarian systems.

All these views about the proper criteria of political development have contributed to what is an increasingly accepted understanding of the concept. In this particular volume, as with the other works in this series of "Studies in Political Development," we have not tried to adhere to a rigid definition of political development. We have instead sought to incorporate in our analysis most of the dimensions of political change and modernization which students of the new states tend to refer to when speaking of political development. The authors of the papers in this volume thus tend to reflect the view that there is, in a generic sense, a phenomenon of political development and modernization. The key elements of political development involve, first, with respect to the population as a whole, a change from widespread subject status to an increasing number of contributing citizens, with an accompanying spread of mass participation, a greater sensitivity to the principles of equality, and a wider acceptance of universalistic laws. Second, with respect to governmental and general systemic performance, political development involves an increase in the capacity of the political system to manage public affairs, control controversy, and cope with popular demands. Finally, with respect to the organization of the polity, political development implies greater structural differentiation, greater functional specificity, and greater integration of all the participating institutions and organizations.

Clearly no matter what particular aspect is emphasized political development strikes at the roots of people's beliefs and sentiments about politics, and hence the process of development must be profoundly affected by the character of the political culture of a society. This is why through the analysis of how different political cultures have reacted to the pressures of change we may hope to gain greater understanding about the forces supporting and inhibiting development and modernization.

These potentialities of the concept of political cultures were among the considerations which led to this study and the production of this book. In seeking to carry out this experiment in the comparative analysis of political cultures in relation to the dynamics of political development it seemed best to emphasize more the existing richness of area studies than the potential advantages of systematic schemata for defining and classifying political cultures. Authors having deep and thorough acquaintance with particular political systems were invited to analyze national political cultures in the light of the country's experiences in political development. Some uniformity was requested of the authors as all were asked to include in their chapters some historical treatment and some evaluation of the significance of various socializing agents in shaping their particular political culture.

Out of this experiment have come sophisticated introductions to ten political systems. The diversity of approaches and the choices in emphasis represent in part the distinctive styles of the individual authors and in part the unique traditions of scholarship specific to the study of each of the countries. We are still convinced that the subtlety and richness of analysis guaranteed by providing latitude to the authors outbalances any returns that might have come from more restrictive but uniform instructions. And, of course, established scholars expect and deserve freedom in following their creative bents.

Along with examining the relationships between political culture and political development in countries at various stages of development we have also been concerned with working toward a more rigorous generalized theory of political culture. Thus the last chapter of this volume is an essay by Sidney Verba on the theory of political culture. Some readers may want to go directly to this essay in order to gain clarification on the concept of political culture before turning to the more empirical chapters that constitute the rest of the study. It did not seem appropriate to place this chapter before the country chapters because such an arrangement might unintentionally suggest to readers that the various authors of the country chapters might properly have been expected to follow the schematic categories basic to the theoretical chapters, when in fact the country chapters were all initiated, and most were concluded, before the theoretical essay was available to the authors.[2]

Possibly the most striking conclusion which emerges from bringing together these studies of ten countries is an appreciation of the diversity of man's experiences in creating and ordering his political life. Differences abound; and even with respect to certain common broad themes, such as democracy and authoritarianism, there is remarkably little similarity. On more detailed examination, however, we can become equally impressed with the number of common themes which all or at least most of the authors felt compelled to stress. It may therefore be appropriate in introducing this study to comment on some of these general themes involving the relationship of political culture and political development.

---

[2] In a few instances the final revisions of the country chapters were done after the authors had seen an early version of the final theoretical chapter, and this explains some use of common terminology.

It might also be noted that several of the authors arrived at a common terminology because of their reliance upon the pioneering study of Gabriel A. Almond and Sidney Verba, *The Civic Culture*, Princeton, Princeton University Press, 1963. This is particularly so with respect to the chapters on England, Germany, Italy, and Mexico, since *The Civic Culture* deals specifically with the mass political attitudes in these four countries, plus the United States. Robert E. Ward, before writing his chapter on Japan, had access to *The Civic Culture* in manuscript form.

LUCIAN W. PYE

The Structure and Configurations of Political Cultures

In spite of the great diversity among the countries, we find certain common generalizations about the structure of political cultures. The first of these is the observation that in no society is there a single uniform political culture, and in all polities there is a fundamental distinction between the culture of the rulers or power holders and that of the masses, whether they are merely parochial subjects or participating citizens. Those who must deal with power and have responsibilities for the decisions of government invariably develop outlooks on politics different from those of the people who remain observers or marginal activists. Even in the most democratic societies this distinction remains in spite of almost heroic efforts of leaders to pretend that they are of the same spirit as the common citizenry, and of citizens and commentators to feign that they are intimately knowledgeable about the inner workings of government. This of course says nothing about the relative importance of the two political cultures, a matter which depends entirely upon the kind of problem confronting the society.

Although all the authors acknowledge in one fashion or another this division, some chose to concentrate on the elite culture and others on the mass political culture. For some countries the decision reflects the relative importance of the two cultures with respect to the problems of development. In writing about the Soviet Union Frederick Barghoorn has chosen not to deal exclusively with the elite culture and the doctrines of Marxism-Leninism but rather to focus on how the reactions of various segments of the Russian people and particularly of the intellectuals to the formal ideology may affect future Soviet developments. In general for the less developed countries there is a fundamental crisis of leadership, and since the prospects for development depend so heavily upon the capabilities of leadership it is understandable that in our studies of Turkey, Egypt, and Ethiopia attention is directed more to the elite cultures. In the more advanced countries the principal issue tends to become one of whether democracy will survive and whether popular sentiments will support continuing development. Thus the studies of Germany and Italy are more directed to the mass culture. It should be added that relative emphasis is also governed by the availability of data: for most of the emerging countries we have little information about the attitudes that make up the mass culture and much greater access to the ideas of leaders, while for the European countries we have the results of opinion polls and sample surveys.

Quite different methods of research are called for in the study of the two cultures. Work on the elite political culture involves skill in interpreting ideologies, in characterizing operational codes, and in defining the spirit and calculations that lie behind high-risk political behavior. The study of mass political cultures depends, on the other hand, upon the advanced techniques of survey research and modern methods of measuring public opinion. The conditions of research and the availability of information in different countries set quite different limits upon possibilities for studying one or the other culture.

The fact that the two cultures of the elite and the mass exist in all political systems means that systems can be readily classified according to the character of the relationship between the two. Political systems significantly differ, for example, according to the degree of homogeneity between the two cultures, and within each of them separately. Donald Levine informs us that in Ethiopia the elite culture is intimately associated with the general culture of a particular ethnic community, the Amhara; and thus the ways of the rulers are completely identified with the social life of this sub-culture, but they are deeply separated from the ways of the other sub-cultures which make up the Ethiopian population. Thus with respect to the elite culture there is a high degree of homogeneity, and indeed cultural integrity, but the same is not true in the relations between the elite and the mass cultures.

With respect to India, Myron Weiner describes the case of a relatively homogeneous elite culture and of a mass culture extensively divided and fragmented according to caste, religion, and linguistic communities. Weiner raises the interesting prospect that India may eventually find a greater degree of integration not through the triumph of the current elite culture but through a complex historical process whereby the various sub-divisions of the mass culture, clashing and competing with each other, will in time produce a new homogeneous culture for the entire nation.

It should be noted that neither stability nor degree of development seems to be a simple function of the degree of difference between the two cultures. Indeed, in highly developed systems, as Richard Rose points out for England, it is ever more necessary to train increasingly specialized people to manage public affairs, and there is less and less a place for generalists. On the other hand, Dankwart Rustow for

Ottoman Turkey and Robert E. Ward for Tokugawa Japan explain that in spite of the lack of social mobility in these traditional systems the leaders and commoners shared many views about the nature of politics.

Stability and development appear to be more affected by differences in the socialization processes that support the two cultures than by the degree of difference in the content of the cultures. In the more traditional systems, such as Ethiopia, India, and Mexico, we find the existence of two quite separate socialization processes which independently induct people into the two different cultures. On the other hand, in the more developed systems, such as England, Germany, and the Soviet Union, we find that those people who occupy places of political influence were all first inducted into a version of the mass culture before being recruited and socialized into the elite culture. As long as there is such a sequential pattern of socialization into the two cultures it appears that the increasing esoteric attitudes essential to a highly developed system will not place too great a strain on the over-all stability of the political culture.

Patterns of Cultural Change

In addition to the division between elite and mass political cultures the process of political development tends to create a second division in all political cultures. This is the division which separates those more acculturated to modern ways from the people who are still closer to the traditional patterns of life. The relationship between these two divisions in political cultures and the relative gap between them appear to be decisive factors governing the total course of national development.

In some countries, as in India and Egypt, the two divisions tend to coincide, with the elite culture consisting largely of people with more cosmopolitan orientations and the mass culture composed of the more tradition-oriented people. As development progresses, the pattern of bifurcation tends increasingly to follow the division between the urban and rural segments of the population, the type of division described in our studies of the Japanese and Mexican political cultures. In other cases the process of cultural change proceeds according to geographic regions, as in Italy, where the sharpest division is between the highly industrialized north and the still traditionalist rural south.

From Myron Weiner's analysis of the relationships between elite and mass cultures on the one hand and the traditional-modern dichotomy on the other we learn that the dynamics of political development does not necessarily call for the persisting spread of the modern views of the elite culture. Instead it appears that in India the political process within the mass culture is producing a "modern" component of the mass culture which may in time replace the "modern" component of the current elite culture and, indeed, become the future elite culture of India. This is one pattern of fusion by which the gaps between traditional and modern, elite and mass, can be reduced.

A somewhat similar pattern of fusion appears to be taking place in Egypt according to the analysis of Leonard Binder. Binder hypothesizes that an "integrative revolution" is taking place under Nasser largely because the modernizing thrust of a new elite culture has been directed toward establishing links with the rural countryside, and that success for the effort is possible because, in the meantime, there has emerged within the rural areas a new form of local leadership capable of cooperating with the national leaders.

The path of development is not often smooth, for change can create conflicts and tensions at various points in the political culture, and particularly by putting out of joint the various socialization processes. Robert Scott's analysis of the Mexican political culture vividly describes the lack of congruence and coherence in the socialization process of a country which has had a revolutionary elite political culture but still a very traditionalist early socialization process. In explaining the fragmented and unintegrated Italian political culture Joseph LaPalombara shows that many of the most important socializing agents, inspired by quite different concepts of development, work directly against each other and thus tend to produce a disturbingly cynical citizenry.

In reviewing the various patterns of change in political culture the example of what has been happening in Germany as interpreted by Sidney Verba is possibly the most significant and encouraging. For though he stresses the difficulties involved in changing a political culture through conscious manipulation, his study of changes in basic political beliefs in Germany since the war suggests that fundamental attitude change among adults is certainly not impossible. We shall want to return to this German experience in democratization in discussing the problems of policy toward political development, but it is appropriate to conclude our review of changes in political cultures by reference to Germany because it is a somewhat reassuring balance to the less happy experiences of many of the other countries.

The Place of Tradition in Modernizing Political Cultures

Although the concern of all the authors is with the dynamics of political development, it is noteworthy that all of them find it necessary to treat the continuing importance of tradition in giving a sense of uniqueness and meaning to the individual political cultures. Political development is not a process in which there is simply a decline of traditional modes of behavior and a rise of rationality and impersonal efficiency. Politics involves the expression of the collective values of a people, the feelings of people about their social and group identities, and above all else the tests of loyalty and commitment. Development in some field of human organization can be usefully conceived of as being the replacement of the particularistic norms, functionally diffuse relationships, and ascriptive considerations of tradition-based societies with the more universalistic, functionally specific, and achievement-oriented patterns of action of more modern societies. In a political culture, however, there is a constant place for particularism, for diffuse identifications, and for attaching importance to nationality and place of birth.

The problems of development, viewed in terms of political culture, involve less the gross elimination of old patterns and values and more the successful discovery of how traditions can contribute to, and not hamper, the realization of current national goals. Effective political development thus requires that a proper place be found for many traditional considerations in the more modern scheme of things. In the concluding essay Sidney Verba discusses in some detail the continuing importance of tradition in the developed polity.

The central theme of Richard Rose's study of English political culture is precisely this problem of the fusion of traditional and modern in giving stability to development. Rose reminds us that in England "modern" innovations have tended, once they are accepted, to become very rapidly a part of "tradition," and thus often an obstacle to further innovations. British innovations of the nineteenth century were once the highest expressions of "modern" forms, but now they have become a part of the tradition of an outmoded Victorian era. Skill in fusing old and new and in making the new so readily a part of the old has contributed greatly to the stability and orderliness of English development. Rose argues, however, that the British have had to pay a price for this stability in the sense that they have over time accumulated such a massive weight of traditions that each new phase of innovating can become increasingly more difficult.

Sidney Verba's study shows that the Germans have followed quite a different course from that of the English as they have had to accept sharp discontinuities between the old and the new. As the consequence of defeat and the policies of the occupation they have had to cast aside many old traditions and keep only the minimum essential for the effective performance of the new democratic order. Contemporary Germany is thus far less weighted down with tradition than England is but, being more open to change, it may also be taking high risks with respect to stability. Verba makes the interesting point that the Germans have been able to take these risks and to achieve democratic development in their country because of their extraordinary efficiency and capacity for organization in the other spheres of life. In particular he suggests that Germany's achievements economically have made it possible for the Germans to create an atmosphere in which the loss of old traditions has not been as unstabilizing as otherwise it might have been.

Both the English and the German studies give emphasis to the fact that modernization and development are not a single act of changing the structure of the polity but a constant and unending process. Countries that have developed earlier historically have some very real problems of keeping up with the demands of continuous change. The British, for example, have had a tendency, according to Rose, to content themselves with existing levels of performance until confronted with the pressures of external competition. Using an analogy from industrial relations, he finds that the British are inclined to follow conservative policies about the modernization of their capital plants and that they cling to existing technologies so long as the machine works, hoping to make up any competitive disadvantages by vigorous and alert salesmanship. This attitude is quite understandable because political systems are usually "machines" of such a questionable nature that if one operates at all satisfactorily it is generally an occasion for self-congratulation.

Turkey and Japan followed a similar pattern in dealing with the need for a continued presence of the past. Rustow informs us that the Turks have persistently given old labels to new practices and thus presented innovations as merely the revitalization of old ways.

Ataturk even used this argument in seeking to replace the religious basis of public affairs with a secular state.

In Japan the relationship of old and new is extremely complex because, as Ward points out, the ground for much of the rapid development of Japanese life was being well prepared during the traditional era. In a sense, many of the Japanese traditional practices and institutions were really "modern" ones disguised in old dress. Thus Japan was able to follow a method of fusing old and new very much like that of England, except that Japan developed at a later stage and thus modernization and innovation inevitably became enmeshed with issues about the acceptance of foreign influences. Ward's analysis of Japanese political culture leaves us with the interesting hypothesis that Japan's remarkable success in adapting modernity may stem largely from the fact that the traditional Japanese culture had within itself a very high indigenous potential for development.

This hypothesis in turn suggests the general but paradoxical proposition that strong and effective traditional systems may provide the ideal basis for subsequent development if they provide a people with a firm sense of identity, but the strength of the traditional order will impede development to the degree that it makes impossible the infusion of any new or modern elements of political culture. Donald Levine's interpretation of Ethiopia's experience supports this view. The extraordinary strength of traditional ways of the Amhara has certainly given Ethiopia many advantages over her African neighbors, and Ethiopia has been a reasonably independent and effective participant in the international community longer than any other African country. Yet, as Levine also points out, the traditions that have made this history possible and have given such stability to the country have also been so strong that it has been extremely difficult to fuse them with much that is explicitly modern.

This conclusion suggests that in examining the patterns of political development it is necessary to go beyond the general categories of traditional and modern and ask about the particular values of a political culture.

Content of Political Cultures

It might seem that there is such diversity among the various political systems that little can be said in general terms about the content of political cultures. In each country the different socialization processes tend to instill in the leaders and followers distinctive mixes of

INTRODUCTION

values and sentiments so that each community is held together with its distinct blends of loyalties and commitments. Yet in spite of these differences we find that our authors in their concern over the relationship of political culture to development tend to focus on many of the same values in describing the various political cultures. In particular there are four themes relating to the presence or absence of four specific values which repeatedly appear in the essays and are apparently related to fundamental issues that arise in the developmental process.

1. The first theme is that of trust and its opposite distrust and suspicion. Political cultures are built either upon the fundamental faith that it is possible to trust and work with fellowmen or upon the expectation that most people are to be distrusted and that strangers in particular are likely to be dangerous. Each political culture differs according to its patterns of trust and distrust, its definitions of who are probably the safe people and who are the most likely enemies, and its expectations about whether public institutions or private individuals are more worthy of trust. The presence of diffuse distrust seems to impede seriously the creation of the kinds of public organizations essential for national development. An equal obstacle to development, however, is the widespread existence of an uncritical and childlike trust in the rulers and in all forms of higher authority.

2 This suggests the second theme which our authors tend to stress, that of hierarchy and its opposite equality. Universally, all political cultures must deal with attitudes toward power, for all politics must involve the relations between superiors and inferiors, between initiators and followers. Traditional societies tended to emphasize and to provide moral justification for hierarchical relationships. Development demands effective leadership, but it also encompasses sentiments about equality and the absence of all arbitrary distinctions in status. How the different countries cope with this dilemma appears to be a central issue in determining their relative successes in development.

3 The third general theme is that of liberty and its converse coercion. Most of our authors tend to place the value of liberty near the center of their interpretations of the democratic political culture. Faith in the power of liberty to build strong nations appears to be extremely low in all except the oldest democracies. Yet few of the countries provide examples of the efficacy of coercion in easily creating national strength.

The last value which most of our authors mention relates to the

22

level of loyalty and commitment, and whether the political culture stresses particularisms in the form of intense and overriding identification with family or parochial grouping, or more generalizable identification such as with the nation as a whole. The process of political development, as seen by the majority of our authors, clearly involves a widening of horizons as people grow out of their narrow parochial views and take on a concern for the entire political system. This process, however, must occur without at the same time causing the people to become alienated from or hostile toward the primordial attachments that give vitality to their parochial associations.

The ten political cultures are strikingly different with respect to these four themes or values, and it is significant that there does not appear to be any fixed relationship among the four. Instead the particular way in which the four themes are combined provides much of the distinctive character of the processes of development in each country.

In the United Kingdom there appears to be a unique blend in which all four values are highly emphasized. The values of both trust and hierarchy are given special recognition in the English political culture, and the emphasis upon liberty is so great that the system also gives great legitimacy to idiosyncratic particularisms. In Germany there is less sense of trust, and the values of hierarchy, liberty, and particularism are muted in favor of the overriding value of efficiency. In Japan, according to Robert Ward, the traditional feudal value of particularism still remains intensely important; and the distinctive patterns of loyalty and obligation which follow from these particularisms tend to govern who should be trusted and distrusted, what hierarchical relationships are acceptable, and what should constitute the limits of liberty.

The political cultures of Italy, Mexico, and Ethiopia appear to be equally low on trust. In Italy distrust is combined with a strong particularistic loyalty to produce a fragmented and hostilely competitive political culture. In Ethiopia the same diffuse distrust is more than balanced by a dominant respect for hierarchy. As Donald Levine points out, Ethiopians generally accept the need for hierarchy, and for almost an arbitrary authority, because they have so little faith in the independent ability of others to hold their aggressive impulses in check. Robert Scott suggests that much the same situation pertains in Mexico in that the general willingness to accept the ultimate authority of the government adequately counters the lack of trust and

INTRODUCTION

the strong parochial sentiments which otherwise would leave the Mexican political culture as fragmented as the Italian is.

The interplay of these four values affects political development in various ways, but possibly most significantly with respect to the problems of increased mobilization and participation. When, for example, there is little basic trust a rapid increase in participants can accentuate suspicion and conflict, as appears to have occurred in both Italy and Mexico. Yet possibly, as Weiner suggests is happening in India, the very process of increased political involvement and competition will in time breed a greater degree of acceptance of other groups and thus produce a decline in suspicion and distrust. On the other hand, in Ethiopia the value of hierarchy appears to be so absolutely fundamental to the political culture that it becomes difficult to conceive of how that system could significantly expand popular participation without destroying the essential characteristics which have given it such a long and stable history.

Democracy and Policies for Development

The problem of change in Ethiopia brings us to the question of effective policies for democratic development. In general our authors show a considerable concern for the prospects of the emergence, or the continued maintenance, of democratic values and practices in the countries on which they are reporting. In various ways they all deal with the large issues of our time, issues about the relationship between democracy and industrial development, and the competition between totalitarian and democratic approaches to bettering the human condition. With respect to these and other important issues our authors are able to present many new insights because of the perspective provided them by the study of political culture.

For example, the conflict between democracy and efficiency in economic development does not appear in nearly as sharp a form as it often emerges in more philosophical discussions, but rather we learn that there are many subtle dimensions to the problem. Richard Rose deals explicitly with this problem for England and demonstrates that various forms of tradition and sentiment, some of which have been artificially associated with the democratic ethos, are more of an obstacle to economic efficiency than democratic decision making and participation are. Apparently, only with the weakening of barriers associated with hierarchy will the British be able to expand their educational and recruitment opportunities enough to meet their needs of increased skills for continued economic advances. Instead of conceiving of a conflict between democracy and efficiency, Sidney Verba suggests that in the German political culture it is specifically the high level of economic performance which has made democracy possible. On the other hand, in the less developed countries we find that expanded political participation may conflict with economic development, not, however, because of the presumed greater efficiency and rationality of the authoritarian governments, but rather because increased popular participation gives more scope to the latent feelings of hostility and aggression which are a part of the general spirit of distrust and suspicion in the culture. In Italy it appears that some forms of arbitrary action by government officials are necessary in order to counter the intense particularism and distrust of important segments of the society.

Our authors generally suggest that there are probably very definite limits to the pace and rate at which it is possible to plan and direct changes in a political culture. Ward, for example, makes it clear that the very rapid rate of development after the Meiji Restoration in Japan was possible only because of a long phase of earlier historical developments. Scott makes the point that the Mexican revolution also had its long-run antecedents, and that considerably more time will be required before the revolution has consummated its goals.

Yet it is also clear from the German, Turkish, and Egyptian examples that historical processes can in fact be greatly influenced and accelerated by appropriate policies. In particular we must be impressed with the potency of education in creating the attitudes and values essential for national development. Above all, it is hoped that a careful reading of these studies will give a greater appreciation of the wise limits and the enormous potentials that exist for building national environments that will be satisfying to the human spirit.

There is no overriding logic that needs govern the order in which these studies can be most profitably read; indeed, as we have suggested, many readers may choose to turn immediately to the concluding theoretical chapter before embarking on the separate case studies. We have somewhat arbitrarily arranged the chapters to begin with Japan, which is such an outstanding model of a rapidly developing political culture. We then turn to the studies of the older political cultures of England and Germany for guidance about earlier historic experiences and for instruction about the continuing problems of redevelopment and planned democratization. Next come the two cases of Turkey and India, in which there have been massive efforts to create consciously democratic institutions, but in which the dynamics of historical processes may still prove to be more decisive in producing national growth. Ethiopia, Italy, and Mexico pose profound problems of integration and development because of the absence of trust within their political cultures. In the study of Egypt we have an example of how some of these fundamental problems of integration are possibly being resolved. Finally, we have the example of the Soviet Union, the model example of the totalitarian system whose political culture seems to be undergoing some changes as a consequence of the dynamics of development.

CHAPTER 2

Japan: The Continuity of Modernization

ROBERT E. WARD

In any comparative study of the developmental experience of modern or modernizing political systems the special interest of the Japanese case resides in two factors: Japan is "modern," and it is non-Western. If one regards the Israeli case as exceptional, Japan is the only society of non-Western cultural antecedents to achieve the higher stages of modernization. It is the only indigenous society in all of Asia and Africa which has succeeded in achieving types and levels of political performance which practically all other Asian and African states either desire or consider essential to their further development.

Under these circumstances the Japanese experience becomes of extraordinary interest. It may not point to the only or to the most effective path to political modernization for other developing societies, but Japan does represent the only mature specimen available for analysis. The Japanese formula has worked for at least one non-Western people, and as a specific and concrete case it affords opportunities for checking and enriching the relatively abstract and theoretical speculations which necessarily bulk large in the early stages of investigation in fields such as this.

The present essay is a highly tentative and experimental attempt to examine a single aspect of Japan's experience with the modernization process, her political culture, by which is meant the internalized cognitions, feelings, and evaluations of Japanese towards their political system and their own roles therein.[1] It is assumed, first, that there is sufficient pattern, logic, and coherence to such psycho-political orientations among Japanese to render at least their major modes crudely identifiable and describable without benefit of detailed survey data or depth analysis; and second, that the state of these orientations bears an important relationship to the developmental capacities and performance characteristics of the Japanese political system as a whole. The primary aim of the paper is to describe in broad and neces-

[1] Gabriel A. Almond and Sidney Verba, *The Civic Culture: Political Attitudes and Democracy in Five Nations*, Princeton, Princeton University Press, 1963, Chap. 1.

sarily superficial terms certain major historical and current aspects of Japanese political culture and to speculate about the light they may shed upon the total course of political development in Japan.

The Emergence of Contemporary Political Culture

To ask how contemporary Japanese political culture emerged is to pose questions as to timing, periodization, and content. How deeply buried in the national history are its origins, along what lines and with what periodicities does it develop, what was its content at earlier stages—in short, to paraphrase Randall, what lies behind the making of the modern political mind in Japan? To begin with, we might take a brief look at the question of origins and periodization.

As one looks back upon the history of political modernization in Japan, one might well be impressed first by the neatness of the manner in which it is usually periodized. In gross terms, for example, one is accustomed to distinguishing periods in Japanese political history called Tokugawa (1603-1868) and post-Restoration (1868+). For somewhat more specific purposes, many distinguish a somewhat overlapping Restoration period (*ca.* 1850-1890) when considering the beginnings of modern Japanese political development. Over the years these convenient denominators for the categorization of historical data have assumed an authority and potential for distortion which was never intended.

The series of events attendant upon the so-called Restoration in 1868 of the Emperor Meiji to the position of temporal authority putatively enjoyed by his distant forebears undoubtedly constitutes the major single turning point in the political modernization of Japan. It marked the initial and critical success of the political forces that underlay and made possible the specific modernizing developments which followed. Despite this, the extent to which that year, or even the Restoration period as a whole, marked a time of new beginnings in an across-the-board political, social, and psychological sense has until very recently been seriously exaggerated by both Japanese and foreign scholarship. So-called revolutionary incidents in any national history seem to share this literary fate. In the earlier stages of analysis the political and social discontinuities to which they allegedly give rise command the attention of practically all commentators. At a later stage—perhaps very much later—the underlying continuities of social fabric and development, which were there all along, are suddenly rediscovered and a revisionist school of historical interpretation is born.

In the Japanese case the emphasis upon the Restoration and its aftermath as a time of revolutionary, i.e., discontinuous, new developments—especially in the political and economic spheres—acquired added force from a subsequent episode in Japanese historiography. This was the widespread practice of interpreting pre-Restoration Japan—the Japan of the Tokugawa period (1603-1868)—in terms of a "feudal" model. Indeed, at a later period this was compounded by the addition of the notion that the Tokugawa shoguns had in effect intervened in the normal course of Japan's historical development and succeeded in refeudalizing the country in the early seventeenth century at a time when its immanent tendencies were modernizing. Thus pre-Restoration Japan came to be viewed not only as "feudal" but, in J. W. Hall's apt phrase, as a "feudal throwback."[2]

One can readily appreciate the consequences attendant upon so dichotomous a treatment of post-sixteenth-century Japanese history. For many the Restoration tended to become a watershed more formidable than the Rockies. What lay behind it was normally viewed as "feudal"; what lay on this side of it became either "modern" or a "feudal survival," that is, an undesirable remnant of earlier practices or attitudes slated for eventual discard. That view was probably reinforced by real ignorance about the actual circumstances of life and society in Tokugawa times. It is only within the past few years that professional research in that period has become at all fashionable, and it is still seriously neglected in favor of more glamorous subjects drawn from the Restoration and later periods. As a consequence the real beginnings of modernization in Japan have frequently been overlooked or dealt with as occurring in much later periods than they actually did.

The degree of literacy and of formal institutionalized education in pre-Restoration Japan provides a case in point. The educational preparation of at least sizeable segments of a population is a basic factor in the modernization of political cultures. Until recently it has been widely assumed that any really critical advances in this sphere waited upon the introduction of compulsory mass education in the 1870's. This is far from true. Consider, for example, the following statement by R. P. Dore in this connection:[3]

[2] John W. Hall, "Feudalism in Japan—a Reassessment," *Comparative Studies in Society and History*, Vol. V, no. 1 (Oct., 1962), p. 46.
[3] Ronald P. Dore, "The Legacy of Tokugawa Education," unpublished paper

THE CONTINUITY OF MODERNIZATION

The first thing to be stressed (with respect to education during the Tokugawa Period) is not simply the kind, but the sheer *amount* of formal education that went on. If the Tokugawa Period was a time of stagnation in some respects and of cyclical fluctuation in others, at least in the field of education there was a steady trend of growth. In Ieyasu's time a samurai who could express himself cogently on paper was a rarity, and total illiteracy was common. But gradually peace "civilized." Saikaku, by the end of the seventeenth century, already speaks of an illiterate samurai as sadly behind the times, and by the middle of the nineteenth century the situation was vastly different. Nearly every fief had its fief-endowed school and there were hundreds of private schools for samurai. Not only was every samurai capable of reading and writing his own language; most of them had undergone a sufficiently prolonged and disciplined intellectual training to be able to read some Chinese as well.

If public provision for formal education was limited to the samurai class, the lower orders were already managing to provide very well for themselves. In the towns a good proportion of the population could read and write Japanese. Parents bought such education for their children, voluntarily and with hard cash, from teachers who derived their total income from fees. In country districts paternally disposed richer villagers did a great deal to supplement the operations of an otherwise private enterprise system. At a very rough estimate it would seem that by the time of the Restoration forty to fifty per cent of all Japanese boys, and perhaps fifteen per cent of girls were getting some formal schooling outside their homes.

This suggests a spread of literacy greater than in most modern underdeveloped countries, and greater than in any European country at a comparable stage of economic development, with the possible exceptions of Prussia and Holland. It even compares favorably with some mid-nineteenth century European countries. As late as 1837 a British Select Committee found that in the major industrial towns only one child in four or five was ever getting to school, and it may have been more than a desire to jolt his fellow-countrymen which prompted one Frenchman to write in 1877 "that primary education in Japan has achieved a

---

prepared for the first seminar of the Conference on Modern Japan, January 1962, pp. 1-2.

level which should make us blush. . . . There is no village without its school, hardly a person who cannot read."

Dore concludes that despite the Confucian orientation of most of the pre-Restoration education "the attitudes to popular education, the sense of the contingency of social institutions on the human will, the training in abstract analysis and the application of evaluating principles to policy, the development of a respect for merit rather than status, the stimulation of personal ambition and the strengthening of a collectivist ideology . . . " represented important contributions to the modernization of Japan, and that all of these had undergone very considerable development long before the Restoration.

In a more specifically political sense the same could be said of the origins and development of another major element in the political and cultural modernizing process—the emergence of a professionally trained, rationally structured, and achievement-oriented bureaucracy. In this connection consider the following statement by Hall:[4]

> If the relationship of shogun to daimyo exhibited a balance between feudal and bureaucratic techniques, the trend towards centralized bureaucratic procedures was conspicuous within the *han* (fiefs). The key institution in this regard was the *kashindan*, or the assemblage of retainers, which comprised the staff of the shogun and the daimyo. In the early years of the Tokugawa Period, the relationship of housemen to daimyo was still in the main personal and voluntary. Though many of the retainers were stipended, the upper strata were individually enfeoffed. But later, with the nearly complete withdrawal of the samurai from the land to live in the castle headquarters towns of the daimyo, the members of the *kashindan* lost their individual identity. Grouped by rank into an army-type organization they were placed under appointed leaders and assigned freely to civil and military duties. Throughout the Tokugawa Period the tendency within the shogunal and daimyo administration was for the central authority to gain at the expense of the independent vassal. Within the *kashindan* the number of landed and high-salaried officers was instantly reduced while the number of dependent and stipended men increased. Eventually even the remaining land allotments were fictionalized. In certain instances daimyo without territory received rice incomes from the shogun's

[4] Hall, "Feudalism in Japan," pp. 47-48.

granary. In the *han,* supposedly enfeoffed retainers actually received only stipends, losing all powers of interference in the affairs of the villages which once comprised their fiefs. By the beginning of the eighteenth century nearly ninety per cent of the daimyo had forced their entire retinues to draw their subsistence from the domain granaries.

These changes were accompanied by important changes in the nature of the bond which tied samurai to daimyo. The pledge of loyalty, once so sacred as to be sealed in blood, became increasingly formalized and perfunctory. In many instances the personally sworn oath was dispensed with and required only when a retainer took an important post in the daimyo's service. Thus in most areas of Japan personal vassalage privately rewarded by enfeoffment was giving way to a system of military statuses which fed into a civil and military bureaucracy. Loyalty was becoming a principle rather than a private commitment. The daimyo became more a legal symbol than a personal despot.

In other sectors of Tokugawa society also authority was being exerted less as a personal right than through institutional or legal channels. The authority of the samurai class, asserted under the feudal system as a privately exercised prerogative over fiefs and cultivators, gave way to a more impersonal and public administrative system. For the farming class the condition of personal bondage gave way to the status of taxpaying tenant of the daimyo. Local administration was absorbed into the daimyo's bureaucracy and no longer subdivided among the daimyo's retainers. Corvée labor and personal indenture was increasingly replaced by paid labor and paid domestic service.

In the light of insights such as these into what was actually taking place throughout the Tokugawa period in Japan one begins to appreciate the long gradual process of institutional and attitudinal preparation for modernization which was well under way at least a century before the Restoration. Comparable preparations may readily be identified at the village level or in the economic sphere;[5] there is nothing unduly selective about these examples. Japanese society during the Tokugawa period may still be appropriately described by such terms as "centralized or nationalized feudalism," but if so, it was feudalism with an important difference. Japan in both institu-

---

[5] See, for example, Thomas C. Smith, *The Agrarian Origins of Modern Japan,* Stanford, Stanford University Press, 1959.

tional and attitudinal terms had come a long way from the hierarchic, personal, loyalty focused relationships and the intricate structure of fiefs and practically enserfed villagers which had characterized the polity in the sixteenth and early seventeenth centuries. On balance the feudal attributes of the society might still have predominated. But mingled with and gradually subverting these were a number of the most salient and potent elements and ideas of modern society. When evaluating the modernization of Japan it is useful to keep in mind this long complex history of covert preparation from which the society benefited.

The modernization of Japan still stands as a unique accomplishment in Asia, but its main roots are buried at least two hundred years deep in the country's social, political, and intellectual history. The florescence of national leadership during the early Meiji period combined with the international circumstances and opportunities of the times had a great deal to do with the amazing speed at which Japan modernized, but in a more fundamental sense Japanese society and the Japanese mind seem to have been prepared for the experience to a degree perhaps still unmatched in some important respects among many contemporary Asian societies. In this context the Japanese preparations for more modern forms of social, economic, and political organization may not be so completely different from their Western analogues as the apparent persistence of a feudal period until 1868 suggests.

Against this background let us next consider the content and development of Japanese political culture since late Tokugawa times. Our theme in general will be restricted to orientations towards the political system and will assume some knowledge of the cultural circumstances of the time.

PRE-RESTORATION POLITICAL CULTURE

Any treatment of pre-Restoration political culture must be based upon the pattern of class stratification prevailing at the time. Beneath a super-class of great military and court nobility—known respectively as daimyo and *kuge*—the great bulk of the population was distributed among four classes: samurai or warriors, peasants, artisans, and merchants. Interclass mobility, although initially proscribed, had become possible in exceptional cases, but in general class status was fixed and inherited in late Tokugawa times. Associated with these statuses were particular political roles. Politics in the high executive and decision-making sense of the term was in theory an exclusive perquisite of the shogun and daimyo, with some provision for limited and ritualized participation on the part of the emperor and *kuge*. Administration, in the bureaucratic sense, and defense of the realm and fief were the proper roles of the samurai, whereas the political roles of the three lower classes—peasants, artisans, and merchants—were restricted to the provision of loyalty, obedience, and support.

The above was of course an ideal dispensation but in a crude way it also represents the actual distribution of political roles and attitudes among Japan's 33 million people during the last years of the Tokugawa era. Political participation and in particular political activism was quite rigorously restricted to the upper classes. The most notable development in this sphere was probably the increasing politicalization of sizeable elements of the samurai class. During the two and one-half centuries of peace and stability which the Tokugawa shogunate brought to Japan this originally military class became progressively more bureaucratized and administrative in function. Their role and importance in the governance of both the nation and its 250-odd fiefs or *han* increased steadily, usually at the expense of the shogun and daimyo. It was discontented and ambitious elements of that class which organized and led the Restoration movement which finally overthrew the shogunate in 1867-1868 and which then provided the leadership of the new Meiji government. Thus it was the samurai, numbering in all somewhat over 2 million or about one-fifteenth of the population, who constituted the prime political class of pre-Restoration Japan.

Political involvement or activism among members of the lower classes was rare and apt to be covert where it did occur. We know very little about it in factual terms. Given the close involvement of a number of the larger merchant houses with the management, marketing, or exploitation of the resources or products of various fiefs, it would be surprising if they did not exercise some form of political influence. Again, there is reason for suspecting that the *Chokaisho* or Townsmen's Associations of Edo during the early nineteenth century had limited political functions. In general the evidence of contemporary literature, drama, humor, and satire would seem to indicate that the cities of Japan were producing at least informed, interested, and critical spectators of the political scene among the lower classes of townspeople well before the Restoration. Among the peasantry, except for occasional spontaneous and short-lived outbursts of anomic violence against local abuses, the political scene appears usually to have been quiet and routinized. Rural administration was carried out by headmen (*nanushi* or *shōya*) appointed from among the wealthier and more influential local peasant families and responsible to appropriate members of the daimyo's staff in the castle town. Opportunities for significant political involvement or action on the part of the three lower classes thus seem to have been few.

While these remarks on the stratified incidence of political involvements and action in pre-Restoration society do not directly tell the story of contemporary Japanese orientation toward their political system, they do provide a framework for its explication. Under circumstances of this sort it was quite natural that political culture too should vary with class status. Among the 90-odd per cent of the population residing in villages, the great bulk of whom were peasants, there seems to have been only a latent and marginal sense of their Japaneseness. Their primary identifications lay with family and community, and these were strong. Judging from the general stability and performance characteristics of the Tokugawa political system, some sense of loyalty and obligation also seems to have been felt towards their feudal lord and his government. In practice, however, one would judge that this was considerably tempered by the nature of their normal contacts with that government. They were largely confined to tax paying, some forms of corvée, and police and judicial matters, all of which were apt to be both costly and distressing to the average peasant. As a consequence, although government was something to be obeyed, it was also something to be avoided by the common man. There emerges from this a situation in which the mass political culture of late Tokugawa times seems to have been characterized by attitudes of habitual obedience and subjugation to duly constituted authority compounded with the sentiment that government is something that is done to the common people and largely at their expense by their socio-political superiors. The average man would be well advised therefore to find and keep to his proper social position in the neo-Confucian sense and leave politics to his betters. The result is what might be called a subject political culture.

So far as any widespread and positive popular identification with Japan as a nation is concerned, the evidence is also scanty, but there seems small reason to believe that it existed on a significant scale. The symbol of nationhood was the emperor, who since the ninth century had lived a cloistered and largely impotent life within the imperial estates at Kyoto. While his existence was generally known throughout the land, he had no meaningful relationship to the lives and aspirations of the average person. This was true in both a political and a religious sense. Imperial Shinto in the popular sense was a creation of the 1870's and 1880's and had no widespread impact before the Restoration. The actual ruler of Japan—insofar as the country had unified national government—was the shogun and his court. But, except for the inhabitants of the Tokugawa family fiefs proper, the shogun stood in no direct relationship to the people of Japan. It was the daimyo and the imperial court which were the objects of his governance, not the people in general. In consequence the shogun never became a symbol of national identity or unity, and his passing in 1868 occasioned remarkably little display of popular interest or concern. Even the advent of foreigners in some numbers and often in menacing contexts did not immediately give rise to nationalist sentiments among the people in general. On the occasion of the punitive international expedition against the Choshu forts in 1864, for example, contemporary accounts depict the local peasantry as standing about on the side lines watching with more or less impartial interest while the European landing forces destroyed the forts and routed their samurai defenders.

The urban lower classes seem to have been somewhat better informed and more interested in political affairs, but there is no very convincing evidence that this gave rise to participatory or activist political attitudes on their part or to any effective sense of identification with Japan as a nation or with either its imperial or shogunal symbols. Some sense of local patriotism or identification with their communities is to be seen, however, expecially in the case of the populace of such major centers as Kyoto, Osaka, and Edo.

One finds very different political orientations among the upper classes of pre-Restoration Japan and particularly among the samurai, their most numerous and important component. Theirs was originally a military class whose monopoly of military training and the right to bear arms underlay and justified their superior status. But two and a half centuries of peace left them in effect technologically unemployed. At the same time, however, the gradual transition of the shogunal and daimyo governments from military camps to rationalized bureaucracies created a need for large professional administrative staffs. The samurai met that need and became a skilled and professional administrative class. Bureaucratic forms of service to their lord became the most honorable, lucrative, and satisfying career open to them, and this involved them increasingly in the government and, inevitably, in the politics of the nation and its several hundred fiefs.

The political culture which resulted from such an experience was of course markedly different from that of the lower classes. A samurai's primary allegiance lay to his lord rather than to family or community. In the course of the Tokugawa period the quality of this loyalty seems to have undergone some rather interesting changes. Initially it was the highly personal fealty of a warrior to his captain, usually symbolized by a blood oath. Gradually, however, the personalized bond appears to have shifted in the direction of a more impersonal and institutionalized loyalty to the lord as a leadership symbol within a political system. Thus, although the primary political identifications of the samurai remained local in focus and feudal in aspect, they were at the same time developing along increasingly rational, impersonal, and institutionalized lines. There can be small doubt that those developments facilitated considerably the more ostentatious shifts in loyalty consequent upon the post-Restoration modernization of the Japanese political system.

The samurai were also quite aware of the national aspects of government and politics in Japan and of the power and operations of the shogunate. Most of them were literate and educated to some degree. Many of them spent considerable time in Edo, the shogun's capital, as members of their lords' retinues during their biennial periods of obligatory residence there. As a consequence they tended as a class to have some conception of Japan as a nation and to combine with it more or less favorable orientations toward the shogunate as a form of national government. Those views were apt to be further qualified by their attitudes toward the emperor and his rightful role in the Japanese political system. It was samurai scholarship which had been responsible during the eighteenth and nineteenth centuries for the revival of interest in historical studies of the nation's past which in turn led directly to questioning the legitimacy of the current position and power of the shogunate and to a movement advocating the restoration of political power to the emperor. These were highly political issues of national stature which were posed by samurai and which enlisted the sympathies or opposition of large sectors of their entire class.

Thus as one surveys our rather meager and imprecise stock of knowledge of Japanese political culture in late Tokugawa times, some of the major structural elements at least begin to emerge. One is impressed first by its dualism. It was made up of two major sets of political attitudes, one held by the lower classes in general—the peasants, artisans, and to a somewhat lesser extent the merchants—the other held by the upper classes consisting largely of the samurai. The lower-class attitudes were characterized by the primacy of their familistic and community loyalties and identifications plus some internalized sense of the legitimacy—or at least of the normality and inevitability—of the government and authority of their particular fief. The sense of legitimacy, however, seems to have been primarily local rather than national in form and passive and apolitical in its consequences. It seems to have engendered obedience but no effective sense of a right to or even a prospect of positive popular or personal participation in the political system. The upper-class set of political values was characterized by loyalties and identifications which, while oriented primarily toward their particular lord and the local system of rule he represented, also possessed secondary orientations toward Japan as a nation. It was these which were aroused from latency by the common challenge to national security presented by the advent of the West during the 1850's and the new opportunities for domestic political change and the improvement of individual and class positions it created. Upper-class political attitudes were highly activist. Government, administration, and politics were at the same time their business and their prerogative. It was their class function and justification to run the state, and in this sense they were well prepared by both practice and aspiration for positions of leadership and command. It might also be noted that the administrative training of the generation of Restoration leaders took place in *han* bureaucracies which, given the feudal and premodern aspect of the Tokugawa system, were surprisingly rational, professional, competitive, and achievement oriented.

The general picture of pre-Restoration Japanese political attitudes which emerges is therefore one of a predominantly subject political culture with an unusually large, energetic, capable, and increasingly dissatisfied administrative class interposed between an apolitical but obedient mass and the formal levels of top political leadership, i.e., the daimyo and shogun. While this is a grossly oversimplified characterization, it is probably accurate in a modal sense. When the Restoration brought the beginnings of massive political change to Japan, innovations proceeded primarily from the samurai sector of the society and were conditioned by that general sort of political cultural background.

Built into the background were certain notable and unusual advantages for the modernization process. There was a mass population which combined diligence, talent, a remarkable degree of literacy, and reliable habits of socio-political discipline and obedience with a lack of any developed propensity towards political action or involvement and with a deep-seated feeling that politics and government were the proper concern of the upper classes. There was a sizable literate and educated upper class trained to leadership roles in terms which contained significant modern admixtures and dissatisfied in part with their own positions vis-à-vis both their particular daimyo and the shogunate. Some rather widely known historical traditions of national unity were reinforced by the country's insularity and racial and linguistic homogeneity. There was a non-politically involved and authentic emperor who could be exploited and manipulated as a symbol and legitimizing agent for types of political change conceived and actuated by a segment of the samurai leadership. The international environment, through the dramatic threats posed or apprehended as a result of the resumption of intercourse with the Western powers, activated and catalyzed the entire system. It created a demonstrable and convincing need for systemwide innovation and change, injected fluidity into a hitherto long-frozen situation and, at the same time, impelled national unity in the face of the foreign threat and argued for the futility and danger of attempting to adjust their domestic problem by means of civil war. This concomitance of elements, unfortunately rare where developing polities are concerned, proved most fruitful for the Japanese.

POST-RESTORATION 1868-1962

Against the background of these remarks about pre-Restoration political culture in Japan we can now turn our attention to the types and patterns of departure and developments from that base which took place in the 1868-1962 period. Again, reliable and precise data on attitudinal changes are both scant and inconclusive, and the account will have to be brief and impressionistic.

In general there seem to have been at least two main and interrelated streams of differentiation and development working upon the above set of base conditions. The first relates to changes in popular political culture, the second to changes in elite political culture, including the emergence of new elites with particularistic cultures of their own. The last will be treated partially here and partially in a later section.

So far as the populace in general is concerned, one might begin by noting the variety of socializing experiences calculated to produce new roles and new political orientations to which they were cumulatively subject. Some such experiences had an explicit and positive impact on political culture, others, only an implicit or potentializing effect.

Among the latter we note the disruption of the traditional family and community systems attendant upon urbanization, diversification of economic activity, and modernization of the industrial system. Not all aspects of this process are readily documentable, but the general thesis is that the existing family system operating in relatively isolated agricultural communities furnished an environment favorable to the survival of the traditional social order and the complex of political attitudes associated with it; and that, as larger and larger segments of the population left family and village for the cities, they encountered new environments and needs which carried with them at least the potentiality of acquiring new political orientations. It seems safe to say that the urban environment and populace has been more receptive to and supportive of political innovation and modernization in Japan than has the rural environment and populace. The reasons have more to do with patterns of social organization and the attitudes engendered thereby than they do with politics. The traditional forms of social organization have been less rapidly and extensively affected by the forces of modernization in the countryside than in the city. Household and community solidarities are more vital forces in the villages, and they carry with them a set of political attitudes and behavior patterns which are conserving and traditional in tendency. The bulk of the urban populace on the other hand is composed of individuals and families who have migrated from the countryside within the last two generations. The fact of migration alone—particularly when individuals rather than family groups are involved—represents a partial but important rupture of the bonds which tie individuals to the traditional forms and attitudes.

Migration to a city does not in itself emancipate or modernize the individual migrant, but it often provides him with an environment in which changes in political as well as social attitudes and behavior are a more practicable and probable development.

Such changes are not necessarily a consequence of movement to the cities, however. It is in fact quite misleading to think of even the major metropolitan areas of Japan as inhabited solely or predominantly by the emancipated in this sense. Even since the war there are sizable segments of the urban population who live in the equivalent of so many "small societies" in the heart of Osaka or Tokyo, and who may be surprisingly untouched by their larger environment and its potentialities for socio-political emancipation or innovation. Despite this, however, it still seems that political development and change in modern Japan are considerably more apt to stem from the urban than from the rural sectors of the population.

If this is so, it becomes especially germane to a developmental account of Japanese political culture to inquire as to the rate at which people actually left the villages for cities in Japan. The available statistics on this question are neither as extensive in time nor precise in character as one might desire, but they do provide some useful insight into the magnitude and timing of the phenomenon. Table 1 indicates, for example, that the urban-dwelling proportion of the population of Japan proper increased from 9.5 to 63.5 per cent in the seventy-year period from 1890 to 1960. The rural reciprocals are 90.5 and 36.5 per cent, respectively.

Table 2 provides a supplementary insight couched in terms of the record of decline in the numbers of small villages and the reciprocal increase of larger centers of population between 1898 and 1955. Note that during that period the number of villages of less than 5,000 population decreased from 12,713 with an aggregate population of 30,518,513 to 1,438 with an aggregate population of 4,577,015, while the numbers and aggregate populations of most classes of cities over 50,000 show decidedly more than reciprocal increases. Incidentally the marked change in the number of smaller units between 1950 and 1955 is due to the partial enforcement during that period of the 1953 Law for the Amalgamation of Cities, Towns, and Villages. By 1960 the number of jurisdictions with populations of less than 5,000 had dropped to a mere 287[6] as a consequence of this law. In any event it is quite clear that the process of urbanization

[6] *Nihon kokusei zue*, Tokyo: Kokuseisha, 1961, p. 48.

alone emancipated, at least potentially, well over one-half of the Japanese population from the more traditional environment of village society and its socio-political concomitants during the seventy years after 1890.

TABLE 1: POPULATION IN URBAN AND RURAL AREAS, 1890-1960

	POPULATION[a]			PERCENTAGE	
Years	Total	Urban Areas[b]	Rural Areas[c]	Urban Areas	Rural Areas
1890	40,453,461	3,863,206	36,590,255	9.5	90.5
1893	41,388,313	4,197,877	37,190,436	10.1	89.9
1898	43,760,815	5,429,009	38,331,806	12.4	87.6
1903	46,732,138	6,809,976	39,922,162	14.5	85.5
1908	49,588,798	8,299,744	41,289,054	16.7	83.3
1913	53,362,682	8,999,264	44,363,418	16.8	83.2
1918	56,667,711	10,842,857	45,824,854	19.1	80.9
1920	55,391,481	10,020,038	45,371,443	18.1	81.9
1925	59,179,200	12,821,625	46,357,575	21.7	78.3
1930	63,872,496	15,363,646	48,508,850	24.1	75.9
1935	68,661,654	22,581,794	46,079,860	32.9	67.1
1940	72,539,729	27,494,237	45,045,492	37.9	62.1
1945	71,998,104	20,022,333	51,975,771	27.8	72.2
1950	83,199,637	31,203,191	51,996,446	37.5	62.5
1955	89,275,529	50,288,026	38,987,503	56.3	43.7
1960	93,418,501	59,333,171	34,084,057	63.5	36.5

[a] Refers to the population of Japan proper, excluding that of Korea, Formosa, the Kuriles and all other overseas territories.

[b] Refers to *Shi* (cities), and *Ku* (wards) as used in the Ordinance for the Establishment of Cities (*shi*), 1888.

[c] All areas other than *shi* and *ku*.

Sources: *Asahi nenkan* (Asahi Year Book), 1961, Tōkyō, Asahi Shimbunsha, 1961; Kōseishō Kenkyujo Jinkō Minzokubu (Ministry of Welfare Research Institute, Population and Nationalities Department), *Jinkō tōkei sōran* (Handbook of Population Statistics), Tōkyō, Kōseishō, 1943; Naikaku Tōkeikyoku (Cabinet Statistical Bureau). *Kokusei chosa hokoku* (Census Reports), 1920, 1925, 1930, 1935, 1940, 1947, 1950, 1955, 1960; *Nihon teikoku tōkeinenkan* (Yearbook of Japanese Statistics), Vols. 11-39.

Another and less readily documentable facet of this implicitly modernizing or potentializing experience in Japan lies in the history of changes taking place within the family and village society. As the modernizing process developed, communications and transportation systems expanded and improved in the countryside as well as in the cities; village children as well as city ones received more and more systematic modern-style education; the legal and actual position of fathers, mothers, and children within the family system changed;

TABLE 2: CITIES, TOWNS, AND VILLAGES, BY SIZE OF POPULATION, SHOWING NUMBER IN EACH SIZE-CLASS, AND AGGREGATE POPULATION IN EACH CLASS, SELECTED YEARS, 1898-1955

Population per Unit (thousands)

Year	Under 5	5-10	10-50	50-100	100-500	500-1,000	Over 1,000	Total
1898	12,713	1,081	213	12	6	1	1	14,027
	30,518,513	6,868,294	3,772,843	772,481	1,236,554	821,235	1,440,121	45,403,041
1903	11,705	1,343	250	16	6	1	1	13,322
	29,903,660	8,589,995	4,502,459	1,077,058	1,654,964	995,945	1,818,655	48,542,736
1908	10,430	1,654	344	19	8	0	2	12,457
	28,107,040	10,736,232	6,009,181	1,352,565	2,124,109	0	3,412,726	51,741,853
1913	10,035	1,852	432	26	8	1	2	12,356
	27,802,064	12,105,244	7,430,708	1,855,550	1,982,375	509,380	3,445,949	55,131,270
1918	9,793	1,912	510	32	12	2	2	12,263
	27,070,684	12,474,669	8,967,606	2,281,879	2,040,334	1,263,077	3,803,022	58,087,277
1925	9,676	1,734	538	51	15	4	2	12,020
	26,408,316	11,475,200	9,667,153	3,444,916	2,538,133	2,092,733	4,110,371	59,736,822
1930	9,306	1,878	584	65	26	4	2	11,865
	25,685,510	12,472,034	10,408,758	4,402,415	776,990	3,279,886	7,424,412	64,450,005
1935	8,893	1,953	612	54	28	2	4	11,546
	24,564,088	12,938,344	10,548,637	3,685,020	4,872,979	1,616,430	11,028,660	69,254,148
1940	8,516	1,888	628	55	39	2	4	11,132
	23,472,463	12,526,032	11,457,374	3,792,373	6,907,208	1,935,325	12,448,954	72,539,729
1945	6,808	2,713	903	76	31	3		10,536
	21,184,960	18,274,682	16,126,175	5,397,034	5,044,569	2,089,088	3,879,969	71,998,104[a]
1950	6,669	2,618	972	91	58	2	4	10,414
	20,671,394	17,622,373	17,272,800	6,306,855	10,135,895	1,716,624	9,473,696	83,199,637
1955	1,438	1,435	1,700	142	91	2	5	4,813
	4,577,015	10,526,488	33,515,574	9,511,893	16,419,671	1,523,617	13,200,971	89,275,529

[a] Includes 1,627 persons not distributed to any size group.

Source: Kōseishō Kenkyujo Jinkō Minzokubu (Ministry of Welfare Research Institute, Population and Nationalities Department), *Jinkō tōkei sōran* (Handbook of Population Statistics), Tōkyō, Kōseishō, 1943. *Nihon teikoku tōkeinenkan* (Yearbook of Japanese Statistics), Vols. 19-59. Sōrifu tōkeikyoku (Office of the Prime Minister, Bureau of Statistics). *Kokusei chōsa hōkoku* (1955 Population Census of Japan), Vol. 1, *Jinkō Sōsū* (Total Population), Tōkyō, Ōkurashō Insatsu Kyoku, 1956.

the village economy became assimilated to the national and even international economies as commuting to urban jobs became first possible and then common, and the regulatory and exhortative arms of government came to penetrate village society to a degree previously impossible and unnecessary. For all their conservatism and relative traditionalism, family and village life and attitudes underwent changes on a variety of fronts, including the political, but the pace of those changes was slower than that in the cities and its quality more piecemeal. The result was, however, a significant modernization of rural as well as urban socio-political institutions and attitudes.

Education. To turn now to the more explicit and positive agencies of political socialization along developmental or modernizing lines, we might look first at the educational system. Considerations of both space and data preclude any but the briefest survey of the impact of the public school system on Japanese political culture. It is crystal clear, however, that the government from the beginning considered political socialization to be a prime function of mass public education. "In the administration of all schools," wrote Mori Arinori, Minister of Education, in 1885, "it must be kept in mind that what is to be done is not for the sake of the pupils but for the sake of the country."[7] The state-centered tone of this official concern with the inculcation of proper political attitudes into Japanese youth through the public school curriculum is perhaps even better conveyed by the Emperor Meiji's famous Rescript on Education of 1890, which set the tenor of the entire Japanese educational system until 1945:

"Our Imperial Ancestors have founded our Empire on a basis broad and everlasting.... Our subjects ever united in loyalty and filial piety have from generation to generation illustrated the beauty thereof. This is the glory of the fundamental character of our Empire, and herein also lies the source of our education. Ye, our subjects, be filial to your parents, affectionate to your brothers and sisters; as husbands and wives be harmonious, as friends true ... pursue learning and cultivate arts, and thereby develop intellectual faculties and perfect moral powers; furthermore, advance public good and promote common interests; always respect the Constitution and observe the laws; should emergency arise, offer yourselves courageously to the State; and thus guard and maintain the prosperity of our Imperial Throne coeval with Heaven and Earth...."

[7] Quoted in Herbert Passin's chapter on education and political development in Japan, *Education and Political Culture*, ed. James S. Coleman, Princeton University Press, 1965, pp. 272-312.

There was obviously no dearth of concern in high places over the indoctrinational effect of the school system on youthful political attitudes, and it was continuous from the outset to 1945. Of course the actual consequences for Japanese political culture do not correlate precisely with the degree of the official concern or even with the rather heroic attempts made to implement it. But given, against the Tokugawa background described earlier, the rapid rise and strong persistence of mass sentiments of patriotism and nationalism, the widespread willingness to sacrifice personal to national advantage, and the numerous other signs of really general popular identification with the nation and its goals so amply demonstrated by the entire course of Japanese history from 1868 to 1945, it seems probable that the school system made significant contributions to this result. The post-1945 emergence of a more democratic Japan has not altered this type of official concern for the school system as an active agency of political indoctrination. Only the techniques and values have changed. These are now more diffuse, low-keyed, and democratic.

For present purposes, then, it is of some interest to establish some of the cruder and more basic facts about the impact of this school system on the youth of Japan during the years since its establishment. In a popular sense the most important elements in the system were the primary and secondary schools. They alone had the opportunity of affecting the political orientations of any sizeable proportion of the school-age population. Table 3 sets forth the basic facts on enrollment at these levels for the period 1873-1957. Perhaps the single most revealing columns in this table are those for "percentages of eligible school-age children enrolled." Note that male enrollment was almost 58 per cent as early as 1878 and was practically total by 1903. The enrollment of girl children also mounted rapidly after 1898 and was practically total by 1908. These are impressive figures by almost any national standard of comparison.

Having established the extent of exposure of the youth group to the program of political socialization provided by the primary and secondary schools, it is germane to inquire as to the nature of the curriculum to which they were exposed and the part played in it by political indoctrination. Courses subsumed under the label "morals" played a prominent role in both primary and secondary public school curricula from at least 1873 until their abolition by the Allied Occupation in 1945. They had from 1881 onward a very high systematic and explicit loading of political indoctrination. The original morals courses of 1871 were innocuous affairs using a direct translation of a French Second Empire text of 1867.[8] But after the revised education regulations of 1881, and especially after a further revision in 1891, the emphasis underwent a marked change. In R. P. Dore's words:[9]

"... the Imperial Institution [became] the fount and origin of all morality. In the Rescript [on Education of 1890] all the virtues it enumerates—loyalty and filial piety (which are one and indivisible inasmuch as the Emperor is father to his people), brotherly affection, marital harmony, charity, diligence, public spirit, respect for the laws, willingness to die for the Emperor in battle—are identified as part of the Way . . . bequeathed by our Imperial Ancestors, of which the Emperor is the guardian and the embodiment. Thus all the private virtues became subsumed under the general virtue of patriotic loyalty, and the Rescript became until 1945 the basic sacred text of

TABLE 3: NUMBER OF STUDENTS, PERCENTAGE OF ENROLLMENT, AND ATTENDANCE IN PRIMARY AND SECONDARY SCHOOLS, 1873-1957

NUMBER OF PRIMARY SCHOOL PUPILS

	Ordinary Primary School			Higher Primary School		
Date	Totals	Male	Female	Totals	Male	Female
1873	1,326,190	1,008,011	318,179			
1878	2,273,224	1,671,276	601,748			
1883	3,055,844	2,065,631	990,212	181,664	150,727	30,937
1888	2,748,868	1,914,710	834,158	179,000	146,643	32,357
1893	2,985,602	1,980,249	1,005,353	351,958	285,776	66,182
1898	3,360,915	2,039,041	1,321,874	701,503	543,236	158,167
1903	4,032,885	2,082,455	1,950,430	1,051,214	750,593	300,621
1908	5,363,942	2,896,906	2,467,036	632,197	434,635	197,562
1913	6,466,398	3,369,011	3,097,387	629,357	433,642	195,715
1918	7,411,779	3,816,549	3,595,230	725,568	492,344	233,224
1923	8,012,483	4,093,214	3,919,269	1,124,677	727,326	397,351
1928	8,353,478	4,237,360	4,116,118	1,327,254	828,873	498,381
1933	9,479,977	4,799,208	4,680,769	1,555,301	927,922	627,379
1938	10,116,925	5,123,553	4,993,372	1,861,758	1,076,799	784,959
1943	10,623,557	5,379,699	5,203,858	2,224,669	1,194,115	1,030,524
1948	10,774,652	5,459,296	5,315,356			
1953	11,225,469	5,695,181	5,530,288			
1957	12,956,285	6,609,351	6,346,934			

(continued)

[8] See R. P. Dore's chapter on education in Japan in *Political Modernization in Japan and Turkey*, eds. Robert E. Ward and Dankwart A. Rustow, Princeton, Princeton University Press, 1964, p. 190.
[9] *Ibid.*, pp. 36, 190-91.

TABLE 3 (continued)

NUMBER OF SECONDARY SCHOOL STUDENTS (OLD SYSTEM)

Date	Middle School Totals	Ordinary Middle School	Higher Middle School	Vocational School Totals	Male	Female	Girls' High School
1873	1,767[a]	1,767					
1878	29,018	29,018		1,210	1,202	8	
1883	14,763	14,763		743	741	2	450
1888	14,380	10,441	3,939	2,363	2,363		2,599
1893	24,046	19,563	4,483	2,810	2,810		3,020
				11,392[b]	10,900	492	
1898	66,296	61,632	4,664	6,975	5,573	1,402	8,589
				28,384	28,197	187	
1903	103,074	98,000	5,074	60,828	46,690	14,138	25,719
				38,530	38,240	290	
1908	120,473	115,038	5,435	192,321	153,926	38,405	46,582
				46,524	46,120	414	68,367[c]
1913	138,355	131,946	6,409	384,983	318,095	66,888	14,920
				65,179	64,580	599	94,525
1918	165,766	158,974	6,792	812,935	674,319	138,616	24,417
				129,304	128,090	1,214	216,624
1923	260,473	246,739	13,734	1,024,774	739,051	287,723	22,777
				228,193	191,411	36,782	331,757
1928	363,341	343,709	19,632	1,181,907	808,016	373,891	27,512
				276,981	228,222	48,759	347,180
1933	347,561	327,261	20,300	1,271,530	855,255	416,275	24,627
				428,434	323,650	104,784	448,818
1938	397,515	380,498	17,017	2,307,022	1,482,435	724,587	30,607
				794,217	619,380	174,837	
1943	633,750	607,114	26,636	3,063,638	2,118,080	945,558	756,955
1948	29,459	798	28,661	4,890	1,649	3,241	3,413
1953							
1957							

(continued)

the new religion of patriotism, memorized by all school children, the subject of endless commentaries in school ethics courses, its ceremonial incantation on all national holidays a feature of school rituals conducted in an atmosphere of impressive solemnity."

From 1883 until 1945, morals courses were usually allotted several hours of curriculum time in all grades. Furthermore, one must also recognize the degree to which the Japanese language and literature courses and those on history and geography which filled much of the rest of the curriculum time, were also utilized as media of political

TABLE 3 (concluded)

	NUMBER OF SECONDARY SCHOOL STUDENTS (NEW SYSTEM)						PERCENTAGE OF[d] ELIGIBLE SCHOOL-AGE CHILDREN ENROLLED		PERCENTAGE OF CLASS ATTENDANCE	
	Lower Secondary School			Upper Secondary School					Ordinary Primary School	Higher[e] Primary School
Date	Total	Male	Female	Total	Male	Female	Male	Female		
1873							39.90	15.14		
1878							57.59	23.51		
1883							67.16	33.64		
1888							63.00	30.21		
1893							74.76	40.59		
1898							82.42	53.73	80.17	88.38
1903							96.59	89.58	86.60	92.94
1908							98.73	96.86	92.45	94.53
1913							98.74	97.54	92.78	95.40
1918							99.12	98.58	93.43	94.74
1923							99.32	99.15	95.37	95.63
1928							99.48	99.42	96.44	96.07
1933							99.59	99.58	96.81	96.45
1938							99.60	99.63	96.88	96.19
1943							99.75	99.77		
1948	4,792,504	2,468,130	2,324,374	1,203,963	744,419	459,544	99.62	99.67	96.20	93.68
1953	5,187,378	2,628,989	2,558,389	2,528,000	1,500,412	1,027,588	99.75		96.8	94.5
1957	5,681,190	2,876,785	2,804,405	2,897,646	1,621,715	1,275,931	99.78[f]		97.6	96.7[f]

[a] The figures for 1873-1888 include girl students.
[b] The lower rank of figures refers to supplementary vocational schools and includes youth schools after 1935.
[c] The lower rank of figures refers to girl students enrolled in practical course girls' high schools (i.e. home economic schools).
[d] "School Age" covers the 6-14 year-old age groups.
[e] After 1948 higher elementary schools became the new lower secondary schools.

[f] These figures are for 1956.

Sources: Mombushō (Ministry of Education), Mombushō nempō (Annual report of the Ministry of Education), Tōkyō, Mombushō, 1874 Annual. Mombushō (Ministry of Education), Gakusei Hachijūnenshi (History of eighty years of the educational system), Tōkyō Ōkurashō Insatsukyoku, 1954.

indoctrination.[10] In particular was this true of the graded series of national language readers used in uniform format throughout the nation during the first six years of primary instruction from 1903 on. The impact of all this systematic political indoctrination was further heightened by a steadily increasing degree of centralized national control over the school system and its curriculum as such, the training and indoctrination of teachers, and the writing, selection, and approval of text books.

Given so wholehearted a dedication of the educational resources of the state over a sixty-four year period to the task of inculcating the nation's youth with a particular form of political culture, it is important to note the qualified nature of the results. Judged from the standpoint of most pre-1945 Japanese governments, the effort was on balance successful. Looked at in terms of political results, the bulk of the citizenry either genuinely acquired political attitudes of the sort intended or at least adopted attitudes which minimized serious domestic discord and dysfunctional consequences for the regime for most of the period between 1872 and 1945. But distributed on the flanks of the majority response were sizable groups of dissentients of the right and left. The former felt that the official definition of political orthodoxy was too moderate, compromising, and wishy-washy. The variants were many, but in general the right-wing elements agreed that the times called for a more nativist, austere, dedicated, and collectivist form of political culture than the current regime considered practicable or perhaps desirable. On the other flank stood an equally heterogeneous group representing a variety of individualistic, democratic, liberal, socialist, or Communist forms of dissentient opinion. Both flanks represented failures or miscarriages of the official program of political socialization through the school system. Both flanks had sizable numbers of adherents and, in terms of political

[10] Data on this subject can be found in: Baron Kikuchi Daigaku, *Japanese Education* (lectures delivered at the University of London), London, John Murray, 1909; Kindai Nihon Kyōiku Seido Shiryō (Society for the Editing of Historical Data Concerning the Modern Japanese Educational System), *Kindai Nihon Kyōiku Seido Shiryō* (Historical data concerning the modern Japanese educational system), Tokyo, Dai Nihon Yūbenkai Kodansha, 1956——, Vol. II; Mombushō (Ministry of Education) *Gakusei Hachijunenshi* (History of Eighty Years of the Educational System), Tokyo, Ōkurashō Insatsukyoku, 1954; Mombushō (Ministry of Education). A General Survey of Education in Japan, Tokyo, The Herald of Asia Press, 1926, 1930, 1935, 1937; Tōkyō Gyōsei Gakkai (Tokyo Administrative Science Council), *Yōryō taishō genko kokumin gakkō rei oyobi kankei hōki soran* (Annotated Conspectus of the Current Primary School Ordinance and the Related Statutes), Tokyo, Genbunsha, 1942.

results, both flanks included ranges of dissentient political attitudes which have subsequently become dominant for limited periods at least—the right-wing element from 1938 to 1945, and the more liberal deviants since 1945. These longer-term consequences are moderately encouraging to the democratically inclined. As Herbert Passin put it, " . . . perhaps the life of thought has its own momentum and logic. Once you start to educate people, it is very likely that some of them are going to reach their own conclusions about the nature of life and society."[11]

Suffrage. The gradual expansion of the suffrage has provided still another potent and explicit agency of political socialization in post-Restoration Japan. Before 1889 there had been no provision for even limited popular participation in the government of Japan, and popular attitudes in general, though changing, were still congruent with such a situation. The introduction in that year of a very restricted suffrage for male citizens of twenty-five or older who paid 15 yen or more in direct national taxes thus marked a major new departure in Japanese practice. Table 4 indicates the manner in which the initially limited suffrage expanded.[12]

TABLE 4: EXPANSION OF SUFFRAGE IN JAPAN, 1890-1960

Election Year	Size of Electorate (in thousands)	Population (in thousands)	Electorate as Per Cent of Population
1890	450.9	39,902	1.13
1924	3,274.6	58,350	5.61
1928	12,405.1	62,070	19.98
1946	36,878.4	75,800	48.65
1960	56,554.5	93,540	60.46

The electorate had thus risen from 1.13 per cent of the population to 60.46 per cent in 1960. The principal steps involved were, first, the successive lowering of the tax requirements for male citizens and, thereafter, granting of universal manhood suffrage in 1925 and introduction of universal adult suffrage and lowering of the voting age to twenty in 1945. Each of these steps marks the induction of additional segments of the adult population into at least limited formal participation in the political decision-making process and each

[11] Passin, *op.cit.*, p. 311.
[12] A. W. Burks, *The Government of Japan*, New York, Crowell, 1961, p. 94.

thus carries with it an attitudinal dimension of new political rights and expectations on the voters' part. It is not claimed that these cohorts of new voters in Japan were in general any more sophisticated or less manipulatable than were their analogues elsewhere, but from the beginning significant segments of them showed a surprising degree of independence vis-à-vis the government in power. Furthermore the granting of the suffrage provided the political basis for legalization and expansion of political parties, while successive expansions of the franchise, by inducting new socio-economic strata of the population into political action, kept changing and complicating the terms of political competition. For example, the adoption of universal manhood suffrage in 1925, by giving the vote to urban and rural workers for the first time, made proletarian parties a practicable political proposition in Japan. Thus an entire new range of political alternatives was opened to the voter.

The grant of suffrage and its gradual expansion would seem therefore to have had several consequences for mass political orientations in Japan. Over a period of time it gradually encouraged significant segments of a hitherto non-participant population to view themselves as having a more positive and participant role in the political process. It also slowly familiarized them with the concept and practice of political parties as aggregators and representatives of popular political desires. In this sense the very concepts of open and legal political opposition and minority rights and a bargaining polity are partially linked to the suffrage. The same is true of the concept of government as a responsible agent of the electorate. It would be too much to claim that any of these basic democratic precepts gained general acceptance and secure status in Japan during the period under consideration, but certainly all have been accepted to some degree by important segments of the populace and, as practical political propositions, all have been linked to and supported by the suffrage as an agency of political socialization.

It is also noteworthy that in the Japanese case universal adult suffrage was not granted until 1946. Fifty-seven years intervened between the initial grant of a very restricted franchise and the advent of universal suffrage. This gave to the government, for good or ill, a certain freedom of maneuver which might otherwise have been difficult to achieve. Japan's experience in this respect is thus more comparable to that of the West than to the newer states of Asia and Africa.

War and Occupation. Both the years of war (1937-1945) and years of Occupation (1945-1952) provide further socializing experiences of profound importance to an understanding of the development of mass political culture in Japan. While Japan has never been a truly Fascist or totalitarian state in the European sense of these terms, she did achieve new levels of political, social, and economic mobilization during the war years. In general the people seem to have accepted the war as legitimate and to have supported their government's efforts to wage it successfully. The war thus brought mass sentiments of patriotism and shared sacrifice and suffering to a new height in Japan. Against this background the popular reactions to defeat were complex. Relief that it was finally over mingled with anger and frustration over the futility of the nation's sacrifices. The search for a scapegoat was general, and the prewar military leadership filled the bill nicely. Added to this one finds a massive revulsion against and fear of any further involvement in international warfare and a new measure of skepticism about the wisdom, competence, and integrity of governments in general.

Into this scene came the Allied (really American) Occupation of Japan, usually called SCAP after the initials of General MacArthur's headquarters. Its most ambitious undertaking was nothing less than the democratization of Japan. The strategy and tactics of this endeavor are far too complex for description here, but it should be noted that the attempt was not confined to the reform of Japanese political institutions. SCAP aimed at the reconstitution along democratic lines of Japanese political attitudes and behavior patterns as well as of the nation's statute books. In general this was to be achieved by vesting major segments of the population with new and valuable political, economic, and social rights with the expectation that they would subsequently support the over-all structure of democratic reform in their desire to preserve intact their own particular gains. Thus women were enfranchised and given new legal and social status; labor was encouraged to form unions and to bargain collectively; tenant farmers were converted into freeholders; youth was given expanded educational opportunities and the voting age was reduced to twenty; and localities were given new rights of autonomy and home rule vis-à-vis the national government and its previously omnipotent ministries.

Without claiming anything like complete success for these endeavors of the Occupation, it is still undeniable that they succeeded in precipitating an unprecedented political ferment in Japan. The elite structure was drastically altered, entire new socio-political strata of the population were pushed upon the political stage, old values and institutions were superseded, and for a time no one quite knew when or in what form the new Japan would emerge and settle down. The process of settling down is of course still going on, and a description of its consequences for mass political culture in Japan would impinge upon the subject matter of the next section. Suffice it to say here that the Occupation and its aftermath have had an important effect on Japanese political orientations.

The foregoing paragraphs on urbanization, changes within village society, the educational system, the suffrage, and the years of war and Occupation constitute a very partial résumé of some of the more salient socializing agencies and experiences working toward the development of new sets of political attitudes and expectations among the Japanese people in general. Other agencies and experiences such as the conscription system, industrialization, or the media of communications have perforce been neglected. For an account of how far the actions of such agencies have moved mass political culture in Japan from its base point in late Tokugawa times the reader is referred to the next section. Before turning to a description of contemporary Japanese political culture, however, it is necessary to say a word about the changes in elite culture which were taking place during that period.

Changes in Elite Culture. The Tokugawa political elite, it will be recalled, consisted of the shogun and daimyo at the level of formal top leadership assisted by a large and hierarchically organized class of samurai whose administrative role steadily bulked larger and more important in the governance of both Japan and its several hundred fiefs. The Restoration itself brought about the first major reconstitution of that situation. The shogun was eliminated from the scene, the fiefs liquidated, and the daimyo largely pensioned off, the samurai as a class were abolished, and gradually a new unified national government headed by a small group of former samurai drawn principally from the Satsuma and Choshu houses, plus a few court nobles, took over the highest political offices. There was always factionalism within this new political elite group, but the exigencies of the Restoration itself and subsequently the urgency of both domestic and international threats to the national security and their own position sufficed to hold the original group together until the Korean crisis of 1873, at which time there emerged a smaller and more compact leadership group often identified as the "Meiji Oligarchy" which, despite obvious personal rivalries, managed to preserve a species of effective working unity until the late 1890's. Thereafter there set in a process of elite differentiation which in time produced quite a constellation of leadership groups. A professional military element split off quite early, while another group concentrated on control of the civil bureaucracy. A group centered upon the administrative apparatus of the Imperial Court and the person of the emperor also emerged. Some hold the view that the House of Peers provided a focus for the activities of still another leadership group, while quite obviously others sought power through the instrumentality of political parties based in the House of Representatives. Later still, about the time of World War I, big business began to acquire an increasingly important voice in political decision making. Since none of these six groups of political elites was in fact solidary, a very significant and steadily increasing degree of pluralism and competition was injected into the Japanese leadership situation from a quite early point.

Where the over-all history of the modernization of Japan is concerned, it is probably the professional civil bureaucracy, among all the elite groups, which has made the outstanding contributions and provided the largest and most continuous share of the country's political leadership. It is germane to note therefore that, although the civil bureaucrats too are subject to pronounced factionalism, its effects are moderated and regulated by a process of educational preparation for their careers which is shared by the great majority of higher bureaucrats.

Tokyo Imperial University was established in 1877 largely as a means of providing within Japan the types of higher education and skills so desperately needed by a modernizing society. By the 1890's it was the principal source of recruitment for the members of Japan's higher civil service. The situation developed to the point that in prewar years it was widely estimated that approximately 80 per cent of Japan's higher bureaucracy—section chiefs, *kacho*, and above—were Tokyo University graduates, predominantly from the Faculty of Law. Despite the Occupation's vigorous attempts to change the situation, circumstances are not much different today. A recent survey in 1954 found that 75 per cent of the current higher bureaucracy fell in the same category. Throughout most of its modern history, therefore, the most important single element among Japan's political leadership groups has shared a common higher educational experience, a single old-school tie, and a tendency to conceive of government and their own role in it in the highly legalistic and formalistic terms usually taught by Tokyo University's Law School. This is an important unifying factor.

But it is the specifically political orientations of these elite groups which are of present concern. Any complete analysis of them is beyond the scope of this paper, but it is possible to identify a few of their shared characteristics which seem of particular importance where the development of Japanese political culture is concerned.

First, all significant political elite groups—this excludes a small number of Communists and left-wing Socialists who were politically unimportant—were, until 1945 anyway, strongly Japanese and nationalistic in their identifications. Not only were their attitudes generally homogeneous at this level but also, after 1877, all accepted the results of the Restoration and later the general form and system of government established by the Constitution of 1889. There was in this sense a fairly general acceptance of the rules of the political game.

Second, given the prevalence of factionalism within even the highest circles and the Japanese preference for collective forms of leadership, there was never any real probability of introducing truly autocratic or totalitarian rule in Japan. Bargaining and compromise within the circles of the elect has steadily been the style and the preference of Japan's political elite.

Third, given this disposition and consequent upon the demonstrations from 1890 to 1898 by the political parties of their ability seriously to compromise the efficiency of government operations, the ruling oligarchy was open-minded enough to incorporate political parties into the bargaining nexus which underlay political decision making in Japan. They were not unalterably opposed to limited forms of popular participation in the political process, and in practice the shifting terms of political competition forced it upon them in larger and larger measures down to the outbreak of the China Incident.

Finally and perhaps most important of all, the political leadership of Japan in modern times has always possessed a sense of national service and obligation to a degree most unusual among developing societies. It was particularly marked during the critical early years, but it is steadily present. It by no means precludes corruption, nepotism, or other political abuses, but these have usually been kept within manageable bounds. The sense of civic duty and responsibility has sometimes focussed on the emperor, sometimes on the nation, but it has been steadily operative.

With this much attention then to the emergence of modern political culture and to the nature of some of the socializing agencies which affected it, let us turn next to a description of contemporary political culture in Japan which may be contrasted with that already sketched for pre-Restoration political culture.

Contemporary Political Culture in Japan

Despite the superior quantity and quality of the data available it is far more difficult to analyze and explain the political culture of contemporary Japan than that of late Tokugawa times. Impressive strains of continuity are to be found, but in general it is the degree of differentiation and the increased complexity of the developmental process which strikes the observer. This is particularly true since the defeat of 1945 and the American Occupation. Before this the political orientations of the nation were notably more solidary and more congruent with their Tokugawa and Meiji antecedents. But defeat and Occupation and the over-all course of liberalization and democratization in postwar Japan have had a markedly disruptive effect upon the political attitudes of the Japanese people. In important degree Japan is today a nation in search of new and more satisfying political orientations. This greatly complicates the problem of distinguishing clearly between the stable and the evanescent, the emergent and the obsolescent elements of contemporary political culture. An attempt will be made in the following paragraphs, however, to sketch at least some of the more salient features of current Japanese political culture. This will be organized into sections devoted to orientations toward the nation, the political process, political output, toward the self as political actor, and toward other political actors.[13]

ORIENTATION TOWARD THE NATION

One of the most operationally crucial aspects of any political culture is the manner and degree of popular identification with the nation. In the Japanese case, how uniformly, how positively, and how reliably do the people identify themselves as Japanese in a national political sense? We have seen that in Tokugawa times the norm was

[13] This schema is derived from S. Verba and G. A. Almond, "Political Process, Political Structure and Political Culture," an unpublished memorandum for the SSRC, Committee on Comparative Politics, July 1962, pp. 5-12.

a sort of passive and limited identification with a locality and the daimyo who ruled it rather than with Japan itself.

Japan's combination of insularity and racial and linguistic homogeneity makes under modern circumstances for a high degree of ingroup feeling and national unity vis-à-vis the non-Japanese world. Particularly since the loss of her empire the country has had natural frontiers sharply demarcated from foreign territory—except the Russian frontiers—by sizable bodies of water. Historically these have given to the Japanese people a degree of national security unprecedented among major states. They have also until recently sharply limited any opportunity for massive contact or interaction with foreign peoples, enhanced and supported the popular sense of the uniqueness of being Japanese, and have encouraged a sort of narcissistic absorption with their own culture, problems, and viewpoints. This last attribute has persisted throughout all of the country's recent periods of intense acculturative experience and has invariably reasserted itself. These centripetal tendencies are reinforced by practically complete linguistic uniformity, qualified only by a few dialect problems, and by a degree of racial homogeneity unmatched among major states. Japan is 99.3 per cent pure in terms of racial composition, having fewer than 700,000 identifiable aliens among her populace. Immigration by non-Japanese peoples has never been a problem of serious proportion in the past two thousand years.

Factors such as these, particularly when historically reinforced, first, by real and fancied threats to the national security and, second, by large-scale imperialist aspirations of their own, have combined to make of the Japanese during most of their recent history a markedly nationalistic and unified people. They have had few problems of identity that have affected the solidary character of their nationalism. In a somewhat different sense, however, they have as a people experienced cycles characterized by massive feelings of inferiority towards the more developed peoples and cultures of the West. But these cycles have normally been followed and resolved by an equally pronounced swing towards the exaltation of their own culture, accomplishments, and ideals.

Some rather strange things have happened to the quality of this nationalism since 1945, however. The martial and aggressive qualities of prewar Japan appear to have been replaced by a spirit of pacificism, withdrawal, and absorption with commercial and peaceful pursuits.

Some would argue from this that nationalism is dead or dying in Japan. Such a judgement seems dubious.

Japanese nationalism in the sense of a strong in-group feeling on the part of the average person and the extension of his loyalty to Japan rather than to any competing object of political identification is still vital. What has changed is its focus and mode of expression. Neither Japan's capacities nor inclinations will at present support a posture of aggressiveness or imperialism. Japan is weak, disarmed, pacifist in inclination, and desperately anxious to avoid any commitments that might again involve her in war. Under the circumstances her nationalism is channeled along defensive rather than aggressive lines; it manifests itself in support of the independence, territorial integrity, and military disengagement of the country and, interestingly enough, is often mobilized by left-wing groups of ostensibly internationalist persuasion rather than by the right-wing ultranationalist of yore. The occasions are apt to be demonstrations against atomic bomb testing, the security treaty with the United States, or the maintenance of American Air Force and Navy bases on Japanese territory. Thus the focus and media are different, defensive rather than aggressive, but the underlying force is still a deep and widespread feeling of popular identification with Japan as a nation.

One can also tell something about the quality and extent of national identification among the Japanese people by examining the symbols of national unity. The contemporary Japanese inherit a myth of national unity at least twelve-hundred years old. Despite the fact that much of the history of that period was marked by localism, civil strife, and the emergence of powerful clans and nobles with high degrees of independence within their own territories, the tradition and forms of national unity and of a Japanese state have always been maintained. The symbol—some would claim the embodiment—of this tradition has been the imperial institution which, although its fortunes and authority have varied widely, has existed continuously and has continuously asserted both its own legitimacy and the essential unity of the state. The Restoration brought about a great and purposive enhancement of the potency of the imperial institution as a symbol of nationhood and a means of evoking mass loyalty and support. Japan's defeat in World War II and the political developments which have flowed from it have somewhat diminished the efficacy of the imperial institution as a legitimizing and unifying force, but it would be a mistake to assume that it is either obsolete or impotent as a symbol of the nation's unity. Among the nation's political parties only the Communist Party has ever openly advocated the abolition of the throne. In a series of national polls conducted between 1946 and 1948, for example, positive support for the imperial system never fell below 87 per cent of the population and normally exceeded 90 per cent.[14]

Although the quotient of mass identification with the nation and its symbols remains very high in postwar Japan, there has been a decrease in its intensity and an increase in the volume of principled dissent. In literary and professional intellectual circles in particular one hears a good deal of discussion of the obsolescence of the emperor as a suitable symbol of modern Japanese nationhood and of the wisdom of converting to a republican system. Associated with and heavily overlapping this are the allegiances to competing and extra-Japanese political systems and groups held by at least some of the more dedicated members of the Japanese Communist and Socialist Parties. These dissentient views are of some political importance in present-day Japan, but it seems improbable that they are now shared in any positive way by much more than 10 per cent of the population. However, since significant segments of college educated youth, as well as left-wing elements, are to be found among the dissenters, it is a figure which may very well increase.

Perhaps more serious than this really small incidence of positive support for a republican rather than imperial form of government or for some vaguely internationalist and pacifist form of socialism rather than nationalism is the postwar weakening in the intensity of popular identifications with the nation and its imperial symbol. In the past these were important sources of the spirit of sacrifice and the sense of discipline and the common good which explain so much of Japan's remarkable success. There is a widespread feeling in Japan that such attributes are now regarded as old-fashioned and illogical. So long as peace and prosperity continue, their demise—if this premise be accepted—may have no important national consequences. But if Japan should be subjected to more difficult circumstances for any prolonged period, one wonders about the strength and resilience of popular political identifications. In a sense the Japanese people may to an indeterminable degree have outgrown or outmoded their prewar sense of

[14] Allan B. Cole and Naomichi Nakanishi, eds., *Japanese Opinion Polls with Socio-political Significance, 1947-1957*, Fletcher School and Roper Public Opinion Poll Research Center, n.d., pp. 431-442.

identification with the nation and its symbols, but to the extent that this is true, they have certainly not succeeded in developing any very satisfactory substitutes therefor.

ORIENTATION TOWARD THE POLITICAL PROCESS

A second important aspect of a nation's political culture is orientation toward the political process. It is primarily the structure rather than the content or output of the decision-making system which is involved. Are people satisfied with the manner in which decisions are made within their political system or do they want to make organizational or structural changes of some sort?

This is a complex question when asked about present-day Japan. The structural characteristics of their political decision-making system have been drastically altered in quite recent times as a result of their defeat. Furthermore the nature of the changes was largely determined by foreigners—specifically by Americans on the staff of SCAP, who even devised and wrote most of the present Japanese constitution. Despite the adaptations which have subsequently been made there is bound to be considerable dissatisfaction with a political structure of this sort—if only on the grounds of its alien authorship.

One might begin a discussion of this issue in Japan on a level somewhat higher than the structural. How do the Japanese view their government from the standpoint of its legitimacy? Does its authority over their lives and actions seem to them to be based upon some right and proper title; does it produce in them the feeling that its commands ought to be obeyed? If one excepts a relatively small group of dedicated Marxists and an even smaller element of extreme right-wingers, the general answer to this question is certainly, "Yes." In most regards the legitimacy quotient of government in general is high in Japan—even though that of particular governments may not be. As a people—either historically or at present—the Japanese do not tend to hold contractual or conditional views of the relationship between government and subject. Government is accepted as part of the fundamental order of things and therefore as a phenomenon as natural as the family system, after which indeed the older orders of government in Japan were quite explicitly patterned.

At a lower level, however, there is an appreciable amount of dissatisfaction with the structure of the political system. The sources and grounds for this differ considerably, as does the intensity with which the dissentient views are held. Practically speaking, the issue reduces largely to the problem of constitutional revision. Should the constitution of 1947, the so-called MacArthur Constitution, be changed, and if so, in what ways and under whose auspices?

The particular revisions involved—which include legislative structure and representation, the position of the Emperor, rearmament, civil rights, and judicial review—are too complicated to go into at this time, but certain general aspects of the problem do relate to political culture and should be mentioned. In the first place, one should note that, despite the highly bitter and controversial nature of the struggle, very little of the agitation for major structural change is revolutionary in character. Apart from the Communist Party and some of the more extreme-left Socialists few Japanese consider a revolutionary solution to this problem as either practicable or desirable. The actual contest therefore is between reformers and advocates of the constitutional status quo. This terminology is somewhat misleading, however, since it is the right-wing or conservative parties which are in general supporting revision and the left-wing or reformist parties which advocate the status quo. The explanation is simple. The latter fear that any changes made under conservative auspices would be retrogressive in nature and politically dangerous to left-wing interests. The resultant struggle, however, takes place for the most part at the parliamentary and party level and, with a few notable exceptions, within the bounds of legal and parliamentary process.

It is difficult to determine the extent to which this bitter struggle at the party level represents an equivalent commitment of public opinion in general over the question of basic structural changes. A series of national public opinion polls on this matter between 1952 and 1957 usually indicated that more than 40 per cent of the population favored some form of constitutional revision while around 30 per cent opposed it.[15] Given the absence of just what types of change were favored or opposed, however, it is difficult to attach much importance to these responses.

Beyond this question of orientations towards the substance or structure of the political process in Japan, it should also be noted that there exist variant views as to an appropriate style for the political process. The question of decision making is a case in point. In the United States we espouse an adversary system of decision making which accepts and values opposition and proceeds by the public posing, sponsorship, and debate of alternative solutions to a problem to

[15] *ibid.*, p. 447.

reach an ultimate decision by open voting. Such a system provides a constructive place for minority and oppositional elements but entails for them the obligation of abiding by decisions legally arrived at and confining their subsequent opposition to legally approved channels. The traditional Japanese system of decision making is different. It operates by consensus, that is, by unanimous agreements. A problem is posed and is then discussed by the group concerned with a minimum of open commitment to positions by participants. Eventually a sense of generally acceptable compromise emerges from the discussion; this is formulated by a senior member of the group and is then adopted by unanimous consent. In such a system no one is openly defeated or humiliated, "face" is preserved, at least the semblance of unanimity achieved, and group harmony is thus maximized. Also the explicit recognition of minorities is avoided. Reciprocally, if the system is to operate along traditionally approved lines, it becomes an obligation of the majority faction not to ignore or ride roughshod over the opinions of the minority elements which do in fact exist. If they do so, the minority can then raise the cry of tyranny of the majority and solicit and obtain public sympathy on this ground.

It is interesting to see the extent to which this traditional preference for a consensual system of decision making still commands understanding and support in Japan. The Western system of adversary procedure is of course known and to a degree used in formal political circumstances, but it is apt to be preceded or at least influenced by consensual considerations. The present Socialist Party, as a more or less permanent minority, has frequently made use of this fact as a tactical weapon of some potency. They evidently feel that their claims of being victimized by a tyranny of the majority bring them sympathy and support from the voters.

One can also find other current Japanese examples of orientation towards the political process in terms of style rather than structure. Their preference for collective rather than individual decisions is one case in point. The quality of leadership in both an ideal and a practical sense seems to be somewhat different in Japan from that in the United States. The Japanese seem to be more comfortable with and to value more highly decisions reached by some sort of committee process than they do the fiats of individual leaders. This may only amount to a more advanced degree of "organizationmanship" than we have yet achieved, but there is a notable difference in the degree of emphasis placed on individual leaders and on leadership and initiative in Japanese society and in our own. Traditional Japanese feelings about the role of violence in politics might provide another case in point, but their current viability is more dubious. Violence and use of force to achieve political ends have long and not dishonorable histories in Japan. And the tendency of the people has often been not to denounce such recourses as ill advised or evil but rather to look to the announced motives and subsequent conduct of the users of violence as a key to judgement. If their motives and they individually were held to be sincere and, above all, if they showed a disposition to prove it and simultaneously to atone by some form of self-punishment—classically by *seppuku* or *hara-kiri*—then the initial act of violence was apt to be viewed with sympathy if not outright approval. Something of this sentiment undoubtedly survives in some quarters in present-day Japan, but it is difficult to say how general it may be.

ORIENTATION TOWARD POLITICAL OUTPUT

An increasingly instrumental view of the political system is perhaps one of the main hallmarks of a modern society. Is government viewed as a producer or guarantor of the good life? In Tokugawa times we have seen that it was not. Government then was a species of legitimized exploitation of the masses on behalf of a limited ruling class. It took much, gave little beyond the maintenance of peace and order, and the people expected little more of it. That situation has changed drastically. Most political observers would grant that a very large share of the present government's hold on political power in Japan is attributable to the popular credit and support it has acquired as the self-proclaimed creator and sustainer of a boom economy. Perhaps the strongest plank in its platform is that which commits it to a doubling of Japan's 1960 national income within a ten-year period. The people now look to government as a normal means of producing or ensuring a vast variety of goods and services ranging from peace and order through transportation and communications to a broad range of welfare and social security measures, as well as serving as a planning and regulatory mechanism for the maintenance of general and increasing economic prosperity throughout the society. The popular image of government has thus been in substantial part inverted. Whereas earlier they viewed government as an essentially exploitative operation at their cost and thus as something to be shunned, now they tend to view it as productive in their behalf and thus as something to be placated, influenced, or controlled. The Japanese view of their political system has in this sense become output oriented.

This change has occurred gradually and has perhaps progressed most rapidly in the periods of ferment and innovation which followed World Wars I and II, particularly the latter one. Concomitantly with this basic shift in outlook upon politics there has occurred an enormous proliferation of political elites and of interest groups in general. Each of these elite and interest groups is concerned in some degree with the output of the political system and is seeking to influence or control the characteristics of this output in its sphere of activity. The result is an enormous broadening of the total sphere of political action and a tremendous increase in and complication of the number of actors involved and their patterns of interaction. This makes it practically as difficult as in the case of the United States to describe with any accuracy and adequacy the various orientations toward and degrees of satisfaction with political output to be encountered in contemporary Japan. A few grossly oversimplified but possibly useful characterizations may be ventured upon however.

If one looks first to the political outputs of the system in terms of the distribution of power, it is not hard to distinguish crudely among satisfied and dissatisfied groups at the activist and elite level. In general the satisfied comprise the Liberal-Democratic Party and their allies, the dissatisfied, the opposition composed in party terms primarily of the Socialist, Democratic-Socialist, and Communist Parties. A more discerning analysis would have to introduce, however, the issue of levels of satisfaction and dissatisfaction and in particular what specific level of dissatisfaction is apt to be critical in inducing action dysfunctional to the existing party units of organization and the present distribution of power. If one does this, it soon emerges that in varying degrees all existing Japanese parties are coalitions of contending factions largely held in present constellation by shrewd but far from unalterable calculations of competitive advantage. The party in power, for example, consists of some eight major factions all competing energetically for the premiership, cabinet posts, and other spoils. The two Socialist Parties and even the Communists are similarly factionalized, and the majority of the factions involved in all parties feel themselves seriously deprived of their proper rights and opportunities. There is obviously a significant degree of instability and a good deal of dissatisfaction, both open and suppressed, in a situation of this sort.

In practice, however, it has proved surprisingly stable over an impressive period of time. The important issue would seem to be therefore not so much the extent of dissatisfaction with political output among the party leaderships but rather how much more would have to be added to the present situation to induce disruptive action. In the absence of alternatives viewed as feasible and preferable an established and working system of power distribution can apparently tolerate a great deal of dissatisfaction both from its political opponents and from its own ranks.

When one looks beyond the output of power distribution by a political system to its more tangible products such as regulations, goods, and services, the question of satisfaction and dissatisfaction with existing outputs becomes even more complicated. In general in a complex, modern, output-oriented society practically everyone is more or less seriously dissatisfied with some aspects of government output and performance. Few if any get all they want or feel they deserve. Again, then, the practical question becomes what is the critical mass of dissatisfaction both in particular cases and for the political system as a whole.

In Japan some groups are critically dissatisfied with the present outputs of the political system, a few to the point of harboring revolutionary aspirations. Fortunately such groups are small in both numbers and influence and confined largely to the more dedicated Communists and left-wing Socialists. Organized labor as a group tends to be critical of government output on a variety of scores. Besides the general political hostility which organized labor, as the mainstay of both Socialist Parties, feels towards the non-socialist government in power, they also complain constantly on the score of alleged government hostility to and harassment of their organization and activities. It is difficult to say to what extent their official policies and views in these respects command the approval and support of their members but, this issue aside, the unions and their federations at least claim to represent a substantial part of the population. In 1960 about 7,662,000 persons—some 34.7 per cent of the industrial labor force—belonged to labor unions. Of this total 3,745,000 (48.9 per cent) were members of Sohyo, a staunchly left-wing and strongly anti-governmental federation of unions, and another 924,000 (12.1 per cent) belonged to Zenro, the second major national federation, which is more moderate in both its brand of socialism and its opposition to the government. Some 61 per cent of unionized labor in Japan was in

1960 thus formally committed to open political opposition to the government in power and to a number of its policies.

Another sizable group dissatisfied with government output in Japan are the intellectuals. Here the antipathy is primarily ideological and based upon the socialist proclivities of large parts of the university educated sector of the population. Associated with the intellectuals in this attitude is an unknown proportion of the youth of Japan. It is hard to say what proportion of the approximately 26 million persons in the fifteen- to thirty-year-old sector of the population is opposed to the government on ideological grounds. Most of the rather unsatisfactory available evidence relates specifically to college youth in major cities. There seems to be little doubt that they are predominantly socialist and anti-governmental in their political attitudes. But the extent to which rural youth or the less-educated strata of urban youth share these views is far more conjectural. Moreover the extent to which youth as a group with increasing age and responsibilities abandons these stands for more conservative and satisfied allegiances and attitudes is uncertain. A good deal of political recidivism of this sort is encountered. As a consequence one can only say in rather vague terms that a very sizable proportion of Japanese youth are ideologically alienated from their government and its political output, and that it is uncertain as to how stable a phenomenon this is.

A pronounced and serious degree of dissatisfaction with government outputs in the areas of credit, banking, industrial, and export policy is also to be found in the small and middle industrial sector of the economy. Of an industrial labor force of approximately 22 million in 1957, almost 13 million (59 per cent) worked for establishments having less than thirty employees, while another 3,600,000 worked for establishments having between 30 and 100 employees. It is primarily the members of this small and medium sector of the industrial economy who feel, with considerable justice, that they have not shared proportionately in the nation's recent prosperity. They blame this upon government neglect of and discrimination against their interests.

These groups—organized labor, intellectuals, youth, and the small and medium industrial sector—represent the major sources of fairly continuous and wide-ranging dissatisfaction with the political output of the government. They receive support from the professions, salariat, and women on many particular issues, but it would be wrong to consider these latter groups as dissatisfied in anything approximating an across-the-board sense. Despite numerous particular and often quite serious complaints the other major sectors of the population such as those in agriculture, industry, and commerce tend to be on balance satisfied and supportive of the present political outputs. Of course the unprecedented prosperity of the Japanese economy since 1955 has had a great deal to do with this. It is hard to predict what effect a serious depression would have on the situation.

ORIENTATION TOWARD THE SELF AS POLITICAL ACTOR

One of the most interesting dimensions of political culture is the attitudes of the citizenry toward their own roles as both participants in and subjects of their political system. Which of these roles receives the greater emphasis? What degree of competence, confidence, and comfort do the people feel in their roles as participants in the political decision-making process? How fair and responsible do they consider their treatment as subjects? We have seen that the average Japanese in Tokugawa times probably lacked almost completely any sense of right or competence to participate in the political decision-making process of his day. There is also evidence indicating widespread, if sporadic, sentiments that government treatment of its subjects was not infrequently both unfair and irresponsible. Our question relates essentially therefore to the extent of the changes one finds in such attitudes in present-day Japan.

Several factors have combined to bring about significant changes in Japanese orientations toward the self as political actor. Prominent among those have been the above-described expansion of the suffrage, the new systems of government introduced first by the constitution of 1889 and subsequently by that of 1947, the democratic experience rather broadly shared in the 1920's and early 1930's, and the even more massive democratic indoctrination since 1945. In general the changes have been in the direction of a more positive conception of the self as a political participant. But the rate of change has varied from segment to segment of the population, and the stage of development achieved in general is still considerably below that encountered in the United States.

Formal political participation through voting has always been high in Japan. It amounted, for example, to 70 per cent of the qualified electorate in the general election of 1960—incidentally, the lowest turnout since 1947—and averaged above 90 per cent in recent town and village assembly elections. But these figures do not correlate well with any index of meaningful political participation. In the villages in particular, where the electoral turnout is regularly highest, voting is often more a function of social organization and pressures for group solidarity than it is of positive orientation towards the self as a political actor. The same is true of sizable sections of the urban electorate as well. One concludes that there is a good deal of political apathy combined with negative or low estimations of the role of self as political actor to be found in both rural and urban Japan.

This impression is reinforced by the attitudes displayed by large sectors of the citizenry in their dealings with the bureaucracy. The tradition of bureaucrats as public servants has not yet become firmly established in Japan. There is small indication in many contexts that the citizen approaches government with the expectation of receiving courteous, prompt, and efficient service as a matter of right. In fact his attitude is apt to be compounded more of elements of servility, resignation, and supplication. The feeling that bureaucrats are superior beings with favors to be bestowed—which, incidentally, is to a very appreciable extent shared by the bureaucracy itself—is an aspect of the traditional political culture which dies hard in Japan.

Traits like these indicate a considerable amount of continuity in the Japanese attitude towards the self as political actor. But they represent but one side of the coin. There is also a most respectable history in modern Japan of political dissent, principled and otherwise, which argues for the existence on a significant scale of courageous and far more positive attitudes towards the political competence of individuals and groups. The Freedom and Popular Rights Movement (*Jiyuminken Undo*), for example, followed hard on the heels of the Restoration. The early political parties were established in the cause of more extensive—if less than universal—participation in the political decision-making process. The early history of Japanese socialism is also closely associated with the cause of popular, civil, and human rights against governmental rights. All of these and many more, while enlisting the active participation of only small minorities of the total population, enjoyed sizable popular support. And all of them were based explicitly or implicitly on the proposition that dissentient minority groups did possess the right and some degree of capacity to meliorate the stands of a hostile government.

In more recent times the development of associational interest groups argues the same sort of conclusion. Interest groups are founded upon the assumption that individuals in association possess the capacity, if not the right, to influence the decisions and actions of government or public. Their premises are essentially positive with respect to the proposition that individuals can participate effectively in the political process. Interest groups in this sense have developed rather slowly and intermittently in Japan and often—in their early stages at least—in circumstances which rendered them more a means of facilitating governmental action than an instrument for bringing external influence to bear thereon. The history of modern interest groups in Japan may be considered as beginning with the establishment of the Tokyo Chamber of Commerce in 1878 and slowly proliferating from this point. The World War of 1914-1918 and its aftermath brought the first major expansion in the numbers and sphere of action of such groups, but it was really only with Japan's defeat in 1945 and the Occupation that they may be said to have achieved a major role in either the economy or the polity. Today, with a few qualifications, the interest group scene in Japan is coming to bear a close resemblance to that in most developed Western democracies. Such groups have not yet penetrated Japanese rural society to the degree they have urban society, but even there they are making rapid progress. The cities of Japan, however, show patterns of incidence, activity, and success by interest groups markedly comparable to those encountered in American cities, and most of these groups have interests which impinge in some degree upon politics. They are thus mobilized and active on the political as well as the economic front. Their record in this sector constitutes one of the most convincing testimonials to the development by the Japanese citizenry of more positive attitudes towards the feasibility and efficacy of popular participation in the political process.

In a sense interest group activities may provide a more meaningful indicator of the present and potential development of a sense of the citizen's competence vis-à-vis the political system in Japan than do the somewhat denigrating remarks made earlier about electoral attitudes. They provide a medium of expression and action which is culturally comfortable for the Japanese, whose preference has normally been for group rather than individual forms of decision making and action. Interest groups satisfy this preference. At the same time their internal organization and their pattern of external contacts and activities are well adjusted to another deepseated Japanese attitude towards politics in general, i.e., that it is a highly personalized process. Programmatic or issue-oriented loyalties and associations are substantially less important in all aspects of Japanese politics than they are in most American contexts. Personal relationships are correspondingly more important. This type of political system lends itself readily to a very high degree of covert, back-stage intrigue and maneuver, which in turn accords well with the pattern of organization and action of most Japanese interest groups. Thus once the rather loose boundaries separating administration and the professional bureaucracy from politics and the society in general were massively infiltrated—or perhaps redrawn—after 1945 the way was prepared for a major involvement of interest groups in politics. This constitutes impressive testimony of the widespread development of new attitudes by citizens towards politics and their individual roles therein. A whole new dimension of informal participation and competence has been opened.

Paralleling developments of this sort has been the more explicit emergence of participant norms among particular sectors of the population. Especially among large groups of the more educated and highly skilled portion of the population the teachings of democracy about the rights of individuals versus government and the concept of government as a servant of the people have been taken with the utmost seriousness. Such groups seem actually to believe in the proposition that individuals should be able to influence political decisions. But in many cases one also gets the impression that they are pessimistic about their ability to do so in fact. Since their political beliefs and causes are apt to be socialist in quality and the government has long been dominated by so-called conservatives, this may well be an accurate perception on their part. But it does give rise to a certain lack of fit between their sense of political rights on the one hand and of political competence on the other.

ORIENTATIONS TOWARD OTHER POLITICAL ACTORS

Political cultures also differ with respect to the attitudes of the average citizen towards the political roles of his fellow citizens and his leaders. Is there a fair amount of mutual trust and confidence present in the system, or is it a dog-eat-dog sort of situation? Again, in what terms is the political game played—low key and moderate, or highly aggressive? In Tokugawa times the question in part did not arise for the average citizen since he was really not an actor in the political process. His attitudes towards his leadership have been described as more or less resigned and acceptive. The situation in present-day Japan is far more complex.

One must start by distinguishing the politically active and involved from the passive and non-involved. The latter are the more numerous. The degree of trust and confidence which they impute to their fellow citizens as political actors is at the outset a function of their view of the political process. If, as is doubtless so for many, they do not consider individual citizens to play a role of any political significance, the question of trust scarcely arises. For the remainder the issue would seem to be normally latent. Politics and politicians in the abstract are not usually regarded as being particularly trustworthy. However, under postwar circumstances this distrust has seldom reached a critical level. A goodly amount of corruption and conniving is more or less taken for granted, but it is balanced by a feeling that the government is ultimately responsible for the well-being of the country and people and that things cannot be allowed to get too far out of hand.

Among the more politically involved and active elements of the population two factors in particular affect the way in which individuals feel about their fellow actors on the political scene. The first is the role of personalism in Japanese politics. Programmatic and policy loyalties and associations figure increasingly in the Japanese political system, but personal loyalties and associations still carry far more weight on balance. This tends to be true even among the ostensibly ideological groups and parties of the extreme left. One advances one's own career and achieves political goals primarily in terms of seniority, ability, and a web of carefully established and assiduously nourished personal connections. In this sense it is still the practice in Japanese politics for the recruit to join *someone* rather than *something*, to select a protector and leader rather than a cause. The bond thus established is apt to be close, durable, and usually dependable. Connections of this sort are not formed lightly in Japanese politics since the mutual obligations entailed are apt to run considerably beyond the range of the working professional relationship. As a consequence a rather high level of loyalty and mutual trust is supposed to—and, one would judge, usually does—characterize this sort of personal political association.

A second factor which has a great deal to do with attitudes toward one's fellow political actors is factionalism. Factions are the basic unit of organization or aggregation for the personally oriented political relationships described above. They pervade all aspects of Japanese politics. Any cross-section of the political system—such as urban versus rural, generational, or right versus left—must in an organized political sense be discounted for its factional characteristics. Factionalism in this sense refers to an informal and relatively small sub-system of political organization based ultimately on personal or parochial loyalties or values and operating within a larger, ostensibly unified political system. The effective ambit of the loyalties and obligations involved is apt to run considerably beyond the specific political goals of the group. Such types of organization have long been characteristic within the Japanese imperial court, nobility, civil and military bureaucracy, political parties, and regional and local elites. They are of course familiar in many societies, including the most politically modern. As societies modernize, however, there seems to be a tendency for this particular type of political organization to be not supplanted but diluted by the more limited, programmatic, and functionally defined allegiances represented by modern interest groups and political parties. In this sense it might be legitimate to regard factions as constituting in part at least a diffusely focused traditional analogue of interest groups.

In postwar Japanese political culture one can quite clearly detect the erosive effect on factionalism of the newer forms of political association, but the process has not proceeded as far as it has in some Western states. Perhaps it never will. In any event, any refined understanding of important decisions and developments within the Japanese political system depends in significant part on one's knowledge of the interplay of factions. These may in recent times have partly shifted their basis of association toward the programmatic or functionally specific end of the spectrum, but even within so rigorously ideological a group as the Japanese Communist or Socialist Parties personally based and widely ranging loyalties still play a remarkably important role. Until recently politics was normally conceived of in Japan as a struggle cast in essentially personal and household terms. It is hard to say with much precision, but it is probable that the concept of limited programmatic allegiances as a basis for political association and action did not really gain an appreciable foothold on a national scale in Japan until after World War I and did not come to compete on anything like equal terms until after World War II. Factions thus continue to be a natural and comfortable form of political organization for the Japanese, and they penetrate and complicate almost all other forms of political association and action.

Factional organization carries with it of course connotations of both loyalty and hostility, loyalty among the in-group, hostility towards out-groups. The former is prized and honored among Japanese politicians. A man's reputation for loyalty and sincerity to and trust in his factional associates is an important element of his professional "face." In fact loyalty to the faction is usually a considerably stronger impulsion than loyalty to some vaguer concept of public trust. Hostility toward out-groups is also a normal factor in Japanese politics. Competition is keen and increasing at the intra-party factional as well as the inter-party level. With this inevitably goes a certain amount of suspicion and distrust of one's extra-factional rivals.

In practice, however, this is somewhat mitigated by several factors operating at the level of personal rather than factional relationships. Party and factional loyalties do not preclude close friendships and associations outside of or across party and factional lines. One of the most conspicuous examples of this in Japanese politics is the continuing effectiveness of friendships formed at the high-school and college levels. These are prior to factional allegiances and are often maintained despite the fact that one friend may subsequently become identified with an extreme-left socialist group and the other with a conservative clique in the Ministry of Finance. Indeed, such personal connections have proved to be of great practical value for many Socialists who, being members of a more or less permanent minority party, lack almost completely any official access to sources of information or patronage. Inherited family connections and obligations or, to a lesser degree, shared local or regional antecedents can have a similar effect.

It is important to note that despite such mitigating factors at the personal level the over-all character of political competition in Japan is aggressive and bitter. The principal engagement is between the Liberal-Democratic and the Socialist Parties. With the exception of one brief nine-month period in 1947-48 when a Socialist prime minister led a shaky coalition government, political power has rested solely with the present Liberal-Democrats or their earlier variants. In quite sincere and strong terms Liberal-Democratic leaders regard their socialist opposite numbers as an almost unmitigated—and un-Japanese—form of national calamity. The Socialist leadership, which has often inclined toward a highly ideological and doctrinaire brand of politics, reciprocates in kind and publicly views the Liberal-Democratic leaders as a species of crypto-Fascists busily engaged in selling the country to big business and the United States. The resultant debate is couched in highly acrimonious terms and is only saved from becoming more serious by the continued inability of the Socialists to poll much more than one-third of the vote. The situation could become very serious if, say, under circumstances of prolonged economic depression the left-wing Socialists were to score an electoral victory and set about the formation of a government. It is bad enough as it is, given the propensity of some Socialists to compensate for their status as a semi-permanent parliamentary minority by ignoring the rules of democratic and legal procedure and instigating disorders on the floor of the Diet and rioting in the streets of Tokyo over issues which they believe to be of fundamental importance to the party and the country.

Yet in what on the face of it seems to be an extremely bitter and hostile situation lines of communication have not completely broken down nor are political relations quite as polarized as they often appear. To some degree the battle lines are bridged by the types of personal connections described above. Moreover the very multiplicity and overlapping quality of the socio-political groups and circles in which a politically active Japanese is involved adds a further dimension of melioration to the situation. Perhaps most important of all, however, are the terms of political competition in postwar Japan. Electoral support is a major dimension in the political struggle, and what a given party or faction can do successfully is to a marginal but important extent contingent upon its effect at the polls. The electorate as a whole may under normal circumstances be relatively apathetic and uninvolved in the ideological and power struggles which are so crucial to the activists, but their support at the polls can no longer be taken for granted by any particular political party and by fewer and fewer individual politicians. As a consequence it has not usually been good politics to press the terms of the political struggle among the activists too far. Extremism in action seems to alarm the electorate, and they have on several occasions given edge to this alarm at the polls. As a practical matter, therefore, the extent of the mutual hostility and distrust which seems to characterize the political struggle in Japan can easily be exaggerated. There are countervailing and meliorating forms of some strength and promise at work below the surface.

Political Culture and Political Development

We have seen in the preceding two sections something of the elements of cultural continuity and change which are involved in roughly the last century of Japan's political history. During that period the dominant modes of the Japanese political system have shifted from the centralized feudalism of late Tokugawa times through several stages of authoritarianism to the democratic order of postwar days. Japanese political culture in the sense of attitudinal orientations toward the political system has also undergone notable changes during the same period. At the popular level, for example, it has moved from a predominantly locally focused, non-participant and resigned view of the political system to a nationally focused, much more participatory, instrumental, and output-oriented attitude. A considerable psychological distance separates these two sets of political orientations although it is mitigated in practice by certain continuities of view which persist throughout the period. Given parallel variations of this sort in political structure and political attitudes, the question naturally arises: are these variations causally related, and if so, in what manner?

This is a most difficult and complicated question which unfortunately can never be sufficiently isolated from the total web of historical causation in which both structural and attitudinal changes are enmeshed to permit of more than speculative response. However, the Japanese experience does suggest a few such speculations which may be of some larger significance.

In the first place, when confronted with the problem of moving their political system from a feudal to a more modern basis of organization Japan's political leaders clearly attached more importance to changing some aspects of the contemporary political culture rather than others. At the level of fairly self-conscious attempts at the manipulation of mass political attitudes they gave first priority to the creation of an effective sense of general popular identification with Japan as a nation. The systematic building of the imperial institution as the embodiment of national unity, the establishment of Imperial Shinto, and the content and emphasis of the new system of compulsory public education all testify to this. Given the international and domestic threats to both the national security and the position of the Meiji leadership, there was obvious wisdom in that emphasis. In this instance then one gets the impression that at the outset, where this important attitudinal dimension of national identification is concerned, the stream of causation ran primarily from the government to the desired attitude, that in effect—and with due deference to the favorable circumstances of the environment—the

Meiji leadership more or less created modern Japanese nationalism.

It is of equal interest to note the negative dimension of governmental policy in early Meiji times toward the altering of the popular political culture inherited from the Tokugawa period. If on the one hand the government officials were anxious to create a general sense of national identification among the Japanese people, on the other they were equally reluctant to encourage the development of more participatory attitudes toward the political process. Although knowledge of parliamentary institutions and of the theory of representative government gained wide currency in Japan during the 1870's and 1880's, and the government was continuously under pressure to broaden its base and institute some form of participatory and representative politics, the general policy of early governments was to give as little as possible as slowly as possible in terms of institutions which would make effective even limited popular participation in the political decision-making process. Thus the policy of government was to prevent or at least retard changes in the non-participatory popular political attitudes of Tokugawa times. In this instance, however, it was far less successful than in its attempts to create nationalist attitudes. Conceptions of their right to participate in politics developed gradually but steadily among more and more sectors of the population, political movements espousing such participation grew in numbers and strength, and the government was obliged to make a series of concessions along these lines. So in this case it seems that the stream of causality flowed primarily from political culture, that is, from attitudes, to political structure.

The causal relationship between political structure and political culture is therefore not unidirectional. It can come from either source or from both at the same time. Changes both planned and unplanned—by the formal political structure at least—thus occur in political culture.

Second, the Japanese experience demonstrates that political culture can have a life and logic of its own even in circumstances where a practically all-powerful government is making strenuous efforts to determine and control the channels along which it should flow. The consequences of the Japanese attempt to indoctrinate youth with "correct" political ideas through the school system and other types of suasion provide a splendid example of this. Even with a practical monopoly of formal opportunities for political indoctrination it was at the level of the better-educated youth that the government perhaps failed most notably to impose its own political ideology.

One might carry this a bit further and note also that the long ascendancy among the bulk of the Japanese people of the official and authoritarian version of political culture has not in fact prevented the subsequent adoption by what seems to be a solid majority of the population of democratic values and attitudes. To be sure, the shift raises questions about the stability and reliability of these new orientations or, for that matter, any other set of broadly held political values at the popular level. But they have been current in Japan for seventeen years now, seem to have gained both wide acceptance and support, and have provided the foundation in popular political attitudes and expectations which the government needs to function stably and effectively. In these senses the new political culture is working in Japan, and judgments as to its durability under stress are perhaps best left to the arbitrament of some future test case.

Third, this investigation in some depth of Japanese political culture calls attention to what Almond and Coleman have termed the "dualism" of political institutions.[16] All modern political cultures and structures contain substantial admixtures of traditional elements which are frequently not confined to isolated or backwater areas but may play a prominent and functionally important role in the modernization process.

In the Japanese case this is well illustrated by our earlier account of the historical development of a professionally trained, rationally structured, and achievement-oriented bureaucracy in Japan. In this instance it was pointed out that what seemed to be a purely feudal institution performing functions of major importance in a predominantly feudal society was at the same time gradually acquiring more and more of the basic characteristics of a modern professional bureaucracy. In a historical sense therefore the late Tokugawa bureaucracy played a Janus-like role. It faced both backward toward the truly feudal institutions and times of the sixteenth century and forward toward the emergent modern society of the twentieth. It also served in gradually shifting proportions the purposes of both waning and emergent societies, and it continued to do this for upwards of one hundred and fifty years. In other words the possibility of peaceful coexistence and even mutual supportiveness of feudal or traditional

---

[16] Gabriel A. Almond and James S. Coleman, *The Politics of the Developing Areas*, Princeton, Princeton University Press, 1960, pp. 20-25.

with modern elements within a given institution and also within a society is well demonstrated by the Japanese experience.

But the context has shifted since Tokugawa times. First, it was the existence of modern elements and tendencies within a feudal environment that seemed noteworthy. Now it is the survival of numerous so-called feudal or traditional traits within the predominantly modern context of present-day Japan which seems striking and gives rise to comments which are apt to be emotionally charged. To some these survivals represent the old, the real, the quintessential Japan and are to be treasured and savored; to others they represent discreditable vestiges of an outmoded, or "Asian," or feudal past which should be given speedy burial.

The explanation of such reactions would seem to be in the dichotomous way in which the terms "traditional" and "modern" are usually related in our thinking. They tend to be viewed as mutually exclusive or polar opposites. The institutions and attitudes associated with one come to be regarded as antipathetic to the other. From here it is but a step to the conclusion that any given traditional survival is fated for elimination from a modern society through some fairly inexorable process of social purgation impelled by a drive towards institutional self-consistency.

The history of the modernization of Japan challenges the tenability of any such thesis. It demonstrates in many ways not only the ability of modern institutions and orientations to coexist with traditional ones for very substantial periods of time, but also the manner in which traditional attitudes and practices can be of great positive value to the modernization process.

The modernizing experience is a strenuous one for any traditionally organized society. If successful, it demands sacrifice, discipline, initiative, and perseverance in quantities and for periods of time which are certain to place the people concerned under very severe strains. One of the greatest problems of leadership under these circumstances is to devise conditions and motivations which will liberate and focus an appropriate amount of popular energy, initiative, and resources and at the same time minimize dysfunctional behavior on the part of all significant elements in the population. Consider briefly some of the techniques used in Japan to achieve these goals, and note the role played therein by traditional elements.

Most obvious of all, perhaps, was the use made of the emperor. This is not to say that there was not some measure of sincerity and philosophic or ethical commitment in the movement to restore the emperor to at least the semblance of temporal power. But the subsequent revival and institutionalization of Shinto and the cultivation of mass loyalty, obedience, and reverence for the emperor were too systematic and innovational to be anything but a deliberate and very clever attempt by the Meiji leadership to channel popular attitudes and conduct along lines which they considered constructive. In this instance the appeal was to an institutional complex which was traditional not only in terms of the circumstances of the 1870's but would have been equally so in terms of those of 1603. The tradition of imperial rule, with very few exceptions, had possessed little validity since approximately the ninth century, while Imperial Shinto as a national cult had been moribund for at least as long, if indeed it had ever before existed in comparable form.

Again, one of the real keystones to the successful modernization of Japan was the device of holding constant, i.e. traditional, the circumstances and attitudes of life in rural and agricultural Japan while at the same time using and exploiting the countryside as a means of building and rapidly developing the urban, commercial, industrial, and military sectors of the society. Modernization is an expensive undertaking, and the costs must be borne by some segment of the population. In Japan in the early and critical years it was the peasantry who through the land tax bore the bulk of this burden. A docile and productive agrarian labor force was therefore an element of crucial importance to the leaders of a modernizing Japan. In a social engineering sense they strove to insure this result by altering the actual sociopolitical-intellectual circumstances of the pre-Restoration countryside as little as possible. Land reform was assiduously avoided; the existing political, social, and economic elites of the villages were insofar as possible confirmed in their status and authority; the traditional community and family systems were not only maintained but in a number of ways were also reinforced and given new legal status and sanctions.

A systematic endeavor was made to insure the tranquillity, obedience, and loyalty of the countryside, and the control devices utilized were almost without exception traditional. This not only assured the government of a maximal flow of food, revenue, recruits, and urban-bound migrants from the countryside but also left it free to concentrate its attention and resources on building the more critical urban aspects of the national economy and defense establishment. This was a strategy of enormous importance to the rapid development of Japan, and its success rested ultimately on the effective enlistment of traditional institutions and appeals in the service of the modernizing process.

If one looks to the contemporary rather than the historical scene in Japan, many examples of this type of "reinforcing dualism" may still be discerned. The most reliable and important element in the long political dominance of the Liberal-Democratic Party in the postwar period has been its control of the rural vote. Below the surface of this phenomenon one will find a political support system compounded of largely personalized allegiance and loyalties reaching downward through the prefectures to roots in every farm hamlet in Japan. The ultimate approach of this apparatus to the voter is based upon a very shrewd admixture of appeals to personal and local advantage phrased in terms of traditional values and relationships. Again, the primacy of personal and hierarchical relations and loyalties in Japanese politics is obvious and well known. The persistence of *oyabun-kobun* and similar forms of traditional fictive family relationships is but an extreme form of this trait. It would probably also be proper to regard the national predilection for consensual rather than adversary forms of decision making and the dualistic nature of the national economy as other examples of the continued vitality and real functional importance of traditional attitudes and practices in the Japan of 1962.

In short, post-Restoration Japan has continuously represented a very complex amalgam of traditional and modern elements, a sort of mutually supportive or "reinforcing dualism" in which the relationship between the two sectors has often been symbiotic rather than antagonistic. This has been true to such an extent that it is probably accurate to claim that Japan could not have been successful in modernizing so rapidly and effectively had it not been for the many planned and unplanned ways in which traditional political culture and behavior positively contributed to and supported the process. Furthermore, there is a good deal of evidence indicative of the continued vitality of some segments of the traditional sector. It is still too early to predict even their gradual displacement by what we regard as more modern traits.

In view of the urgent concern with modernization of traditional societies two aspects of the Japanese experience with changes in political culture should be stressed in conclusion. The first is that changes in Japan's political culture have involved what might be termed the phenomenon of delayed payoff. During the thirteen years which have elapsed since the end of the Allied Occupation of Japan there have been many surprised comments upon the continued support by the Japanese people and government for the democratic institutions and practices imposed upon them by the Occupation. These have not been discarded or subverted in the manner which many confidently expected. Although it cannot be proved, one suspects that the fundamental reason for this is the fact that Japanese political culture is not really as antipathetic to democratic norms and values as it has been believed to be. In this case so much depends upon which stream of Japanese political culture one chooses to emphasize: the officially and normally dominant prewar authoritarian stream; or the at least proto-democratic stream which has survived and expanded its influence and strength since the 1870's and which was by no means expunged by the ultranationalism of the late 1930's and the war years. Actually the democratic reforms of the 1945-1952 period were built, consciously or otherwise, upon the foundations of Taisho democracy and upon the popular political attitudes and values derived from this experience. This is not to claim that all or the majority of Japanese were latent democrats in 1945, but only that the political culture of democracy had taken sufficient hold on enough strategically placed elements of the population during the 1918-1932 period to render the Occupation's reforms a feasible undertaking. This native reservoir of democratic aspiration and experience represents the delayed payoff of Japan's own liberal tradition in politics which so many considered to have been expunged by the political experiences of the 1930's and early 1940's. The Occupation could not have been so successful in the absence of such a tradition.

A second important aspect of culture change deals with the relationship of political culture to political structure. In Japan the developmental process on both sides has been gradual. We are surrounded today by attempts to make over and modernize the minds and institutions of so many peoples through a series of five-, six-, or ten-year plans. The experience of Japan casts some doubt upon the feasibility of such undertakings. If one takes contemporary Japanese political culture as a point of departure, it is necessary to remember that it has in the most immediate sense taken practically a century of slow, piecemeal, and gradual development plus something as massive as military defeat and almost seven years of American occupation to produce the present constellation of political values and attitudes in Japan. If one looks deeper to the roots of these developments in Tokugawa times, it is necessary to add another century or so of pre-takeoff preparation and tooling up. This does not argue that more rapid development of a modern political structure and the popular values and attitudes associated therewith is impossible. But it does point out that there is no historical support for such a thesis in the experience of the sole non-Western society which may be said to have achieved the higher levels of modernization.

CHAPTER 3

England: A Traditionally Modern Political Culture

RICHARD ROSE

ENGLAND is outstanding in the field of comparative politics as an example of stable, representative government. For centuries, cultural attitudes, political institutions, and socioeconomic characteristics have combined to maintain an effective and competitive political system. The experience of England is worthy of study because modern societies with stable governments are rare in the world today, and most of the small number of fortunate nations which have long combined both these characteristics owe much to the direct influence of England.[1] Unlike the United States but like most developing nations, England began to modernize with an agrarian, aristocratic society as its basis. Unlike European neighbors such as Germany, France, and Russia, England achieved modernization without revolutions or recurring departures from constitutional government. The experience of England is important also because it illustrates that modernization is not, as some writers suggest, the consummation of a nation's history. The attainment of certain social, economic, and political characteristics marked the crossing of an important threshold for the English, but it did not make an end to the strains and conflicts of political change. England, like India, Egypt, and Turkey, is a society in transition.

The persisting ability to solve political problems without breaking the continuity between past and present and without making temporary divisions permanent meant that the English people, unlike many ex-colonial peoples today, began industrialization with a secure national identity. England's island position and strong navy has kept the country free from foreign invasion since the eleventh century. The identification of the nation with the government was

[1] In Phillips Cutright's classification the seven leading countries are America, England, Canada, Australia, New Zealand, Switzerland, and Sweden. See "National Political Development," *American Sociological Review*, Vol. XXVIII, No. 2, 1963, p. 258. See also, Gabriel A. Almond, "Comparative Political Systems," *Journal of Politics*, Vol. XVIII, No. 3, 1956, pp. 392ff.

achieved in medieval times, and the break with the Roman Catholic Church sanctified patriotism with a national religion. The Civil War of 1644-1660 involved religious differences; it was not followed by severe persecution, but by toleration acts. Religious non-conformists were not regarded as aliens in the community; the great religious enemy—Roman Catholicism—lay outside the English nation.[2] The Industrial Revolution profoundly altered English society but it did not represent a challenge from a foreign culture, as the coming of European colonizers and Western technologists did in Afro-Asian nations. In England rising industrial leaders could and often did resolve personal status insecurities by the relatively simple means of changing their religious denomination, buying land, and educating their sons as gentlemen. Neither industrial nor aristocratic leaders regarded the differences between them as unbridgeable, and many old status leaders secured protection for their position by profitable investment in industrialization. When nationalism was a disruptive force in many European societies in the nineteenth century, the English had already so well integrated the Scottish and Welsh people into the government of Great Britain that separatism was no problem. (The Irish struggle for Home Rule is, as always, an exception.) Industrialization further strengthened the predominance of England and the English within the United Kingdom of Great Britain and Northern Ireland; hence, this essay is concerned with the relationship of English society to British government.[3]

Any attempt to date the point at which England became a modern society shows the weakness of giving a rigid, technological definition to what is a relative concept. As Stanley Rothman has rightly argued, "England had developed many of the characteristics of a modern nation before the economic and social revolutions of the eighteenth and nineteenth centuries."[4] From the Norman Conquest of 1066, the rudiments of a nationwide system of public administration began to develop, reaching a relatively high stage of complexity and differentiation by the fifteenth century. Yet from the Magna Carta

---

[2] A point ignored by Everett Hagen in his analysis, *On the Theory of Social Change*, Homewood, Ill., Dorsey, 1962, Chap. 13. Cf. Ursula Henriques, *Religious Toleration in England, 1787-1833*, London, Routledge, 1961.

[3] The government itself has never adopted a consistent policy in differentiating the parts of the United Kingdom for purposes of legislation, administration, or statistical reports.

[4] "Modernity and Tradition in Britain," *Social Research*, Vol. XXVIII, No. 3, 1961, p. 299. See also Harry Eckstein, "The British Political System" in S. H. Beer and Adam Ulam, eds., *Patterns of Government*, New York, Random House, 2d edn., 1962, pp. 81ff.

of 1215 there also began to develop a set of legal and political restraints upon the exercise of absolute authority by the monarchy. In medieval times England had a Parliament which was in crude form a representative assembly. Since then the constitutional history of the country has recurringly involved the adjustment of the balance of power between the parts of a strong central government and between this government and organized groups and local leaders claiming freedom from central authority unless it acted with their assent. In Tudor times central authority was strengthened; Henry VII and his sixteenth-century successors repaired the harm the Wars of the Roses had done to the monarchy. The separation of the Church of England from the jurisdiction of the Roman Pope and the establishment of a national church based upon Erastian principles, subordinate to the state rather than competing with it for power, further strengthened the monarchy. The seventeenth century was a period of unrest and Civil War, yet one which ended not in chaos but in a restoration. By the deposition of James II in favor of William and Mary in 1688, the English demonstrated their ability to manage peacefully and successfully that most difficult of tasks, the transferring of legitimacy from one ruler to another, and the resolution of the conflicts of civil war. By the late seventeenth century, the age of Sir Isaac Newton, Sir Christopher Wren, and John Locke, commerce and scientific studies had begun to flourish. Legal institutions with strong traditional roots supported belief in the orderliness of life, and that belief in order was a central tenet of neo-classical thinking in the eighteenth century. Thus, before its Industrial Revolution began, England had a stable, legitimate government with a centralized executive subject to recognized legal restraints and working with an elected representative assembly. This achievement is the more impressive when comparison is made with the state of other European, and of non-European nations at the time.

Of key importance in analyzing the modernization of English society is the different timing of development in analytically separate but mutually related parts, the socioeconomic system, and the political system, the latter further divided into political institutions and the political culture. The criteria for measuring modernization in each of these parts differ, as does the nature of change. These three parts, and the processes of political socialization, must each be analyzed separately and then together in order to understand the complex process which has made England an outstanding instance of political development.

I. *Industrialization and the Adaptation of Political Institutions*

The most succinct way in which to date the modernization of the socioeconomic system is to apply theoretical criteria to the readily available resources of quantitative data about the Industrial Revolution in England. In this essay the criteria of James S. Coleman are employed.[5]

"*Widespread literacy.*" More than half the population was literate by about 1840, and virtually complete literacy was achieved by 1893, notwithstanding the slowness of the government to institute free compulsory education. Of great importance is the fact that the language of the engineer, the clergyman, the administrator, and the intellectual was the same, and the same as the language of the literate or illiterate manual worker. The cult of working-class self-improvement through literature, sanctioned by religion and encouraged by middle-class leaders, further strengthened common values cutting across class lines in society.[6]

"*An extensive and penetrative network of mass communication media.*" Throughout the eighteenth century, political discussion had been carried on by the politically active in clubs and coffee houses and also in a corrupt and sometimes harassed press. The consumption of printing paper began to rise in the 1780's. Mechanical improvements speeding up printing were followed by rises in newspaper circulation by the 1840's, before the repeal of the stamp tax on newspapers in 1855 withdrew the last formal restraint upon the mass circulation of newspapers.[7]

---

[5] See "The Political Systems of the Developing Areas" in Gabriel A. Almond and James S. Coleman, *The Politics of the Developing Areas*, Princeton, Princeton University Press, 1960, pp. 532-533. Coleman calls the first of the two sets of criteria employed criteria for a modern society. Here the term society (or social system) is used to refer to the sum of all the sub-systems, of which the political and socioeconomic sub-systems are major examples. The problem of establishing criteria of modernization for the whole society is discussed in the concluding section of this essay.

[6] On literacy generally see Raymond Williams, *The Long Revolution*, London, Chatto & Windus, 1961, pp. 156ff.; on the influence of the middle-class literary culture upon working-class leaders, see "The Labour Party and the Books that Helped to Make It," *Review of Reviews*, Vol. XXXIII, No. 198, 1906, p. 198.

[7] See B. C. Mitchell, *Abstract of British Economic Statistics*, Cambridge, University Press, 1962, pp. 263-264; and A. P. Wadsworth, *Newspaper Circulations, 1800-1954*, Manchester, Statistical Society, 1955.

"Extensive geographical and social mobility." Because few points in England are more than 100 miles from the sea or a few miles from a river, geographical movement has always been comparatively easy, internally and also internationally. The boom in canal building in the 1790's improved inland transportation for industry. By 1814 there were 21,449 ships registered in the United Kingdom; the introduction of the steamboat greatly increased the tonnage of ships, but not the number, so well developed had been the maritime fleet previously. Railways were quickly developed following their invention; by 1850, there were 6,000 miles of track in a country where trips of 150 miles were and are relatively long journeys. Because the ownership of land was concentrated in few hands, and that concentration was increased by enclosure acts in the eighteenth century, agricultural laborers were not tied to the land by owning it or by serfdom and could thus readily move into industrial areas in response to the demand for labor. Preindustrial social stratification was not inflexibly inhibiting to social mobility, particularly by the co-option of men of economic achievement into the aristocracy or gentry. Industrialization greatly increased opportunities for social mobility through achievement and also modified methods of stratification in ways that did not lead to a breakdown of the older structure.[8]

"A comparatively high degree of urbanization." Industrialism transformed an agrarian society with no large city outside London into an urban society. In the process Englishmen whom Polanyi has dramatically described as "the detribalized, degraded natives of their time" migrated from rural into industrial areas.[9] In that period English cities were the scene of political riots, and political leaders feared the danger of urban uprisings during the Chartist troubles of the 1840's and intermittently for two generations thereafter. By 1851 half the population was urban and many agricultural areas were dotted with coal mines and cotton and woollen mills. By about 1880 urbanization was being followed by suburbanization.

[8] See Mitchell, *op.cit.*, pp. 212-227; J. H. Clapham, *An Economic History of Modern Britain: The Early Railway Age*, Cambridge, University Press, 1930, 2d edn., Chaps. 3 and 9; G. Kitson Clark, *The Making of Victorian England*, Cambridge, Massachusetts, Harvard University Press, 1962; and Alexis de Tocqueville, *Journeys to England and Ireland*, London, Faber, 1958 ed., pp. 59ff.

[9] Karl Polanyi, *The Great Transformation*, Boston, Beacon, 1957, p. 290. See also Phyllis Deane and W. A. Cole, *British Economic Growth, 1688-1959*, Cambridge, University Press, 1962, pp. 9-12, 108-109; and Asa Briggs, *Victorian Cities*, London, Odhams, 1963.

"*A relatively high degree of commercialization and industrialization of the economy.*" As studies of the origins of modern capitalism have shown, commercial activity of considerable significance was taking place in England centuries before industrialization. By 1821 the numbers employed in manufacturing, mining, and industry were greater than the numbers employed in agriculture, forestry, and fishing,[10] and the basis for England's early pre-eminence in international commerce and industrial production was already established.

"*Comparatively high per capita income.*" The continuing debate among economic historians about the "real" value of wages received by different categories of workers during the course of industrialization cannot be resolved by reference to statistics, because it is essentially a political and ideological controversy.[11] Early industrialization meant that England was not only rich in comparison to other nations but also rich in comparison to previously established expectations. The rapid development of inventions such as the railway outstripped rather than lagged behind popular expectations. Unlike leaders of developing nations, the political leaders of England in the course of industrialization were free from the pressure of rising economic expectations, though subject to demands to protect traditional ways of life. Thus demands for political changes could be met more easily by legislation than can economic demands in economically backward nations today.

"*Widespread participation and involvement by members of the society in modern social and economic processes.*" This broad standard is best regarded as a general description of a modern socioeconomic system. On the basis of other changes discussed above England can be said to have had a modern socioeconomic system for more than a century, for it was radically transformed in the period from the late eighteenth century until the middle of the nineteenth century. Insofar as a landmark date is symbolically useful, one might take 1846, the year of the repeal of the corn laws; the repeal meant formal political acceptance of the shift from an agrarian to an industrial society.

---

[10] The increase in non-agricultural workers reflected the increase in the population, for the absolute number of those in agricultural occupations continued to rise until 1861. See Phyllis Deane and W. A. Cole, *op.cit.*, pp. 142-143, and, more generally, the multitude of studies and criticisms provoked by Max Weber's *The Protestant Ethic and the Spirit of Capitalism*, London, Allen & Unwin, 1930.

[11] See especially R. M. Hartwell, "Interpretations of the Industrial Revolution in England: a Methodological Inquiry," *Journal of Economic History*, Vol. XIX, No. 2, 1959, p. 240.

Political institutions also went through major changes in the nineteenth century, but dating those changes is difficult. In the lengthy process of institutional adaptation, the changes in function were not always matched by simultaneous changes in structures. For instance, there was no formal change in the House of Lords between 1800 and 1900, yet its function in the political system altered considerably. Often the conclusion must be that the changes were not clearcut.

Socialization. In a modern society socialization involves the direct impact of the political system upon the individual and the penetration of primary social structures by secondary ones. Since feudal times English government has been able to make an impact upon its subjects, but often its activities have been mediated by placing administration in the hands of personages who, by virtue of feudalistic loyalties and social deference, could claim authority in primary group relationships in addition to that conveyed by offices in secondary structures. The strength of legal institutions and the cultural value placed upon legal procedures in preindustrial England helped to regulate and limit arbitrary personal authority. By the end of the seventeenth century the divine right claims for monarchy were no longer part of the constitution. By the mid-nineteenth century industrialization had created a large urban population with no personal ties to agriculturally based social leaders. However, it did not put an end to the interpenetration of primary and secondary loyalties. In less industrial areas and in face-to-face relations in national politics, primary, personal loyalties can still take precedence before more formal and impersonal secondary ties.[12] In industrial areas a different kind of class relations also involves the interpenetration of primary and secondary relationships for, as T. H. Marshall has emphasized, class reflects "the way a man is treated by his fellows." Thus, although impersonal political institutions had become extremely important by the latter half of the nineteenth century, it did not mean that they had become, or are now, so important as to exclude primary social influences.[13]

Recruitment. Ascriptive qualities have always been important in

---

[12] Particularly good examples are the case studies of Margaret Stacey, *Tradition and Change*, London, Oxford University Press, 1960; and Tom Lupton and C. Shirley Wilson, "The Social Background and Connections of Top Decision-Makers," *The Manchester School*, Vol. XXVII, No. 1, 1959.

[13] See especially T. H. Marshall, *Citizenship and Social Class*, Cambridge, University Press, 1950; Elizabeth Bott, *Family and Social Network*, London, Tavistock, 1957, pp. 159ff.; and Gabriel A. Almond and Sidney Verba, *The Civic Culture*, Princeton, Princeton University Press, 1963, p. 287.

recruiting national politicians in England, though never to the complete exclusion of individuals with great acquired wealth or of great talent but humble birth. Industrialization brought forward in society a large group of men whose status rested primarily upon achievement in the economic system, whether as industrialists, engineers, or trade union leaders, though rarely have such men reached highest Cabinet offices. Industrialization also resulted in an increase in the technical complexities of public administration and thus stimulated recognition of the importance of achievement in appointments to public offices. Because men of ability sometimes have ascriptive advantages as well, and because those with ability but lacking ascriptive advantages may seek to be assimilated into traditional society, it follows that recruitment on ascriptive and achievement grounds are not necessarily in conflict. Today, there is still debate concerning whether ascriptive or achievement criteria are more influential in the recruitment of people to elected and appointed political office.[14]

Pressure Groups. The function of associations performing "a system-wide regulatory role by processing raw claims and directing them in an orderly way and in aggregable form" is consistent, as S. H. Beer has shown, with eighteenth-century attitudes toward Parliament as a forum for aggregating the interests of all with a stake in society. By the last quarter of the nineteenth century, business and trade union pressure groups had begun to gain national recognition.[15] Since the rapid decline in the importance of religious pressure groups after World War I, almost all pressure groups have presented demands capable of settlement by bargaining, negotiation, and compromise.

Party System. Political groups which may be labeled parties have operated as "competing, pragmatic and bargaining parties" in England at least since the middle of the eighteenth century. The Conservative Party has been a party of situational conservatism for many generations, never allowing its opposition to reforms in one decade to cause it to ossify and become rigidly reactionary subsequently. In

[14] For historical background see W. L. Guttsman, *The British Political Elite*, London, MacGibbon & Kee, 1963; for a contemporary analysis, Richard Rose, *Politics in England*, Boston, Little, Brown, 1964, Chap. 4.

[15] See S. H. Beer, "The Representation of Group Interests in British Government," *American Political Science Review*, Vol. LI, No. 3, 1957; "Political and Economic Planning," *Industrial Trade Associations*, London, Allen & Unwin, 1957, pp. 3ff.; J. M. Baernreither, *English Associations of Working Men*, London, Swan Sonnenschein, 1893; and B. C. Roberts, *The Trades Union Congress, 1868-1921*, London, Allen & Unwin, 1958.

a complementary fashion, nineteenth century Liberals, while often advancing reforms, were always prepared to bargain about introducing them when holding political power in the Commons. Only the Irish Nationalists, a minority party flourishing from about 1880 to 1922, have presented demands incapable of assimilation within existing political institutions. The Labour Party, unlike some European Socialist counterparts, has always emphasized its readiness to work through existing political institutions. At least since the time of Disraeli and Gladstone, the party system has been characterized both by competition and cooperation between parties with meaningfully different but reconcilable programs.[16]

Political communication. The creation of "autonomous and specialized media" transmitting "a steady flow of information within the polity" in many respects had to wait until industrialization made it technically possible to distribute national mass circulation newspapers daily. By late Victorian times, newspaper subscribers throughout the country were able to read exhaustive accounts of political controversies and to attend meetings where political issues were discussed in detail. Today, the small size of the island and the economics of the communications industry combine to make available throughout England every day a large supply of information about politics by means of the press, radio, and television. Yet only about one-tenth of the population regularly subscribe to those publications that provide political information in any detail; the great majority of the population ignore political communication and prefer to get entertainment from the media.[17]

Governmental machinery. The complex structure of government in England can be traced back to medieval roots. At least by the eighteenth century there may be said to have existed a measure of "differentiation, explicitness and functional distinctiveness" characteristic of modern political institutions. Yet the traditional idea of concentrating authority in one place never died out, though the locus of authority has shifted during the centuries from the monarchy to Parliament, to the Cabinet and, some would argue today, to the

[16] See e.g. Sir Lewis Namier, *The Structure of Politics at the Accession of George III*, London, Macmillan, 2d edn., 1961; R. O. Bassett, *Essentials of Parliamentary Democracy*, London, Macmillan, 1935, pp. 60ff.; and Richard Rose, "Parties, Factions and Tendencies in Britain," *Political Studies*, Vol. XII, No. 1, 1964.

[17] See Francis Williams, *Dangerous Estate*, London, Longmans, 1957; *National Readership Surveys, 1962*, London, Institute of Practitioners of Advertising, 1963; and D. E. Butler and J. Freeman, *British Political Facts, 1900-1960*, London, Macmillan, 1963, Chaps. 17 and 18.

Prime Minister. Simultaneously, increasing demands for governmental output have led to the maintenance and development of a wide range of governmental and quasi-governmental advisory committees, boards, royal commissions, and offices outside the main body of departments headed by ministers of Cabinet rank. In part this differentiation has been explicit and purposeful, and in part it has arisen from the partial adaptation of anachronistic bodies and procedures.[18] Although the organization of central government has tended to explicit, functional distinctiveness for about a century, this influence has not been exclusively predominant.

Dating the achievement of modern political institutions in England cannot be done with any preciseness. Most modern political institutions have recognizable roots in traditional English society. For example, the monarchy has been an important institution for a thousand years. Parliament, of medieval foundation, has been important as a representative assembly for at least 350 years—but the definition of who was represented and in what form, as well as the recruitment and management of Parliament, has changed greatly during that period. Although in the late nineteenth century the traditional importance of corruption and family was greatly circumscribed, traditional influences remain important in recruiting and promoting some M.P.'s (cf. Table 2, below). The year 1885 might be chosen as a landmark date in the process of modernization, for in that year the first general election was held in which the majority voted (though not all men were eligible to vote) and representation was based upon the enumeration of individuals rather than upon traditional communities; by that time too the modern party system had begun to flourish. The date could hardly be placed earlier, and it might be said to be as late as 1918.[19] It is certain that political institutions were not modernized until some decades after the socioeconomic system was, and even today the political institutions cannot be said to be completely modern. The characteristics of political institutions cannot be precisely and quantitatively measured as the characteristics of the socioeconomic system can be.

---

[18] See especially Lord Campion and others, *British Government Since 1918*, London, Allen & Unwin, 1950; and J. P. Mackintosh, *The British Cabinet*, London, Stevens, 1962.
[19] Not until the latter date was the property qualification removed from the franchise, the veto power of the House of Lords curbed, and the Labour Party a major party in the nation.

II. Values and Symbols: the Mixture in the Culture

Measuring and dating the development of cultural outlooks can be done only approximately. The chief sources are literary, or inferences can be made from the patterns of behavior of those in national political roles and of those who refrain from taking them. In a society as hierarchical as England has been there is considerable justification for concentrating attention upon attitudes found in the active minority rather than upon those of the peripheral public.[20] The following points do not represent a coherent and consistent outlook; they are a catalogue of attitudes, both implicitly and explicitly expressed, which gain in interest just because they are not a unified and systematic philosophy.

VALUES

Government as beneficent. The positive value placed upon government as beneficent can easily be traced back to medieval times, when the monarchy was more central to the structure of society than it is today. Until the middle of the nineteenth century the government was regarded as a source of benefits, if not for the whole population then at least for some groups. The rising support given to laissez faire economic beliefs at that time led to strong political resistance to governmental distribution of economic benefits and beneficial intervention in society, but the strength of this value began to be eroded in the late nineteenth century, and there has since been increasing support for the belief that government benefits are constructive and necessary for society.

Liberty. The value placed upon liberty at times supported skepticism or active opposition to increases in governmental activity; for instance, there was vociferous opposition to the introduction of full-time policemen in the 1820's. Since the defeat of Stuart absolutism in the seventeenth century, no anti-libertarian political creed has been of major political significance in England. The legislation which confirmed the libertarian trend in the late seventeenth century had not, according to Keir, "made any substantial change in the law of the constitution."[21] So strongly have libertarian attitudes been internal-

---

[20] Cf. the classic literary analysis of Walter Bagehot, *The English Constitution*, London, World's Classics edn., 1955; the study based on national survey data by Gabriel Almond and Sidney Verba, *op.cit.*; and the emphasis upon partisan influences on culture in Rose, *Politics in England*, Chap. 2.

[21] D. Lindsay Keir, *The Constitutional History of Modern Britain, 1485-1937*, London, Black, 3d edn., 1946, p. 268.

ized by Englishmen that there has not been the need to protect them with the elaborate legal guarantees provided in the United States since its foundation. Yet the liberty of Englishmen to do as they wish was for centuries restricted in politics by the narrow basis of the electoral franchise as well as by great social and economic inequalities. The horror Bagehot expressed in 1867 of "rule by mere numbers" was characteristic of the period which followed immediately upon socioeconomic modernization. *Universal suffrage* was not provided for all men free from property qualification until 1918, and the principle of "one man, one vote" was not made completely binding until 1948.

Deference. The limitation of voting rights was closely related to the importance placed upon deference in a hierarchical society. The values commanding deference have slowly modified through the centuries, yet traditional bases have not been completely eroded. In preindustrial English society birth was of special though not exclusive importance, conferring recognized political rights and duties. In the nineteenth century, systematic provision was made for public boarding schools to transmit gentlemanly manners and political status. The passage of the 1944 Education Act greatly increased scholarships for further education, and embodied the increasing respect given to educational achievement, whether in gentlemanly or technical subjects. Insofar as equality of educational opportunity is thought to exist today, deference to education can claim added legitimacy. Deference to educational achievement has supplemented but not entirely supplanted the traditional deference to inherited social status and wealth.[22] The claim to deference on a multiplicity of grounds is particularly notable in the Conservative Party. As Edward Shils has argued, deference is not necessarily opposed to liberty and may underpin it by enhancing the security of leaders and nonleaders. But it is opposed to the value of *equality*. Conservatives have always rejected equality as impossible and undesirable. Since 1945 party leaders have placed less emphasis upon inequalities of birth and more upon the respect and rewards which are said to be due to inequalities of achievement. The Labour Party, since its foundation in 1900, has given some support to egalitarian beliefs, in particular seeking to improve the material welfare, the oppor-

---

[22] See especially Bagehot, *op.cit.*; R. T. McKenzie, "Bagehot and the Rule of Mere Numbers," *The Listener*, November 19, 1959; Rupert Wilkinson, *The Prefects*, London, Oxford University Press, 1964; and Michael Young, *The Rise of the Meritocracy*, Harmondsworth, Penguin, 1961, Part I.

tunities, and the social status of manual workers, who form two-thirds of the population and (including agricultural laborers) have always constituted the "bottom half" of English society. Yet the Labour Party has never gone so far as to argue that absolute material or social equality is practicable, notwithstanding support for its desirability.[23]

The ambivalence regarding egalitarian norms is reflected in the divisions of the electorate. Both major political parties seek electoral support from all levels of the social hierarchy. The Conservatives are able to do this because the working class does not have as high a level of political cohesion as the middle class, and the Labour Party is forced to do so for the same reason. The leadership of both parties similarly reflects the deference paid to particular social characteristics (cf. Table 2, below). Ambivalence is reflected in the behavior of individual politicians, particularly among working-class Labour leaders whose high political office gives them a status inconsistent with their social origins. Ramsay MacDonald is the classic example of a Labour politician who resolved this incongruity by moving to the right politically. Some men, such as Ernest Bevin, manage with little difficulty, but others may retreat into the rhetoric of aggressive class consciousness or turn to drink.[24]

Trust in fellow citizens is a basic cultural belief. The Civic Culture survey found trust in social relationships particularly high in England and reflected in politics. The legal maxim, "The Queen can do no wrong," echoes this belief. At the level of national political activity this trust can be traced back to feudal conceptions of loyalty, which mixed personal honor and the obligations of office. The mixture still occurs. The shock of the Profumo affair in 1963 arose from the fact that a minister would lie to the House of Commons in a personal statement. Significantly, his colleagues preferred to trust the word of this ex-officer and gentleman rather than cross-examine Profumo on the basis of available evidence.[25] Only through the mutual trust of partisan opponents can respect for the conventions and customs of

---

[23] Cf. Edward Shils, *The Torment of Secrecy*, Glencoe, Ill., Free Press, 1956; Marshall, *op.cit.*; and C.A.R. Crosland, *The Future of Socialism*, New York, Macmillan, 1957, Part IV.

[24] See especially Egon Wertheimer, *Portrait of the Labour Party*, London, Putnam, 1929; and V. L. Allen, "The Ethics of Trade Union Leaders," *British Journal of Sociology*, Vol. VII, No. 4, 1956. Cf. the biographical appendix of Catherine Ann Cline, *Recruits to Labour*, Syracuse, N.Y., University Press, 1963.

[25] *Lord Denning's Report*, London, Her Majesty's Stationery Office (henceforth cited as HMSO), Cmnd. 2152, 1963, para. 181ff. Note also, Almond and Verba, *op.cit.*, Chaps. 4 and 10.

British government be maintained. The depth of this trust is evidenced by the maintenance for centuries of a stable system of government without a written constitution.

Privacy. Trust does not lead to frankness in discussing policy making in public; instead it makes tolerable the making of policy in considerable privacy. Little of the deliberations between ministers, civil servants, pressure group spokesmen, and experts is published before the announcement of major decisions, and strictly enforced laws concerning official secrets, ministerial private papers, and the anonymity of civil servants help to maintain privacy after decisions are announced. Certain parts of the deliberations may be published, but often they can be understood only against the background of private discussions. Sometimes key points may be published in "code," that is, in a form meaningful only to those in government circles. The outlook is succinctly summed up in a quasi-governmental report on public expenditure: "Limits are quickly reached in the practicable disclosure of the government's judgments of future uncertainties and intentions in detail for several years ahead in defence, major economic policy and, of course, in social policy and in legislation."[26] The respect for the privacy of government has an origin planted centuries before in the time when the business of government and the king's personal and private business were inextricably joined. The persistence of the belief in privacy also reflects a pragmatic judgment concerning the advantages it gives to government officials, advantages now enjoyed by elected ministers and civil servants and not by the Crown.

Diffuse leadership. This has been important in England since medieval times. Traditionally, political skill has been regarded as a quality possessed by English gentlemen. Because leadership was so largely the duty of men of diffuse status, few needed to use politics as a means of gaining status. Today M.P.'s are still disproportionately drawn from the diffusely educated gentlemanly strata, and their salary traditionally has been kept low to prevent the job of M.P. from becoming an occupation which provides a good livelihood. Men with diffuse leadership credentials have a head start in becoming political leaders, and those with inherited wealth or extra-political income predominate among leaders. They can easily afford a full-time politi-

---

[26] *Control of Public Expenditure*, London, HMSO, Cmnd. 1432, 1961, para. 74. Cf. the translation of this report by W.J.M. Mackenzie, *The Guardian*, Manchester and London, May 25, 1963. More generally, see Rose, *Politics in England*, Chap. 8.

cal career. Insofar as office is a consequence and confirmation of diffuse status, rather than an instrument by which individuals realize political programs, then it follows that the content of governmental legislation may be less important than retention of office. In this context it is significant that R. T. McKenzie in his study of party leadership emphasizes retention of office, rather than advancement of programs, as the main goal of party leaders.[27] Historically, political leaders of diffuse high status have often been lazy rather than autocratic when in office.

Limits on government. Political leadership outside the circle at court developed in an effort to place limits on government; this might be traced back to Magna Carta. By the eighteenth century the threat of royal domination had lapsed, but weak and restricted government was still valued as a protection against tyranny. In the mid-nineteenth century proponents of industrialism sought to use their rising political influence to circumscribe the activities of government and to maintain a free market in trade. But their influence was fading perceptibly by the beginning of the twentieth century. The rise of the Labour movement resulted in some political support for the belief that politics could transform English society. Especially since experience of government in the 1920's, Labour leaders have emphasized that they do not wish to politicize the whole of English life, but rather to adjust the boundaries separating what is a legitimate field for governmental action from what is not.[28]

Collective consultation. Consultation has roots in English medieval history, for from early times collegial organs such as Parliament and royal councils have been deliberative bodies which might by advising inhibit the powers of the executive. This value is important in restricting the possibility of unilateral action by those who command simultaneously the chief political institutions—the Cabinet, Parliament, and the majority party. For instance, in 1963 the government accepted "the main responsibility for national economic policy" but it admitted that success would result only from collective consulta-

---

[27] R. T. McKenzie, *British Political Parties*, London, Heinemann, 1955. Cf. the discussion of the effects of diffuse leaders in the Army by Simon Raven, "Perish by the Sword," in Hugh Thomas, ed., *The Establishment*, London, Blond, 1959.

[28] See, e.g., the debate on whether Labour should support legislation prohibiting parents from privately educating their children, *Report of the Fifty-Seventh Annual Conference of the Labour Party*, London, Labour Party, 1958, pp. 85-114. On laissez faire generally, note especially J. B. Brebner, "Laissez Faire and State Intervention in Nineteenth-Century Britain," *Journal of Economic History*, Vol. VIII, 1948.

tion influencing how the "government, management and unions carry out their respective functions."[29]

Welfare benefits. The value placed upon the collective provision of welfare benefits, reflecting organic beliefs about social relations, also can be traced back to medieval times. For instance, objectives stated in the Act for the Relief of the Poor of 1598 were substantially restated more than 300 years later in the Poor Law Act of 1930. When England entered industrialization in the late eighteenth century, there already existed a rudimentary network of institutions providing food, shelter, and care in old age. That network proved increasingly inadequate and was attacked by exponents of laissez faire; it underwent major reform, most notably in the Poor Law Amendment Act of 1834. The welfare system was not, however, abolished. Thus, when some began to demand, early in this century, more and better welfare services, they did not raise completely new questions of fundamental values; it was the range and standard of benefits that were in dispute. In this century, there has been a growing value placed upon welfare, and the range and standards of services have reflected the increased importance of welfare values in politics.[30]

Military defense. Although military defense has been a prime political value in almost all societies, in England there has not been cultural consensus about it for a century. Traditionally, a standing army had been regarded as unnecessary and suspect because of England's island position. By mid-Victorian times men such as Richard Cobden had fully developed a set of ideas which gave international free trade greater importance than military strength. In both the Boer War and World War I small but significant groups opposed fighting. After 1918 the value of military defense was challenged by believers in pacifism, Marxism, international law, and appeasement. Consensus was achieved during World War II, but since the late 1950's the Campaign for Nuclear Disarmament has provided an institutional focus for fundamental dissent from the predominant beliefs of foreign policy.[31]

---

[29] National Economic Development Council, *Conditions Favourable to Faster Growth*, London, HMSO, 1963, para. 217ff. See also K. C. Wheare, *Government by Committee*, Oxford, Clarendon Press, 1955; and S. H. Beer, "Pressure Groups and Parties in Britain," *American Political Science Review*, Vol. L, No. 1, 1956.

[30] Maurice Bruce, *The Coming of the Welfare State*, London, Batsford, 1961, p. 20. See also, Asa Briggs, "The Welfare State in Historical Perspective," *European Journal of Sociology*, Vol. II, No. 2, 1961.

[31] See, e.g., J. A. Hobson, *Richard Cobden, The International Man*, London, Unwin, 1918; A.J.P. Taylor, *The Trouble-Makers*, London, Hamilton, 1957; and

A static society. Belief in an essentially static society is characteristic of the outlook of a traditional, agrarian society. Although the rapid industrialization of England in the nineteenth century prompted a widespread belief in and attachment to progress, by the end of World War I faith in dynamic social development appears to have been waning. Support for the status quo could readily be found in a situation in which England's fortune was subject to strong challenges from other nations. During the present century standards of living have been rising, but the rise has not eliminated "traditionalistic" beliefs in maintaining society as it is. From 1939 until 1954, wartime and postwar rationing and material shortages greatly affected economic conditions and attitudes. The concern expressed by politicians about economic growth since the establishment of the National Economic Development Council in 1962 is a sign of a desire among leaders for change, but it is also an attack upon prevailing attitudes unconcerned with growth.[32]

Evolution and assimilation. Particular value is placed upon changes occurring, when necessary, in evolutionary ways, and new developments being gradually assimilated into older practices of the political system. Not since the Civil War of 1644-1660 has government in England involved sharp and sudden discontinuities. In reaction against the challenge of the French Revolution and of industrialization, Whigs and Conservatives in the 1820's and 1830's altered anachronistic features of the constitution and showed a readiness to assimilate middle-class industrialists, just as later, manual workers were assimilated into active political roles. The contemporaneous radical Benthamite attempt to rationalize the institutions of government met with only limited success. The rise of the Labour movement in this century has been notable because the Labour Party rejected Marxism and has preferred what Sidney Webb called "the inevitable gradualness of our scheme of change." Evolutionary values facilitate change at a slow tempo. The willingness of old leaders to assimilate new ideas and new groups, in conjunction with the desire for assimilation by politically mobile groups, muffles the chain-reaction effect of particular reforms. As G. Kitson Clark shrewdly notes of the old leaders' achievement in the great nineteenth-

---

Richard Rose, "The Relation of Socialist Principles to Labour Foreign Policy," unpublished D.Phil. thesis, Oxford University, 1959.

[32] English attitudes thus contrast markedly with those delineated in America by David M. Potter, *People of Plenty*, Chicago, Phoenix, 1961 edn.

century crisis, "After 1848 their position was stronger than it had been before, for they had abandoned what was indefensible in their position and retained what was material for their power."[33]

SYMBOLS

In politics, as in many aspects of English society, emotional affect is carefully contained and channeled. Emotional disturbances of individuals do not cause political disruption, and political controversy is rarely intense enough to create individual emotional disturbances. In particular, those socialized in youth as potential political leaders receive strict instruction in disciplining and sublimating their emotions.[34] As Bagehot recognized a century ago (and British monarchs have studied this text since), the use of dignified symbols of government can be of value insofar as they "excite and preserve the reverence of the population."[35] Emotions can be aroused as an overtone or by-product of many political activities; in what follows, attention is concentrated upon symbols that stir political emotions, because they are relatively easy to isolate and describe analytically.

The monarchy. The origin of the emotional appeal of the monarchy is lost in antiquity. Yet the continuity in form masks a major change in function. For many centuries, the monarchy was not only a symbol but also the executive branch of British government. Late in Queen Victoria's reign affection for the monarchy rose simultaneously with the final decline of the monarch's efficient role in government. Today the monarchy gives institutional focus for emotional loyalties which in some countries fix upon a president or other executive official. The emotional support for the monarchy, surveys indicate, is favorable yet shallow and a response to the impersonal symbols of office rather than to the person of Queen Elizabeth.[36]

Past traditions. Affection for past traditions is a characteristic of a traditional, agrarian society. Industrialization challenged the institutions and the values of rural England. The depth and the suddenness of industrialization stimulated an intellectual reaction against industrialism in early nineteenth-century England. This was ex-

---

[33] Clark, *The Making of Victorian England*, p. 43. See *Report of the Twenty-third Annual Conference of the Labour Party*, 1923, pp. 198ff. for Webb's views; and more generally, G. M. Young, *Victorian England*, New York, Anchor, 1954 edn.

[34] See especially B. M. Spinley, *The Deprived and the Privileged*, London, Routledge, 1953.

[35] Bagehot, *op.cit.*, p. 4.

[36] See the detailed analysis in Rose, *Politics in England*, Chap. 10.

pressed in the Romantic movement in literature and in the revival from about 1840 of Gothic architecture and Catholic liturgy in religion. Exponents of Socialism in late Victorian England, such as John Ruskin and William Morris, were also prominent in glorifying medieval society. Today, Victorian England is far enough in the past, and industrial society so widely accepted that it too can be a source of traditional symbols—though the tradition represented is an integral part of what was once modern. Traditions, while important, are selectively preserved. For instance, in Parliament, emotions associated with traditional procedures are zealously guarded—but not the traditional role of Parliament as a strong restraint upon the executive.

The English community. Judging by literary sources, the community of the English people has been an important stimulus of political emotion at least since Shakespeare's time. At no date since the seventeenth century has any large group of Englishmen identified with a foreign power. At times, community solidarity has been strengthened by opposition to a foreign church (the Roman Catholic), to the ideology of an unfriendly foreign power (revolutionary French ideals), and by the challenge of other nations to its Imperial possessions (the Boer War). The absence of a large immigrant population and the failure of Welsh and Scottish politicians to develop strong nationalist parties has resulted in a situation in which the ethnic differences of English, Welsh, Scots, and Ulstermen do not detract from the emotional strength of symbols of the British community since the violent settlement of the Irish problem in 1922. In this century community ties have increased as the religious differences which intensified ethnic differences during the nineteenth century have lost political salience.[37]

The Empire and Commonwealth. The Empire is a relatively recent source of political emotion. Though England had possessed overseas territories for centuries, it was not until the latter half of the nineteenth century that the administration and the ideology of Empire became of continuing major political significance. From late Victorian times until World War II, symbols of Empire were pervasive throughout the political system, affecting education, the mass media, and the programs of parties. Yet the transformation of the Empire into the Commonwealth since World War II has proceeded without any great political reaction within England. This suggests

[37] See Robert Alford, *Party and Society*, Chicago, Rand, McNally, 1963, Chap. 6.

that the symbol of Empire, though prominent, was perhaps not so effective in stirring emotions of the general population as it was in a small group actively concerned with Imperial activities. The substitution of the symbol of the Commonwealth has helped absorb the shock of abrupt change and provided a substitute focus for emotional loyalties. Today, Commonwealth members may divide over the Cold War and problems as important to England as the Suez War, but Commonwealth conferences, royal tours, state dinners, and the sending out of Governors General continue to serve as symbolic tokens of a now vanished Imperial authority.[38]

England as a world power. The emotional importance of England's world power status has fluctuated during the centuries. Because of an island position, Englishmen have always been able to remain partly detached from European affairs and, by developing sea power, to build loyalties in continents far from Europe. The detachment (and the advantages of early modernization) have sustained a sense of superiority to other nations without inhibiting international activity. The military basis of England's world power began to decline before World War I; its decline was sealed by the North Atlantic Treaty of 1949, which brought the United States in to maintain a balance of power in Europe which England could no longer hold. Yet since then the Conservatives, by emphasizing thermonuclear weapons as a symbol of world power, and Labour, by emphasizing the country's moral strength, have shown that the emotional appeal of world power status remains strong, strong enough to survive the shocks of the loss of Persian oil fields in 1951, of the Suez Canal in 1956, and the rebuff on entry into the European Common Market in 1963.

Parliament. Since its medieval foundation, Parliament has aroused emotional loyalties as well as performing efficient functions in government. In recent decades, and particularly since World War II, its efficient role has declined. Yet the institution remains prominent as a chief symbol of government in the mass media, in formal teaching about government, and in conversation; M.P.'s are much more

---

[38] On contemporary cross-currents arising from the immigration of colored Commonwealth citizens to England see House of Commons *Debates*, 5th ser., London, Vol. 649, cols. 687-820, November 16, 1961, *et seq*. On the historical background see especially A. P. Thornton, *The Imperial Idea and its Enemies*, London, Macmillan, 1959; S. R. Mehrota, "On the Use of the term 'Commonwealth,'" *Journal of Commonwealth Studies*, Vol. II, No. 1, 1963; and as a case study of the decline of Imperial attitudes, Leon Epstein, *British Politics in the Suez Crisis*, London, Pall Mall, 1964.

visibly a part of government than are civil servants or pressure group officials. The only national elections are those for Members of Parliament. The presence of M.P.'s provides symbolic assurance to voters that government is responsive and responsible to its subjects, although in practice the government (that is, the Cabinet) informally dominates Parliament.[39]

Socialism. Since the latter half of the nineteenth century, Socialism has been a symbol arousing deep political emotions, first of revulsion and then, after the formal adherence of the Labour Party to this cause in 1918, arousing emotional conflicts between active supporters of the major parties. Between the wars, Socialists such as Harold Laski and anti-Socialists such as Winston Churchill indicated, by the extremes to which they carried their political arguments, that this symbol could arouse emotions strong enough to affect greatly certain values and beliefs. The co-operation of the parties in the Coalition government from 1940 to 1945 and the subsequent Labour government greatly reduced the extreme affect of this symbol. But Socialism and anti-Socialism remain important sources of emotional attachment to the major parties, and Socialism is a symbol which both unites and divides active members of the Labour Party. Although the emotions aroused among political activists are strong, they are rarely strong enough to inhibit personal relations between Socialists and non-Socialists.[40]

Outlining the historical origins of the contemporary political culture, as in Table 1, gives only a very approximate picture of a complex process; yet this simplification also underscores certain basic characteristics. The outline illustrates that any attempt to date the point at which a political culture became modern is misleading. The majority of attitudes prominent in the culture today can be traced back to traditional, preindustrial English society. Yet this long lineage does not make them incompatible with the activities of a twentieth-century industrial society. The Industrial Revolution resulted in a complete transformation of the economy, but not in a comparable change in the political culture. Some norms of the traditional culture failed to survive, some were adapted, and some have remained im-

---

[39] See, e.g., A. H. Birch, *Representative and Responsible Government*, London, Allen & Unwin, 1964, Chaps. 12-13.

[40] Cf. Graham Wallas, *Human Nature in Politics*, London, Constable, 1948 edn., pp. 92-94; the debate on nationalization launched by Hugh Gaitskell, in *Report of the Fifty-Eighth Annual Conference of the Labour Party*, 1959, pp. 105ff.; and Almond and Verba, *op.cit.*, Chap. 5.

TABLE 1: THE HISTORICAL ROOTS OF ENGLISH POLITICAL CULTURE

Value or Symbol	Pre-Industrial	Early Industrial ca. 1832-1918	Post-1918
Beneficent government	X	-,/	/,X
Liberty	X	X	X
Universal suffrage	-	-,X	X
Deference	X	X	X,/
Equality	-	-	-,X
Trust	X	X	X
Privacy	X	X,/	X
Diffuse leadership	X	X	X,/
Limits on government	X	X	X,/
Collective action	X	-,/	X
Consultation	X	/	X
Welfare benefits	X	/,-	X
Military defense	X	/,-	X,-
Static society	X	-	/,X
Evolution and assimilation	X	/	X
Monarchy	/,X	X	X
Past traditions	X	/	X
Community	X	X,-	X
Empire and Commonwealth	O	-,X	X
World Power	/	/,X	X
Parliament	X	X	X
Socialism	O	-	-,X

Symbols: X = Positively affirmed.   / = Partially affirmed.
 - = Rejected.   O = Not relevant.
More than one sign indicates sharp divisions.

portant. In this century there appears to have been a resurgence of emphasis upon certain attitudes from preindustrial England, such as welfare and past traditions. The result is a political culture which is neither traditional nor modern, but a mixture.

Since the mixture of traditional and non-traditional attitudes is, as Almond has argued, a characteristic of all political systems, the important point is the way in which contrasting values, beliefs, and emotions are combined within the system and within individual Englishmen. Writing of the English culture, Almond describes the combination as fusion: "In other words, all the way from right to left among the British public, the modern and the pre-modern attitudes are combined in such a way as to produce a homogeneous political culture, secular and traditional in content."[41] This broad definition blurs important distinctions between different processes of cultural

---

[41] "Introduction" in Almond and Coleman, *The Politics of Developing Areas*, pp. 24-25. Cf. the later and more complex discussion of this point in Almond and Verba, *The Civic Culture*, Chap. 15.

mixing. Outlooks rooted in different though not necessarily conflicting periods of English history coexist within the national society, within regions, and within local communities. Margaret Stacey has shown in a study of Banbury, a country town which had an aluminum factory built in it, that very different cultural outlooks can be held by people who, while living in the same small town, are "so widely separate socially that in practice they rarely meet face-to-face."[42] Political parties, social organizations, and trade unions institutionalize support for differing cultural attitudes; individuals thus may hold differing attitudes because of membership in organizations. They may also differ in outlook because of age, sex, education, and social class differences. Within an individual Englishman a mixture can result from an individual holding attitudes which are logically inconsistent, or which reflect preferences for competing political programs. Some individuals have no consistent attachment to particular norms. For instance, there appears to be considerable ambivalence among Englishmen in their support for the conflicting values of deference and equality; this ambivalence is important. Because of the variety of possibilities for combining support for norms, it would seem advisable to distinguish between instances in which apparent inconsistencies are integrated or fused in practice, and instances in which differences remain salient—as in Banbury or in contacts between competing pressure groups. In the latter instances, there is coexistence rather than fusion.

The persistence of differing outlooks, both in sub-cultures and in inconsistent outlooks of individuals, has been important in the peaceful and stable growth of the political system, because it has prevented abrupt breaks with tradition. Ties to the past, however, could be maintained in a transformed socioeconomic system only because preindustrial English society and its political leaders were predisposed to accommodate and assimilate social and political change. The result is a political culture which by its very mixture of values, beliefs, and symbols, provides a wide range of mechanisms for maintaining the legitimacy of the political system.[43]

III. *The Effects of Socialization*

In the course of initiating successive generations of Englishmen into the political system the agencies of political socialization both

---

[42] Margaret Stacey, *Tradition and Change*, p. 175.
[43] For illustrations of the ways in which traditional aspects of the political system help to legitimate governmental authority see Rose, *Politics in England*, Chap. 10.

perpetuate and modify major norms of the political culture. A mixture of attitudes from different times is strengthened because institutions important in political socialization are not wholly traditional or wholly modern.

The political influence of the family is a stabilizing one. Because of historically early industrialization and urbanization, the traditions of the parents are those of an urban, industrial society. Children learn in the family to take industrial society for granted, and strong face-to-face ties can coexist in communities with advanced industrial technologies. For instance, studies in older and in newer communities in the London area indicate that the ties between grandparents, parents, and children are strong. Social change does not stand between the generations of a family, as can easily happen in developing nations. Strong family beliefs in mutual aid appear to strengthen support for welfare values. The concern for the welfare of old-age pensioners, shown by all age groups in society, particularly illustrates this link. Indirectly, the family influences political attitudes and recruitment by the consequences it has for a child's education and his adult role expectations. In part this results from the fact that parents transmit to their children the relative advantages or disadvantages of their position in the class structure. But studies have also shown that within a given social class differences in attitudes of parents can be important in influencing the socialization of their children.[44] Furthermore the value placed upon assimilation—both by those with established high status in politics and by those seeking it—makes it possible for parents and children to think in terms of high mobility between generations. The influence of family is not as important as the influence of caste in other societies.

The influence of the class structure upon the development of political attitudes is not a phenomenon unique to England, although it appears to be more important there in its influence upon party and party loyalties than in societies such as America, Canada, and Australia.[45] The mixture of the culture is reflected in the variety of class structures which coexist within the political system. There is a structure involving deference to those at the apex of an organic hierarchy

[44] See, e.g., Michael Young and Peter Willmott, *Family and Kinship in East London*, Harmondsworth, Penguin, 1962; Almond and Verba, *op.cit.*, Chap. 12; Brian Jackson and Dennis Marsden, *Education and the Working Class*, London, Routledge, 1962; and D. V. Glass, ed., *Social Mobility in Britain*, London, Routledge, 1954.

[45] See Alford, *Party and Society*.

based upon the traditional social relations of preindustrial England. Its political significance can be found not only in agricultural areas, but also in the deference which many urbanized, middle-class persons pay to upper-class politicians and, to a much lesser extent, in that paid by a minority of industrial manual workers. Intensive studies by Elizabeth Bott indicate that Englishmen who have had a variety of social experiences have a conception of class which involves many kinds of social discrimination. In practice, this can be an implicit use of role analysis. Since roles can be taken, or changed, much more easily than class identifications, this model makes for political adaptation and flexibility in the system. Studies have shown that some Englishmen conceive of class relations as reflecting conflicting interests between workers and those in leadership positions; this model of class relations is often explicitly linked to politics by respondents in interviews. In its extreme form this produces the political subculture represented in the Labour left-wing and in right-wing Conservatives. In studying subjective aspects of class stratification F. M. Martin found that both manual workers and middle-class respondents tended to be inclusive rather than exclusive in their assignment of others to social classes; the respondent's own class was often regarded as embracing most of society, and the opposing class was perceived as small. Politically the Labour Party has sanctioned this ambivalence by emphasizing the importance of class in politics, yet defining its class basis so broadly—"the workers by hand or by brain" —that only *rentiers* are excluded.[46]

By segregating and stratifying young people into markedly different institutions for education the initial influence of family and class upon the formation of complementary political attitudes and role expectations is usually strengthened. The educational system has three main divisions. The public schools, expensive boarding institutions, educate about 3 per cent of young people from the age of 8 or 13 to 18. Although the numbers so educated are very small, they form a large portion of those in national political roles, both in elective and appointive offices and in the higher civil service. The public schools emphasize character building and educational achieve-

---

[46] Quoted from Clause IV of the Labour Party constitution. Cf. Elizabeth Bott, *Family and Social Network*; F. M. Martin, "Social Status and Electoral Choice in Two Constituencies," *British Journal of Sociology*, Vol. III, No. 3, 1952; J. M. Goldthorpe and David Lockwood, "Affluence and the British Class Structure," *The Sociological Review*, Vol. XI, No. 2, New Series, 1963, and the forthcoming study of deferential Conservatives by R. T. McKenzie and Allan Silver.

ment. The character model includes diffuse qualities valued as symbols of eligibility for national political office. Some public schools have maintained a tradition, often enjoined by their founders, of training young boys to accept the duty of public office, either within England or in the Empire. The emphasis upon duty, rather than privilege, has succeeded in internalizing self-restraints. Such restraint has been further stressed by the extent to which, within a school community, boys have been expected to conform to group norms, a conformity which, at least one author has argued, is a disincentive to question existing social institutions or to seek to innovate.[47] The grammar schools provide, at state expense, an academic education up to university entrance standards for about one-quarter of the population today, a group normally selected by examination at the age of 11. Those recruited come from a very wide range of social backgrounds, and similarly occupy a wide range of positions in the political system. For a minority of the very able the grammar school can be the means of mobility from an ordinary middle-class or skilled working-class family into a professional or upper-class social and political position. Studies suggest that for the majority at grammar school, the emphasis there upon accepted character values leads them to be strong supporters of existing political institutions and attitudes. This is not, however, true of the small fraction who go on to the universities.[48] About two-thirds of the population attend secondary modern schools, which provide a non-academic terminal education from the age of 11 to 15. (A variety of specialized schools absorb the small remainder not educated in these three major institutions.) In colloquial language, pupils at secondary modern schools are said to have "failed," that is, not to have won a place at a grammar school. The majority of the electorate left school before World War II, when this stigma was less important because youths from working-class homes were not expected to have had any secondary education. The extent to which education is important in recruitment into elective office is indicated in Table 2, which shows the relationship between secondary education and membership of Parliament. The table illustrates how egalitarian political institutions such as popular elections can be combined with deferential cultural attitudes.

[47] Rupert Wilkinson, *op.cit.*
[48] See Frances Stevens, *The Living Tradition*, London, Hutchinson, 1960; Jackson and Marsden, *Education and the Working Class*, and *Students in Society*, Man-Manchester, University Union, 1963.

TABLE 2: THE EDUCATION OF M.P.'S ANALYZED BY PARTY
(in per cent)

Education	Estimated Population	M.P.'s Conservative	Labour	All
Public school/public school and university	3	72	18	50
Grammar school and university	2	12	23	17
Grammar school only	16	14	23	18
Elementary school only	79	2	36	15

Note: Data adapted from D. E. Butler and Richard Rose, *The British General Election of 1959*, p. 128.

Today the majority of Englishmen leave school at the age of 15; before the last war the age was lower. The job as much as the school is the place in which formative adolescent years are spent. Because of the influence of family background and of education upon occupational choice, for the great majority of youths going to work does not involve a major change in their position in society.[49] At work, both manual and non-manual workers are subjected to a variety of forms of organizational discipline which affect their sense of political competence. The majority of male manual workers join trade unions and, studies show, union membership strengthens support for characteristic labour attitudes.[50] The trade unions are politically the most important of a number of class-specific institutions, including council house estates, co-operative societies, mutual-benefit funds, and working-mens' clubs. These institutions can reinforce face-to-face ties in industrial communities and furthermore they can represent these ties in national politics, providing countervailing influence against organizations in which upper- and middle-class outlooks predominate. Although the political interest of individual members of working-class organizations is often limited, this does not prevent organization officials, especially in class-specific trade unions, from deeply involving themselves, their organizations, and by

---

[49] In the writer's opinion the social mobility analysis of D. V. Glass, ed. *Social Mobility*, p. 183, can be interpreted to support this statement, for most of the movement which Glass reports is of only one rank in a stratification model composed of seven ranks.

[50] *Trade Unions and the Public in 1964*, London: British Institute of Public Opinion, 1964; Almond and Verba, *op.cit.*, Chap. 12.

implication their members in national politics by pressure-group activity, work within the Labour Party and negotiations with government departments. The class-specific trade unions have provided since the late nineteenth century an important channel especially reserved for recruiting manual workers into national politics. Although the unions stress performance criteria and seniority in selecting officials, the class basis of membership ensures that all potential officials will have ascriptive qualifications as well. (Similarly there is a concealed class bias favoring the well born and expensively educated in civil service examinations nominally testing for intellectual achievement.) There are a large number of local government authorities and Labour parliamentary seats which consistently nominate and elect working-class men as representatives. Because class ties are important, more manual workers are elected to Parliament than are elected in the United States to Congress.[51] Yet for the majority of the working class in the Labour Party, membership is indirect, and trade union as well as face-to-face class ties mediate between the party and five-sixths of its members. In a complementary fashion, individual Conservative Party members may be joined by social ties and ties of class with others in the party. Intermediate loyalties rooted in class-specific organizations and relationships are restraints against the party dominating the life of its members, yet simultaneously they can strengthen emotions of party loyalty by reinforcing them with emotions associated with face-to-face loyalties.[52]

Party organizations are socializing institutions for a minority active in politics. Parties have branches in every community and membership is open to all. Approximately one-quarter of the electorate are nominally party members, although only a small fraction of this number are actually active members. The greater an individual's activity in a political party, the greater the chance that the party itself will be a significant institution of political socialization for him. Party doctrines might suggest that the parties stimulate the development of ideologically conflicting cultural attitudes. Sometimes that does happen, but the analysis of policy resolutions forwarded to the

[51] Cf. e.g., D. R. Matthews, *United States Senators and their World*, Chapel Hill, University of North Carolina Press, 1960, Chap. 2; and Table 2, *supra*. See also D. C. Miller, "Industry and Community Power Structure," *American Sociological Review*, Vol. XXIII, No. 1, 1958.

[52] See especially Egon Wertheimer, *Portrait of the Labour Party*, pp. 112ff. For theoretical background see William Kornhauser, *The Politics of Mass Society*, London, Routledge, 1960.

annual conferences of the parties by constituency association activists suggests that it is not often the case: half the resolutions lack any significant ideological content, and only one-quarter might be classified as immoderate.[53] Activity in local parties at the leadership level is more likely to provide socialization into the political ethic of compromise and bargaining. Local parties are usually governed by collegial means and not by autocratic ward leaders. Election of a local activist to the city council will introduce him to the need for compromise with other elected representatives as well as to the difficulties of reconciling party principles with the problems of public administration. In both the Conservative and Labour parties there has been a clear tendency for party members rising to positions of authority and importance to adopt a bargaining approach to policy making; partisans who unwaveringly insist upon rigid ideological principles usually remain in the political wilderness.

Parties are not the only political institution socializing adult recruits into the specific norms of particular political roles. The administrative class of the civil service has for generations emphasized the importance of socialization to role, and has most thoroughly bureaucratized procedures for ensuring that those in leading positions will have already spent half their life or more in subordinate positions in the administration internalizing the outlooks of older men, before they are promoted to positions where they have much personal leeway. Similarly, the highest offices in trade unions and other pressure groups are usually awarded on a basis of seniority. In promoting M.P.'s into the ranks of Cabinet ministers, a wider variety of achievements may qualify persons for high office, but the clear tendency of the parliamentary system is to put a high premium upon the successful adaptation to ministerial norms while in subordinate and junior ministerial office. For instance, in this century the average Prime Minister has spent 26 years in Parliament before reaching that office.[54] The length and intensity of role socialization is particularly significant in integrating the activities of those in

[53] See Richard Rose, "The Political Ideas of English Party Activists," *American Political Science Review*, Vol. LVI, No. 2, 1962; and similar conclusions in A. H. Birch, *Small-Town Politics*, London, Oxford University Press, 1959, Chaps. 4-6.

[54] On the career length of M.P.'s see P. W. Buck, *Amateurs and Professionals in British Politics, 1918-1959*, Chicago, University Press, 1963; on civil servants, see, e.g., C. H. Sisson, *The Spirit of British Administration*, London, Faber, 1959. On role socialization in political parties and government see Richard Rose, "The Emergence of Leaders," *New Society*, No. 55, October 17, 1963.

central government, because implicit customs and traditions are disproportionately important.

The cumulative effect of the agencies of socialization upon the majority of the population appears to reinforce existing political attitudes. Family background, education, and work experience tend to be consistent, and churches are no longer so important as institutions dividing society politically. It is relatively simple for most Englishmen to acquire a sense of political identity; the instabilities of an ex-colonial nation are unknown, nor are there the variety of religious, racial, and ethnic differences which inhibit status crystallization in America. Institutional arrangements exist in the educational system, in the economy, and particularly in party politics and pressure groups for a few individuals to become highly mobile both politically and socially. Equally important is the fact that class-specific institutions make it possible for politically interested manual workers to occupy important political roles without any greater degree of mobility than that involved in promotion within a trade union. The provision made for deviations from modal patterns of political socialization allows for the assimilation of many kinds of aspirants into national political roles. As an aristocratic Conservative M.P., Lord Balniel, has remarked, "The entire Establishment is preserved not so much by the conscious efforts of the well-established but by the zeal of those who have just won entry and by the hopes of those who still aspire."[55]

IV. *The Interaction of the Political Culture, Institutions, and the Socioeconomic System*

An important influence upon a nation's political development arises from the interaction of the several parts of the social system which have heretofore been treated separately. A case study of the changing criteria for recruiting high-level civil servants can illustrate the complex nature of this interaction. The problem of recruiting an efficient bureaucracy is one common to all political systems undergoing modernization, because of the importance of the civil service in maintaining political stability, adapting the institutions of government, and attaining policy goals. The development of the British civil service is particularly significant because of its impact upon the civil

---

[55] "The Upper Class," *The Twentieth Century*, Vol. CLXVII, No. 999, May 1960, p. 432. See also Ralph Turner, "Sponsored and Contest Mobility," *American Sociological Review*, Vol. XXVI, No. 3, 1961.

service of many former colonies;[56] in fact, crucial innovations were adopted in British India before being applied to the home civil service in the mid-nineteenth century. Furthermore some of the major features of Victorian modernization are today challenged as inadequate to meet contemporary needs.

While the socioeconomic system was becoming industrialized, civil service recruitment took place through traditional procedures of patronage or the purchase of offices. Office holders did not necessarily perform the duties of the office; some hired substitutes at a fraction of their official income. These methods of appointment were not peculiar to the political system; they also existed in the Church, in the universities, and in the army as well. They reflected cultural values so strong that critics such as Edmund Burke did not attack the assumptions of recruitment but only particular abuses. In part, patronage functioned as a means of securing support for the government from those with electoral influence. Insofar as promotion went according to merit and seniority, the operation of patronage in initial recruitment handicapped, but did not impose insuperable difficulties upon the work of the departments of government, with small staffs and few tasks. Appointment to profitable sinecures had the latent function of reducing the pressure for patronage appointments to offices in which appointees were required to be regular and efficient in their work. Traditional procedures as well as traditional offices remained important for centuries. For instance, the Treasury did not adopt completely the use of the English language and Arabic numerals until compelled to do so by legislation in the 1830's.[57]

Industrialization did not depend upon the initiative of the governments of George III. The reform of administration followed socioeconomic change, and socioeconomic changes influenced cultural values. The political economists of laissez faire criticized the economic waste of patronage, and the Benthamites, dedicated to the rationalization of political institutions, objected to its administrative inadequacies. These inadequacies were highlighted by the new burdens imposed upon government administration by legislation

---

[56] See in particular Ralph Braibanti, "The Civil Service of Pakistan," *South Atlantic Quarterly*, Vol. LVIII, No. 2, 1959; L. W. Pye, *Politics, Personality and Nation-Building*, New Haven, Yale University Press, 1962; and Ronald Wraith and Edgar Simpkins, *Corruption in Developing Countries: Including Britain Until the 1880's*, London, Allen & Unwin, 1963.

[57] See, e.g., Emmeline W. Cohen, *The Growth of the British Civil Service*, London, Allen & Unwin, 1941, Chaps. 2-4.

designed to meet demands arising from industrialization. Between 1797 and 1841 the civil service had not shown a net increase in size, but between 1841 and 1851 the numbers more than doubled, rising from 16,000 to 39,000. In the words of a senior civil servant about 1850, "Official habits have become inadequate to the urgency and volume of modern business."[58] Great administrative reforms were needed and they were underway.

The irony is that administrators recruited by traditional means were leaders in the effort to adapt political institutions to cope with problems resulting from changes in cultural expectations and in the socioeconomic system. The crisis occurred in the decades around 1850 —before the modernization of recruitment took effect. Three points are crucial. Under the patronage system important administrative posts were sometimes given to men who had not undergone intensive role socialization in the prevailing traditionalistic norms of the civil service at a time when it was necessary to reject many traditional attitudes. It enabled outsiders—men described by G. Kitson Clark as "known and mature and often obstreperous experts"—to be given key positions at a time "when the traditions were unsettled but the needs of government expanding." Furthermore those strong-minded appointees, intent upon change, were supervised by political ministers —also recruited in traditional ways—who were uncertain of their policies concerning administration, and lacked strong party and government support. Hence the outsiders brought in to fill posts inside government managed to get away with intriguing and lobbying unceasingly for their reforms, though this was not entirely consistent with the attitudes of the time. The reformers proceeded to institutionalize their outlook, moreover, by achieving the reform of methods of recruiting civil servants, including the appointment of technically competent men to new specialist jobs such as factory inspectors.[59]

Once the administrative machinery had been adapted, the task of government became that of maintaining the new institutional arrange-

---

[58] Quoted by Edward Hughes, "Sir Charles Trevelyan and Civil Service Reform, 1853-1855," *English Historical Review*, Vol. LXIV, No. 250, 1949, pp. 56-57. For statistics on growth see W. J. M. Mackenzie and J. W. Grove, *Central Administration in Britain*, London, Longmans, 1957, Chap. 1.

[59] See especially G. Kitson Clark, "'Statesmen in Disguise,'" *The Historical Journal*, Vol. II, No. 1, 1959, pp. 35ff. On the institutionalization of reform see especially Oliver MacDonagh, *A Pattern of Government Growth, 1800-1860*, London, MacGibbon & Kee, 1961. For a local study of reform see David Roberts, *Victorian Origins of the British Welfare State*, New Haven, Yale University Press, 1960, Chap. 10. Roberts dates the great change as completed by 1854.

ments then in existence. At this point the veteran publicists and controversialists who had contributed to introducing reforms began to disappear or to be pushed out of office. The *Northcote-Trevelyan Report*, published in 1854, laid down the basic principles for a "modern" recruitment policy to replace the traditional system. The report recommended the recruitment of young graduates for the highest positions in the civil service. Young men were recommended on both grounds of economy and of their "superior docility." (Docility, that is, readiness to accept existing attitudes toward administration, was also a characteristic of many appointed in youth on patronage grounds.) The report recommended appointment on the basis of diffuse merit, tested by examinations of the academic type measuring general ability, with the difficulty of the examination graded to match the difficulty of the work. The centralization of appointments in the hands of a Civil Service Commission was also recommended as a safeguard against ministers' continuing to exercise patronage power.[60]

The recommendations of the report were adopted. The changes, though great, were not abrupt. The chief points concerning recruitment were not put into effect until sixteen years after the report was published, and the process was not completed until the end of World War I. That meant that a few senior officials serving in the government after World War II had been recruited on prereform bases.[61] Furthermore, as new recruits entered established departments they did not immediately make their influence felt; they were first trained to perform duties by those recruited in traditional ways. Even recruits to new departments had to learn to work with established departments, particularly the Treasury. The introduction of achievement criteria did not end ascriptive advantages, because examinations for the administrative class home civil service presupposed a university education, and that was then the prerogative of the well born and the wealthy. In 1854 William Gladstone argued that the reform would "strengthen and multiply the ties between the higher classes and the possession of administrative power. As a Member of Parliament for Oxford, I look forward eagerly to its operation."[62] A later Socialist critic called the reforms "rational class nepotism."

---

[60] The *Northcote-Trevelyan Report* is conveniently reprinted in *Public Administration*, Vol. XXXII, Spring 1954.

[61] See, e.g., Robert Heussler, *Yesterday's Rulers*, Syracuse, N.Y., University Press, 1963; and Sir Ralph Furse, *Aucuparius*, London, Oxford University Press, 1962.

[62] Quoted by Edward Hughes, "Civil Service Reform, 1853-1855," *Public Administration*, Vol. XXXII, Spring 1954, p. 28. Cf. H.R.G. Greaves' comment, *The*

The reforms were important in strengthening influence of political institutions upon the socioeconomic system, since the maintenance of efficient administration is a prerequisite for government intervention in the economy and in the social services. The reformers also believed that the government, by recognizing educational merit, would encourage greater attention being given to examination success at Oxford and Cambridge, then intellectually at low ebb. Furthermore, the creation of a unified and efficient civil service was important in developing Treasury control of expenditure, the institutional device by which the laissez faire value of keeping government expenditure to a minimum was achieved. Government expenditure as a percentage of the gross national product actually fell from 11 per cent to 9 per cent between 1792 and 1890.[63]

Today recruitment to the administrative class of the civil service still reflects values of the Northcote-Trevelyan report. English critics of the civil service attack procedures which were thought modern a century ago on the ground that they can be justified only by an appeal to tradition. Of particular significance in this dispute is the concern with the relative advantages of recruiting young graduates on the basis of general or specific expertise. The dispute is invested with strong emotional overtones inasmuch as diffuse and non-technical education has historically been associated with gentlemanly status, and technical and specific skills have not. The proponents of nineteenth-century reform were clear in their views. Lord Macaulay argued that general intellectual ability was so much more important than specific training that, "If astrology were taught at our universities, the young man who cast nativities best would generally turn out a superior man." The Northcote-Trevelyan report however contained the suggestion that examinations in modern subjects such as economics, as well as in classical subjects, would encourage the study of modern subjects. But Benjamin Jowett, soon to become the influential Master of Balliol College, Oxford, wrote in a letter appended to the official report, "The knowledge of Latin and Greek is, perhaps, upon the whole, the best test of regular, previous education." In the debate on the report, a government inspector of educa-

---

British Constitution, London, Allen & Unwin, 2d edn., 1948, p. 164; and the statistical analysis of R. K. Kelsall, *Higher Civil Servants in Britain From 1870*, London, Routledge, 1955.

[63] See Alan T. Peacock and Jack Wiseman, *The Growth of Public Expenditure in the United Kingdom*, London, Oxford University Press, 1961, pp. 35ff.

tion, the Rev. Canon Mosley, argued for greater attention to be given in examinations to modern and technical subjects. He feared that classics graduates would have learned "not to accept the present of human knowledge or to look to the future, but hark back to the past." Jowett triumphed.[64]

The debate about the relative value of examining for general intellectual ability or for specific expertise continues today. Most administrative-class civil servants are still recruited on grounds established a century ago. This is especially true of those recruited before World War II and now holding leading positions in the service.[65] Since the war, the number of recruits with a generalist's classical education has been about equal to the total with expert training in social studies, mathematics, science, and engineering combined (see Table 3). Because intensive academic specialization begins in England

TABLE 3: EDUCATIONAL SPECIALIZATION IN CIVIL SERVICE RECRUITMENT
Administrative Class, Home Civil Service
(per cent)

Special Subject	1948-1956	1957-1962	Total
English history	32.4	33.4	32.8
Classics	20.9	24.7	22.2
Economics and politics	10.5	10.5	10.5
Philosophy, politics and economics	9.5	6.9	8.6
Modern languages	8.7	6.9	8.1
English literature	5.7	5.0	5.5
Law	4.0	4.7	4.2
Mathematics	2.3	0.7	1.7
Science and engineering	1.1	2.5	1.6
None	0	0.7	0.2
Other subjects	4.9	3.6	4.5
	(N = 527)	(N = 275)	(N = 802)

Source: *Recruitment to the Administrative Class*, London, HMSO, Cmnd. 232, 1957; and Civil Service Commissioners, *Annual Report*, London, HMSO, 1957-1962.

[64] Cf. *The Life and Letters of Lord Macaulay*, London, Longmans, 1923 edn., Vol. II, pp. 585-586, 609-610; Jowett's letter, printed with the original report, C. 1713, 1854, p. 27, and Canon Mosley's comments, both in *Papers Relating to the Re-Organization of the Civil Service*, London, Eyre & Spottiswoode for HMSO, 1855, p. 39.

[65] The subsequent discussion and statistics do not include persons promoted into the administrative class from lower grades in the civil service because few entrants by promotion in fact reach the politically most important posts. See R. K. Kelsall, *Higher Civil Servants*, Chap. 3.

by the age of 16, the choice of subjects of study by civil service candidates also involves the avoidance of other fields of knowledge. Today, as in the nineteenth century, recruits come very disproportionately from upper- and middle-class families, from public schools, and from Oxford and Cambridge. (Unsuccessful candidates have similar social and educational characteristics.) Great changes in university education have not been reflected in great changes in recruitment. Today three-quarters of undergraduates do not attend Oxford or Cambridge and do not specialize in the liberal arts at their universities. Nonetheless, the processes of preadult political socialization continue to work in long-established ways, so that only a relatively small number of graduates identify themselves as potential administrative-class civil servants.[66] The great majority do not expect or wish to go into the administrative class, notwithstanding efforts of the Civil Service Commissioners to get a wider variety of graduates to compete for appointments. The expectations established by Victorian reforms remain predominant. Particularly significant, in view of the contribution made a century ago by mature men recruited from outside the civil service, is the fact that only in the exceptional circumstances such as wartime does recruitment of men in middle age now occur.

The value of recruiting on the basis of general intellectual ability rather than special skills is defended and criticized today on much the same grounds as those used in the 1850's. According to Lord Bridges, former head of the civil service, there is always the need of laymen in key positions ready "to call a halt when the departmental enthusiast shows signs of getting out of hand." Insofar as specialist knowledge is useful, it is argued that such specialized knowledge can be acquired only on the job; therefore, no formal academic preparation is necessary. Insofar as classical education requires individuals to learn a very unfamiliar body of specialized and remote knowledge that education might be said to be useful training for administrators who will quickly have to assess complex and unfamiliar problems in their work. In practice a young recruit with a generalist's education may spend his government career acquiring highly specialized knowledge within one or two departments while lacking knowledge of extragovernmental viewpoints both because of his education and his devotion of a lifetime to one job. The result is, in the opinion of one

---

[66] See *Recruitment to the Administrative Class*, London, HMSO, Cmnd. 232, 1957; *Returns from Universities and University Colleges, 1961-1962*, London, HMSO, Cmnd. 2135, 1963, and for interpretative comments, W.J.M. Mackenzie, "Problems of Administrative Reform," *The Listener*, February 28, 1963, pp. 367-368.

student of comparative administration, "members of the administrative class have very narrow horizons."[67]

Because of high intellectual standards for recruits, young administrators have no difficulty in learning the difficult and complicated business of managing the coordination of routine governmental affairs and coping with *ad hoc* crises when they arise. (A crisis on the scale of a major war, however, has usually required the drafting of many recruits from outside the established service, including specialists.) Yet the administrators, and *a fortiori* the political ministers supervising them, often lack the results of expert research needed to foresee the long-term consequences of existing policies in changing conditions. For instance, when a Cabinet minister wishes an analysis of social change, he can entrust to a journalist the task of writing a memorandum for his colleagues. In the opinion of D. N. Chester, a wartime civil servant and now an Oxford academic, only the Colonial Office and the Home Office have made adequate provision for carrying on expert research relevant to their responsibilities.[68] The utility of expert knowledge in framing government policy has become more widely recognized in the 1960's, but the generalist outlook (often called the amateur outlook) is still predominant.[69]

The difficulties of the Treasury in recruiting and utilizing economists in making economic plans is particularly significant as an example of generalist-expert relations. The Treasury has always been a pre-eminent department of government, and it has enjoyed special responsibility for staffing the civil service and promoting and posting members of the administrative class. Many of the most able young recruits have sought and obtained posts in the Treasury; it does not lack men of high general ability. In the context of late nineteenth-century English society it proved efficient in the negative task of limiting expenditure, in Gladstone's words, "the saving of candle ends." The Treasury remained an institutional bastion of the

[67] Brian Chapman, *British Government Observed*, London, Allen & Unwin, 1963, p. 23. For the tribute to the power of the generalist to restrict action, see Sir Edward (later Lord) Bridges, *Treasury Control*, London, Athlone Press, 1956 edn., p. 22.

[68] D. N. Chester, "Research as an Aid in Public Administration," *Public Administration*, Vol. XL, Spring 1962. On the survey of social change, see House of Commons *Debates*, Vol. 671, cols. 406-416, February 5, 1963; and the survey, reprinted in *New Society*, No. 13, December 27, 1962.

[69] The distrust of specialists in part reflects the social gulf between many academic social scientists and Conservative Cabinet ministers. On this see Timothy Raison, "Towards a Tory Sociology," *Crossbow*, Vol. VII, No. 25, 1963, and articles in the special number on sociology of *The Twentieth Century*, Vol. CLXVII, No. 999, 1960.

value of minimizing government expenditure until World War II. Yet the Boer War and then World War I resulted in the recognition of the Treasury's need for more expert economic skills; in particular, the first World War had required much expert ability to cope with complex socioeconomic problems. In 1917 the government began to experiment in various ways to provide an institutional basis for economists to contribute their skills to policy-making. As socioeconomic problems increased in difficulty, and cultural demands for government management of the economy increased in intensity, successive Prime Ministers and Chancellors of the Exchequer have tried first one arrangement and then another. After forty-four years of government attempts to integrate economists into the Treasury a committee headed by Lord Plowden, a former official planner, reported in 1961 that "the traditional system in this country as it developed in the nineteenth century" still prevailed: "the system is one of piecemeal decisions."[70] According to critics, successive failures of Treasury efforts to plan in part reflect a failure of the Treasury generalists to make best use of expert planners.[71]

The political institutions, however, have not remained inflexible. The repeated attempts of the Treasury to use economists indicate that even this conservative department has been seeking to adapt. The Conservatives' attempted solution, establishment of the National Economic Development Council in 1962 independent of the Treasury and other administrative departments, is characteristic of the British pattern of institutional adaptation to meet changing cultural expectations and socioeconomic conditions.* The NEDC straddles the boundaries between the political and economic systems; its members include the government economic ministers, business spokesmen and trade unionists. Most significantly, the full-time staff has been re-

---

[70] *Control of Public Expenditure*, para. 8.
[71] See, e.g., D. N. Chester and F.M.G. Willson, *The Organization of British Central Government, 1914-1956*, London, Allen & Unwin, 1957, pp. 292ff., 321ff.; P. D. Henderson, "Government and Industry" in G.D.N. Worswick and P. H. Ady, *The British Economy in the Nineteen-Fifties*, Oxford, Clarendon Press, 1962; Thomas Balogh, "The Apotheosis of the Dilettante," in *The Establishment*, and Hans Daalder, *Cabinet Reform in Britain, 1914-1963*, London, Oxford University Press, 1964.

* Harold Wilson, upon installation as Labour Prime Minister in October 1964, left the formal structure of NEDC in existence, but transferred functions and staff from it to a specially created Ministry of Economic Affairs. By careful use of appointive powers the new Prime Minister installed anti-traditionalist outsiders in key jobs at the Treasury. These changes, made after the above was written, further illustrate the strong differences of political opinion in England today about the best method of re-organizing the machinery of economic planning in order to "re-modernize" the economy.

cruited from outside the administrative-class civil service; it is largely recruited on grounds of expertise. The NEDC is in this respect typical of many boards, agencies, public authorities, and committees which have been established by or taken over by the government without being integrated into the structure of government departments. The nationalized industries, with approximately 2 million employees, form the largest single group in the twilight world between central government and private organizations. Bodies such as the Atomic Energy Authority and the Medical Research Council are examples of institutions established to serve specialized needs. In some instances, however, the administrative heads of these specialist bodies are not experts but generalists, or even ex-civil servants, for the Treasury exercises influence in the nomination and appointment of individuals to some of these extra-departmental extensions of government. In a complementary fashion, many specialist grades exist within the established departments; a recent estimate was of about 640 specialist classifications, some dating back to the middle of the nineteenth century. The officially described "highest" ranks of the civil service, numbering 171 men at the top of the salary scale, divides into 44 per cent in specialist classes and 56 per cent in the administrative class. The scientific officer grade comparable to the administrative class is about one-third larger than is the generalist grouping. In a sense the increase in the number of specialists and in the number of specialist agencies outside the departments increases the problems arising from the generalist bias in recruiting for the administrative class. Reasons are that the latter class provides by far the largest number working closely with the political ministers in charge of the government, and it dominates the Treasury, which by its budgetary authority and control of personnel enjoys a pervasive influence throughout government. The specialists are to a great extent segregated from generalists and tend to occupy fewer strategically important positions. The result is tension between contrasting kinds of individuals recruited for government employment on contrasting definitions of achievement. Occasionally, as in C. P. Snow's lectures on science in government, the tension erupts into public controversy.[72]

The changes in recruitment to the senior civil service—and the

[72] *Science and Government*, London, Oxford University Press, 1961. Cf. Z.M.T. Tarkowski and A. V. Turnbull, "Scientists vs. Administrators," *Public Administration*, Vol. XXXVII, Autumn 1959; and the comments of businessmen Conservative M.P.'s in *Change or Decay*, London, Conservative Political Center, 1963, pp. 17ff. For basic statistics, see W.J.M. Mackenzie and J. W. Grove, *op.cit.*, Chaps. 3 and 7.

absence of changes—indicate the way in which the cultural value of assimilation is expressed in the processes of politics. Industrialization caused great socioeconomic changes and changes in attitudes toward the activities of government. These resulted in legislation which greatly expanded the tasks of central government—though at first much of the burden remained with local authorities—and the resulting pressure led to the reform of methods of recruiting senior administrators. Yet, though achievement criteria were introduced, the leading positions have remained largely the preserve of a socially small strata of generalists and gentlemen. Institutions of government have expanded enormously in size in this century, and multiplied in number too. Both changes have enabled the government to benefit from expert skills without dislodging the administrative generalists from their central, strategic position. The recurring difficulty of the Treasury in integrating especially skilled economists into its structure provides a particularly striking example of the limits beyond which new recruits have not been assimilated. Today the work of the economy is influenced by the combined efforts of officials in three public bodies: the Treasury, recruited on grounds of general achievement; the National Economic Development Council, recruited for expert skills; and the Bank of England, which appears to employ ascriptive criteria because of the predominance of a small group of bankers related by family, by schooling, and by marriage. What is traditional in the political system assimilates change, and what is once modern can itself become neotraditional.

V. The Political System and Socioeconomic Change

From the point of view of political leaders the crucial question concerning the interaction of parts of society is: To what extent can those in public office play an important part in stimulating and carrying out major socioeconomic changes? The experience of modernization in England indicates that there is no simple answer to this question.

Many major developments in English society have had counterparts in other European nations and in older nations of the Commonwealth. An extreme interpretation of some similarities is that social change has been inevitable; developments in England have been only the working out of influences common to all societies at a particular stage of historical development. A comparative perspective is valuable in emphasizing that major events in English history have not been unique. But an international perspective also shows that, notwithstanding common influences, there have been very wide and significant variations in the nature of political change within countries subject to common influences arising from industrialization. For instance, the growth of welfare services has been a common feature of modern industrial societies in the past century. Yet the content and range of welfare services, the pace at which they have expanded, and the attitude toward such services vary considerably, and these variations appear to reflect political as well as socioeconomic influences.[73] Changes have not occurred with the gradual, almost imperceptible movement of, say, demographic changes. Instead they have followed prolonged political agitation and negotiation, resulting in the adoption by legislation of particular services at far from predetermined rates of benefit. Today the argument of inevitability is often used in discussing economic growth. Yet the dogmatic assurance that the economy will "inevitably" double its gross national product in 25 or 40 years does not help a Chancellor of the Exchequer faced with immediate problems concerning the rate, pace, timing, and nature of economic expansion in the short run.

The impact of war upon twentieth-century England provides a striking example of the influence unprecedented events can have upon the course of political development. The impact has been traced with some precision by Alan Peacock and Jack Wiseman in their study of national expenditure; in particular, they emphasize the extent to which the costs of war expand the limit of popular acceptance of higher tax rates. Once current war costs have been met, the increased revenue can be devoted to new programs as well as financing the long-term costs of wartime measures. Yet in what these economists take as a key field—welfare services—not only has expenditure risen directly in response to wartime innovations, but also it increased in the comparatively peaceful period of 1925-1935 and in the 1960's.[74] Furthermore, although the two World Wars and the Boer and Korean Wars have all influenced public policy, the nature of the influence has not been constant. For instance, welfare expenditure rose following both World Wars I and II, but the most important devel-

---

[73] See, e.g., a special number on the welfare state of the *European Journal of Sociology*, Vol. II, No. 2, 1961; and C. W. Pipkin, *Social Politics and Modern Democracies*, New York, Macmillan, 1931, 2 vols.

[74] See Alan T. Peacock and Jack Wiseman, *The Growth of Public Expenditure*; the appendix of J. Stirling, "Social Service Expenditure During the Last 100 Years," *The Advancement of Science*, Vol. VIII, No. 32, 1952; and *Public Expenditure in 1963-64 and 1967-68*, London, HMSO, Cmnd. 2235, 1963, p. 5.

opment was the change in the method of judging welfare needs, a change caused by the second war, but little affected by the first. Today global war is not raging, but England's political system is perhaps more dependent upon events in the international political system than it has been in past generations, when involvement did not cause so much dependency because of the country's greater international strength. In economics, in defense policy, in colonial affairs, and in diplomacy political leaders in England are often at the mercy of decisions and events outside the nation's control. For instance, in the six years of the 1945-51 Labour government, self-consciously committed to economic planning, fluctuations in the international economy three times caused major crises with wide repercussions throughout the social system. General de Gaulle's veto of The United Kingdom's application to join the European Common Market in January 1963 is an even more dramatic instance of the extent to which decisions taken in foreign nations can influence the country's political course.

In considering the role the government plays in social change it is important to distinguish between the intentions of politicians and the consequences of their decisions. In retrospect a historian may impose pattern and logic upon a policy decision, but in prospect, politicians may make *ad hoc* decisions without regard for long-term consequences. The point is particularly well documented by a case study of the drafting of the National Insurance Act of 1911. In retrospect, it can be seen to have been the basis of the expansion of welfare services because it introduced the insurance principle—a by no means inevitable outcome. The political decision was made by David Lloyd George, Chancellor of the Exchequer, in response to very immediate and short-term political influences. In the words of one of his civil service advisors, "We were embarking upon an unknown sea. No one could say what would happen with universal compulsory insurance and everyone held different views."[75]

The welfare services today continue to reflect the long-term consequences of the accretion of many *ad hoc* attempts to solve problems. Changes in circumstances can change the effects of decisions even when the decisions formally remain unaltered. For instance, in welfare services legislation may establish fixed benefits, but the amounts paid can vary by the amount of demand (as in unemployment in-

[75] W. J. Braithwaite, *Lloyd George's Ambulance Wagon*, London, Methuen, 1957, p. 127.

surance), in real purchasing power (as in government pensions), by changes in cultural expectations (demand for further education), by changing patterns of socioeconomic activity (as in the use of roads), or in the accumulation of subsidies (as in the case of an annual grant of a small number of housing subsidies cumulatively becoming large since each house is subsidized for 40 years). In some fields of policy, government departments can, in the course of improving the administration of existing laws, become active initiators of legislation expanding their scope of activity. Oliver MacDonagh has provided an intensive study of this process in the period 1800-1860. Analysis of legislation annually presented to Parliament today indicates the importance of government departments as sources of bills, many perhaps of a minor nature, but cumulatively of considerable significance.[76] Usually the departments introduce legislation only after consulting fully with quasi-governmental committees and extra-governmental pressure groups, and these consultations restrict the autonomy of the departments. Insofar as Cabinet ministers and their administrative advisors exercise initiative their problem is not so much whether their actions can have long-term consequences, but rather whether the consquences can be accurately predicted and controlled by governmental action. The point emerges with particular acuteness in economic planning.

Changes in cultural attitudes also appear to be of some importance in introducing alterations in the political system and the socioeconomic system. For instance, changes in attitudes toward government intervention in the economy, beginning in the latter half of the nineteenth century, gradually broadened the limits within which a government was expected legitimately to act.[77] Notwithstanding the magnitude of the impact of World War I upon the political system and society generally, attitudes toward the legitimate scope of government did not alter dramatically. The point was underscored by the election of two Labour governments in the 1920's, both of which had little desire to expand greatly the work of government. During World War II attitudes toward the role of government in

---

[76] See J. Stirling, *Public Expenditure*; Oliver MacDonagh, *op.cit.*; and the *Times*, London, September 19, 1963, "Many Bills Compete for Priority in Next Parliamentary Session," and similar stories in other years at about the same date.

[77] See, e.g., A. V. Dicey, *The Relation Between Law and Public Opinion in England During the Nineteenth Century*, London, Macmillan, 1962 edn.; Henry Parris, "The Nineteenth Century Revolution in Government; A Reappraisal Reappraised," *The Historical Journal*, Vol. III, No. 1, 1960; and D. N. Chester and F.M.G. Willson, *op.cit.*, pp. 24ff.

society changed greatly and swiftly. Wartime studies by Mass-Observation have documented the growth of this diffuse desire for radical political innovations; these focused toward the end of the war upon the Beveridge Report and were important in causing the election of a Labour government in 1945. However, these new expectations continued to coexist with older attitudes expecting little of government. Mass-Observation found that many of its respondents were ambivalent at the end of the war: they hoped for great changes but were partially discounting the prospects because of the memory of their prewar beliefs.[78] That ambivalence meant that the partial frustration of popular expectations during the economically difficult period after 1945 did not lead to discontent, since cultural ambivalence meant willingness to accept either the status quo or change. The extent to which changes in attitudes in the early 1960's have taken place and are putting political pressure upon the government to initiate social change has not been measured with any precision. Evidence from surveys conducted in 1958-1960 suggests that the increase in national wealth and in popular consumption in the 1950's had not been matched by a corresponding change in cultural expectations. In intensive interviews conducted in 1960 as part of the civic culture survey the great majority of respondents did not see political action as altering their own lives; when changes were perceived, they were seen as coming from primary relationships—marriage, the death of parents, widowhood, etc.[79] Nearly half could not suggest anything that the government could do to improve conditions for the people, and suggestions volunteered usually referred to improving existing welfare services and not to demand for great changes. Respondents regarded both parties as equally unlikely to stimulate change. Since then some national politicians and intellectuals have again begun to talk publicly about the need for major changes in political attitudes and in the socioeconomic system.[80] Whether such changes at the elite level, including the election of a labour govern-

---

[78] See Mass Observation "The World of Politics," London, typescript, ca. 1949, and data from that period in the files of the British Institute of Public Opinion. Note also, R. M. Titmuss, *Problems of Social Policy*, London, Longmans and HMSO, 1950.

[79] Responses tabulated by the author from unpublished life history interviews collected by Almond and Verba, *op.cit.* See also Peter Willmott, *The Evolution of a Community*, London, Routledge, 1963, Chap. 10; and F. Zweig, *The Worker in an Affluent Society*, London, Heinemann, 1961, pp. 189ff.

[80] See, e.g., "Suicide of a Nation," a special number of *Encounter*, No. 118, July, 1963; and Harold Wilson's speech, *Report of the Sixty-Second Annual Conference of the Labour Party*, 1963, pp. 133-140.

ment in 1964, have affected mass attitudes is doubtful; a sample survey conducted by the author in Stockport in March 1964, found few respondents who articulated strong desires for major changes.

SOME CONCLUSIONS

In attempting to assess the relative importance of such a variety of influences in the past and, by implication, their future importance one faces questions arising from England's experience that are generally relevant to nations in many phases of political development.

The relationship between the socioeconomic system and the parts of the political system. The foregoing analysis has shown that changes in the socioeconomic system, in political institutions and in the political culture have not been closely synchronized in modern English history. The case study in Part IV illustrates the way in which contrasting outlooks coexist. For instance, industrialization did not lead to recruitment for the highest-rank civil services on the basis of performance criteria and specialist skills, as in industry; instead, when recruitment changed, it was to emphasize qualities of general intelligence. Insofar as many features of the contemporary political system antedate industrialization in their origins, the experience of England suggests that the modernization of the socioeconomic system is not essential for stable, representative government, and that developments in the political system can take place in a time sequence more or less independent of socioeconomic development. Thus, the nature of any conclusion that a political scientist reaches about modernization in England is greatly influenced by the relative weights given to the socioeconomic system, the political institutions, and the political culture in defining modernization.

Modernization as a phase or a final goal. Because many comparative political studies concentrate upon nations yet to be developed, certain implications of a three-stage model of traditional, transitional, and modern societies are not always discussed. When the criteria by which modernization is usually measured are applied to English history, then it is found that some 50 to 100 years ago the nation reached the goal toward which most nations still strive. Yet the achievement of modernization by the late nineteenth century did not mean the end of political difficulties, as is often implied by the use of modern criteria as if they were absolute rather than relative measures. The landmark date of 1885 coincides almost exactly with the eruption of communal and religious strife in Ireland, which continued for nearly

40 years, threatening the legitimacy of the parliamentary regime and the Englishman's conception of national identity. Industrial unrest began to develop in the 1880's and culminated in the General Strike of 1926. Successive Conservative governments in the interwar years gave legislative expression to fear of industrial and political disorder. The fear was exaggerated but social and economic difficulties were real. They were exacerbated in the 1930's by the threat of world war. In the crucible of World War II many problems were solved, yet in postwar England new difficulties in the structure of industry, in foreign policy, and defense have emerged. The unprecedented decision of the Conservative government in 1961 to seek entry into the European Common Market, though aborted, is evidence of the radical diagnosis of national problems by the government.

The problem of "remodernization." In terms of its own history and its own future, England is a society in transition. Insofar as it has already become a modern society then the transition is toward a phase of history which might tentatively be labeled postmodern. Contemporary discussion in England reflects concern with the problems arising from the inherited burdens of nineteenth-century modernization—the need to replace the housing, now slums, provided for early industrial workers; the need to rejuvenate regions that grew as a consequence of early industrialization but are today in decline; and the need to reorganize the structure of the economy to compensate for the decline of such traditionally modern industries as coal, railroads, and shipbuilding. The need for changing cultural attitudes and political institutions is also a topic of discussion. In the judgment of the harshest English critics of the nation's position today, what is needed is a complete remodernization of society involving the removal of things once modern but now regarded as traditional. In order to separate the elements mixed together in such discussions, it is important to distinguish between what is traditional, rooted in eighteenth century preindustrial England; the traditionally modern introduced during the great changes of a century and more ago; what is contemporary, and what is, in the circumstances of contemporary England, situationally modern.

Political values and situationally modern goals. Politicians as well as social scientists are concerned with defining what are the situationally modern goals toward which government should aim in contemporary England. The controversy between the Labour and the Conservative Parties reflects the importance of values in answering what is initially posed as an academic question. An economist might emphasize economic growth as the chief goal in the contemporary situation. But a Socialist might argue that the redistribution of existing wealth and social advantages is the chief test of advance. Some might argue that modernism consists in greater humanitarianism and stress the importance of government provision of services for the underprivileged, the old, the mentally retarded and mentally ill, and criminals. Yet another standard might be rates of individual participation in politics—though social scientists might disagree as to the consequences for society of raising or lowering rates of popular participation. Even if maintenance of the existing political system is stated as the prime goal, questions of a technical nature still arise concerning the amount of adaptation required and desired to preserve in changing world conditions the existing situation of England.

The contrast between such questions and the questions that usually arise in studies of political development underscores the deviant position of England in the world today. Now, as for generations past, it is a society which stands apart from its neighbors. Its cultural outlook can best be characterized as a particular and peculiar mixture which merits the ambiguous description of traditionally modern.

CHAPTER 4

GERMANY: THE REMAKING OF POLITICAL CULTURE*

SIDNEY VERBA

THE problems of nation building and rapid change in political culture are most sharply focused in the newly independent nations. In these nations the problem of the creation of new political attitudes is particularly pressing, for so much must be accomplished at once. Not only must people not used to politics be brought into some stable pattern of political participation—for though the skills involved in political participation may not always be present, the demand for such participation is almost universal—but the very sense of national identity must be created at the same time. And this must all be accomplished while the battles of economic development and political independence are being fought.

In the more developed parts of the world the problem of citizen making is not so pressing and complicated, but it exists nevertheless. There is in the first place the need to create citizens out of each new generation. Even where the pattern of political attitudes in a nation remains relatively stable from generation to generation, each society must socialize young people into this pattern. But even stable nations do not merely transmit a set of political attitudes from generation to generation; they are also faced with the problem of the creation of new political attitudes. This may be because the nation is faced with a new set of problems; if former colonies have been faced with the problem of creating attitudes appropriate to their status as free nations, so have their former rulers been faced with the problem of creating new attitudes appropriate to their status as ex-colonial powers. Or an established nation may be faced with the problem of the creation of citizens out of new arrivals, as was the United States in the nineteenth century. Or the more established and industrialized nations may be faced with the problem of creation of new political attitudes to fit the problems of change and transformation in their postindustrial society—for change does not end with the industrial revolution.

* *Note*: The author is grateful to the Center of International Studies of Princeton University and to the Center for Advanced Study in the Behavioral Sciences for providing the opportunity to prepare this paper.

This is not to argue that the formation of a political culture is a constantly new and revolutionary process in the developed countries of the world. The point is, rather, that one cannot consider the issue settled. If a new culture is not being created at each moment, there are still aspects of the existing culture that are probably undergoing considerable change.

For those interested in the problem of the creation of a political culture a study of postwar German political attitudes is a valuable exercise. In the past decade and a half Germany has been faced with the problem of the remaking of a political culture. If there is uncertainty about the future of German democracy, it is not so much uncertainty about the constitutional structure of the Bonn Republic as about the political attitudes that lie behind the Constitution. The government institutions of a stable democracy exist, as do the non-government political institutions. But have German political ways of thinking been reshaped to provide a basis for a democratic political system?

There are several reasons why the analysis of German political attitudes since 1945 ought to be rewarding to the student of political culture and political change. In the first place, Germany is a highly modern, industrialized nation. It has a relatively high standard of living, an expanding economy, a highly developed system of mass media, widespread literacy, and a good school system. If, as some recent students have argued, stable democracy and high levels of economic development are closely related, Germany becomes an interesting deviant case.[1] Second, a study of German democracy in the Bonn Republic can be easily put in a comparative framework, for we have the previous attempt to create democracy in Germany with which to compare it. We may ask, as many others have, "Is Bonn Weimar?" But perhaps the most important reason why the question of German political culture is so interesting has to do with the intellectual history of attempts to understand Germany. To a large extent the psycho-cultural study of politics has its origin in German experience. Many of the classic works on the non-political roots of political attitudes—works that delved into psychological and social variables—were written by men trying to answer questions raised by German National Socialism. One thinks immediately of Adorno, Horkheimer, Lewin, and Fromm, as well as of the postwar studies

[1] See Seymour M. Lipset, *Political Man*, Garden City, Doubleday, 1960, Chap. 2.

of German political character.[2] While more traditional explanations of politics in terms of constitutions, issues, and institutions might have been satisfactory as an explanation of the failure of German democracy in the early 1930's, they appeared quite inadequate to explain the particular type of political system and ideology which replaced it. The explanation of Nazism required deeper social and psychological probing. In studying German political attitudes, therefore, we shall be studying an interesting part of the history of political analysis as well.

It may be, furthermore, that the experience of Germany with the problem of political culture change is more relevant to the problems of the new nations than is the experience of many other Western nations—though whether the experience of any Western nation is particularly relevant remains an open question. In some respects the position of Germany in 1945 resembles that of the new nations. Not only was Germany faced with the problem of the creation of new basic political attitudes; it was also faced with the more pressing problems of rebuilding an economy and a nation. The Germans had not merely to create new citizens but to create a new political and constitutional structure and find a position in world society at the same time. There was not only the problem of changing the schools but of rebuilding the schools. And within the realm of attitude change itself the number of crucial new attitudes that were needed was large. The legitimacy of the old political system was shattered with no new one to take its place, and the fundamental problem of national identity was unsolved. Of course the parallel should not be pushed too far. Germany in 1945 was by no means an underdeveloped new nation. But it was faced with a cumulation of problems in many ways similar to those confronting new nations.

The study of German political culture since World War II ought to be instructive for another purpose. Rarely has a nation undergone so self-conscious an attempt to change and remold politics and political attitudes in a democratic direction. Much of this change began under the auspices of the occupying powers, but it has been the continuing explicit concern of many Germans—particularly German educators—ever since. The study of Germany thus becomes a case

---

[2] See among others Bertram Schaffner, *Fatherland: A Study of Authoritarianism in the German Family*, New York, Columbia University Press, 1948; Henry V. Dicks, "Some Psychological Studies of German Character," in T. H. Pear, ed. *Psychological Factors of Peace and War*, New York, Philosophical Library, 1950; and David Rodnick, *Post-War Germans*, New Haven, Yale University Press, 1948.

study of the possibilities of the conscious manipulative change of fundamental political attitudes, in particular of change in the direction of more democratic attitudes.

The question I raise in connection with German political attitudes since the war is whether or not there has been created a stable democratic attitudinal base upon which a stable democratic political system can be built. But before one can look at German attitudes to see if in fact there is such a base, one must deal with the thorny question of what exactly such a base would look like. Is there a set of political attitudes that is requisite for a democratic political system or, if not requisite, at least conducive to the maintenance of democracy? The question is a difficult one. Almond and I, in our study of the civic culture, deal with two models of democratic political culture—the "rationality-activist" political culture and the "civic" political culture.[3] The former is the political culture one would expect to find in a successful democracy if its citizens were living up to the norms prescribed in most civics textbooks. Citizens would act rationally on the basis of a combination of general principles and calculated self-interest. They would be active in politics, concerned, and informed. The "civic" culture, on the other hand, while containing parts of the "rationality-activist" culture, is a more mixed political culture. Political activity, rationality, and involvement are balanced by passivity, traditionality, and political indifference. The citizen is neither so deeply involved and active in politics as to destroy the ability of the government to make authoritative decisions nor so inactive and indifferent as to give political elites complete free rein in making decisions. This more balanced civic culture is based upon a more general set of non-political social norms and attitudes—norms of trust and interpersonal cooperation that penetrate the political system. And this political culture, we argue, is conducive to the maintenance of democratic stability.

Is the civic culture the standard one should use in assessing the democratic potential of German political attitudes? The model derives from an analysis of democratic institutions as well as examination of the experience of two relatively stable democracies, the United States and the United Kingdom. The latter fact makes one pause before coming to the conclusion that Germany would have to develop a civic culture if it is to build its democratic political structures

---

[3] See Gabriel A. Almond and Sidney Verba, *The Civic Culture*, Princeton, Princeton University Press, 1963, especially Chaps. 1 and 15.

on a firm attitudinal base. Though the civic culture is conducive to the maintenance of democracy where it is found, there have been just too few cases studied to allow one to assume that it is the only feasible pattern for democratic politics. Other patterns of political attitudes may work as well. And the appropriate set of attitudes for the United States or Britain may be a less appropriate basis for democracy in a nation which has undergone the political shocks of German political history. Furthermore the type of political attitudes that developed within the older democracies may be neither feasible nor the most useful to late-comers to the democratic scene. The pattern of relatively free economic development pursued by the nations that industrialized in the nineteenth century worked well for those nations but may not be the pattern most conducive to rapid growth in the twentieth. And the same may be true of political development as well. What led to stable democracy in an earlier age may be less relevant today.

But use of the civic culture as a model for comparison of German political attitudes does have an advantage over the rationality-activist model. The latter, with which most democracies including Germany are usually compared, sets standards of political participation, involvement, and rationality that are probably unattainable and—even if attainable—might not be the most conducive to democratic stability. Thus consideration of the civic culture will keep us from the despair others have expressed if we find that not all the German population is politically active or politically interested. There may be other reasons for despair, or at least concern, but they are not these.

One further point must be made about the criteria to be used in looking at German political attitudes. Those who deal with the question of the future of German democracy may be concerned with one or more of three different questions. One question has to do with the level of democracy Germany has attained or will attain in the future, the extent to which there are diffusion of political power and guarantees of basic freedoms. Another question deals with the stability of German democracy, the extent to which the current pattern of German democratic government has a potentiality for survival. Thus, in connection with the first question, we ask how good a democracy Germany is; in connection with the second we ask how likely it is to last. There is a third question that also deserves separate consideration: if German democracy does not survive, what is the likelihood that it will be replaced by the extreme form of government created in the 1930's rather than by some more conservative and limited authoritarian system?

These questions are clearly related—but different. For instance, if one is interested in the chances that the Bonn democracy (however adequate or inadequate a democracy it is) will survive and not be replaced by an authoritarian political system, one would concentrate on those aspects of political culture one would assume to be the minimum requisites for survival; if one is interested in the extent of democracy in Germany, one looks for more than that. But, more important, it may be that the factors that maximize the chances of survival differ from those that maximize the extent of democracy—just as the economic strategies that would maximize the chances that a firm will stay in business may differ from those that will maximize profits. If one wants to maximize profits or the extent of democracy, it may be that one has to take more risks than if one merely wants to remain in business or prevent the collapse of a democracy. The question of the optimum level of political involvement by the ordinary man may be an example of an area in which one would pursue different strategies depending upon one's goal. Whereas high levels of involvement may increase the extent of democracy in a nation— a passive citizenry is hardly conducive to democratic government— such high levels may also entail somewhat greater risks: issues may become more intense, and the "last groups" mobilized into politics may be those whose political attitudes when they become politically involved are least conducive to the maintenance of democracy.

Similarly, the question of the possibility of a return to Nazism in Germany is related to, but not the same as, the question of the extent and stability of democracy in Germany. For the latter questions, evidence of political apathy and lack of commitment to democratic values may be quite important; for the former question what may be important is that, though the commitment to democratic values may not be too high, the opposition to any radical political movement is even higher. And again, the strategies one might pursue in attempting to increase the extent of democracy or in trying to foster the survival of democracy might be different from those one would use in attempting to prevent the return of Nazism. In a sense Weimar is instructive here, for one can at least argue that a more authoritarian system in Germany after World War I, though it would obviously not have maximized democracy, might have been less likely to degenerate into Nazism.

The Remaking of Political Culture
German Political Attitudes Since the War

Postwar prognostications of the future of Germany were gloomy. However difficult it had been to create a viable democracy in Germany after World War I, the situation after World War II was worse. Destruction and disillusionment were much greater. Furthermore students of Germany had come to the conclusion that the roots of Nazism and German authoritarianism were more than political; that they lay within German character and social structure.[4] In particular the German inability to achieve democracy was traced to the family. Within the family the German child was brought up to expect relationships of domination from authority figures. The father-dominated family (one writer wrote of the mother-dominated family,[5] but the impact on the child was the same) created submissive and dependent individuals. The expectations for the future of Germany were particularly gloomy with respect to youth. They had been raised under the Nazis and knew no other value system; yet this value system and the society based on it collapsed in 1945. And with the collapse came physical destruction and disruption of family life. The prediction for the future was a German youth made up of Nazi fanatics and aimless anomic youth bands.[6]

One was faced then with a picture of a Germany in which a vicious ideology either lived on to create havoc for the society or had disappeared, leaving a vacuum in its place; in which the basic formative institutions of society, family, and school produced citizens who yearned for domination; and in which the physical destruction was so great as to suggest that little energy would be available for political reconstruction. Yet the gloomy predictions about the future of Germany have not been fulfilled. In this paper we shall examine some data on postwar German attitudes in order to describe how those attitudes have developed since the war, to suggest some reasons why they did not develop as predicted, and to assess the relationship of these attitudes to the potentiality for democracy in Germany.

In describing the state of German attitudes toward politics since World War II the researcher has available to him a wealth of material. The interest of the occupying powers in the potentialities for German democracy led to a long series of public opinion polls by

---

[4] See Schaffner, *op.cit.*, and David Abrahamson, *Men, Mind and Power*, New York, Columbia University Press, 1945.
[5] Rodnick, *op.cit.*
[6] See Howard Becker, *German Youth: Bond or Free*, Gary, Ind., Norman Paul Press, 1950.

the military government and, later, by the office of the High Commissioner for Germany. These have been supplemented by numerous studies of German political attitudes by German scholars. In fact, in terms of the amount of data about basic political attitudes the researcher is probably better equipped to deal with Germany than with any other nation. There is a large volume of survey material available for Britain and the United States as well, but little of it displays the constant, self-conscious concern with questions of basic political orientation and the acceptance of democracy. (The fact that so many introspective questions are asked about problems—attitudes toward democracy, the state, politics in general—which are presumably not considered problematic in other nations is in itself a significant bit of information about the nature of German political culture.)

But though there is no shortage of material, a few words are in order about some problems of interpreting these data. It is hard to say what the implication of the response to any particular public opinion poll question means for the problem of democracy in Germany. If one finds a substantial proportion of the population responding in ways one would assume are not supportive of democracy, one can point out that in democracies more successful than Germany one also finds political attitudes that do not fit the expectations one would have as to democratic attitudes.[7] On the other hand, the meaning of answers which indicate adherence to democratic norms and practices may also be hard to interpret. Does the expression of agreement with normative propositions of democratic theory represent lip service to what is assumed to be a proper norm, or does it involve a commitment with significant behavioral implications?[8] The former is not unimportant, but it is obviously quite different from the latter. There are no easy answers to these questions, but the reader is forewarned

[7] Studies of voting behavior in the United States have consistently shown relatively low levels of political knowledge and political involvement. See in particular Angus Campbell *et al.*, *The American Voter*, New York, Wiley, 1960, Chap. 10. See also Samuel A. Stouffer, *Communism, Conformity and Civil Liberties*, Garden City, New York, Doubleday, 1955, for some disturbing data on the support among Americans of certain civil liberties. See also James W. Prothro and Charles M. Grigg, "Fundamental Principles of Democracy: Bases of Agreement and Disagreement," *Journal of Politics*, Vol. 22, 1960, pp. 275-294.

[8] How, for instance, is one to interpret the fact that 63 per cent of a sample in the American Zone of Germany in 1948 said "yes" to the question, "In the future, should the people have more influence on political activities or not?", when in the same sample 75 per cent of former members of the Nazi Party said, "yes," to the same question. See Office of Military Government for Germany (U.S.), Surveys Division, Report 88, January 20, 1948. (Reports of this sort will hereafter be cited as *OMGUS*, Report No. ———.)

that the response to any particular question must be interpreted with caution. To give responses some framework, we shall deal at several points with some problems for which comparable data exist from other nations (particularly the data gathered by Almond and myself in *The Civic Culture*) as well as with problems for which one can trace changes over time so that we can see in what direction the system is moving.

The German Citizen Views the Political System

The most obvious characteristic of contemporary German political attitudes—especially in the light of the postwar predictions—is their conservative nature. The electorate has supported the moderate and broad-based parties of the middle, while the more radical right-wing and narrowly oriented refugee parties that appeared to be gaining strength at the beginning of the Bonn Republic have dropped in strength. The political attitude of "no experimentation" is reflected in a general security-consciousness and conservatism of German youth, the group from which one might have expected the greatest degree of volatility. In a 1956 study of German youth 79 per cent of the respondents reported that they would prefer a secure and low-paying job to a less secure but higher-paying one;[9] and in a similar survey 68 per cent of German youth said they would prefer a job with a lower salary and a pension plan than a higher salary and no pension plan.[10]

This conservatism is reflected in the lack of intensity of German attitudes toward politics. Consider for instance the attitudes toward the particular regime in power. A series of polls taken over a decade indicates a striking stability in the public's evaluation of Adenauer's performance as Chancellor. Both the proportion that considered his work "very good" and the proportion considering his work "bad" have hovered around 10 per cent going neither much higher nor much lower, while the bulk of the population fell in between.[11]

---

[9] *Basic Orientation and Political Thinking of West German Youth and Their Leaders*, Frankfurt am Main, DIVO Institut, 1926, p. 31 (hereafter referred to as *DIVO Youth Study*).

[10] Elisabeth Noelle Neumann and Erich Peter Neumann, *Jahrbuch der Öffentlichen Meinung, 1957*, Allensbach am Bodensee, Verlag für Demoskopie, 1957, p. 135 (hereafter referred to as *Jahrbuch, 1957*). Karl Deutsch and Lewis Edinger report a similar caution and conservatism in relation to attitudes on foreign policy. See their *Germany Rejoins The Powers*, Stanford, Stanford University Press, 1959, Chap. 2.

[11] *EMNID Information*, October 1958, No. 42. If one looks at less intensely phrased responses than the responses that Adenauer's policies were "very good" or

These results do not indicate overwhelming support for Dr. Adenauer but neither do they indicate strong opposition. And what is most important—given the history of intense partisan rivalry in pre-Nazi Germany—is the fact that expressions of support are often found among supporters of parties other than Adenauer's own CDU. Perhaps this attitude of neither strong support nor strong opposition toward Adenauer is the same as the German attitude toward the Bonn Republic and to democracy in general.

Since the formation of the Bonn Republic the numbers favoring a democratic form of government or a multi-party system over a single-party system have steadily increased. The proportion saying that democracy was the best form of government for Germany increased from 57 per cent in 1953 to 74 per cent in 1960, though a fairly steady 20 per cent replied that they do not know what government is best for Germany; and the proportion thinking it is better to have more than one political party rose steadily from 61 per cent in 1951 to 76 per cent in 1956.[12] And the proportion perceiving the Bonn political system as democratic—for instance, the proportion believing that one can speak his mind freely in Germany—also consistently goes up.[13] Figures of this sort are hard to interpret. Which is the significant finding—that "as many as" 70 per cent of the German respondents say that democracy is the best form of government, or that "as many as" 30 per cent say they think some other form is better or they do not know? Information of this sort tells us little about the state of German political opinions.[14] Perhaps more important than the reaction to the word "democracy" is the nature of democracy Germans believe they have or would like to have.

In one of the first postwar sociological studies of German youth

---

"bad," one finds a larger proportion supporting him. Thus, during his tenure of office, the proportion saying they "generally agree" with his policies stayed around 40 to 50 per cent with only a few fluctuations above or below. See Erich P. Neumann and Elisabeth Noelle, *Statistics on Adenauer*, Allensbach, 1962, pp. 40-44.

[12] *EMNID Information*, May, July, September and October (Nos. 19, 28, 35, and 40) 1960, and *Jahrbuch*, *1957*, p. 259.

[13] *Jahrbuch*, *1957*, p. 165.

[14] Less structured questions may be more useful. The more unstructured the question, the less chance there is for individuals to answer with slogans. On unstructured questions the proportion favoring democracy tends to be quite a bit lower. In an analysis of a large series of systematic group discussions, for instance, it was found that about 10 per cent of the statements were prodemocratic; about 67 per cent were mixed, and about 27 per cent antidemocratic. See Friedrich Pollock, *Gruppenexperiment: Ein Studienbericht*, Frankfurt am Main, Europaische Verlagsanstatt, 1955, pp. 139-140.

by a German, Gerhard Baumert wrote that "when the American army brought great quantities of the basic necessities that the Europeans needed for survival, the notion 'democracy' became closely connected in the minds of German youth with the notions 'food, clothing, abundance.' "[15] This quotation suggests that "democracy" and what has come to be called the "economic miracle" are closely interconnected in German attitudes, and the evidence supports this proposition. It is not so much an intellectual connection between the terms democracy and economic progress. When asked to name the most important characteristics of democracy, less than 2 per cent of respondents in each of five different polls conducted from 1953 to 1959 mentioned economic advancement, and most respondents mentioned various freedoms or rule of the people.[16] The connection between democracy and the economic miracle lies in the fact that a good deal of the orientation of the individual to the state in Germany is a rather pragmatic orientation in which the economic services the state can provide are considered important. In 1947 Germans were asked, "Which of these two forms of government would you personally choose as better: a government which offers people economic security and a chance to make a good living, or a government which guarantees freedom of speech, suffrage, press, and religion?" Sixty-two per cent replied that they favored a government which provided economic security, while 26 per cent preferred a government which guaranteed freedom. (The rest had no opinion.)[17] It is probable that the dichotomy is a false one and that there is hope one would not have to choose, but it is instructive to note that, forced to choose, German respondents chose economic security. When an identical question was asked at the same time in the United States, 83 per cent chose freedom, while 12 per cent chose economic security.[18] Given the state of the German economy in 1947, one would expect answers of this sort, but three years later an almost identical percentage answered the same question the same way.[19] However, this still may reflect more a positive need for economic progress than a negative reaction to democratic government. In 1950, for instance, 58 per cent of the

[15] Gerhard Baumert, *Jugend der Nachkriegszeit*, Darmstadt, Edward Roether Verlag, 1952, p. 198.
[16] *EMNID Information*, January 1959, No. 5.
[17] *OMGUS* Report 74, October 27, 1947.
[18] National Opinion Research Center, *Opinion News*, August 1, 1948.
[19] Office of the High Commissioner for Germany, Office of Public Affairs, Reactions Analysis Staff, Report No. 50, Ser. 2, November 30, 1950 (hereafter referred to as *HICOG* Reports).

employed respondents wanted a government that stressed economic security, whereas 74 per cent of those unemployed considered this most important. (There is a less clear relationship with income level.)

The fact that Germans tended at the time of the founding of the Federal Republic to view the government as an economic and social service agency rather than as a guarantor of freedom and democracy has led to concern about the future of democracy in Germany. An attachment to a particular form of government based upon the economic performance of that government is too fragile. If the economic level falls, so may the government. Long-run political stability probably depends upon a more general commitment to the political system as legitimate over and above its day-to-day performance. But the fact that at the time of its founding the Bonn government was looked on as a system with mainly an economic task is not in itself cause for despair. Such a political orientation is to be expected in a situation in which economic needs are great. Furthermore it may be that through experience with the political system as an effectively functioning unit—one under which the economic demands of individuals are satisfied—a more general, positive attachment to the political system can be created. One would not, for instance, expect Germans after World War II to become suddenly converted to democracy in the normative and affective sense—that is, suddenly to come to accept democratic values as the proper ones to follow and suddenly to come to feel a strong and diffuse attachment to democracy per se. The political attitudes that would support democracy are not of a form to which one can suddenly become converted—as one might be converted rather quickly to a more comprehensive and inclusive ideology. Rather, the political culture which would support democracy is a complicated mixture of norms, perceptions, and behaviors—a mixture in which many of the components are implicit and some are indeed inconsistent with others. It is not through formal teaching that one learns what is the right system (though teaching plays a role), but through a long and often indirect socialization process as well as through experience with participation in a democratic system.[20] Thus experience over an extended period with a government which is adequately performing the task it is primarily expected to perform (in the German case maintaining the economy)

---

[20] This argument about the nature of the democratic political culture is developed much more fully in Almond and Verba, *The Civic Culture*, see in particular Chaps. 1 and 15, as well as Chap. 12 for a discussion of socialization processes.

may create other forms of attachment to the system over and above the pragmatic one based upon performance. If the economic recovery can retain the luster of a miracle and if the political system can operate in a way that fosters participation and adherence to democratic norms, then it may be possible to transfer the pragmatic attachment toward politics to a more thoroughgoing acceptance of the democratic system.

How long does it take for this transfer to take place? It is hard to say since it depends upon so many factors, but it may well be a slow process. The question one can ask about Germany is whether there is any evidence for the beginning of a generalization from the economic performance of the system to a more general political attachment. The decline of radical parties and of ideological politics suggests that the performance of the system has reduced any sharp rejection of the Bonn government. But it is less clear that there has been developed any more diffuse positive sense of attachment to the political system. For one thing, though economic reconstruction was considered the task of the new German government, there is less evidence that the government is given direct credit for the economic miracle. When asked to name the factors underlying the economic miracle about 12 per cent of a German sample credited it to the activities of the government. Most respondents talked of the industriousness of the Germans (41 per cent) or of foreign aid (21 per cent)—though perhaps the latter should be considered an indirect praise of the Bonn government.[21] This in itself may not be that significant. It may be more important that the economy in Germany creates a stable environment in which political attitudes can develop and change than that the government itself be given credit for the economic environment.

The kind of commitment to the political system that one finds has two characteristics: (1) it involves a certain pragmatic—perhaps even cynical—view of politics, combined with (2) the absence of the kind of intense rejection of politics that this pragmatic detachment might engender. In 1953 a sample of Germans was asked if they believed that the representatives in Bonn considered first the interests of the people or whether they considered first other interests. Thirty-nine per cent replied that Bonn considered the interests of the people first, 41 per cent mentioned other interests (personal interests, party interests, or specific interest groups), and 24 per cent said they did

[21] *HICOG* Report, No. 236, June 19, 1956.

not know. It is hard to say how high a level of cynicism toward the Bonn government this represents, but what is significant is that in surveys carried on in the three succeeding years the results remained remarkably stable. By 1956, 38 per cent of the respondents said that the representatives in Bonn are interested primarily in the welfare of the people, 36 per cent said they have other prime interests, and 28 per cent "do not know."[22] Unlike the responses about the desirability of democracy, which did change noticeably even within that short period, the responses that indicate respect for the actual operation of the government in Bonn do not change appreciably. Furthermore the answers about the prime interests of the representatives in Bonn appear to reflect closely the German citizen's own view of what is of prime importance. When asked how they would vote if they had to choose between a vote that would benefit themselves but not Germany, or Germany but not themselves, 37 per cent said they would vote so as to benefit themselves, 33 per cent so as to benefit Germany, and 30 per cent did not know.[23]

The pragmatic and perhaps cynical view of the political system reflected in the above data can best be appreciated in a comparative context. In our study of political attitudes in five nations Almond and I dealt with two types of attachment to the political system, what we call "output affect" and "system affect." The former refers to the level of satisfaction the individual expresses with the specific performance of the government; the latter, to his more general and diffuse attachment to the political system as a whole without reference to any particular aspect. In Germany one finds an expression of satisfaction with specific governmental performance more frequently than an expression of attachment to the system as a whole. This fact is highlighted by the comparable data from the other nations studied. In terms of output satisfaction the German data roughly resemble that in the United States and Britain; in terms of system affect the

[22] *Jahrbuch*, *1957*, p. 177. In 1950 a sample of 3,000 Germans in the American Zone were asked: "Do you find that the West German Government keeps the welfare of the West German people in view or do you believe that they primarily follow the aims of their parties?" At that earlier date a higher proportion answered that it kept the views of the West German people in view (52 per cent), but the different phrasing of the question makes the comparison over time a bit difficult (see *HICOG* Report, No. 28, Ser. 2, July 1950).

[23] Elisabeth Noelle and Erich Peter Neumann, *Jahrbuch der Öffentlichen Meinung 1947-1955* (Allensbach am Bodensee: Verlag für Demoskopie, 1956), p. 123 (hereafter referred to as *Jahrbuch, 1947-1955*).

differences are sharp.[24] The absolute levels of system affect are, however, not what is of greatest interest here. Considering recent German history, it is to be expected that a much smaller proportion of individuals would report that they take pride in the political system of their nation (to take the specific measure of system affect used) than would so report in Britain and the United States. Nor is it unexpected that the nations would be more alike in the frequency with which satisfaction with specific governmental performance is expressed; the latter form of satisfaction can obviously develop more rapidly. What is of greatest interest is whether the level of system affect—of stable and diffuse attachment to the political system not based upon performance—is developing out of contact with the specific activities of the German government. Are contact with the government and participation within the political system leading to greater system affect? If so, one can predict that over time the stable functioning of the Bonn government will lead to the development of citizens committed to it over and above its specific performance at any particular time—a form of "rain or shine" commitment that may be necessary for long-run stability.

Data collected by Almond and me are relevant here. We divided our respondents into three groups depending upon the extent of their subjective sense of ability to participate in and influence the government. This was done on the basis of scores on a scale of "subjective competence." Those who score high on the scale consider themselves capable of influencing the course of government action; those who score low consider themselves incapable.[25] The question we raise is: does a citizen's satisfaction with the government increase, the more he considers himself able to participate in the government? In our data we find that those who consider themselves competent to influence the government are more likely to express satisfaction with the specific output of the government in the United States, in Britain, and in Germany as well. For instance, 75 per cent of the respondents who scored high on the subjective competence scale in Germany (n:244) reported satisfaction with governmental output, in contrast with 62 per cent (n:233) of those who scored low.[26] Thus the individual who believes he can participate in decisions is more likely to express satisfaction with the output of the governmental

---

[24] For the specific measures used and the data see Almond and Verba, *op.cit.*, Chaps. 3 and 4.
[25] For a description of the scale used for these purposes see *ibid.*, Chap. 9.
[26] See *ibid.*, Chap. 9, Table 4.

decision-making process. The relationship between sense of ability to participate and more general system affect produces a sharp contrast to the above pattern. In the United States and Britain general system affect (as measured by the frequency with which individuals express pride in their political system) increases with the level of sense of ability to participate. Those high in sense of competence are more likely to express pride in the political system and less likely to say they are proud of "nothing" as citizens of their nations. In Germany, on the other hand, the pattern is quite different. There is apparently little relationship between an individual's sense of political competence and the likelihood that he will express pride in the political system. High scorers on the subjective competence scale are not more likely to say that they are proud of a political aspect of their nation than are low scorers. Furthermore, although those respondents high in subjective political competence are less likely to say that they do not know what they are proud of as Germans than are those low on subjective competence; they are just as likely to give a rather alienated response that they are proud of "nothing." In Germany the sense of political competence does not appear to be related to a more general sense of system affect.[27]

In Germany, though there is some opportunity to participate and there are some respondents who consider themselves competent to participate, the participation does not lead to a greater sense of identification with the political system. This point must be qualified, however, in that there is a positive relationship between sense of political competence and system affect among those Germans who have attained an educational level beyond the primary school. This suggests that the translation of ability to participate into attachment to the political system may be beginning among those who have attained some higher educational level. Since our data support the proposition that the attainment of a sense of political competence develops earlier among those with higher educational attainment, the fact that it is among these people that the translation into attachment to the political system takes place supports the point that time is what may be needed for experience with the performance of the Bonn government to be translated into a more stable commitment.

But in general the data for Germany suggest that whatever attachment there is to the political system is mainly a pragmatic one. The individual who believes himself capable of participating within

[27] *ibid.*, Chap. 9, Table 5.

the political system is more satisfied with the system, but his satisfaction tends to be with the specific outputs of the system. If the hypothesis about the greater significance of system affect for the long-run stability of a political system is correct, it would appear that the sense of ability to participate in governmental decision processes that has developed since the war in Germany will foster the stability of the system so long as the performance of the system remains at a high level. If the performance of the system lags, the fact that some individuals feel capable of participating may add little to its capacity for survival.

These data as to contemporary German political attitudes must be evaluated, however, in the light of recent German political history—and when seen in this light, the picture is quite a bit brighter. A purely pragmatic politics that involves no emotional or ideological commitment is not a firm basis for a stable democracy, but then neither is its polar opposite. What is needed is a combination of pragmatism and deep commitment. Given the history of Germany's first attempt at democracy during the Weimar Republic—a republic torn by politically intense, and irreconcilable ideologies—the rather stolid pragmatism of politics under Bonn can only be welcomed. The crucial point may not be the fact that there is little deep attachment to the system, but that there is little deep rejection of it. That Germans have a detached and somewhat cynical view of what goes on in politics is important, but it is more important that they do not totally reject the political system because of this— as Weimar politics was often rejected as a rather dirty form of horse trading. One of the reasons Weimar was rejected may be that it was expected to be an ideal democracy, and when it did not live up to that ideal, the rejection was total.[28] If contemporary Germans can see the blemishes in the Bonn democracy and yet not totally reject it, they may have learned a significant political lesson indeed.

The German Citizen as Political Actor

We have thus far considered the views of Germans about their political system. In general one finds a view of a system as an instrument. Germans are concerned with the output and performance

---

[28] See the discussion of the critical view held by many intellectuals of the system of parties and interest groups under Weimar, in Karl D. Bracher, *Die Auflösung der Weimarer Republik*, Villingen-Schwarzwald, 1960, pp. 37-44. By setting up an ideal image of a democracy in which the selfish interests of political parties and special groups played no role these writers were able effectively to discredit the parliamentary system under Weimar.

of the government. There is little hostility to the government and little radicalism, but no strong sense of attachment either. This general picture of an almost apolitical attachment to the political system is reflected in what material is available about Germans as participants in their political system. If we switch our perspective from what Germans think of their political system to what they think of their own role in politics and what they in fact do in politics, we can observe the pattern. We shall consider the role of the Germans in politics from three points of view: the nature of their participation in politics; their sense of obligation to participate in politics; and their sense of ability to influence political decisions.

The relationship between levels of political activity and the stability potential of a democracy is complicated. In the United States activity and participation in politics are usually considered desirable, whatever the content of that participation. "Vote for the party of your choice" (it does not matter which) is a slogan heard frequently around election time. And it is true that a passive populace uninterested in the vote and apathetic about politics would hardly maintain the level of control of elites by non-elites needed in a democracy. But the notion of voting for the party of one's choice is a policy with little danger for democracy only when those parties are pretty much limited to the Democrats and Republicans (or their equivalents elsewhere). If the party of one's choice is likely to be a radical, anti-democratic party, a high level of participation, rather than implying a solid democracy, may be an indicator of weakness in a democracy. A high level of participation may then have contrary implications at different times. It may indicate that a democracy is functioning at a high level of elite responsiveness to non-elites (certainly a major goal for an effectively functioning democracy) or it may mean that the democracy is in trouble.

What about German political activity since the war? One can argue that, though the level of activity is in a number of areas quite high, it neither represents a challenge to democracy nor indicates an effectively functioning democracy. Voting participation, for instance, has been quite high in Germany since the war. In 1957 it went up to 88 per cent of those eligible to vote, a very high figure compared with those of most nations and a figure even higher than the voting participation in the hectic elections in Germany in the last years of Weimar, when the sudden increase of the vote had serious unstabilizing effects on the political system.[29] But there is clear indication that the increase in voting turnout that has gone on since the war does not represent the unstabilizing radicalization that the voting turnout increase in the late Weimar republic represented. Instead of the increase in votes going largely to the radical left- and right-wing parties, the increase in voting in Bonn has been going to the moderate center parties.[30] The interesting characteristic of the German vote is that, though it is high in frequency, it tends to be relatively low in intensity. German elections are carried on in comparative peace compared with the elections of the early 1930's.[31] In the 1957 election more than half of the voters for each of the major parties thought that nothing would change if the SPD (Social Democratic Party) was elected to replace the CDU (Christian Democratic Party), and a similar pattern was discernible in 1961.[32]

On the other hand, the high level of voting in the Bonn Republic does not mean a high level of effective participation in the political process, nor is it necessarily a reflection of a decline in the political passivity of which Germans have so often been accused. The high frequency of voting, coupled with the low involvement in the results, is probably an indicator of the relatively passive view of the vote in Germany. Rather than a means of control by non-elites over elites, it is considered more often to be an obligation to be discharged. Thirty-one per cent of German respondents reported that voting is one of the obligations they owe to their nation—a figure higher than that in any of the other four nations Almond and I studied. Furthermore many respondents explicitly stated that their obligation to participate in politics is exhausted by the fulfillment of their voting obligation. For instance, a German worker said that one's responsibility to the local community was to "choose a mayor at election time. That's all you need to do. The mayor takes care of everything." Or as a German housewife put it: "The people in the council are cleverer after all. They'll do a good job. You just have to vote for the right

[29] On German election participation see Erwin Faul, *Wahlen und Wahler in Westdeutschland*, Villingen, Ring-Verlag, 1960.

[30] Thus in 1949 the two major parties received 60 per cent of the vote; in 1953, 74 per cent of the vote; and in 1957 and 1961, 82 per cent of the vote (see Dolf Sternberger, "Mutation des Parteisystems" in Faul, *op.cit.*).

[31] See Uwe Kitzinger, *German Electoral Politics*, Oxford, Clarendon Press, 1960, pp. 270-272.

[32] DIVO Institut, *Untersuchung der Wahlerschaft und Wahlentscheidung*, Frankfurt am Main, DIVO, 1959. See also Klaus D. Eberlein, "Die Wahlentscheidung vom 17 September, 1961, Ihre Ursachen und Wirkung," *Zeitschrift für Politik*, Vol. 9, 1962, pp. 237-257.

ones." Similar results are reported in a recent study in Hamburg. Over half of the respondents reported that one ought to vote even if one were completely indifferent as to the outcome of the election; and among those who thought one ought to vote under these circumstances the major reason given for voting was that one had an obligation or duty to do so.[33]

The attitudes toward the vote thus reflect the paradox of German political culture and are evidence for the point made earlier that the problems of the survivability of the Bonn democracy and the level of democracy under Bonn are different problems. That German voters are not intensely involved in the outcome of elections and that they do not anticipate radical changes if the opposition party is elected suggest that there exists in Germany the limited commitment to political controversy and the willingness to turn power over to political opponents that are needed for the stability of a democratic political system.[34] On the other hand, the orientation to the vote as an obligation that one owes one's country rather than an instrument that might affect the way in which the nation is run does not suggest a high level of democratic performance. Whereas the notion that the vote may have a real effect on governmental policies or on the incumbents of governmental office is compatible only with a democratic form of government, the notion that one performs a duty to one's country by voting is a view of the vote quite compatible with authoritarian forms.

The combination of high frequencies of formal participation and a passive orientation to that participation is reflected in other data on German political activities. If one compares levels of activity in the United States and Britain with those in Germany, one finds that

[33] Wolfgang Hartenstein and Günter Schubert, *Mitlaufen oder Mitbestimmen. Untersuchung zum demokratischen Bewusstsein und zur politischen Tradition*, Frankfurt am Main, Europäische Verlagsanstalt, 1961, pp. 36-37. Similar results are reported in a study of students at Frankfurt University. Habermas reports that even among the most unpolitical of the students studied—those who consider political affairs to be none of their business, who know nothing about politics, and who prefer not to be involved—most replied that one had an obligation to vote in elections. See Jürgen Habermas *et al.*, *Student und Politik: Eine Soziologische Untersuchung zum Politischen Bewusstsein Frankfurter Studenten*, Neuwied, Hermann Luchterhand Verlag, 1961, pp. 85-86.

[34] Under Weimar voters probably also believed that the outcome of elections made little difference. But this was because, under Weimar, governmental coalitions were created within the closed confines of the *Reichstag* and were in fact little affected by electoral results. Under the Bonn regime, where the question posed refers to the possibility of a CDU dominated government being replaced by an SPD dominated one, the meaning of the belief that the outcome of the election would make no difference is clearly different.

the more passive and formal the activity, the more similar the three nations are. The greater the degree of active intervention by the individual involved in the particular activity and the less the activity is clearly formally structured, the more Germany tends to differ. Thus, in terms of exposure to communications about politics, information about politics (particularly about the formal structure), and participation in elections, German respondents report such activities as frequently as, if not more frequently than, do respondents in Britain and the United States. But when it comes to more active and informal participation—such as engaging in political discussion—the differences between Germany on the one hand and the United States and Britain on the other increase. Similarly, when asked how they would go about attempting to influence the government, Germans more frequently mention working through a formal organization and much less frequently talk of the possibility of forming some informal group.[35] One of the sharpest indicators of the passive nature of participation in Germany can be found in data on membership in formal organizations in the three nations discussed above. German males, British males, and American males are almost equally likely to be members of some formal organization. (The figures are 68 per cent among American males, and 66 per cent among British and German males.) But if one considers the proportion of organization members who have ever taken some active part in the operation of their organizations, a sharp difference appears among the nations. In the United States 41 per cent of the males who belong to some organization have taken some active role in that organization; in Britain the corresponding figure is 32 per cent; in Germany it is only 18 per cent.[36]

The passivity of the German involvement in politics is reflected also in the nature of the obligations to participate felt by Germans. Thus fewer German respondents say that the individual ought to take some active part in the affairs of his community than say so in Britain and the United States. In the United States 51 per cent of the respondents said that the individual ought to be active in the affairs of his community—attend meetings, join organizations, and so forth—as did 39 per cent of the British respondents; but only 20

---

[35] For these data see Almond and Verba, *op.cit.*, Chaps. 4 and 7.

[36] *ibid.*, Chap. 11. Furthermore the degree of participation in an organization has an effect on political activities. Those who are active members of their organizations are also more likely to be active politically than are those whose organizational role is more passive.

per cent of the German respondents agreed with that viewpoint. In contrast, more respondents in Germany than in the other two nations said that the individual ought only to take some more passive part in the affairs of his community—keep informed, or just take an interest, or vote—(39 per cent in Germany, 31 per cent in Britain, and 27 per cent in the United States).[37] And there is little evidence that this sense of obligation to take an active community role has increased from a lower level since the formation of the Bonn Republic. When asked in 1949 whether "you would be willing to take a responsible position in the political life of your community if you were asked," 24 per cent of the respondents in the American zone said, "yes"; and when the question was repeated a year later, slightly under 20 per cent of a sample of youths (aged 15-25) said, "yes"—figures which closely resemble those found a decade later.[38] The extent to which Germans are oriented to participation in their national life in terms of the pragmatic rewards of such participation rather than in terms of the political rewards of the diffusion of political control is best illustrated by comparing the 24 per cent who said they would be willing to take an active political role in community life with the 76 per cent in the same survey who said they would be "willing to work an hour daily without pay for the economic rebuilding of Germany."[39]

If one may generalize from the above data: the orientation to politics in Germany is in terms of the specific outputs of the political system, and the individual sees himself as either the beneficiary or not the beneficiary of that output. He is less likely to consider himself a participant in a political process in which groups engage in peaceful conflict and bargaining about the government's activities. His view of himself as a participant tends to be rather passive—one fulfills obligations rather than participates in the decision-making process of the government. Furthermore, insofar as an individual attempts to take some active role in connection with the government, he acts not as a democratic citizen actively attempting to exert political influence on the government, but rather as the subject of a *Rechtsstaat*

---

[37] *ibid.*, Chap. 6.

[38] *OMGUS* Report No. 191, December 8, 1949; and *HICOG* Report No. 50, Ser. 2, November 20, 1950. It is interesting that when one compares the respondents aged 15-25 in the 1950 survey with their age cohorts in the Almond-Verba survey of 1959—i.e., those who were 25-35 years old in 1959—one finds almost no change in the frequency of expressed willingness to take an active part in the affairs of the community; just under 20 per cent express willingness in both cases.

[39] *OMGUS*, Report No. 191, December 8, 1949.

defending his rights under the law—rights in the establishing of which he did not participate as an influential citizen. Almond and I found, for instance, that of the five nations we studied, only in Germany were respondents more likely to manifest what we call "administrative competence" (a sense of ability to have one's voice heard in bureaucratic situations) than "political competence" (a sense of ability to influence the legislature and other rule-making bodies at the time rules and laws are made).[40]

In general one finds a heavier stress in German political attitudes upon the more formal aspects of politics. Participation tends to be formal, and knowledge of governmental activities tends to be more of the formal-legal structure of government than of the actual operation of politics.[41] Furthermore Germans appear to be more at ease and competent in administrative situations. Though they express cynicism about the operation of the legislature, they are more sanguine about the sort of treatment they will get in administrative offices.[42]

Otto Kirchheimer has written of the "juridification of human relations" in the German Republic, by which he means the tendency to formalize and depersonalize political relationships—in a sense, to depoliticize them.[43] This tendency toward a dependence on explicit formal-legal rules to regulate political relations rather than on practices that have evolved more flexibly over time—what Spiro has called the "legalistic political style"[44]—is reflected here in the orientation of the ordinary man to his political system.

The other most striking characteristic of postwar German political culture suggested by the data on the German citizen as political actor is the lack of deep ideological commitments and divisions in Germany. The bulk of the electorate votes for the two major parties. The lack of ideological commitment of these parties is also reflected in

[40] Almond and Verba, *op.cit.*, Chap. 8.
[41] German university students are more likely, for instance, to have information about formal aspects of the government structure than they are to understand the workings of actual politics. See Habermas *et al.*, *op.cit.*, pp. 54-57.
[42] Almond and Verba, *op.cit.*, Chap. 8.
[43] Kircheimer, "German Democracy in the 1950's," *World Politics*, Vol. 13, 1961, pp. 254-266.
[44] Herbert Spiro, *Government by Constitution*, New York, Random House, 1959, p. 181. This orientation is reflected also in the attitudes one finds toward conflict resolution. The tendency in Germany is to seek expert and objective means of resolving conflict rather than allowing the solution to emerge from the confrontation of the competing parties—a tendency to find a non-political rather than a political solution. See the discussion of German legal procedure and the procedures for settling labor-management disputes in Ralf Dahrendorf, "Demokratie und Sozialstruktur in Deutschland," *Archives Européennes de Sociologie*, Vol. I, 1960, pp. 50-85.

the campaign appeals. The emphasis in both the Christian Democratic and Social Democratic Parties is upon symbols and tactics that appeal to as wide a range of voters as possible and that de-emphasize social conflict along ideological lines—as the SPD campaign slogan in 1961 put it, "With each other, not against each other." Recent studies of German electoral behavior suggest that the great ideological currents which in the past divided Germans along religious or class lines play little role in elections.[45] Compared with the politics of Weimar Germany, it is clear that German political culture has undergone a significant degree of *Entideologisierung*.

The patterns of attitudes that have been sketched out above are different from what was expected at the end of the war. There are no strong ideologies, no radicalism, no bands of werewolves, no violent anti-democratic forces attempting to overthrow the government. Rather, if the pattern of attitudes is not what the pessimists expected, neither is it what the optimists would have liked to create. The politics of Germany reflects a pragmatism and passivity to governmental authority. Not that these are not useful and in fact necessary traits for the maintenance of democracy, but unless they are balanced by some degree of political activity and involvement and by some more general commitment to the political system, the commitment to democracy may be fragile. But the development of commitment may have its dangers. It has been suggested that political commitment in Germany has gone through sharp fluctuations. It has at times been very strong and matched by high levels of activity and involvement; at other times, weak and matched by passivity and unconcern. As Laqueur has put it, "patriotism has usually been all or nothing—either ultra-nationalist or nihilist, without roots or loyalties."[46] If this cyclical image of German political commitment is an accurate one, it is clear that politics in the first decade and a half of the Bonn Republic represented a period of low commitment. The essential problem is whether a pattern of commitment and activity can be created to assure that the stability of the system is not threatened by too sharp conflicts or by too intense involvement in politics. It is of course a difficult question to answer, but the greater political involvement apparent in Germany since the erection of the Berlin wall and, in particular, in connection with the affair of *Der*

---

[45] See Eberlein, *op.cit.*, n. 32, above, for some material on studies of the 1961 election.

[46] Walter Z. Laqueur, *Young Germany, A History of the German Youth Movement*, New York, Basic Books, 1962, p. 221.

Spiegel—and the relative responsibility of this involvement, seeking redress but not radical redress—suggest that such a balanced involvement in politics may be possible.

Indications that there may be a future trend in this direction are found in the comparison of the attitudes of young and old in Germany. Passivity and political indifference do characterize young and old alike, but young differ from older citizens in that they are more likely to support democratic values and are less likely to think of political participation as involving essentially the fulfillment of an obligation.[47] But the future level and form of German political involvement are unpredictable because the issues of German politics—issues connected with both the German past and the German future—are so important. German political attitudes have been affected by the Eichmann trial, the affair of *Der Spiegel*, and the Berlin wall—issues involving the history of Germany, the present internal politics of Germany, and its future as a nation. And in the reaction to these events, youth has been particularly involved. Future developments in any of these areas might produce a radical change in the pattern of German political culture.[48]

Political Socialization in Germany

As was suggested earlier, postwar analyses of the German political future concentrated heavily upon socialization processes, particularly upon the schools and the family, as an explanation of German authoritarianism. If there was to be a revolutionary change in German political attitudes, it would have to begin with these basic institutions. It will be useful therefore to look at these institutions briefly, to see if one can find within them some explanation for the particular kinds of political attitude developments that have taken place in Germany since the war.

THE GERMAN FAMILY

Compared with the picture of the German family painted just after the war, contemporary studies of German family relations indicate a great liberalization.[49] There are two aspects of this liberaliza-

---

[47] See Hartenstein and Schubert, *op.cit.*, pp. 41, 57, and 63.

[48] For a discussion of some recent data which contradicts the earlier material on the withdrawal from politics in Germany see Walter Jaide, "Not Interested in Politics?" in Walter Stahl, ed. *The Politics of Post-War Germany*, New York, Praeger, 1963, pp. 363-376.

[49] See Rolf Frohner, Maria von Stackelberg, and Wolfgang Eser, *Familie und*

tion of authority structure: the role of the wife and the role of the child. The male-dominated family no longer appears to be the standard German model. Rather, studies of the German family agree that there is a greater emphasis on *Partnerschaft*. Similarly, though the evidence is not as clear, there has been a liberalization of the family from the point of view of the role of the child. Both Wurzbürger and Baumert report a large number of "child-centered" families, in which the views of the children are considered important. Furthermore there is evidence that this is a pattern toward which the German family is continuously moving. In a survey conducted in 1957 respondents were asked their opinions on the most important lesson that children ought to learn. Twenty-five per cent chose obedience and respect (in contrast to the 32 per cent who chose independence and free will), but the important point is that younger respondents were much less likely to consider obedience the most important trait in children than older respondents were. Only 15 per cent of those between 16 and 25 years and 22 per cent of those between 25 and 30 thought obedience most important, whereas 38 per cent of those over 65 thought it was.[50] The emphasis on independence of the child appears to be growing in Germany, both as an explicit norm of behavior and in actual behavior itself.

This pattern of authority is quite different from that found in the immediate postwar years by such investigators as Rodnick and Schaffner. Several reasons may be adduced for this change. Nazism itself challenged the traditional authority structures of which the family was the prime example. The upset caused by the overthrow of the Nazi authority system, the physical destruction of Germany, the absence of the father from home for extended periods, the influx of refugees, all the great turmoil and confusion of the end of the war had significant impacts upon the structure of the family. The main

---

Ehe, Bieiefeld, Maria von Stackelberg Verlag, 1956. They found that 2/3 of the 1753 families they studied had a partnership form of husband-wife authority. Gerhard Wurzbürger, *Leitbilder Gegenwartigen Deutschen Familienleben*, Stuttgart, 1953, found that 74 per cent of the families he studied had this pattern as well. Similar findings are reported in independent studies by Helmut Schelsky, *Wandlungen der Deutschen Familie in der Gegenwart*, Stuttgart, 1955; Gerhard Baumert, *Deutschen Familien Nach dem Krieg*, Darmstadt, 1954; Rene König, "Family and Authority: The German Father," *Sociological Review*, Vol. 5, 1955, pp. 107-127.

[50] *EMNID Informationen*, No. 29, July 1957. There is also rather strong evidence that the degree to which children can participate in family decisions has been increasing over time. See Almond and Verba, *op.cit.*, Chap. 12.

effects of the social upheaval were a weakening of the role of the father, a strengthening of the role of the mother, and a turning in upon the family. The family as an institution played a major role during the transition after the war. With the political and ideological disillusionment and with the great demands for day-to-day survival, the family became a central institution for the maintenance of society. The absence of the father and the greater demands on the mother for leadership had significant effects upon the authority structure within the family.[51]

But the changes in the German family derive from more long-term forces as well. In fact one can argue that the extreme postwar conditions had their major impact through the acceleration of what was a long-run change in family structure—a change not limited to Germany but apparent in most modernizing nations of the world. The postwar German authoritarian family described, for instance, by Schaffner was not unfamiliar in the United States of a few generations back, or more recently in Switzerland.[52] The breakup of the extended family as the economic functions of the family decline, the greater emphasis on education and youth rather than on hard-earned experience as an economic asset, the introduction of women into the labor force thereby opening the family to non-traditional influences, the introduction of old-age benefits modifying the dependence of parents in later life upon children—all these factors and many others that accompany economic modernization, it is argued, better account for these changes in the German family than do specific postwar events.[53]

Recent evidence can be adduced to support the contention that the changes in the German family are due more to long-run social forces than to the specific impact of the war and the postwar era. For instance, if one considers the frequency with which individuals report that as youths they had the opportunity to participate in family decisions, one finds a gradual increase in frequency of such reports as one moves from older to younger respondents. Respondents raised at an earlier period are less likely to report that they had the chance

[51] See Schelsky, *op.cit.*, and Baumert, *op.cit.*
[52] Robert H. Lowie, *Toward Understanding Germany*, Chicago, University of Chicago Press, 1954, has pointed quite clearly to the fact that the Swiss family—in that highly democratic country—shares in many ways the "authoritarian" pattern of the German family (see Chap. XIII).
[53] See Baumert, *op.cit.*, König, *op.cit.*, and Lowie, *op.cit.* In this connection it is interesting to note that much of Schaffner's data about the German authoritarian family is based on interviews with people raised under the Second Empire.

to take part in family decisions. But the interesting point is that one finds a steady change in the direction of more participation, ranging back to those who were socialized before World War I—not a sudden and discontinuous increase in participation among those socialized since 1945.[54] Studies of the German family before World War II cast doubt upon the existence of a pattern of male dominance in the family. In studies made around 1930 of both rural and urban families in Germany one is struck by the mixed pattern of family authority that is found—some families dominated by the father, but many not—as well as by the frequently expressed complaint that family authority is breaking down, that children are no longer as respectful as they used to be.[55] Furthermore, that the liberalization of the family is due to long-run modernization is also suggested by the fact that such liberalization is most apparent in families that are more involved in the modern economy. Whereas 15 per cent of all families in the EMNID Institute's study of 1,753 German families were listed as father dominated, 50 per cent of the farm families were so listed. And Almond and I found that the frequency of reported participation within the family increases with the educational level.[56]

Further evidence for the long-run nature of the changes in the German family can be adduced if one looks at the role of women in German politics. One characteristic of a more modern family structure and economy is that it tends to bring women out of the home and into the larger social environment—a change that plays a major role in interrelating the structures of the family with the structures of society.[57] In Germany this pattern of increased female participation in politics can be traced at least back into the Weimar period and is not merely a post-World War II phenomenon. Table 1 reports the difference in voting turnout for men and women in different age groups for the 1924 Reichstag election and the 1953 Bundestag election.[58] The smaller the difference, the more we may assume women are playing a political role, and—more inferentially—that norms of male domination are weakening.

[54] See Almond and Verba, *op.cit.*, Chap. 12.
[55] See Gunter Krolzig, *Die Jugendliche in der Grossstadtfamilie*, Berlin, 1930; and Alice Salomon and Marie Baum, *Das Familienleben in der Gegenwart*, Berlin, 1930, cited in Lowie, *op.cit.*, Chaps. 14 and 15.
[56] Frohner *et al.*, *op.cit.*; and Almond and Verba, *op.cit.*
[57] On this general topic see Almond and Verba, *op.cit.*, Chap. 13.
[58] The difference between the two sexes in the percentages voting is selected as an indicator of female participation in politics rather than as the absolute level of female participation in order to correct for differences in over-all turnout due to the nature of the election.

TABLE 1: DIFFERENCES IN VOTING TURNOUT BETWEEN MEN AND WOMEN BY AGE GROUP IN 1924 REICHSTAG ELECTION AND 1953 BUNDESTAG ELECTION

(per cent)

Age	1924 Election	1953 Election
21-30	2.8	0.7
30-40	5.0	1.2
40-50	5.7	1.4
50-60	8.7	2.7
60-70	12.0	6.3
Over 70	20.6	14.6
Mean difference	6.4	3.1

Note: Adapted from Gabriele Bremme, *Die Politische Rolle der Frau in Deutschland*, Göttingen, Vandenhoeck and Ruprecht, 1956, p. 41. The data are based on a special government survey of sex and age factors in the two elections and both are based on close to 400,000 cases.

The data make quite clear that the difference between male and female participation in Germany has declined since the Weimar period. Whereas there was in 1923 a difference of 6.4 per cent in the turnout of men and women at the polls (to be precise, 87.9 per cent of the eligible males voted and 81.5 per cent of the eligible females), in 1953 the difference declined to 3.1 per cent; and a similar pattern is seen within each age group. But though the evidence is clear that the degree of female participation is greater in Bonn than in Weimar, the evidence also suggests that it is a matter of changes that began in the Weimar period. In each election there is a consistent pattern of greater male-female similarity as one moves from older to younger age groups. This indicates that not merely has there been a general change in atmosphere between the two republics but also that there has been a steady change in attitude toward female participation, with the females in each succeeding age group appearing more and more like the males in their voting behavior.

The data allow us to deal a bit more closely with the question of the nature of political modernization in Germany (if we may consider female participation an indication). The question we can raise is whether the change in the political status of women over time is largely a function of changes in the socialization processes (the liberalization of relations in family and school) or a function of general changes in the political atmosphere which affect all people—not merely those who are being socialized in the new atmosphere but also people who are already adult. The data in Table 1 present a strong argument for the formative impact of socialization—an effect that remains strong throughout adult life. At least in terms of the problem of female participation in political life it appears that patterns of behavior acquired when a person first enters politics remain throughout life, though the general set of social attitudes is changing. Consider the "age cohorts" in Table 1 (the percentages linked by lines).[59] Among those who were just entering politics about the time of the 1924 election (those 20-30 in 1924) the difference between male and female voting turnout is 2.8 per cent. Thirty years later, in 1953, we find the same group (they are now the 50-60 age group) with an almost identical difference, 2.7 per cent. That the pattern set at the time of entry into politics persists and probably plays a larger role than the "temper of the times" is emphasized if we compare relations between the same age cohorts over time with the relations among the various different age groups in each time period. The group that was 20-30 years old in 1924 is much more like its age cohort thirty years later than it is like the group a bit older than it (30-40 years old) in 1924. Similarly, those who were 50-60 in 1953 resemble their age cohort in 1924 more closely than they resemble those older or younger in 1953. A similar pattern exists for the next-older age cohort, the people who were 30-40 in 1924 and 60-70 in 1953. They are not so similar to each other as the younger cohort, but they are more similar to each other over the thirty-year span than they are to three out of four of the adjacent age groups in each respective time period.[60]

The data on relative voting turnout have been presented in some

[59] For a discussion of the uses and logic of cohort analysis see William M. Evan, "Cohort Analysis of Survey Data," *Public Opinion Quarterly*, Vol. 23, 1959, pp. 63-72.

[60] The generalization does not hold for the next age group largely because the male-female difference in 1953 was so large among those over 70. But the data for both 1924 and 1953 suggest that in this rather old group differences undergo an almost qualitative change, perhaps because of specific social and physical problems among the very old.

The major qualification as to the validity of such a comparison over a thirty-year period involves the question whether the age cohorts have the same social composition in the two time periods. Differential rates of mortality among social classes, for instance, might bias the results. The cohorts might be more heavily weighted toward upper social strata in 1953 than in 1924 if there were differential death rates among classes, and this might affect the data. There is, however, little reason to believe it would alter the results substantially.

detail because they clearly illustrate the point that there has been a long-term secular liberalization of the German pattern of political participation (and, inferentially, of the family structure) and that we are not dealing with a new pattern of behavior brought on by the destruction in the post-1945 period or with a pattern imported by the British and American armies. Those events probably accelerated the change but did not initiate it. Moreover the data present striking evidence for the importance of socialization processes in the formation of certain basic patterns of political behavior.[61]

THE GERMAN SCHOOL

The school is, along with the family, one of the basic socializing agencies of a society and is one of the prime sources of political attitudes. In fact there is evidence that its impact on political attitudes tends for a variety of reasons to be stronger than that of family experience. Furthermore education has an impact on political attitudes in a great variety of ways. The skills learned, the social status

---

[61] That this liberalization is a function of the gradual modernization of society over time is supported by the fact that male-female differences are also a function of urbanization. In each time period the male-female differences were greater in smaller communities than in larger, as shown in the tabulation below.

DIFFERENCE IN VOTING TURNOUT FOR MEN AND WOMEN BY SIZE OF COMMUNITY IN 1928 AND 1953

Size of Community 1928	1928 Election (per cent)	Size of Community 1953	1953 Election (per cent)
Under 2,000	29.7	Under 3,000	4.4
2,000–5,000	14.8	3,000–50,000	2.9
Over 5,000	10.8	Over 50,000	2.5

Source: Data from Bremme, op.cit., pp. 45-46. The 1928 data are for the Reichstag election in Hesse. The 1953 data are from a UNESCO survey throughout West Germany.

More striking is the fact that in 1953 the difference among the communities of different size is much smaller than in 1928. This suggests a gradual spreading out of the more equal role of women from the urban areas into the countryside. (The data are not exactly comparable due to the different size-of-town categories. But if anything, the difference would bias against the conclusion drawn here—i.e. the 1953 data with the larger differences in size of town produce the smaller difference in male-female voting turnout.)

What this section is arguing is not the absence of male-female political distinctions in Germany. Almond and I argue elsewhere that they are greater in Germany than in Britain and the United States (see *The Civic Culture*, Chap. 13). What I am arguing here is that there is a clear pattern of change over time in this dimension.

The data presented above do support the importance of political socialization during the formative years, but they should not be taken to imply that on all political attitudes one would find this persistence of patterns learned in early life. It may be only on certain types of attitudes, like the difference between men and women, that socialization plays a dominant role.

achieved, the content of the education, as well as the general structure of the educational environment—in particular, the authority patterns within the school—all have a significant impact on an individual's political orientation.[62]

It is significant in this regard that those who tried to remake Germany after the war—both the occupiers and the Germans themselves—viewed the German educational system as the most important challenge and opportunity. Unlike Weimar, where a democratic constitution was placed upon an unchanged non-democratic base in the schools—where if there was not positive hostility to the new government, the subjects taught and the general authoritarian atmosphere in the schools certainly did little to support democracy—the founders of the Bonn Republic consciously attempted to form a school system that would teach the type of citizenship needed in a democracy. Furthermore they approached the problem from a broad point of view. Not only was the content of instruction to change, but also the method of instruction as well as the general social atmosphere of the school would be reformed. There were to be specific courses in civic education as well as other courses with civic content, the classroom was to be more democratic, and student participation in the administration of the school was to be fostered.[63]

Much of the desire to change the atmosphere in the schools was a reaction to the attempts at political education under Weimar—an education which tended to stress formal and legal principles rather than the actual working of the government. "One of the few memories which remains in the minds of those who went to school at the time [under Weimar] is being given on leaving a copy of the Weimar Constitution, which they never subsequently opened."[64] In contrast, those interested in current German political education stress the need for practical experience in cooperation with one's fellows, a stress not on abstract ideals but on practical application.[65] There is

[62] For an extensive discussion see Almond and Verba, *op.cit.*, Chaps. 12 and 13.

[63] See, for instance, the set of guiding educational principles drawn up by the Ministers of Culture of the various Lander in 1950, *Bürgerverantwortung in der Gemeinde*, Frankfurt am Main, Institut zür Forderung Öffentlicher Angelegenheiten, 1950. See also the "Gutachten des Deutschen Ausschusses für das Erziehungs- und Bildungswesen zur Politischen Bildung und Erziehung," cited in Thomas Ellwein, *Pflegt die Deutsche Schule Bürgerbewusstsein?*, Munich, 1955, p. 300.

[64] Richard Hiscocks, *Democracy in Western Germany*, London, Oxford University Press, 1957, p. 27.

[65] The strongest statement is in Friedrich Oetinger, *Wendepunkt der Politische Erziehung: Partnerschaft als Politische Aufgabe*, Stuttgart, 1951. See also Fritz Borinski, *Der Weg zum Mitbürger*, Düsseldorf-Koln, 1954; as well as Walter Stahl,

evidence that there have indeed been changes within the German schools. Between 81 per cent and 87 per cent of the students in Frankfurt University reported they had had some social science or civics courses before coming to the university;[66] and students whose education took place within the past decade are more than twice as likely as students whose education took place at any other time in German history to report that they had an opportunity within the schools to engage in classroom discussions and debates on current issues.[67]

Socialization and Political Attitudes

This long excursion through German public-opinion data and material on the German family and the German schools poses a problem. At the end of the war it was believed that the German nation could be fashioned with stable democratic underpinnings only if there were fundamental changes in the family and the schools. The difficulty of changing such basic institutions made one wonder and despair at the chances of rooting democracy firmly in Germany. There have been changes in these institutions. But though the changes have taken place in the underlying structures, political attitudes are still in many ways unchanged from those of an earlier period. True, the radicalism and stress on ideology of the late Weimar years has been replaced by a pragmatic and perhaps cynical attitude toward the operation of the government; but this is combined with an orientation to the formal and legal aspects of government operations rather than the political ones; a certain passivity in types of political behavior; a greater ease with the role of the subject who is affected by government than with the role of the citizen who affects the government; and a lack of strong attachment to the symbols of the political system.

There are several reasons that may be suggested to explain why the substructure of political attitudes has changed while political attitudes have shown less fundamental alteration. In the first place, it may be that the importance of liberalization of the family struc-

---

ed. *Education for Democracy in Western Germany*, New York, Frederick Praeger, 1961.

[66] Habermas, *op.cit.*, p. 268.

[67] Almond and Verba, *op.cit.*, Chap. 12, Table 12. Thirty-eight per cent of those aged 18-25 reported that they had such opportunities to participate, in contrast with an average of under 10 per cent for the rest of the German sample.

ture has been overrated in terms of its impact on politics. As suggested earlier, democratic politics have been pursued in nations with authoritarian families. The patterns of family authority, though not irrelevant for political attitudes, may be so distant from politics—distant in terms of time and in terms of type of social structure—that the impact is limited.[68] Furthermore the type of impact that one would expect upon political attitudes from experience with a more participatory family structure—essentially a transfer of experience to politics leading to the expectation of being able to participate in politics—may be one that takes a long time to develop. What is being learned, after all, is not a lesson that may be cognitively learned and then followed in practice, but rather a habit of participation—and such habits are longer in developing.

The difficulty of transfer of family training to political attitudes is not unexpected. In all societies one would expect a gap between family training and the secondary structures of society, including the political. And this gap can cause strain when the individual is forced to shift from the more affective, diffuse, and particularistic standards of the family to the more affectively neutral, specific, and universalistic standards of the polity. In this sense family socialization is always inadequate as a preparation for politics. And this inadequacy will be greater, the greater the gap between the standards of behavior within the family and those within the polity. In a traditional political system in which the particularistic standards of the family are also found in the polity such strain would be minimized. But in a society such as Germany, with a political system stressing relatively universalistic and achievement norms, some such socialization gap is unavoidable.[69] In such a situation the size of the gap and the attendant strain may be determined by the extent to which the family system incorporates some of the standards of the secondary institutions of society. The evidence from a variety of studies comparing German and American family structures suggests that the socialization gap is

[68] See Almond and Verba, *op.cit.*, Chap. 12 for some data on the effects of family experiences on political attitudes. We suggest that though there is some effect, it is not as great as the impact of experiences in other social situations—school and workplace, in particular.

[69] On this general topic see Schelsky, *op.cit.*; S. N. Eisenstadt, *From Generation to Generation*, Glencoe, Ill., The Free Press, 1955, Chap. 3; Almond and Verba, *op.cit.*, Chaps. 12 and 15; and Harry Eckstein, *A Theory of Stable Democracy*, Princeton, Center of International Studies, 1961. Lucian Pye's study of Burma suggests that this strain may be greatest in societies just beginning to modernize. See his *Politics, Personality, and Nation-Building*, New Haven, Yale University Press, 1962.

greater in Germany than in the United States. The German family appears to stress close affective and dependency relationships between parent and child more than the American family does. There is in the former a slower development of motives for autonomous achievement. And what may be most important, there is less opportunity within the German family structure for the development of relations with autonomous peer groups—the kinds of relations that would train a child for the greater range of cooperative and participatory activities that the political system presents.[70] In this sense, though there has been in Germany a liberalization of the family making the transition from family roles to participant roles in politics probably quite a bit easier than it was in the past, the socialization gap and the attendant strains may still be relatively great.

One aspect of family development in postwar Germany, on the other hand, may have had an important effect on political attitudes—an effect not so dependent on the kind of transfer of attitudes discussed above. The turning in upon the family for support that took place in Germany when its institutions failed may have a close relationship to the pragmatism of postwar German politics. This turning in upon the family involves a rejection of larger social forces as guides to conduct—a rejection of ideology and a rejection of politics. German democracy, as Kirchheimer has put it, "is characterized by its stability, depoliticization, and privatization";[71] and the emphasis upon the family reinforces those qualities. This brings us back to our earlier discussion of the difference between those factors that might make for stability of the present regime in Germany and those that might make for the greater democratization of the regime. The privatization and turning in upon the family do not make for the sorts of active and participant citizens needed in a democracy, yet they do make for high-level stability. It may in fact be, as some have argued, that it was the family that carried the German social

[70] See Urie Bronfenbrenner, "Patterns of Parent Behavior in the United States of America and the Federal Republic of Germany: A Cross-national Comparison," *International Social Science Journal*, Vol. 14, 1962, pp. 488-506; David C. McClelland *et al.*, "Obligations to Self and Society in the United States and Germany," *Journal of Abnormal and Social Psychology*, Vol. 56, 1958, pp. 245-255; McClelland, *The Achieving Society*, Princeton, Van Nostrand, 1959, p. 346; Don C. Rapp, "Child Rearing Attitudes of Mothers in Germany and the United States," *Child Development*, Vol. 32, 1962, pp. 669-678; and Fritz Süllwold, "Empirische Untersuchung über die Sorgen und Probleme von Jugendlichen in Deutschland und den USA," *Psychologische Rundschau*, No. 10, 1959, pp. 49-66.

[71] *op.cit.*, p. 262.

structure from the destruction and turmoil of the postwar era to its more stable present state.[72]

The changes in the German schools also appear to have wrought few fundamental changes in German political attitudes. Again, one can suggest some reasons for this. For one thing, the changes within the German school may be changes that are more apparent on the level of the ideology of German education than they are real changes within the schools. The Frankfurt University students who in large numbers reported having had training in civics and the social sciences before entering the University also reported that the training was heavily weighted in the direction of descriptions of the formal and legal structure of the political system. There was less stress on the practical side of politics, and the attempts made to introduce *Partnerschaft* and participation were reported by the students as having had little effect. They reported that attempts by teachers to introduce these new approaches seemed forced and out of place. Furthermore, those who reported civics training differ relatively little from the students who had no experiences with the new civics education. The students who did experience civics training were somewhat more likely to report interest in politics, but they were no different from other students in terms of their commitment to democratic values, their readiness to participate in politics, or their degree of actual participation.[73] Despite the explicit desire to change the nature of the program, the above data from Habermas, as well as the constant complaint by professional educators about the difficulty of changing the traditional patterns of teaching in the schools,[74] suggest that formal aspects of politics still predominate.

The general social environment of the schools may also play a role in the development of a stress on the formal aspects of politics. The characteristic German orientation to a formal set of rules rather than to a set of practices learned through experience may be something developed quite early in life before entering the political arena. One way in which people learn to engage in political activities with others—learn the political skills of flexibility, cooperation, and bargaining—is by having experience in cooperative groups. German youth, however, give little evidence of opportunities for such ex-

---

[72] See Schelsky, *op.cit.*, and Baumert, *op.cit.*
[73] Habermas, *op.cit.*, p. 273. See also Theodore Heubener, *The Schools of West Germany*, New York, New York University Press, 1962, pp. 85-96; and Ellwein, *op.cit.*, pp. 118-124.
[74] See Stahl, *op.cit.*, *passim*.

perience. In a comparative study of German and American high school students David McClelland and his associates found a sharp difference in the types of activities students engaged in. When asked how they spent their time outside of school, American students on the average mentioned five group activities; German students on the average, one. German students were more likely to engage in individualistic activities. Furthermore McClelland indicates that this differential experience with group activities has an effect on the sense of interpersonal obligation developed in youth. Among American youth such obligations are governed by patterns of behavior learned by participation with others in groups; among German youth, where such interaction is less frequent, the norms governing interpersonal relations tend to be based on a more explicit and rational set of norms derived from general principles rather than from experience. In a sense, then, one has the beginning of the formalistic orientation to politics and interpersonal relations in early experiences.[75]

But again, as with changes in family patterns, it may be that not enough time has elapsed to allow the ideology of school training to affect actual practices—it is easier to change the philosophy of education than to change the educational system—and for the practices to affect political attitudes. Transfer of attitudes of this sort may take a long time. We have seen that this transfer may be inhibited by differences between the primary socialization processes and the processes in the world of politics. Another factor that may interfere with the transfer of a sense of ability to participate from the family and the schools to the political sphere is the lack of interest and involvement in politics. Insofar as Germans have turned away from politics, they may have little opportunity to test out and use in the political sphere that which is learned in the family and the school. Almond and I have shown, for instance, that there is some tendency in each of the five nations we studied for individuals to transfer experience in participation within the family and the school in a sense of competence to influence the government.[76] But in Germany this transfer seems to be mediated by the extent to which an individual is involved in politics. If we consider those respondents

---

[75] McClelland *et al.*, *op.cit.* That the political results of school experience are more consistent with the informal peer group relations than with formal teaching agrees with findings in the United States as to the greater impact on student values of the peer group culture compared with the content of courses. For a summary of the literature, see Alex S. Edelstein, "Since Bennington: Evidence of Change in Student Political Behavior," *Public Opinion Quarterly*, Vol. 26, 1962, pp. 564-577.

[76] *op.cit.*, Chap. 12.

who reported that they consistently follow political affairs (the involved) and those who reported that they consistently do not follow political affairs (the uninvolved), we find that the tendency for experience with participation in non-political settings to be reflected in political competence is found largely among those who are involved in politics. As Table 2 points out, among those German respondents who do not follow political affairs (left-hand column) it makes no difference to their sense of political competence whether or not they had a chance to participate in decisions within the family

TABLE 2: PROPORTION OF GERMAN RESPONDENTS RECEIVING THE HIGHEST THREE SCORES ON THE SUBJECTIVE POLITICAL COMPETENCE SCALE, BY FAMILY AND SCHOOL PARTICIPATION, WITH LEVEL OF POLITICAL INVOLVEMENT HELD CONSTANT

	Percentage Level of Political Involvement	
	Low	High
Participants in the family	30 (91)	66 (213)
Non-participants	30 (171)	58 (159)
Participants in the schools	31 (94)	71 (173)
Non-participants	29 (178)	57 (179)

Source: For a definition of the measures used, see Almond and Verba, *op.cit.*, Chap. 12.

Note: Numbers in parentheses refer to the base upon which percentages are calculated. Each percentage refers to the proportion of the group high in subjective political competence.

or within the school. Among those whose involvement in politics was low both 30 per cent of those who reported that they *could* participate within the family and 30 per cent of those who reported they *could not* participate within the family are high on political competence. On the other hand, among those who reported a high level of involvement in politics (right-hand column of the table) the extent to which they had an opportunity to take part in family and school decisions does appear to play a role in the level of their political competence. Among this high involvement group 66 per cent of those who participated in the family are high in political competence, in contrast with 58 per cent of those who could not participate in the family. And a similar difference between those high and low in political involvement is seen in connection with participation within the schools.

Changes in the family and schools therefore have had little impact on political attitudes because of a gap between the more primary institutions of society and the political system—a gap maintained by the lack of commitment to politics in Germany. There is a compartmentalization of the polity and the society. Germany has often been described as a democracy that is developed at the top only, in the rules of the constitution and in the conduct of elections. But there may be some development of democracy at the bottom as well, within the family and, perhaps over time, within the schools. What is missing is the connecting link—a set of political attitudes that can facilitate transfer from one level to the other. For this to happen one would need a set of attitudes in which politics was not looked at as an alien sphere, to be manipulated for one's benefit but not to be trusted. There would have to be developed a more stable commitment to the system, a commitment not based merely upon pragmatic interest but more firmly rooted, and it would have to include an acceptance of the system on the symbolic level.

Culture Change and German Democracy

When one looks at the attempts to create a political culture more conducive to a stable democracy in Germany, one is struck by the difficulty of such an enterprise. The set of attitudes to be striven for—the sense of political competence, the willingness to engage in politics, to bargain, to cooperate—are not attitudes that are easily taught. They are habits that must be created over time through experience, both in the political realm and in analogous relations outside of politics. Great Britain stands out as a sharp contrast to Germany in this respect, for in Britain the habits are learned but there is no explicit attempt to teach them. There is little in British schools to match the German self-conscious *Bürgerkunde*, nor are there elaborate philosophies of what British children ought to be taught to give them the proper citizen attitudes as there are debates in Germany on what makes for the proper *Bürgerbewusstsein*.

Does this mean that such efforts at the creation of citizens are useless? Not necessarily. It merely means that for them to be of use will take time. The non-pragmatic attachment to the state, for instance, takes time to develop. One may self-consciously plant the seeds of a political culture, but it needs time to grow. One needs experience with democratic politics for democratic attitudes to become firmly rooted.

And what does this all mean for the future of democracy in Germany? As the question is always put, "Is Bonn Weimar?" The answer to this question must be mixed. On the one hand, the radicalism and ideological politics of Weimar are gone;[77] and the events of 1933-1945, as well as the close experience with Communism, may serve as a preventive against any turning toward totalitarianism.[78] But the passivity of the German citizen, the pragmatic orientation to politics (bordering on cynicism), the lack of political involvement of the bulk of the population, the legalism, the subject orientation—all these indicate a political system in which firmly democratic attitudes are as yet not established. What this suggests is that for the growth of a democratic political culture Bonn needs what Weimar did not have—time. It needs time for the experience with democratic politics to produce political involvement and a sense of political competence. It needs time for the changes in the schools, that are now more a matter of ideology than of genuine liberalization, to take root and for these changes as well as the changes in the family to penetrate the political system through the creation of attitudes conducive to democratic participation. For this the absence of radical attitudes in Bonn may be important as a means of giving the Bonn Republic time to develop these new political orientations—and change in this direction is apparent.

The problem is complicated in Germany by the fact that some of the basic issues of political culture are still unresolved. The major unresolved issue is the one that plagued German politics in the nine-

[77] But perhaps even here the contrast ought not to be drawn too sharply. As Deutsch and Edinger put it, "German politics today looks remarkably sober, even pedestrian; no startling changes appear at all probable. Yet it is worth remembering that German political life presented a similar appearance during the heyday of the Weimar Republic between 1925 and 1929, only a few years before its collapse and the National Socialist seizure of power" (*op.cit.*, p. 32).

[78] The experience with Nazism may not have made democrats out of the Germans, but it may have sensitized them to certain undemocratic practices. Hartenstein and Schubert, in their recent study found that 52 per cent considered it unequivocally a bad idea to denounce to the authorities any person whom they suspected of being a Communist, and only 11 per cent considered it a good idea (*op.cit.*, p. 64). In contrast, Stouffer found in the United States that 73 per cent of his sample thought it a good idea to report to the FBI any person they suspected of being a Communist and that only 19 per cent thought it was a bad idea. (Samuel A. Stouffer, *Communism, Conformity and Civil Liberties*, Garden City, Doubleday, 1955, p. 45.) A good deal of the contrast between the American and the German response patterns may have to do with the greater salience of domestic Communism as a threat in the United States in 1953, when Stouffer's study was conducted, than in Germany in 1960. Furthermore we are comparing a national sample in the United States with a sample from Hamburg—a city that may be atypical in this respect. But the contrast is still striking.

teenth century—the problem of national identity. The problem of the *kind* of political system to which individuals would be committed was subordinated in nineteenth-century Germany to the problem of the *scope* of the system. Forces that would have pressed for a liberal democracy in Germany were diverted by the forces pressing for unification. And one can argue that until a political culture includes a stable and secure sense of national identity all other problems will be subordinate. In present-day Germany the problem of the scope of the nation is not clearly resolved, as the Berlin wall symbolizes. But the effect of this unresolved problem on the potentialities for the formation of a liberal democratic culture in Germany is less clear. On the one hand the division of Germany plays a salutary role in the support of democratic attitudes by acting as an insulator against Communism within West Germany, by giving the West Germans a sense of unity, and perhaps by removing from West Germany some of the politically more authoritarian sections. On the other hand the carefully cultivated tentativeness of the present Bonn Republic may inhibit the development of a strong sense of commitment to the system. Above all, the fact that such a basic political cultural question as the boundaries and identity of the nation remains unresolved introduces a great potential volatility into the German political culture. The development of German political attitudes in the past fifteen years or so would lead to a prediction of continued political restraint and the gradual development of a more balanced political commitment rather than to a prediction of a return to the radical shifts in the past from extreme detachment to extreme commitment. The reactions to the highly salient political events of recent years suggests the validity of the prediction. The Berlin wall, the Eichmann trial, and above all the affair of *Der Spiegel* have led to an increased awareness and interest in politics, but not to a radical change in the kinds of demands placed on the system. Yet, while the nation remains divided, the volatility will remain.

CHAPTER 5

Turkey: The Modernity of Tradition

DANKWART A. RUSTOW

The Emergence of Contemporary Political Culture

THE DISTINCTION between modern and traditional political systems has gained currency in recent decades as comparative politics has expanded its horizons in two directions—from a parochial preoccupation with Europe and its overseas offshoots to a systematic study of the politics of all continents; and from exclusive concern with legal institutions and formal organization to increasing attention to the cultural, social, and psychological setting of politics. Like any dichotomy applied to empirical reality, it has had to be expanded, refined, and modified. Although tension between modern and traditional politics is readily perceived in most parts of contemporary Asia, Africa, and Latin America, closer examination suggests a number of revisions of the original concepts.

First, tradition turns out to be something of a residual category. It lumps together vastly different types of political behavior—of the Arabian bedouin, the farmer in the Mekong rice paddy, the Bolivian tin miner, and the Greenland Eskimo—and these acquire some unity only as they are confronted, in reality and in concept, with the historically unique culture of industrial society that had its roots in the Europe of the Renaissance. Second, historical research quickly dispels the somewhat naïve assumption that modernity is the only dynamic factor injected into an otherwise static traditional scene. Third, it becomes clear upon closer reflection that modernity and tradition are never fully distinct in reality, that the political culture of even the most modern countries is in fact a blend of traditional and modern traits.

The political evolution of Turkey from Ottoman Empire to national republic offers excellent opportunities for testing the adequacy of various concepts and theories of political modernization. There is no question that the Ottomans in their 600-year history developed a distinct and recognizable tradition. Furthermore the program of conscious borrowing from a European culture perceived as somehow superior, which began piecemeal in the late eighteenth century and wholesale in the mid-nineteenth, may quite properly be described as an example of Europeanization, Westernization, or modernization. But once we push beyond these elementary generalities, matters become more complicated. Of all major non-Western regions, the formerly Ottoman Near East is the one geographically and historically closest to Europe. Unlike the Americas or Japan, it did not have to be discovered or opened up by the dramatic arrival of ships from distant shores. Islam grew out of the same Judaic and Hellenic roots as did Christianity. The Arabs learned their science and philosophy from the ancient Greeks and taught them to the medieval Europeans. By established conventions of geography, Turkey is partly in Europe and mostly in Asia. The Ottomans ruled in Athens, Sofia, and Belgrade before they conquered Ankara, Sivas, and Kayseri; Budapest fell into their hands a few years after Adana. Their governmental institutions and culture were profoundly influenced by those of the Byzantine Empire. The Ottoman ruling elite of the classical period was composed mainly of Christian converts from the Balkans, just as the most prominent Young Turks and Kemalists in our own century were Muslim natives of Macedonia. In short, there has been continuous political interaction and cultural interchange between the Near East and Europe since long before migrant tribes of Central Asian horsebreeders made Anatolia the country of the Turks.

In Turkey itself, even during the periods of most rapid Westernization, political and cultural change was always directed by indigenous elites. The dialectic of colonial conquest and liberation, which breaks historic continuity in most non-Western countries, is absent. There is an uninterrupted chain that links the Kemalists to the Young Turks, to the men of the Tanzimat, and to the classical Ottoman Empire—the sponsors of modernity in the twentieth century with the founders of tradition in the thirteenth. It is symbolic of this continuity that Mustafa Kemal after his victory over the Greeks in the Turkish War of Independence (1919-1922) was given the title of Gazi ("Victor")—the very name that had been the common designation of the Seljuk frontier warriors who first established the Ottoman state in victories over an earlier generation of Greeks on the same Bithynian battlefields.

As we apply the concepts of tradition and modernity to the

Ottoman and Turkish setting, we must remember therefore that we are in fact dealing with a single continuous stream of history. We also must guard against the usual Western condescension in viewing the history of other world regions. It is true that the Ottomans' accomplishments in science, literature, and most of the arts were limited and lacked originality. It is also true that by the nineteenth century the empire had fallen (with a powerful assist from the European powers!) into a state of political disarray that seemed to earn it the contemptuous sobriquet of "The Sick Man of Europe." But there can be no doubt that in its *politics*, the empire of Mehmed the Conqueror (1451-1483) and Süleyman the Magnificent (1520-1566) was far more "modern" than the realms of any of their contemporaries in Europe. (Significantly, the Ottomans' most notable artistic achievements, like those of other state builders, were in architecture.) In fact Ottoman Turkey ranks with Rome, China, Russia, and the United States among the most populous and durable overland empires in all human history. In the early sixteenth century it stretched from Algiers to the Caspian Sea and from Hungary to Aden, setting new standards of effective communications and orderly administration. Any discussion of political modernization in Turkey therefore must include an examination of the "modern" elements of Turkish "traditional" culture as well as of the "traditional" features surviving into the "modern" period.

The classical Ottoman Empire was a highly dynamic political structure. The state was in essence a military camp and an educational institution. Out on the battlefields Ottoman armies expanded the frontiers of the realm into Europe, Asia, and Africa. Back home in Istanbul an elaborate system of palace schools trained young men for the army, the revenue service, and the many branches of the Sultan's lavish household. The system was for its time remarkably rational, purposeful, tolerant, and adaptable. Indeed, Albert Lybyer, the founder of Ottoman historiography in the United States, saw in Süleyman's realm the closest historic approximation of Plato's concept of a philosophic state.[1]

The religious establishment of the Ottoman Empire always remained clearly distinct from the military-administrative structure. The pupils of the palace schools were recruited chiefly from among Christian subjects on the Balkans or Muslims from the Caucasus, and

[1] Albert H. Lybyer, *The Government of the Ottoman Empire*, Cambridge, Mass., 1913.

the legal status of the graduates remained that of slaves—thus minimizing the disruptive effects that attachment to family and property would have had on the Imperial service. By contrast, the *ulema* or "learned men," i.e. teachers and practitioners of Islamic law and theology (the singular is *alim*) were free-born Muslims. Although no hereditary nobility was ever recognized or established, the legal-theological profession commonly—and particular offices frequently—passed from father to son. Since the sources of Islamic law—mainly revelation and the recorded practice of the Prophet—were beyond the competence of temporal rulers, the *ulema* enjoyed extensive autonomy. Nevertheless they remained clearly subordinate to secular authority. An *alim* received his diploma from other *ulema*, but he held his office of mufti (jurisconsult), teacher, or prayer leader by appointment of the sultan or his local representatives. Since Islam recognizes no sacerdotal function, the *ulema* could become a clergy but not a priesthood.

The rationality of administration and the emphasis on public education and on military service may all be considered "modern" elements of Turkish traditional culture. But there were at least two important respects in which the Ottoman political tradition was distinctly premodern—the lack of any concept of universal civic obligation or equality before the law, and the relative lack of governmental concern with economic matters.

The classical Ottoman political culture described in the previous paragraphs belonged in fact to a small political elite which ruled over a vast congeries of largely autonomous local communities. The empire throughout its history included a great diversity of religions and languages among its subjects, and the relations among its nationalities were a mixture of amalgamation and segregation, of guaranteed privilege and habitual oppression. The emperors had considered themselves the foremost defenders of Islam, but over the centuries they had come to rule over millions of Christian subjects. The Koran prescribed toleration of the "People of the Book" (i.e. Christians and Jews) if they recognized a Muslim ruler's authority. (It is due chiefly to this Islamic tradition of toleration that Christian peoples in the Danubian–Balkan areas retained their religious-national identity under four centuries of Ottoman overlordship—in sharp contrast to the fate of Muslims after the Christian conquest of Spain and Sicily.) Religion, law, and ethics are largely fused in Islam; hence, just as the Muslims were expected to live by the Islamic *shariʿah* as interpreted by the *ulema*, so it was assumed that Christians were to live by Christian law and Jews by Judaic law as applied by their priests and rabbis. Where under the Arab Caliphate Muslims had mingled freely with Christians and Jews, the Ottomans promoted an increasingly strict social segregation among the faiths. They also recognized the principle of religious diversity of law in the so-called *millet* system. Christians of various confessions (Greek Orthodox, Armenian-Gregorian, and later Maronite and Bulgarian) as well as Jews were recognized as *millets* (denominations) within each of which the clerical hierarchy, headed by a Patriarch or Chief Rabbi, were responsible for judicial matters and for the collection of taxes.

The administrative *millet* system was reinforced in the social and economic spheres by an ethnic division of labor. In the Balkans, for example, the vast majority of Serbs, Bulgarians, and Albanians were farmers or shepherds whereas the Greeks were chiefly traders and the Turks, government officials and soldiers. The Jews in Istanbul and other large cities pursued commerce and handicrafts. In Anatolia the majority of farmers were Muslim Turks, yet there were prosperous Greek farming communities on the Aegean and Black Sea coasts, and Armenian ones in the East. Throughout Anatolia the crafts and trades were almost exclusively in Greek and Armenian hands. The Kurds in Southeast Anatolia and Northern Iraq were shepherds with a clear patriarchal tribal organization. Among the Arab-speaking populations in Syria and Iraq, Muslims predominated in agriculture and Christians in urban crafts and trade. In addition to these major ethnic and religious groups there were other numerically smaller elements, such as the Lazes, a seafaring people on the northeastern Anatolian Coast speaking a Caucasian language related to Georgian, and the Druzes, Arabic-speaking mountain tribes in Syria professing a secretive religion derived from a medieval Islamic heresy. The empire's complex ethnic composition, moreover, was further diversified by a small but steady trickle of immigration— and in politics and society these new arrivals often played a role out of proportion to their numbers. Among these may be mentioned the Circassians, a Muslim people from the North Caucasus, who escaped in large numbers in the 1860's after the collapse of their resistance to Czarist conquest and were settled in various parts of Anatolia and Syria. (Other Muslim refugees from the Caucasus included Ossetians, Chechens, and Abaza.) An earlier group of immigrants were the *Dönmes* ("converts"), members of the seventeenth-century Jewish messianic sect of Sabbatai Zvi who were persuaded to convert to Islam, were settled in Salonica, but despite their conversion have long maintained a distinct social identity.[2]

The most important single effect of modernization—or, more specifically, of the European impact—on this traditional social-political system was the advent of national consciousness. The conversion of the nationalities of the empire to nationalism was a gradual process in several waves from the early nineteenth to the early twentieth centuries. It spread first to those parts of the empire closest to Europe in geography and culture—that is, the Christian Balkans—and only later to Anatolia and Arabia. In each region the larger national groups with compact areas of settlement were converted to nationalism earlier than the smaller ones or those who were widely scattered among neighbors with different faiths or languages. And finally those groups who enjoyed distinct political, social, or economic advantages in the multi-national empire were among the last to be converted to nationalism. Specifically, the Serbians and Greeks asserted their national independence in the early nineteenth century—the former encouraged by Russian Pan-Slavism, the latter by British Philhellenes such as Canning and Byron. The Romanians and Bulgarians followed suit in the second half of the nineteenth century. Nationalist aspirations among the Armenians, who were mainly prosperous traders and farmers scattered widely in Anatolia, began in the 1890's; because of the slim prospects of territorial nationhood, agitation took the form of terrorist tactics which resulted in ruthless countermeasures and the eventual near-extinction of Turkey's Armenian population. The Muslim Albanians, long considered the empire's most loyal supporters, did not opt for independence until 1911-1912, when the Ottoman position on the Balkans was hopelessly shaken. The first stirrings of Arab nationalism began in the mid-nineteenth century—significantly among Christian Arabs in Lebanon. The movement did not become a major political force among the political elites in Syria and the Hijaz until the eve of World War I and came out in the open so late as 1916. Smaller Muslim groups, such as the Kurds and Circassians, remained among the most dedicated bitter-end supporters of the Ottoman Empire. The small Jewish community of Istanbul never was converted to any nationalism of its own; a few of its mem-

---

[2] See H.A.R. Gibb and Harold L. Bowen, *Islamic Society and the West*, Vol. 1, Part 2, London, 1957, pp. 241ff.

bers, in fact, actively participated in the Turkish nationalist movement of the early twentieth century.

Among the Turks themselves national consciousness was slow to spread. The Ottoman civil-military ruling class was an ethnic conglomerate. Its language was a refined and modified form of Turkish in which a vast amount of Arabic and Persian vocabulary was superimposed upon a Turkish syntactic structure. Down to the late nineteenth century the members of this ruling class used the term "Turk" mainly as a contemptuous epithet for the unlettered peasant from Anatolia. The adherents of the constitutionalist movement which was responsible for the basic law of 1876 and then went into opposition against the absolute regime of Abdülhamid II (1876-1909) were known in Europe as the "Young Turks." Significantly, they themselves adopted this name only in the form of a French loan word, "Jön Türk." In the Ottoman Empire they were known as "New Ottomans," a usage that reflected the attempt of the reformers of the Tanzimat period to create an ideal of Ottoman citizenship regardless of language or religion. But the divisions of the past proved too engrained. Under the impact of successive defeats, culminating in the loss of the empire's European provinces in the Balkan Wars (1912-1913), the Turkish-speaking elite was gradually converted from an Ottoman to a Turkish national consciousness. Significantly, Turks from the Balkan border provinces and refugees from the scattered Turkish settlements in czarist Russia were among the earliest and most vocal advocates of this new tendency. The gradual conversion of Ottomanism into Turkish nationalism further accelerated the secessionist tendencies among the non-Turkish populations. The collapse of the Ottoman Empire in World War I completed the transition to Turkish nationalism. Yet so late as May 1920 Mustafa Kemal (Atatürk) himself felt compelled to intervene in the proceedings of the newly convened National Assembly to discourage the use of the term "Turk" as too controversial and to assert that "we are all Ottomans, we are all Muslims."

The historical process just reviewed has resulted in the transformation of a vast multi-national and dynastic empire into a small nation-state, the substitution of intensive mutual loyalties among a small population for dynastic obligation among a thinly spread ruling elite. Yet this process occurred at a recent date and its results are still precarious. The urban educated groups in Turkey are thoroughly converted to nationalism. But among the rural population religious consciousness still vies with national consciousness, and the term *"millet,"* which to the city-dweller denotes "nation," still is used in the older meaning of religious community. When asked, "What is your *millet?*" the Anatolian peasant is as likely to answer "Islam" as "Turk." Even in the city a Greek, Armenian, or Jew is considered a Turkish citizen but not a Turk. Despite 40 years of official secularism a non-Muslim Turk is still a contradiction in terms.

The extension of governmental functions in the legal and economic spheres was a second major result of the European impact since the late eighteenth century. The earliest stimulus to reform was military defeat, and the first changes therefore were in army organization and military training. "Yet," as I have written elsewhere, "by a compelling logic the program slowly spread. The army could not be reformed in isolation from the rest of the body politic. The new soldiery needed officers schooled in mathematics, French, and geography, and army surgeons with *alla franca* medical training. Military conscription required a tightening of administration in the provinces where powerful vassals ruled in increasing defiance of the sultan. The costs of the new army and administration had to be borne by systematic taxation. An entire new school system was instituted to prepare the future officers, administrators, and tax collectors for their tasks. The schools required more money—and yet more schools for the training of teachers."[3] The net result was an unprecedented flood of orders, decrees, and laws which gave to the mid-nineteenth century the name of the Tanzimat period (1839-1876), the period of regulations. In the classical Ottoman period the sultan and his ruling establishment were considered the guarantors of the *shariʿah*, the unchanging Holy Law, and of the religious-legal systems of the subject non-Muslim *millets*. Those bodies of religious law were supplemented by commercial agreements, known as capitulations, which regulated the activities of European traders resident in Istanbul and other port cities. Now, however, the sultan and his ministers became officially the main source of new legislation. The most important law code of that period, the *Mecelle* or Civil Code of 1869-1876, attempted to summarize in systematic fashion the traditional tenets of the *shariʿah*. But the mere fact that it owed its validity to proclamation by the sultan was a departure from legal precedent. The constitution of 1876—the first written fundamental law adopted in

[3] See my chapter, "The Military: Turkey," in Robert E. Ward and Dankwart A. Rustow, eds. *Political Modernization in Japan and Turkey*, Princeton, 1964, p. 353.

a country outside the European tradition—firmly established the principle of secularization and Europeanization of the legal system. The wholesale adoption of European law codes in the 1920's was the logical culmination of that trend.

The involvement of the government in economic matters proceeded apace. Railroads and telegraph systems were constructed, notably during the reign of Abdülhamid, who found in them convenient means to maintain his autocratic rule in distant provinces. Yet these public works programs carried out by European concessionaires continued the old pattern of ethnic division of labor whereby commerce and trade were predominantly in Christian hands whereas warfare and administration were the exclusive, and farming the preponderant, preserve of Muslims. In fact, as a result of the empire's bankruptcy, the collection of customs and many other revenues was turned over in 1881 to a European-administered *Dette Publique*.

World War I made the first decisive inroads in the old dualistic economic structure. The capitulations were abolished in 1914. Wartime government requisitioning and other economic controls were used to create for the first time in history a Muslim-Turkish business class in competition with Greek, Armenian, Jewish, and Levantine establishments. The same policies were continued under the early republic. The *Dette Publique* regime was abolished. The Greek-speaking population of all areas except Istanbul itself was exchanged. Foreign-owned railroads and utilities were bought out by the state. By 1928 tariff sovereignty was attained and it soon was used for the protection of domestic industry. Even earlier, leading members of the Kemalist ruling circle had set up the İş Bankası (Business Bank) as a major industrial holding concern. In the early 1930's *étatisme*, or government enterprise to supplement private economic activity, was launched as a major new program. The discriminatory property levy (*varlık vergisi*) of 1942 ruined many Greek, Armenian, and Jewish concerns and transferred an even larger share of trade to Turkish hands.

The gradualism of Turkish political evolution may easily obscure the enormity of the change which had occurred in the nineteenth and early twentieth centuries. The sultan's slave household, which had been the early Ottoman ruling establishment, had given way to a bureaucratic state. National welfare rather than dynastic conquest had become the principle of statecraft. Law, once rooted in immutable religious precept, was now the preserve of an omnicompetent secular legislature acting in the name of the sovereign people. Subjects had been transformed into citizens, empire into republic. The plural economy based on ethnic division of labor had been transferred to Turkish nationals, and the state had assumed a major share in its development. By about 1930 this entire transition from "traditional" to "modern" politics was firmly established in the law of the land and in the consciousness of the urban educated class—though the task of spreading it to the practice of the countryside was still largely ahead.

The Contemporary Political Culture and Its Sub-cultures

Turkish social structure today can best be understood as being divided into three groups or classes—the urban educated class, the rural lower class, and the urban lower class—and each of the three has its distinct political sub-culture.

The major social divide in contemporary Turkey is a high school (lycée; in Turkish, *lise*) education, and all who have traversed it are members of the urban educated class. Above this line there is a good deal of social mobility, below it there is some, but across it practically none. If a peasant or laborer can manage to send his son to a lycée, he may see him rise to the highest positions in society. For the talented lycée graduate the government provides university scholarships, and a university degree provides access to the officers' corps, the civil service, and the professions of law, medicine, and teaching. More recently there have been widening opportunities in business, and the larger firms are willing to reimburse the government for a young graduate's scholarship so as to release him from the obligation of two years' government service for every year at the university. In any of the professions inherited wealth or family connections promote rapid social ascent, but native talent and application may outweigh these advantages. The Young Turk and Kemalist periods confirmed the pattern of social mobility within the lycée-educated class. Enver (1881-1922), leading member of the so-called Young Turk triumvirate which ruled dictatorially from 1913 to 1918, was of humble and indistinct origin. His colleague Talât (1874-1921) began his career as a telegraph clerk but rose to the rank of Paşa and grand vezir. "When I became minister," he once remarked, "everyone began nursing the same ambition."[4] Mehmed Emin Yurdakul (1869-1944), the most celebrated nationalist poet of the

---

[4] Quoted in İbnülemin Mahmud Kemal İnal, *Osmanli devrinde son sadriazamlar*, Istanbul 1940-1953, p. 1962.

early twentieth century, was a fisherman's son. Ex-President Celâl Bayar's father was a small-town mufti from near Bursa. Few Turkish political figures can trace their ancestry for more than two or three generations, and only some *ulema* and landowning families (e.g. Cenani, Karaosmanoğlu, Mardin) for several centuries.

By contrast, the village boy who must help his father in the fields instead of going to the lycée in the far-away town and the laborer's son who must shift for himself at an early age will always remain in the (rural or urban) lower class. The ambitious peasant boy may set up a barbershop, a filling station, or a coffee house in his village. Or, like his urban cousin, he may take up a craft or trade in the city. But only exceptionally, such as in the role of labor leader, can he aspire to any position of power or influence on the national scene.

This basic social distinction is reflected in everyday speech and etiquette. Although a law of 1934 requires use of the uniform titles of *bay* and *bayan* ("Mr." and "Miss/Mrs."), actual practice continues the older forms of *bey* and *hanım* for educated gentlemen and ladies (with *beyefendi* and *hanımefendi* reserved for persons of greater dignity and *paşa* for generals) and *efendi* or *ağa* for men of the lower class. Similarly members of the upper class are commonly addressed in the second person plural, those of the lower class in the singular. *Beys* and *hanıms* dress in the Western middle-class styles. *Efendis* wear a variety of traditional costumes or riding breeches, jackets, and caps; their womenfolk hide their legs in baggy trousers gathered at the ankles and when outdoors wrap their heads with a black or colored cloth that falls over the shoulders. The city policeman will push around any *efendi* but stand at polite attention in addressing a *bey*.

Members of the urban educated class are conscious of being a ruling elite. Competition for prestige, for power, for wealth within this elite is fully accepted, in thought and private conversation, as a natural consequence of human appetites, as a basic fact of social life. Individual success in this universal competition is viewed as the result of connections, of personal ingenuity, and of good fortune; at any rate it is a risky affair subject to sudden reversal. Personal motives and traits of character are considered the most important determinants of political events—and in view of the small size of the educated class the personalities of the prominent members are well known to most of the rest. (The annual number of lycée graduates was 1,000-4,000 in the 1930's, 4,000-6,000 in the 1940's and by 1959 rose to 9,414. The cumulative total for the period from 1930 to 1959 was 135,645; living lycée graduates therefore must amount to less than ½ of 1 per cent of the population. Over the same period the number of lycées increased from 22 to 182; of the latter, 84 were in Istanbul, Izmir, and Ankara provinces.)[5]

The only political ideology that enjoys universal respectability and commands wide allegiance among this educated class is Turkish nationalism as formulated by Kemal Atatürk, but the essence of that ideology is a direct continuation of Ottoman political traditions. In the conclusion of his monumental *Six-Day Speech* of 1927 Kemal summed up his flexible and pragmatic creed by asserting that "we make use of every means solely and exclusively for one purpose: to bestow upon the Turkish nation that position which is its due within the civilized world."[6] His formulation was a direct echo of the words used by the authors of the 1914 decree abolishing the capitulations in reviewing the nineteenth century reform efforts: "The Ottoman Empire . . . continues to march in the path of renaissance and reform which it entered upon [with the Tanzimat decree of 1839] . . . in order to assure for itself the place which was due it in the family of the civilized peoples of Europe."[7] Although the Kemalist dictum just cited is an explicit commitment to political modernization, its formulation reveals once again the historic continuity from Ottoman Empire through Tanzimat and Young Turks to Kemal and the present.

From this inner core of doctrine outward, differences of emphasis and disagreements as to specific means increase, as may best be seen by examining briefly the "Six Arrows," or slogans, which Kemal's Republican People's Party (RPP) inscribed upon its program in 1931. Republicanism and Nationalism enjoy universal acceptance. The downfall of the Ottoman Empire may be welcomed by ardent Kemalists as relief from an incubus or viewed with wistful regret by more conservative minds; since by both it is considered irrevocable, even in the earliest days of the Kemalist republic no "legitimist" opposition ever arose in Turkey or in exile. There are vastly differing interpretations of *İnkılâpçılık* (a term denoting rapid and fundamental, although not necessarily violent, political change, and hence variously translated as "reformism" or "revolutionism") and of Secularism. To some conservatives, *İnkılâpçılık* means acceptance of

[5] See *İstatistik Yıllığı, 1959*, p. 159.
[6] *Nutuk*, 1934 edn., ii, 336.
[7] Cited in J. C. Hurewitz, *Diplomacy in the Near and Middle East*, Princeton 1956, ii, 2.

the Kemalist reforms as salutary or at least necessary in their time but subject to modification and revision in our day. To the most radical Kemalists it means a continuing cultural and social revolution aimed at complete Westernization and social-economic equality of all strata. Secularism, to the staunch Kemalists, means firm control of the Muslim religious establishment by an agnostic government. Religious conservatives, who are an insignificant minority among the educated but have wider appeal among the lower classes, pay lip service to the concept while advocating a gradual restoration of Islamic education and, possibly, law. To a broad moderate trend of opinion Secularism is compatible with either of these extremes or any intermediate position as long as it has majority endorsement at the polls.[8] The last two tenets, Populism and Etatism, have been considered the RPP's distinguishing characteristics. Etatism was explicitly repudiated by the Democratic Party (DP) when it challenged the RPP's monopolistic power position after 1945; yet when the DP itself came to power in the 1950's the over-all proportion of public to private investment did not appreciably change. Among a small group of intellectuals Etatism today is interpreted as socialism of a Fabian or even Marxist tinge. Populism can be variously understood as government *for* or *by* the people, that is, as benevolent dictatorship or as majoritarian democracy, and both positions have found adherents in all major political camps (although the term itself is a monopoly of RPP adherents, who are known as Populists—*Halkçılar*—for short).

Many of the differences and controversies just surveyed can be attributed directly to the characteristic ambivalence of countries engaged in rapid modernization or Westernization.[9] Secure for Turkey its due place in the civilized world? Yes, definitely! Accept Europe and North America as the foremost representatives of that world civilization? Yes, agreed! But do modernization and civilization require faithful acceptance and imitation of European ways or, on the contrary, assertion of the distinctive essence of national culture and tradition? Can Western majoritarian ideas of politics justify surrendering power to a traditionalist and culturally anti-Western peasant majority, or should such a transfer be delayed until the majority has been thoroughly re-educated in the minority's image?

---

[8] On these three trends see my article, "Politics and Islam in Turkey, 1920-1955," in R. N. Frye, ed. *Islam and the West*, The Hague, 1957, pp. 101-107.

[9] See my essay, "Politics and Westernization in the Near East," reprinted in Richard H. Nolte, ed. *The Modern Middle East*, New York, 1963, pp. 67-71.

It is over these latter questions that the Turkish modernizing elite tends to fret, waver, and divide.

The political sub-cultures of Turkey's rural population and of the urban lower class are far more difficult to describe, both because we lack detailed preliminary studies and because these, in contrast to the urban elite, are not specifically political classes; they also are far less homogeneous. Hence only a few tentative generalizations will be attempted.

The peasantry is the stronghold of traditional values. Education in the home or at the feet of the imam emphasizes Islamic ethical principles of cleanliness, of respect of the young for the old and the female for the male, of loyalty to family and village. The quest for power and wealth is fully sanctioned, for God has promised to the righteous both prosperity on earth and eternal bliss in the hereafter. The nationalist-secularist ideology of city-trained school teachers or government administrators is viewed with suspicion, or cautiously incorporated into religious lore, with Mustafa Kemal emerging as a latter-day Islamic saint in direct line from the early Caliphs, from Osman and the good sultans. The age-old exactions of central government—taxes and conscription—are evaded by all available means. City politicians who flock to the village in quest of votes are a source of puzzlement. Voting behavior is determined more by the advice of imams, village elders, and family chiefs than by examination of abstract issues. After some initial hesitation, material benefits bestowed by a benevolent government or promised by an ambitious opposition—feeder roads, water wells, new mosques, wheat subsidies, dams, factories—are eagerly accepted and rewarded with new political loyalties. Adnan Menderes, the visible fount of such recent benefits, is readily accepted into the canon of saints. Did not God himself save Adnan when his plane crashed at the London airport? And when his envious detractors were putting him on trial for his life on Yassıada, did he not ride nightly on a white stallion to the sacred mosque at Eyub (built in honor of the Prophet's companion who died a martyr at the wall of Istanbul), a mosque richly redecorated by Adnan's lavish donations in his luckier days? Stories of unconstitutional shenanigans, of financial corruption, of sexual libertinism are unlikely to tarnish this affectionate image. For the peasant knows that women and easy living are the tangible rewards that would send him to the distant city in quest of power and glory if he had the chance.

What more likely awaits the migrant to the city is a precarious existence as a construction worker or an unskilled factory hand, a squalid life in squatters' shacks—and all this in full sight of luxury automobiles, of palatial hotels, of women half undressed in the Frankish, unbelieving fashion. It is among the urban lower classes that traditionalist protest movements such as the Nation Party and smaller groups of the right-wing lunatic fringe find their best recruiting ground. It is among them that a few purposeful organizers can start occasional riots such as the orgy of anti-Greek destruction in Istanbul and other cities in September 1955.

The Culture and Political Performance of Specialized Elites

The specialized elites which play a major role in the modernization and socialization of Turkish political culture may conveniently be divided into three groups. The first, including the military, the bureaucracy, and the parliamentarians, represent, in one form or another, the continuing tradition of the Ottoman ruling class. The second group, including the communications elites (journalists, writers, poets), party politicians, and educators, tend to mediate between these ruling elites and the rest of society. The remaining group, including interest groups and other socioeconomic elites, still play only a limited role in politics.

THE MILITARY

The military have played a leading role in Ottoman and Turkish modernization. Army officers were the first group to receive a systematic education outside the traditional Islamic syllabus of Arabic grammar and theology in such subjects as mathematics, history, and French. By the second half of the nineteenth century the military cadets and younger members of the officer corps became the foremost spokesmen for liberal-constitutionalist ideas. And with the victory of the military-civilian conspiracy in the 1908 revolution the prominent role of military officers on the political stage or in the wings became firmly established. The military coup of 1913 in particular brought to prominence such officers as Enver and Cemal, who in alliance with the key civilian organizers of the Union and Progress Party, notably Talât, ruled the country dictatorially for the next five years. The collapse of 1918 re-emphasized the political role of the officer corps. Civilian resistance groups formed in the provincial towns, but their consolidation was achieved by military leaders, foremost Mustafa Kemal Paşa, with the connivance and support of the General Staff in Istanbul.[10] Following the victory in the Turkish War of Independence (1919-1922) and the establishment of the Republic (1923) Mustafa Kemal himself (President of the Republic until his death in 1938) insisted on a clear separation of military and civilian affairs. The most prominent military-political leaders of the War of Independence followed his example in doffing their uniforms and assuming leading positions in government. These included, among many others, İsmet İnönü (Prime Minister 1923-1925, 1925-1937, 1961– ; President 1938-1950); Refik Saydam (Minister of Health 1923-1937, Interior Minister 1938-1939, Prime Minister 1939 until his death in 1942); and Recep Peker (Minister with various portfolios 1924-1930 and 1942-1943, powerful secretary general of the Republican People's Party 1923-1924, 1925, and 1931-1936, Prime Minister 1946-1948).

During the decades from 1923 to 1945 the Turkish army was developed as a disciplined, professional, non-political force—although its armory still was filled with miscellaneous European equipment of World War I or pre-World War I vintage. With the proclamation of the Truman Doctrine in 1947 a large-scale program of U.S. military assistance was instituted. This has involved a reduction in numbers of men under arms (from about 750,000 at the beginning of the program to half that number in 1962) together with introduction of latest mechanical and electronic equipment.

The officer corps represents the most concentrated embodiment of the Kemalist ethic of service to state and nation, of radical and rapid social change in a Westernizing direction. It also is the only group in Turkish society with Spartan and ascetic values. Its orientation to politics in recent years has been ambivalent. Kemal Atatürk's doctrine and practice required abstention of the army from politics and obedience to civilian authorities. But what if the civilian superiors abandon and betray the Kemalist heritage of reform—as the Menderes government did at an accelerating pace in the 1950's? The events of 1959-1960 forced the army's hand in this dilemma. The civilian superiors, after gradually undermining the secularist ethos of the Atatürk reforms, were now systematically violating the constitution which the soldiers were duty-bound to uphold and were attempting to use the army as a tool in these designs. General Gürsel's parting advice in resigning his army post in April 1960 echoed

---

[10] See my article, "The Army and the Founding of the Turkish Republic," *World Politics*, Vol. 13, No. 4, July 1959, pp. 513-552, and the essay cited in note 3, above.

Atatürk's precept of soldierly abstention from politics. But in fact the army by then had no choice about abstaining: if it obeyed the orders issuing from Menderes, it would be deeply in politics on his behalf; if it refused to obey, it would be even more deeply in politics against him. In the revolution of May 27, 1960 the army chose the second alternative. Although a civilian constitution was restored in the fall of 1961, the sentiment persists among younger military officers that Turkey is not politically mature enough for competitive parliamentary politics, and that only an authoritarian regime under military aegis can accomplish the necessary tasks of social, cultural, and economic reform.

Army hierarchy still reflects Turkey's fundamental two-class division. The officers are gentlemen, members of the urban educated class. The recruits are peasant boys subject to barked commands without back talk. Nevertheless the latest wave of cultural change under military auspices—that initiated by the postwar U.S. aid program—is beginning to affect these traditional patterns. Whereas the reforms of Selim III (1789-1807) and Mahmud II (1808-1839) gave the new officer corps access to Western learning, the current program of military service gives the privates as well an intensive exposure to mechanical training. Conversely, there are some indications of a reduction in the social status of the officer corps. Increasingly, prestigious opportunities in such fields as engineering and business compete with an army career. And whereas earnings in private enterprise keep in step with or ahead of inflation, the fixed salaries of officers, as of other public servants, have periodically declined in purchasing power. Upon American advice the armed forces in the 1950's adopted a new set of regulations allowing for the possibility of promotion of qualified sergeants into the officers' corps. Little use has as yet been made of this possibility, but it may be a first indication of a future trend.

Nowhere else are the rapid cultural changes of mid-twentieth century Turkish society as sharply reflected as in the experience of the army recruit. Back in the village the ideals of manly courage and martial valor are inculcated in him at a tender age. "A future pasha!" is the most common compliment to the proud mother of a newborn male. "A soldier doesn't cry," the tearful toddler is admonished. Circumcision, commonly performed at age 7 or 9 and often without anesthesia, is considered a first major test of courage for the future soldier. And a threat, "The Moskovs will get you," keeps the rebellious youngster in line. Once in the army, the young adult is transferred abruptly from the age-old technology of the stick plow and the squeaky ox-cart to that of the jeep, the automatic rifle, and the armored car. In addition a far-flung literacy training program, planned by Georgetown University experts, has been instituted for army recruits.

In the late eighteenth-century reforms, in the Young Turk and Kemalist revolutions, and again since 1960 the military have been in the forefront of political and cultural change. At the same time they embody more clearly than any other social group the historic continuity between modern Turkey and its Ottoman tradition. The course of Turkish modernization in the foreseeable future once again is likely to be intimately related to the role of the military in society and politics.

THE BUREAUCRATS

The bureaucracy, like the army, is one of the important links of continuity between the Ottoman Empire and the Turkish Republic. Whereas Europeanizing reform began with army reorganization, it spread in the mid-nineteenth century to the administrative establishment. The great reforming ministers of the Tanzimat period—Reşid (1799-1857), Âli (1815-1871), and Fuad (1815-1868) Paşas[11]— were diplomats and administrators trained in Western ways in the translation chamber of the Sublime Porte and the early embassies at Paris and London. Although they are best known for the various Imperial rescripts (1839, 1856, etc.) which promised civic equality to all subjects regardless of language and creed, their most notable achievements were in the administrative and educational fields. A permanent diplomatic corps, composed primarily of Turkish-speaking Muslims, replaced the *ad hoc* foreign missions and the Greek Phanariote dragomans of an earlier period. The collection of revenues was taken from private entrepreneurs (known as tax farmers) and transferred to a revenue service. Following the assertion of central authority over peripheral feudatories under Mahmud II, local administration was set up on a hierarchical basis, separate from military organization, of provinces, departments, districts, and sub-districts (the Turkish terms being *Vilâyet, Liva, Kaza,* and *Nahiye*). The judiciary was reorganized on a similar basis. The Civil Service School (*Mekteb-i Mülkiye*) was instituted to provide administrators and judges, the central government offices placed under cabinet ministers,

[11] On these figures see Roderic H. Davison, *Reform in the Ottoman Empire*, Princeton, 1963.

and a Council of State set up to supervise the administrative machinery. In the late nineteenth century the ministry of education was provided with resident field inspectors. By 1900, various economic ministries (Posts and Telegraphs, Public Works, Forests and Minerals) rounded out the list.

The Turkish bureaucracy to this day retains much of the flavor of this late Ottoman period with its conscious adaptation of French patterns. A citizen's errand to a government office typically begins with a written request. A series of initials and signatures must be scribbled on the left and lower margins as the document is passed up the hierarchical ladder. An official evaluation, disposition, or reply is prepared at each step and fastened to the growing bundle with an ordinary steel pin. Each successive paper collects its quota of initials and signatures, of stamped seals, and of tax stamps. If a fee is payable, an invoice must be prepared by an accountant and initialed by an auditor, and a receipt prepared by the cashier, and several more tax stamps must be duly licked, affixed, and cancelled. The experienced petitioner has bought an ample supply of such stamps in all conceivable denominations at a cigarette store before venturing into the labyrinth of offices—for to stoop to trafficking in these magic bits of gummed and perforated paper with lowly subjects would be far beneath the dignity of august state authority. Its stamps and signatures in place, each document now is carefully numbered according to two different indexing systems. Each signature is duly dated, each incoming and outgoing document carefully inventoried in a folio register. The language of requests, dispositions, and other official correspondence reverberates with the reverential circumlocutions of the Ottoman Imperial chancery. Each incoming paper, and a carbon copy of each one going out, are duly placed in pronged cardboard files. In the perennial twilight of asthmatic offices dossiers upon dossiers slant in glass-doored cupboards or teeter on high piles on the creaky floor. The harried clerk now can tug contentedly at the green visor on his forehead and smooth out the black sleeve protectors on his forearms. His task is well done. When a document is needed a month later only the most assiduous and extensive search is likely to extract it.

These exacting procedures were once devised no doubt in the hope of protecting both citizen and state from arbitrary and capricious action by individual administrators. They do effectively tend to stifle the civil servant's initiative, and they even more surely dilute his responsibility. But the intricate system engenders its own antidotes and immunities. Documents are carefully drafted but hastily read. Signatures are uniformly illegible. The fees for most tax stamps barely repay the time and effort of purchasing, licking, and cancelling them. Above all, the system puts a premium on "connections." The lowly petitioner starts to wind his way upward from the Secretariat for Incoming Papers through a tedious progression of antechambers. Not so the well-connected citizen, who instead sips a trayful of amicable cups of coffee with his cousin or classmate or cousin's classmate who, as luck will have it, occupies the well-upholstered armchair in the director-general's office—while a bevy of lesser spirits at the mere flick of a hand scurry back and forth with the growing pile of necessary papers.

Nor does the system of itself prevent corruption. Small-scale bribery seems to have declined steadily in recent decades, but when and where it was prevalent the plethora of signatures simply meant a multiplicity of palms to be greased. During the Atatürk era some of the more notorious cases of corruption were brought to trial—resulting even in the impeachment of one cabinet minister. With the increase of government economic activities and regulations during World War II and under Menderes the opportunities for corruption increased—favoritism in the issuing of licenses and exchange permits, kickbacks on government contracts, profitable real estate dealings in areas due for municipal development. And prosecutions were conspicuously absent—until the prolonged mass trials following upon the 1960 revolution. Even so (and although it is patently impossible to give reliable estimates in such matters) it would seem that bureaucratic corruption in Turkey at its worst was far less widespread than it was in neighboring Near Eastern countries and hardly more so than in some machine-ridden cities in the twentieth century United States.

THE PARLIAMENTARIANS

Under the constitution of the First Republic (1923-1960) the Grand National Assembly was the embodiment of national sovereignty, and each of the members—some 300 at the beginning and over 600 at the end of the period—thus enjoyed his pro-rata share of the plenitude of political power. The deputies ranked in social prestige after army generals and provincial governors (*valis*) and somewhat ahead of university professors. By simple majority they elected the President of the Republic and confirmed the cabinet; by a three-fourths vote they could amend the constitution. Salaries were higher than those of any civil servants and were supplemented by other perquisites, such as frequent free trips on the state railways and liberal advances on the Treasury.

The lists of candidates for the parliamentary elections were made up by the central party leadership, including the President, Prime Minister, and Minister of the Interior (often doubling as the governing party's secretary-general). During the period of exclusive dominance by the Republican People's Party (1923-1945) nomination was tantamount to election. Once in office, the legislators were allowed much freedom of debate on details, especially within the party caucus. Even occasional "nay" votes were tolerated in public session as long as they represented no concerted bid for power. A spontaneous opposition split off in 1924 and was suppressed the next year. In 1930 a 13-man loyal opposition group was formed in parliament with Kemal's sanction, but the experiment was called off after four months when the opposition proved too popular.

Open party competition was allowed after 1945, and in 1950, the Democratic Party of Bayar and Menderes won a sweeping victory, confirmed by a wider margin in 1954 and a smaller one in 1957. Nominations on the Democratic ticket were freely dispensed by central headquarters, although local popularity now became a factor of account. The deputies began to act as channels for favors to constituents. The Republican People's Party, now in opposition, went so far as to leave four-fifths of the nominations to elected party conventions in the provinces. In parliament the minority parties (the DP before 1950 and the RPP afterwards) suffered from periodic defections to the majority or to splinter groups. Increasing centralization of power in Menderes' hands led to a series of expulsions, especially in the late 1950's. In the meantime the scramble for ministerial offices and Menderes' habit of periodic cabinet shuffles created an atmosphere of sycophancy.

The advent of competitive politics brought about a notable change in the Assembly's social composition. Whereas once it had been filled primarily with senior government officials—army officers, civil servants, judges, professors—members of the free professions (notably lawyers), businessmen, and large land owners increased in all party delegations.[12]

[12] See Frederick W. Frey, *The Turkish Political Elite*, Cambridge, Mass., 1965.

The legislature of the Second Republic (first convened in November 1961) is divided into two houses—a Senate elected by majority and a House by proportional representation. The result has been a temporary loosening of the two-party system. The first coalition was formed by the two largest groups, the Republican People's Party and the Justice Party, chief successor of the defunct Democrats. The coalition of inimical groups dissolved after seven months of inaction and stalemate, to be replaced after laborious negotiations by a coalition of the RPP with the two smaller groups. In social composition there seems to be no basic change from the 1950's, although the Senate contains a contingent of lifetime military members from the 1960-1961 junta. By 1964, the tendency toward a two-party alignment had reasserted itself, although the military's presence in the wings contributed a sense of uncertainty to the political drama.[13]

THE POLITICIANS

The successful politicians are those in parliament, whose role has just been discussed. The unsuccessful or aspiring ones are those defeated in elections and the many lesser figures who work in the central and local party machineries. The process of party competition has brought politics from the capital to the provincial towns and the villages. The small-town merchant and lawyer and the large and middling landowner in the country now are involved in politics and set their sights on office in party or parliament. The small peasant is content to troop to the polls and to choose among more prominent names. Although on a nationwide basis the RPP tends to have stronger support in the cities and the old DP and new Justice Party in the rural areas, local party alignments often follow patterns of family relationships and clan enmity. A well-known candidate is likely to line up a heavy vote for his home province ticket whatever the party—Menderes in Aydın, Bayar in Bursa, İnönü in Malatya. Where the politicians of the one-party period under the aegis of Atatürk and İnönü conceived their task as one of educational and economic development of a backward country, the competing party organizations are eager to become the spokesmen for economic and sectional interests.

[13] See my article, "Turkey's Second Try at Democracy," *The Yale Review*, Summer 1963, pp. 518-538.

THE EDUCATORS

Of all the Westernizing innovations of the nineteenth century, those in higher education have proved most durable and fruitful. The reformed army suffered more disastrous defeats than the old Janissaries. The centralized tax system could not stave off bankruptcy. The 1876 Constitution was suspended from 1878 to 1908 and superseded after 1920. The ponderous *Mecelle* was replaced by European codes in 1926. But the *Mülkiye* (transferred to Ankara and renamed Faculty of Political Sciences) still is the most important source of recruitment for the civil, judicial, and diplomatic services. The lycée of Galatasaray, set up in cooperation with the French ministry of education in 1868, still is the most prestigious preparatory school, rivaled only recently by Robert College (founded in 1863) as a training center for businessmen and engineers.

The curriculum in secondary and higher education started from a French-inspired basis—much emphasis on literature, history, mathematics, on memory work, on formal lectures, on formal examinations. German influence was strong in the military schools (Colmar Freiherr von der Goltz-Paşa was their inspector at the turn of the century), and at the university level there was a brief influx of German scientists in 1917-1918 and a more prolonged one of anti-Nazi refugees in the 1930's and 1940's. Some American influence began with a brief advisory junket by John Dewey in the 1920's. Since World War II, English has replaced French and German as the favorite foreign language, and it is spoken with an American accent. "Colleges" with an English-language curriculum have been set up by resourceful entrepreneurs eager to extract tuition fees from the children of affluent and gullible social climbers, and more recently by the government.

In the universities the faculties of law and letters have traditionally attracted the largest enrollment, although engineering and agriculture have vastly increased in the last two decades. Atatürk's predilection for the (real or presumed) pre-Islamic history of the Turks gave an impetus to research in such esoteric subjects as Altaic and Chinese philology and Hittite and Sumerian archaeology. Arabic and Persian philology are almost totally neglected; Ottoman historiography has a few devoted adherents. Turkish history and politics of the twentieth century as a serious subject is largely the preserve of a few retired staff colonels and high-school teachers.

The elementary and high-school teacher in the country town still is the most influential missionary of modernization, of secularism, of Kemalist nationalism. His greatest handicap is that he is likely to feel in exile and to wish for an early return to the city. During the People's Party period a number of Village Institutes were set up, where youngsters from the country were trained as school teachers without exposure to the beguiling influence of the big town. The stirring and well-known account by Mahmut Makal[14] reveals the frustrations that awaited the graduate on his first assignment: suspicion of parents, competition and slander from the imam, cultural isolation. During the Menderes period, moreover, the Village Institutes came under attack from conservative rural legislators who found coeducation repugnant and equated social reform with Communism. Even before 1950 the secularist elementary school curriculum was diluted with lessons (first voluntary, then compulsory) in Islamic religion. Nonetheless education remains (and is regarded by most upper-class Turks as) a major vehicle for progressive modernization. It seems likely that a peasantry more firmly enmeshed in the market economy will increasingly perceive the more tangible benefits of the three R's for their sons—and ultimately even daughters.

COMMUNICATIONS

Turkey belongs to the highly verbal Mediterranean-Near Eastern culture, and journalists, writers, poets, and pamphleteers play a great and highly vocal role in society and politics. The military and bureaucratic modernizers of the early nineteenth century were soon joined by men like İbrahim Şinasi (1824-1871), who was sent to Paris to study finance but returned an ardent admirer of Hugo and Lamartine to become the Turkish founder of daily journalism and of romantic poetry. The 1876 Constitution was drafted by Midhat Paşa, the reformist administrator from the Balkans, Namık Kemal, Şinasi's poetic-journalistic disciple, and Ziya Paşa, a poet and civil servant.

After the enforced silence during Abdülhamid's absolutism the Young Turk period (1908-1918) brought an unprecedented efflorescence of journalism and political writing. Organized partisan opposition suffered periodic repression, especially after the coups of 1909 and 1913. But writers of all descriptions continued to advocate and elaborate their contradictory remedies to the foundering empire's plight: Panturkism, Islamic traditionalism, Westernization, national-

[14] *A Village in Anatolia*, London, 1954.

ism. Following the abolition of the caliphate (1924) and the suppression of the Progressive Party (1925)—both of which had been ardently supported by most of the Istanbul press—a period of enforced monotony ensued. For years the official People's Party organ, called first *Hakimiyeti Milliye* ("National Sovereignty") and then *Ulus* ("The Nation") in Ankara, and the semi-official *Cumhuriyet* ("The Republic") in Istanbul dominated the scene. In the midthirties new dailies were founded, while the People's Party tried to direct this semi-free press through an officially inspired National Press Association. Another period of untrammelled press freedom began during the years of party competition after 1945, and in the 1950 election campaign even the government radio made time available to opposition parties. During the later years of Menderes' premiership (1950-1960) libel laws became increasingly stringent, journalists accused of harming the government's reputation filled the jails, and news-print quotas and official notices were allocated so as to muzzle free expression in the Istanbul press and subsidize sycophantic weeklies in the provinces. After the 1960 revolution a new degree of freedom, unprecedented since 1908 and 1946, has been established—although interludes of states of siege have provided minor restrictions.

During the single-party period many poets and prose writers converted their long-standing interest in public affairs into propagandistic advocacy of Kemalism. Others withdrew into a nostalgic lyricism (e.g. Yahya Kemal Beyatlı, 1884-1958), or attempted to develop a philosophy of social reform vaguely inspired by Bolshevism (e.g. Yakub Kadri Karaosmanoğlu, b. 1888). Beyatlı, Karaosmanoğlu, and others were rewarded for their pains with honorable exile as ministers to minor capitals such as Tirana, Warsaw, or Bucharest. Nazım Hikmet (b. 1901), widely acknowledged to be the most gifted poet of his generation, was jailed on charges of being a Communist in 1935. Released under a general amnesty of 1950, he escaped to Russia, where he took to reading rhymed diatribes against Foster Dulles, Wall Street, and the Korean War over Radio Moscow. Since World War II there has been an upsurge of lyrical poetry liberated from the older clichés—e.g. Orhan Veli Kanık (1914-1950)—of novels realistically portraying village life—e.g. Yaşar Kemal (b. 1922), whose *Memed My Hawk* recently appeared in English translation—and social satire—e.g. Aziz Nesin (b. 1915), who bitingly portrays the moral and esthetic incongruities of half-digested democracy.[15]

ECONOMIC ELITES AND PRESSURE GROUPS

Pressure groups are notably absent from the Turkish political scene. The customary candidates for such activity, business and labor, have lagged each for their own reasons. Effective labor organization is handicapped by the pervasive feeling of class distinctions, by the prevalence of unskilled over skilled labor, and by the steady influx into the industrial labor market from the overpopulated rural areas. Few labor leaders as yet have the necessary determination, and even fewer the required poise, to speak effectively to the gentlemen employers. As soon, on the other hand, as a labor leader becomes familiar with gentlemanly etiquette, he may become less zealous in defending the interests of his working-class constituents. The first nationwide system of trade unions was established by government legislation in the late 1940's. Throughout the 1950's one of organized labor's major aims was to obtain the right to strike, by friendly petition to the Labor Ministry for permissive legislation. Well-intentioned legislative welfare provisions often backfired in a situation of oversupply of labor—e.g. the requirement of severance pay after six months' service caused some employers merely to lay off their entire work force twice a year. Fear of class politics has led to stringent provisions against political activity by unions—although by the mid-1950's individual labor leaders were eagerly courted for parliamentary nomination by the major parties. The labor legislation of 1963, legalizing the right to strike and collective bargaining for the first time, can be expected to bring about a consolidation of labor organization as a major political and economic force.

Among businessmen there is a widespread attitude of mutual distrust. Small craftsmen have their associations continuing earlier guild traditions. Modern manufacturers, on the other hand, are more likely to use their individual connections in the bureaucracy to secure favorable application of individual rules than to band together with their competitors to influence the legislative formulation of those rules. The large sector of government-owned industries further limits the field for collective organization. In the 1950's, however, individual

[15] For an excellent sampling of contemporary Turkish prose and poetry, by these and others in English translation, together with a perceptive interpretive essay by Kemal H. Karpat, see *The Literary Review*, Vol. 4, No. 2, Fairleigh Dickinson University, Winter 1960-1961.

"self-made men," such as Kâzım Taşkent and Vehbi Koç, have put together powerful industrial-commercial empires; as a result their individual voices carry weight in politics. The Chambers of Industry and Commerce, set up years ago by law on the continental European pattern, have recently played a role of accredited spokesmen of business interests. Their statistical publications in the 1950's enjoyed a better reputation among economists than those of the government, and thorny issues such as the allocation of import quotas were turned over to them by law or decree.

Agricultural producers have not even progressed to the rudiments of political organization. The large landowners are likely to be included, or well connected, in the ruling circles of the upper class. The peasants are scattered among thousands of villages. Collectively they hardly require any pressure group organization. Since they constitute three-fourths of the electorate, their most effective pressure is brought to bear at the polls, not in the lobby.

Continuity and Change

The evolution of Turkish political culture since the eighteenth century offers a remarkable combination of continuity and change. The Ottoman state, it was suggested earlier in this essay, was essentially a military camp and an educational institution. Although Turkey's political culture has changed in most particulars since the onset of Westernization in the eighteenth century, the change has been directed at all times by indigenous elites within which army officers and educators have continued to play a leading role. The destruction of the Janissary corps, the Young Turk revolution of 1908, the transition from empire to republic in 1919-1923, and the revolution of 1960-1961 probably constitute the decisive turning points. But the Janissaries were replaced by a European-style army trained by the Sultans for a generation, the Young Turks restored a constitution suspended thirty years earlier, and Mustafa Kemal and his followers, throughout most of the War of Independence that laid the foundations for the republic, averred their loyalty to the Sultan and Caliph. When the political elite changed most drastically, political institutions remained stable in their major features; when political institutions were thoroughly refashioned, the political elite remained unchanged in its social composition. The Westernized officers and bureaucrats of the Tanzimat period were trained to buttress the traditional sultanate. This new elite come to power in

1908 and presided over the Kemalist transformation. In the years after 1945 new social groups have become active within political institutions which have remained stable—except for the restorative revolution of 1960-1961.

The alternating continuity of institutions and personnel has preserved for later generations and diffused among wider strata the sense of political responsibility that the small imperial elite of the sultan's slave household accumulated over several centuries. This sense of responsibility and pragmatism helped solve for Turkey the problem of defining its national identity when the multi-national empire collapsed in 1918. While Turkey has had a series of governmental coups, notably in 1807-1808, 1876, 1908-1913, 1960-1961, there have been no outbreaks of endemic uncontrolled violence and no sudden social revolution. Instead, the circle of rulers and of politically active citizens has broadened gradually and steadily. As much as Turkey's social structure and political orientation may differ from those of Britain and Japan, the combination of progressivism and conservatism, of continuity and change is characteristic of these three political cultures as it is of few others in the world.

CHAPTER 6

India: Two Political Cultures

MYRON WEINER

The Indian elite which won power from the British in 1947 took steps to create a new political order, and India became one of the few new nations in which power was deliberately and successfully dispersed and democratized. The result has been that on the local level less educated, more traditional, and less national-minded individuals have acquired political power and have brought with them attitudes toward power and government which the national leadership often finds distasteful.

There thus have emerged in post-independence India two political cultures operating at different levels of Indian society. One culture is in the districts. It permeates local politics, both urban and rural, local party organization, and local administration. It is an expanding political culture which reaches out into the state legislative assemblies, state governments, and state administrations. Although it is permeated with traditional elements, it is not wholly traditional, for it has many modern components.

The second political culture predominates in New Delhi. It is personified by India's planners, many of the national political leaders, and the senior administrative cadre. It is also widespread in the army and it is shared by most of the English-speaking intelligentsia. It becomes less evident as one moves into state capitals, though it can be found there too, and almost disappears as one moves into rural areas or municipal government. It is a defensive political culture. It is critical of the emerging, more popular, mass political culture which in large measure is its own creation. But though this culture is expressed in modern language and is permeated with elements which we ordinarily think of as modern, it is not wholly modern, for it has many traditional components.

The first political culture can be characterized as an emerging mass political culture; the second, as an elite political culture. It would be quite misleading, however, to describe one as traditional and the other as modern, for these two terms would not only oversimplify two complicated sets of attitudes but would also lead to quite incorrect judgments that one is bad, the other good, that one is inappropriate to modernization and the other appropriate. In this paper I shall suggest that, although there are many aspects of the emerging mass political culture which are adaptive and appropriate for the goals of democratization, political stability, and perhaps, though less clearly, modernization, it also has some aspects which are inappropriate to these goals. I shall also suggest that the political culture of the elite, though it appears to be extraordinarily modern and is generally characterized as being modern by those who belong to it, is often quite inappropriate and unadaptive to these goals. And it will also be suggested that while some of its attacks against the emerging mass political culture are in order, its understanding of that culture is limited, and therefore its solutions are permeated with utopianism and an incipient authoritarianism.

The Impact of The Elite on the Mass Political Culture

Political attitudes in a country as large and complex as India are bound to be diversified. Alongside the gentle, Gandhian style of politics in the state of Gujarat in the northwest one finds both the more emotional, violent, and calculating politics of the delta of Andhra in the south and the uncompromising ideologically oriented politics of West Bengal in the northeast. However, even in a country as diverse as India, there are some general patterns of political culture.

The literature on India—by Indians or foreigners—abounds with arguments concerning the degree and character of diversity in Indian life and the kind of societal links which exist. While some scholars stress the extraordinary variations in India's social organization, others note that some form of caste organization is always present and that hierarchical relationships are a pervasive element of social life. Some scholars stress the wide variations in local power structures, while others note that almost everywhere there are dominant and subordinate castes and powerful local bureaucracies. Religious beliefs too appear to be infinitely diverse, but scholars of the "higher" traditions point to characteristic beliefs shared by the three-quarters of the population who are Hindus. Some scholars stress the diversity of culture and language among the sixteen states and within each state as a divisive element in political life, while others point to the socializing effect on Indians throughout the subcontinent of Moghul and British-introduced institutions: a national university system, a relatively uniform administrative system in the country's more than four hundred districts, the use of English as the language of the educated elite, a politically independent press and a national radio system, and of course a national government.

The image—and reality—of extraordinary diversity on the one hand and the obvious fact on the other that there are shared attitudes and behavioral patterns in India which distinguish Indians from other nationalities have led scholars to explore the nature of the linkages and common influences in Indian society. In place of earlier notions concerning the economic self-sufficiency of the village there has developed a more sophisticated awareness of the place of the village economy in a wider market.[1] In place of notions emphasizing the unique social and cultural features of villages there has developed a picture of the role of marriage patterns, pilgrimages, and the like in linking each village to a larger environment, and the role of traveling sadhus (religious mendicants), bards, and peddlers in bringing external cultural influences into the village.[2]

The impact of national political institutions and national political activities on local attitudes and behavior has been less clear. Most anthropological studies say little about peasant attitudes toward the nationalist movement or toward the secular, democratic, and federal institutions which guide the country's political life. They make little mention of the peasants' awareness of India's national leaders—the late Nehru, members of the cabinet, or even the state leaders. In recent years, however, there has been a growing awareness of the effect of central government policies on the political behavior and attitudes of virtually the entire population.[3]

[1] M. N. Srinivas, "The Myth of Self-Sufficiency of the Indian Village," *Economic Weekly*, Vol. 12, 1960, pp. 1375-1378.

[2] Bernard S. Cohn, "Networks and Centers in the Integration of Indian Civilization," *Journal of Social Research*, Vol. 1, 1958, pp. 1-9; V. Raghavan, "Variety and Integration in the Pattern of Indian Culture," *Journal of Asian Studies*, Vol. 15, August 1956, pp. 487-506; M. N. Srinivas, "The Nature of the Problem of Indian Unity," *Economic Weekly*, Vol. 10, 1958, pp. 571-577; Milton Singer, "The Cultural Pattern of Indian Civilization," *Journal of Asian Studies*, Vol. 15, 1956, pp. 23-36.

[3] For an examination of the impact of factors external to the village on the power structure of a village, see Alan R. Beals, "Interplay Among Factors of Change in a Mysore Village," in *Village India*, McKim Marriott, ed. Chicago, University of Chicago Press, 1955. In the same volume, David G. Mandelbaum summarizes village studies containing data on the views of villagers toward their external world ("The World and the World View of the Kota"). He describes the complicated maneuvering for social standing and the importance of factional strife as an element in the struggle for the establishment and maintenance of personal status as characteristic of rural India, and concludes that in spite of considerable variations in world views, "there appeared to emerge some views common to the diversity of villages represented in this volume" (p. 253).

The nationalist leaders who took power from the British in 1947 set out to remake India in their own image. Their policies and actions are well known to those who have followed political events in Asia—five-year plans for economic development, the community development program, a spate of land reform legislation, new institutions of local government, a national constitution, free state and national elections, the abolishment of the princely states, the reorganization of states along linguistic lines. What is less known is the impact which these various policies have had upon the attitudes and behavior of Indians toward the state and toward politics generally. The changes caused by them are important new socializing forces. Indeed, one might argue that in India, as in many other new states, the changing character of political attitudes and the political process is increasingly the consequence of the introduction of new governmental institutions and of governmental activities.

Clearly the most significant change is the increase in the amount of contact between individual Indians and their government, with a consequent change in the character of their relationship. Three aspects of governmental activity have been vital in this changing relationship: the expanding activities of all levels of government, the dispersion of power, and the democratization of power. In the pages that follow we shall show how these changes have brought into political life large numbers of Indians with attitudes and purposes often at odds with those who wield national power. We shall explore too the relationship between the new emerging mass political culture and the older national political culture of the political and bureaucratic elites and the possible consequences of this relationship for subsequent political development.

THE EXPANDING NET OF GOVERNMENT: REGULATION
AND DISTRIBUTION

The most important element at work in changing India's mass political culture is the large number of directives emanating from the state and central governments, most of them of a regulatory nature. To import a commodity, to open a shop, or to purchase certain scarce supplies, one must obtain permission from some administrative agency. In India economic planning has largely meant that investment targets and production goals have been set; the over-all strategy has been to establish a series of regulations concerned with allocating scarce resources, such as steel, coal, power, and foreign exchange. On some commodities, moreover, prices have been fixed, new taxes imposed and permits for purchasing required.

Economic planning in India has also meant controls over the activities of specific business firms and individuals. Such controls and regulations are not inherent in economic planning. Planning may rely mainly on fiscal and monetary measures intended to have an effect on the market environment in which businessmen and consumers freely make their choices to buy or sell. Such measures are quite impersonal in character and, though they have profound consequences for the individual and for the economy as a whole, they do not involve government directly in the lives of individual citizens as does a system of direct controls. Though among socialists and capitalists the great controversy has concerned the forms of industrial management—whether industry is to be in the public or private sector—among economists concerned with economic growth the more important choice is between planning which seeks to regulate and control individual economic decisions and to supplant the free market by preventing the forces of supply and demand from determining the prices and quantities of goods and services bought and sold, and planning which seeks to affect the market so as to encourage or discourage buying or selling, lending and investing.

Both types of planning occur in India, but there is a strong element of direct controls and regulation. The reasons for this choice are many, not the least of which is that the new Indian government drew its experiences from a wartime government. The bureaucracy was already predisposed toward such regulations, and many intellectuals—including the Prime Minister—drew their notions of planning from one country which had made economic planning a central goal of national government policy, the Soviet Union.

A policy of direct controls has important consequences for individual relations with government. Complex regulations are formulated to be administered and adjudicated by a large army of administrative personnel. Increased competition among individuals takes place, not within the free market, but within the administrative apparatus. There is competition not only among individuals, but also among communities and regions for a larger share of governmental allocations to either the public or private sector. Moreover the fact that government uses its own resources for development activities—for the construction of roads, schools, telegraph and telephone facilities, irrigation and power schemes, steel mills, fertilizer plants, machine tools, and other heavy industries—increases such competition.

Decisions that were formerly made within the village now involve a level of governmental activity which may be ten miles or even a thousand miles away from the village. And competition which once occurred within the free market now takes place in the political market place or within the governmental apparatus. There is thus a substantial and growing flow of communication between individuals and the district towns on upward to the state and national capitals. Buses from villages to district towns routinely carry cultivators on government "business," and flights from Calcutta, Madras, or Bombay to New Delhi are full of businessmen on government "business." The ultimate aim of this communication is to influence administration, for both villagers and businessmen are generally more concerned with influencing the application of government policy than bringing about a change in policy.[4]

THE DISPERSION OF POWER

In one sense power has always been dispersed in India. Before British rule India was governed by the imperial Moghul powers in Delhi who had established an intricate pattern of relationships with Moghul governors, Hindu rulers, and at a lower level a network of local kingdoms.[5] While national and most regional powers were eliminated or absorbed by the British rulers, local powers often persisted by adapting themselves to British rule. In fact, in an effort to find ways of exercising authority in such a vast country the British were not only prepared to sustain many of the local powers but often took steps to create such powers. Under British rule therefore there existed thoughout the country local powers who worked with, influenced, and were in turn influenced by the British-created administrative system. These men had many titles—jagirdars, zamindars, watandars, talukdars—but everywhere their local power was based on their control over land, their position as a high or "dominant" caste, and the fact that such groups were often lineages under the guidance of leading men.

Under the British, however, formal governmental authority at

---

[4] For a discussion of the relationship of the business community in India with policy makers and administrators, see Myron Weiner, *Politics of Scarcity*, Chicago, University of Chicago Press, 1962, Chap. V, "Organized Business."

[5] For an analysis of levels of political systems in pre-British India, see Bernard S. Cohn, "Political Systems in Eighteenth Century India: The Banaras Region," *Journal of the American Oriental Society*, Vol. 82, No. 3, July-September 1962, pp. 312-320.

the local level was in the hands of district administration. In the latter part of the nineteenth century the British set out to create institutions of local government. In large parts of the country, district local boards—partly elected and partly appointed—were established, and at a lower level limited powers were extended to elected village councils. Under Moghul rule a system of provincial governments had already existed, and with some modifications this was continued by the British. At the time of independence therefore Indians were ruled by many levels of government. The new Indian constitution, which was based primarily on the British constitutional act of 1935, provided for the establishment of a federal system in which the states would have considerable power over education, welfare, and agriculture, while the center would have jurisdiction over defense, foreign affairs, transportation, and industrial development in its broadest aspects. Many of the planners were eager to centralize power as much as was feasible and at a minimum to press for national policies even regarding such state matters as agriculture and education.

Other national leaders, profoundly influenced by Gandhi's convictions that strong democratic local governments should be the basis of India's politics and village self-sufficiency the basis of her economy, pressed for the transfer of administrative powers to local governments. In the latter part of the 1950's the influence of the "decentralists" grew as it became apparent that the central government program for mobilizing the peasantry to participate in the community program for the development of sanitation, education, improved health, village industries, and agriculture was far from a success. There was increasing criticism that the program had failed to arouse public participation.[6]

After investigating this problem a government committee proposed that rural development activities be placed in the hands of new institutions of local government, and in 1959 two states, Andhra and Rajasthan, inaugurated a new system of local government known as *Panchayati raj* or democratic decentralization. Under this program a three-tiered system of local government was established which is now being extended throughout India. At one level is the village *panchayat*, an elected council with enlarged powers of local govern-

[6] In 1957 a team was appointed by the National Development Council to look into the shortcomings of the Community Development Program. The report of the team on Community Projects and National Extension Service, under the leadership of Balvantray Mehta, was issued later in the year recommending a program of decentralization.

ment. At a second level is a *samiti*, usually consisting of the heads of village panchayats and covering an area of about 60,000 people, and at the third level there is a *zilla parishad*, or district council made up of the samiti presidents. (In some areas the zilla parishad is directly elected.) The area of the samiti coincides with the geographical area of the government-sponsored community development program, and the parishad has as its major responsibility the coordination of all development activities within the entire district, an area encompassing more than a million people. The samiti and the parishad thus constitute not only units of local government but also rural development units with substantial budgets for primary and secondary schools, medical dispensaries, road construction, wells, and agricultural development programs, including minor irrigation works.[7]

An increase in the power available to villagers has also occurred with the large-scale expansion of rural cooperatives during the past decade. These cooperatives are actually government created, regulated, and financed but have a voluntary membership. In any district there may be 500 or more cooperatives providing loans and services to small-scale village industries, and seeds, fertilizers, and storage facilities for the cultivators. Since the limited money made available by the district cooperative bank is offered at a lower rate of interest than can be obtained from village money lenders, and fertilizers and cement are sold through cooperatives at government rates fixed lower than those prevailing in the open market, the pressure of demand on these bodies from cultivators is considerable.

From the government's viewpoint these new institutions of local government and the cooperatives are important instruments for facilitating economic development in the countryside. Local politicians in the Congress Party, and men of local power generally, are strong advocates of a policy of dispersion, for it obviously enhances their position vis-à-vis local administration and the local citizenry. As we

[7] The literature on community development programs and on panchayats is enormous, but relatively few studies deal with the relationship between the rural power structure and the development program. One of the best accounts of village politics is Ralph H. Retzlaff, *Village Government in India*, Bombay, Asia Publishing House, 1962. For a critique on the use of panchayats for development purposes, based upon an assessment of village power structures, see Daniel Thorner, "The Village Panchayat as a Vehicle of Change," in *Economic Development and Cultural Change*, Vol. 2, October 1953, pp. 209-215. For studies of the development of political leadership at the village level, see the papers in *Leadership and Political Institutions in India*, Richard L. Park and Irene Tinker, eds., Princeton, Princeton University Press, 1959, Part 8.

have noted, for the Gandhians this dispersion is viewed as an expression of an economic, social and political philosophy. But whatever the intent of those who support decentralization, as we shall see, the establishment of these institutions has had important consequences for the character of the political culture at the local level.

THE DEMOCRATIZATION OF POWER

While most other new nations of Asia and Africa have generally been moving in the direction of greater authoritarianism, India has moved toward a greater democratization of power. By 1950 several hundred princely states were absorbed into the Indian union and their powers turned over to the newly elected state legislative assemblies. The princes were permitted to retain limited privy purses during their own lifetime, and a few of the larger maharajas were given honorific positions as state governors, although their actual powers were eliminated.[8]

In most of the states land reform legislation was passed which eliminated some of the worst concentrations of rural economic and political power. Zamindars, jagirdars, watandars, and talukdars were all deprived of their major landholdings and, though most of these men continued to be substantial property owners, they no longer held the vast powers and influence over administration which characterized their position before independence. The recent establishment of panchayati raj has also meant that new units of elected government now have power in the spheres of agriculture and education which in the past were often controlled by powerful local men, by local administration, or by state governments.

But perhaps the most important aspect of the program of democratization has been the establishment of universal adult suffrage, which has made the new institutions subject to popular control and thus caused a shift in power from administration to popular government. This shift, first in the states and central government, and in recent years with the establishment of panchayati raj at the local level has had, as we shall see later, profound consequences both for the relationship between the individual and the Congress Party organization and for the relationship between the individual and the bureaucracy.

[8] For a historical account of the process by which the princely states were absorbed, see V. P. Menon, *The Story of the Integration of the Indian States*, London, Orient Longmans, 1956.

The Emerging Mass Culture

The expansion, dispersion, and democratization of power in India have led to an increase in public participation. Of the 176,000,000 eligible voters, 88,600,000 or slightly more than 50 per cent, actually voted in 1952. In the 1962 elections the number of actual voters increased to 114,000,000. The turnout for state assembly elections generally exceeds that of national parliamentary elections, and in most parts of the country participation in elections for village councils involve even larger turnouts.

In the last ten years most of the major political parties, and particularly the Congress Party, have been increasing their memberships, and the rush for public office—to be a Member of Parliament, in the state assemblies, district councils, or village panchayats—has been unprecedented. Four or five candidates will commonly run for each seat to the state legislative assembly, and often a half-dozen contenders or more will compete for the Congress nomination. In the 1962 elections 1,593 candidates contested 489 seats for Parliament, and 12,627 candidates contested about 2,800 state assembly seats. If one considers that there were probably an average of five contestants for each Congress ticket and perhaps two for most other parties, one reaches the staggering figure of 30,000 to 35,000 contenders for public office in India, not counting contenders for office in local government bodies.

STATUS POLITICS

One might explain the rush for office on the grounds that an elected office is after all a job and educated unemployment in India is great, if it were not that the amount commonly expended by candidates for public office far exceeds the remuneration received by a legislator. And while a few legislators may supplement their incomes illegally (it is popularly believed that many do), probably only a handful run for public office with this in mind. Nor is the rush related to serious differences in public policy, since policy conflicts play almost no part in India's general elections. Clearly the struggle is simply for power and the status associated with power in India.

The rush for office is bound to be great in a hierarchical social system. Furthermore, where authority is esteemed, as it almost universally is in traditional societies, individuals in a hierarchical system look with covetous eyes on all positions of power accessible to them. Struggles for power become particularly intense and emotional when other criteria for status become fuzzy. Caste in changing rural India is no longer as clear a mark of status as it once was. The power and status held by a handful of large landowners, petty rajas, and maharajas has been reduced or eliminated, and education is no longer the exclusive possession of a small elite. Many villagers say that in the "old days" it was not necessary for men to contest panchayat elections since everyone recognized who the village leaders were. That this is becoming less and less so suggests that the criteria for status are no longer clear; today men must often stand for public office to assert their claims to status.

The transfer of power to many levels of government also intensifies the struggle for office. The older panchayats had fewer legislative and executive functions. Samitis and zilla parishads were of course non-existent, and state legislative assemblies in the British era had fewer powers. In any political system, when power is transferred to old bodies or new bodies of power are created, there is invariably an increase in political conflict.[9]

As important as status considerations are, one should not underestimate the material gains associated with the holding of office, at least within local bodies.[10] By controlling the panchayat one not only enhances the status of one's faction but also has greater access to government money. Precisely where the new village road is to be located, near whose fields irrigation channels are to be built, where a new tube well for irrigation or drinking water is to be dug are no small matters within the village. Moreover the politically dominant element may exercise great influence over the allocation of credit and the distribution of limited supplies of fertilizers, seeds, or cement.

"CASTEISM, COMMUNALISM, PROVINCIALISM"

Another consequence of the dispersion of power is that new elements have entered into the political arena. In many instances polit-

[9] Some Indians have attributed the rush for office to the presence of political parties, but there is no evidence for this argument. Village panchayat elections are intensely political even where political parties do not participate. The principle is simple: where there is power, there is always politics. If you want to eliminate politics from local government, or any level of government, then you must take away power. If there is nothing to fight over, then politics will wither away.

[10] Field investigations of village politics in India are divided on this point. Some emphasize the central concern of the dominant castes for maintaining control over land; others stress the struggle for status. For the former case, see Daniel Thorner, *The Agrarian Prospect in India*, Delhi, University Press, 1956. The two—status maintenance and control over land—are clearly interlocked.

ically ambitious individuals have found their caste, tribe, or religious group a natural political unit. The creation of a modern parliamentary system based on universal adult suffrage has encouraged the organization of interests on the basis of ethnic loyalties. Part of the demands of these ethnic groups are quite modern—more educational facilities, economic assistance, housing sites, and so on; but others are of a more traditional character, e.g. that community affiliation, not merit, should be the criterion for admission into schools, colleges, and administration. Since in the judgment of local politicians, which is probably correct, voters are inclined to give preference to a member of their own community, the major parties take caste, religion, tribe, and other ethnic affiliations into account in nominating candidates for elective office; and in the conduct of the election campaign, it is common for candidates to make appeals to their own community.

In terms of widening the bases of consent within the new democratic order loyalties along ethnic lines have had mixed consequences. The political demands of some groups have sometimes threatened the geographical unity of the country, but in the main their effect has been marginal since India and Pakistan were partitioned in 1947. Some of the Naga tribesmen in the hill areas near Assam have demanded a separate state, and there is a movement in parts of Madras state calling for a separate south Indian state. But in most other instances the demands have simply been for more facilities for a particular ethnic group. Indeed, the very success with which some of the politically organized communities have won special privileges by obtaining more jobs in administration, more seats in colleges, and more posts in government has reduced the likelihood that these groups would be alienated from the political system. In the south, for example, many non-Brahmin communities which had opposed the national movement for a long time before independence only gradually entered the Congress movement in the 1930's, in some areas not until after independence. In Madras, Mysore, Andhra, and Maharashtra the nationalist movement eventually fell into the hands of non-Brahmin communities which then took steps to strengthen their position in administration and government and to expand educational facilities for their own communities. In some areas the movement has gone so far that many Brahmins have become alienated from the political system and have started to lament the decline in merit standards on which they rested their ambitions. But the non-Brahmins have replied, with some force, that the application of the principle of equal opportunity on merit alone would further entrench the position of the Brahmins and that not until non-Brahmins achieve a higher educational and income level will it be possible for merit alone to be the criterion for appointments and promotions.

There is no reason to think that politics based on ethnic loyalties is likely to disappear or even be reduced in the years ahead. As anthropologists have pointed out,[11] the improvement of transportation and communication has widened the opportunity for contacts within the various ethnic groups. Many castes now publish their own newspapers, hold conferences of a social and often political nature, and in general have become increasingly conscious of their own identity. But these ethnic groups are not necessarily those about which the anthropologist speaks, for the new "caste" groups are often not the older endogamous groupings. A low caste association of Harijans, for example, may consist of a large number of endogamous Harijan castes. In Gujarat one finds that the politically powerful Kshatriya Sabha actually consists of a number of related castes which together constitute as much as half of the population in some areas. Similarly, the Jharkhand Party in Bihar, which has demanded a separate tribal state within the Indian union, consists of a large number of diverse and distinctly endogamous tribes.

While loyalty to the ethnic community may in and of itself be paramount, it is often strengthened by some common economic interests. Though there is rarely complete occupational and income uniformity within these communities, there is often enough unity to cement further the ethnic ties. The Nadar community in the south, for example, consists of many shopkeepers and small businessmen; the Sourashtra community in Madurai is made up predominantly of individuals involved in the production and distribution of hand-loomed cloth; in most areas Harijans are mainly agricultural laborers. Not until there is greater occupational diversity within these ethnic groups is there likely to be a reduction in ethnic loyalties and, even then, if the American experience is of any relevance, ethnic loyalties are still likely to play an important political role.

"Balancing" tickets has become as delicate a political task in India as in the United States. In addition the Indian politician has to make

[11] See M. N. Srinivas, *Caste in Modern India*, Bombay, Asia Publishing House, 1962, especially pp. 15-41; see also Lloyd I. Rudolph, "The Political Role of India's Caste Association," *Pacific Affairs*, Vol. 33, 1960, pp. 1-22.

adjustments to other types of village conflicts. It is quite common for villages in India to be torn by factional conflicts which cut across both class and caste loyalties. Two leaders of the same caste and occupation (landlords or large cultivators, generally) may struggle for political power and status within the village. Each will have the support of his own kinsmen and friends and of others with whom he has economic ties. The transfer of new financial powers and new functions to the elected village councils thus provides a new arena within which the factions may contend. In elections for the state legislative assembly each faction may ally itself with a candidate of a political party, often because it provides them with some outside financial and political support to strengthen their own hold within the village. Furthermore it is not uncommon for factional leaders to extract promises from candidates to the state assembly that special assistance will be given to the village in return for their political support. Village leaders often use the struggle between political parties as an opportunity to strengthen their own positions of political power within the village.

The Congress Party at the local level is infused by rural leaders who emphasize factional and ethnic loyalties, are sensitive to status considerations, and look upon government and the party as something to be used. It is no wonder then that the local and state party is torn by factional struggles and that there is so much indifference in the local party to a consideration of issues of public policy. Party leaders at the local level therefore find it easy to give public endorsement to resolutions passed by the national party although in private they may be indifferent and even hostile to the proposed policy. The party is faced with serious problems of cohesion, but not because of any ideological or policy differences. Indeed, a toleration for policy differences and the avoidance of major conflicts on public policy or ideological questions is a source of the party's strength. Though competition for power within the state and district party organization is often so intense that individuals who fail to get party nominations will leave the party or privately oppose the official candidate, men who have left the party have often returned. For though language, caste, religion, and tribe divide men, politicians of diverse ethnic and occupational background will often join together in a common desire for patronage and power. In this sense politics is often a great unifier. In fact it can be argued that if political parties did not exist at the local level in India, struggles might be exclusively ethnic.

Moreover the pattern of ethnic loyalties is far from fixed in India. Since a typical villager has many affiliations—to his village, kinsmen, faction, caste, religion, language, sect, and occupation—he must constantly make choices, and the choice he expresses in one election may not be repeated in another.[12] Thus during some elections the appeal to language has overridden all other loyalties in some localities, while in subsequent elections in the same area, caste and even party loyalties have prevailed. In general, however, one might say that at the village level neither loyalty to political movements on the basis of policies nor loyalty to India in a territorial sense is well developed. On the other hand, though loyalty to ethnic groups is increasing, it has taken on a new meaning and function in a new and increasingly modern context.[13]

CONFLICT RESOLUTION

Methods for the resolution of conflict are still another aspect of the emerging mass culture in India which is partly derived from the traditional political culture. Conflict of course is part of any modernization process. Industrial growth invariably brings labor-management conflict. Old conflicts over land rights continue, but they are sometimes intensified by the intrusion of new irrigation schemes, new inheritance legislation, and legislation directed at the consolidation of land holdings. The modification of land tenure systems as a consequence of land legislation also results in landlord-tenant conflicts. The growing mobility of ethnic groups, resulting from their increased access to education and government jobs and the introduction of the right to vote, often leads to an intensification of old ethnic conflicts and the development of new ones. Historical antagonisms are often "squared" when a numerically large low caste takes control over a

[12] Villagers actually play political roles simultaneously in a number of political systems. For a study of the interrelationship of these political roles and allegiances—within a tribal community—see F. G. Bailey, *Tribe, Caste and Nation*, Manchester, Manchester University Press, 1960, which deals with the Kond tribes of Orissa. Bailey shows that the Konds have allegiances to tribe, caste, and nation. To achieve social purposes—status, or power, or control over land—Konds will pick and choose among these political systems (p. 271). What was once fought out in the village—the struggle for control over land, for example—may now be fought in a larger political arena. For a study of the relationship between village and state politics, see the recent book by Bailey, *Politics and Social Change: Orissa in 1959*, Berkeley, University of California Press, 1963.

[13] For two conflicting views on the political significance of ethnic loyalties for national integration in India, see Selig S. Harrison, *India: The Most Dangerous Decades*, Princeton, Princeton University Press, 1960; and Myron Weiner, *op.cit.*, Chap. 3, "Community Associations."

village panchayat or even of a state government. The feeling is that some non-Brahmins may try to "get even" with Brahmins for real or imagined grievances.

The traditional method for resolving conflict in India has been through arbitration. Bernard S. Cohn has pointed out in his study of law in a north Indian village that the traditional way of dealing with a dispute was to recognize that a dispute did not involve simply one issue but a network of controversies; that no man told the truth with respect to the facts of a controversy but looked upon his presentation as a means of indicating his support for one side; and finally, that those who settled the dispute recognized that the parties had to continue to live side by side within the community and therefore that any settlement must be ambiguous enough to satisfy both sides. The introduction of English courts, with their notion that a dispute consists of one issue rather than a vast network, that evidence presented by an individual must be truthful, and that in a dispute one side is right and the other wrong in accordance with law or legal precedent, did not fit easily into the Indian pattern. The result, Cohn points out, is that the legal system became a method not for settling disputes but often for furthering them.[14]

The traditional hamlet and caste panchayats were essentially arbitration bodies. And even when disputes were inter-caste it was customary to call in a respected, generally upper-caste individual to arbitrate them. In many villages one particular community provided the arbitrators. Consequently even today the notion that arbitration is the appropriate method for the resolution of conflict is widespread throughout contemporary Indian society.

The national government, for example, does not believe that labor and management should openly battle or that it is a function of government to provide a framework within which industrial conflict and bargaining can be resolved. While management, labor, and government in India give lip service to the British and American notions of collective bargaining, in practice all three parties are committed to the present industrial relations legislation in India which provides an elaborate machinery for conciliation and arbitration.

Within the Congress Party too arbitration is the accepted method for the resolution of conflict. When conflict arises within the district party unit, the state party organization sends an officer to arbitrate

[14] Bernard S. Cohn, "Some Notes on Law and Change in North India," *Economic Development and Cultural Change*, October 1959.

the dispute. Similarly when the state is torn by factional conflict, the national party sends an arbitrator or observer from another state or from the central office. This pattern is widely accepted by those involved in the controversy. Indeed, it is often the strategy of weaker factions to press for external intervention in the hope that they can get better results than they might otherwise obtain through their own bargaining power.

Arbitration also enters into the relationship between the party and the village. Local Congress Party workers, especially respected and prominent district leaders, often play an arbitrational role within the village. If a dispute arises between a landlord and tenant or between two villagers over land rights or stray cattle, a Congress worker may visit the village to try to end the dispute. The local Congress Party leadership, however, tries to avoid tying itself too closely to particular village factions (though this is not always possible) since this would diminish their electoral appeal in other villages.

The outsider thus plays an important political role in India. Men who are insiders with respect to one dispute may of course be outsiders with respect to another and therefore may be asked to perform an arbitrational role. But to some extent the role is a specialized one, so that within the district and even within a village there are individuals who are ordinarily outside all controversies and are constantly asked to perform the role of arbitrator. Within the Congress Party the national President and the general secretaries perform this role. Mr. Nehru had frequently done so, as Gandhi did before him, and in recent years Mr. Lal Bahadur Shastri, as Home Minister, and Mrs. Indira Gandhi, the Prime Minister's daughter, have served as arbitrators within the party. Retired court judges are often used as arbitrators in industrial disputes and on government commissions appointed to resolve disputes between states or between states and the central government. The foreign consultant or an international team of experts is often used by the government to resolve conflicts between government ministries.[15]

Although bargaining in India is increasing, it is not ordinarily a part of the political culture. Individuals and groups customarily make immoderate demands on the assumption that a third party will make the compromises. Furthermore it is quite common that the bodies

[15] Much to the understandable dismay of the national leadership, the leader of the Sikh Akali Dal (a political party in the Punjab), suggested in 1961 that an Englishman be called in to arbitrate the dispute over whether the state should be bifurcated into Punjabi- and Hindi-speaking states as the Akali Dal had demanded.

appointed to resolve a conflict will not contain any of the disputants and also that the disputants not communicate with one another. As a means of settling disputes among groups, arbitration can be as workable a system as bargaining. It does not, however, lend itself easily to settling conflicts between organized interests and the government. Similarly, in other dominant-subordinate relationships there is no easy opportunity for the application of arbitration, and the result is often an uneasy relationship between those who are in positions of authority and those who are not.

Many opposition parties and organized interest groups in India have taken the position that the "people" have the right to violate the law if the government has committed an injustice. Formulated as an ethical principle, this position might be stated as follows: "Truth and justice are more important than law, and when truth and justice are violated by government, then it is only right that the public violate law." Under Gandhi's guidance the principle was applied with great solemnity and much forethought, but today opposition groups often use it to justify the launching of civil disobedience movements on a wide range of issues: a decision by the central government to build an oil refinery in one state rather than another; the question of merging two linguistic areas or of transferring a district from one state to another; a decision by a state government to increase agricultural taxes, or by university authorities to increase tuitions.[16]

The frequency and vitality of these movements stems from two factors: opposition parties often use civil disobedience as a means of strengthening their own political position by eliciting mass support; and large numbers of people often support such movements when other channels for influencing public policy are closed. The initial response by government to most of these movements is to treat them as threats to its authority. Firmness, sometimes accompanied by police firings, follows. Though these tactics have often brought about the collapse of the movement, they have perhaps more often abetted the growth of the mass movement, with the result that government has frequently backed down in the midst of a controversy. Several major policy decisions or reversals of decisions by the states or the national government have been made under these pressures: the decision to create a separate Telugu state (and ultimately to reor-

---

[16] This issue has been discussed in more detail in Myron Weiner, *op.cit.*, Chap. 8, "Political Groups and the State."

ganize the states along linguistic lines), and the decision by West Bengal and Bihar to cancel their intended merger.

The responsiveness of governments to civil disobedience movements has led many organized groups to look upon such movements as a legitimate method for influencing public policy. In the absence of a more understanding, responsive, and bargaining attitude on the part of the government, many of these groups argue, there is no alternative but to commit civil disobedience. In many instances the charge is an accurate one, for even when it has not been in the public interest for the government to accede to demands, little effort has been made to educate the public on the issues involved in the controversy through closer consultations with the affected public. Two examples come to mind. The Assam government and organized political groups in Assam demanded that the central government build an oil refinery in their state on the grounds that their area was particularly backward and oil had been found in the state. During the controversy the national government in effect refused to recognize that there was a contradiction in its own position that investments should be based on economic criteria and that at the same time special attention should be given to the more backward regions. When the government finally did agree, under massive pressure, to give Assam a refinery, it claimed that it had reconsidered the technical arguments and decided to award Assam the refinery on the basis of economic considerations. Since this was patently untrue, the government's decision was widely received as a concession to political pressures from Assam. Thus the controversy did little to clarify what is indeed an important issue of public policy. The second example which comes to mind is the decision by the University of Calcutta to raise tuition fees. The students launched a massive protest movement, boycotted classes, and even destroyed government property until the university, with government support, finally backed down. No effort was made either before the decision or during the controversy to raise as a public issue the question of how to finance the university and whether it was possible without further financing to admit more students without seriously lowering university standards.

In the absence of a greater effort on the part of government leadership to establish a more responsive relationship with organized groups and to use demands as an opportunity to clarify public policy issues (rather than as a threat to authority) the use of civil disobedience is likely to continue as an institutionalized instrument for influencing public policy.

RULER AND SUBJECT: PUBLIC SERVANT AND CITIZEN

The difficulties in establishing an easier relationship between authority and the citizen in India grow partly out of the persistence of pre-independence patterns. The British, as alien imperialist rulers who did not subscribe to an equalitarian tradition, pursued a policy of bureaucratic aloofness from those whom they governed, justified on the grounds that it was necessary to maintain authority and impartiality. An occasional British bureaucrat did demonstrate warmth, though rarely intimacy, with his Indian subordinate, but his relationship with the public was one which called for great deference on the part of the people. The British official was obviously not a servant in the modern administrative sense but a ruler. This pattern of ruler-subject relationship could easily be adapted to a hierarchical social system in which local power had been in the hands of a large network of local rulers legitimizing their power by reference to their caste or their clan. The local raja was often helpful to his subjects; he might remit revenue to tenants in bad years, assist a man in the marriage of his daughter, and in other ways bestow gifts upon his subjects. But the subject was to approach the ruler with great deference and, in turn, all wielders of power were to remain aloof—fathers from their sons, teachers from students, ruler from subject, bureaucrat from petitioner.

The shift from subject to citizen is not easy, nor is the shift from the role of ruler to public servant. Although the new government created a democratic system in which those who were elected were to be responsible to the voters, and though the elected politicians announced that the administrative system would now serve the public instead of being its master, the older patterns often persisted. Indeed, the newly elected elite often adapted itself to the older patterns. The President of India was to live in the old Viceroy's palace, and the pomp associated with that office (the regal carriage, turbaned bodyguard, etc.) was to continue. Ministers, both in the center and in the states, were given and indeed demanded elaborate residences. Great attention was paid to the accoutrements of power—the number of peons, size of residence, number of deputy ministers and personal assistants, the size of the minister's automobile, seating at public functions, invitations to social functions at the Prime Minister's or Chief Minister's residence.

Under the new democratic structure political leadership is often torn between the attractions of the older pattern of aloofness and the new requirement of intimacy with the citizens. A few well-known politicians—the former Chief Minister of Madras comes to mind—are able to mix freely with citizens, but others find the new role a difficult one. The dilemma is a highly personal one and extends to authority at many levels in the society. Teachers are reluctant to establish intimate relations with students for fear that to do so would reduce their authority. Similarly, a minister often fears that too much intimacy with his subordinate would reduce his authority, and too intimate contact with a voter might destroy the mystery and charisma associated with his power.

It is important to note, however, the increasingly active role being played, particularly at the state and local level, by the Congress Party as a link between the public and administration. Party officials assist agriculturalists and businessmen in obtaining permits or licenses from government officials and help villages to obtain wells, roads, schools, and other facilities from the government. Since the Congress Party controls not only the state and national governments but most of the local governments and the new quasi-governmental development bodies (such as cooperatives), as well, the party has been able to establish extensive control over patronage. Through the use of patronage the party leaders serve as a link between the villager and the complex administrative and governmental machinery.

The new power of the local party bosses has been of considerable concern to many members of the bureaucracy. A thin line exists between reporting grievances and requesting developmental assistance from administration, on the one hand, and "interference" in administration on the other. In at least two states, Punjab and Kerala, where the line has often been crossed, there has been considerable demoralization within the bureaucracy. Some have argued that the process has gone so far that merit and achievement as standards for bureaucratic action are rapidly being replaced by notions of ascription and, above all, patronage. They argue that while the bureaucracy is still being recruited on a merit basis (though reservations for various ethnic communities cut into this principle), the actions of the bureaucracy are increasingly being controlled by local politicians, who use administration to benefit their own ethnic groups or their own political supporters. There is much truth to this argument, though perhaps by the standards of nineteenth-century America, or even of many contemporary American municipal governments, the administrative system is far from being politicalized. But clearly the process is well under way.

Perhaps it would be more accurate to say that powers are being transferred from administrative to political bodies. Whereas decisions concerning the location of schools, roads, and irrigation schemes, and even which cultivators should receive loans were once made by administrative officers, the decisions are now being made by elected local officials. One important consequence of this change, and of the greater developmental activities pursued by government, is that the punitive image of government which was so prevalent in the pre-independence era is rapidly being replaced by a more instrumental view. Rural people are developing high expectations with respect to the services government can perform for them, so much so that many rural people, and especially rural politicians, look upon the community development program as a kind of patronage or pork barrel program for rural India. One increasingly finds village leaders speaking with pride of their ability to get things from government for their village —a new road, school, panchayat hall, enclosure for stray animals.

Village attitudes toward government and particularly toward the local bureaucracy are conditioned by the kind of adaptation bureaucrats have made to the government's developmental activities. The rural citizen often encounters administrators, particularly in the lower echelons of administration in the districts and in the state secretariats, whose attitudes and behavior are inappropriate to the new developmental activities. It is not simply, as many have argued, that local administrators are not interested in development, but rather that the local administrator is often limited by his own rigid adherence to formal administrative rules rather than being oriented to the solution of problems. The administrator is truly "rule oriented" in a highly formal sense, and he is generally concerned with an inflexible adherence to "channels." Bureaucrats hesitate to make decisions which involve making any judgment or taking any responsibility if it is possible to find someone else in the administration who can make the decision.[17] Bureaucrats thus often appear to be most adept at finding

[17] According to the findings of the Mysore Resources and Economy Committee— which reported on administrative reforms for the state—it normally takes 272.2 days on the average for a file to be processed in the secretariat. A study of 7,157 petitions

...local bureaucrat knows that punish-
...inaction, and that praise is not given
...einterpret rules so as to bring about
...n. The system of rewards and punish-
...es not encourage a shift in attitude
...rations found in official studies that
...rn to accept greater responsibilities.
...nistrator is generally more oriented
...nan serving the public. In pre-inde-
...large part of the administration was
...inistration. Though, as in any admin-
...increasingly a larger and larger part
...deal with the public since independ-
...of administration have substantially
...udes, in the lower echelons of admin-
...ble indifference. The bureaucrat, by
...and above all by virtue of his power,
...hus even in the post and telegraph
...find the clerk behind the counter
...before turning to his customer.
...vernment is judged by the behavior
...he interest of the party to speed the
...ions. Furthermore the indifference
...onal societies have toward the pro-
ducers of wealth, whether they be merchants or agriculturalists, is partly remedied by the democratization of power. Local government bodies, which are invariably controlled by producers of wealth, can be constant prods on administration. And the fact is that with all its limitations, the Indian administration does perform more services than ever before, especially, one might add, in those areas where there is an effective district party organization.[18]

There has, moreover, developed a class of "expediters" both within and out of the administrative services who are skillful at assisting

---

presented to the Revenue Department in the state capital showed that 6,111 of these petitions could have been dealt with at lower levels of the government.

[18] Some Indian politicians have argued that administration is most unresponsive in some of the largest states, like U.P., Madhya Pradesh, and to a lesser extent Bihar, not simply because these areas were not as well administrated by the British as the Presidencies of Bengal, Bombay, and Madras, but also because the states are so large that the ministers cannot effectively watch over local administration. If this theory is correct, then the establishment of panchayati raj is likely to improve the responsiveness of local administration.

businessmen and agriculturalists in getting around the rigidities of administration. Political party leaders at the district level often perform this function. So do many party members of the state legislative assemblies, members of Parliament, and at a lower level, members of the zilla parishads and non-official representatives of the district cooperative bank and other quasi-governmental developmental bodies.

The low level of motivation in the performance of work and the inflexibilities often present in administration have given rise to a widespread system of bribery and corrupt practices in dealing with government officials. It should be noted that not all corruption is dysfunctional to the goals of economic development, nor does corruption necessarily destroy confidence in government since it may simply involve making payment to local administrators to do what they ought to be doing and what the rules permit them to do but they would ordinarily do through "channels" and after extraordinary delays. A businessman waiting for an import license, and often entitled to it, but unwilling to wait months before he is informed is prepared to make payment to a bureaucrat to speed the decision, as well as to get a favorable one. He is thus paying a price for saving time. One might view such payments as simply a way citizens have found of building rewards into the administrative structure in the absence of any other appropriate incentive system.

The system of corruption, or what is widely known in India as the payment of *bakshish*, is a highly stable one. It is a regularized relationship. Businessmen and agriculturalists often regard the payment of *bakshish* to be as much a part of the application for government service as filing a government form. The rates of payment are generally based upon the rank of the officer, the character of the services being requested, and the financial means of the claimant. The rates are thus more or less predictable and on the whole (there are notable exceptions, however) moderate. Caste affinities and family relationships can often facilitate the individual's contact with local administration, but since the administrative and entrepreneurial communities in India are generally recruited from different ethnic groups, and since bureaucrats, even at the lower levels, are transferred frequently, nepotism is moderate compared to what is prevalent in many other transitional societies. Thus there is among businessmen a feeling of equity with respect to dealing with administration, a feeling that anyone with money and good contacts can get action more or less irrespective of caste and kin. Under such conditions it is possible to have a substantial amount of corruption without extensive alienation from the system.

The expediter may not be a man with any official power, but he is always someone who is familiar with the intricacies of administration. His skill lies in knowing who is the senior officer with the authority to make a decision and in getting access to him. The skilled expediter tries to by-pass lower-level officials, to reduce the number of individuals to whom *bakshish* must be paid, and in general to speed the process of administrative decision making. The expediter in a developing society may thus perform functions ordinarily performed within the administrative system of a modern society.

It would be quite unfair and incorrect to imply that the pre-independence administration performed no developmental functions or that the post-independence administration has not adapted itself to the new political environment. The British administration did sponsor much development work, especially in the Presidency areas of Madras, Bengal, and Bombay; and the present administration has made a remarkable adjustment to the transfer of power not only to the Indians but to publicly elected officials. But in the pre-independence era too it was not uncommon to pay officials for the performance of their work, and in some departments (especially the village officers) it was assumed that these payments would supplement the low salaries. With the expansion of government activities and an increase in regulations, more citizens have had to come into contact with government, and so more transactions that require payment take place between the bureaucrat and the citizen.

As we have seen, the expansion of government functions since independence, combined with increased political participation at all levels of the political system, has had profound consequences for the attitudes which rural Indians have toward government and administration. The attitudes are not necessarily new, but they are more strongly held and they affect the behavior and expectations of a larger part of the population, including many who only a decade ago had little expectation that they could personally benefit from governmental action. In the absence of systematic survey research data it is not possible to indicate how great these expectations are and among which social and economic groups such views are most strongly held. Nor is it possible to be precise concerning the effects which increased corruption within local administration has had upon local attitudes toward government. Personal impressions and a number of scattered field reports suggest that while there are positive notions concerning the functions which government ought to perform, there is considerable local cynicism with respect to the way local officials actually do perform. What is of particular long-term interest is whether those who, for whatever reason, fail to gain access to local administration become disaffected from the political process as such and are prepared to employ methods viewed by others as illegitimate.

RULING CULTURES

Thus far we have so oversimplified our discussion of the relationship between traditional political cultures and the emerging mass culture that one might assume that at the local level all Indians share the same traditional outlooks and respond to stimuli in the same way. In actuality there is considerable variation in response to the new developments not only from one locality to another but, more importantly, from one ethnic group to another. Here we might only briefly call attention to one ethnic group, or collection of ethnic groups, which shares a common attitude toward the dispersion and democratization of power. These groups can be described as those who shared a common "ruling culture." In fact some of these ethnic groups did hold power in the recent past: the Muslims in most of northern and central India, before the British arrived and afterwards, in a number of important princely states; the Maratha caste, which held power under the great warrior Shivaji, in large portions of western India; the Sikhs, a religious community which under the famous warrior Ranjit Singh controlled sections of northern India through the beginning of the nineteenth century; and the many Rajput kings who governed princely states until Independence, in Gujarat, Madhya Pradesh, and Rajasthan. There are many people in these communities who clearly had no hold on power themselves and were not even related to those who did, but who share the same outlook. Thus, for example, the Rajputs of northern India share a martial tradition which emphasizes loyalty, bravery, sacrifice, and authority.

The historic memories of being rulers, or being part of a ruling class (in the cultural sense), is often reinforced by a religious tradition which sanctifies a martial outlook and justifies the wielding of power by the community. Wilfred Cantwell Smith in his writings on Islam in South Asia argues that this attitude was a major factor in the

Muslim demand for a separate state of Pakistan. There is some evidence that a religious attitude reinforces the demand by many members of the Sikh religious community in the Punjab for a separate state of their own. And John Hitchcock points out in his anthropological writings on the Rajputs that this community's attitude toward power has propelled it into active politics in much of northern India.[19]

The most extreme attitude of a ruling culture is its unwillingness to share power with others. This attitude characterized the outlook and behavior of many Muslims in pre-independence India and distinguishes that of many Sikhs in the Punjab today. Among other ruling cultures there is deep aversion toward the present trend to distribute power widely to other classes, with a subsequent loss of power to the ruling culture. At the local level especially Rajputs lament their loss of power to numerically larger communities which, from their point of view, do not grasp the meaning of authority. One interesting response of the Rajputs has been to try to increase the size of their communities so that they can more readily win elections. In Gujarat, for example, a number of Rajputs (or more precisely a sub-caste of the Rajputs) formed an organization called the Kshatriya Sabha. This organization declared that it welcomed all those who shared the martial outlook of the "Kshatriyas," a Vedic term which encompasses a large number of castes which traditionally define themselves as martial. This organization was attractive to a great number of numerically large but poor lower castes who welcomed the opportunity to increase their status through closer political and social contacts with upper-caste Rajputs. This rapidly growing organization was first associated with the Congress Party, but when it failed to win more power within the local Congress, it left to join the newly formed Swatantra Party. In the 1962 elections the Kshatriya Sabha-backed Swatantra Party won a majority of seats in the district in which it is most active.

In fact a large part of the strength of the Swatantra Party in the states of Gujarat, Madhya Pradesh, and Rajasthan comes from the Rajput community, which is increasingly seeking support from other Kshatriya communities. It is important to note, however, that the Rajputs in the Kshatriya Sabha argue that an individual becomes a

---

[19] John T. Hitchcock, "The idea of the Martial Rajput," in *Traditional India: Structure and Change*, Milton Singer, ed. Philadelphia, the American Folklore Society, 1959.

Kshatriya not by birth or blood but by his martial spirit of sacrifice. As one Rajput Member of Parliament put it, "We say that if the Bhils (a tribal people in central India) are brave enough, we shall call them Kshatriyas". The Kshatriya Sabha thus represents an attempt by the Rajputs to democratize and modernize their political culture without giving up their central values.

Were the traditional elites of India and traditional ruling cultures openly hostile to the forces for secularism, nationalism, modernization, or democracy, then one might expect the open confrontations characteristic of a number of African states. In the years which immediately followed independence those who had earlier been maharajas tended to withdraw from politics almost entirely. Under the settlement which the new Indian government negotiated with each of the former princely rulers the rulers were not debarred from political activity at all, but it was quite clear that the new government would not look with equanimity on any effort on the part of the princes to reassert their power by new means. Many of the princes joined the Congress Party, a few joined some smaller opposition groups (particularly in the states of Orissa and Rajasthan), but the bulk abstained from political activity.

Among the ruling cultures the response was not uniform either. As I have already indicated, the Rajput community has begun to adapt itself to the new political environment. The Sikhs have been very much divided. One section—perhaps the larger part—has joined the Congress Party, and in the Punjab it is predominantly Sikh leadership which controls the state. A smaller group—but a highly vociferous one—has thrown its weight toward the creation of a separate Sikh-majority state which would not have to share power with non-Sikhs and which would seek to recreate the glories of the powerful Sikh kingdom of an earlier era.[20]

The Muslims, India's largest single religious minority, were largely with the Congress Party after independence, since they viewed Congress secularism as a major source of security. Most of the prominent leaders of the Muslim community had migrated to Pakistan. Increasingly, however, Muslims have been defecting from the Congress fold, and there are reports of growing disillusionment among them as they are denied access by local Hindu leaders to local power and influence. In West Bengal and in U.P.—two areas with

[20] For a fine account of the struggle within the Sikh community, see Baldev Raj Nayar, "Political Leadership in the Punjab," University of Chicago doctoral thesis, 1963 (unpublished).

large Muslim populations—the Congress vote among Muslims has declined, and in both Andhra and Kerala, Muslim communities have put up their own candidates for office, sometimes through a Muslim political party. But the Muslim community in India clearly does not have the advantages of either the Rajputs or Sikhs, for the Rajputs can redefine their status so as to enlarge their support, and the Sikhs are sufficiently concentrated in one state that they can exercise considerable influence in that area. In contrast, the organization of the Muslims precipitates counterorganization among Hindu castes which would otherwise be divided; and the Muslims are now too scattered throughout India to exercise more than a marginal influence in any one state.[21]

The discussion has tried to show that the expanding activities of government, the dispersion of power, and the democratization of power have resulted in a growth in popular participation in local, state, and national politics. The entrance of new social groups into politics has brought into modern political life elements partly derived from the traditional culture—a politics based in part on status relationships, loyalties to caste, linguistic and religious community, traditional patterns of dispute settlement, difficulties in establishing a public servant-citizen relationship to replace the older ruler-subject relationship, and the peculiar adaptation of traditional ruling cultures to a political system in which power must be shared.

The new mass political culture is clearly neither wholly modern nor wholly traditional, but an amalgam. Its future depends in good measure upon how the national leadership interprets and reacts to it. It is their attitude and response toward the emerging mass culture that we now turn to.

The Elite Culture

In new nations it is often those who fought for freedom and created the new political order who have become most alienated from the political system. Military take-overs are almost always carried

---

[21] The two best accounts of the political role of Muslims in pre-independence India are Wilfred Cantwell Smith, *Modern Islam in India*, London, Victor Gollancz, 1946; and Ram Gopal, *Indian Muslims: A Political History (1858-1947)*, Bombay, Asia Publishing House, 1959. For a discussion of the psychological difficulties of the Muslim community in adjusting itself to a position of permanent minority in India after independence, see Wilfred Cantwell Smith, *Islam in Modern History*, Princeton, Princeton University Press, 1957, Chap. 6, "India: Islamic Involvement." "Muslims," writes Smith, "have either had political power or they have not. Never before have they shared it with others" (p. 287).

out with the blessing of many important political groups and often almost the entire intelligentsia. The shift from democratic to authoritarian political frameworks has come about not because of mass upheavals but because of attitudes and behavior of sections of the ruling elite—in political parties, the bureaucracy, and the military.[22]

Many writers have noted the sense of frustration that educated sections of society feel in the new states when they encounter the problems and frustrations of freedom. The unity imposed by an alien ruler now has to be converted with some difficulty into a unity based upon consent. Administration can no longer depend upon being reinvigorated by the skills of foreigners. And, finally, economic prosperity does not occur merely because the foreign "exploiters" have been removed. But perhaps even more alarming to the intelligentsia than the slow rate of growth is the character of the emerging political process.

Well-educated Indians and those who hold power in the central government have virtually arrived at a common critique of the emerging political culture, and this critique is in itself based upon a common political orientation. There are of course many aspects of the mass political culture which have penetrated into the elite and, similarly, many of the attitudes of the elite are shared by some of those who are active participants in the mass political culture. But there are "model" types. Just as the District Congress Committee President, the President of the Village Panchayat, and the village factional or caste leader are representatives of the mass political culture, so the members of the Indian Civil Service or Indian Administrative Service, the members of the Planning Commission, and members of the Working Committee of the Congress Party are representatives of the elite political culture.

How this elite political culture arose and how it is strengthened by the socialization process will be explored later. Let us first examine the reaction of this leadership to the mass political culture which, as previously noted, is in good measure its own creation. We shall discuss the perspective of the elite on ethnic loyalties, the increasing importance of patronage as opposed to "sacrifice" as a motiva-

[22] It is a popular though unfounded myth in the United States—largely growing out of the notion that poverty is the cause of political "evils" in the world, corruption, communism, authoritarianism, etc.—that the collapse of party government in such places as Pakistan, Burma, and Sudan was a consequence of mass illiteracy and poverty.

tion for political action, the impact of the mass culture on the implementation of policy, and the role of conflict in the political system.

PERSPECTIVE ON ETHNIC LOYALTIES

From the viewpoint of the elite the most serious defect of the mass political culture is that political action seems to be so heavily based upon loyalty to caste, religion, tribe, and region at the expense of national loyalties. Castes and religious groups oppose one another. States quarrel over their boundaries and over the distribution of water from rivers which cut across state lines and compete for public sector investments by the central government. Castes demand representation in state cabinets and in state assemblies. And some states even try to discriminate against the investors and workers from other states. Furthermore many of these loyalties are exploited by politicians who try to win power by appealing to irrational, traditional, feudal sentiments. The elite consider that such ambitions and loyalties have no place in a modern democracy and that if they continue they could destroy the democratic system and the national state. India can be a united nation, feels the elite, only when each ethnic group or region recognizes that its interests must be subsumed under national loyalties and goals, and democracy can function only if individuals are guided by a more rational concern for issues and ideologies.

This perspective is clearly heavily influenced by the British view of politics, which educated Indians generally use as their model. To the Indian, British political history is one of struggle between two or three political parties quarreling over fundamental ideas: Whigs versus Tories, and now Labour versus Conservatives. It is a politics of ideas and of men who personify ideas. There is room for personal foibles, but not for irrational and irrelevant ethnic loyalties. The perspective of the Indian intellectual is also very much influenced by his own changing ideas toward caste and other ethnic loyalties. Caste was subjected to rigorous British attacks, especially by missionaries, in the nineteenth century, and under the impact of those attacks many Indians reinterpreted their own historical and religious tradition to prove that caste was a medieval intrusion which had to be eliminated from the Hindu religion. Educated Indians argued that individuals should be able to enter temples and to seek any kind of employment they wished without suffering the disabilities of caste. India's constitution formally bars discrimination on any basis.

The national movement certainly strengthened the ideal of India as one nation, and men became willing to sacrifice for a common cause without concern for the parochial loyalties to caste, religion, tribe, or language. The great struggle between the Muslim League and the Congress Party over whether India was one nation or two, the partition of India in 1947, and the bloodshed which soon followed strengthened the conviction of India's national leaders and intellectuals that ethnic loyalties of any sort would destroy the possibilities of building India as a unified, democratic, modern society.

It is in this context that one has to view the post-independence controversy concerning the linguistic reorganization of states. For several decades there had been movements at the state level, often within the Congress Party itself, for the remapping of political boundaries so that each major linguistic group in India would have its own state. The Congress Party, in fact, endorsed this position, and it was generally understood that as soon after independence as feasible the reorganization would be brought about. Shortly after 1947, however, Nehru and other national leaders moved to the position that a reorganization would be undesirable, partly because the administrative burden of reorganizing state boundaries would be great, partly because it might result in such administrative dislocations that economic development activities would be disrupted, and partly because it was felt that a reorganization of states along linguistic lines might intensify provincial sentiments at the expense of national loyalty. But despite Nehru's efforts the demand for reorganization increased, particularly from the linguistic groups in southern and western India, where states were multilingual. Each linguistic group argued that democracy could best function if government and the people shared the same language, and this would be possible only if states were linguistically homogeneous. Several major linguistic organizations with strong mass emotional backing launched civil disobedience movements until finally, in 1956, legislation was passed by the central government providing for a large-scale reorganization of the states more or less along linguistic lines.[23]

For many intellectuals and national leaders the reorganization was considered to be a great defeat, and evidence of continued linguistic and other ethnic loyalties was viewed with alarm. During the general

---

[23] For an account of the state's reorganization controversy see Joan V. Bondurant, *Regionalism Versus Provincialism: A Study in Problems of Indian National Unity*, Berkeley, University of California Indian Press Digests Monograph Series, No. 4, December 1958.

elections in 1962 the national leadership, concerned with the growing tendency of political groups, including the Congress Party, to select candidates for public office on the basis of their caste, and of candidates to make appeals to caste during the campaign, called a National Integration Conference. Leaders of various political organizations were invited, but interestingly enough, spokesmen for some of the more important ethnic associations and parties were excluded. Some national leaders suggested that appeals to caste and religion by parties or candidates should be declared illegal, and in the absence of such a basis they urged all political parties not to appeal to the electorate in such an irrational fashion. But caste, tribe, and religion did play a part in the national elections. It is true that some of the more heated ethnic issues were not as important in 1962 as they had been earlier—the demand for linguistic states had of course disappeared; and parochial parties in Bihar (the Jharkhand Party), Maharashtra (the Samyukta Maharashtra Samiti), and the Punjab (the Akali Dal) did not do well. But in Assam and Madras caste and tribal parties flourished, and throughout the country candidates regularly appealed to voters on the basis of ethnic loyalties.

The national elite continues to find it difficult to accept the possibility that a democratic modern system can function in the midst of such parochial political loyalties and, though the Congress Party won the election, many of its national leaders felt that the elections had further unleashed disintegrative tendencies. Thus, while the district and state leadership generally take ethnic divisions in their stride as a fact of social life and seek to adapt the political system to it, the national leadership continually looks for ways either to change the social system or, at the very least, to make it an irrelevant factor in political life.[24]

PERSPECTIVE ON THE SPIRIT OF SACRIFICE

The national elite feels that the spirit of sacrifice is rapidly disappearing from political life. The great leaders of the past, who left

[24] The passion for eliminating caste, religion, and tribe from political life is so intense among the national leaders that it often leads to utopian proposals from men who are otherwise politically sophisticated. A general secretary of the Congress Party recently suggested that these loyalties could be eliminated if the party decided as a matter of principle to give tickets to individuals from minority communities in every possible constituency. I pointed out that district and state leaders would not accept such a proposal—and they after all more or less decide who will get the party nomination—for the simple reason that to pursue such a policy might be political suicide. His reply to this was, "But then I am prepared to see us defeated on this issue."

their private fortunes, their occupations, and even their family life to take part in the national movement, are disappearing from public life and are not being replaced by men who share their spirit of sacrifice. Instead there is growing in public life a struggle for power by men who are concerned with patronage and power for its own sake. The result is a bitter struggle for the fishes and loaves of office, and intense factionalism within the governing party based not on differences in policy but on competing personal loyalties and ambitions. Thus the party functionaries are less concerned with the specific policies and ideology of the party than they are with access to power.

The hunger for power, the elite feels, is also in conflict with India's hopes of building a new society. A good society, it is felt, can be built only on the foundation of a class of sacrificial individuals who work for the good of the whole society and not on a class of individuals who operate on selfish profit motives. It is this perspective which strengthens the elite's distaste for the profit motive and the private sector and attracts it to socialist ideals.[25] Thus the efforts by businessmen to obtain licenses, permits, and contracts, the receptiveness of bureaucrats to illicit remuneration, and the struggle by petty politicians for office are seen as fundamental failures in the Indian character.

The elite shares a belief, or at least a predisposition, to judge men by their motives rather than by the quality of their work. The right or wrong of a fast or of a civil disobedience movement may be discussed on the basis of the motivation of those involved rather than on the issue concerned or on the consequences of the action. The activities of Gandhian organizations—the Gandhi Memorial Peace Trust, the Harijan Sevak Sangh, and other such groups—are not subjected to any public scrutiny, for it would be considered wrong to criticize the activities of individuals whose motives are pure.

The elite recognizes that it is difficult to inculcate a spirit of sacrifice, particularly when businessmen and politicians appeal to baser motives. It exhorts young people to develop the spirit of sacrifice, but there is the feeling that this spirit may wither away as the present generation of leadership disappears. There is therefore a pervasive melancholy among the older generation of national leaders,

---

[25] For a discussion of popular attitudes toward business, including some data from surveys conducted by the Indian Institute of Public Opinion, see Myron Weiner, *op.cit.*, pp. 123-129.

and one occasionally hears an ominous voice among intellectuals noting that only the army effectively inculcates the spirit of sacrifice.

PERSPECTIVE ON IMPLEMENTATION

Planning and implementation must be closely related. Obviously no plan for a country's economic development can have any relevance unless attention is given to the complex of political, administrative, social, cultural, and economic factors at work either for or against a proposed course of action.[26] Economists often point out that there are more or less basic economic laws which planners can ignore only at the risk of destroying the effectiveness of their plans. An attempt to implement a proposal in violation of some economic law is likely to fail or to have unintended consequences, and one would conclude that the error is in the policy, not simply in its implementation. Similarly, a proposal which fails to take into account some fundamental political factors or cultural values may also fail, and it would be equally wrong to attribute the failure to inadequate implementation.

Although India's Five Year Plan is prepared by the Planning Commission of the central government, much of its implementation depends upon the state governments. Land reform policy, for example, was formulated by the Planning Commission, but its implementation is dependent upon state government legislation. The Community Development Program was developed by the central government, but the implementation of the program is completely in the hands of the state governments. Similarly, the implementation of central government proposals with respect to small-scale enterprises, fisheries, forests, and smaller irrigation works relies heavily upon policy decisions by the state governments.

The greatest difficulties in planning in India, Prime Minister Nehru said, lie not in policy but in implementation. India, he went on to say, thinks and speaks in one way but behaves in another. Many members of the central government share the Prime Minister's view and feel that state governments have all too often failed to implement recommendations made by the center, partly because the states privately oppose central government proposals and partly because they lack the skill or are inefficient, but often because they lack the courage or will to do those things which are necessary for the development of the entire country. For example, state govern-

[26] Although there is a vast literature on planning in India, there is remarkably little on the relationship between planning and implementation.

ments have often failed to tax sufficiently (especially land revenue and agricultural income) to finance their own development plans and have had to turn increasingly to the central government for financial assistance. Land reform legislation proposed by the Planning Commission has been delayed and diluted by state governments under pressure from local agrarian interests. The number and size of colleges and universities have been increased at a far greater rate than the central government's educational body, the University Grants Commission, has recommended. Central government planners could make a long list of recommendations and policy decisions by the center which have been diluted or ignored by state governments and state administrations.

Still another aspect of the gap between policy and implementation, from the viewpoint of some of the national leaders, is the greater concern by state and local leaders for the distribution rather than creation of wealth. Thus panchayat samitis and zilla parishads, local government bodies empowered to take steps to increase the country's agricultural production, are more interested in building roads, schools, wells, assembly halls, and nurseries than in getting cultivators to employ new methods to increase production. And state governments, simply on the ground of the backwardness of their areas, press the central government to locate new industries within their boundaries regardless of national economic considerations. However, on these issues it should be noted that the national leadership is itself ambivalent. Equality has been a cardinal principle of the national leadership and, where this principle has run into conflict with the goal of maximizing the nation's wealth, the latter has often been submerged.[27]

In spite of difficulties in implementing policy the national leadership of India retains a remarkable confidence in the efficacy of law. Indeed, there are few countries where so much hope rests on legal action and so much change is assumed to flow from legal action. According to the law the dowry system has been abolished, discrimination on the basis of caste is illegal, women have equal inheritance rights, absentee landlordism is abolished, ceilings exist on land holdings. Some Indians conclude that the dowry system is disappearing, caste disabilities are no more, women have equal rights, and the tiller owns the land. More sober and realistic Indians recognize

[27] For an extended discussion of the impact of the doctrine of equality on Indian public policy in the fields of economics and education, see Myron Weiner, "The Struggle for Equality in India," *Foreign Affairs*, July 1962.

that the legislation for such reforms is a set of hopes but argue that it serves as an educational force. Thus the educational and aspirational rather than regulatory aspects of legislation are stressed, and often little attention is paid to the problems of implementation.

Indeed, the national leadership sometimes behaves as if policy and implementation are separate, the one to be planned without prior consideration of the other. The very skill with which India's economic planners can create new planning models, develop more rational schemes of taxation, propose new input-output models, and new methods for computer research intensifies the distaste for politics, for bargaining, and for the non-economic elements in planning which are of the very essence of implementation. To many of the planners, politics represents the irrational in Indian life—particularistic loyalties, an indifference to issues of public policy, lethargy in administration, and demands which may only impede economic planning and growth.

PERSPECTIVE ON CONFLICT AND TENSION

For reasons which must lie deep in the psychology of Indians, India's national party leaders, intellectuals, and bureaucrats look upon conflict within their society as intrinsically undesirable. While the notion of competition and conflict is central to American political life and thought, notions of cooperation, harmony and, to use a favorite Indian word, "synthesis" are central to Indian thought. This is not to say that there is more cooperation and less conflict in India than in the United States, but simply that while in general Americans easily adapt to situations of conflict, the Indian elite generally finds such situations intolerable.

The passion for harmony and synthesis is clearly seen in Indian historiography. Indian historical writings tend to stress the unities of the past and minimize the conflicts and the struggles over power.[28] Indian intellectuals generally envision the pre-British village as a harmonious social and political unit. And contemporary historical writings on the struggle for independence tend to underplay the great internal dissensions which existed.

Most of the national leadership believes that every effort should be made to eliminate conflict within rural India. No progress, so the argument goes, can be achieved in the villages without a spirit of harmony and cooperation. Similarly, conflict should be minimized or

[28] The historical writings of K. M. Pannikar are a notable exception.

eliminated at all levels of society, for it is only as the country is united that it can move forward.[29]

This view—and it has been stated in its most extreme form here—has many subscribers, and many proposals have been made to eliminate conflict within the society. Efforts to get political parties to agree not to participate in village panchayat elections have been somewhat successful, and one state, Rajasthan, offers a bounty to any village which elects its panchayat unanimously.[30] Of course local Congressmen are nevertheless drawn into village panchayat elections, but the national party has urged state and local party units to avoid creating partisan political spirit in the village.

Some intellectuals further argue that since parties divide the country, efforts should be made to create a partyless democracy. One such movement was in fact begun at the time of Independence by M. N. Roy, a Bengali who was at one time one of India's leading intellectual Marxists. Today the most active exponents of this viewpoint are associated with various Gandhian organizations and movements. Their most prominent spokesman is Jayaprakash Narayan, also a one-time Marxist, who some years ago in a dramatic gesture renounced his political career, left the socialist movement, and became a *jeevandani*, that is, one who has made the gift of his life to the service of others. Jayaprakash has become a strong exponent of what he calls a "communitarian" society, in which party politics

---

[29] The notion that politics, in village, or state, or nation, is based not on individuals and socioeconomic units each with their own interests, but on the family conceived as a harmonious unit, is presented by S. K. Dey (Minister for Community Development) in *Panchayati Raj: A Synthesis*, Bombay, Asia Publishing House, 1961. "Marriage," writes Dey, "like the administration in the State, is a social function. It calls for community-joint family action. Discussions are free and frank. They become warm, even hot at times. A consensus emerges in the end. . . . The affairs of State conducted in a democracy should move like the marriage in a joint family" (p. 123). Dey feels that such order is absent in parliament and in state legislatures and that "if order and not chaos is to be the rule, decentralization whether of thinking or action, can only take place in a balanced organism in which all components are related to one another by clearly defined laws which are understood, accepted and honoured" (p. 125).

[30] In order to win the bounty, some villages conduct informal elections before the regular elections. A survey conducted by the Rajasthan government, however, showed that in spite of the bounty only a small fraction of the villages held unanimous elections. A few state Congress politicians have privately expressed doubts about the political wisdom of abstaining from village elections for they have noted that where opposition parties gain control of the panchayats, these villages tend to vote against Congress in state and national elections. Moreover, many of the villages in Rajasthan which "unanimously" elected their panchayats were those which contributed to the near-defeat of the Congress Party in the state election of 1962.

would be eliminated, and where popular elections would be replaced by a system of indirect elections from village councils up to the national parliament. This position is derived from what Morris-Jones has aptly referred to as India's "saintly" tradition. This tradition, which pre-dates Gandhi but of which he was a great exponent, disapproves of struggle for power (for any purpose) and stresses the importance of harmony, unanimity, and sacrifice in public life.

During the past few years Jayaprakash and many of his followers have carried his critique of parliamentary democracy to many parts of India. Parliamentary democracy, he has argued, with its system of political parties, has intensified conflict at all levels of Indian society, divided India's villages, aggravated caste and communal tensions, and encouraged men to seek power for its own sake. He fervently believes that it is possible to increase the powers of local government (a position he strongly advocates) without at the same time increasing local conflict if only political parties would voluntarily abstain from participating in village life. One might argue that in any political system the dispersion of power simply means the dispersion of political conflict; but Jayaprakash Narayan and his supporters believe that a spirit of self-sacrifice and detachment can be inculcated into all those who wield power at any level.

Even those who reject Jayaprakash's solution as utopian are prepared to accept his criticisms of the parliamentary system and his basic assumption that harmony is a prerequisite for national development. There are several other versions of this view which find support among some intellectuals and national leaders. One popular variation, which is likely to grow as party conflict in India increases, is that the present system of party government should be replaced by a "national" government which would consist of all of India's political parties. The argument that a more diversified government than now exists would simply mean that political conflict would be transferred from outside of government to within government is countered with the reply that in a "national" government all the political parties would have to give up their own political ambitions in order to serve the common goal of national unity and national development.[31]

---

[31] This position was argued by the President of the Indian Political Science Association at a recent national convention.

IV
Political Socialization of the Elite Culture

The attacks against the emerging mass culture come from a wide variety of sources ranging from the Marxists in the Communist and Socialist Parties to the Gandhians in and outside of Congress, from senior bureaucrats to national politicians, from university professors to working journalists. That men of such diverse occupations and otherwise such diverse viewpoints should share a common view toward the kinds of political attitudes and behavior emerging at the local level is surprising and suggests that some common influences are at work. In the absence of any systematic survey data on the socialization processes at work in India one must turn for evidence of such influences to biographies and autobiographies and to the descriptions and insights of historians and anthropologists.

Much has been written on the differences between a "great" tradition and a "little" tradition or, to use another phrase of Redfield's, between the "hierarchic and lay culture."[32] Indian culture has always combined the great Sanskritic tradition with that of many folk traditions. Though cultural specialists (priests, learned men, village bards) have perpetuated their own traditions, each tradition has interacted with and transformed the others.[33]

In the realm of political authority as well there has always been a sharp division between the Sanskritic and village traditions. As one scholar of Sanskritic political theory, Charles Drekmeier, has written: "In European theory the political has traditionally been viewed as that which is shared by the people as a whole; society is commonly understood as an arena of competing interests seeking to influence the formation of public policy. In ancient India the political was thought to be the province of one particular segment of society—a society broken into castes, for whom the idea of political competition would have been unthinkable. Indian political philosophy is preoccupied with the problem of order; it is a philosophy of caution, a warning against the unfortunate consequences of any disturbance of tradition and the institutions in which it was embodied."[34]

---

[32] Robert Redfield, *Peasant Society and Culture*, Chicago, University of Chicago Press, 1956.
[33] McKim Marriott "Little Communities in an Indigenous Civilization" (in *Village India, op.cit.*) has characterized the process whereby the folk tradition enters the great tradition as "universalization," and the process whereby the Sanskritic tradition enters into and is modified by villagers as "parochialization."
[34] Charles Drekmeier, *Kingship and Community in Early India*, Stanford, Stanford University Press, 1962, p. 7.

The gap between rulers and ruled is an accepted part of the classical Hindu tradition. "Hindu thought," writes Drekmeier, "assumes that there is a peculiar Brahman mentality, a shudra mind, and so forth, and that the basic social group is composed of those of similar mental configuration. The caste system—the fundamental sociological context of Hindu polity—aimed at providing the individual with a milieu of like minds in which to fulfill the obligations of his social station."[35]

Nineteenth-century Indian intellectuals, seeking to find in traditional political and social thought a philosophy and tradition conducive to modernization and one worthy of confrontation with British thought, turned to the Vedanta tradition. The efforts of Ram Mohan Roy and those who followed him to revive and reinterpret the monotheistic tradition are too well known to discuss here.[36] The later nationalist movement did not attack tradition but sought to make it relevant to its political, social, and economic goals. In any event, as Edward Shils has noted, the impact of traditional patterns of thought on the minds of Indian intellectuals is far greater than one might suppose. Brahmanical notions of duty (dharma), the emphasis on civil obligation rather than civil rights as the basis of subject-state relations, and the importance of order are all important elements in contemporary elite thought. Nineteenth-century British thought often reinforced Brahmanical conceptions and Indian intellectuals who visited and studied in England found much to admire there. British Marxist thought influenced an important group of young Indians in England in the 1920's and 1930's,[37] but it is striking that so many Indians also found the viewpoint of the earlier nineteenth-century British and French utopian socialists appealing. Gandhi himself turned to the Victorian romantics—Ruskin and, in America, Thoreau.

The impact of British thought on Indians both in England and in India through English-established schools and colleges in the nineteenth century has been well documented and need not detain us here.[38] What is less obvious is the extent to which young Indians

---

[35] *Ibid.*, p. 299.

[36] See William Theodore DeBary, *Sources of Indian Tradition*, New York, Columbia University Press, 1958, especially part VI, "Modern India and Pakistan."

[37] For a discussion of Marxist influences and social background of twentieth-century Bengalis see Myron Weiner, *Political Change in South Asia*, Calcutta, Firma K. L. Mukhopadhyay, 1963, Chap. V, "Changing Patterns of Political Leadership in West Bengal," and Chap. VI, "Notes on Political Development in West Bengal."

[38] Perhaps the best account of British influence on India during the nineteenth century, focusing particularly on land tenure and law, is Eric Stokes, *The English*

of upper-class and bureaucratic family backgrounds are today being educated and socialized into the traditions of the elite culture of British India. Though the content of English education and the use of the English language itself has diminished in Indian public schools, this is not so for the private schools.[39] In Bombay, Calcutta, Madras, and Delhi members of the upper classes commonly send their sons to English-language schools; and the number of Indians studying in colleges and universities abroad has increased since independence. While it is commonly argued that the quality of spoken and written English has substantially declined in India since independence, the fact is that the English-language press has increased its circulation at a faster rate than all but a small part of the regional-language press.

Many members of the younger English-speaking intelligentsia have even less contact with rural India than their fathers did. As families have become more urbanized—and many of the national politicians have lived with their families in Delhi or in the state capitals for twenty years or more—younger people have fewer opportunities to return to their ancestral homes. Land reform too and the animus increasingly associated with absentee landlordism have cut still one more link—tenuous though it may have been—with rural India. Paradoxically, the improvement in transportation facilities has not increased but has decreased personal contact between the elite and the country's villagers. A class system on the railroads and the increasing use of air transport does not facilitate such contact. The more frequent use of automobiles and jeeps by district collectors and other district officials as well as by senior politicians eliminates the need to spend the night within a village. There is now much quick touring, and communication is more often likely to be in one direction.[40]

Utilitarians and India, Oxford, Clarendon Press, 1959. For an account of the Indian reaction to British policies, see William T. DeBary, *op.cit.*

[39] Though Hindi and the regional languages are increasingly being utilized in the schools, even those who have some responsibility for implementing such a policy are often strong advocates of English. See, for example, the book by Humayun Kabir (former Minister for Education), *Education in New India*. N.Y.: Harper and Brothers, 1955, especially Chap. 6, "The Study of English."

[40] "The state in early India," concludes Drekmeier (*op.cit.*, p. 297), "was believed to be instrumental to the attainment of the spiritual goal. This ultimate purpose was itself so conceived as to presuppose an elite responsible for defining and interpreting the values that ordered the world and regulated even the actions of the king. *This elite maintained its purity by remaining more or less apart from political life, which was tainted by the sin inherent in political and military roles.*"

The elite culture is thus sustained by its own socialization process, one which separates the elite from the society at large. The sons of the elite are often even more hostile to the emerging mass culture than their fathers are, and their opportunities for extensive contact with village life are even less. The gap between elite and mass—one which, after all, characterizes many societies—is significant largely because it is the emerging mass culture which is gaining in power and the elite culture which is losing its political hold.

Conclusion: Traditionalism, Modernity, and the Two Cultures

Criticisms of India's emerging political culture come from many quarters. The bureaucrat and national politician lament the growth of irrational loyalties, the absence of a sense of a public interest, and the high degree of emotionalism that characterizes state and local politics. The planner resents the intrusion of political demands on his efforts to plan rationally. The political idealist is alarmed by the growth of political conflict at all levels of the society and by the emergence of men more concerned with the patronage and power of office than with sacrificial service for the poor and underprivileged.

As we have pointed out, the emerging political culture, with its emphasis on particularistic loyalties, its growing stress on the importance of power and patronage, and its highly charged and emotional quality, cannot be called traditional even though it has traditional components. But there is nothing traditional about the demands for more schools, roads, wells, fertilizers, and jobs. The claim to power on the part of a candidate for the assembly or Parliament is increasingly based on the concept of "service" in the patronage sense as well as on the more traditional claim for support on the basis of caste, religious, or tribal affiliations. Even traditional power cultures have put aside their appeals on the basis of blood and kinship and have found a new basis for winning political support by trying to persuade others to share their orientation toward politics. The corruption of local officials, while often of ancient vintage, is now frequently used for quite modern purposes. Those who are now rising to positions of local power are not necessarily large landlords or men of high caste, but others who increasingly come from lower classes and castes who have discovered that numbers are an important source of power. Thus the emerging mass political culture is an amalgam of traditional and modern elements.

The elite's distaste for a politics in which ethnic loyalties play an important role is based on a peculiarly British model of the political process. So is its unwillingness to recognize that state demands on and conflicts with the central government are simply characteristic of a federal system. The intellectual's perspective on the developing political order is often profoundly affected by his lack of knowledge about the way in which the social, economic, and political system actually functions.[41] The nostalgia for harmony and unanimity is essentially a product of traditional notions. Thus the struggle between the elite and the mass political cultures is not simply between a modern and a traditional political culture, for there are aspects of both modernity and traditionalism penetrating both views.

The important point is that with all its limitations, the emerging mass political culture does work. Older, punitive notions of government are gradually disappearing. Masses of people have come to accept and work within the new democratic process. And above all, the governing party, with all its limitations, has united people who are divided by all else except the desire for power, patronage, and office and has done this so effectively that India is one of the few countries in Asia which has been able to maintain an effective, stable, democratic regime. Moreover the emerging political system shows considerable viability. The greater responsiveness and adaptiveness of state and local Congress politicians to the local political, social, economic, and administrative milieu in which they operate has made it possible for the Congress Party to build one of the most effective district and state party organizations to be found in all of Asia or Africa.

This is not to say that the emerging mass political culture does not

[41] Many writers on India have noted that the Indian intellectual tradition is a non-empirical one. The most systematic recent exposition of this view is Edward Shils' *The Intellectual Between Tradition and Modernity: The Indian Situation* (Comp. Stud. in Soc. and Hist., Suppl. 1, paper, 1960). Shils notes that Indian scholars have been attracted by modern mathematics, the theoretical aspects of physics, and modern Western schools of philosophy, rather than the empirical areas of the physical and social sciences, which require a concern for the study and handling of concrete phenomena. Shils concludes that this lack of concern for the concrete inhibits the development of a civic tradition on the part of the intellectual classes. I might only add here that in my experience the local members of legislative assemblies and the district Congress Committee bosses have an intimate and concrete knowledge of their districts that in the recent past one might have found among the senior civil service and especially district collectors. It is, in fact, this intimate knowledge which has strengthened the power of the local politician vis-à-vis the local bureaucrat. I might also add that on the other hand foreign-trained Indian intellectuals, with a few notable exceptions, do not absorb the Western concern for the concrete since American and British training of foreign students often sharpens the passion for logic and theory rather than facts.

have its difficulties, or that it is always conducive to modernization or to stable democratic government. How to get states to increase their revenue through heavier agricultural taxation; how to stimulate the interest of local politicians in measures to increase agricultural productivity; how to improve the motivation of the lower levels of administration; how to find an alternative reward system to the present system of bakshish; how to provide greater educational and job opportunities for lower castes without recourse to ascriptive criteria; how to establish a relationship between organized groups and government which will reduce the use of civil disobedience; and finally, how to raise the level of civic competence by discussions of public policy—all these remain crucial questions. The danger exists that solutions to these genuine problems will be offered which are essentially utopian, that is, which fail to recognize that conflict is a normal part of the political process, that ethnic loyalties are inevitable in an ethnically diverse society, that the struggle for patronage and power is part of the democratic process, and that political parties and pressure groups are also an essential part of that process. The danger of a utopian perspective is that it is conducive to authoritarian solutions. While in principle the Indian elite is committed to the democratic process, it is so concerned about the development of the new mass political culture that a situation could arise when, in the midst of a national crisis, it might welcome the establishment of a more rational, even if authoritarian, military regime.

Fortunately there is no great likelihood of such a crisis occurring. Power has become so dispersed in India that strong interests now exist which would seek to preserve the democratic framework. The state chief ministers, who have already played a decisive role in the selection of the present Prime Minister, will find it in their interests to avoid a national crisis. The chief ministers recognize that a military take over in the center would surely affect their own positions. While on the one hand the growing power and independence of the chief ministers presents great problems for the central government, on the other hand it means a strengthening of stable democratic government in India.

But it is not enough to maintain stable democratic government. If the national elite continues to misunderstand the nature of the political culture which it itself has helped to create, the consequence could be a deepening disillusionment and a widening gap between ideals and implementation. In the long run India's success at maintaining a modernizing and democratic system may depend upon the closing of the gap between her two cultures.

In the past India's cultural tradition has involved an interplay and mixture of elite and mass cultures, though in the realm of politics a sharp division was maintained. The dispersion and democratization of power which has occurred in recent years in India makes it impossible to maintain such a division. Today the elite culture—even while it maintains itself through its own socialization processes—has been losing political ground to the mass culture. It is possible that there can be recruited from within the upper classes individual leaders who can bridge the two cultures, as Gandhi and, to a lesser extent, Nehru once did. But the expansion of the mass culture and the entrance of rural leaders into state and national life suggests that if the gap is to be bridged, it is more likely to be done by creative leadership from the countryside. At the state level there has already emerged a number of leaders who promise to perform this critical role. Madras and Bombay—two states which have been strongly influenced by the West—have already produced such leaders in the form of K. Kamaraj, former Chief Minister of Madras and now a national Congress leader, and Chauvan, former Chief Minister of Bombay and later Defence Minister in the central cabinet. Such men, with essentially rural backgrounds, often (as in Kamaraj's case) of lower caste, deficient in Western education (only in recent years has Kamaraj learned to speak English fluently), and whose political careers have largely been in the local party organization, are often capable of breaking from their parochial backgrounds to assume positions as national leaders. If men such as these ultimately take control over the national government, they will have the formidable task of making the emerging mass political culture acceptable to the national elite while at the same time modifying that culture so that it is truly conducive both to modernization and to stable democratic government.

CHAPTER 7

Ethiopia: Identity, Authority, and Realism

DONALD N. LEVINE

I

THE POLITICAL systems of nearly all the nations of Asia and Africa are "new" in one of three respects. In the extreme case, illustrated by Malaysia and Nigeria, they comprise entirely new political entities, the more or less arbitrary invention of state makers who have drawn a line around a piece of territory and given it a name. In other instances, such as Burma and Morocco, they represent a restoration to autonomous status of former nations whose rulers were displaced or subordinated by European powers. A third type of novelty is represented by countries like China and Egypt, which both have a national history and were self-governing by the end of World War II but have since experienced a revolutionary change of governmental form.

All these societies are now working to cope with the consequences of a fairly sharp break with the recent past. Insofar as they are committed to economic and social modernization they are aided by the freshness of their political institutions and the climate of dynamism in which their governments came into being. At the same time their viability as national societies is made problematic by the fact that the concept of themselves that they now seek to sustain is at such variance with their prior experience and culture.

Precisely the converse constellation of circumstances is faced by a smaller group of nations whose distinguishing feature is a conspicuous degree of continuity with the past. These are the proud old nations, traditional monarchies with rich national cultures and long histories, whose indigenous leadership was never effectively dislocated by outside forces or structural change. In this group we find Afghanistan and Thailand, Iran and Ethiopia. For these countries the attainment of a national identity in the modern world has been relatively unproblematic, while the effort to modernize has been arduous and halting, palpably artificial in the context of customary national life.

When Ethiopia is examined in this comparative perspective, it is apparent that the tendency to represent Ethiopia as one of so many African nations is highly misleading despite the fact that her political and cultural ties with the rest of the continent have of late become increasingly prominent. It is true that to most of Africa's aspiring nationalists and Christian separatists Ethiopia has stood for decades as a symbol of African autonomy. It is noteworthy that the Imperial Ethiopian government, spurred by the international developments of the past decade, has turned from a policy of virtually complete alignment with the Western powers and aloofness from pan-Africanism toward a policy of greater neutralism and outspoken solidarity with the other nations of Africa, a change marked by the establishment of the UN Economic Commission for Africa in Addis Ababa in 1958 and the convocation there in 1963 of the Conference of Heads of Independent African States. It is likewise notable that the emphasis on Ethiopia's extra-African ties which has characterized most Ethiopianist scholarship in the past, an emphasis on the numerous culture complexes absorbed from Mediterranean and especially Semitic cultures during the past three millennia, is slowly giving way to an appreciation of Ethiopian culture traits which are of African origin and character. Yet for all this upsurge of interest in perceiving Ethiopia as an African nation, from the point of view of comparative politics it is clear that now, more than ever, Ethiopia is "in Africa but not of Africa."

II

To say this is to draw attention to a number of particular aspects of Ethiopia's situation that contribute to the distinctiveness of her political system.

1. The Ethiopian polity of today is continuous with political institutions that have a recorded history of some two thousand years. Ethiopia has not shared the *élan* and the agonies that accompanied the birth of the new states of Africa. She has experienced in much milder form and more leisurely pace the problems and stimulation that come with building a contemporary state: establishing the legitimacy of national political authority, securing recognition from other states, devising the machinery of national government, and so on.

2. Unlike the other African states which were independent in 1945—unlike Liberia and South Africa, whose elites represent alien elements, and unlike Egypt, whose native elites identify with supra-

national Islam or pan-Arab nationalism—Ethiopia has traditionally been governed by indigenous elites connected with her antique institutions and bearers of a national culture. They have been custodians of a written tradition which, though partly foreign in origin, was thoroughly Ethiopianized in character and became a primary repository of Ethiopian national sentiment. However much divided by differences of region, dialect, custom, theology, and interest, they shared faint memories of ancient national glories and the symbols and practices of a national religion.

3. The Imperial Ethiopian Government has evidently never dogmatically opposed the principle of imperialism. Though the Ethiopian version of this state's name is, literally, Government of the King of Kings—and hence connotes a personal regime rather than territorial empire—it is a conspicuous fact that the Ethiopian state has emerged through the ascendance of one of the peoples in the country, the Amhara, over all others.

The Amhara came to the fore in Ethiopia by the thirteenth century. Since the beginning of what is known as the restored Solomonid Dynasty (1270) virtually all the emperors of Ethiopia have been Amhara. In the centuries following their ascendance they maintained a prosperous and expanding kingdom. After severe setbacks in the sixteenth and seventeenth centuries they began a comeback which eventuated in the victories of Menelik II (1889-1913), under whom the area subject to Amhara rule was tripled. Throughout most of the past seven centuries Amhara emperors, nobles, soldiers, and colonists have maintained their political supremacy in Ethiopia and have made their tongue, Amharic, the national language.

4. The Amhara hegemony is upheld by a number of beliefs and sentiments which in their anti-egalitarian character are likewise not typical of contemporary African ideologies. According to an Amharic saying, "The Amhara is to rule, not to be ruled." This presumptive right is legitimated, in Amhara minds at least, by fairly intense feelings of ethnic and cultural superiority. Thus the Amhara have carried on "cultural imperialism" to a limited degree as well: Amharization via the school system, the spreading of Amhara customs and religion through settlers, traders, and occasional missionaries. The most recent example of this process has been the substitution of Amharic names for indigenous place names in many parts of the empire.

5. Ethiopia was never effectively colonized. During the brief period

of foreign rule (1936-1941) many if not most Ethiopians who were politically aware did not define the situation as that of being in a colony, but rather as that of suffering temporarily under an enemy invader. Furthermore, numbers of Ethiopian patriots, mostly Amhara, carried on an underground resistance during the whole period, while many others spent the years in exile. The fact that Ethiopia has been a non-colonial country distinguishes her from most other African nations in a number of respects:

a. Ethiopians do not have the psychic scars that come from having grown up as an alien in one's own country. Rather, they enjoy a high degree of self-esteem and pride in their long tradition of independence.[1]

b. Ethiopian public life has not experienced the rise of modern agitational politics, nor the related phenomenon of political movements or parties. There has thus been no serious threat to the rule of the traditional elites.

c. The Ethiopian public has not been exposed to oratory promising dynamic and economic changes for the benefit of the people. There has thus developed no mass base of support for populist leaders who might seek to promote more rapid forms of change.

One may summarize the distinctive aspects of Ethiopia's situation just enumerated by observing that, unlike all other African states, the Ethiopian state represents a historic nation which has largely preserved its own institutions, elites, and culture from displacement by Western forms and authorities, chiefly through the agency of one of a large number of ethnic groups which has partially imposed its rule and its language upon the others. It is clear that any attempt to understand the nature of the Ethiopian political system must begin with the fact of Amhara dominance.

Considered numerically, the Amhara are a minority group in Ethiopia today. They are concentrated in four of the fourteen provinces of the Empire—Shoa, Wallo, Gojjam, and Bagemder—each of which contains sizeable non-Amhara populations. All together the Amhara comprise perhaps one-fifth of the total national population of some 20 to 25 million people.

Their disproportionate influence on the course of Ethiopian politics appears first of all in the fact that not only the Crown but also

[1] This point begs the question of the extent to which non-Amhara peoples in Ethiopia have suffered because of their subordinate status, a question concerning which the author does not possess reliable data.

the great majority of important positions in the government and the armed forces are in Amhara hands (for the most part Amhara of Shoa Province, homeland of the present imperial dynasty). The Amhara are also over-represented in the one area of Ethiopian life where competition is not affected by ethnic considerations, the school system. Due to their fortunate economic position and perhaps to the location of primary schools, Amhara students make up approximately 55 per cent of all Ethiopians registered in secondary schools and colleges.[2]

Without denying the significance of this factor of differential access to influential positions, it may be suggested that a more revealing measure of Amhara influence on Ethiopian political life is the extent to which the ideas, symbols, and values which govern Ethiopian politics are drawn from Amhara culture. The national politics of Ethiopia have on the whole been shaped in accordance with what may be called *Amhara political culture*. It is the task of the pages which follow to develop the meaning of this concept and to ask what it implies for the understanding of Ethiopia's political development.

Political culture, simply stated, consists of the complex of meanings given by a people to the objects in their political system. Yet this simplicity of definition is a hollow victory, since social scientists are far from agreement on how to define a political system and have yet to produce a viable schema for the systematic analysis of cultural meanings. Whether, in analyzing political culture, one chooses to focus on the cultural aspects of a political system or the politically relevant aspects of a culture, one is treading on unstable conceptual ground.

In keeping with the rudimentary state of our facility to deal with this concept, I shall forego the temptation to set forth a coherent and systematic account of Amhara culture and dwell instead on three themes that are of compelling relevance to any consideration of political culture: orientation to authority, to human nature, and to the polity.[3] The first two themes represent very general, basic orientations that connect with other aspects of Amhara culture as well as the narrowly political. Their content is much the same at all levels of Amhara society and presumably has changed very little

---

[2] This figure is based on a survey conducted by the author in 1959-1960.

[3] Using somewhat different terms and evolving a richer framework of distinctions, Verba's concluding essay discusses some of the grounds of this relevance.

over the centuries. The third theme, that of nationhood, has been somewhat more prominent in the outlook of the Amhara elites than of the masses and has undergone a historical development which we shall attempt to reconstruct.

III

The complex of beliefs, symbols, and values regarding authority constitutes a key component of Amhara political culture. Throughout Amhara culture appears the motif that authority as such is good: indispensable for the well-being of society and worthy of unremitting deference, obeisance, and praise. Every aspect of Amhara social life is anchored in some sort of relationship to authority figures, and the absence of such a relationship evokes feelings of incompleteness and malaise. The chief exceptions to this are those activities which are defined as outside the pale of society—as in the solipsistic worlds of the anchorite and the outlaw.

The psychological roots of these attitudes toward authority lie of course in the Amhara family. Although Amhara kinship rests on the principle of bilateral descent, and women enjoy substantial rights with regard to inheritance and divorce, the character of the family is unmistakably patriarchal. The father is endowed with considerable powers and is entitled to the utmost respect and obedience. His jurisdiction handily includes the area of physical punishment, which he may apply to wife and servants as well as children, and which, whenever inflicted, is usually considered to be deserved and productive of salutary effects.

Obedience is the prime objective in the socialization of Amhara children. They are taught to be inconspicuous and respectful and to respond readily to any parental commands. An illustration of this ethic is the Amhara practice during mealtime, whereby children are expected to stand quietly, facing the wall, while their elders are eating, and are only fed afterwards, with what is considered second-rate food. Adolescence, although a period for learning the skills and norms related to adult self-sufficiency, is also a time when paternal authority is heightened and demands for obedience are greatly multiplied.

This experience in the family is continuous and consistent with the rest of Amhara culture. Children and adolescents acquire a disposition to respect and obey authority which is generalized to all other spheres of their life. Even in children's play groups there is a pronounced tendency to define someone—usually the eldest—as an authority figure and to submit willingly to his ideas and impulses. Amhara students in the secular government schools, even when separated from their families by boarding arrangements, retain this traditional orientation to a large extent. In a survey of attitudes of secondary-school seniors which I conducted in 1959-1960, 67 per cent of those who identified themselves as Amhara maintained that *one should always obey the order of a superior*. The main reasons given for this response were that, "it is one's duty," "things would not go right otherwise," "the Bible says so," and, "obedience is a virtue."

Ethiopia is not a "political society" in Shils' sense inasmuch as involvement with the goals of the total society is not widely dispersed throughout the populace. But the nature of life among the Amhara *is* highly "political" in that the wielding of authority is a basic and pervasive feature of their social relationships and in a manner that is broadly similar for all institutional contexts. Theirs is an authoritarian and a politicking society.

Perhaps a better way of approaching this phenomenon is to say that there is but a very tenuous distinction between the occupation of high status on the one hand and the possession of authority on the other, whether the latter be conceived as the legitimated capacity to influence the actions of others or as a legitimate agency for allocating values. Men who possess a good measure of one or more of the qualities for which high status is ascribed in Amhara society—family, age, wealth, ecclesiastical rank, and political rank—are esteemed throughout the society, and their judgments and decisions are binding in their local contexts. Family patriarch, parish chieftain, wealthy landlord, ecclesiastical dignitary, political dignitary, military officer—all are perceived in the imagery of fatherhood; all are the objects of comparable attitudes regarding the obeisance which is due them and the benefits which may be expected from them.

Amhara culture provides numerous forms for indicating deference to superiors. Some of these are linguistic, the numerous respect forms used in reference and address to superiors. There are in addition many non-verbal gestures of respect towards superiors. For example, an inferior rises to speak when addressed by any authority figure. If eating in his home, he must rise when water is brought for washing his hands. If riding a mule, he dismounts and bows until the superior has passed. When entering his home, he twists his toga in a respectful manner and bows low to the ground, his arms crossed over his chest.

The praise of authorities is an activity which makes use of some of the most elaborate symbolic forms in Amhara culture. These include formal hymns of praise, at times composed in the classical Ethiopic language Ge'ez, in which extravagant religious imagery may be used to glorify secular authorities, as well as extemporized laudatory verses in the vernacular Amharic rendered by minstrels.

Similarly, ready compliance with the wishes of any authority figure is expected of the Amhara, at least in appearance. If the subordinate disagrees with the decision of some authority, he does not express that disagreement openly—certainly never in public. If he has some public criticism to make of any authority, he may voice it only through the obscure, double-edged witticisms or verse which are the genius of Amhara culture. Related to this is a very important aspect of authority relations: acceptance of the pronouncement of a judge. Although the Amhara is quick to assert his claims and grievances in litigation, once a judge, at whatever level, has pronounced his verdict, the decision is instantly acquiesced in. If the loser is dissatisfied, which is often the case, he will go outside and appeal to a higher-level judge at a later time.

In their turn, most authority figures are looked upon as sources of certain benefits for the people. One of these is the provision of food. The function of "feeder" is closely associated with the role of father, and "big men" generally are expected to feed numerous relatives and retainers regularly and to institute annual feasts for the benefit of the poor and indigent in their area as well as for wider circles of kin and friends. Prosperous clergy sometimes do the same. The confessor, or "soul father," moreover, performs this function in reverse as it were, checking the observance of fasting requirements by his confessants and imposing additional fasts as punishment for transgressions.

Another service commonly performed by authority figures is the dispensation of justice. Local chieftain, priest, elder, landlord, as well as judges and administrative officials are continually being requested to reconcile antagonists or pass judgment on litigants. It would be considered highly improper for them to refuse such requests. Still another is the ceremonial function. The presence of "big men" in places of honor is an indispensable aesthetic ingredient on such occasions as the celebration of annual religious festivals and, more recently, of secular national holidays.

There is, finally, a sort of magical function connected with the higher political authorities. Their presence is regarded as a source of well-being in the country, a precondition for order and prosperity. This attitude is reflected in an Amharic proverb which attributes fertility of the land to the nobility, and in the story of the deposition of one local Amhara ruler in the eighteenth century because of a severe drought which occurred during the first year of his rule.

All of these themes are realized in the most complete form and on a grand scale in connection with the highest authority figure of all, the emperor. The incumbent of this role has been the recipient of the most extreme forms of obeisance. It has been customary, for example, for Ethiopian subjects to prostrate themselves and refrain from lifting their eyes in his presence. Earlier records document a comparable show of deference when royal messages were received from afar; the recipient had to hear the message outside his home, standing, and naked above the waist. Similarly, eulogies of the emperor were expressed in numerous literary forms. In royal chronicles and hymns of praise which span seven centuries the emperors are celebrated for superlative beauty and superhuman powers. In splendor of countenance they are likened to the sun; in awesomeness of power, to the lion; in religious character and divine force, to the kings of Israel and, at times, to God Himself.

Expectations of service from the emperor were on a comparably grand scale. Hundreds and at times thousands of men were periodically nourished at his feasts. Numerous cases of litigation—appeals from lower judicial levels, as well as disputes originating at the highest level—were judged by him in periodic court sessions. His appearance in any part of the country at any time was itself a momentous ceremonial occasion. And his magical function was, according to some students, the most important of all—a transcendent source of social euphoria. For this reason, again, the death of an emperor has usually been a time of acute social malaise, often bordering on anarchy, and the news of his death has often been concealed as long as possible from the public.

While it is meaningful thus to regard the orientation toward the emperor as a continuation and projection of the orientations toward authority figures at all levels in Amhara society—he is the greatest father figure of all—there are however certain discontinuous and unique elements in Amhara political culture concerning the imperial role and person. For the role of emperor is bound up with beliefs and values that are *sui generis* and that are directly connected with other more fundamental aspects of Amhara culture. These relate primarily to the conception of the emperor as a sacred personality, as "Elect of God."

This conception, probably deriving ultimately from pre-Christian notions of divine monarchy and subsequently anchored in beliefs concerning Solomonic ancestry and the transfer of divine mission from the Kings of Israel to the Kings of Ethiopia, is closely connected with the self-image of the Amhara people. By virtue of the beliefs on which the charisma of his office is grounded they are able to view themselves as a chosen people and to affix some of that charisma to themselves. On the one hand they identify themselves as descendants of the ancient chosen people of Israel. Nobles related to the imperial line have in fact traditionally been referred to as "chiefs of Israel." On the other hand they identify themselves as the unique bearers of the Christian faith, and to this day many if not most Amhara regard themselves as the only authentic Christians in the world. These beliefs provide the ideological basis for the superiority which the Amhara feel vis-à-vis the other peoples of Ethiopia (except the Tigre, with whom they share this cultural legacy) and for their claims to be the just rulers of the land.

Because of the important symbolic function of the royal office, certain extraordinary qualifications have been required for entry into that office. One is that the emperor actually be descended from persons identified as members of the Solomonic line. Another is that his body be free from any physical defect, in order as it were to serve as an adequate symbol for the integrity of the body politic. Finally, legitimate accession to the throne has depended on two rites, anointment by oil and bestowal of the crown. Authority to conduct these rites was vested in the archbishop who, until the election of an Ethiopian to that station in 1950, had always been an Egyptian monk sent by the Coptic Patriarch at Alexandria. The act of coronation transformed the status of the new emperor, who assumed a new name and accoutred himself with such insignia as a red silk parasol and special drums, trumpets, and flutes.

The unique status of the emperor relates to other aspects of Amhara culture which are particularly important for understanding the nature and scope of the Ethiopian monarchy today. One of these is the peculiar responsibility placed on the emperor for the welfare of the Orthodox Church. Most emperors have in fact been active in one way or another in supporting the religious institutions of the country. For some the Christianizing role has been a key component of their identity—those, for example, who selected the throne name of Constantine. They have frequently granted lands to the church, constructed church buildings and monasteries, and bestowed gifts of silk robes and other precious items. Several emperors have been particularly involved in some specialized aspect of religious affairs, whether the composition of religious writings and the revision of liturgies, like Zara Yaqob (1434-1468); working to resolve theological controversies, as did Yohannes the Pious (1667-1682); stimulating, like Iyasu the Great (1682-1706), religious cultural activities and education; or waging campaigns to convert the heathens, as did Yohannes IV (1872-1889).

The authority to invest the highest ranks was another distinct attribute of the emperor's position. Ethiopia did not possess a hereditary aristocracy such as those developed in most European countries. To be sure, there developed a quasi-hereditary nobility, based on the tendency for lands, office, and titles to be given to members of the same families. In practice the emperors frequently let such possessions pass from father to son, either because they were in too distant a region or because there was no good cause for taking them away, and on occasion drew up written charters assigning grants of land to a man and his future descendants. But titles never passed directly from father to son without the approval of the emperor, and however much a man might qualify for political appointment or honorific title by virtue of his father's standing, he could attain the highest distinctions only through the agency of royal favor. Thus two kinds of variables were always involved in the assignment of status to an authority figure: the intrinsic factors of family background, wealth, and local military strength, and the extrinsic factor of investiture by the sovereign. The relative importance of these two sources of high status depended on the actual political strength of the emperor at a given time and the degree of proximity to his court.

Still another distinctive feature of the emperor's pre-eminent position was his authority to introduce culture change. While the Amhara are basically resistant to innovations of any sort, they have expected the emperor to do what is necessary to ensure the welfare of the realm and have tolerated his deviation from precedent when that has not conflicted with their ultimate values, such as allegiance to the Ethiopian Orthodox faith. At times such changes have been introduced by direct proclamation, as in the institution of new religious holidays by Zara Yaqob or the introduction of smallpox vaccination by Menelik. At times they have been introduced through suggestion or by providing models for the populace to follow, as in the effort of a number of monarchs of the past century to combat the Amhara's repugnance for manual labor by themselves engaging in arduous physical work on occasion. More recently they have included the establishment of new institutions, such as the State Bank and the secular school, introduced by Menelik.

IV

Another aspect of Amhara culture highly relevant to an understanding of Ethiopia's political development is its approach to human nature. This phenomenon may be examined first of all by inspecting the variety of semantic usages connected with the generic word for "man," *saw*. Perhaps the most common connotation of this term is the concept of "others." An object which is described as *ya-saw*—literally, "of man"—means an object belonging to *someone else*. So used, the word *saw* tends to have unpleasant overtones. It means someone outside the circle of kin; it means neighbors or outsiders, and thus conveys a negative or at best sternly neutral sentiment. The adage that "the affairs of man [i.e. other people] are grief" illustrates this. An extraordinary instance of this negative use of the generic word for man appears in the expression *ya-saw ayn*; literally, "the eye of man," or "the eye of others." *Ya-saw ayn*, however, is an idiom which signifies the "evil eye," one of the most feared and despised objects in Amhara culture.

By adding the suffix "*ya*," *saw* takes on the meaning of a particular man. The word *sawya* is used in narrative in a neutral, descriptive sense: *and sawya nabara*, "once there was a man." But it is also used in a vocative sense, like the American *man*! or the German *Mensch*! Unlike these latter, however, it conveys no positive sentiment based on the friendly assumption of solidarity between two members of the same species. On the contrary, the term *Sawya*! tends to be spoken in a somewhat domineering tone and might best be rendered by the American expression, "Hey you!"

In other contexts *saw* takes on a more affirmative meaning. It may signify a free man as distinguished from a slave. It may also signify a human being, a fully formed member of the species. But here the Amhara attitude toward human nature is expressed in a common and very characteristic saying, *Saw yallam*—"there is no human being"; in other words, an individual who fully embodies the concept of humanity does not exist. In this sense of the term human nature in the abstract is admirable, but in actuality never so.

Extending our examination beyond such narrow semantic analyses, we find that these negative associations of the word *saw* are supported by two sets of negative ideas concerning man: the attribution of inferiority to various human types due to their possession of certain ascribed qualities, and the assumption that man is dominated by certain fundamental negative propensities.

The Amhara's conception of humanity is radically unegalitarian. A person's chief characteristics, in the Amhara view, are whether he is male or female, elder or youth, Amhara or non-Amhara, Christian or non-Christian, free or slave, and well born or poor. Each of these dichotomies falls into a superior-inferior pattern. Women are considered inferior because of their alleged infidelity and the triviality of their conversation. With respect to age categories, children are considered inferior because they are governed by ignorance and passion; adolescents because, like wind, they are flighty and never settled; young men because, like fire, they are hot in picking quarrels and chasing after women. Non-Amhara people are disdained, partly on a racial basis—the "ashen-faced" European and the black man with Negroid features, both the traditional objects of racial ridicule—and partly on a cultural basis, with occupational hunters and pastoral nomads at the bottom of the status hierarchy. The distinction between Orthodox Christian and all other religions is all-or-none; Catholic, Protestant, Muslim, and pagan are, to the traditional Amhara, virtually interchangeable as inferior, infidel types. Finally, slaves, ex-slaves, and poor folk generally are considered inferior by definition. Because of this strong unegalitarian ethos the Amhara have but a very dim feeling that the simple fact of being a human being is sufficient to entitle an individual to respect.[4]

Part of the reason for this is that the particular features which

---

[4] Such egalitarian sentiment as they have is manifest primarily in the notion that all men are to be judged impartially before God and in the (structurally unimportant) social form known as *māhebar*, a kind of religious fraternal association.

dominate the Amhara's image of generic human nature are man's inherent aggressiveness and his untrustworthiness. Amhara culture does not support the belief that unformed human nature is good raw material. It holds, rather, that without strict punishment for nearly a dozen years of his life a person will not grow up properly. He will be rude, untrained, tending to trample on others.

Once a person reaches adulthood, moreover, his hostility must constantly be kept in check. This belief is illustrated by the Amharic concept of *Ṭagābegnā*. The literal meaning of *ṭagābegnā* is "one who has been sated," who has had his fill of food and drink. In common usage, however, the word signifies a person who is disposed to insult and pick fights with people. A servant who becomes "uppity" or a soldier who opposes his superior's command may be called *ṭagābegnā*, implying that the arrogant behavior in question comes from having been too well off. A number of Amharic couplets begin with the lines, "When a peasant gets sated, he beats with his stick." In the Amhara view the specific effect of drinking alcohol is to release not Eros but the aggressive instincts. The following proverb about the Ethiopian barley-beer, *ṭallā*, states this forthrightly:

> One [glass] whets the appetite;
> Two quenches it;
> Three heats one up;
> Four makes one quarrel;
> Five brings fighting;
> Six causes killing.

The Amhara view of human nature thus conceives of aggression as a response to abundant gratification, not frustration. A corollary to this is the belief that deprivation is the proper prophylaxis against aggression. The Amhara refer to fasting as the most important part of their religion, and indeed, with respect to the number and harshness of the fasts it prescribes, Amhara custom is probably the strictest in the world. This custom is explained on the grounds that by weakening one's body thus, one is less likely to commit some wrong against others, like assaulting or insulting them.

Related to this view of man's powerful latent hostility is the notion that man is untrustworthy. *Sawan māmman ba-kantu naw*, "It is futile to trust in man"—so runs an Amharic epigram sometimes woven ornamentally into wool rugs. In part this is an expression of the otherworldly orientation of Ethiopian Christianity; the world is transient, all things pass away except God, and so it is futile to place one's trust in anyone other than God. But this epigram also expresses a very deep-rooted secular disposition, a disposition to be suspicious of everyone outside the narrow circle of kin and often within that circle as well. This disposition is institutionalized in the custom known as *wāss*, according to which virtually any sort of secular transaction—hiring a servant, lending money, litigating in court, and so on—requires as the initial step the securing of a guarantor who agrees to make good for any damages caused by the man he is backing.

The Amhara's essentially pessimistic estimate of man's potentialities does not, however, imply a dogmatic or emotional rejection of man, such as has been experienced in some other developments within the Christian tradition. The Amhara's approach to human nature may be characterized, rather, as a sort of realistic humanism. Man is accepted, with all his frailties, for what he is assumed to be. The institutions and norms of the Amhara are shaped not to overwhelm man with guilt for his shortcomings, not to pressure him into personal or social reform, not to deprive his worldly existence of all enjoyment and significance, but rather to accommodate human realities and transcendent values to one another in such a way that neither is seriously compromised. The negative propensities of man are simply acknowledged and taken into account. Where feasible, they are controlled; where not, their free sway is accepted.

The latter alternative is followed in instances where certain Christian ideals are upheld at the same time as the normal human inclination to flout them is recognized and accepted. With respect to the use of violence, for example, the Christian pacifist ideal is embodied in the requirement that those who officiate in the celebration of the Mass—priests and deacons—must never have shed human blood; and an Amhara who has been ordained as a priest must not even shed the blood of an animal. This does not mean that the clergy have constituted a social force working to oppose violence as such. Priests have gladly accompanied military expeditions and assisted the efforts of combatants by their divinations and their prayers. But by virtue of the norm that they themselves abstain from violence, the clergy have kept alive in this traditionally martial society a faint echo of the Christian ideal of non-violence.

The Amhara arrangements with respect to the Christian ideal of monogamy are equally discriminating. The Ethiopian Church recognizes as legal only those marriages which have been sanctified by a ceremony in which the husband and wife partake of the Eucharist. The parties to such a marriage, known as a *qurbān* type of marriage, are thereafter forbidden to commit adultery, to divorce, or to remarry upon the death of one of the partners. Such rules are clearly oppressive to the majority of Amhara, who prefer to contract a civil marriage and live their lives technically excommunicated by their church, which they may do and still remain fully respected members of the society. Marriage according to this church law is, however, a prerequisite for ordination to the priesthood, and the most important single prerequisite at that. In other words, the Christian ideal of monogamy is embodied in the careers of those whose vocation is ritual purity, while the rest of the society is relatively free to follow the inclinations of the old Adam.

Still another sociological arrangement which embodies the Amhara's forbearance toward human frailty concerns the role known as *dabtarā*. The *dabtarā* is the literatus of Amhara society, and his functions as chorister, scribe, and religious poet are essential to the working of the Church. In this role the Amhara have instituted a religious vocation which requires the attainment of special knowledge but does not expect pious behavior. The *dabtarā* can be a man who has marched on the warpath or who hunts wild game. His marital life is as free of restrictions as the ordinary layman's. The role of *dabtarā* thus provides an outlet for religiously oriented Amhara who do not choose to be tied down by the strict conditions of the priesthood and for priests who, finding these conditions to be too much to live with, have divorced or remarried.

Other aspects of Amhara society and culture are organized so as to set limits to the acting out of man's presumed asocial and disruptive tendencies. One of these we have already mentioned: the subjection of all Christian Amhara to a stringent regime of fasting. The Amhara acknowledge the appropriateness and efficacy of this custom in a matter-of-fact way. They say, when questioned, that man is susceptible to the temptations of the devil, and that by weakening their bodies through fasting they will be better prepared to withstand these temptations and to refrain from committing some wrong against their fellows.

Another source of control is the subordination of all individuals to the authority of various superiors. Here two understandings are at work. One is the feeling that centrifugal and mutually destructive impulses will play themselves out unless checked by some figure of authority. As a number of secondary school and college students noted when justifying their response that "one should always obey the order of a superior," "things would not go right otherwise," and "this is necessary for people to cooperate." The other is the expectation that some judge-figure will always be available; that it is all right to unleash complaint and accusations against one's neighbor because sooner or later the antagonism will be brought into control and channeled through the agency of customary judicial procedures. The Amhara view of human nature thus complements the previously discussed orientation to authority in buttressing a disposition to respect and obey figures of authority.

The realistic acceptance of and adjustment to what are perceived as man's inherent shortcomings is an expression, furthermore, of a more general orientation to the universe that may be described as a kind of fatalism. The concept of fate—*eddel*—is invoked by Amhara to account for the various accomplishments and peripeties of their lives. *Eddel* is the working of divine will as it affects human purposes, and it is believed to be more important than human effort in attaining any end. Amhara culture thus provides little justification for efforts to introduce change. On the contrary, received habit is tenaciously kept because of its association with the authority "of our fathers." Nature is regarded as a set of conditions to be accepted as found and carefully adjusted to, not to be conquered or transformed. Time is conceived as cyclical, not linear, and ordered in terms of months, years, and sequences of years of which the characteristic feature is not historical uniqueness but indefinite repetition. This cyclical feeling is mirrored in the Amhara's organization of space, which is marked by the repeated use of concentric circles.[5]

The chief political implication of all this is that society no more than human nature is to be made the object of systematic efforts to apply transcendent principles or to transform the *status quo*. The task of political authority is to accept such conflicts and strains as exist and to work, by skillful manipulation, adjudication, and occasional coercion, to maintain a minimum of order and retributive justice. Another implication of some importance is that, because human beings are considered so untrustworthy, the degree to which Amhara are disposed to unite in pursuit of a common cause is a priori quite limited.

---

[5] Cf. D. Levine, "On the Conceptions of Time and Space in the Amhara World View," *Atti del convegno internazionale di studi etiopici*, Rome, 1960.

V

Neither at the local nor the national level does Amhara culture place a high value on the notion of civil community.[6] Indeed, the concept of "community" can scarcely be rendered in idiomatic Amharic. Social cohesion has been attained not by the attachment of solidaristic sentiment to communal symbols or the organization of activities in behalf of communal ends but through the sharing of common religious, territorial, and linguistic identifications on the one hand and subordination to individual authority figures on the other. When individual and presumed communal interests come into conflict, Amhara culture tends to place greater weight on the defense of individual interests. Similarly, it values the pursuit of local, para-dynastic interests more than the subordination of parochial goals to the interests of the nation. Most of the stories which Amhara like to tell of their national history thus take the form of anecdotes related to internecine warfare and political conflict, and the substance of their history has been to a large extent as described by an Amhara literatus: "Always the same old thing—one lord fighting another to gain more power."

Nevertheless some sense of national community, however rare, has never been wholly absent from the Amhara consciousness. It rests on a number of national memories, symbols, and aspirations that are an inalienable part of Amhara experience.

Ethiopian nationality has for millennia been designated by the term Habasha by Orientals. The term apparently derives from the name of one of the South Arabian tribes which migrated across the Red Sea in the first millennium B.C., the Habashat. Although Ethiopians frequently use the term *hābashā* among themselves—if for no other reason than that it is simpler to pronounce than the cumbersome *etiopiyāwi*—they resent the use of the term (and its European counterpart, Abyssinian) by outsiders because of alleged pejorative overtones.

It is difficult to determine at what time the name Ethiopia gained currency as a symbol of national identity. In Aksumite antiquity it referred not to their own country but to Nilotic kingdoms to the west. The earliest recorded use of the appellation "King of Kings of Ethiopia" was by Yekuno Amlak in the late thirteenth century, and

[6] Cf. D. Levine, *Wax and Gold: Tradition and Innovation in Ethiopian Culture*, Chicago, University of Chicago Press, 1965, Chap. 7.

all emperors since him have followed suit. Yet whatever name it went by, some sense of nationality must have preceded this usage, and contemporary national sentiment refers back to two cultural sources which clearly antedate the rise of the Amhara as rulers of the country: the tradition of the monarchy and that of the Church.

Native king lists connect the present dynasty with a genealogy that stretches back literally to King Solomon. Associated with the antique monarchy in the national memory are the former seats of royal power which were embodied in enduring architectural constructions: the stelae of Aksum, the churches of Lalibela, and the castles of Gondar. The sense of Ethiopian nationhood is thus in part the effect of identification with a legendary and historical national dynasty shared by all Amhara.

It is also the effect of common membership in a national religion. Introduced by King Ezanas in the fourth century, Christianity has expressed and stimulated the development of a national sentiment among those who have adopted it. It is in connection with her religion that Ethiopia has undergone some of the most unifying experiences in her history.

1. Although the political center of Ethiopia shifted southward from Aksum toward the end of the first millennium A.D., the cathedral of St. Mary of Zion at Aksum remained the first sanctuary of the land until the latter part of the nineteenth century. Thus some sense of an underlying unity of north and south, of Tigre and Amhara, was kept alive by the Amhara's respect for the sanctuary in the north and the custom of holding the rite of coronation of the Amhara emperors at Aksum.

2. Through a spontaneous process of geographical division of labor Ethiopia developed over the centuries a nationwide system of higher religious education. Ethiopian youth who sought a greater mastery of the religious traditions than that afforded in their local parishes left home and tramped across mountains to one or another of the more specialized centers of instruction. For study of the liturgical chants the best schools were in Bagamder and Tigre provinces; for the art of religious poetry they went to one of the monasteries in Gojjam; for religious dance and the study of the holy books the best masters were to be found, in recent centuries, at Gondar. Thus virtually all parts of the country were linked in the minds of Amhara as parts of a unified, national system for the transmission of religious culture.

3. The greatest collective trauma remembered by Ethiopians was the effect of a *jihad* led by an imam from the eastern kingdom of Adal, Ahmad Gragn. In a series of campaigns that began in 1527 and continued for fifteen years, Ahmad Gragn, fortified by firearms from the Ottoman Turks and hordes of Somali fighters, laid most of the Amhara country waste, looted and burned churches, and forced most of the inhabitants to embrace Islam. His eventual defeat was followed by the return of most of the forced converts to the Christian fold and a slow and painful reconstruction of the church. This first serious invasion of Ethiopia by an outside power thus connected the themes of national defense and Christian identity in an intimate way and stamped upon Ethiopian consciousness the self-image which was later to be made famous in the remark of Menelik, who characterized Ethiopia as "an island of Christians in a sea of pagans."

4. In the course of seeking to recover from the destruction wrought by Gragn's *jihad* a number of emperors turned to European Christian powers for religious association as well as political support and technical aid. Some of the emperors became converts to Catholicism and, encouraged by Jesuit missionaries, attempted to promote the Roman faith among their subjects. This policy in turn provoked a strong nationalist reaction, particularly during the reign of Susneyos (1607-1632). Susneyos was forced to abdicate, the Jesuits were expelled from the country, and the new emperor secured the agreement of the pashas on the coast to execute all priests who tried to enter the country. Thus, as one historian has put it, "it was the Muslims who now became the [Ethiopians'] allies . . . against what seemed to them the greater menace—the attempt of Europeans to undermine their national religion, the very embodiment of their national spirit."[7] Through this second trauma, then, just as through the assaults of the Muslim invader, adherence to the traditional religion provided a rallying point for the crystallization of a greater sense of national unity and identity.

It was only in the nineteenth century, in response to the acute civil disorder brought on by a century of feudal separatism and the growing external threat—first from Muhammed Ali's Egypt, then from Mahdism in the Sudan and the expansion of European imperialism—that a more secular concept of nationalism began to

[7] J. Spencer Trimingham, *Islam in Ethiopia*, London, Oxford University Press, 1952, p. 101.

germinate in Ethiopia. The agent of this germination was Emperor Tewodros II (Theodore, 1855-1868), whose tortuous career was devoted to the goal of unifying the country and upholding its dignity as a nation. In the words and deeds of Tewodros the two secular aspirations which form the hard core of modern Ethiopian nationalism—territorial integrity and self-rule—received a classic formulation.

Territory has overriding emotional significance to the Ethiopian because virtually all the ideas and values of his secular national culture are derived from peasant experience. The Amhara peasant's deep attachment to his land and his readiness to defend it by fighting are projected at the national level into a determination to protect the territorial boundaries of the nation at all costs. This attitude is reflected in one of the mottoes of the Imperial Bodyguard, "Bitter as aloes for a handful of earth." In the case of Tewodros it was expressed in the story of his dealings with two British explorers who had been accused of making maps of the country. When they were about to depart, Tewodros gave them many jewels as a farewell present but sent a servant along to wash their boots before they embarked. His explanation: "Far more precious than jewels is a single grain of our country's soil."

Yet if Tewodros is remembered for anything in Ethiopia, it is for his proud determination not to be subjected to foreign rule, capped by his dramatic suicide—a highly unusual act in traditional Ethiopia—when faced with the prospect of capture by the chiefs of the British expedition in 1868. In his famous remark to M. Lejean, the French Consul, Tewodros expressed the pride of sentiment that lay behind that final act: "I know the tactics of European Governments when they desire to acquire an Eastern State. First they send out missionaries, then consuls to support the missionaries, then battalions to support the consuls. I am not a rajah of Hindustan to be made a mock of in that way: I prefer to have to deal with the battalions right away."[8] The resurgence of interest in Tewodros by Ethiopians during the past decade, the plays written and performed about him, and his increased popularity as a national hero are based on his perfect incarnation of the Amhara wish: Give me freedom from foreign rule or give me death. Because of their long history as rulers of the country, moreover, and their deeply ingrained belief that "the

[8] Cited in L. Woolf, *Empire and Commerce in Africa*, New York, Macmillan, p. 145.

Amhara are to rule, not to be ruled," the Amhara are, of all Ethiopians, most sensitive to the encroachment of foreign powers.

The elemental goals of secular nationalism were further pursued by the Tigre emperor Yohannes IV (1871-1889), who also sought to revive the association of Ethiopian nationality with Orthodox Christianity. By his time, however, the numerous Muslims in the country made such a concept no longer feasible. Yohannes' brutal policy of forcing conversions to Christianity was foredoomed to failure. The religious component of Ethiopian nationality was thereafter reduced in importance, particularly after the national boundaries were expanded to their present extent under Menelik, an expansion which added millions of Muslims and pagans to the population of the country.

In the course of Menelik's reign, on the other hand, the concept of national self-determination reached a new level of importance. Indeed, it may be said that the modern concept of Ethiopian nationhood was born of Menelik's defeat of the Italian troops at Adowa in 1896. That event represented a tremendous national undertaking, in which Tigre and Galla as well as Amhara generals played important parts. It also gave the Ethiopian nation a considerable increase in prestige, moving European powers to acknowledge Ethiopia as a force to be reckoned with seriously and so to increase or establish diplomatic representations at Addis Ababa. The year following Adowa witnessed the adoption of an official version of the tricolor Ethiopian national flag[9] and opened a decade of negotiations with European powers in which nine border treaties were signed.[10] On the basis of this quickened intercourse with European states Menelik began to introduce a number of modern Western institutions into his country, including, as one of his last major acts, the establishment of governmental ministries.

Because of the crucial importance of the victory at Adowa in establishing Ethiopia's identity as a nation in the modern world it is not surprising that the annual commemoration of that victory constitutes one of the five national secular holidays celebrated in contemporary Ethiopia. The other four commemorate events that have occurred during the reign of the present Emperor, Haile Selassie I.

[9] S. Chojnacki, "Some Notes on the History of the Ethiopian National Flag," *Journal of Ethiopian Studies*, Vol. I, No. 2, July 1963.
[10] Harold Marcus, "A History of the Negotiations Concerning the Border between Ethiopia and British East Africa," *Boston University Papers in African History*, Vol. II, 1964.

VI

There have been no radical changes in the Amhara orientation to nationhood under His Imperial Majesty Haile Selassie I. The values which informed this orientation under Menelik have remained much the same: the Solomonic monarchy as the locus of sovereignty, territorial integrity, national self-determination, and a tempered emphasis on Orthodox Christianity as an embodiment of the national spirit. What has happened during Haile Selassie's long and eventful regime is that these themes have been enriched by new experiences and the accretion of new meanings. The net result has been a slow but continuous evolution of a sense of Ethiopian nationhood consistent with the traditional Amhara beliefs and values.

The idea of the Solomonic monarchy as the locus of Ethiopian sovereignty has been raised to a new level of importance. It has been given legal expression in the two constitutions which Haile Selassie presented to the people of Ethiopia, in 1931 and again in 1955. Both constitutions affirm the genealogical basis of imperial legitimacy, proclaiming that "the Imperial dignity shall remain perpetually attached to the line of Haile Selassie I . . . whose line descends without interruption from the dynasty of Menelik I, son of the Queen of Ethiopia, the Queen of Sheba, and King Solomon of Jerusalem." They further assert that "By virtue of His Imperial Blood, as well as by the anointing which He has received, the person of the Emperor is sacred, His dignity is inviolable and His power indisputable. He is consequently entitled to all the honours due Him in accordance with tradition and the present Constitution . . . The Sovereignty of the Empire is vested in the Emperor."

The person of the Sovereign has been publicized to a degree hitherto unimagined. Haile Selassie has been the subject of an unremitting cult of personality. The paraphernalia of royalty have been refined and multiplied through the incorporation of modern facilities. The image of an august, benevolent sovereign has been projected throughout the empire by means of modern media. Celebration of the anniversary of his birth and the annual commemoration of his coronation have been institutionalized as national holidays. The country has thus been permeated with the image of a legitimate national authority and has thereby moved somewhat closer to the sense of itself as a single political entity.

The main international event of this reign, the war with Italy and subsequent five-year Occupation, likewise produced and diffused a more substantial sense of nationhood. The consequences of this event were not unmixed, to be sure. Some tribal groups welcomed the Italians as liberating them from Amhara suzerainty, and many ambitious parties joined the Italian cause as collaborators. Yet for most of the Amhara, and many Tigre and Galla, the invasion of their territory and the usurpation of their government by an alien power was not to be borne. Numbers of them spent the Occupation years as exiles in Kenya, Somalia, Sudan, Israel, or Europe; and many others conducted an effective campaign of resistance on the home front. Like Adowa, moreover, the repercussions of the Italian invasion were such as to heighten the importance of Ethiopia in world opinion. Ethiopian prestige was at an all-time high in the international sphere in the decade following the liberation, and some awareness of this condition likewise boosted the sense of national identity at home.

A new set of national symbols and memories was one of the legacies of the Italian era. The annual holiday in honor of the "Ethiopian Martyrs of 12 Yekatit" commemorates the massacre of educated Ethiopians and clergy carried out in February 1937 in retaliation for an attempt on the life of the Italian viceroy, Marshal Graziani. Liberation from the Italian rule is the theme of another holiday, falling on May 5. This anniversary upholds the identification of the monarch with the state, for actually it is defined not as an anniversary of national liberation but rather as "His Imperial Majesty's Triumphant Return to Addis Ababa." Still another symbolic event was the martyrdom of Abuna Petros, the Ethiopian bishop who chose death rather than collaboration with the Italian regime. An imposing statue of this venerable monk was erected in the capital to commemorate, as the *Ethiopian Herald* put it, "the martyrdom of an Ethiopian patriot," a subject also commemorated in the form of a verse drama by a distinguished Amhara writer.

The case of Abuna Petros leads us once more to the question of the relationship between religion and Ethiopian nationality. The traditional Orthodox faith has remained a national religion under Haile Selassie in some very important respects. The 1955 Constitution states that only adherents to this faith may be counted as members of the imperial family and prescribes that the Emperor, in the oath taken upon coronation, swear to "profess and defend the Holy Orthodox Faith based on the doctrines of St. Mark of Alexandria, professed in Ethiopia since the Holy Emperors Abreha and Atsbiha." Article 126 explicitly sets forth that "The Ethiopian Orthodox Church . . . is the Established Church of the Empire and is, as such, supported by the State."

In practice, however, a pluralistic approach has been in evidence. Haile Selassie has not attempted to force conversion to the Orthodox faith, but has adopted a policy of toleration. His conciliatory attitude toward the large Muslim minority and efforts to integrate them into a national community are indicated by his construction of mosques, bestowal of honors and benefits upon selected Muslim notables, and support of a newspaper published in Arabic as well as Amharic— a paper whose name refers to the Ethiopian national flag. He has adopted the practice of inviting leaders of the Muslim community to the palace at the close of the fast of Ramadan.

While the main Ethiopian Christian holidays are still observed as national holidays, some of them have become occasions for the expression of a more secular national spirit. On the festivals of Masqal (Finding of the True Cross) in September and Temqat (Epiphany) in January members of various tribal and religious groups congregate to perform their respective traditional dances and songs. These holidays have to some extent become media for the stimulation of feelings of national solidarity rather than divisive sentiments.

VII

Where, as in the case of Ethiopia, a traditional culture has not been subjected to radical transformation through the agency of alien powers or internal revolutionaries, it may be expected that the most general beliefs and values concerning the political system will remain efficacious, guiding and limiting the variety of immediate adjustments in governmental structure and popular political action. Thus in Ethiopia the political culture of the Amhara, dominant in the land for many centuries, remains today the chief determinant of Ethiopia's political orientation as she is pushed by history in the direction of modernization.[11] How do the features of Amhara political

---

[11] This is perhaps the place to refer, however briefly, to the largely unexplored problem area defined by the relationship between Amhara culture, as the dominant national culture, and the political cultures of other native traditions in Ethiopia. Since the Galla constitute the largest ethnic group in the country, a word about Galla political culture may be in order.

The classical Galla social system is oriented around a system of temporally differ-

culture we have discussed affect the course of political development in Ethiopia?

To answer this question we must first specify what will be meant here by "political modernization," underdeveloped though our understanding of that complicated notion may be. Three ideas are commonly regarded as central to this concept. One is that the authority of government be firmly established in the structure of a sovereign nation-state—not in a clan, a tribe, a church, a duchy, or a trust. The modern polity is first of all headed by a national government which both possesses a preponderance, if not a monopoly, of the means of physical coercion and is recognized as legitimate by a substantial majority of those living under its regime.

The second idea essential to the notion of political modernization is that of rationalization. Rationalization, an integral part of any conception of generic modernity, refers to the sustained and systematic effort to subject man's environment to rational control; more specifically here, to maximize the efficiency of operation of the various parts of the political system. With respect to the organs of government this is usually understood to entail the establishment of a bureaucratic form of public administration and a division of labor involving the separation of judicial, executive, and legislative functions. With respect to the governed it is usually understood to entail the establishment of procedures whereby their interests can be known and their support can be mobilized.

A third and related constituent of political modernization may be

---

entiated social classes, called *gadā*, which move through a series of ten periods, or grades, of eight years duration (cf. Asmarom Legesse, "Class Systems based on Time," *Journal of Ethiopian Studies*, Vol. I, No. 2, July 1963, p. 2).

For present purposes what is relevant about this system is that it is highly "democratic," involving the periodic election of government authorities by the members of a *gadā* class whenever it reaches the fourth period, and its subsequent transmission of electoral sovereignty to the succeeding class when it has reached the fifth period. The Galla ethos, moreover, is relatively egalitarian: relations between the father and the rest of the family tend to be friendly and informal, and provision is made for the incorporation of strangers into local communities.

In these respects nothing could be further apart than the political cultures of Amhara and Galla. Yet the latter has had virtually no impact on the national political culture of Ethiopia. Amhara culture has worked rather—partly unwittingly, partly through conscious policy—to disintegrate the Galla *gadā* system. In so far as classical Galla culture has survived at all in national politics, it may be reflected in the fact that, of the small percentage of Ethiopians who incline to a republican form of government, the Galla appear to be overrepresented—an inclination also furthered by the fact that the Galla have most to gain from a political system based wholly on majority rule.

designated as the institutionalized capacity to generate and absorb change. A modern or modernizing polity is thus one which is disposed to experiment, to innovate, and to react to social change not as a threatening, extrinsic phenomenon but as a normal, expected feature of political life.

So conceptualized, the course of political modernization in Ethiopia may be seen to have been affected in diverse ways by the continuity of Amhara political culture. Speaking very generally, one may say that this culture has furthered the establishment of legitimate national government, has obstructed the process of rationalization, and has affected both positively and negatively the receptivity to social change.

Several features of Amhara political culture have favored the establishment of a national government accepted as legitimate by a substantial majority of the Ethiopian people. The principal one is of course the traditional belief in the transcendent dignity and authority of the King of Kings of Ethiopia. This belief has been preserved over the centuries, even when (during the "Age of the Princes," *ca.* 1769-1855) the emperor was a mere puppet, a shadowy figure, having no perceptible impact on Ethiopian political life. It has been sustained by the high value accorded to the Solomonic genealogy and to the sanctity of anointment. It has been used by the emperors of the past century to justify their efforts to establish autocratic authority over the entire country. Acceptance of this authority has been furthered by the Amhara's emphasis on obedience to authority figures generally. The relevance of this orientation to authority is shown by the fact that although the present emperor has numerous opponents, no one has dared to criticize him publicly. As one high official once told me, "Whether we like him or not, we must not criticize him." The tenacity of this mentality was dramatically illustrated by the behavior of the rebels of December 1960; they did not presume to stage a coup d'état while the emperor was in the country, and in all of their revolutionary pronouncements during their brief stay in power the emperor was not once mentioned directly.

It is difficult to determine what proportion of the total population of Ethiopia accepts the suzerainty of the Amhara monarchy. It must be assumed that many Muslim and pagan tribesmen remain alienated from it. But the politically relevant elements of the population certainly accept it, even where they are critically disposed toward the present incumbent; and this has made it possible for Haile Selassie to eliminate once and for all the semi-autonomous strength of the powerful provincial nobles and to centralize power and prestige in his person to a degree never before realized in Ethiopia.

While the authority of national government in Ethiopia thus rests primarily upon a solid base of allegiance and subordination to the office of the emperor, it also gains support from the aspirations of the people of Ethiopia to maintain their national territory and freedom from alien domination. No political issue has aroused Ethiopians of all classes more in the past decade than the dispute over the Somali border. Except for the Somali elements in the population, most Ethiopians who have any awareness of the issue are passionate nationalists when it comes to the prospect of having to relinquish a single acre of the vast Ogaden desert. Furthermore, as a result of the Italian Occupation and more recently the spread of ideas about the white man's imperialism elsewhere in Africa, the Amhara passion to avoid being dominated in any way by aliens provides a further channel for the expression of nationalist sentiment.

The authority of the national government is thus further upheld by its acceptance as a spokesman for and defender of national political interests, interests which are deeply valued in Amhara political culture. It is true that the national government is scarcely perceived as an embodiment of the will of a united Ethiopian people; for feelings of solidarity among the peoples of Ethiopia are still very weak. Regional, ethnic, and religious differences remain the paramount foci of orientation for the vast majority of the population. Such differences are accentuated by the traditional notions of Amhara superiority and sense of exclusiveness. Even so, it can be said that Amhara culture provides some bases for the development of a greater sense of Ethiopian nationality.

One of these is, paradoxically, the continued association between church and state—paradoxically, because the religious composition of the Ethiopian populace is so very mixed. A rough estimate, based on Trimingham's figures,[12] would be: Christians, 49 per cent; Muslims, 27 per cent; pagans, 23 per cent; Jews, 1 per cent. Other estimates make the Christian and Muslim proportions very nearly equal. Despite this mixture the close connection between church and state may be seen as furthering the sense of Ethiopian nationality and the authority of the central government in two ways. On the one

[12] Trimingham, *op.cit.*, p. 15.

hand it provides a basis for uniting the political leaders of the country, nearly all of whom are Christians though stemming from diverse ethnic, tribal, and linguistic backgrounds; and it gives them a greater self-esteem through the feeling that they are first-class citizens and associated with the peculiar historical mission and traditions of Ethiopia. On the other hand it contributes to a growing sense of nationality at the popular level through the secularization and universalization of some of the Christian holidays.

Another feature of Amhara culture which has not been discussed in this context is the use of Amharic as a national language. Although less than half of the population know Amharic, it is slowly becoming a lingua franca in the empire by virtue of its required use as the language of instruction in the elementary grades as well as for purposes of administration and judicial records. Some groups may resent or be disadvantaged by the suppression of their native languages in such matters, but Amharic is clearly the medium of communication in Ethiopia's future and as such a strong nationalizing factor. Even among those who are not native Amharic speakers those who are aware of the situation elsewhere in Africa tend to take pride in the fact that their national language is indigenous, not, as is true of most other African countries, an alien tongue.

It may also be noted, finally, that Amhara culture has traditionally subverted its ethnic snobbishness to some extent by favoring intermarriage for purposes of political harmony. The example set by many Amhara notables, including the present Emperor, in marrying into families of non-Amhara stock has mollified the bans against ethnic intermarriage, which were never extremely rigid anyway. When asked if they would marry someone from another tribe, 67 per cent of the Amhara secondary students and 74 per cent of Amhara college students replied affirmatively. In responding to a more general question on the relative strength of their tribal and national identifications 60 per cent of all secondary and 75 per cent of all college students indicated that their identification as Ethiopians took priority.

VIII

With respect to rationalization, the second characteristic of political modernization as we have proposed to understand it here, Amhara culture is as much of an obstacle as it is an asset in regard to the goal just considered. For if the main criterion of rationalization in the political realm is the development of relatively specialized structures appropriate to the performance of the several functions of a political system, nothing could be further removed from this standard than the aspects of Amhara culture which define the character of Ethiopian politics. The political system as it has developed under Haile Selassie, an extrapolation from but fully consistent with traditional Amhara beliefs and practices, is designed for anything but differentiation of function. With respect to the performance of all seven functions of the political system identified by Almond— rule-making, rule application, rule adjudication, interest articulation, interest aggregation, political communication, and political recruitment[13]—it may be said that Emperor Haile Selassie has been a key agency.

In the first three, the governmental functions, this functional diffuseness is self-evident from a reading of the Ethiopian Constitution. While the 1955 Constitution represents some movement in the direction of differentiation, in that it delegates greater prerogatives to the Parliament and provides for the popular election of the Lower House, it continues to invest the monarch with supreme legislative, executive, military, and judicial powers. The Emperor is given the right to appoint the members of the Senate, to initiate legislative proposals, and to veto any legislation passed by the Parliament. He has the right to determine the "organization, powers, and duties of all Ministries, executive departments and the administrations of the Government, and appoints, promotes, transfers, suspends, and dismisses the officials of the same." He likewise appoints the heads of all municipal governments. As Commander-in-chief of the Armed Forces, he reserves the right to determine their size, organization, and duties. He appoints the members of the judiciary, and "has the right and the duty to maintain justice through the courts, and the right to grant pardons and amnesties and to commute penalties."

All this only renders explicit and in detail what have been the normal traditional functions of the Amhara emperors. Historically this diffuseness of function likewise characterized the roles of provincial governors and lesser authorities, all of whom combined rule-making, administrative, military, judicial, and ceremonial functions as well. The situation has been changed at the local level under Haile

[13] "A Functional Approach to Comparative Politics," *The Politics of the Developing Areas*, Gabriel A. Almond and James Coleman, eds. Princeton, Princeton University Press, 1960.

Selassie, who has deprived provincial notables of their traditional military functions and has attempted, through the distinct organizations of the Ministries of Interior, Finance, and Justice, to differentiate administrative and judicial structures. But the fusion of roles at the pinnacle of governmental authority has been a conspicuous and tenacious feature of the present regime.

This pattern, while supported by certain factors peculiar to the contemporary political situation and the actors involved, has proved especially resistant to change because it is grounded in two features of Amhara political culture discussed above: the high estimation of authority and the low estimation of human nature. The Amhara habitually look to the person of highest status in whatever hierarchy they belong to for all authoritative decisions, whether of a rule-making, administrative, or judicial nature. To delegate authority elsewhere is to deprive the functionary involved of the power and dignity that have been ascribed to him by virtue of his high status. The Emperor has been unwilling to delegate any of his basic powers and has been supported in this by a good segment of the Amhara people because of the feeling that his dignity would thereby be somewhat diminished. On the other hand he has also been reluctant to do so because of an inability to trust those to whom he might confer powers which he has wielded himself. While this intense suspiciousness and caution might reflect idiosyncratic factors, there can be no doubt that it is in some part a cultural phenomenon expressive of the typical Amhara orientation to human nature.

These factors likewise are part of the reason for the absence of structures that might serve the articulation and aggregation of interests. It is true, and important, that Amhara culture respects the rights of any individual to air his grievances or pursue his interests in litigation and to ask for mercy or special favors from a superior. But the form in which these interests are expressed is crucial: it is a context of complete deference and obedience to authority. The individual in Amhara culture has an inalienable right to present his claims, but no inalienable rights regarding the substance of his claims. The sole legitimate manner of interest articulation in Amhara culture has been the respectful *petition* of a man or spontaneously formed group of men before an authority.

This remains the dominant pattern today in the capital as in the provinces, with interesting implications for the political process. It accounts in part for the reluctance of the Amhara people to make use of the opportunities for interest articulation afforded by the electoral provisions of the new constitution. When faced with the prospect of electing parliamentary representatives in 1957 and 1961, most Amhara responded with indifference or cynicism. In some instances local officials actually had to force citizens to register to vote even though there was a plurality of candidates from whom they were free to choose. In few Amhara districts was the ballot understood as a possible vehicle through which to agitate in behalf of popular interests. Among those who did accept the new machinery the most common attitude was probably the very passive one expressed by a petty provincial governor who told me he would like to run for Parliament some time. When I asked why he wanted to run, and what he would do if elected, he replied: "I will go to the Government in Addis Ababa and tell them what the people of my district need. If they agree, they will give it to me; if not, they will not." In other words, being elected to Parliament meant being in a position to present a petition to the Emperor.

Despite the existence of Western-educated individuals who have promoted the idea of parliamentary representation in Ethiopia for more than sixty years, the idea runs so counter to the authoritarian cast of Amhara political culture that electoral procedures are simply not taken seriously. All serious articulation of interests has been in the form of petitions to His Majesty, either directly or through the mediation of a high-ranking official or member of the imperial family. An important implication of this is that the articulation of interests has been carried out in private through channels directly managed by the Emperor. The ban on the public articulation of interests has been virtually complete.

Those who have had recourse to these channels have for the most part been individuals, not groups. To a limited extent the leaders of the church and the military forces have represented institutional interest groups, but the Emperor's intimate association with both institutions has meant that they have rarely stood apart and voiced demands autonomously. The chief exception to this was the Army's march on the palace in 1961 in demand for a pay raise (which they obtained). Spontaneous interest articulation in the form of riots and demonstrations has likewise been avoided, except for one or two polite demonstrations by students, because of the population's deep-seated respect and fear regarding authority as well as fairly effective security controls. Overt expression of the interests of regional or ethnic groups has also been rare. It appears only on the occasion of some acute problem, such as the local crisis over land rights in the Galla Province of Wollega in 1962, which was solved typically by the sending of a delegation to the palace to petition and the royal appointment of a committee to produce some reconciliation. The establishment of associational interest groups, finally, has simply been forestalled for as long as it has been politically feasible to do so. Prior to the 1960 rebellion virtually the only formal associations permitted in the country were welfare organizations like the Y.M.C.A. and Red Cross and popular savings and welfare associations. Professional associations did not emerge until after the rebellion, and labor unions were suppressed until 1963.

In general the government's attitude toward the collective expression of interests has been that conveyed by a government official when explaining, some years ago, why the students of a certain school who wished to voice their approval of a certain government policy were not being permitted to do so: "If they were allowed to express their agreement without being told to, they might sometime want to express their disagreement."[14] This attitude applies a fortiori to the process of interest aggregation. As Parliament enters its seventh year of deliberations under the new Constitution, political parties are still not permitted by the government. On the contrary, it has been the steadfast policy of the Emperor to forestall efforts toward the aggregated expression of interests in any form. Through techniques of *divide et impera*, frequent reshuffling of appointments, and systematic political surveillance, emerging coalitions of interests have typically been disintegrated well before they have reached a stage where positive political demands could be set forth.

The lack of organizations for the articulation and aggregation of interests in Ethiopia is the result not only of the authoritarian character of the regime, supported as this is by traditional Amhara attitudes toward authority. It also reflects the difficulty Ethiopians have in undertaking any sort of concerted action, particularly in the political sphere. Here again the Amhara conception of human nature is a factor of more than academic significance. The mutual distrust and lack of cooperation which inform the political climate of the country are directly related to a very low regard for man's

[14] William Seed, "Ethiopia's Iron Curtain" (pamphlet issued under the name of the "Ethiopia Freedom Committee"), p. 32.

capacity for solidarity and consensus—*saw yallam*. The idea that it is possible to transcend the prevailing atmosphere of anxiety and suspicion by trusting one another, by taking some risk based on a belief in human potentialities, has been slow to appear and extremely rare.

To say that the Emperor plays a key part in the performance of the functions of interest articulation and aggregation, then, is to say, perhaps somewhat poetically, that all serious expressions of interest have typically been brought under his direct purview sooner or later and co-determined by his intervention. The chief high-level organs of the government—the Crown Council, the Council of Ministers, and the Private Cabinet—may be seen as advisory councils assisting him in this as in other functions. When we speak of the Emperor's important role with regard to the functions of political communication and recruitment, on the other hand, no poetic license is involved.

Political information is transmitted to the government chiefly through a series of communications networks under the direct or indirect control of the Emperor: the formal intelligence networks, and informal networks operating through various officials who report to him more or less regularly. A further source of information consists of disclosures from various individual parties who hope to ingratiate themselves by reporting something incriminating about someone else.

Apart from these channels the central authority has relatively little access to information about current realities. The Emperor, though in a position of supreme power, has thus been at the mercy of those who control the communications channels to him. To a large extent he remains isolated from the real condition and aspirations of his people. It is possible to argue that the 1960 rebellion was as much as anything else the effect of a faulty communications system. Improvement of the channels for political communication has been at the forefront of the demands of the proponents of political modernization in Ethiopia, as illustrated by the following passage taken from a leaflet circulated by one underground agitational group in 1961: "The purpose of founding a government is to serve the people. To serve the people it is necessary to know the desires and ideas of the people ... To know the thoughts of the people, it is necessary to give them freedom of thought, freedom of speech, and freedom of press. A people oppressed by spying and police is a slave; one may not truly call it a people. If the oppression becomes excessive, an explosion is inevitable. It is necessary for the people to have the power with which to control the government and the services they desire, and the opportunity to define the conditions of administration. Freedom of thought, speech, and press provides the means of gaining this opportunity."

The channels of political communication to the public are similarly circumscribed. The mass media are under the moral control of the government when not subjected to direct and unremitting censorship. They serve two purposes, neither of which has to do with the attempt to present objective, neutral, and thorough reporting on matters of domestic political interest. One is to produce propaganda, usually highly unsubtle, in support of the regime, a task that has been described by one of the employees of an Ethiopian newspaper as follows: "I am employed by the Government to help edit one of its papers and to write interpretive articles. My job is to commend the Government, and specifically the Emperor. My job is to inject this praise into every conceivable news item. But that is not all; I am also an advocate, a lawyer, for the Government. If, for example, a bad epidemic breaks out in the slums, and it comes about through the negligence of the Government's health services, then my job is to cover up this fact. But I go one step further, I will write how the Government had mobilized its forces to wipe out the epidemic, regardless of whether this is true or not. And then I praise the Emperor and His Government for their humanitarian action."

The other purpose served by the press has been to air some of the problems and frustrations of transitional Ethiopia through the medium of contributed articles and verse and editorial commentaries. Dealing with such questions as marriage among educated Ethiopians, the status of traditional medicine, the high cost of living, the immorality of modern life, and so on, these items skirt but do not penetrate directly political issues. When politically controversial matters have been touched on in the press, it has not been in the form of dispassionate or detailed analysis but through vague expressions of alienation or else *ad hominem* attacks, which are conveyed not openly but in the form of parables or secret messages apprehended, for example, by reading the initial syllables of each line of a long poem. In recent years sober articles critical of the performance of some governmental ministry have appeared once in a while. But all such ventures are carried out at the author's and editor's risk: punishment from the palace—for example, loss of a week's salary—is readily imposed for any wanton display of critical sentiment.

It is obvious that the orientation toward authority which characterizes Amhara culture must preclude the development of an autonomous and differentiated medium of political communication. For, as we have seen, Amhara culture proscribes direct and honest public criticism of any authority. In authoritarian relationships—and again, all political interaction among the Amhara is contained within authoritarian relationships—there are only three alternatives: complete deference, acquiescence, and flattery; criticism by devious and covert means; or outright rebellion. Government and public will remain poorly informed about political realities until Ethiopian norms are changed to permit development of public discussion of controversial issues and a pattern of loyal opposition.

To deal even cursorily with the function of political socialization and recruitment would entail entering into the complex question of stratification and mobility patterns in Ethiopia, which space does not permit.[15] Suffice it to observe that the Emperor personally has been the dominant agent of political recruitment since the time his power was secured, and that his appointments have been made primarily with an eye to maximizing loyalty and submissiveness and minimizing the chances for the coalescence of interests. This again represents the traditional orientation of authority figures in Amhara culture, the difference here being that Haile Selassie has for the first time in Ethiopian history been able to carry out this pattern fairly effectively throughout the whole empire.

IX

As observed in the previous discussion of the Amhara approach to human nature, Amhara culture is not sympathetic to efforts to transform human society in accordance with abstract principles. On the contrary, its fatalism, its patriarchalism, and its "realistic humanism" dispose its people to look askance at innovation. The basic outlook of the Amhara is thus one which is fundamentally incongruent with the ethos of dynamism inherent in the goal of political modernization.

On the other hand, we have also seen that the pre-eminent authority of the Emperor has provided a mechanism for the deliberate introduction of culture change. By virtue of this authority Haile Selas-

[15] Cf. *Wax and Gold, op.cit.*, Chap. 5.

sie has been able to effectuate a number of social and cultural changes in nearly every year of his reign. He has established a number of institutions without precedent in Ethiopian history, including a national parliament, an electoral system, military academies, technical schools, colleges, and a university—not to mention the written Constitution. He has, by direct proclamation, effected a number of specific changes in the customs of the country, including the formal abolition of slave trading and slavery, and modification of certain excesses with regard to traditional practices of mourning, arrest, and punishment. Through various indirect means he has promoted a number of other reforms, such as encouraging the preaching of sermons in church, removing some obstacles to ethnic and religious harmony, and eliminating archaic practices like the use of a drugged boy in cases of theft to identify the thief. Perhaps the greatest source of change for which he has been responsible has been importation of hundreds of European teachers and sending more than a thousand Ethiopians abroad for college and graduate study.

The consequence of the Amhara's ambivalent posture regarding change is that, while the initiation of change by imperial decree and recommendation is passively accepted, the desirability of change as a basic feature of contemporary life is not. With its penchant for equilibrium and its disdain for change stemming from non-authoritarian sources, Amhara culture supports no comparable mechanism for seeking to assimilate and plan for change. The Emperor, for his part, has insisted on the full prerogatives of his position and has thus tried to maintain a monopoly over the initiation of change and to retain control over its various ramifications. This has necessarily resulted in a crippling of energies, demoralization, and the obstruction of modernization.

Whether the rationalization and dynamism now sought by some educated Ethiopians can be attained by redefining the relevant beliefs and values of Amhara culture; or whether their goals will require more radical changes in political orientation, thus possibly endangering the stability of legitimate national authority; or whether the very goal of political modernization will be undermined by the persistence of traditional Amhara beliefs and values—these are the questions history now waits for Ethiopia to decide.

CHAPTER 8

Italy: Fragmentation, Isolation, Alienation

JOSEPH LAPALOMBARA

SPEAKING of the central mission of the Italian government immediately following unification, Massimo d'Azeglio, a *Risorgimento* leader, mused, "*Fatta l'Italia, bisogna fare gli Italiani*" ("Having made Italy, we must now make Italians"). A century later the typical resident of the Peninsula is likely to react to inclement weather with the telling remark, "*Piove. Governo ladro!*" ("It's raining. Thief of a government!").

The striking truth about Italy is that, except at a somewhat superficial level, the leaders of the country have failed to "make Italians." In his attitudes toward government, his identification with the nation and its political institutions, his reactions to public policy, his views concerning third persons and voluntary organizations, and his sense of involvement in the political process, the Italian is far removed from the kinds of citizens one finds in countries like the United States or Great Britain. He is not, for example, a meaningfully participating citizen. The fact that he votes should not be misinterpreted to mean the existence of strong support for the political system, for it is the mildly compulsory voting laws which impel him to the ballot box. Nor is he even a subject in the sense of accepting as legitimate or justifiable the institutions and the outputs of the political system. He is, rather, often parochial, strongly tied to his identifications with traditional institutions and structures that have themselves been only imperfectly integrated with the political system. Moreover the Italian is frequently more than merely parochial in his response to politics. He is, in addition, isolated into mutually antagonistic sub-groups of the society, basically disinclined to engage in the pragmatic bargaining—the give and take—of a pluralistic democratic polity and at times completely alienated from the political system. His attitudes and behavior therefore do not generally contribute to the maintenance and growth of a stable democracy.

In this important sense, then, the symptoms of political malaise which are dramatically apparent in Italy today cannot be ascribed merely to existing formal institutions of government or to the failures of Italian political leadership. The Italians themselves, in their attitudes and behavior toward politics, contribute significantly to the present state of affairs. This fact is frequently noted by Italian observers and often leads them to insist in bitterness that their countrymen get exactly the kind of political system they deserve.

This latter judgment is much too harsh. I shall seek to point out that Italy's political culture grows out of a number of historical, institutional, and situational factors over which the individual Italian can at best exercise only extremely limited control. I shall also try to suggest that there are certain indications that a viable pluralistic democracy may actually emerge in Italy, particularly if those leaders who are involved in the "Opening to the Left" confront with realism and resolution some of the central problems that reinforce—indeed, actually increase—the fragmentation, isolation, and alienation so typical of the political culture.

I. Manifestations of Political Culture

As Verba's concluding chapter in this volume suggests, there are various bases for judging a society's political culture. We can ask such questions as these: What are the attitudes of Italians toward the political system, toward other actors in it, toward the output of government, and toward the political input processes? What is the political style of the country, that is, to what extent, in what manner, and with what expectations do Italians participate in the political process? What kinds of values affecting public policy are expressed, and how firmly are they held? How much information about political problems and the political system do Italians possess, and how does it impinge on political behavior? Responses to queries such as these permit us to speak of political cultures as essentially fragmented or cohesive, integrative or isolative, allegiant or alienated, parochial, subject, or participant. Although any political system, including Italy's, will include citizens who fall into all these categories, it is possible to detect a central tendency so far as political culture is concerned, and it is this central tendency which presumably will have the most telling impact on the operation of a political system.

The concept political culture as I am using it here refers not to behavior but to perceptions and attitudes—not only toward the political system but also toward the self as someone involved in the political process. As formulated by Sidney Verba in this volume, and developed by Almond and Verba at greater length elsewhere,[1] these perceptions and attitudes can be classed as "cognitive, affective, and evaluative orientations toward the political system in general, its input and output aspects, and the self as political actor." Although my comments will not adhere strictly to that particular formulation, all the following observations concerning Italian political culture can be viewed logically as falling into one or another of these categories.

Turning first to a consideration of the Italian attitudes toward the political system, it is abundantly apparent that feelings concerning the Republic are anything but unanimously positive. In the referendum of 1946, when the voters were asked to choose between the Monarchy and the Republic, nearly half of those who voted on the question opted for the Monarchy, support for which was strongly concentrated in the South, while the North voted heavily in favor of institutional transformation. Thus the present Italian Republic came into being against the wishes of a considerable portion of the electorate; and although few now seriously feel that the Monarchy can be restored, the persistent electoral appeal of the Monarchists in places like Naples and in the region of Piedmont is striking. It can be added with confidence that nostalgia for monarchical government also characterizes considerable numbers of voters who support the conservative Italian Liberal Party (P.L.I.) and the right-wing of Christian Democracy (D.C.). It is apparent that in the elections of 1963 most of the heavy losses suffered by a disintegrating Monarchist Movement (P.D.I.) were absorbed by these two parties.

On the extreme right of the political party spectrum one finds the Italian Social Movement (M.S.I.), a party made up of a combination of unreconstructed Fascists of the older generation and younger voters who share an essentially antagonistic attitude toward the Republic. The neo-Fascists mince no words about present political institutions. In the furtherance of myths and symbols such as *nation*, *order*, and *discipline* they would quickly support the actual destruction of the Republic and its replacement by some form of totalitarianism.

On the extreme left we find the Italian Communist Party (P.C.I.), which in the 1963 elections surprised almost everyone by adding over one million voters to its lists and reaching the striking figure of over

---

[1] Gabriel A. Almond and Sidney Verba, *The Civic Culture*, Princeton, 1963, Chap. 1.

one-quarter of the Italian electorate. Of course it is hazardous to infer a complete set of attitudes from the mere act of voting, and I certainly do not wish to suggest that all of the more than seven million Italians who voted for P.C.I. are in favor of the overthrow of the Republic and the creation of the dictatorship of the proletariat. This would impute a degree of ideological content to the P.C.I. vote that survey research data assure us is not there. Nor do I wish to ascribe to all of the seven million Communist Party supporters an attitude of protest against the present political system and therefore a tendency to support P.C.I. which is purely negative in its underlying motivation. Given the striking lack of information about politics and the downright absence of concern with political issues, it is clear that large numbers of Communist voters support P.C.I. for varying reasons that do not imply political attitudes or judgments. It is also probable—particularly in view of P.C.I.'s movement away from a revolutionary orientation toward an essentially electoral, even revisionist, posture—that many who support the party do not view this act as a renunciation of the existing political system. Indeed there are many Communists and Communist Party supporters who believe that a P.C.I. in power is the only efficacious means of giving concrete meaning to the Republican Constitution and the political institutions it brought into existence. There are obviously others, living at the margins of society, who support P.C.I., not because they expect it to come to power, but simply to reinforce in parliament the party that seems to be most earnestly committed to opposition on behalf of such groups.

Having introduced these reservations and cautions, it remains necessary to emphasize that since 1946 nearly one-quarter of the Italian electorate has consistently supported at the polls a party widely described by non-Communist political leaders and the mass media as inconsistent with and inimical to the Republic. The least one would infer from this phenomenon is that the attitudes of many P.C.I. voters toward the existing political system are indifferent and certainly not positive. Beyond this it is possible to suggest that the persistently strong P.C.I. vote reflects a degree of alienation from the political system which is basically out of step with a stable democracy.

Were we to conclude at this point that the three-fifths of the Italian voters who supported the Socialist Party (P.S.I.), the Christian Democrats, Republicans (P.R.I.), and Social Democrats

(P.S.D.I.) are positively oriented toward the political system, the picture painted here might not be so stark. Indeed this is exactly the inference suggested by those in and out of Italy who seek to minimize the markedly increased electoral prowess of the P.C.I. It is suggested that the impressive aspect of the 1963 election is that so many voters supported parties that are favorable to the existing political system and that explicitly make clear their intention to support and to fortify existing political institutions.

Two observations must be made regarding this conclusion. First, it is apparent that the Socialist Party is neither unanimous nor consistent in its support of the present political system. As has been true of most of its history, P.S.I. contains a Maximalist wing which, in its pronouncements at least, is even more revolutionary than the Communist Party. Indeed in January 1964, following P.S.I. collaboration in the Government led by Aldo Moro, a portion of the extreme left created a schism and formed another Socialist Party (P.S.I.U.P.), led by Tullio Vechietti. Within leadership circles this faction has until recently counted for almost one-half of those who occupy governing positions in the party. Presumably these anti-system leaders reflect the views of the party militants and much of the rank and file. Presumably, too, their views are supported by those who cast preferential ballots for the Maximalist candidates in national elections. In 1963 it is apparent that in regions like Emilia-Romagna, Tuscany, and Umbria a considerable number of these extreme Left voters moved over to support P.C.I. Nevertheless, if attitudes toward the political system are to be inferred from the act of voting, it is simply untenable to conclude that P.S.I. voters are essentially pro-system in their attitudes.

Second, and more critically, we now know not merely that Italians are overwhelmingly ignorant about political affairs and basically uninterested in the political process but also that their identification with the political system is minimal and their attitudes toward it startlingly negative. Lack of knowledge of and interest in political issues has been many times demonstrated by postwar opinion surveys. In April 1947, following the 1946 referendum on the Monarchy and in the midst of the campaign to get the new constitution ratified, 68 per cent of the Italians had not read the document and 38 per cent of those surveyed said they had no intention of reading it.[2] Ten years

---

[2] Pierpaolo Luzzatto-Fegiz, *Il volto sconosciuto dell'italia: Dieci anni di sondaggi DOXA*, Milan, 1956, p. 419.

later a study of 3,000 Italians between the ages of 18 and 25 years revealed that a decisive 72.7 per cent of them had little or no interest in national and international affairs. In the case of women, notoriously uninvolved in the political system except when they vote massively as they are instructed by their priests, the figure reaches a striking 86 per cent.[3] A collaborative study of the 1958 national elections revealed that a strikingly large number of Italians were unexposed to the political campaign, uninformed concerning major political issues, and either uninterested or actually antagonistic toward the activities of the national legislature. Although these parochial and alienative characteristics were much more pronounced among Italian women, they were significantly present among men as well.[4]

The most impressive recent evidence of this phenomenon comes from a five-country study (including Italy) of political culture conducted by Almond and Verba,[5] who found among Italians exactly the widespread rejection of the political system that is typical of a parochial, fragmented, isolative, and alienative political culture. For example, not more than one-half of the Italians surveyed felt that the national government affected them in any way. Among the five populations surveyed, Italians scored lowest on the dimension of following political affairs regularly and highest by far in responding that they *never* followed accounts of political and governmental affairs.[6] Only 16 per cent of the Italians indicated that they followed newspaper accounts concerning politics as often as once a week, while the next lowest figure was twice that number for Mexicans.[7]

More is involved here than the finding that Italians scored lowest on the amount of political information they possess. For example, a study of the relationship between level of political information and attitudes toward the political system points up the fact that lack

[3] Joseph LaPalombara and Jerry B. Waters, "Values, Expectations and Political Predispositions of Italian Youth," *Midwest Journal of Political Science*, Vol. 5, February, 1961, p. 47.
[4] Alberto Spreafico and Joseph LaPalombara, eds. *Elezioni e comportamento politico in Italia*, Milan, 1963. See especially the chapters by Alberto Spreafico, Paolo Ammassari, Mattei Dogan, and Joseph LaPalombara.
[5] Almond and Verba, *op.cit.* Countries included in this study are Italy, the United States, Great Britain, Germany, and Mexico. The data derive from national surveys of approximately 1,000 respondents plus a smaller number of intensive life-history interviews. For a discussion of the methodological problems of the study, see Chap. 2 and Appendix A.
[6] The percentages, by country, of those who never follow accounts of political and governmental affairs are: Italy, 62 per cent; Mexico, 44 per cent; the United Kingdom, 32 per cent; Germany, 25 per cent; and the United States, 19 per cent. *Ibid.*, Chap. 3.
[7] *ibid.*

of information seldom inhibits the Italian from making evaluative judgments of the political system and its output—evaluative judgments that are frequently negative and destructive.[8] Almond and Verba also found that 42 per cent of the Italians were alienated toward governmental output and 63 per cent of them alienated toward the input activities of the political system. This sense of alienation is dramatically depicted by the Italians' responses to the open-end question: "Speaking generally, what are the things about this country that you are most proud of?" The percentage distribution of some of the responses obtained by Almond and Verba by country and by some of the more salient categories are given in the tabulation below.[9]

	Country				
Category	U.S.A.	U.K.	Germany	Italy	Mexico
Government, political institutions	85	46	7	3	30
Social legislation	13	18	6	1	2
Economic system	23	10	33	3	24
Contribution to the arts	1	6	11	16	9
Physical attributes of country	5	10	17	25	22
Nothing or Don't Know	4	10	15	27	16

One is impressed by the small number of Italians who spontaneously mentioned pride in political and governmental institutions and by the relatively high proportion who replied either "nothing" (8 per cent) or "don't know" (19 per cent). Only Germany, similar to Italy on many dimensions, manifested a similar lack of pride in the political system, although there was a marked difference between attitudes toward the economic system, notwithstanding that Italy has also experienced a postwar economic "miracle" and that the Italian rate of economic growth in recent years has been nothing short of spectacular.

I would suggest that not even the 25 per cent figure concerning the physical attributes of the country is a sign of national integration. What the Italian often means when he boasts about the beauty of Italy is his perception—sometimes accurate, sometimes grossly

---

[8] See Paolo Ammassari, "Opinione politica e scelta elettorale," in Spreafico and LaPalombara, *op.cit.*, pp. 733-779.

[9] Source: *ibid.* Chap. 4.

romanticized—of his village, province, or region. Thus I would suggest that his favorable responses in many cases represent a manifestation of the very parochialism, or *campanilismo* as the Italians call it, that is consistent with the kind of political culture I am ascribing to Italy. If the titles of popular songs can be used as a rough index of this phenomenon, I would point out that very few of them deal with the physical or other attributes of the country as a whole but focus rather on the towns, cities, and regions. *"Come sei bella Roma"* or *"Sorrento"* are symbolic of the Italian's tendency not to conceptualize politically beyond his home town.

There are many other indicators of Italian political culture that we might cite. For example, Italian attitudes toward the bureaucracy combine feelings of disdain, hostility, frustration, and hopeless resignation.[10] To some extent these are deeply engrained attitudes born of centuries of arbitrary action from governments far removed from the people and scarcely in a position to understand their needs. For many Italians the government remains the heavy-handed police, the tax collector, and the omnipotent prefect. For others it is an inefficient and insensitive bureaucracy heavily featherbedded and staffed by men and women who prefer to think of people as subjects rather than citizens. This general dissatisfaction with the bureaucracy is widely reflected in the verbal and written outpourings of intellectuals who have thus far insisted in vain on a major reform of public administration. Persistence of present patterns therefore serves to reinforce the antagonism toward public authority, the strong belief that government is essentially corrupt, and the resigned acceptance that little or nothing can be done to rectify an unwanted situation.

Among intellectual circles too there is growing hostility toward Italy's political parties. The intellectuals complain that Italy is politically run by a party elite—a *partitocrazia*—in which the party bureaucrats—the *apparato*—dominate to the point of dictating to lawmakers and making or unseating governments. Some of these observations are valid, as demonstrated for example in the sharp increase in the national legislature of deputies who are professional or career political party leaders.[11] Nevertheless the way in which the problem itself is treated in Italy suggests on the part of writers a preference for a solution of the De Gaulle type which adds to the quantum of

[10] For trenchant criticisms of the Italian bureaucracy, see the following two books by Ernesto Rossi: *Lo stato industriale*, Bari, 1953; *Il malgoverno*, Bari, 1955.

[11] For a minute documentation of this, see the excellent and ground-breaking study by Giovanni Sartori, ed. *Il parlamento* (Naples, 1963), pp. 323-331.

antagonistic attitudes toward the present political system. The point is that even among those Italians who claim to want to support and invigorate Republican political institutions there exist toward parties (presumably vital on the input side of the political process) attitudes that are inconsistent with a pluralistic democracy.

Closely associated with the attitudes toward parties are the views held concerning other actors and groups in the political process. These views make it obvious that the general atmosphere is one of fear, suspicion, distrust, and hostility. As Almond and Verba discovered, more than two-thirds of the Italians report that they *never* discuss politics with other people.[12] To a degree, of course, this phenomenon is to be explained by the wholesale lack of information about and interest in politics already noted. However, it is also an important reflection of the distrust and suspicion with which the Italian views the political process. Italian peasants, for example, are strongly socialized in the belief that it is safer to keep one's affairs and political views strictly to oneself. This attitude which is essentially endemic in Italy (although Italians with more education and from higher social strata feel greater freedom to engage in such discourse) is natural in a society in which jobs are awarded or denied, business with the government expedited or impeded, passports and emigration permits issued or refused, and other values distributed or subtracted in part on the basis of one's political affiliation. It is no accident therefore that in all public opinion surveys relatively large numbers of Italians flatly refuse to divulge their political party affiliations, to indicate how they voted in past elections, or to suggest which political party they intend to support in a given election.[13]

The fact is that the typical Italian feels that elections are contests among mutually and fundamentally antagonistic groups—between the "we" and "the enemy." It is assumed that the winners will take advantage of and exploit the losers. For many the election is described

---

[12] Almond and Verba, *op.cit.*, Chap. 4. The comparable and really striking percentages for the other four countries are: U.S.A., 24 per cent; United Kingdom, 29 per cent; Germany, 39 per cent; and Mexico, 61 per cent.

[13] The problem of either refusals or "don't know" responses to such questions in survey research has been a thorny one throughout the postwar years. Not even the obvious projective question, "Which party do you think is most worthy of support in this election?" loosens up the Italian respondents' reticence. See Luzzatto-Fegiz, *op.cit.*, and LaPalombara and Waters, *op.cit.* Almond and Verba, *op.cit.*, Chap. 4, found that almost one-third of their respondents would provide no information on this score. Comparable figures on the remaining four countries are: United States, 2 per cent; United Kingdom, 2 per cent; Mexico, 1 per cent; and Germany, 16 per cent.

as essentially a life-and-death struggle between opposed and irreconcilable ways of life.

One consequence of this at an organizational and participatory level is extreme polarization of feeling which is in part reflected in the proliferation of political parties. The most serious breaches are between the Communists on the Left and the Christian Democrats, who represent the expression of Catholic ideology. Even though the strongest polarized utterances involve the relationships between Communists and neo-Fascists, it is obvious that the basic postwar political struggle is the one being fought between Marxism and Catholicism. Communist militants and supporters do not easily abide Catholics and readily articulate their antagonism toward them. Catholics in turn—and particularly the militants in the branches of Catholic Action—are quick to make clear that the battle against Communists is essentially a modern crusade.

Such highly charged views toward other actors in the political system characterize the other parties as well. The Radicals, for example, broke from the Italian Liberal Party because of the alleged reactionary economic views of the latter. Relationships between the two groups are intensely antagonistic. Both Radicals and Republicans are also strongly anti-clerical and keep up a rapid-fire assault against religious interference in secular affairs. The Social Democrats (P.S.D.I.), who emerged from an earlier schism within the Socialist Party, manifest not merely the usual revisionist opposition to the Communist Party but also great antagonism toward both P.C.I. and P.S.I., based on issues of foreign policy. Those who support M.S.I. are basically alienated from all other political parties, reject Republican institutions, and assume that only the neo-Fascists are reliable custodians of the nation's honor and integrity. Thus opponents are not viewed simply as such but really as traitors, fifth columnists, and otherwise sinister persons. It is partly because of attitudes such as these, held by many among the political elite and the masses, that incidents of physical violence occur not merely in the public squares but in the national legislature as well.

The fragmentation that grows out of this mutual suspicion and antagonism is dramatically portrayed when we look at Italy's secondary associations. In the field of labor, for example, the largest confederation recruits primarily Communist and Socialist workers, another appeals essentially to Catholics, a third is basically Social Democratic and Republican in membership, and a fourth is openly neo-Fascist. These organizations are deeply involved in politics, and their activities extend considerably beyond those concerning wages and working conditions.[14] They reproduce and intensify in the arena of organized labor the intense feelings that characterize interpolitical party relationships. Policies are recommended, tactics are devised, and positions are assumed on the basis of ideological considerations or strategic decisions designed to favor not the Italian worker as such but a particular isolated sub-group of the society.

The suspicion and distrust that this basic orientation generates are evidenced in the polemics engaged in by trade union leaders. Communists and Socialists accuse Christian Democrats of "white" trade unionism, meaning a form of Catholic intervention in the labor field designed to deny meaningful gains to the working class. Christian Democrats in turn accuse the Communist and Socialist leaders of using organized labor strictly as a political instrument in the interest of fomenting chaos and possibly revolution at home and of making the Italian worker a slavish object of Soviet foreign policy. Christian Democrats also criticize the Social Democrat and Republican labor leaders for fragmenting the labor movement on weak ideological grounds at a time when the need for a unified front against the extreme left is paramount. And so it goes in the endless arguments among the labor movement's elite.

The Italian workers respond to this fragmentation and isolation in a variety of ways. Many of them have simply withdrawn in disgust from any kind of trade union affiliation. Of those who remain, many develop exactly the kind of sectarian isolation and antagonism toward "outsiders" that is typical of their own leadership. Some of them, according to labor organizers who have talked with me, hedge their bets by accepting membership cards in several of the competing unions and paying their dues to none. This is the counterpart in the trade union field of the alleged practice of shrewd South Italian families of sending one son into each of the major competing political parties, thus assuring survival no matter which group achieves power.

It is needless to prolong this recitation. The point is that whenever one is speaking of agricultural organizations, professional associations, athletic clubs, youth groups, women's federations, university student movements—really the entire gamut of voluntary associa-

[14] See Joseph LaPalombara, *The Italian Labor Movement: Problems and Prospects*, Ithaca, 1957; Daniel Horowitz, *The Italian Labor Movement*, Cambridge, 1963.

tions—one is likely to find them fragmented into at least Communist, Socialist, Catholic, and Fascist factions. Thus to some extent each of the parties tends to create its own exclusive infrastructure of functional and auxiliary organizations which serve both to inculcate and also to reinforce the kinds of attitudes toward politics and political actors just discussed.

It is important to understand that the manner in which people perceive the environment has much to do with the style of political behavior that characterizes individuals and organizations. Industrialists and leaders of industrial organizations such as *Confindustria* correctly perceive the Italian environment as extremely hostile toward the private entrepreneur. Many of these men whom I interviewed[15] stressed that Italians do not sufficiently appreciate the vital creative role played by the private entrepreneur. Rather than welcome the dynamic role in the nation's development played by the industrialist, the Italian considers him a callous exploiter of labor and someone who should be subjected to constant harassment. These presumed attitudes are said to permeate even the political leadership groups of the country so that the parties, in dealing with industrialists, behave demagogically, fomenting hatred and aggressiveness against the industrial class. Thus the industrialist sees himself as involved in vicious class warfare from which there is no escape and in which the posture of the industrial group remains largely defensive.

Perceptions such as these among industrialists date back to the beginning of Italian industrial development and were intensified after the turn of the present century when Socialist mass movements became a major factor in Italian politics. In 1922, and later, that fear of the working class led the industrialists to support the rise of the Fascist party. There is no question that many of the violent and punitive escapades of Fascist *squadristi* against leaders and followers of the political left were financed by contributions from industry. Once the industrialists got into the political driver's seat, they in turn proceeded to behave exactly as the workers expected: the industrialist was glorified, freedom of speech was curtailed, the trade union movement was placed under tight totalitarian control, strikes were outlawed, rival secondary associations were driven out of existence, and a wide spectrum of sanctions was applied against deviants and dissenters. In short, the industrialists demonstrated that their op-

---

[15] See LaPalombara, *Interest Groups in Italian Politics*, Princeton, 1964, Chap. 11, for a detailed elaboration of the point I am making here.

ponents were to be treated fundamentally as enemies. As a consequence the hostility that the industrialist now feels is real; it stems from empirical experience.

In the present era the Italian industrialist has largely withdrawn from overt participation in the political process. While some of *Confindustria's* leaders lament that the legislature contains too few industrial leaders, they add that the typical entrepreneur has no stomach for the rough and tumble of Italian political campaigns. One of them, for example, insists that the industrialists would be quite willing to engage in physical combat with the Communists but that they will not demean themselves by coming before the public in search of votes that will never be awarded. Thus the industrialist and his professional associations prefer political activities that have low visibility: financing reliable individual candidates and political parties, intervening in the bureaucratic labyrinth rather than in the legislature, placing certain high-level bureaucrats and politicians on hidden retainers, and so on. It is the proliferation of this kind of activity in recent years that leads increasing numbers of Italians to speak disgustedly of *il sottogoverno*—the under-government—as the pervasive morass in which political institutions are corrupted.

The industrialists are but one illustration of the fact that there is an intimate connection between perception and political style. Essentially the same point could be made concerning organized Catholicism. Italian Catholics view society as lying in an almost hopeless state of damnation, owing to a denial of Christ and his teaching which, by a complicated route, can be traced to the Protestant heresy. Liberalism, Socialism, and Communism are direct emanations of this heresy, and it is natural therefore that these movements should manifest an unremitting antagonism toward the Catholic Church. Notions of class conflict and attitudes of anti-clericalism are typical outcomes of man's failure to understand Christ's message as interpreted by the Catholic hierarchy. As in many times in the past, a besieged Church has no alternative except to seek to protect itself by any means available.

There are many ways in which organized Catholicism in Italy responds to this perceived challenge. In the political sphere it has been massively involved since 1948, when Civic Committees were created to save the country (i.e. the Church) from the threat of Communism. Thus, as noted above, there are Catholic organizations corresponding to every facet of the Italian's existence. In providing this kind of infrastructure for millions of Italians the Catholic Church seeks to isolate them from other groups and organizations in society whose values and possible influence the Church considers damaging.

Moreover Catholicism is not satisfied merely to provide associational opportunities for workers, farmers, peasants, men, women, children, doctors, lawyers, nurses, artists, writers, actors, and so on. Through a tightly disciplined secular arm—Catholic Action—consisting of over four million members, it exercises influence over the Christian Democratic Party, infiltrates the bureaucracy, exercises a veto over provincial and local governmental affairs—and does all of this on the basis of the central assumption that all those in Italy who are not positively *for* the Catholic Church are dangerous enemies.[16]

One might expect Catholics to be less distrustful of others—or at least less rigid in their partisanship—than, say, the Italian Communists. The evidence at our disposal suggests that exactly the opposite is so. When Di Renzo applied a modified version of the Rokeach dogmatism scale to a sample of national legislators, he found that those representing the political left were less dogmatic, less closed in their views of others, than any other group. Those who scored highest on the scale were the Christian Democrats and the neo-Fascists.[17] Similarly, Almond and Verba sought to discover the degree of "open" or "closed" partisanship, but, once again, it was the Catholic Christian Democrats who scored significantly higher on this measure than Communists and particularly Socialists. These authors found in Italy an extreme form of clerico-traditional conservatism. They thus conclude that:

"Italy presents us with the curious anomaly of a political system in which the formal democratic constitution is supported in large part by traditional-clerical elements who are not democratic at all, and not even political in a specialized sense of the term, and opposed by a left-wing which, at least in part and at the rank-and-file voter level rather than among the party elite, manifests a form of open partisanship which is consistent with a democratic system."[18]

---

[16] For a detailed documentation of Catholic Action's role in Italian politics, see *ibid.*, Chaps. 8-10.

[17] Gordon Di Renzo, "A Study in Political Dogmatism," unpublished Ph.D. dissertation, Notre Dame University, 1963.

[18] Almond and Verba, *op.cit.*, Chap. 5.

FRAGMENTATION, ISOLATION, ALIENATION

Although those of the political left may be less rigidly partisan, there is little question about their sharing the sense of mutual distrust that is endemic on the Peninsula. It is this distrust that leads to the conclusion, widespread in Italy, that it does not pay to participate in politics and that it is not possible through peaceful and regularized channels to have much of an impact on public policy. This sense of frustration and hopelessness in turn leads to a political style in which the language of demand is dangerously inflated and in which there are periodic manifestations of anomic political behavior.

In a strict sense, anomic political behavior—riots, demonstrations, revolutions—should be spontaneous, and there are examples of this that one could cite for Italy. Thus it is certainly true that on occasion the forceful occupation of farm land by Italian peasants is generated spontaneously out of a sense of desperate futility concerning attempts to get ameliorative private or public policy. As a matter of general practice, however, most such occurrences are the premeditated work of political parties or interest groups. Pregnant women, for example, do not spontaneously appear lying prone on roads leading from Montecatini sulphur mines in order to keep scab-loaded trucks from passing. Mutilated veterans who converge on Rome en masse and wave their artificial limbs in protest over pension policies do not get there because of the widely shared intuition that a demonstration before a ministry will bring immediate results. Italians who demonstrate and riot over alleged germ warfare in Korea, over the execution of the Rosenbergs, or over the killing of several workers by trigger-happy Italian police rarely come together in violence without some sort of deliberate leadership.

Even though cases of violence are more infrequent now than a few years ago, it would be a mistake to obscure the important and persistent role that anomic political behavior has played in Italy's history. Although not so deeply involved in such a destructive political style as are many Latin American countries, Italy is still far removed on this dimension from what one generally finds in the Anglo-American political system.[19] Periodic violence is exactly what one would expect to find when the degree of intergroup antagonism,

---

[19] I do not wish to push this last distinction too far in view of the violent occurrences in the United States over the issue of racial integration. However, I do believe it is possible to say that violence plays a more important role in Italy than in Britain or the United States. Indeed, there are many Italians who fear that the present political system may still someday be destroyed by violent means.

fragmentation, and of alienation from the political system reaches the proportion it has in Italy. The Italian who is compelled by law to vote sees no rationale for engaging in other peaceful participatory activities affecting politics. At best his views toward his political system are those of disinterested neutrality; at worst he is in some way available to take part in exactly the kinds of aggressive activities that may bring present political institutions toppling to the ground. This is as true of the intellectual who is a rigid Marxist, a Catholic Corporativist, or a critic of political parties, as it is of the distraught peasant or the professional party bully who is impelled toward violence.

This picture of Italy's political culture is admittedly stark, and it will be objected to by many Italians who would say that the mere survival of the Republic since 1946 is a miracle in itself. There will also be those in Italy who object to a description of Italian psychology which is essentially Hobbesian and not sufficiently attuned to the "positive" aspects of Italian cognition, affects, and evaluations concerning the political system and those who are actors in it. Regarding the first point, I would respond that I am aware of some forces working toward change and shall discuss them later. Regarding the second observation, I am compelled to assert that on the basis of the evidence at my disposal the attitudes Italians maintain are essentially Hobbesian and that the history of the country suggests that, when the state of nature becomes too intolerable, it is also a Hobbesian solution concerning government to which Italians turn. The fact that republican government remains relatively intact means neither that d'Azeglio's Italians have materialized nor that the Republic can survive many more years on its culturally uncertain and problematical foundations.

II. The Sources of Italian Political Culture

We may now ask what are the conditions that help to bring a fragmented, isolative, and alienative culture into existence—and to maintain it. For it is only if these conditions or factors are reasonably well understood that one can hope to effect changes in the cultural dimensions of a political system. In this section I shall seek to relate Italy's political culture to certain conditions of the environment and then to certain other salient features of the political system.[20]

[20] For a more detailed discussion of the factors that are treated in this section, see my *Interest Groups in Italian Politics*, op.cit., Chaps. 2-4.

IMPERFECT INTEGRATION

All nation-states at some point in their evolution and continuing forward in varying degrees of intensity must confront the crisis of national integration. When we speak of a nation, it is necessary to conceive of it as something more than a given set of physical boundaries, political institutions, and related political behavior. Before we can speak of a nation as being more or less well integrated politically it is necessary to explore exactly those feelings and attitudes discussed in the previous section. It seems obvious that another way of describing Italy is to observe that the nation is badly integrated politically or that the crisis of integration initially confronted over a century ago remains intense and unsolved today.

In understanding why this is so it is necessary to recall that the unification of Italy was never a mass movement. With rare exceptions the *Risorgimento* attracted not the man on the street but primarily the attention and the ideological and organizational fervor of elements of the northern middle and upper classes. Moreover, as events immediately preceding and following formal unification dramatically attest, there were serious differences among the *Risorgimento* leaders as to the kind of nation-state that should be created. It is significant, for example, that what emerged under the guiding spirit of Count Cavour and the House of Savoy was not the Italy desired by either Giuseppe Mazzini or Giuseppe Garibaldi—two names which loom significantly in the movement for unification. In any event, we know that the new state began its troubled journey without the widespread or meaningful participation of the masses, with only the half-hearted support of the people south of Rome, and with the virulent, unrelenting hostility of a Catholic Church outraged over the loss of its secular powers. It was not an auspicious beginning.

It is true that the House of Savoy managed to "Piedmontize" Italy in a relatively short time, although the two major strategies utilized to accomplish that mission served to assure inadequate political integration so far as Italians in general were concerned. First, the Napoleonic administrative system, based on centralized ministries and a network of strong prefects responsible to Rome, was extended to cover the entire Peninsula. On the one hand the extension of bureaucratic power—strongly opposed by those who wanted greater regional decentralization—served to create a sense of an existing national government where none had previously existed. On the other hand the concentration of decision in a centralized authority resulted in denying Italians that very experience with political participation at the local level which is now so strikingly lacking. In their single-mindedness drive to forge a nation-state the central architects of unification lost sight of the fact that the nation is necessarily something more subtle than a constitution and a set of formal institutions. The point is that not sufficient attention was paid to the remark by d'Azeglio quoted in the opening lines of this chapter.

Second, in exchange for a central governmental posture that left the South pretty much to its own devices, Piedmont was able to "buy" the support of the southern "notables" who saw their region as a place to exploit for personal gain and certainly not as an area to develop at a pace that would someday permit the South to catch up with the North. The deals between southern prefects and those "notables," whereby the latter were returned to legislative office at Rome, are too notorious to require enumeration or analysis here. It is certain that they served to inculcate in the southern masses a gross disrespect for political institutions which has not been significantly modified over the years. Thus, just as the "notables" at the beginning of nationhood continued activities of neglect and corruption typical of Bourbon administration, contemporary activities of a newer generation of southern officeholders remained lost in that same mold. A group of political leaders seriously dedicated to the task of integration would surely have dealt differently with the South. Instead, the policies of a century have made of that area the most alienated segment of Italian society.

To be sure, with the exception of some important southern riots in the first months following unification, Sicilian restiveness following World War II, and the lingering South Tyrol problem, Italy has not been plagued with serious separatist movements. Yet the sense of national identification remains tenuous and makes it difficult for the average Italian to conceptualize about national problems, national goals, and his own role concerning them. Fascism stepped in with a desperate effort to reinforce the sense of the nation, promising in the process to recapture some of the glory that was Rome. What it delivered instead was tragicomic economic enterprise and a devastating and unwanted war. World War II gave rise to yet another major event in Italy's history—the armed anti-Fascist Resistance—which was essentially divisive rather than integrating in its consequences. Like the Renaissance and the *Risorgimento*, the Resistance was primarily a northern phenomenon serving further to increase the psychological distance between North and South.

Another vantage point from which to view imperfect political integration is that of the degree of localism or parochialism which persists in a society. Although parochialism is especially strong in the traditional South, it is also still very much in evidence north of Rome, where the localizing influence of city-states and independent duchies still survives. Thus far the mass media of communications are only partly successful in breaking down these parochial barriers. In a relatively modern region such as Tuscany, for example, residents still feel and react to the ancient hostilities among cities like Pisa, Florence, Lucca. The residents of these towns are Pisans or Florentines first and foremost, then Tuscans as distinguished from other regions of Italy, then northerners as opposed to southerners, and finally—perhaps divinely—Italians. Sentiments like these are present throughout Italy, born of centuries of political fragmentation, inadequate communications, a succession of invasions by foreign and competing powers, and by strong local political and cultural traditions. Even linguistically Italy remains divided, with the Italian language indigenous only to the regions of Tuscany and Umbria. Thus, although Italian is taught in the schools and is now understood by all but several million illiterates, local dialects, often unintelligible beyond a radius of a few kilometers, display amazing survival power. *Companilismo* has many facets; all of them working together amount to a formidable barrier against national integration.

We cannot fully understand the imperfect integration of Italy without noting the contribution to it emanating from the Catholic Church and the controversies concerning the Church's appropriate role in Italian society. It is well known that the Church strongly opposed the creation of a united Italy, that it was active in its opposition in every conceivable way, and that the final wresting of temporal power from the Vatican led directly to the *Non Expedit*, the papal prohibition against Catholics' participation in the affairs of the new state. For fifty years the Catholic Church kept its faithful isolated from the Italian state. When it finally lifted the ban against involvement in national politics, it was in no sense out of a conscious and willing acceptance of Italy. Rather, permission to enter the field of politics was a defensive gesture designed to afford the Church added protection against the growing forces of Socialism.

In the years since World War II Catholicism has loomed as the dominant force in Italian politics. The party over which the Vatican exercises often uneasy control has led the country, alone or in coalition, uninterruptedly since 1946; a vast network of Catholic interest groups is active in every conceivable political arena; within each diocese it is widely believed that nothing can happen politically that does not have the bishop's sanction; the extent of the Vatican's involvement in social welfare activities and in the vital economic and financial activities of the country is generally conceded to be vast; overt attempts by the clergy to orient the political attitudes of the masses—even to dictate legislative, administrative, and judicial decisions—often reach alarming and widely publicized proportions. Even if, as some Italians assume, the impact of the policies of Pope John XIII and Pope Paul VI will be that of forcing the Christian Democrats toward a more liberal policy, the weight of Catholicism on the Italian political system will not be substantially diminished.

That weight continues to be used primarily to protect the necessarily sectarian needs of Catholicism. In the years since World War II the political intervention of the Church has been justified on the basis of the threat to its spiritual mission represented by Marxism, primarily as fostered by the Communist Party, but also as advocated by the Socialist Party of Pietro Nenni. The rationale for this intervention was put by a recent writer in these words:

"The only case in which the church, by reason of its doctrine, descends to the level of ideology is when She finds Herself confronted by systems in which the principles of the promotion of the common good, of the salvation of the person, of the extraterrestrial end of all human action, of the origin and substance of natural law and authority, are substituted by a philosophical, ideological and therefore political platform that excludes all idea of God. This is the reason that leads to the condemnation of liberalism, for example, and of Communism, which systems, however opposed they may be to each other, are both naturalistic conceptions of human destiny."[21]

The author goes on to stress that when the Catholic Church is compelled to intervene it does so by condemning the principles of a political system and not the system's empirical institutions. This

[21] Alfonso Prandi, "L'insegnamento politico della chiesa," *Il Mulino*, Vol. 11, February 1962, p. 130. I am aware that Italian Catholicism does not represent an ideological monolith, that there are conservative and liberal—even socialist—groups that are Catholic in origin. However, it is the polarizing impact of Catholicism as a whole, and not its internal ideological divisions, that is of primary concern to us here.

may or may not be true. My point would be that in stepping into Italian politics in a massively organized way the Catholic Church intensifies the isolative character of Italian political culture at least as much as was the case when the Vatican insisted that good Catholics remain apart from the critical activities of the Italian state. By its ideologically governed intervention the Church gives rise to fundamental and essentially irreconcilable clashes between those Italians who support the Church's presence in politics and others who view such involvement as a threat to democratic institutions or to their own interests.

It is obvious of course that the kind of ideological polarization I refer to is also the outcome of the historical advent of Marxism and its permeation of Italian society. As it developed in Italy, Marxism took on a peculiarly Italian flavor, influenced in part by the fact that the philosophy's arrival in a profound sense predated Italian industrial development and in part by the powerful influence on Italian intellectuals exercised by the anarchist Bakunin. For these and other reasons Italian left-wing thought, attitudes toward existing institutions, and demands for change have generally been of the extreme variety. The Socialist Party, over most of its history after 1892, was dominated by the fire-eating "Maximalists," and not by the milder and more reasonable and compromising revisionists. The Italian Communist Party, now much stronger than P.S.I., was in part the direct outgrowth of the unwillingness of revisionist Socialist leaders to plunge Italy into revolution following World War I.

Recruiting large numbers of workers and peasants who were historically marginal to Italian society—outside the system so to speak —the parties of the left quickly developed the kinds of demands and organizational devices that served to preserve working-class isolation and sectarianism. In these isolated sub-cultures, beliefs and attitudes concerning the Italian political system were inculcated by Marxist and Anarchist political and trade union leaders. Italy's oppressed and bedeviled working class constituted a vast reservoir into which could be poured the disintegrative notions of capitalist oppression, corruption of bourgeois political institutions, class war, anti-clericalism— the whole gamut of myths and symbols, including the proletarian revolution, that make up a basically antagonistic and alienative attitude toward politics and the state. On one side, then, was the Catholic Church, molding a basically negative and distrustful view of the liberal state; on the other side, a virulent left-wing movement having essentially the same impact. In between there existed a few groups and political parties that served to counterbalance that type of impact. Thus from its beginnings as a nation-state and throughout its turbulent history Italy has been influenced by historical occurrences and crises that serve to fractionalize rather than to cement the political system, to intensify rather than to diminish the sense of divisiveness that is inimical to the achievement of national integration.

DUAL CULTURE AND ECONOMY

Another major factor strongly affecting Italian political culture is the striking difference between North and South. South of Rome the basic structures of society are "traditional"; in the North they are much more "legal-rational."[22] To be sure, neither the traditional nor the legal-rational ideal types are ever found in reality. What we find are particular cultural "mixes" in which some structures reflect particularism, some universalism; some ascription, others achievement; some which are essentially secular, others in which sacral values or considerations predominate; some that reflect the primary groups as having the highest priority and value, others that ascribe a strong place to secondary groups and associations. Despite these mixes, however, it is possible to speak of central tendency and of nuances, and it is in this last sense that we can characterize Italy as encompassing two major cultural configurations.

It is apparent that in southern Italy traditional structures and values have a strong impact on people's orientation to politics. When examining any aspect of politics in southern regions it is of the utmost importance to ask what is the impact of family, obligations of friendship, identification with a person's town or village, obligations to his religious group, and so on. It is not without reason that students of Italian politics unanimously agree that southern politics remains the politics of "notables" and their electoral clienteles. These leaders are often able to shift personal followings from one political party to another almost at will. In the political sphere the notable is the functional equivalent of the "padrone" in agriculture, the priest in the parish, or the "protector" in dealing with the government. One manifestation of this highly personal and traditional approach to political

---

[22] The terminology here is essentially Max Weber's. It is also used by Gabriel A. Almond and James Coleman, *The Politics of the Developing Areas*, Princeton, 1960, Chap. 1. Another interesting effort to provide a triadic taxonomy of bureaucratic (and presumably political) systems is in Fred W. Riggs, "Prismatic Society and Financial Administration," *Administrative Science Quarterly*, June 1960, pp. 1-46.

participation is in the relative weight of the *preference vote* which gives the Italian elector the opportunity to vote not merely for a party list but also for several individuals of his choice who appear on the selected list. Evidence at our disposal shows that use of such votes in the South is several times their use in the North.[23] Whereas the northerner tends to vote for the party, the southerner votes for the man.

Indexes of the force of traditionality in the South could be multiplied at some length. They include the place of the woman in society, the stress on the family, a curious combination of Catholicism that combines relatively modern religious practices with others based on ancient superstitions and pagan practices, primitive agricultural methods, the heavy incidence of "crimes of honor," the heavy incidence of particularism and ascription in recruitment to political and economic roles, and so on. No one who travels in the South—even in some of its larger cities—could fail to note that this vast region of Italy is at best only at the threshold of political modernity.

It is true of course that there also exist strongly traditional rural areas in the North. But, as one of Italy's better students of this problem points out, in the North the rural institutions have felt the strong impact of the urban, industrial, secular, and legal-rational centers that surround them.[24] Another way of putting this is to note that in the North the primary structures have been penetrated and influenced by secondary structures and that there is in general better integration of both primary and secondary structures with the political system, the result of which is that the political process in the North is much more characterized by achievement and universalistic norms, is more secular and rational.

The division of Italy into two major sub-cultures is a critical datum. Northern Italy differs from the South on almost every significant variable. Culturally the North is European, the South is Mediterranean; the North was exposed directly to eighteenth- and nineteenth-century European thought; these ideas permeated the South later and very imperfectly. The North is heavily industrialized, with much of Italy's national wealth concentrated in the Industrial Triangle formed by Milan, Turin, and Genoa; the South is still largely rural, with significant industrial enterprise limited to areas around Naples, Bari,

---

[23] See Giovanni Schepis, "Analasi statistica dei risultati," in Spreafico and LaPalombara, *op.cit.*, pp. 329-406.
[24] Achille Ardigò, "Le trasformazioni interne nelle campagne settentrionali e l'esodo rurale," in *Aspetti e problemi sociali dello sviluppo economico in Italia*, Bari, 1959, pp. 39-54.

and Catania. Administratively the North was strongly influenced by the French and Austrians who occupied that area; the South, on the other hand, acquired the less dynamic ways of the Spanish Bourbons, who contributed little to economic development and who encouraged the rigid preservation of class and caste which is apparent to this day.

By comparison to the North, the South is desperately poor, and the data indicate that during recent years of rapid economic development the gap between the two regions has actually widened. The mean economic plight of the *bracciante*—the agricultural day laborer—rivals what one would find in some of the most underdeveloped countries in the world. The southerner produces more children than the northerner, is the victim of more disease, travels on inferior roads, is exposed to inadequate schools and inferior teachers, does not have adequate public services, and is much more the victim of the elements, whether they be physical or human.

Whether one thinks of diet or recreation, transportation or agricultural tools, indoor plumbing or medical care, income or working conditions, the per capita quality or availability of these amenities is always superior in the North. The notion that the South Italian is essentially a philosopher, inclined to sing happy ballads in the face of his plight, is a grotesque invention of the travel posters. In the face of conditions such as these the southerner is much more likely to invade large landholdings or to become completely anomic. At the very least he develops toward politics both an abject willingness to be manipulated by men of wealth and power and a total disrespect for the political institutions of the country.

Thus the South is not unlike many of the so-called underdeveloped countries. It is deeply steeped in tradition; it is economically backward; it lays great stress on the importance of family, religious, and village primary structures. As Banfield found in one southern Italian village, loyalty to the nuclear family can be so extreme as to make it impossible for the southerner to engage in cooperative civic activity. Where "amoral familism" prevails, where the nuclear family's gain must be maximized at the expense of everything else and all those who are not family members are considered enemies, attitudes toward politics and the political system are likely to be essentially disintegrative. In addition, such extreme traditional loyalties will inhibit the development of voluntary associations that are important as instruments of secondary political socialization. These critical means of responsible induction into the political system are notoriously lacking in the South. People who seek to develop trade unions, professional associations, and similar organizations south of Rome encounter primarily frustrating obstacles.[25]

North and South are hostile toward each other, and this fact contributes considerably to the country's lack of political consensus and integration. The northerner describes his countrymen to the South as indolent and shiftless, *furbo*, or crafty in their human relationships, illiterate or at least ignorant and therefore incapable of developing or managing modern economic or commercial enterprise, politically corrupt and prone to use public administration as a dumping ground for sons who are incapable of doing anything else. As in all stereotypes, there are some elements of truth in this description. Centuries of having to deal with ruthless absentee landlords and dishonest land managers have made the southern peasant somewhat crafty and suspicious, characteristics which have not been modified in the least by land reform laws that continue to be administered particularistically on the basis of religious, social, and political considerations. Similarly, what appears to be a certain amount of indolence (e.g. the *siesta*, a slower pace in most physical activity, loitering in the public squares, and so on) can be ascribed to such things as climate, dietary deficiencies, unemployment, and the like.

It is also true that southerners are found in public administration in greatly disproportionate numbers. The causes of this are mixed. In the first place, the southerner inherited from the Bourbon invaders the notion that the highest status occupation was that of the public administrator trained as a lawyer and given real power over the lives of many people, a notion directly comparable to what one now finds in many of the post-colonial new states. Second, where land is not sufficient to occupy all members of relatively large families some of the sons of large landholders naturally filter into the bureaucracy, treating it either as a sinecure or as an opportunity for corruption, or both. Third, public employment serves in part to alleviate unemployment, in part to absorb the excessive number of college graduates trained in the law. Finally, in an industrially underdeveloped area public employment is preferred as offering the greatest security.

On this last point we found marked differences between northern

---

[25] For a discussion of the differences between North and South so far as the incidence of interest group organization and membership is concerned, see LaPalombara, *Interest Groups in Italian Politics*, *op.cit.*, Chap. 5.

and southern youth. A sample of almost 3,000 Italians between ages 18 and 25 were asked: "If you could choose, would you in general prefer to work for a private firm or be an employee of a state agency?" A significant 44 per cent of all respondents opted for public employment and indicated that the security or lack of risk afforded by such employment was the principal maximizing factor. When the number of responses is broken down by geographic region, however, the results shown in Table 1 are obtained.[26]

TABLE 1: PERCENTAGE PREFERENCE FOR PRIVATE OR PUBLIC EMPLOYMENT, BY MAJOR GEOGRAPHIC REGION

Preferred Employment	*North* (N = 1,288)	*Central* (N = 491)	*South* (N = 860)	*Insular* (N = 323)
Private Firm (869)	38.0	28.6	21.4	17.0
Public Agency (1,308)	31.8	46.9	55.2	59.8
No Preference (779)	29.8	24.5	23.3	23.8
No Response (6)	0.4	0.0	0.1	0.0

Thus the farther South one moves, the greater the tendency to seek employment in the bureaucracy. This preference is directly related to the lack of alternative job opportunities, to poverty, and to grim expectations about one's economic future. As a result it is true not only that the Italian bureaucracy recruits primarily from among southerners, but also that, for many who go into the bureaucracy, the step is not a positive one but one dictated by necessity and limited expectations regarding alternative employment. It is little wonder, then, that Italian bureaucrats tend unduly to emphasize status, to treat Italians with scorn and disrespect, and therefore to reinforce the widely held negative view of the bureaucracy.

Moreover there is evidence that the "southernization" (*meridionalizzazione*) of the bureaucracy is actually on the increase. Northern university graduates are easily finding employment in industry, particularly if they are trained in technical or scientific fields. Some bureaucratic positions remain unfilled; many others are quickly absorbed by southerners trained in law. Another aspect of this situation is that, because of their traditional dominance of Italian administrative agencies, southerners have managed to capture a disproportionate number of top-level administrative positions. Thus one student finds that 50 per cent of the important directors general in the ministries

[26] LaPalombara and Waters, *op.cit.*, pp. 44-45.

come from cities and towns with populations of less than 20,000. Furthermore, when one looks at these men in terms of their geographic origin, the results shown in Table 2 obtain:[27]

TABLE 2: PERCENTAGE DISTRIBUTION OF DIRECTORS GENERAL, BY GEOGRAPHIC ORIGIN, COMPARED WITH PROPORTION OF ITALIAN POPULATION RESIDING IN EACH REGION

Geographic Region	Directors General	Resident Population
North	11.5	36.8
Central	26.0	25.6
South	46.9	25.2
Insular	15.6	12.4
Total	100.0	100.0

In some of the ministries the prevalence of southerners as directors general is overwhelming. It is 75 per cent or above in the ministries of the treasury, labor and social security, public works, and the interior. It reaches 67 per cent in the ministry of industry and commerce and 100 per cent in the ministry of tourism and entertainment. Furthermore the situation is not likely to change in the near future, for as one moves from the oldest to the youngest directors general, the presence of southerners among them actually increases![28]

There is, then, some justification for the northerner's assumption that the bureaucracy is shot through with men who represent the most backward and traditional areas of the country. The Italian expects to find—and frequently does—that the bureaucracy is particularistic in its distribution of value, that both its internal rewards and its response to citizens are not based on achievement norms, and that its heavy reliance on those trained in the law makes dealing with the bureaucracy a bedlam of formalism and legalistic norms. For the northern entrepreneur bent on developing or exploiting the country economically the bureaucracy looms either as an inimical, unwieldy machine or as something to be corrupted in the interest of moving ahead. The upshot of it all is that the antagonism between North and South is frequently translated into antagonism toward the political system as a whole.

Interregional antipathy is fully reciprocated by the South and also has its political cultural consequences. Generations of southerners

[27] See Alessandro Taradel, "La burocrazia italiana: provenienza e collocazione dei direttori generali," *Tempi Moderni*, Vol. 6, April 1963, pp. 12-13.
[28] *ibid.*, pp. 10-15.

have lamented the crass way in which governments dominated by northerners ignored the nagging problem of southern economic development.[29] True, it is recognized that the South failed to develop the kind of political leadership that would have made development the price of unification or of continued support for the House of Savoy. Instead southern deputies were usually corrupt men whose support was made available to the highest bidder. Nevertheless it was a northerner like Giovanni Giolitti who perfected the notorious practice of parliamentary *trasformismo* when he might have turned more of his extraordinary energies to the solution of what was and remains the country's major problem. In the face of this history there are many in the South who argue that the economic expansion of the North took place at the South's expense, and that all of that exploitation was both encouraged and facilitated by legislative and administrative intervention. The general attitudes toward the political system that emerge from this bitter reflection are not those associated with a healthy democratic state.

RIGID SOCIAL STRATIFICATION

The antipathy Italians feel toward each other, which is so intimately a part of Italian political culture, is closely related to the system of social stratification. By American standards Italy evinces a fairly rigid stratification system with low mobility and high class conflict. Class lines are not easily crossed, and the social barriers and distance in the country result from attitudes and behavior patterns which have been institutionalized over several centuries.

As in everything else, the North and South differ on this dimension. The North continues to feel the impact of industrialization and of the changes in the social system that accompany it. A heavier incidence of skilled and reasonably well-remunerated labor, mechanized agriculture, better communications, greater use of educational facilities, and the like induce a degree of social dynamism that cannot be detected in the South. As one would expect about an industrial society, a middle class of growing proportions and importance does exist in the North. It consists of highly skilled industrial workers, independent artisans, small businessmen and shopkeepers, white-collar workers engaged in service and industrial occupations, and intermediate-level public servants. Turin is called the "Detroit of Italy"

[29] There is a vast literature on "the problem of the South." The interested reader can fruitfully consult, Bruno Caizzi, *Antologia della questione meridionale*, 2d edn., Milan, 1955.

not merely because both cities produce automobiles but also because Turin manifests sociocultural patterns typical of large industrial communities.

Analogies are dangerous, however, and should not be pushed too far. For example, the P.C.I. vote in Turin in 1963 was 4.6 per cent greater than in 1958, better than the net gain registered by the Communists in Italy as a whole.[30] This suggests that the extreme in politics continues to appeal to considerable numbers even in areas where the rate of economic growth in recent years has been most spectacular. It suggests too that one should not lose sight of the fact that the industrial North contains tens of thousands of semiskilled or unskilled workers, peasant sharecroppers, agricultural day laborers of the Po Valley, desperately poor farmers who occupy the hilly and mountainous regions, and the unemployed. These groups on the lowest strata of the social system do not see many channels of future social mobility.

At the top of the North's social hierarchy one finds industrial owners and managers, absentee landlords from the South, top-level bureaucrats, operators of large-scale agricultural enterprises, affluent merchants, financiers, and the more successful members of the liberal professions. Italians are self-consciously concerned about the moral degeneration of the socioeconomic elite, as is evidenced by such motion pictures as *La dolce vita* and Antonioni's caustic and bitter trilogy, *L'Aventura, La notte*, and *L'eclisse*. Motion pictures like these seem in part to reinforce the view that great social distances separate the classes in Italy.

Despite its relative economic affluence and growing modernity the North is not free of the symptoms of virulent class conflict. The industrial worker tends to see the industrialist in negative terms—as an exploiter of human labor who refuses to recognize man's dignity. The industrialist in turn has not yet evolved into the type of enlightened capitalist to be found in Anglo-American societies. At best, management's attitudes toward labor is condescending. At worst, management will see the plant as personal and inviolable property and consider trade union leaders as revolutionary upstarts bent on closing the social distance between the *padrone* and the worker.

It is apparent that rigid class differences in the management-labor relationship grow in part out of the basic structure of Italian industry.

[30] For a very interesting comparative figure on the Italian parties over several elections and by geographic region and major city, see the tables in *Tempi Moderni*, Vol. 6, April 1963, pp. 75-86.

With the exception of such giant enterprises as FIAT, Pirelli, Montecatini, Marzotto, and Italcementi, Italian industry is extremely fragmented. The 1951 Census revealed that Italy's 4,300,000 workers are spread over 680,000 firms! Of the latter, only 312 employed over 1,000 workers. Eighty-nine per cent of all of the firms were classified as the property of a single owner.[31]

Thus, while Italian industry is dominated by a handful of giants, most industrial workers find themselves in work situations that are tailor-made for the Marxist propagandists. In this context one of Italy's leading sociologists finds essentially three kinds of relationships between management and labor. The first of these is *authoritarian paternalism* wherein a single family owns the enterprise and is therefore the only source of power within it. The owner demands from his employee absolute and undeviating loyalty, and any effort to organize a trade union in this setting will be considered an act of personal betrayal. The worker is expected to be grateful for his work, to know his place, and to maintain traditional distance between himself and the padrone. There is no question that to the latter the system of social stratification which differentiates him from the worker is more important than possibly higher profits. As Ferrarotti notes, "The key value in this first type of rapport is obedience or pure subordination."[32]

Ferrarotti also cites *manipulative paternalism* and *democratic paternalism* as other types of labor-management relationships, but the evolution of either requires a breakdown of the single-family ownership of the plant.[33] For our purposes it is sufficient to note that the overwhelming proportion of Italy's industrial workers find themselves in work situations that continue to reflect the class structure and social conditions of a preindustrial society. Moreover it is important to recognize that both managers and workers understand this fact, even find security in the norms of stratification, and behave toward each other on the basis of the class-conflict formulations that grow out of the system.

As one would expect, class lines are even more rigidly maintained in the South. There the extremes of wealth and poverty are more pronounced than in most countries of the West. An enormous gap

---

[31] See Franco Ferrarotti, "L'evoluzione dei rapporti fra direzioni aziendali e rapprasentanti operai nell'Italia dell doppoguerra," in Atti del IV Convegno Mondiale di Sociologia, *Aspetti e problemi sociali dello sviluppo economico in Italia, op.cit.*, pp. 137-138.

[32] *ibid.*, p. 142.

[33] *ibid.*, pp. 142-144.

separates the worker and peasant from the clerk or salaried person. An even greater one divides all of these from the southern nobility and landowners. Class differences can be easily detected from the way people dress, the food they consume, the manner in which they address each other, the kind of recreation they enjoy, and so on. The social elite demand—and get—deference from the masses even when it is given sullenly. A peasant stands in the presence of a gentleman, removes his hat, bows a little, and is obsequious. Although the Republican Constitution abolished titles, they are in widespread use in the South. A *barone* or *principe* remains such. If the lower-class peasant is unsure of the noble status of a person wearing a tie or giving other evidence of education or opulence, he can always have recourse to the terms *commendatore* or *dottore*. Even where he resents it, centuries of experience have taught the southerner to be abjectly deferential in the face of social, economic, or political authority, often wrapped up in the same person.

The striking thing about the South's social system is the absence of a middle class. Viewed in its broadest terms, the social hierarchy is topped by the nobility, bishops, large landowners, a few industrialists, the political "notables," and the top-level bureaucrats like the prefect. Below them exist a small middle group of liberal professionals, shopkeepers, middle-level bureaucrats, teachers, and a few highly skilled artisans and workers. Below them come the undifferentiated mass of peasants, unskilled workers, petty bureaucrats, small shopkeepers, clerks, agricultural day laborers, and the unemployed. Even among the latter the efforts at effecting some basis of social differentiation are extreme.

In a narrower sense one can think of the social hierarchy of a typical small rural town in the South. There one will find a local elite usually consisting of the pharmacist, the notary, the doctor if there is one, the teacher, possibly the priest, the mayor, and the petty officer of the *carabinieri*. Everyone else is lower class, living in the meanest of conditions and developing toward the political system—indeed, against all of society—feelings of total alienation.

Until it is radically transformed the Italian educational system will continue to perpetuate rigid stratification and low mobility. Relatively early along the educational route, and at several junctures, students are separated into groups based essentially on socioeconomic class. There are, for example, postelementary curricula that do not lead to regular secondary school, and contain courses of study that permanently exclude the opportunity to go on to university training. The surest passage to a university degree is through the *liceo classico* or *liceo scientifico*, and recruitment into these particular secondary schools is heavily class-based.

The 1951 Census revealed Italy's educational hierarchy to be as follows: There were only 422,324 university graduates, of whom 340,873 were males. Almost one-fourth of these were graduates in jurisprudence, and an almost equal number received their degree in letters. Only 51,000 graduates were trained in the sciences, another 64,000 in medicine, and 48,000 in engineering. A mere 1,379,811 persons had completed upper secondary school; 2,514,474 were graduates of lower secondary school; and 24,946,399 persons had successfully completed the five elementary school years. A striking 13 million Italians had secured no diploma at all, of whom 7.6 million persons were classed as literate and 5.4 million as illiterate. As one would expect, the South has smaller proportions of educated at all levels, and throughout the country women pull away from the educational pyramid much more precipitously than men do.[34]

The marked class basis of educational achievement can be seen when we examine data concerning graduates from secondary schools and university student populations. Of the 73,362 students graduated from upper secondary school in 1956-1957 the breakdown of the social condition of the father is shown in Table 3.

TABLE 3: GRADUATES OF HIGHER SECONDARY SCHOOLS, 1956-1957, BY SOCIAL CONDITION OF FATHER[35]

Social Condition	Number of Graduates
Owners, managers, professionals	7,945
Self-employed	29,271
Workers	12,569
Assistants	188
Not indicated	1,869
Non-professional	488

The composition of 43,140 first-year university students in 1957-1958 and 19,489 university graduates for the year 1956-1957 is shown in Table 4.

[34] See Istituto Centrale di Statistica, *Annuario statistico italiano, 1960*, Rome, 1961, p. 89.
[35] *ibid.*, p. 104.

TABLE 4: FIRST-YEAR UNIVERSITY STUDENTS, 1957-1958, AND UNIVERSITY GRADUATES, 1956-1957, BY SOCIAL CONDITION OF FATHER[36]

Social Condition	First Year	Graduates
Owners, professionals	5,460	3,193
Managers and white collar	19,181	8,502
Self-employed	10,961	5,254
Workers	5,117	1,465
Assistants	104	31
Not indicated	2,014	836
Non-professional	303	208

It is abundantly apparent that the Italian working class is grossly unrepresented not merely in the universities but in the upper secondary schools as well. Moreover the data concerning university graduates suggests that university students from working-class families fall away in significantly larger proportion than students of any other group do. It is not very impressive evidence of social mobility that the university system awards degrees to 1,400 students from working-class backgrounds. The Italian who evaluates the opportunity for development afforded by the political system will surely not rate the educational aspect of it very positively.

The depressed South of course is much less dynamic in this area than is the North. This is detected not merely in the significantly smaller proportion of the population to reach any given level of educational achievement; it is also apparent in the kinds of things studied by those who do somehow manage to filter into the universities. Thus in the very sector of Italy in greatest need of graduates with scientific and technical skills the overwhelmingly greatest number of university students study law and letters. As recently as 1959, for example, from one-fourth to over one-third of all of the students enrolled at the universities of Rome, Bari, Naples, Palermo, and Catania were studying law. Quite apart from the illogic of this from an economic development standpoint, I would suggest that the situation is basically designed to increase the sense of political alienation among the Italian intelligentsia. The economy simply cannot absorb these legions of lawyers. They will therefore gravitate to the bureaucracy, where their disgruntlement will affect the image that Italians develop of the government; they will in many cases become

[36] *ibid.*, pp. 110-111.

intimately involved in the corrupt politics of the South, using their legal skills to prevent the development of a democratic political system; and some of them will become extremely hostile journalists, free lancers, and even political leaders, using their education to add considerably to an inflated language of politics that has already reached dangerous proportions.

As to the young Italians' expectations regarding the future, in a 1958 survey of almost 3,000 Italian youth (ages 18-25) we found that over 50 per cent were dissatisfied with their present economic condition and that fully two-thirds expected their condition to improve "little" or "not at all." About 25 per cent of the sample fall into the last category, and we can consider them to be Italians who see absolutely no hope for personal betterment originating in existing social or political institutions. Dissatisfaction reaches its highest point in the South and on the Islands, where over 70 per cent of the youth express little or no satisfaction with their present economic status.[37] Our data also indicate that there is a direct and positive relationship between degree of dissatisfaction and support for the extreme left in politics.[38] It is certainly plausible, after all, that when one's expectations concerning the future are essentially negative, when the social system is perceived as so rigidly structured as to make advancement unlikely or impossible, identification with political parties that offer revolutionary change is a natural one.

One can suggest other ways in which the system of social stratification bears on the political culture. On the one hand it is possible to suggest that the stratification system aids and abets notions of extreme class conflict, contributes to a sense of futility that spills over into men's attitudes toward and evaluation of the political system, helps to perpetuate patterns of leadership in the legislature and bureaucracy that are direct causes of disdain and hostility toward the political system, and so on. On the other hand it is also possible to stress that the social system may actually inhibit the growth of secondary structures that might facilitate more efficacious participation in the political process. Thus the continued dominance of the one-family industrial firm serves to inhibit the development of a widespread trade union movement. Not only does it deny many of Italy's industrial workers an important means of induction into politics; it also serves to widen the cognitive and evaluative gap between workers who are members

---

[37] LaPalombara and Waters, *op.cit.*, pp. 42-43.
[38] *ibid.*, p. 57.

of trade unions and those who are not. Similarly, the rigid class structure of the traditional South inhibits the growth of any kind of voluntary associations. It is significant that the most important organization in the rural South is one which recruits the agricultural day laborer and is dominated by the Communist Party. It is this organization which from time to time inspires not responsible participation in the political process but violence and other forms of anomic political behavior. Without a widespread system of secondary associations, the southerner's attitudes toward the political system—and the actors within it—will continue to be based on parochial values and on perceptions of the nature of government born of centuries of maltreatment and exploitation. Presumably it is exactly these perceptions which might be somewhat modified if greater mobility were introduced into the Italian social system.

IMPERFECT POLITICAL SOCIALIZATION

It is well understood that all political systems tend to perpetuate their cultures and structures through time. This is not a static but a dynamic process in which many institutions are more or less intimately involved. If we can think of a political system as requiring a certain set of attitudes toward institutions and process, it is both reasonable and important to ask how these attitudes might be generated. It is equally important to rate the extent to which the attitudes created do not conform to the requirements of a given political system. Thus we know, for example, that a critical problem for the so-called developing areas is that the attitudes and behaviors instilled by the institutions of traditional society make economic, social, and political change extremely arduous. If it is agriculture that planners wish to mechanize, some means of changing age-old attitudes toward the use of land must somehow be devised; if it is mass public education that is the end in view, such traditional norms as the use of child labor on the land and the role of woman in society must be changed. Similarly, if it is a pluralistic democracy—or simply a developmentally capable bureaucracy—that is the major political goal, something must be done to assure that the dominant political culture that emerges in the society is consistent with such aspirations. This fact is true no matter what may be the specific goals in the political sector. Thus the Italian Fascists were greatly concerned with the schools because they rightly saw them as an important means of creating basic values consistent with those of the regime. Thus too the Bolsheviks early recognized that the schools would have to be remade to assure not merely the technical skills needed to bring about rapid economic change but also the kinds of basic attitudes toward the state that would be consistent with the goals and the ideology of Bolshevism.

Political socialization is not a process that is limited to the nuclear family, the neighborhood, the village, and the schools. Of course many of the attitudes toward politics a person evinces in his adulthood can be traced back to the manifest or latent political impact of these primary associations; but the socialization process is continuous, involving secondary associational activity in later years as well as such obvious phenomena as exposure to the mass media. These later experiences may either challenge or reinforce attitudes acquired in childhood. It is therefore a combination of both early and later—and in any event continuous—political socialization which determines what the individual feels toward the political system, how he views other persons and actors in the political process, the amount of affect he manifests toward the nation and its governmental institutions, how he participates or does not participate in politically relevant activities, and the kind of self-image he develops about his place and role in the political system, to cite only a few of the more important considerations. In this sense, then, we can say that the nature of political socialization helps to define the limits—to set the parameters—within which political organization and behavior evolve.

What we know about the family and the school in Italy is not encouraging for those who desire the evolution there of a healthy and vigorous democracy—or what Almond and Verba call the civic culture. To some extent, which I shall not attempt to specify in a quantitative way, the fragmented, isolative, and alienated political culture which currently characterizes Italy grows out of experiences in the family and in the school. It will be useful therefore to look at some of the more salient characteristics of these two important institutions.

We have already noted that in the South primary and essentially exclusive loyalty is owed to the nuclear family. As Banfield points out, in this kind of society "no one will further the interest of the group or community except as it is to his private advantage to do so." Family loyalty tends to be antagonistic to participation in public affairs except insofar as participation itself can help to aggrandize the family's fortunes. Thus Banfield suggests that the southerner's inability to transcend the nuclear family loyalty creates a milieu that favors authoritarian politics.[39]

It seems reasonably apparent that the Italian family fails to provide its members with a coherent view of the national political system or with a sense of effectual involvement concerning it. Although the South probably produces such inadequately socialized persons in much greater proportions, the phenomenon is significantly present throughout Italy, and certainly in the rural sectors of the North. Beyond this aspect of socialization, however, one can rightfully ask whether, as Banfield suggests, family experiences prepare adult Italians to accept and support authoritarian rather than democratic political structures. Obviously, establishing a tight relationship between early socializing experiences and subsequent political behavior is a hazardous enterprise.[40] The difficulty is immediately apparent for any country when one stops to consider that out of basically similar family experiences emerges a very wide spectrum of political behavior. Such differences are surely to be explained in part by the fact that the individual in his adult years is subjected to a continuing series of secondary and intervening socializing experiences. With this important caveat in mind, we can offer some suggestive comments on the relationship between the Italian family structure and the nation's political culture.

I realize that it is commonplace to say that the Italians never accepted Fascism, that they are basically not authoritarian, and that, particularly in the South, Italians would have defeated Fascism simply by not taking it seriously—even laughing it out of existence. While there may be grains of truth in such observations, they are grossly oversimplified. There is much in the Italian personality that Fascism managed to reach and touch deeply, and there is much about the Italian family concerning which Fascism was in part a macrocosmic manifestation.[41]

The Italian family, urban and rural, is fundamentally authoritarian in character. It is organized around the central idea that children must accord unquestioning obedience to and respect for parents and grandparents. Particularly in rural sectors, familial au-

---

[39] Banfield, *The Moral Basis of a Backward Society*, Glencoe, Ill., 1958, pp. 85-97. The whole of this chapter is a fascinating commentary on southern local politics.

[40] On this score, one would simply recall the critiques of T. Adorno *et al.*, *The Authoritarian Personality* contained in Richard Christie and Marie Yahoda, eds. *Studies in the Scope and Method of the Authoritarian Personality*, Glencoe, Ill., 1954.

[41] On the more fundamental meaning of Fascism for Italians, see Costanzo Casucci, *Il Fascismo*, Bologna, 1961.

thority is hierarchically structured, descending from the male parent to the oldest male sibling and so on down through the entire family membership. Decisions are rarely taken on a democratic basis; children are not expected to participate in decisions concerning themselves, nor are they often permitted even to complain about actions they consider basically unfair. When complaint does occur it is likely to be in the form of an emotional protest, or even in the form of violent behavior. With rare exceptions there is little training in the kind of pragmatic give-and-take that a democratic polity requires.

The same Italians who are noted for the loving and demonstrative affection they bestow on children are capable of administering severe physical punishment. A high degree of apparent permissiveness toward the young is coupled with frequently capricious and arbitrary parental behavior toward them. The Italian child quickly comes to understand that those in the family who wield power will use it physically and readily in order to exact obedience.

It would be misleading, however, to view the Italian family as rigidly patriarchical. Overtly authority appears to reside in the father, and there are indeed myriad ways in which Italian society is largely a man's world; yet, despite her formally inferior role in the family, the mother is of critical importance. In both the cities and the countryside Italians will explain that such things as the financial management of the family center in the mother. Beyond this she plays a major role in the early education of the children, she sees to their initial religious observances, and she acts as an important mediating influence between the children and the father. It is not a matter of chance that the most important religious figure in Italian Catholicism is the Virgin Mary, or that the country is referred to as the "Madre Patria," the Mother-Fatherland. Because of this factor—and if the projection from family to politics makes any sense at all—Italians in politics are probably less authoritarian than, say, the Germans. On the other hand it is also probable that they are more authoritarian than, say, the British or Americans.

It should be added that the basically inferior status accorded women in the family transfers directly to the political realm. Women are not expected to be very knowledgeable about political affairs, and the facts demonstrate conclusively that they are not. Women generally accept this inferior status; over 60 per cent of the same women who go to the polls at each election indicate in cross-section surveys that women should not concern themselves with political issues or public affairs. Curiously enough, the same women who fade into the background in family affairs quietly participate in elections and account for the continued dominance of the Christian Democratic party.[42]

Whatever authoritarian values are instilled by the Italian family and by the Catholic Church, from the earliest years rigid discipline characterizes the Italian schools, both public and private. Except in those few primary schools that experiment with the methods of Dewey and Pestalozzi the pupils are exposed to a teacher-pupil relationship in which the former is the accepted and unquestioned authority. I have personally watched a form of discipline administered to pre-school children in one of the most "progressive" schools in Rome: the children are compelled to sit silently and with hands folded for periods up to forty-five minutes. I was told that this helps to prepare the youngsters for the kind of atmosphere they will find on entering the primary grades.

The social gap maintained between teacher and pupil actually widens as one moves up through the secondary schools and the university. In the latter the professor is a remote and austere person, strongly impelled in many ways to demonstrate to the students their intellectual inferiority. His well-made lectures are frequently brilliant, displaying impressive command of the subject matter. On the other hand he brooks no interruption in the classroom, refusing to encourage discussion, and actually considering any attempts at it as dilatory or downright impertinent. Advanced students generally do not work out their projects on the basis of discussion and compromise; the professor involved "gives" the student a dissertation topic. More often the student never sees the professor at all but has his work dictated to him through the *assistente*, who is yet another symbol of the hierarchical and dictatorial structure of Italian education. Thus the teacher at all levels is the counterpart of the father in whom all wisdom and authority reside and concerning whose wishes and commands the only socially acceptable response is submission.

Italy's school system retains a strong Roman Catholic authoritarian flavor. Highly centralized under a national Ministry of Education, it serves to instill values closely attuned to conservative Catholicism

---

[42] For a most impressive analysis of the voting behavior of Italian women, see Mattei Dogan, "Le donne italiane tra il cattolicesimo e il marxismo," in Spreafico and LaPalombara, *op.cit.*, pp. 475-494.

and is staffed by largely pro-Catholic teachers. Students are exposed to officially chosen text books that contain such passages as these:

> The fourth commandment—honor thy father and thy mother—orders us to respect and love our parents and all who have authority over us, that is, our superiors: the Pope, the bishops, the priests, the civil authorities, and our teachers. ...
>
> There is much social change because parents fall prey to stupid ambitions for their children. The shoemaker wants his son to become an accountant; the sausage vendor wants his son to become a physician. Just imagine such foolishness.[43]

Forces are at work in Italy designed to effect fundamental changes in the school system at all levels. The demand for reform encompasses teaching methods, concentration and distribution of subject matter, more widespread opportunities for educational mobility, greater secularization, and a more democratic and permissive atmosphere in the classroom. Until such changes occur—and as Italians themselves have publicly recognized—the school system, from the earliest grades through the university years, will continue to reflect traditional values as well as attitudes toward authority that were institutionalized under Fascism. Italian education therefore is hardly an impressive means of preparing the individual for active, questioning, and responsible participation in the political system.

Authoritarian values of the family and the school are of course mightily reinforced by the Catholic Church in almost all its manifestations. Catholicism openly asserts the necessity to exercise full control over its adherents in all matters that involve their spiritual salvation. Although it is true that Catholic doctrine distinguishes among the kinds of subjects on which the Pope can speak with infallibility, such fine distinctions are lost on the millions of Italians who hear authoritative clerical figures comment on legislation, on the relative merits of political parties and voluntary associations, on education, on the proper relationship between church and state—on literally all the problems and occurrences that touch a man's role as a citizen.

There is really no major category of the Italian population left untouched by the organized campaign of the church in the political sphere. Millions of politically illiterate women cast their ballots

[43] From John Clarke Adams and Paolo Barile, *The Government of Republican Italy*, Boston, 1961, p. 234.

exactly as they are instructed to do by parish priests. Several million more Italians are encompassed by units of Italian Catholic Action that instill conservative—even reactionary—political attitudes. Although other Catholic organizations may be much more liberally inclined than Catholic Action, they too contribute to the creation of a view of society which sees it made up of the "good" and the "evil," of "friends" and "enemies," of the "saved" and the "damned." In this sense the impact of the effort to maintain a Catholic sub-culture intact and isolated from contaminating influences serves to increase the amount of fragmentation apparent in the Italian political system.

Moreover, central to the doctrine of Catholicism regarding man's relationship to religious authority is the concept of *obbedienza*—obedience. The Catholic's duty is not to question religious authority but simply to obey. It is reasonable to suppose that this posture of the individual toward his religious governors is relatively easily transferred to the political sector and results in exactly the predisposition toward authoritarian politics we have noted above.

Finally, in evaluating the impact of Catholicism on the political systems it is well to note that pronouncements of the clergy and its lay representatives regarding the politics and political institutions serve primarily to intensify isolative, negative, and alienative views. Bureaucracy is depicted as a haven of corrupt practices and a refuge of freemasonry; the government is accused of providing subsidies for the production of motion pictures that are immoral and otherwise unacceptable to Catholicism; political parties are described as dangerous forces of the kind of laicism that the Church considers to be a mortal threat to its existence; civil marriage is condemned as an institution that places the Italian outside his religion, and on occasion its civil validity is challenged; political leaders who wish to reform the school system are described as anti-clerical architects who wish to undermine man's moral edifice and expose him to damnation. Thus where the Church does not encourage basic passivity and submission in the face of authority it helps to create virulent antagonism toward political institutions.

III. Change and Development

Thus far I have tried to concentrate attention on the central tendencies of Italian political culture and on some of the major environmental factors that help to create and perpetuate it. The picture I have painted is to some degree deliberately distorted; it is intended to highlight those aspects of Italian society that are most inconsistent with the maintenance of a pluralistic democratic system. My particular concern, which I share with many in Italy, is not merely that of understanding the dynamics of political development but also that of predicting—even of influencing—the particular direction political development might take.

For those who share the desire to have Italy move from a parochial and subject culture to a participant, civic one—or from unstable to stable democracy—some recent occurrences are potentially very encouraging. The most striking of these are rapid economic growth, growing urbanization, apparent changes in the Vatican, and the political "Opening to the Left."

ECONOMIC GROWTH

It is impossible to quarrel with the assertion that since 1948 Italy has experienced a miracle of economic reconstruction and development. In the first years of the recovery outside assistance such as that offered by the Marshall Plan played a determining role; in more recent years growth and development have resulted from a combination of the internal dynamics of the Italian economy, the impact of Italy's membership in the European Common Market, and a flourishing tourist trade which helps to redress an unfavorable balance of payments.

Whatever may be the total list of propellants, growth itself cannot be ignored. It is evident in the index of industrial production, which increased over 50 per cent since 1953; it is even more apparent in such specialized sectors as hydrocarbons, fuels and combustibles, chemicals, transportation, synthetic fibers and plastics, where the index numbers of production since 1953 range from 170 to 300.[44] Growth is also reflected in national income statistics. In constant lira values, annual national income rose from 47 to 146 billion lire between 1861 and 1939. Between 1945 and the present, however, national income—drastically reduced by the war—went from 71 to almost 300 billion lire. During the last dozen years per capita income registered a level of increase more than double the growth between 1861 and 1938.

Economic progress is also evident in the greater number of automobiles on Italian streets, the rapid expansion of the distribution of television around the country, the number of new dwellings con-

[44] Istituto Centrale di Statistica, *Annuario Statistico Italiano, 1959*, Rome, 1960, pp. 191-209.

structed in recent years, dramatic improvements in daily diets, the amount of per capita expenditure on entertainment, and so on. Italians are better off economically than they have ever been in their national history.

Insofar as antagonisms toward the political system can be associated with poverty, unemployment, and negative expectations regarding personal economic future the economic occurrences of recent years should be encouraging. Even though development has been uneven—and has actually widened the gap between North and South—Italy does not seem to be sitting on the short-fused political powder keg of a few years ago. Even the Communist Party, which came close to triggering revolution in July 1948, seems to recognize this fact. We thus find Palmiro Togliatti insisting not that the existing regime is hopeless but that the Communists have a right to participate in directing the future peaceful development of the country.

If industrial expansion can be maintained at its recent pace, if the Common Market can provide additional occupational opportunities, and if the problem of the South's economic development can be massively attacked, unemployment and related causes of political disaffection can be substantially reduced. Future generations of Italy's youth might then have greater positive expectations toward the future than those noted above, and fewer of them might turn in bitterness either to extreme political movements or to alienated withdrawal from the political system.

URBANIZATION

Just as dramatic as recent economic growth is the level of urbanization registered since World War II. The migration is everywhere apparent, although it is particularly directed toward the major industrial cities of the North. During the last twenty years places of over 100,000 inhabitants have grown more than 30 per cent, while Italy's general increase in population has been only half that much. If one compares the capital cities of each province with all other lesser cities, it is striking that increases in population in the former exceed increases in the latter by 29 times.[45] So important is this phenomenon of in-migration that it is one of the most discussed—and recently most investigated—problems in Italy.

[45] See Manlio Rossi-Doria, "Aspetti sociali dello sviluppo economico in Italia," in *Atti del IV Congresso Mondiale di Sociologia, op.cit.*, pp. 9-35. Note especially the table on page 25.

If we can generalize from one important study,[46] urbanization should carry with it profound changes in Italian political culture. As Lerner puts it, the movement from the rural to the urban center should make the individual better able to empathize about other persons and groups in the society. As an urbanite, his literacy should increase, he should become a more frequent consumer of the mass media and, finally, he should engage in more meaningful participation in the political process.

In the terms I have been using here we might say that urbanization will make the individual less parochial; less tied to traditional institutions such as the family, church, neighborhood, and village; more prone to affiliate with secondary associations that provide additional political socialization; potentially, at least, more open in his political partisanship and less aloof from or hostile toward political institutions.

Although I believe this may be the long-run impact of Italian in-migration, it is necessary to record several reservations. In the first place, both the southern and northern migrants to northern industrial cities tend in large measure to be dirt-poor peasants who settle on the outskirts of Bologna, Milan, Turin, and Genoa and live in isolated squalor. The natives of these cities are anything but pleased about these new arrivals and have made their antipathy known through their newspapers as well as by acts of violence. The native residents resent the intrusion, are fearful of competition for jobs, look with alarm at increased problems of law and order and social welfare, and are generally not prepared to cope with these and other problems created by sudden growth in population.[47]

Thus many who migrate to northern cities languish in poverty that may be even more intolerable than what was left behind because the impersonal city provides few of the security-giving institutions of the countryside. Bitterly disappointed at their lack of good fortune, and exposed for the first time to the organizational efforts of extreme political parties, these migrants become a prime recruiting ground for P.C.I. Thus Achille Ardigò suggests that, if the situation at Bologna can be generalized, the immediate consequence of movement from the countryside to the central industrial city is a marked

---

[46] Daniel Lerner, *The Passing of Traditional Society*, Glencoe, Ill., 1958.

[47] For an excellent treatment of these problems by one of Italy's most knowledgeable students of the phenomenon, see Francesco Compagna, *I terroni in città*, Bari, 1959; cf. Goffredo Fofi, "Meridionali e settentrionali attraverso lo' specchio dei tempi," *Nord e Sud*, Vol. 8, June 1961, pp. 81-105.

increase in the electoral support for the Communist Party.[48] This surmise is strongly supported by analyses of voting patterns at Genoa and Turin in the national elections of 1963.[49] Thus it is possible that, for some time at least, attitudes toward the political system that were initially parochial will be transformed into those that are primarily alienative.

Second, it is important to recognize that much of the urbanization that occurs in the South is not associated with industrialization. What develops there is the "peasant city" about which Compagna says: "As is known, the characteristic of 'peasant cities' is that of hosting, like a true 'dormitory,' a high percentage of agricultural population, always greater, and sometimes much greater, than fifty per-cent of the active population."[50] These peasants gravitate to dormitory cities not because they are offered new occupational opportunities but, rather, because they are in search of better administrative services and other amenities that urban centers can provide. The peasant therefore does not better his economic status but may actually find it deteriorated. Moreover such cities in no way contribute to the economic growth of the region; they become parasites, serving to delay rather than to spur economic modernization.

One might argue that urbanization itself, whatever its causes, will necessarily bring some changes in political culture. It is obvious, for example, that urban living will necessarily change a man's conception of his physical and spatial surroundings. In addition new and different associative patterns are encouraged, which will inevitably impinge on parochial and traditional values and attitudes. In this sense one may say that the Italian South is very much in ferment, that the southerner who goes from rural village to central city is somewhat freed from the binding ties of family and religion, and that he has at least a reasonable opportunity to learn the ways of responsible participation in the political process. Whether this will in fact be the outcome of southern urbanization, however, will depend in part on the speed with which the economic "miracle" of the North makes itself felt and visible south of Rome.

[48] Achille Ardigò, "Il volto elettorale di Bologna," in Spreafico and LaPalombara, *op.cit.*, pp. 801-849.
[49] See Pino Crea, "Il voto degli immigrati: Torino," *Tempi Moderni*, Vol. 6, April-June 1963, pp. 87-91; Alfredo Livi, "Il voto degli immigrati: Genova," *ibid.*, pp. 92-95.
[50] Francesco Compagna, "Dopo i primi anni di esodo rurale," *Nord e Sud*, Vol. 8, October 1961, p. 12.

CHANGES IN THE VATICAN

It is unnecessary to detail at great length what may be the consequences of an apparently less antagonistic view of the Vatican toward international and national secular forces. The work of Pope John XXIII in lessening international tension is now widely known and applauded. In Italy his liberalizing policies were felt within Catholic Action, where some of the most extreme leaders were quietly removed, and within the Christian Democratic party, where it was learned that the Vatican would lift its previous rigid opposition to collaboration in domestic affairs between Catholic and socialist forces. It is expected that Pope Paul VI will continue, perhaps even more resolutely, along the paths opened up by John XXIII.

Obviously if Catholicism decreases the level of its antagonism toward liberalism, socialism, and other laical forces, the impact on Italian political culture should be profound. If Catholics are told that the problems of contemporary Italian society require at least a peaceful dialogue and possibly active cooperation between Catholics and Socialists, the Roman Church will have taken its first significant step in reducing the degree of mutual distrust and hostility that the Church itself was so instrumental in creating. There is literally no predicting how far such a change in posture would carry Italy in the direction of greater political stability.

Moving along such a path will be an arduous exercise. Decades of the kind of rigid leadership provided by Pius XII are not easily reversed; strong forces within organized Catholicism will not easily succumb to the kinds of policies regarding that the Vatican may now desire. The history of Christian Democracy itself—as well as the contemporary occurrences within the party—clearly indicates that those who would perpetuate what exists remain very powerful. The Vatican will need all the creative support that laical forces, as well as the more enlightened groups, can provide.

OPENING TO THE LEFT

Finally, in the sphere of politics itself one must note the momentous "Opening to the Left" effected by Amintore Fanfani and Pietro Nenni, and renewed in 1963 when P.S.I. actually joined a coalition government for the first time in history. Both Nenni for P.S.I. and Fanfani, and then Moro, for the D.C. had to overcome intensive opposition both within and outside of their respective parties in order to hammer out a basic agreement. Nenni was confronted by his party's extreme left, the Maximalists, who prefer close ties to the Communist Party and who do not want to share power until it is wrested completely from the political center. It was a portion of this extreme left (or "Chinese") faction that broke with P.S.I. in 1964 creating even further political confusion. He was also under severe attack by the Communist Party, which accused him of wanting to sell out the working class and of seriously jeopardizing working-class unity. That the Socialist Party paid a price for its movement toward the D.C. is evidenced by Communist Party gains and Socialist Party losses in the regions of Emilia-Romagna, Tuscany, and Umbria in 1963, and by significant Socialist party losses in regional and local elections in 1964.

Fanfani, who bulldozed the "Opening" through his party, was also confronted by strong opposition from the center and right wings. In addition he was stridently attacked by the liberals, monarchists, and neo-Fascists for his willingness to collaborate with a Marxist party. The losses suffered by the D.C. in 1963 and in 1964, the gains registered by the Communists, and the gains won by the liberals were all ascribed to Fanfani's (and, incidentally, John XXIII's) apparent willingness to bargain and compromise with a Marxist party. In short, there are those who argue that if Socialism gets a foot in the door, Communism will not be far behind; or that if the Pope accords an audience to Khrushchev's son-in-law, Italian Catholics will no longer see the logic and necessity of denying their votes to parties on the Left.

Aldo Moro, although more "center" than Fanfani, faced the same sort of internal party opposition in late 1963 when he sought to bring the P.S.I. into his government. Conservative Christian Democratic factions led by Mario Scelba and Giuseppe Pella openly threatened not to support another "Opening to the Left," and only open intervention by the Vatican through *Osservatore Romano* brought them reluctantly into line. By December 1964, on the occasion of Giuseppe Saragat's election to the national presidency, ideological differences in the party had reached the point of schism, thus threatening further progress.

If the new "Opening to the Left" turns out to be something substantial in terms of policies and achievements, it is difficult to understand why it should not have a profound influence on Italian political culture. For, above all else, the "opening" promises to effect some profound changes in Italian society. If the Socialists have their way, the government will have to consider national economic planning. More important, the Socialists will insist that the sections of the Constitution anticipating greater regional autonomy will actually be implemented. Greater regional autonomy should at least in theory afford the Italian citizen the opportunity of more direct and meaningful participation in the political process.

Also implicit in the "Opening to the Left" is a major reform of the educational system and of the Italian bureaucracy, two institutions which, as I have noted, contribute strongly to the kinds of attitudes Italians manifest toward politics, political institutions, and public authority. In addition planning should facilitate further an integrated economic development, desperately needed in the South. To put this succinctly, those in Italy who support the *apertura* are fully aware of the causes of political disaffection and instability and are capable of devising both the short- and long-term means of reducing it.

It would be preferable to conclude this paper on an optimistic note. Although most Italians would argue that the country's history might make such a gesture ill advised, if not downright foolhardy, I prefer to think—perhaps blindly to believe—that a nation which has produced so much else that is civilized will somehow create a civic culture.

CHAPTER 9

Mexico: The Established Revolution

ROBERT E. SCOTT

ALONG with Japan, Turkey, and the Soviet Union, Mexico was one of the first countries during the present era to attempt consciously to throw off the shackles of traditionalism and to seek a place in the modern, industrialized world, with its economy of mass production and consumption, its society of mass national integration, and its polity of mass participation. Because Mexico sought to modernize politically without resort to totalitarianism or a rigid ideological framework, its experience provides a case study of fifty years of relatively unhampered interaction among the diverse factors affecting and affected by the progress of a political culture from the parochial to the subject and toward the participant stage of development.[1] The patterns of political activity that emerged during this period point up very effectively the reciprocal influence of political culture on political modernization and of modernization upon political culture.

In the political as well as in the economic and social sectors Mexico has experienced many of the changes that mark the advent of mod-

[1] This terminology, like most in the study, is based on concepts of functional analysis presented by Gabriel A. Almond and James S. Coleman in *The Politics of the Developing Areas*, Princeton, 1960, Lucian Pye in *Politics, Personality, and Nation Building*, New Haven, 1962, and G. A. Almond and Sidney Verba in *The Civic Culture*, Princeton, 1963. The concept of identity is adapted from E. H. Erikson's works, *Childhood and Society*, New York, 1950; and *Young Man Luther* New York, 1958.

The terms parochial, subject, and participant refer to the manner in which individuals relate to the political process. The parochial is a member of the traditional society, unaware of (or in a very few cases rejecting for emotional reasons) the national political system. If he has any reaction to the activities of national government, it probably is suspicion or mistrust. The subject and participant, on the other hand, do relate to the national political process but in very different ways which have to do with their function in the input and output activities of government. Input refers to those activities that concern the articulation, structuring, and formulation of public policy; output to those activities concerning the implementation of public policy. The subject identifies primarily with the output functions of government—services, such as road building, education, police protection, and national defense, and responsibilities, such as paying taxes, obtaining licenses, and performing military obligations. The participant identifies with governmental outputs but also with the input functions of the political process—membership in interest groups and associations, membership in political parties, voting, sharing to a greater or lesser degree in the articulation of interests and the formation of public policy.

ernization in countries throughout the world. Superficially many of its formal and informal political structures resemble those found in other polities. The formal constitutional agencies, for example, are modeled upon those of the United States. But like many of the rapidly changing states in Asia and Africa, Mexico has concentrated authority in a single dominant political movement—a revolutionary party—in order to resolve more easily some of the problems of continuity and integration inherent in the transition process. The operational political action patterns, however, reflect deeply ingrained values and understandings which are part of the political culture. It is these patterns that determine the functioning of the political structures and produce a distinctive political system with a clearly defined Mexican political style.

Mexico shares much with the other modernizing countries discussed in this volume, not only the common experience of rapid modernization but also somewhat similar approaches to the problems associated with change and, in some cases, outwardly similar political structures to deal with these problems. Japan too has avoided adopting a single formal ideology of modernization but, unlike Mexico, operates through a multi-party system. Like the Soviet Union, Mexico acts through a monopolistic political party, but unlike Russia Mexico accepts no highly systematized formal ideology. Egypt is somewhat more analogous to Mexico in that its "official" modernizing movement is not bound to a single theoretical framework, but the Arabs have not yet had enough time under Nasser's rule to evolve a predictable and participatory political system.

For an even closer parallel, compare Mexico with Turkey.[2] Revolutionary leaders in both countries sought for over thirty years to impose modernization upon the populace by means of a chosen instrument, an official party that was not ideologically oriented. In each case the original impetus toward development and integration brought large numbers of persons into national awareness, but in the political sphere neither the Turks nor the Mexicans have been able to consolidate change completely or to move easily from a subject-dominated into an effective participatory political system. The reader must decide for himself whether the reasons were basically similar in the two countries. Whatever that decision may be, and despite

---

[2] In addition to Rustow's study in this volume, see Robert E. Ward and D. A. Rustow, eds. *Political Modernization in Japan and Turkey*, Princeton, 1964; and Kemal H. Karpat, *Turkey's Politics*, Cambridge, 1959.

greater or lesser degrees of similarity between Mexico and each of these countries, in the final analysis it is clear that their political systems are not identical.

The lesson to be learned here is important. The imperatives of transition seem to force many basically very different types of countries to adopt certain patterns of political action or particular kinds of political structure to combat the disintegrative and dysfunctional effects of rapid change. But as modernization proceeds, the imperatives of its own basic political culture, coupled with the accidents of history, endow a country like Mexico with a political system that if not completely unique is at least markedly different from that of any of the other developing states.

The commonly accepted and most convenient symbol for the beginning of Mexico's modernization process is the Mexican Revolution of 1910, although the pressures of both economic and political change had been building up for some time before. Since that date, considering the number and complexity of the problems involved, Mexico has progressed amazingly in its evolution toward modernity. A high degree of control is exercised over the physical and social environment. The ratio of inanimate to animate energy is expanding constantly as industrialization and commercialization of agriculture replace handicrafts and subsistence farming. Urbanization replaces rural isolation, specialization and professionalization replace unskilled labor, and achievement rather than ascription becomes the basis for high status. The literacy rate grows as popular education spreads, and the circulation of mass media rises apace. The middle- and upper-class sectors of the population increase in size, and improved social mobility opens their ranks to the more ambitious and able of the masses. Secularization of values begins to pervade most phases of life. By almost any of the recognized indicators, Mexico rapidly is becoming modernized both socially and economically.[3]

[3] The Mexican process of modernization has proved so intriguing that in preparing a study of this sort one is hampered by the very volume of available publications, all providing some information on the subject at hand. To list, much less cite, all of the general works providing background data is impractical, as is any attempt to supply here all of the information required for an understanding of modern Mexico and its politics. The reader is urgently requested to consult the following sources: Howard F. Cline, *The United States and Mexico*, Cambridge, 1953; and *Mexico: Revolution to Evolution, 1940-1960*, London, New York, Toronto, 1962. Oscar Lewis, *Life in A Mexican Village: Tepoztlán Revisited*, Urbana, 1951; *Five Families: Mexican Case Studies in the Culture of Poverty*, New York, 1959; *The Family of Sánchez*, New York, 1961; *Pedro Martinez: A Mexican Peasant and his Family*, New York, 1963. Sol Tax, ed. *Heritage of Conquest*, Glencoe, Ill., 1952. W.

The political system, on the other hand, has not kept pace in the modernization process. Of necessity, given the level of social and economic development, government performance is broad in range and high in volume, and political authority is sufficiently effective to assure the stability essential for economic growth. While the decision-making process is becoming increasingly rational and secular, however, it remains mainly in the hands of a small governing group because involvement in politics and popular interest in the input functions of government still are at a relatively low level. Functional differentiation of political structures and specialization of political roles has begun, but development of a plural society and a self-regulating polity has been slowed down by the need to establish and maintain a centralizing authority which can control the disruptive tendencies of a partially mobilized and as yet inarticulate population. The single-party, non-dictatorial political system centering in the revolutionary party and the presidency has provided an apparently necessary authority and assured political stability, but the very presence of these informal but effective diffuse political structures between the predominantly subject-oriented citizenry and the more formal and differentiated legal governmental structures has made it

---

P. Tucker, *The Mexican Government Today*, Minneapolis, 1957. Robert E. Scott, *Mexican Government in Transition*, Urbana, 1959. William Glade and Charles Anderson, *The Political Economy of Mexico*, Madison, 1963. Raymond Vernon, *The Dilemma of Mexico's Development*, Cambridge, 1963. Frank R. Brandenburg, *The Making of Modern Mexico*, Englewood Cliffs, N.J., 1964. Victor Alba, *Las Ideas Sociales Contemporáneas en México*, Mexico, D.F., 1960. José E. Iturriaga, *La Estructura Social y Cultural de México*, Mexico, D.F., 1951. Samuel Ramos, *Profile of Man and Culture in Mexico*, Austin, Texas, 1962. Octavio Paz, *The Labyrinth of Silence*, New York, 1962. See also the four volumes of *México: 50 Años de Revolución*, Vol. I, *La Economía*, Mexico, D.F. 1960; Vol. II, *La Vida Social*, Mexico, D.F., 1961; Vol. III, *La Política*, Mexico, D.F., 1961; and vol. IV, *La Cultura*, Mexico, D.F., 1962; as well as novels such as Carlos Fuentes, *Where the Air is Clear*, New York, 1960; *The Good Conscience*, New York, 1961; or Luis Spota, *Almost Paradise*, New York, 1963.

In addition to these publications and my own investigations, a major source of data on the Mexican's cognition and evaluation of, and sense of participation in, government is a survey study of a national cross-section of Mexicans in towns and cities of over 10,000 population taken for the previously cited Almond and Verba study, *The Civic Culture*. Although the findings of this survey are based on a relatively small sample of 1,007 Mexicans and clearly underrepresent the rural inhabitants, they do reflect quite accurately my own observations on the politicized population. Some indications of accuracy and inaccuracy can be suggested: for example, the cross sample showed 20 per cent of the respondents without schooling while the 1950 census placed the figure for persons over 25 at 43 per cent. Conversely, the survey indicated 85 per cent of the respondents supporting the revolutionary party to some extent, compared to a vote of 90.4 per cent for the party's candidate in the 1958 election. This is a remarkably small difference.

harder for Mexico to take the next giant step toward a participant political system, much less beyond to a more nearly "civic" system.

The difference in degree of development between society and polity can be attributed partly to lack of agreement on where the emphasis of modernization should lie. Long before 1910 some Mexicans equated modernization with constitutionalism while others stressed social and particularly economic advance. Since the Revolution a similar dichotomy of attitudes has existed and the revolutionary ideology, which is a great deal more pragmatic than theoretical, has embraced both sets of values. The Revolution stands for modernization, but on balance economic development and social change has taken priority over political evolution, though not simply because the national leadership was interested in maximizing its financial position or protecting its government monopoly.

The fact is that while most Mexicans share a common understanding about the economic and social goals of the Revolution, they can not easily agree on political norms because of cross pressures engendered by the political culture. A high premium is set on eventually achieving government based on democratic and constitutional forms, but at the same time the most compelling norms of the Revolution support integration of the entire population into effective national life, including the on-going political system based on strong central authority. The political culture inculcates acceptance of both these goals, but to date at least it has stressed values offering stronger support for the second at the expense of development of a participatory system.

This study is concerned less with political modernization as such, however, than with the difficulties inherent in building a congruent relationship between a political culture and the political structures when both are being affected by change in the entire environment, economic and social as well as political, but at different rates. In this study we shall see how the modernizing and nationalizing effects of economic and social change altered the demands made on government, shifting the need for political structures from those suitable for a primarily parochial or traditionally oriented system to others more suitable for a subject or government output-oriented system. We shall see too that the Mexican political culture was able to accommodate this shift, but that it has had much more difficulty in adjusting to further change that would allow the political structures to accommodate themselves to a participant political system. It will be apparent that change in the existing political structures or development of new ones is strongly conditioned by corresponding change (or lack of change) in the political culture. Finally, we shall see that although the political culture as a whole was much less responsive to change than some other factors involved in the political process were, certain political values involving formally learned attitudes toward government have adjusted to some degree to the new conditions; and even the more basic, deeply internalized political norms which are most inelastic very recently have begun to react to the new conditions growing out of modernization.

The Emergence of a National Polity

On the eve of the 1910 Revolution Mexico appeared to offer a classic example of a stable, systemically mixed parochial-subject political culture in quite strong congruence with the operational political structures if not with the formal, participatory structures described in the 1857 constitution, which had been copied from the United States document. Some 90 per cent of the population, in the lower class, seemed to be parochials—tradition-bound, village-oriented, and content to continue the isolated, localistic, and essentially passive way of life they had known for centuries. The remaining 10 per cent of the citizens—aware of the nation, tied to a money economy, and not entirely ignorant politically—consisted of a tiny aristocratic upper elite and a thin stratum of small businessmen, professionals, bureaucrats, and other traditional middle-sector elements dependent on and servicing the well to do. For the most part this national group accepted the authoritarian centralization imposed upon the country by General Porfirio Díaz and his *científico* followers. Of the few who did not, probably the majority either preferred some more locally dispersed governmental system in which they could feel more free to dominate their own region or felt that some other incumbent than President Díaz should occupy the presidential chair—preferably one of them. No more than 1 or 2 per cent, however, were active enough politically to share in the input or governmental policy-determining functions as participants. Generally speaking, few Mexicans thought seriously of implementing the formal participatory structures established in the constitution, and even fewer could have imagined an impending social and economic revolution with profound political consequences.

Within the next decade, however, the old patterns had been

altered irrevocably and the first tentative steps were being taken toward a new, more open society and a more efficient and modern governmental system. Despite the near anarchy of that period a new constitution had been adopted in 1917, one that reiterated the formal participatory norms and structures of its predecessor and added an impressive new class of government rights and responsibilities in social and economic matters, expanding enormously the output functions of the central administration as well as the expectations of a recently multiplied though still tiny sector of politicized and nationally minded citizens. Hopes ran high that the country had laid a firm foundation for the construction of a modern nation.

More careful analysis of the situation points up two vital variations on this rather idealized theme of Mexico's revolutionary development. First, pre-1910 politics were hardly so traditional, static, and monolithic as the "Porfirian" peace made it appear. Next, in spite of the rapid social and economic progress achieved since the Revolution and notwithstanding the political stability of recent decades, political modernization has not yet accomplished perfect fusion of traditional and more modern modes of behavior.

Most of the patterns of traditional life which carry over to the present have their roots deep in the three hundred years of Spanish colonial rule before Mexico obtained formal independence in 1821. For the vast majority of Indian[4] and *mestizo* people, rural and parochial in outlook, replacement of the *peninsulares* by local *criollo* governors meant little change from the semi-feudal system of landholding under which large numbers of *peones* were for all practical purposes bound to land controlled by absentee landowners. These peons, together with a few Indian groups which had managed to retain ownership of their own land, lived physically in Mexico but were not really part of the polity in the sense of participating or even being aware of national affairs. Their sole contributions were labor on the land, paying taxes (usually indirect and therefore not easily recognizable as such), and, occasionally, conscription into the army or the private military forces of local leaders.

During the colonial era the thin veneer of Hispanic-European institutions and values introduced by the conquerors had fused gradually with the multitude of Indian cultures to produce a fairly stable

---

[4] The terms Indian and *mestizo* refer to culture traits and not blood lines; the latter is a person of mixed Indian-Western norms. An Indian can become a *mestizo* by changing his habit patterns, just as a *mestizo* can become a "white" or fully modernized Mexican by doing the same thing.

and self-perpetuating traditional culture which set a high value on isolation, adjustment to environment, and rejection of novelty.[5] The Spanish missionaries who acted as principal disseminators of European norms spread the Roman Catholic faith by syncretizing adoration of the indigenous gods with simplified and debased forms of Christianity, leaving the masses not only in religion but in most aspects of life with a sense of mysticism, resignation, and the hope for some outside agency rather than personal efforts to resolve problems.

This sense of stoic fatalism carries over in the political system as one element in the political style of even nationally aware Mexicans, who are notably lacking in the sort of political motivation that might encourage them to participate very actively on the input, policy-making side of the political process. Reinforcing this pattern is the anomie growing out of a lack of self-esteem produced by the difficulties of resolving the personal identity problem, which will be considered presently.

In politics both physical isolation and the natural tendencies of an oppressed people heightened the sense of inwardness, of *localismo*, leading each community to evolve its own parochial-style government. Even after Mexico became independent the inhabitant of this sort of community had little or no consciousness of a national political system because, with the exception of sporadic instances of military conscription or the legalized stealing of his lands or water rights, the operations of formal government hardly touched him. In most cases where government did affect him the villager was more likely to see the act, as he did many other calamities in his life, as the personal whim of a local political leader allied with the *hacendados* than as the action of a legitimate government.

The degree to which the individual villager might be able to conceive of government or to which conservative and xenophobic attitudes were inflexible depended of course upon the stability of his culture or upon his general attitude toward the wide world. In large measure cultural stability and the closed society coincided most fully in the more Indian areas, those states of the central plateau and the south where the largest number of close-knit Indian communities had managed to salvage their own lands. Being mainly subsistence farmers, they were least dependent upon and least susceptible to out-

---

[5] A helpful discussion of pertinent culture traits among traditionally oriented Mexicans can be found in Sol Tax, ed. *Heritage of Conquest, passim.*

side modernizing influences. The Indian who worked the land of a *latefundista*, on the other hand, had little choice about becoming aware of some aspects of government activity, for it was government in the form of soldiers or rural police which collected taxes, enforced the debt bondage system, and put down his protests at inhuman conditions.

In the northern and western states, where Indians were few and the somewhat more westernized *mestizo* worked the large cattle ranches and commercial agricultural haciendas, the villager was apt to be slightly more aware of the nation, to recognize the effects of outside influences upon his own life, and to consider the possibility of bringing pressure himself. He usually understood national politics only imperfectly. If he became desperate enough, he might resort to anomic action to resolve his problems. It was no coincidence that most of the political revolts during the past century came from the north and west.

Despite differences in degree of awareness of the nation and of receptivity to change, neither Indian nor *mestizo* really participated in any meaningful way in formal politics until economic development brought about social change and pressures which ultimately forced more Mexicans into the main stream of national life. Even then the greatest part of the population looked upon innovation with suspicion and mistrust because for most of them experience taught that change always seemed to be for the worse. Psychologically the tendency toward withdrawal was strengthened by the dual pressures of culture-change anxiety and a deeply internalized sense of personal insecurity which continues to manifest itself in inverse form as *machismo*, with its characteristic suspicion, violence, and emphasis on male sexual prowess. The very fact that pressure for change came from outside authority may have caused the parochial villages to close in on themselves in order to maintain their identity. In many cases subject awareness characterized by such government outputs as taxation, conscription, or legal confiscation of property seemed to work in reverse, reinforcing parochial orientation rather than national integration.

A surprising number of persons from the tradition-bound rural mass nonetheless did make the transition into national political life, both individually and collectively. Some, full-blooded Indians but *mestizo* or European in culture, like Beneto Juárez and Porfirio Díaz, became Presidents of the Republic. Others represented an anomic reaction to the intolerable pressures on the poor imposed by Díaz and his *científicos*—Emiliano Zapata and Pancho Villa, for example. In fact, as Levy suggests,[6] when conditions became appropriate a surprising number of members of the lower-class traditional group participated in the Mexican Revolution of 1910, a very few as leaders but many more as fighters.

This is an excellent example of how men's implicit assumptions about their ability to control their environment, including political environment, can and do shift as examples of change become available. Note how what must have been a growing disposition toward and pressure for greater participation in the national life was held in abeyance until a crack in the facade of control imposed by the old system appeared. At the same time, however, we have seen already that a shift in that assumption was not accompanied by a change in the general assumptions about the possibility of the individual's participating actively in policy making. Change in one facet of culture is not necessarily accompanied automatically or immediately by changes in other, related values or understandings about politics.

After the military phase of the Revolution many of those who had traversed the country fighting—women (*soldaderas*) as well as men—remained a part of the national political life, but many more returned to their home villages, some to revert to the old traditionalism and others to provide the nucleus around which future modernization could build when economic development provided roads, schools, and other innovating influences.

For every example of a modernizer, however, there remained a large number of persons bound to the traditional way of life, the norms of which interacted to form a highly integrated and stable system that could be changed only with great difficulty. Nevertheless, change has occurred not only among the already less rigid *mestizos* but even among the Indians, so that both the total number and the proportion of pure parochials is falling steadily. In fact a recent spurt in the number crossing over into national life has brought with it problems of adjustment and integration which make the development of a single democratic political culture more difficult.

Technology and its by-products have assisted the leaders of the

[6] See Marion J. Levy, "A Philosopher's Stone," *World Politics*, Vol. 5, July 1953, pp. 555-568. A careful review of the evidence that parochials did participate in Mexican national politics under appropriate conditions was prepared by Donald Herr in "Political Acculturation: Mexico Since 1910," a graduate seminar paper at Yale University, 1962.

Mexican Revolution to begin the process of inculcating modern values in the population and to incorporate one-time parochials into the national life.[7] In a material sense the country has accomplished near-miracles in providing the requisites for successful transition to economic and social modernization. Using W. W. Rostow's terms, the preconditions for economic take-off were established during the early post-revolutionary period up to the late thirties; the actual take-off occurred during the 1940's and 1950's, hastened no little by the impact of World War II; today Mexico is beginning the drive for economic maturity. In support of the process of quick development the revolutionary government has followed a policy of heavy public investment, particularly in social overhead activities. Although these expenditures were made primarily with social and economic ends in mind, inevitably they have political consequences.

Materially the bases for a modern, balanced, internally oriented economy are clearly evident. Money crops, both food and fiber, are rapidly replacing subsistence farming, and mechanization of food processing permits a more efficient national market. Industrial production and processing of petroleum for domestic use are surpassing mineral extraction, trade, and services as producers of wealth. As the source of the national product shifts, gross national product and per capita income increase, though benefits are by no means distributed evenly throughout the population. For a small rural segment, in fact, per capita income probably has fallen since the Revolution.

Transportation and communications of all sorts have multiplied rapidly, tying the population together and opening the possibility of interaction on a national scale. Urbanization, with its opportunities for social contact and improved political awareness, has been marked. The proportion of population in cities of over 10,000 inhabitants rose from 12.2 per cent in 1900 to 37.5 per cent in 1960. The Federal District, with over 5.5 million inhabitants, and Mexico City proper, with some 3 million citizens, had more population than the next seven largest cities combined, providing a principal focus for political socialization and activity.

Literacy rates and formal education also have improved remarkably, opening new opportunities for mass participation in national life and politics. Between 1910 and 1960 literacy rose from 30 per

---

[7] These generalizations on social and economic development are based on detailed data which have been eliminated from this study but which appear in my text on Mexican politics in Little, Brown's Series in Comparative Politics.

cent to 62 per cent. Between 1950 and 1960 school attendance rose from 48.5 to 65 per cent of the children of primary school age. By 1971 the government plans to provide enough schools to care for all primary students, despite the terrible burden of increases in the national population of over 3 per cent each year. Dropouts, particularly in rural areas, continue to limit the role of education in national integration and political socialization. During 1963 the Secretary of Education pointed out that of each 1,000 children who enter primary school 983 drop out before completing the six-year cycle. In the same year only about 10 per cent of all Mexicans students attended some kind of educational institution more advanced than a primary school. Despite these limitations, expanding educational opportunities, spreading influence of the mass media of communications, and increasing ease of transportation are exposing more and more Mexicans to the national sphere.

The relative success of this economic and social transition points up just how difficult is the process of political modernization even under generally favorable government auspices. Many, perhaps most, of the factors of material and social modernization appear to be present in the Mexican environment. Involvement of large numbers of the population in national life is strong; specialization of economic and social activities has produced apparently skilled social groups. There is a fairly high rate of information flow within the society and between the populace and the government, which has the means of penetrating both the society and the economy. But the final step toward a participatory political culture and a modern integrated polity seems very difficult to take. The majority of individual Mexicans have not yet lost their suspicion of fellow citizens or of government; neither individuals nor social groups and functional interest associations as yet act independently upon the input functions of the political process. Other than the government's revolutionary party, political movements or parties are neither very numerous nor very effective. Most of the nominal anti-government organizations and their leaders are related to the governing faction in some way, making them a not merely "loyal" but supine opposition. One gets a feeling that the give and take of authentic pluralism simply does not exist.

In short, despite the involvement of an ever-increasing proportion of the population in the national life and economy, even the vast majority of urbanized *mestizos* have been unable to resolve the problems of national and personal identity which might enable them to act as fully effective participants in the political process. If this is true of the urban Mexicans, it is much more true of their rural counterparts. Nonetheless change—that slow, uneven, and politically not very constructive change already mentioned, but change for all of that—is occurring. More and more persons have been made aware of and drawn into the national life, and for many of them opportunities for social intercourse and political interaction are greater than they ever have been before. Perhaps the most graphic indication of the implications of change that can be offered is a review of the shifts occurring in the class structure. While it is impossible to offer a detailed breakdown of change by political culture groups, comparison of social change by classes (see Table 1) suggests the trend away from parochial and toward nationally oriented political norms.[8]

Some idea of the composition of each of these classes is available in

TABLE 1: THE CHANGING CLASS STRUCTURE IN MEXICO, 1895-1960
(per cent)

Classes and Sub-classes	1895	1940	1950	1956	1960 (est.)
Upper					
Leisure	0.4	0.4	0.5	1.0	1.5
Semi-leisure	1.1	2.5	1.5	4.0	5.0
Sub-total	1.5	2.9	2.0	5.0	6.5
Middle					
Stable	6.1	6.1	8.0	15.0	17.0
Marginal	1.7	6.5	17.0	15.0	16.5
Sub-total	7.8	12.6	25.0	30.0	33.5
Transitional	—	6.5	20.0	20.0	20.0
Popular	90.7	78.0	53.0	45.0	40.0

[8] See Cline, *Mexico: Revolution to Evolution, 1940-1960 . . .*, *op.cit.*, pp. 122ff. for a discussion of how these classes were derived. Hugo Pompa Estrada, in "Niveles Socioeconómicos de un Pueblo," *Hoy*, January 5, 1963, pp. 37-39, offers an interesting confirmation of Cline's findings based on 1960 census data. Estrada breaks down socioeconomic classes as follows:

Classes	Percentages
Alta } Media Superior }	—10
Media Inferior	—30
Baja Superior	—35
Baja Inferior	—25
Total	100

Cline's accompanying breakdown of the classification by occupation of economically active persons as presented in Table 2. Using these two

TABLE 2: SOCIAL CLASSES AND OCCUPATIONS: SUMMARY, 1950-1956
(thousands employed)

	Estimates, 1950			Estimates, 1956	
Class or Category	Number	Per Cent	Proportion	Number	Per Cent
Upper					
Managerial			All	77.4	
Professional			⅓	137.7	
Sub-total	124.5	1.5		215.1	2.0
Middle					
Stable					
Professional-technical			⅔	274.6	
Office workers			½	452.8	
Small tradesmen			⅓	456.7	
Sub-total	830.0	10.0		1,184.1	12.0
Marginal					
Office workers			½	452.8	
Small tradesmen			⅓	456.7	
Artisans			⅓	662.3	
Sub-total	1,535.5	18.5		1,571.8	16.0
Sub-total	2,365.5	28.5		2,755.9	28.0
Transitional					
Small tradesmen			⅓	456.7	
Artisans, semi-skilled			⅔	1,324.5	
Miners, petroleum			All	42.2	
Service employees			⅔	619.6	
Sub-total	1,760.0	20.0		2,443.0	24.8
Popular					
Service employees			⅓	309.8	
Manual day labor			All	383.8	
Agriculturalists			All	3,559.0	
Unknown			All	194.0	
Sub-total	4,150.0	50.0		4,446.6	45.2
Economically Active	8,300.0	100.0		9,860.6	100.0

tables and the other descriptive materials presented earlier, it is possible to analyze Mexico's contemporary political culture and to estimate the size and composition of its three identifiable sub-cultures and to suggest the trend of their development.

Since the Revolution Mexico has developed what must be called a single political culture even though it is made up of three overlapping and interpenetrating but analytically identifiable political sub-cultures—parochial, subject, and participant. Dominant among these is the subject political sub-culture. The greatest part of the country's inhabitants are aware of and accept the centralizing national authority, albeit reluctantly, and relate most directly to the output performance of government rather than to input functions or to citizenship participation responsibilities. The norms which motivate the members of the smaller parochial and participant political sub-cultures are not completely distinct from those influencing the subjects, however, nor are the subjects unaware of or unaffected by traditional and participatory values. In fact each of the political sub-cultures share some of the values motivating the other two, and the interrelationship among all three is so fluid and so intertwined that we cannot consider them systemically mixed and interpenetrating only slightly but must classify them as different tendencies of a single political culture. This is especially true of the two "national" sub-cultures, the subject and the participant.

The persistence of this tripartite division in the political culture and the continued intermingling of more or less incompatible norms in all three sub-cultures suggest that Mexico has found it difficult to fuse traditional value patterns into an integrated political infrastructure which includes more modern values and which can relate constructively with modernizing national political structures. Among the increasingly large proportion of citizens who think in terms of the nation few can be classed as pure subjects or participants; instead, as each individual tends to emphasize one rather than another set of norms, he leans toward the subject or participant sub-culture but does not necessarily reject all the values of the other. At the same time he probably carries with him disrupting influences in the form of stubborn parochial value patterns which can hamper his full integration into modern political life. All of this leaves the average Mexican with a blurred and confused understanding of acceptable modes of political action and a broad range of dysfunctional reactions to national government no matter what form the political structures may take.

In Mexico, as in other transitional polities, one is struck by the ambivalence concerning political attitudes held by most nationally conscious persons. An obvious surge toward ordered, rational, and systematic politics is counterbalanced by what appears to be a continuation of nearly endemic resort to violence, mistrust of other people—both as individuals and as political leaders—lack of self-assurance, and seeking after warmth in interpersonal relations, all reinforced by strong feelings of rejection of authority in any form. The positive and modernizing political norms are institutionalized in the revolutionary ideology and accomplishments, while the negative personal sentiments and action patterns are so deeply embedded in the general as well as the political culture that they carry generic and widely understood names—*machismo, dignidad, personalismo*.

Quite clearly this ambivalence is a direct result of political culture fragmentation brought about by the shift from diffuse and localized norms to differentiated national values inherent in modernization, a fragmentation intensified both by the high rate of change and by differences in the ability of socializing agencies to accommodate themselves to change. In the Mexican experience the rate of adjustment to modern conditions has been much faster in areas of formally learned actions and the values stemming from the cognitive processes through which individuals approach the operations of their political system and much slower in areas of deeply internalized motivation, cooperation, and associational norms which shape the personality in its attitude toward political life. That is, political socialization and particularly recruitment into active political participation are slowed and distorted by basic values inculcated by the general socialization process.

This is not to say that change, however uneven, is not taking place. The number and proportion of pure or nearly pure parochials who are unaware of the nation is shrinking at a rapid rate; at present it probably does not exceed 25 per cent of the population, all in the popular or lowest sector and of which about one-third are Indians. Those who might be classed as sharing the subject political sub-culture make up about 65 per cent of the whole, including the remaining 15 per cent of the popular class, the 20 per cent of the transitional group, most of the marginal middle and many of the stable middle class, and even a few from the upper class. The 10 or so per cent who share participant political culture norms are found primarily in the upper and in the stable middle class; of these no more than 1 or 2 per cent could be characterized as viewing politics from the perspective of the more nearly democratic "civic culture" of Almond and Verba.

Considering how imprecise the boundaries are, this classification of political sub-cultures may be overly simplistic. While the facts suggest that rather basic shifts are taking place in the social and occupational patterns, important because political competence increases to some extent as one moves up the social and economic scale, the breakdown cannot indicate more than gross categories. In discussing parochials, for example, one lumps together tribal Indians who never heard of Mexico as such, emerging traditionals who are about to make the transition to some more nearly national status, and emotional parochials who reject national life for normative rather than rationalistic reasons in a kind of residual category that includes every Mexican who by definition is not a subject or participant. It is similarly impossible to indicate where along the continuum of political development any given portion of the 65 per cent of subjects may be located.

From the viewpoint of theory this classification has other and possibly more important weaknesses. It appears to suggest that the modernization process is both unilinear and unidirectional when in fact it cannot be proved to be either. From the evidence supplied in this study it is obvious that each of the three political sub-cultures is made up of numerous very different groups and that they do not necessarily follow any single orderly progression in their reaction to the stimuli that result from modernization. Although with the exception of a very few psychologically induced rejections almost all Mexicans undoubtedly will respond to these stimuli by becoming nationally oriented, the precise nature of their national being may well depend on the diverse elements in their backgrounds. As already suggested, in some cases the carry-over from earlier, less "modern" patterns may continue to pervade the political culture of large numbers of nationally aware citizens and, conversely, more modern attitudes may affect portions of the population who are not yet integrated into the modern world.

Although this description of the Mexican political culture and its sub-cultures admittedly is not entirely satisfactory pragmatically and theoretically, it does serve the purpose of this study in the sense of showing how, as modernization progressed, a national polity evolved. The information presented indicates how rapidly and in certain instances how unevenly formerly isolated traditionals are being absorbed into Mexico's national economy and society. It does not indicate how quickly or even whether such persons ever will become participant or democratic citizens or suggest why this next step should be so difficult. For some insight into these problems we must turn to another kind of analysis.

ROBERT E. SCOTT

The Process of Political Socialization

Induction into the political culture is a psychological process, the end product being a set of attitudes. In traditional cultures it is essentially an unplanned and implicit process; in more modern cultures socialization continues beyond this into a whole sequence of manifest politically socializing experiences through the primary and secondary structures of society. As a consequence the attitudes of every Mexican toward the polity is a product of his whole life experience. Early socialization, learned ideas about politics, exposure to the political process, and his own reactions to all these events combine to give each person a particular image of the society and of his role in it. For a sense of completeness, of full personal identity, all these experiences should be reasonably consistent and integrated. But in a transitional society there is no single set of accepted norms or of political realities. The Mexican brings to his image of society and of the political system and to his conception of personal political role a wide range of conflicting and sometimes mutually incompatible attitudes.

Almost inevitably therefore progress toward political modernization in the sense of development of a single and effective participant political culture with appropriate political structures has been agonizingly slow and uneven. Both individually and as a nation the Mexicans long have suffered what Erikson and Pye term the identity crisis. For nearly a century an ever-growing number of persons have searched for a sense of personal integrity based upon a consistent set of political norms which would enable them to relate to national government. But there is no single set of norms that encourages all of the modernizing and nationalizing traits and restrains the traditional and localizing values, any more than there is a single legitimate and workable set of national political structures. The various agencies that socialize the individual into social and political life are as diversified as the culture in which they operate, so that all too often the deeply internalized values which control motivations or attitudes of social cooperation reflect traditional sentiments incompatible with learned skills which seek to mold competent modern citizens. In the same way, the formal constitutional agencies suitable for a participant political culture must compete with operational auxiliary political structures such as the revolutionary party which act as control devices over the dominant subject political sub-culture.

Having no single broadly accepted political culture to which he can relate confidently, the incompletely acculturated Mexican finds himself in what seems to be a vicious circle. Without widely shared norms to provide acceptable boundaries for the development of consistent and integrative patterns of individual values and acts no sense of personal identity can evolve, but without some reasonably consistent set of shared personality traits neither can any sense of a single national identity emerge. In fact, of course, neither the problem of national identity nor the problem of personal identity is incapable of solution. Other countries have resolved them, and as conditions become more propitious Mexico is beginning to do so also.

Of the two problems, that of national identity is closer to solution because it is affected by more general and observable factors. The material advances brought about by industrialization, for example, have multiplied opportunities for induction into national life through improved transportation and communication and for indoctrination through education, reinforced by such nationalizing symbols as the country itself and particularly the Revolution of 1910. Nonetheless the problem of national identity will not be solved overnight, for the difficulties to surmount are many and varied.

Clearly in Mexico there is no single all-embracing national character, nor can one talk properly of modal personality types because such a concept presupposes a certain degree of cultural stability which is not very widespread in the country's fluid social environment. Here the insights provided by Almond's conception of political culture, with its formulations of cumulativeness and interrelationship among analytically separable sectors in the society, are helpful. Despite identification of three political sub-cultures which reflect distinct individual reactions to the polity, we know that some of the norms involved are shared with greater or lesser intensity by all (or at least the greater part) of the members of the community. The degree of intensity with which each individual holds each of several sets or clusters of values, beliefs, and symbols makes him primarily a parochial, subject, or participant. In present-day Mexico, we know, the largest part of the population emphasizes the cluster of attitudes which reflect subject political culture norms.

Lack of general agreement on political culture norms, indeed lack of consistent individual attitudes, is a direct result of anomalies in the socialization pattern. Unlike polities with a more nearly integrated political culture, where all three stages of the political socialization process—basic socialization, political socialization, and political recruitment—show a high level of consistency and continuity, reinforcing each other and strengthening the sense of political coherence, in Mexico fundamental contradictions are inculcated by the several stages. Many, perhaps most, of the basic norms supplied by early socialization continue to resemble values appropriate to a more diffuse parochial political culture, while later and more formalized political socialization provides the dual subject-participant norms already noted.

The cleanest break between the passive subject and the more influential participant comes, however, at the level of political recruitment, for only recruitment into some sort of explicit political role really is tantamount to full participatory socialization. This does not necessarily mean running for elective office or holding an appointive public position. It also could mean voting or having opinions on questions of public policy in specific or general matters, or both. Probably as a least common denominator it means being aware of the possibility of influencing the input or policy-making side of the political process and being willing to support leaders who do attempt to influence the making or the implementation of government decisions. The total number of Mexicans so completely politicized is small because notwithstanding expansion of the number of potentially influential specialized political roles the proportion of persons who compete for them and who participate actively in politics is still remarkably limited.

It may be too drastic to suggest that the traditional patterns of behavior which help mold the social and political infrastructure undermine and disrupt the more modern patterns which provide the superstructure of the national political system, but the traditional patterns certainly do not fuse easily with or reinforce the more modern ones. Social and economic modernization have produced conditions under which the formal and technical skills of civic competence and manipulation of complex government can be learned, together with incentives for acquiring and applying such skills. But the motivations impressed upon the average person by the pre-adult socialization process inhibit the tendency to move wholeheartedly into what to him is a cold, achievement-oriented, and highly competitive modern political system with concomitant requirements of submission to impersonal authority.[9] Closely related to this are built-in

---

[9] While Glade and Anderson, *The Political Economy of Mexico, passim,* cite several authorities, including Wilbert Moore and John Fayerweather, as offering evidence that Mexican entrepreneurs are moving in the direction of David McClelland's achieving society, it should be emphasized that only a tiny number of persons have

inhibitions against development of associational sentiments and values conducive to cooperative collective political action. As we shall see presently, these inhibitions result from the average Mexican's widespread mistrust of his fellow citizens and his need for a dependency relationship with particular individuals, both products of an authoritarian environment.

This barrier to effective participation in politics arises because two important components of cultural outlook—basic motivation and capacity to relate to others—are defined and inculcated by the earliest stages of general socialization and therefore are more deeply internalized than the cognitions and formally learned social-political skills with which they compete. As a consequence it has proved difficult for a majority of Mexicans to adjust their attitudes fully to the demands of a modern participatory political system. This presents a particularly tenacious problem because there is a kind of circularity of influences at work. The non-cooperative action patterns have produced authoritarian operational structures, and these structures in turn define and reinforce the norms of suspicion, mistrust, and rejection of collective action. These operational structures range all the way from very basic, highly personal family and primary groups to informal political agencies like the revolutionary party.

To put it another way, the traditionally oriented sentiments and action patterns implanted in most Mexicans by the primary socializing structures—family, friends, Church, even workplace experience and social contacts—do not relate very well with those supplied by the secondary components of the modernizing political infrastructure—the voluntary and functional interest groups and associations, the political party, the mass media of communication. Transmission of individual and primary group impulses, needs, preferences, and desires into the general political system is weak, because the diverse goals are poorly articulated and inefficiently aggregated.

This does not mean that as modernization occurs no change whatsoever has taken place in the processes of socialization, including political socialization. Several vital changes which presage gradual shifts in political values and understandings are apparent. In prerevolutionary Mexico socialization tended to result mainly from primary contact—the family, village group, *patrón*, or local political boss—rather than through secondary agencies which might integrate

---

made the transition even in the economic sector. In the general social and the political sectors the process is still less apparent.

the individual into the national political system. Membership in the nation, if stressed at all, was through diffuse secondary institutions such as Church or school with essentially non-political and hardly participatory norms. Although such diffuse primary and secondary socializing agencies continue to operate, modernization has provided a whole new set of socializers. Not only are these new agencies more numerous and differentiated, but also the experience gained in exposure to mass media of communication, in tremendously expanded social and physical mobility, new work situations, in participation (no matter how minimal) in functional interest associations and political movements changes expectations about government and about participation in the political process.

Inevitably, but much more slowly, that experience leads also to changes in the norms of the more traditional primary socializing agencies. We know that the most deeply internalized values inculcated by the family, Church, certain aspects of the educational process, and the like—authoritarianism, inhibition of easy collective action—continue to fuse poorly with the learned patterns of cooperative political life that represent modernization. Nonetheless generalizing and modernizing norms are beginning to penetrate the primary as well as the secondary social structures, and some of them actually have begun to reinforce national consciousness and the process of political modernization.

It is scarcely necessary to point out that the nature of the political culture mix depends directly upon the conditions that obtain during the socialization process. While it is true that modernization has brought with it greater opportunity for any Mexican to acquire the skills of modern politics—since education, communications, and economic interdependence make the learning process easier and the rewards higher—the rural Mexican remains less likely to be exposed to the most meaningful politicizing influences of advanced education, specialized occupational roles and groupings, mass media of communication, or social mobility, not to mention active participatory political experience. Consequently he is inclined to reflect action patterns based on the aggressive and essentially socially uncooperative norms inculcated by the traditional and primary socializing agencies. In most cases he carries these patterns with him to town or city, as so many have in past years, particularly if he becomes a part of the shapeless marginally employed popular or transitional group exposed only slightly to new secondary socializing mechanisms.

Even those more successful migrants, with greater opportunity to participate in collective action organizations such as labor unions or social action groups, face difficulties in adjusting and in utilizing their memberships as acculturating agents because of the insecurities they feel from the rapid culture change involved in moving from rural to urban environment. There is also the factor of cultural lag; the attitudes learned earliest are deeply embedded and hardest to change.

The urban population is much more conveniently situated for exposure to the modernization process, but even among this group the pattern is uneven because of the lag of the primary socializers in adjusting to the norms of modern politics. Throughout the country but particularly in the larger cities those who appear most positively oriented toward modern participant and democratic values are the young men. They are exposed to a higher proportion of cognitive-type socializing agencies and their experience with the basic socializing influences of family, primary group contacts, and school experience has been demonstrated to be considerably more open and even more democratic than that known by their parents.

Women and girls also tend more toward modernity as they are urban and younger, but as a group they lag appreciably behind the males. The culture tends to treat women as second-class human beings intellectually and economically and therefore as second-class citizens as well. Easy integration into modern life, including politics, is limited for them by lack of opportunities to participate in the broadening experience of advanced education, specialized occupations, or responsible social roles. This marked inferior status, mainly but not solely in the family, leaves women frustrated and often with neurotic tendencies which they pass on to their children in the form of anti-social attitudes.

These barriers to effective politicization are highest for the majority of Mexicans in the popular and transitional social-economic class, whether rural or urban, because all of the negative factors seem to combine and conspire against allowing them to move easily into modern political life. But even the middle and upper sectors face the problem of uneven political acculturation which produces the anomaly of a tripartite political culture.

One striking fact which emerges from our review of social and economic change is the obvious growth of the middle sector. Between 1940 and 1960 this classification has multiplied three times until now it represents a third of the whole population.[10] If many of these people continue to operate at an extremely low level of economic productivity and social-political awareness, they are at least attuned to national life and provide the intermediate elite leadership necessary to indoctrinate the parochials and the less fully socialized subjects into the modern polity.

As modernization has reached down and out to the once submissive lower class, the traditional fabric of social controls has weakened, but no new pattern of controls based on formal constitutional norms has been constructed to replace it. The newly aware Mexicans look upon government in highly unrealistic terms. Lacking experience in political participation and rejecting government authority on psychological bases, they begin with little or no sense of loyalty to the nation or its formal political norms and even less conception of the operation of governmental input functions or their role in them. On the other hand, they relate strongly to the output function, identifying government—or, more likely, the president—with the old *patrón* upon whom so many relied for indoctrination. In the modern setting they expect a maximum of government services for a minimum of taxation, absolute protection of their personal freedom with equally absolute lack of interference in personal activities. And they want all this without paying the price of individual participation in the political process, which, as Verba suggests in his Chapter 12 in this volume, tends to include a sense of responsibility and a greater ability to compromise.

Having considered some of the changes occurring in the mechanisms of political socialization that may help resolve the problem of national identity, let us now turn to a problem which makes these shifts less constructive and functional than otherwise they might be, the problem of developing in the Mexican a sense of individual identity. In *The Civic Culture* Almond and Verba characterize Mexico's present-day political culture as having a high rate of cognitive self-appraisal but a relatively low standard of performance. They suggest that this can be attributed to the experience of the social revolution which implanted a sense of expectation by means of its past

---

[10] In addition to Cline's comments on this phenomenon, in *Mexico: Revolution to Evolution, 1940–1960*, Chap. XI, see John J. Johnson, *Political Change in Latin America: The Emergence of the Middle Sectors*, Palo Alto, 1958. Another useful source that collects some North American and Mexican comments on class structure changes is M. Othón Mendizábal *et al.*, *Las Clases Sociales en México* (Mexico, D.F., n.d.).

accomplishments and promise for the future while at the same time inhibiting any sense of freedom to act because of the violence which accompanied the earlier phase of the movement. This interpretation is valid as far as it goes, but the phenomenon rests on more basic factors inherent in the Mexican psyche and reinforced by the socialization process.

Almost endemic in the political culture and in the mind of the individual is a combination of anxieties, personal insecurities, and rejection of authority that not only permeates the basic pre-adult socialization process but also extends into adult social relationships and spills over into the political realm as well. These traits, which affect not only political outlook but political action as well, are responsible for these ambivalences of personality and social-political role.[11]

Speaking of the personality structure of the *machista*, a common Mexican type, one native observer characterized his fellow countrymen as "a childlike people, near adolescence, with few examples of maturity or of productive character. Common attributes are receptivity, dependency, irresponsibility, scorn for human life, physical force, feminine conquest, mourning and death, armed aggression, and maternal reliance that seeks a miracle to resolve problems. Mexicans avoid reliance upon their own resources, do not employ prolonged effort, constancy, and efficiency. They also like facilitation, improvisation, pull, nepotism, recommendation; [they] demand pardon and consideration from everyone else."[12]

Most Mexicans, particularly those in the majority who are most influenced by subject political culture norms, share many of these characteristics. Despite the appearance of entrepreneurial types as the economy matures the low level of personal and political motivation evidenced by most citizens results from the psychologically induced fantasy that some day, somehow, they will be able to receive

---

[11] In addition to the general works on Mexico cited earlier much of the material on personality types and psychological attitudes derives from studies by Mexican psychologists and psychoanalysts, including the following: Ancieto Aramoni, *Psicoanálisis de la Dinámica de un Pueblo*, Mexico, 1961; Francisco González Pineda, *El Mexicano: Su Dinámica Psicosocial*, Mexico, 1961; and *El Mexicano: Psicología de su Destructividad*, Mexico, 1961; María Elvira Bermúdez, *La Vida Familiar del Mexicano*, Mexico, 1955; Rogelio Díaz Guerrero, *Estudios de Psicología del Mexicano*, Mexico, 1961; M. Loreto H., *Personalidad(?) de la Mujer Mexicana*, Mexico, 1961; José Gómez Robleda, *Psicología del Mexicano*, Mexico, 1962. Their observations and those of Mexican and foreign anthropologists and sociologists are reassuringly similar if one takes into account the differing frames of reference. Generally they tend to substantiate the more specifically political findings of journalists and political scientists who have studied Mexico's politics.

[12] Ancieto Aramoni, *op.cit.*, p. 287.

everything as a gift and return to the sweet and simple dependency of their earliest years. This quality is so deeply ingrained in the culture that a generic term—the search for a miracle—has come into professional usage. What strong motivation does exist is sidetracked from effective political activity to the search for personal identity and for a sense of adequacy in the individual's social role. As Alex Inkeles has pointed out, lack of self-esteem is a basic cause of anomie, which helps to explain the relatively low level of political participation and of meaningful partisan opposition which obtains in a political system undergoing rapid change.

The fact that the environment is in continual flux may heighten the sense of inadequacy and insecurity because new perspectives are constantly required. This may help explain the tendency of politicized persons to pull back from modern activities, including politics, where a great deal of personality adjustment may be demanded. The individual may find it necessary to consolidate his character from time to time, just as the country as a whole seemed to do during periods in the 1940's and 1950's when the less dynamic administrations of Presidents Ávila Camacho and Ruiz Cortines followed those of the great social and economic innovators, Cárdenas and Alemán.

The personality problems inherent in an environment subject to continuous change are suggested by the nature of the defense mechanisms which evolve. In a study covering Mexico City, where both speed of change and proportion of persons involved is greatest, Díaz Guerrero found a high rate of neurotics, totaling 33 per cent, especially among women, with a rate of 44 per cent. He found also a high degree of rigidity in toleration of the views of other persons and groups, 34 per cent of the sample tested. Most important, he discovered very little plasticity on acceptance of social change, with over 70 per cent of the adult respondents embracing ideals which apparently interfere with adaptation to an environment in continuous change.[13]

It is my contention that the deep-seated anxieties and need for reassurance as to self-esteem, resulting from a series of mutually reinforcing environmental conditions ranging all the way from early authoritarian family experience to the inquietude accompanying rapid culture change, result in overcompensation that on the social side takes the form of *machismo* and on the political side the naïvely

---

[13] Díaz Guerrero, *op.cit.*, "La Salud Mental, Personal y Social del Mexicano de la Ciudad," pp. 69-79.

high rate of cognitive self-appraisal already cited.[14] To this overevaluation of the individual's role in social and political situations must be added his inability to subordinate personal interest to socially responsible collective activity.

Like Pye's Burmese, the Mexican tends to view reality in a highly subjective manner and to conceive of his actions as ends in themselves. He finds it difficult to understand the notion that phenomena are related or that causal relationships really occur. As a consequence he does not exhibit any strong sense of the existence or operation of social collectivity.[15] This view is institutionalized throughout Latin America and particularly in Mexico as *dignidad,* which is a way of minimizing the individual's responsibility toward the community as a whole or toward its subordinate units while maximizing self-realization. Pre-adult socialization, bolstered by later experience, inculcates the necessity of a man's viewing himself as an entity different from all others in order to enhance the sense of personal identity. Because he views society in this way, he tends to consider other persons similarly rather than as factors in a rational or at least understandable system of relations. Nearly everything in the early socialization process hinders development of a sense of collective responsibility toward the polity at the expense of individual self-fulfillment.

Nor does the growth of material and secular norms of modernization have much effect upon this outlook. The as yet inconsiderable number of persons who have begun to replace subjective sentiments by more objective ones have adopted either passive or rejective attitudes that isolate them from community responsibility and political activity. Or, having been recruited politically, they have adopted an active, exploitative, and often authoritarian view of governing mechanisms. In either case the movement toward a sense of collective responsibility or cooperative competence is very slow.

Focusing more directly on the political implications of these personality patterns, we discover that the lack of a feeling of personal effectiveness affects political competence. Although the sense of inadequacy is masked behind a facade of high cognitive self-appraisal, the performance of most persons in the political process is consistent with their deeper self-image. The sense of and desire for dependency encourages relation to the output functions; the sense of inadequacy

---

[14] Oscar Lewis' studies of Mexican families offer analyses in depth of these phenomena. See his *Five Families, The Family of Sánchez,* and *Pedro Martínez,* cited previously.

[15] Pye, *op.cit.,* pp. 200ff.

reduces evaluation of self as a political actor and limits participation on the input side. In these terms the attitudinal factors that are most influential in the political culture are consistent with the subject sub-culture and its authoritarian centralizing operational political structures. The relatively weak ego-image of the Mexican acts as a deterrent to positive participation in most sorts of collective social functions, carrying over to voluntary groups, functional interest associations, and political parties. Instead, in psychoanalytical terms, the individual identifies with the President of the Republic as a super-ego figure, relating to him personally. In more sociological terms, instead of following a differentiated and policy-oriented motivational pattern, the individual continues to apply a more diffuse, total commitment to the chief executive as symbol of government. Note the analogy to the old *patrón* system. This use of the president as a symbol is an example of the adaption of a traditional component of authority to a new use as the political system changes.

The low level of political performance is reinforced by another broadly based personality trait, the authority syndrome. The greatest part of the population tends to resent authority when in a subordinate position but to exercise it strongly when in a superordinate role. If family authority patterns were the only causal factor, later socialization might reverse the trend. Evidence suggests, however, that authoritarian influences operate not only in the earliest primary structures which least resemble formal governmental structures but also in adult social situations which do equate more nearly with formal and specific political mechanisms. In the social sphere, experiences in family, school, religious, military, and work situations all tend to implant a greater sense of authority than of easy interpersonal relations and free participation. The point to be made here is not that authoritarian family experiences condition political attitudes but that continuing authoritarian situations reinforce and are reinforced by the family experience. If therefore the individual relates his general experience to politics, he carries with him a heavy load of dependent, rebellious, or authoritarian attitudes, depending on the status he enjoys.

This point should not be overstated, however, for we already know that other, more democratic norms coexist in the modernizing revolutionary ideology and that some types of adult socialization, including higher education and for higher status workers certain aspects of work experience, mitigate authoritarian sentiments even though they cannot fully erase them. In the same way, for today's youth family and school conditions are less authoritarian than they once were. Nonetheless, although *The Civic Culture* shows a similar tendency operating in all the modernizing countries studied, the pattern of change in this direction has been slowest in Mexico, suggesting that authoritarian values are deeply embedded in the culture.

In order to understand the Mexican's personality let us look first at some aspects of early general socialization before turning to the more specifically learned patterns and more strictly political experience. A comparison of the data of Almond and Verba on perceived participation with that on actual participation in family and school situations offers a clear picture of the strong sense of subjective competence and weak performance.[16] In the family situation respondents were asked how much influence they had at age sixteen. Mexicans recalled having had some influence to a greater extent than Germans and Italians did, but when asked how freely they could complain about family decisions, and how often they actually did complain, they moved to the lowest point on the scale. In the case of persons who actually did complain level of education appears to have had an influence. The total who did complain was 41 per cent, but only 38 per cent of the respondents with primary or less education ever did complain, compared with 51 per cent of those with some secondary education and 68 per cent of those with some university training. The same general findings were noted for the sense of freedom to participate and actual participation in school.

This is not to suggest that education as such makes the difference between social participation or lack of it, for education relates closely to class, status, economic position or lack of it, and a number of other factors which could be influential but are less easy to isolate. Nor in the case of Mexico does it suggest, as was discovered in the other countries surveyed, that the individual with consistent opportunities for social participation is apt to generalize his experience to politics. Apparently in Mexico the countervailing socializing influences weaken the individual's capacity to generalize, particularly as the operational political structures do not foster participatory activity outside the regular patterns.

Another personality trait which grows out of early socialization relates to the authority syndrome. This is the norm that weakens associational sentiments and inhibits collective action. The tendency

---

[16] See Almond and Verba, *op.cit.*, Chapter XII. Data reported below are taken *passim* from this source.

against participation in politically effective groups—whether voluntary associations, functional interest organizations, or even political parties—is partly a function of the desire to avoid authoritarian situations. Some notion of this tendency is important to our understanding of the political culture and its role in the political system because it is through the activity of such integrating mechanisms that disparate political interests are aggregated and upward articulation of interests into the governmental superstructure takes place. Where the political culture inhibits effective grouping, for whatever reason, an important auxiliary political structure is denied to the political process. It may be in fact that it is impossible or at least much more difficult to make the transition from a subject to a participant political culture without the integrating function which grouping provides.

In Mexico we encounter an intriguing anomaly concerning collective activity. A considerable number of respondents to the cross-section survey spoke of the possibility of employing groups to achieve political goals, but the total proportion of persons belonging to political groups or to potential politically influential organizations and having had experience with collective action in the governmental process is among the lowest in the five countries studied. The authors of *The Civic Culture* found it difficult to account for the Mexican's propensity to speak of forming groups but not to utilize them in the political arena. Unlike most other significant political attitudes—voting, party membership, sense of political competence, and so forth—there appeared to be no relationship between grouping and education, status, or other social phenomena. My guess is that this rather distinct Mexican political style is a direct result of certain traits growing out of the early socialization process and reinforced by later events. By using the cross-section data we may be able to identify these traits.

The clue appears to lie in the fact that unlike citizens of more integrated countries the Mexicans most apt to suggest use of groups to attain political ends are those who do not place a high value upon outgoing social traits and who show lower frequencies of social trust.[17] In general the Mexicans like the Italians do not consider civic interaction as a highly admired quality, nor do education and high occupational status change this attitude very much. For example,

---

[17] For more complete definitions of such terms as "outgoing social traits" or "social trust," as well as some indication of the measures used in evaluating these attitudes, see Almond and Verba, *op.cit.*, Chap. X.

education does increase the individual's confidence in others but, unlike the United States and England, where the number who select outgoing traits rises sharply when controls for higher training are applied, among the tiny percentage of highly educated Mexicans, well over half continue to support the strongest negative statement on trust. This seems to indicate that these attitudes are culturally instilled through the socialization process and very hard to change. The pattern is reinforced by the finding that in relating primary groups to partisanship there is little difference between social trust and cooperative political competence. Again, only 7 per cent of those who speak of using primary groups actually are active politically, as compared with 10 per cent for the whole sample. All this suggests that the group performs a rather special function in the Mexican culture and that this function does not transfer very well into effective political tactics, as the most highly politicized citizens know.

As used by the Mexicans, group seems to refer to a primary, face-to-face relationship the principal purpose of which is to provide constant personal reinforcement of self-esteem for its members, a prime necessity in the insecure and shifting environment. Even in urban situations the most basic ties are likely to be on a primary often individual basis, the so-called dyadic contract in which the participants interact in personal and reciprocal arrangements such as *personalismo* and *compadrazco*.[18] Such groups are apt to be homogenous in membership and function largely to supply an intimate and congenial atmosphere to bolster the insecure individual. In Verba's terminology the relationship of the individual to the group is expressive rather than instrumental.

Primary groups organized around diffuse reinforcement functions of this type are unlikely to shift their function to specific instrumental political purposes and in fact may inhibit their members from active participation in such functional organizations as labor unions. It is precisely the nature of the social role of such primary groups which, tied to the Mexican's low political motivation, makes for the lack of acute political partisanship. These group relationships provide a means of resolving a basic psychological problem which political activity cannot resolve. As a side effect, such grouping inhibits movement toward the input function which produces participants. It is also this factor which makes more difficult the meshing of personal

---

[18] See George M. Foster, "The Dyadic Contract: A Model for the Social Structure of a Mexican Peasant Village," *American Anthropologist*, Vol. 63, No. 6, December 1961, pp. 1173-1192.

and intimate operations of the primary structures with the more impersonal and abstract political structures.

Possibly the strongest evidence that the Mexican's tendency to suggest informal grouping as a political means represents a cultural rather than a tactically based idea results if we compare methods of influencing local as compared with national government. In all the countries surveyed the general population was more likely to suggest operating through informal groups to influence local rather than national policy, but in Mexico informal grouping was suggested almost as often for national as for local policy-influencing tactics. Even among political competents, as defined in *The Civic Culture*, this unrealistic appraisal of appropriate tactics was obvious. Fifty per cent of the local competents felt use of informal groups would be good strategy for local influence, and 46 per cent of the national competents felt the same for influencing national policy, where in practice such groups would be much less appropriate.

On the other hand, the same data indicate that the Mexicans were unrealistically sanguine in their estimate of possible success in influencing both national and local governmental policy, a further sign of high self-esteem unhampered by any great knowledge of political tactics or experience. Compare their view with that of citizens of the other countries involved (Table 3).

TABLE 3: CHANCES OF SUCCESS IN INFLUENCING LOCAL AND NATIONAL GOVERNMENT

	United States Local	United States National	United Kingdom Local	United Kingdom National	Germany Local	Germany National
Probable	27	16	18	12	23	7
Probable, if others join in	25	24	18	12	9	6
Improbable	40	54	50	63	49	73
Other, and don't know	8	6	14	13	19	14

	Italy Local	Italy National	Mexico Local	Mexico National
Probable	19	8	37	29
Probable, if others join in	3	3	0	0
Improbable	52	63	54	62
Other, and don't know	26	26	9	9

The most modernized and politicized citizens tend to suggest use of groups for political ends less frequently because emotionally they have less need of them and politically they are aware that groups of this sort are not likely to have much impact on the political process as it now operates. As a person becomes more nearly adjusted to modern life he is apt to lose some of the anxieties engendered by culture change, and because his own sense of personal identity is more nearly complete he becomes less dependent upon face-to-face assurance and thinks less of group support. At the same time, being more self-assured himself, he becomes less suspicious of the motives of other persons and more apt to value outgoing traits. But this modernizing portion of the population still is small in numbers and does retain some parochial attitudes. And, as noted previously, the early socialization process continues to reduce the sense of collective social and political responsibility, so that even among the modernizing sector in the population cooperative competence is not fully developed.

Moreover the modernizing element must work within the framework of the existing political structures which respond to the action pattern of the large, more nearly parochial mass of the population. Knowing how the political system really operates, the more politicized citizens recognize the difficulty of access to the decision-making process that faces informal groups, because policy is made at the center and hardly more than ratified by the formal elections. They know too that usually the citizen is not tied into the operational political structures as an individual or as part of an informal group but as a member of a functional interest association either within one of the PRI's three sectors or in a semi-official organization dealing with the presidency. In other words, observation and experience in the political system seem to suggest to the more politically sophisticated citizens that Mexico's political style does not provide much payoff for this particular kind of political tactic, *despite the deeply internalized identification with the primary group.* Perhaps the best way to summarize the position is to say that the idea of the primary group is basic to the general culture, but that collective action through such groups is not very meaningful in the political culture, at least not among the majority most influenced by dominant subject political culture norms. This is simply another way of saying that little fusion has occurred between the action norms of the primary groups and the secondary political structures.

Considering the personality inhibitions and the political structural barriers to effective individual participation in and influence over politics, together with the obvious function in the political process of more formal interest associations both in and out of the revolutionary party's three sectors, it might appear somewhat surprising that a larger proportion of respondents did not suggest use of formal organizations to influence government policy. Only 2 per cent suggested this tactic to influence local policy and 3 per cent to influence national policy. Since in most polities such associations are a valuable intermediate agency to supplement the primary group as a means of allowing the individual to articulate his political needs and desires, the very fact that primary groups are not a meaningful resource for intermittent influence ought to strengthen the political function of the more structured mechanisms representing varied interests. In Mexico the individual obviously does not think of unions, farm organizations, or professional associations in these terms. Whether this attitude results from the low level of political motivation, from the lack of collective competence, or from the role of such organizations in the political system as government controlled, captive "protective associations" rather than independent bargaining agencies, or a combination of all three, the result is the same—weakness in the articulation and aggregation process regarding representation of individual interests.

While this relationship to the general political system makes for a high degree of political stability and for a form of aggregation of interests imposed from the top, as well as for a minimum of dangerous pressure for extreme positions, it does little to promote individual participation in politics. It does little also to allow competition among independent interest associations, or to encourage formation of the sort of multiple, cumulative group memberships that limit exclusive loyalties and reduce the possibility of fragmentation when large numbers of citizens become increasingly active and the demands of the revolution of rising expectations surpass the expansion of material productivity. The pattern in Mexico is all too clear. Only 24 per cent of the Mexican respondents said they belonged to any voluntary association, the lowest proportion of all five countries studied and reported on in *The Civic Culture*.[19] Moreover the 2

---

[19] The other countries indicate the following figures for persons with voluntary association memberships: U.S. 57 per cent, U.K. 47 per cent, Germany 44 per cent, Italy 30 per cent. In Mexico memberships are as follows: trade unions 11 per cent, business organizations 2 per cent, professional organizations 4 per cent, charitable

per cent of all Mexicans who belonged to more than one organization also was the lowest among the countries, as was the 8 per cent of organization members who held some sort of multiple membership. As in other modern-style social activities, higher levels of education or of job status increase the probability of persons belonging to at least one voluntary organization, as they do the likelihood of persons having held office in such a group. But even here the percentages remain low. It is interesting to note that 46 per cent of the organization members believed their group was involved in politics. The parochialism of Mexican women is demonstrated by the fact that although 24 per cent of the total sample belonged to some organization, 42 per cent of the men and only 15 per cent of the women did, as well as by the fact that of 33 per cent of the organization members who had ever held office, 43 per cent of the men and 18 per cent of the women had.

So far we have discussed political socialization mainly in terms of traits that might result from basic pre-adult experience. We turn now to the area of learned skills and adult exposure to situations more nearly analogous to the political process. With the spread of educational, communication, and transport facilities, the growth of industrialization and urbanization, and the proliferation of specialized roles—of modernization and secularization in general—more and more Mexicans share appropriate skills and experience which should support an image of self-confidence and encourage participation in all kinds of relationships. If such exposure to modernization were the only factor operating on the personality, we might expect a large minority, perhaps even a majority, to have become politicized and active participants in the governmental system. This we know has not occurred.

While it may well be true that the individual who has consistent opportunity to participate in non-political decision making can generalize his experience in the political sphere, transferring social competence into political competence, in Mexico the most consistent emphasis has been the other way round. At the mature socialization stage as in the pre-adult stage the more common experience is with authoritarian controls and lack of real opportunity to share in policy

---

organizations 1 per cent, religious organizations 5 per cent, civic-political organizations 3 per cent. The bias of the cross-section sample base of towns of 10,000 population and over is evident in the lack of agricultural and cooperative organization memberships despite the existence of a large number of each affiliated with the revolutionary party.

formulation. The parallel to family and school experience is striking, as we can see if we consider workplace participation for an illustrative indication of the difference between the Mexican's self-image of his social role and the manner in which he implements his conception. The individual clearly believes he is consulted quite regularly about decisions concerning his work and feels he is reasonably free to complain about decisions affecting it, but in practice he seldom does complain.[20] The cross-section figures also show that generally as a person moves up the scale in occupational status from unskilled through skilled labor toward professional and managerial positions he is consulted more frequently and feels freer to complain, but the percentage of higher-status Mexican employees who actually are consulted remains the lowest of all five countries studied.

These findings underscore several significant observations about the role of learned skills in the general culture and their relation to political competence. First, the adult workplace experience does little to counter early authoritarian and anti-social influences. Next, work experience reinforces the Mexican's tendency to overestimate his political competence. Last, if there is a relationship between specific learning of orientations toward competence and participation in nonpolitical adult social situations and in politics, the nature of nonpolitical adult socialization generally provides little modern political competence, despite specialization of role and secularization of many aspects of the social and economic culture.

These observations are supported by the cross-section data relating to politics. The Mexican reported more frequently a sense of obligation to participate in politics than did the German and much more than the Italian, but at the same time he tended to consider that government has little effect upon his daily life. Similarly, he tended to feel

---

[20] Without repeating all the pertinent cross-section data, it might be worth comparing the performance in various countries of actual work-decision complaints. To the question "Has respondent ever really complained about work decisions?" the answers, in percentages, are:

Yes: U.S. 62 per cent; U.K. 67 per cent; Germany 57 per cent; Italy 54 per cent; Mexico 36 per cent

No: U.S. 38 per cent; U.K. 32 per cent; Germany 37 per cent; Italy 41 per cent; Mexico 63 per cent

Don't Know: U.S. ——; U.K. ——; Germany 6 per cent; Italy 5 per cent; Mexico ——

It is interesting to note that the rebellious attitude toward authority carries over to the work situation. Díaz Guerrero studied a group of workers over 18 in Mexico City, of whom 68 per cent said they liked their jobs (27 per cent did not, 5 per cent didn't know), but 63 per cent also said they resented being told how to do things (op.cit., pp. 37 and 62).

more frequently than the Italian that he follows accounts of politics and government, but this was coupled with surprisingly little real information on political matters. Nonetheless he was reluctant to admit lack of knowledge (high self-esteem); although Mexicans demonstrated the lowest political information scores, they were as willing to offer opinions and as reluctant to admit they "didn't know" as were the Germans, who had scored the highest. All this and other data from the survey, too detailed to include here, add up to a combination of setting a high value on the appearances of political action and low amounts of knowledge and skills for effective democratic participation which Almond and Verba cite as evidence of a civic aspirational tendency. These findings add up also to a high rate of political alienation, paired with a reasonably high amount of system affect (identification with or pride in the country's political institutions).

One might seek to account for output alienation by noting the low popular expectation of responsiveness and fair treatment by the government bureaucracy and the police. Compare Mexico with the other four countries in the survey. The percentage of respondents expecting fair treatment by the bureaucracy were U.S. 85 per cent, U.K. 83 per cent, Germany 65 per cent, Italy 53 per cent, Mexico 42 per cent. Those expecting unfair treatment were U.S. 9 per cent, U.K. 7 per cent, Germany 7 per cent, Italy 13 per cent, Mexico 50 per cent. Similarly, those anticipating fair treatment by the police were U.S. 85 per cent, U.K. 83 per cent, Germany 72 per cent, Italy 56 per cent, Mexico 32 per cent, while those fearing unfair police treatment were U.S. 8 per cent, U.K. 6 per cent, Germany 5 per cent, Italy 10 per cent, Mexico 50 per cent. Even stronger data can be cited on the Mexican's low expectation of consideration of his point of view, especially by the police. But one would also discover a fairly positive attitude concerning pride in the political system (system affect); 30 per cent of the Mexican respondents evinced this sentiment, as compared with the U.S. 85 per cent, U.K. 46 per cent, Germany 7 per cent and Italy 3 per cent.

Related to all this is the Mexican's sense of subjective political competence concerning freedom to discuss politics. As with other aspects of competence, the individual's impression of what he can do fails to reflect very well what he does do. Half of the respondents reported they could speak freely on political subjects, but of that half 61 per cent reported they never do, 18 per cent felt they can and do speak to most persons, and 20 per cent said they do discuss politics but avoid doing so with many or almost all people.[21]

Considering the ever-growing integration of Mexicans into the national life, some other reason than the existence of pure parochials must be sought to account for this ambivalence—relatively high system affect and positive expectations of one's social and political role on the one hand, and rejection of the effects of government and poor citizenship performance on the other. Perhaps, as Almond and Verba suggest, part of the explanation lies in the fact that Mexicans have a high though diffuse political involvement through the input structure tied to revolutionary experience. I would add what was noted previously, that for many of the most recently activated the President of the Republic represents an image to which they can relate diffusely as a substitute for positive and differentiated input activity, because for this not inconsiderable group the stage of specific policy alternatives has not yet become reality.

On the negative side, and particularly with regard to output alienation, it has been suggested that poor government performance, for example the ever-present graft and the low expectation of consideration from police and bureaucrats—coupled with an overselling of revolutionary accomplishments in school and by the mass media, leading to false hopes for both the spread of material benefits among the masses and the movement toward democratic constitutional norms—result in alienation. I hesitate to read very much into the fact that a higher amount of alienation is found on the output than the input side. The fact of the matter is that many people still do not conceive of government in terms of input functions, as evidenced by the weak individual political participation and ineffectual associational role in the policy-making process already noted. Instead, as we have seen, the basic socialization process inculcates a need for a strong dependency relationship, in this case with government, and at the same time supports the rejection of authority. When these patterns combine with the attitudes engendered by the search for personal identity they total up to tremendous pressures on government performance.

[21] Once again, education makes a difference in attitudes. The number of respondents who reported they discuss politics regularly totaled 39 per cent, but the rate for persons with primary or less education was 34 per cent, for those with some secondary school training 67 per cent, and for those with some university work 65 per cent. Those who felt reasonably free to talk politics totaled 41 per cent; with some primary 39 per cent, some secondary 54 per cent, and some university work 54 per cent.

The foregoing comments may have been unduly pessimistic. In describing factors that limit the possibility of learning political skills or of relating other adult experiences to the political system one must almost of necessity stress the negative. In fact, despite the problems involved, the personality of the modernizing Mexican seems able to struggle against the inhibiting factors of traditionalism. Of course the process is slow, and the resultant mix is not as consistent as it would be if the basic socialization process were able to adjust to modern life more easily. But a gradual expansion of political competence is already evident, with growth both in number of participating citizens and in the intensity of their activities. Equally important, the predominantly subject-oriented populace is starting to show signs of a shift in the nature of its competence. The individual is becoming more aware of himself as a political actor, and the first indications of a move from output to input pressures are becoming evident.

At present, it is true, the low intensity of individual political motivation and the effective controls exercised over the political process by the operational political structures in the hands of the revolutionary party tend to reduce the probability of a great deal of popular influence over government policy on either the input or the output side. But in terms of transition toward a participatory political culture the important fact is that such activity takes place at all, and that most such activity occurs within the frame of reference of the ongoing political system.

It is hardly surprising that the bulk of input initiative comes not simply from politically aware individuals but also from the more structured and semi-independent interests and organizations representing commerce, industry, financial groups, employers' organizations, and even the Church, all of which also exhibit a strong concern about implementation of government policy as it affects them. Significantly, however, in very recent years on specific issues the elites have turned to the masses more frequently to organize a public opinion which can have indirect influence on government policy. This has been the tactic of the Roman Catholic Church in its campaign against Communism, which began with a July 1962 Declaration of Catholic Principles signed by forty-eight members of the hierarchy in their first overt politically inspired public action since the time of the Calles administration over thirty years ago. A similar approach has been followed by Mexican conservatives, mainly but by no means all Roman Catholics, in their battle against free and compulsory primary school texts, which they term Godless and socialist, if not Communist, tinged. Leftist leaders too have taken the initiative in trying to organize popular support in attempts to force the government to adopt policies against the Alliance for Progress and favorable to Castro's Cuba. They too object to the free texts, on the ground that their content is too conservative. Few of these or similar campaigns have been successful in shifting the government from its centrist position, but the very fact that this sort of tactic is seriously considered indicates a change in generally held attitudes about the nature of the political process and the citizen's relation to it.

We shall see presently that among the operating political structures a growing number of organizations and movements representing specialized economic, social, and ideological views are developing, some within the revolutionary party and its functional sectors and some outside it. But, very important, most though not all of these groups attempt to attain their goals through the existing political system. This even includes the three legally recognized opposition national political parties and dissatisfied elements in the government party. In attempting to strengthen their position and to capture greater influence these groups are performing an aggregating function which by its very process reduces their own extremist attitudes and those of other forces. At the same time, they are performing a recruitment function as they move out among the previously unorganized citizens and seek to spur them to political action. Inevitably in reaction to these activities by the opposition the revolutionary party has expanded its policy of attempting to recruit and politicize large numbers of Mexicans, not only to broaden its popular base but also to strengthen the intensity of political action by its members.

Once again, not all of these activities are successful. During 1963, in anticipation of the next year's presidential election, Vicente Lombardo Toledano's *Partido Popular Socialista* absorbed the leftist *Partido Obrero Campesino Mexicano* but could not work out an arrangement with the ultra-extremist *Movimiento de Liberación Nacional* and the Mexican Communist Party. Similarly, the conservative *Partido de Acción Nacional* was unable to form a coalition of the rightist movements and in fact lost a splinter group that wished to follow a more liberal, Christian Democratic line. Previously both parties had contended strongly but unsuccessfully in various state and local elections. This growing organizational and electoral activity is an indication of a gradual growth in popular participation in the political system. If it has not resulted in changes in administration, it has influenced individual government policies and has led to a greater recognition of the possible role of an opposition. The national constitution, for example, was amended recently to assure that any party getting at least 2.5 per cent of the national vote in 1964 would receive a minimum of five deputies, with additional seats for each 0.5 per cent more votes up to twenty deputies.

When the PRI's Gustavo Díaz Ordaz became President of the Republic in December 1964, all Senators and 175 elected Deputies belonged to the official party, with only two candidates of the *Partido de Acción Nacional* and one of the *Partido Popular Socialista* elected to the lower chamber. As a result of the constitutional amendment, however, the minor parties' share of popular votes entitled them to *deputidos de partido* as follows: PAN—18; PPS—9; and PARM (*Partido Auténtico de la Revolución Mexicana*)—5. This enlarged non-organization voice has permitted a more balanced discussion of public policy matters, though it has had little real influence over the formal adoption of legislation.

Within the government's *Partido Revolucionario Institucional* the Left forces grouping around the figure of former President Lázaro Cárdenas and the Rightists who use former President Miguel Alemán as their symbol have become more active in past years, but both appear to be able to accept the moderate center as a bridge to keep the so-called revolutionary family united. Some individuals, such as Braulio Maldonado, ex-governor of Mexico's newest state, Baja California (Norte), may have found their political ambitions frustrated and so moved into active opposition, but the largest number of disappointed members of the official family accept temporary reversals and continue to operate through the PRI. At the state level a number of attempts have been made to reverse central government decisions on who should be governor, and at the local level similar movements to replace official party candidates for municipal president have occurred. Although all of the state-level attempts and nearly all of the local movements have failed, the nature of the political action involved on both sides suggests that a larger and more effective group of participants is operating in the revolutionary party and within the framework of the existing political system.

More generally, William V. D'Antonio's sociological studies of political attitudes of opinion leaders in Mexican border towns,[22]

[22] See W. H. Form and W. V. D'Antonio, "Integration and Cleavage Among

together with voting statistics from recent congressional and local elections, suggest that in regions where the demonstration effect of nearby North American political values has an influence, or in larger towns and cities where the influence of urbanization and of education encourage a greater degree of political interaction, an ever-increasing number of Mexicans are moving—slowly and unevenly, but moving—toward effective participant status. It may well be, as Harold Lasswell has suggested, that the constant repetition of revolutionary slogans about national integration and political equality, together with the careful perpetuation of the forms of democratic elections among several parties, have imbued the Mexicans with a set of expectations about the possibility of political participation and the belief that their votes may some day be counted. Though this viewpoint may not be widespread at present, chances are that it will grow as some of the norms of democratic responsibility and cooperative competence work down into the primary structures where, as we have seen, they are already beginning to affect the socializing function of the family, school, and other basic formative agencies. Slow as this process is, and despite the continued existence of deeply entrenched and inelastic traditional value patterns which disrupt the smooth evolution of a viable and modern political system, Mexico's political culture shows significant trends toward expanded participation and ultimately, perhaps, toward the democracy of a civic culture.

The Political Role of the Elites

Meanwhile, however, Mexico continues to be ruled by a relatively small elite group that, behind a facade of ostensibly democratic constitutional political agencies, utilizes the semiauthoritarian political structures of the revolutionary party and the presidency to dominate the subject-oriented bulk of the citizens. This is possible for a number of reasons. In the first place, as we shall see presently, the operational political structures are reasonably well suited to the dominant subject political sub-culture but flexible enough to allow adjustment as the political culture changes. Secondly, we already know that among the nationally aware Mexicans, even including the alienated subjects, there is a remarkably high degree of positive system affect which apparently grows out of popular identification

---

Community Influentials in Two Border Cities," *American Sociological Review*, Vol. 24, No. 6, December 1959, pp. 804-814; some of D'Antonio's most enlightening data on politics are as yet unpublished.

with the goals of the 1910 Revolution and out of appreciation of the material gains of recent years. This acceptance of the political system may not carry with it a great deal of respect for the ability or the honesty of individual *politicos* but, coupled with the Mexican's low political motivation, it leaves the elites with a relatively free hand. Finally and probably most important, the members of the various elites generally are agreed upon the most basic values affecting modernization and the political process, and that agreement gives them a decided advantage over the unintegrated and inarticulate masses.

After fifty years of revolutionary rule there is a growing tendency toward homogeneity in all of the elites—social and economic as well as political. Almost by definition to be a member of an elite group is to support modernization, although the precise form modernization should take may not always be agreed upon unanimously. Similarly, in spite of disagreements on specific policy questions or attempts to capture control of the central government from within the revolutionary party or through opposition parties, most of the elites operate as part of the ongoing political system. In fact the very nature of the operational political structures reduces the likelihood of violent or even peaceful electoral competition among the elites and the interests they represent, not only by imposing policy decisions from the center but also by determining before the election which functional interest organizations shall have which elective offices. The concentration of policy-making authority in the presidency rather than in other constitutional agencies and the role of functional interest associations in the political system as captive, protective associations interested primarily in the output aspects of government policy rather than in its formulation as independent bargaining units further restricts the potential distinctiveness of the leaders who participate in government and semigovernmental organizations. To a considerable extent most members and prospective members of the several elites seem to be satisfied with this arrangement.

It is significant that the trend toward homogeneity in outlook and values has become apparent just as increasing specificity of roles expands the size and diversity of Mexico's elites. Until quite recently rather a sharp distinction could be noted between (1) the political elite, whose source of status was power amassed through the effective use of violence and the successful manipulation of political strength during the rough-and-tumble postrevolutionary era, and (2) the social and economic elites, the first representing in part a carry over of ascriptive status and the second an entrepreneurially minded type whose status reflected successful economic activity.[23] Though a kind of tenuous and mutually beneficial truce existed between the two, the earlier governing group was uneasy and suspicious in the presence of the others and allowed them little real voice in government policy decisions.[24]

Today, despite continued participation in politics by a number of survivals from the older generation of military politicians, the largest and most influential part of the national elite is composed of a newer stratum which has grown up since the Revolution. This elite group is more broadly based and more diverse both in its origins and in its interests than was its predecessor, and as a consequence tends to think in differentiated terms—of government, commerce, industry, and the like—but it does not look upon politics and government activity as completely separate from or incompatible with private operations. Instead, although the demands of role specialization work to separate the political man from his economic counterpart, the two can and do communicate and interact for mutual benefit and, much of the time, for the national good as well.[25] In fact one is struck by the growing degree of consensus in the key values of the political and the non-political elites, whatever criteria are employed to assign individuals to the classification. On a class basis the new elites share common middle and upper economic backgrounds and experience, with a disproportionate number originating in larger cities and particularly in the capital; status is based primarily but

[23] After the hegemony of the landed aristocracy was broken by the Revolution some of its more progressive members, together with the small group of entrepreneurs who had begun to operate under Díaz, made their peace with the revolutionary leaders and went into finance, commerce, and industry, supplying some of the technical knowledge and specialized leadership needed to accomplish the material aspects of modernization. Over the years an appreciable number of revolutionary politicians joined them, providing access to the governmental policy process.

[24] We shall see that the organization of the revolutionary party still reflects this attitude. The three sectors represent labor, *ejido* agriculture, and the more diverse popular interests. Commercial, industrial, and financial interests, as well as old-line social movements such as those centered in the Church, relate to government in another way, through the presidency.

[25] Studies of the Mexican elites have been very rare. Community influentials have been studied by Form and D'Antonio (see note 22) and by D'Antonio and others, "Institutional and Occupational Representation in Eleven Community Influence Systems," *American Sociological Review*, Vol. 26, No. 3, June 1961, pp. 440-446. Economic elites have been studied by Moore, Fayerweather, and Glade (see note 9). Frank Brandenburg has also conducted extensive studies of economic and other policy influentials, *op.cit.*, *passim*, while Raymond Vernon, *op.cit.*, Chap. 6, offers valuable insights into the motivations and ideologies of Mexico's business leaders.

not entirely on merit and achievement rather than ascription;[26] power position in turn is a function of the individual's role in the political or economic system. While some persons may share one or two of these criteria and lead the good life, to be a full member of the effective political elite one must combine some elements of all three.

As social and economic opportunities widen, the proportion of Mexicans in the politically influential elite group slowly expands, but it is not an easy group to enter, for the qualifications are high and the competition keen. While not impossible, it is no longer so simple to substitute an overwhelming mastery of one of the three criteria for the other two, as military politicians of the immediate post-1910 period did. The demands of a complex society and economy make it extremely unlikely, for example, that a person without advanced education of some sort can operate as effectively as one with this advantage. Considering the restricted educational opportunities and particularly the very high drop-out rate after primary school, the number of persons who can meet even this minimal first requirement is quite small. Those who do, however, will have been exposed to a much wider range of common socializing influences than the vast majority of their fellow countrymen, ranging all the way from more frequent and intensive exposure to mass media of communication to the shared experience of university training, often at the National University.

Upward mobility through education does occur in Mexico, as indicated by the fact that of the nearly 80,000 students at the National University some 52.2 per cent can be classed as poor and 43.8 per cent as middle class.[27] But these figures themselves indicate that the

[26] It should be pointed out that ascriptive status is not unknown in Mexico any more than in, say, Massachusetts. Some retention of social position by members of the old aristocratic families exists, and a new status group consisting of the offspring of early revolutionary politicians has come into being. The sons of ex-presidents Obregón, Rodríguez, Cárdenas, and Alemán, among others, have held appointive or elective positions, some with notable success and others with equally notable ineffectiveness. In at least one case such a person has benefited remarkably in his business ventures because of his relationship. It is clear, however, that for all the obvious advantages involved, unless the individual possesses some sort of ability of his own he will remain on the fringes of the real power group. Some indication of the lack of real status such persons have, in popular terminology such men are known as "Juniors," a derogatory comment on the aping of North American usage by adding the term after their name. Some intermarriage between the older, aristocratic status elite and the revolutionary status elite is beginning to take place.

[27] These figures are cited by Arturo de la Fuente, quoting a high official of the National University, in *Hoy*, No. 1320, September 1, 1962, p. 18. They are given also in the *Guía Oficial de la Universidad Nacional Autónoma de México*, Mexico, D.F., 1962, p. 15.

lower class is greatly underrepresented proportionate to its size, and they do not show how many of each group are in real university-level classes and how many among the roughly one-third in pre-university preparatory work. Nor do they suggest that many, perhaps a majority, of the students are part-time, perennial members of the university community, attracted by the status accorded students and the extremely low tuition of 200 pesos ($16.00, U.S.) a year. On the basis of personal observation and interviews I believe that the majority of serious, adequately prepared students who have a real chance of completing their university education come not from the lower but from the middle sectors.

Perhaps the somewhat ambivalent pattern of recruitment to the elite group can be illustrated if we consider the backgrounds of one class entering the National Military College. In most Latin American countries the officer corps has been characterized as one means by which able and ambitious young men can improve their status. This was particularly true in Mexico during the military phase of the Revolution and to some extent continues to be so as the Army's officer corps becomes more professionalized. Today, however, the multiplication of new sources of status and power for those who can obtain professional, university-level training makes a military career less attractive, leaving the bulk of the competition to the lower-middle class.

Given the egalitarian norms of the Revolution, it is not surprising that a serious effort is made to assure geographic and class representation among the Mexican cadets, but in practice this goal is not always achieved. One restrictive factor is the fact that the competitive entrance examination is based on the assumption that the applicants have completed secondary school or its equivalent, automatically eliminating the vast majority of young persons who do not finish even the primary cycle. For example, the group that sought to enter the National Military College in 1955, on which all of the following tables are based, had an educational background that was completely atypical of Mexicans of their age (Table 4).[28] All but slightly over 4 per cent taking the examination had completed their secondary-level education, and over 13 per cent had begun or completed the equivalent of junior college training.

[28] This material on National Military College cadets is taken from Javier Romero, *Aspectos Psicobiométricos y Sociales de una Muestra de la Juventud Mexicana*, Mexico, D.F., 1956, *passim*.

TABLE 4: ACADEMIC BACKGROUND OF ASPIRANTS FOR
NATIONAL MILITARY COLLEGE, 1955

Level of Training	Students Number	Per Cent
Complete secondary or pre-vocational	369	82.73
Incomplete secondary or pre-vocational	18	4.03
Complete *Bachillerato* or vocational	10	2.24
Incomplete *Bachillerato* or vocational	49	10.99
Total	446	99.99

The relationship between level of education and regions where schools are more plentiful is obvious. If we consider place of birth and residence at time of examination, the correlation between modernity, education, and probability of attempting to move into a relatively mobile status group like the military is obvious (Table 5).

TABLE 5: DISTRIBUTION OF 1955 ASPIRANTS BY ZONE,
ACCORDING TO PLACE OF BIRTH AND RESIDENCE

Zone	Place of Birth Number	Per Cent	Residence During Past 5 Years Number	Per Cent
Federal District	174	39.10	209	46.97
Center (11 states)	127	28.54	97	21.80
South Pacific (4 states)	58	13.03	39	8.76
North (7 states)	40	8.99	28	6.29
Gulf (5 states)	33	7.41	27	6.07
North Pacific (3 states)	12	2.70	6	1.35
States of more than one zone			39	8.76
Non-Mexican	1	0.23		
Total	445	100.00	445	100.00

The predominant influence of the capital is underlined if the period of residence before the entrance examination is reduced to one year, which results in over 51 per cent of the aspirants coming from the Federal District in a period when its inhabitants totaled approximately 10 per cent of the country's population.

The relationship between certain kind of status and tendency to seek entry to the Military College also is enlightening (Table 6). In a country where more than one-half the population live in rural areas and are engaged in agriculture less than 11 per cent of the fathers or guardians of aspirants reflect this background, suggesting

TABLE 6: OCCUPATION OF FATHERS AND GUARDIANS OF 1955 MILITARY COLLEGE ASPIRANTS

Occupation	Fathers	Guardians	Total	Per Cent
Military	63	14	77	19.11
Shopkeeper	66	6	72	17.87
White-collar worker	60	5	65	16.13
Manual laborer	58	1	59	14.64
Agriculturalist (landowner)	28	3	31	7.69
Teacher	11	3	14	3.47
Engineer	12	0	12	2.98
Farmer (non-landowner)	11	1	12	2.98
Railroad worker	12	0	12	2.98
Chauffeur	11	0	11	2.73
Mechanic	11	0	11	2.73
Physician	7	1	8	1.98
Accountant	6	1	7	1.73
Lawyer	4	1	5	1.24
Artist	1	1	2	0.50
Others	4	1	5	1.24
Fathers dead			26	
Guardians dead			4	
No data			13	
Total			446	100.00

the farmer's isolation and lack of opportunity. Similarly, considering their high status and relatively advantaged position, the children of professionals (engineers, physicians, lawyers) and semiprofessionals (teachers, artists, and the like) are underrepresented in the sample, probably because other, more attractive possibilities are available. The largest number of applicants come from among the more modernized and urbanized low-status groups with low education and income levels (military personnel, small shopkeepers, white- and blue-collar workers, lower bureaucrats) who can meet the minimum education standards and are aware of this possibility for upward mobility.

Despite the Revolution therefore in Mexico as elsewhere movement into the elite is hardest for the rural farmer, for the undereducated and unskilled city worker, for the member of the lower class, few of whom ever manage to acquire the understandings and attitudes which might enable them to operate effectively in the national environment. Most of the privileged who utilize their class- and status-provided advantages to reach a power position that places them in the influential elite, on the other hand, achieve success within the operating economic and political system. Though they may not accept all the norms upon which the *status quo* is based, they tend to conform outwardly to most of them or they would not be among the influential elites. Often in fact, as Merle Kling has pointed out, they appear to obtain what Murray Edelman calls "symbolic reassurance" by adhering to nominally opposition parties or movements which do not unduly challenge the system. Some businessmen, for example, reap tangible benefits and simultaneously avoid violating the values into which they were socialized by supporting the *Partido de Acción Nacional*, which they know cannot unseat the revolutionary government. Some leftist intellectuals obtain the same reassurance by participating in futile reformist or what they term "true" revolutionary movements, but they always seem to return to the official party fold in time to line up with the faithful at the public trough, or at least in time to avoid being cast into outer darkness.

Having discussed the influential elite in these general terms, it now becomes necessary to sharpen our classifications. Obviously not all members of the social and economic elites, or even the full-time political activists, exercise the same degree of power over government. This is particularly true in a country like Mexico where there is a very hazy boundary between those members of the elite who are subjects and those who are participants in our technical use of the terms. Generally, however, although some concentrate on politics, some on economic affairs, yet others on humanistic or social matters, enough of the aware citizens share understandings and attitudes to interact systematically and constructively as a controlling elite. Similarly, those who do not yet participate on the input side of policy making but who do have a vital interest in governmental output to date have been satisfied (or at least mollified) by the achievements of modernization accomplished since the Revolution.

A citizen need not be a full-time politician or even formally committed to the revolutionary party to enjoy a satisfactory relationship with government regarding protection of his interests. Consider the growing number of ambitious and able persons who are specializing in technical and more purely economic matters, reflected in the move in university training from traditional professions such as law to engineering and business administration. Conversely, a man can be in the government and not be active in politics. Consider the growing number of professionally trained men working in the government's industrial, transportation, and other activities. This is not to say that political influence has no role in advancement of government employees but that it is not the only or in many cases the most important factor.

As the country modernizes, changes take place not only in the economy and the society but in the power structure as well. There has been a shift in emphasis from concentration on politics and government toward shared influence with those in the increasingly important private sectors. Access to the political process for these new elite groups is through semiofficial channels of their functional interest associations—the *Cámara de Comercio* and the *Cámara de Industrias*, the Bankers' Association, the Employers' Association, which work with and through the presidency.

In fact even more than in two- or multi-party countries full time commitment to politics as a vocation is possible for very few persons in Mexico, particularly among those not connected with the revolutionary party. Only the PRI has an ample supply of appointive and elective patronage positions to support the professional politician, and even among the party faithful competition for such posts is sharp enough to allow a certain amount of selection on the basis of merit, however that merit may be acquired. Few members of opposition parties are assigned elective or appointive posts, but those who are tend to respect the political system as it operates, especially if they are dependent upon their government places or the administration's good graces for a livelihood. Most opposition leadership in the upper as well as the lower echelons is part time and sporadic, but even this sort of *politico* is vulnerable to economic and legal pressures from the dominant official party. If one can believe their campaign pronouncements or deduce their sentiments from the manner in which they conduct themselves between elections, a substantial proportion of the opposition party leadership accepts the present political system, and some are members of the power elite in the sense of participating in and to some extent influencing general policy decisions.

A few opposition leaders refuse to play according to the rules of the game as they have evolved since 1940 and therefore find themselves outside the effective political elite group. But whether they are independently wealthy, inordinately ambitious, supported by outside influences, or simply insistent upon immediate implementation of the formal norms of constitutional democratic government, such persons are apt to find they cannot buck the system. If they depart too far from the established operating norms they may find their political party outlawed, as did General Henríquez Guzmán after the 1952 election, or their business hampered by labor difficulties, or themselves in jail, as David Alfaro Sequeiros of the Communist Party did for several years until granted amnesty after the 1964 presidential election.

In short, Mexico now is governed by a power elite of interlocking political, economic, and status leaders whose interests and attitudes overlap sufficiently to assure a considerable degree of cooperation, but it is neither a closed nor a functionally specialized elite. New persons and representatives of emerging interests can join the elite as individual success or collective pressure makes their participation desirable in order to assure stability. As now composed, the power structure includes several elements which reflect the dominant subject political sub-culture but which may gradually weaken as a larger number of persons acquire participant norms. These subject-oriented elements tend to break the various kinds of public and private elites into three quite identifiable but overlapping classes which wield authority. The three are a ruling class, a governing class, and a mediatory class.

It is my contention that the first and the third of these classes respond to the imperatives of the subject sub-culture. At the present time the ruling class consists of a group of revolutionary politicians including the President of the Republic, the ex-presidents, and a very small number of other persons controlling physical force and economic power. As yet the social and political mechanisms for enforcing self-adjusting and peaceful compromise among the contending interests of the society are not quite strong enough to act automatically, so the ruling group provides the ultimate sanction to require cooperation. The very fact that it exists and that its members are able to reach accord on the difficult policy questions means that it seldom has to act.

Most policy questions therefore are decided and implemented by the governing class, which consists not only of middle-range government bureaucrats but also of commercial, industrial management, financial, functional interest association, social, intellectual, and intermediate political leaders. It is they who carry on the daily tasks of articulation, aggregation, and decision making that are necessary for rational operation of the modern state. Because they do share many understandings about the legitimate function of government among themselves and with the ruling class, they can complete the normal business of society with a minimum resort to the power held in reserve by the ruling group. Like the ruling class the governing class can be considered as participants in the governmental process, though the nature of the matters in which the two classes are most concerned differs to some extent.

The mediatory class consists primarily of the line officers of government and society. It is their function to apply the output activities of government and the services offered by private entities—enforcing the laws, providing the goods, collecting the taxes, manning the mass media of communication, teaching the schools, and in general performing the myriad tasks that gradually turn a state into a nation and an unintegrated mass of traditional villagers into citizens governed by an effective political system. Most of these mediators accept and attempt to encourage the spread of modernization in its economic and (to some extent) in its social aspects, but they are not yet completely aware of the implications of participation in the determination of government policy. In their relationship to the ruling and the governing classes they accept the limitations of the subject; in their relations with the general population they adopt an authoritarian attitude which leads to the negative expectations of fair and considerate treatment from public officials discovered by the survey of Mexican citizens.

In terms of Mexico's political evolution it is interesting to speculate about the future of these three parts of the political elite. My own rather optimistic forecast is that what is now the governing class gradually will expand its role in the political process as the institutional mechanisms for compromise and adjustment become widely diffused throughout the political system. It is already clear that the frequency with which the ruling class is forced to act to resolve what Verba calls the "salient political crises" has shrunk markedly over the years, and that the policy areas in which the ruling class can act without consulting the manifold interests represented by the governing class are decreasing apace. At the same time, the subject orientation of the mediatory class is slowly shifting toward greater awareness of the input function and participation in the policy-making process. As this happens, the former mediators are becoming part of the governing class and should begin to transmit somewhat similar values to the masses of the population with whom they come into contact. When this occurs, the one real unsolved problem of the Mexican Revolution's modernizing function may be solved, and the elites may be able to mobilize more completely the support of the non-elites in their attempts to integrate the nation and to provide a responsible and representative government.

If my prognostication is correct, and unless some major crisis that cannot be resolved should arise to force a regression to earlier, more authoritarian modes of political action, the schema of today's political hierarchy shown in Table 7 gradually should change, with the box representing the governing class expanding as those representing the ruling class and the mediators contract.

As the most sophisticated and knowing section of the population, whether political activists or simply social and economic leaders working within the ongoing system, this political leadership group also includes the highest incidence of influence by participant political culture norms. Here it is that more persons understand the governmental input function and the potential of the citizen as a political actor. As of now the participant norms are not in the ascendancy, because the attitudes of the masses do not require and the values of the governing elites do not yet demand such a development. But we know that the elites act in their roles as heads of the functional interest associations, as political and social leaders, as communicators to the masses. Even if they see their responsibility not as agents for their followers but according to the ethical and ideological standards of the Revolution, the impetus toward participatory values is present. If the true ideology of a movement is measured by the values, motives, and acts of the elites of that movement, we should recall that the ideology of the Revolution includes not only the search for political stability to support material modernization but also the symbol of the constitution and the participant norms it embodies.

Being the most highly politicized of the Mexicans, the members of the political elites best illustrate the inherent ambivalence found in the country's political culture. None of them are parochials, but almost all of them manifest differing combinations of subject and participant political culture norms. If most subject-oriented citizens reject authority, the political elites exercise it—for personal gain, for self-realization, and because it is a component element in the operational political system. A ruling group is as essential to the subject political culture as a ruled if anarchy is to be avoided. In light of their stake in political stability the members of Mexico's power elite incline strongly toward moderation and continuity in the operation of the political process. For most of them this is not inconsistent with

TABLE 7: THE MEXICAN POLITICAL ELITES

Participants

Ruling Class
- The President of the Republic
- Ex-presidents
- Major Policy Advisers
- Cabinet ministers (including PRI chief)
- Military chiefs
- Top financial, commercial, industrial leaders[a]

Governing Class
- Leaders of Specialized Elites (National or General)[b]
- Policy-making bureaucrats
- Managerial group
- PRI functional sector leaders (farm, labor, popular)
- Church leaders (lay leaders as well as hierarchy)
- Mass media owners
- Major intellectuals
- Field-grade military officers
- Opposition party leaders

Subjects

- State Governors[c]
- Leaders of Specialized Elites (local or particular)
- Local politicians heading Popular Sector of PRI
- Leaders of state labor federations or individual unions
- Leaders of state farm organizations (CNC)
- Individual businessmen and manufacturers
- Middle-range public and private bureaucrats
- Owners of local, editors of national mass media

Mediatory Class
- Operational Level Mediators
- School teachers
- Line-service bureaucrats (policemen, tax collectors, public health nurses, postmen, etc.)
- Supervisers and technical workers (foremen, welders, office managers, etc.)
- Parish priests
- Junior-grade military officers and NCO's

[a] Economic leaders may be here as functional interest association representatives or in their own right as major dominators of some sector of economy.
[b] Note that specialization has not fully replaced poly-functionalism. Many individuals are in several of these categories.
[c] Individual governors may stand higher in the hierarchy if they control their own local political machines rather than having control imposed by the central authorities.

their frequently repeated statements about social justice and revolutionary reform, because they recognize the necessity of high government output performance if they are to retain and consolidate their positions. More important, the political elites have worked out a political system in which the operational structures not only are suited to the contemporary dominant subject political sub-culture norms but also appear capable of adjusting to change as participatory norms become more widely diffused throughout the country. This says a great deal for the political elites and about the political style they have evolved on the basis of the values and understandings they have acquired in the socialization process.

Mexican Political Style and the Operational Political Structures

The Mexican political style is just what one might expect from a country in transition toward political modernity which has undergone a basic social and economic revolution to weaken the ties of the past. Some of its political values, those most immediately affected by material change, reflect nationalizing and integrating influences. Others, more personal and deeply inculcated in the individual, retain the stamp of parochialism. As a consequence those aspects of the Mexican political style most directly affected by a movement toward solution of the national identity problem appear more "modern," while those involving the individual or personal identity problem are less so. This is hardly surprising when we recall that the political culture is broken down into two nationally oriented sub-cultures each of which socializes the individual citizen with sets of values of somewhat different patterns.

On the national level Mexico's political style is clearly pragmatic rather than ideological because the values which condition political action at this level are, in Verba's terms, reasonably open, implicit, and (regarding the operational structures at least) informal. At the personal and individual level, on the other hand, most Mexicans remain suspicious, uncooperative, rigid, and insistent upon certain formalities of government in order to protect their own positions and personalities. Throughout this study we have seen illustration after illustration of how incongruent personal and parochial values have intruded themselves into the more modern political processes to give Mexico a political style which is unique. Now let us consider how the revolutionary leadership faced up to this problem of incongruence to produce operational political structures which could effectively organize the modernization of the country.

For a number of years after adoption of the 1917 constitution the revolutionary leaders tried to set up a political system based on the formal agencies of government, but to no avail. The lack of political consensus turned such balancing and limiting concepts as federalism or presidential government into open invitations to anarchy. Abortive revolts by regional strong men, immobilization of the congress by irreconcilable factions, power struggles by ambitious presidential aspirants, and a plague of similar difficulties demonstrated only too clearly the incongruity between democratic and participatory legal structures and an alienated subject political culture. If improved government performance necessary for modernization was to be achieved, some of the formal political norms had to be sacrificed. Once again, as in the previous century, the national leadership had to devise some centralizing mechanism to assure at least a minimum of coherence in government policy, to assert the authority of the nation, and to enforce the legitimacy of the Revolution.

Interesting, but not really a surprise, is the fact that this modernizing group encountered adjustment problems that have historical counterparts in nineteenth-century Mexican experience. Just as the *afrancesados* who supported Maximilian sought to adopt a kind of "instant integration" from Europe to provide a sense of national identity, so the highly exaggerated *indianismo* of the 1930's and the *pochismo* of the 1940's and fifties looked inwardly to the first inhabitants or outwardly to the more highly developed United States to satisfy the same need. Neither succeeded, and it was not until social and political integration had advanced sufficiently to allow a meaningful adjustment with the contemporary national environment that a viable national identity has begun to grow up around the national culture.

In the same way the highly differentiated and specialized political mechanisms of federalism, separation of powers, and the other democratic norms and structures of the 1917 constitution were little more suited to the dominant subject political sub-culture than they had been under the 1857 document, and the effective operational political structures which emerged to provide stability were appropriately diffuse and dependent upon authority backed by force. But another parallel also appears. Just as in the nineteenth century a number of Mexicans favored outward observance of the constitutional forms in order to enhance the country's international reputation and because they looked upon the constitution as a symbol of the nation and its independence, so today an increasingly large number of persons seek implementation of legal forms as a means of expanding political responsibility and restraining the relatively uncontrolled authority of the revolutionary party. The old struggle between freedom and stability, or perhaps between license and dictatorship, continues but in a much more moderate way than previously.

It is not surprising that a parallel between pre- and post-revolutionary political adjustment problems exists because many of the same factors continue to contribute to the make-up of the subject political culture and to the relationship it bears to the political structures. The new, integrative elements provided by technology may change the mix, but until now the change is not so marked that elements of the old political style and its familiar problems have disappeared. Many of the norms that characterized the pre-1910 subject political culture have been absorbed by the newly nationalized group from the existing middle sector, which acted as a reference group, the more easily because the values and attitudes of most Mexicans inculcated by the basic socialization process are consistent with such a political culture. If anything, the problems of establishing a legitimate national political system are greater now than they were a hundred years ago because the speedily multiplying nationalizing group lacks systematic indoctrination into the limits and responsibilities of modern political life. At least during Juárez' lifetime the number of upwardly or nationally mobile persons was so restricted that they could be absorbed by and acculturated into the governing elite with a minimum of disruption to the operating system.

The basic problem of creating a new set of national authority structures was resolved by the gradual development of the revolutionary party.[29] Late in 1929 President Calles set up a confederation of local political machines led usually by revolutionary generals. During the 1930's the attrition of death and politics gradually reduced the number and influence of those leaders until by 1937 the party had become highly centralized, semi-corporative, and dominated by the President of the Republic. Membership in its three corporative sectors—agrarian, labor, and popular—generally was automatic as a consequence of belonging to a functional interest organization, for example, peasant league for *ejidatarios*, labor union for industrial workers, popular organization for small businessmen, cooperative, or a consequence of occupation, as professional politicians, bureaucrats, and later, school teachers.

During the 1940's and 1950's this centralizing mechanism per-

[29] The revolutionary or "official" party has been known variously as the PNR (Partido Nacional Revolucionario, 1929-1937), the PRM (Partido de la Revolución Mexicana, 1937-1945), and the PRI (Partido Revolucionario Institucional, 1945—).

fected its organization, expanding its membership and absorbing new functional interest associations as the society and economy became more complex and as roles of all kinds became more specialized. Interests such as large-scale commerce, heavy industry, finance, and the Roman Catholic Church, which were not subsumed within the sectors of the revolutionary party, were tied to the operating political structures through what became institutionalized dependency upon the office of the chief executive, who also controlled the party. It is significant that few rank-and-file members relate to the official party on an individual basis. Instead the relationship between the functional interest organizations and their party sectors is as what Pye terms "protective associations," which tie into the decision-making process on the output side and attempt to mitigate or reverse policy rather than to influence its adoption on the input side.

Starting in the 1940's, as the political system built around the core of authority provided by the official party became institutionalized, the norms governing the operating political structures have emasculated the legal functions and autonomy of the national legislature and judiciary, of the state and *municipio* governments, subordinating the formal structures to the chief executive in what the Mexicans call *presidencialismo*. Presidential government in Mexican terms has a very different meaning from that in the North American political lexicon; it refers to the overwhelmingly dominant role of the president in the political system as a personification of government in the eyes of the masses and as the ultimate aggregator of interests and wielder of the power concentrated in and about his office by his control over the legal and the auxiliary political structures.

Over the years, as the operational political system has become more structured, the center of power has shifted away from the revolutionary party to the presidency, which has met the demands of the modernizing society and economy by improving the efficiency of the administrative system in a way that the diffusely organized party could not. Especially in the government agencies one notes an increasingly strong differentiation of function, based on more carefully defined and observed norms governing performance, which has improved notably both quantitatively and qualitatively. We already have seen some indication of the degree of impact this improved output performance has had on the polity. On the other hand, the input structures manipulated by the President have not become differentiated as quickly because by the very nature of their policy-determining function they cut across the activities of all sorts of formal agencies and informal groups. If the new Secretariat of the Presidency has taken upon itself formal responsibility for rationalizing the making of policy, it has not provided built-in and assured access for the kinds of differentiated representation that an independently elected congress or competitive interest associations or even a popularly controlled political party could supply.

On the other hand, differentiated representation is less a necessity in a society like Mexico's than it might be in the United States. We know that the North American highly pluralized society, with its multi-membership pattern that reduces the individual's commitment to any one interest or viewpoint, would not meet the emotional needs of many Mexicans. Instead the psychologically satisfying primary interest-group tie and the dyadic relationship between two individuals is to them a more natural kind of pattern. But neither of these is essentially suited to function as an input agency in the political process. As a consequence the ruling revolutionary group has established its own structures appropriate to the situation.

This indicates that despite the existence of differentiated political structures set up by the constitution the imperatives imposed upon the governmental system by the continuing dominant subject norms of the political culture restrict the autonomous operation of such formal mechanisms. The shift of power from the official party toward the presidency does not mean that the chief executive's power results from his legal office any more than it does that the national legislative and judicial branches or the agencies of local government have assumed their full constitutional functions. It does mean that the activities of the authority structures are being rationalized and formalized by the addition of trained personnel and structured administrative agencies. This process satisfies some of the requirements of a complex modern society for improved administration and meets part of the spreading desire for at least token movement toward constitutional, democratic government. But it does so without loss of that hard core of authority needed to control the disruptive tendencies still operating in the Mexican political environment.

The operational political structures which grew up around the centralizing authoritarian core of the revolutionary party are quite consistent with the subject political sub-culture norms most Mexicans share and, at the same time, flexible enough to accommodate some of the more democratic values also operative in the political culture.

They supply the necessary controls over intensely personal or antisocial action but simultaneously permit a certain degree of oppositional political activity as long as it remains within the bounds of the accepted political system. Opposition parties never have been prohibited, though in many ways during the formative period of the 1930's and 1940's their freedom of action was inhibited. Today, with the revolutionary party in apparently firm ascendancy, the sphere within which the opposition may operate and the possibility of free and fair campaigns and elections have expanded enormously, but without much likelihood that the government's opponents would be allowed to win political control if they should capture a larger share of the votes.

Mexico's political system provides a high degree of stability because it neatly balances a need for authority with a minimum of direct control over the individual, taking into account the as yet unresolved inconsistencies in the political culture mix of the majority of nationally aware citizens. Unassimilated parochial tendencies are mitigated by the government's minimal demands made upon the citizen and by providing a mechanism (the revolutionary party) and a symbol (the President of the Republic) to relate the diffuse traditional approach to politics with the differentiated agencies of modern government. At the same time, the nature of individual and group relations with the operating political structures minimizes the necessity of adjusting an essentially insecure and suspicious personality to the demands of collective cooperation. The predominant subject political norms are satisfied by the strong emphasis on effective government output performance made possible by the development of central authority structures. Democratic aspirations are recognized in the preservation of constitutional formality even though the agencies do not really perform their functions as described. Such aspirations also are encouraged by the gradual formalization of function as the center of power moves away from the official party toward the presidency.

Because Mexico has been involved for some little time in the process of general culture change, with related adjustments in political culture, many of the fragmenting effects of the process that were most evident during earlier phases have begun to be resolved and a new phase of cultural fusion is taking place. Unfortunately, as we saw when we considered political socialization more directly, not all of the norms involved are equally plastic, and their inability to adjust easily into the emerging modern pattern results in the political culture incongruence which forces adoption of a hybrid set of political structures. This situation would presage increasing political instability for the country if it were not for what appears to be a degree of flexibility in the political system. The continuous but uneven pattern of culture change has been accompanied by a corresponding continuous pattern of political structural transformation. The principal problem to date has been that change in some norms is so rapid and in others so slow that difficulties arise in working out smooth transitions and adjustments of the new cultural patterns into the ongoing political system.

The problem is complicated by the fact that the entire population is not moving from the parochial into the subject or from the subject into the participant political culture at the same time or the same rate and, as we have seen, many Mexicans operate under some norms from all three categories. Large islands remain to be absorbed into the national mainstream, usually into the dominant subject political sub-culture. If these parochials could skip the subject phase and take on participant values directly, the adjustment problem could be eased, but this is not happening. The majority of the Mexican populace still are subjects, and despite the growing influence of mass socializing agencies acculturation is accomplished most effectively through personal contact. Moreover not all mass media necessarily impart participatory indoctrination, being manned partially by persons who continue to be motivated by dominant subject norms. Finally, the basic socialization process of the average Mexican inculcates within him a tendency toward a subject relationship with government.

Lately this problem has become more rather than less acute as the snowballing effects of modern industrialization telescope the process of culture change into a few short decades, multiplying the number of persons brought onto the national scene and intensifying the dislocations felt by those already there. The speed-up of change since 1910 and particularly since 1940, accompanied as it is by the natural anxieties inherent in moving out of a comforting and well-known traditional environment into a strange and seemingly threatening wider political world, has increased the feeling of threat to the individual's identity, impeding his sense of personal competence, his sense of confidence in others, and his ability to identify with the polity as a whole.

Only during recent years, as the country has begun to take on some semblance of national unity because of the expanding interpersonal involvement made possible by technology and the growing interdependence necessitated by economic development, have a few Mexicans been able to make a more complete personal adjustment with the changed environment. It is extremely difficult to know whether the evolution of a sense of national identity makes possible the fusion of traditional and modern values that produces a personality capable of dealing with national political structures, or whether the growth of a sense of personal identity produces reactions that lead to the formation of a particular set of national political norms and structures. Probably the two are interdependent. As of now only a small minority of persons have been able to consolidate their self-images and their conceptions of the nation sufficiently to resolve the identity crisis, but now that conditions appear suitable and the trail has been blazed, others should follow in ever-increasing numbers.

In the immediate future, however, most of the nationally politicized Mexicans probably will continue to relate to the political culture in the diffuse and overlapping manner they do now, and the national political structures should reflect this pattern. Therefore the three political sub-cultures and at the national level the peculiar mixture of authoritarian and participatory political structures undoubtedly will continue to characterize the political system until a much larger number of Mexicans have passed through the process of resolving the personal crisis of identity. Once having done so, they should be able to relate constructively to the nation as it really is, gradually providing a solution to the national identity crisis also.

In the study of the influence of political culture upon the political system as the latter seeks to move toward the integrated and responsible action patterns of modern government, the concepts and categories of structural-functional analysis offer a useful descriptive model against which to compare change in the political system as a whole and to isolate individual factors affecting the operation of the political culture or the political structures, or their relationship to each other. They do not in themselves, however, provide a theory of political development or analyze the process of political culture change, both of which must be inferred from the differences in the political mechanism described at various stages in the development of Mexico's political system.

The Mexican experience also underlines the fact that utilization of the concept of stages of development does not imply a unilinear or unidirectional progression. Mexico has moved from a fairly simple and stable, systemically mixed parochial-subject political culture before 1910 toward the much more complicated and highly fluid tripartite political culture already described. But the progression has not followed a single clear line of development from the more simple to the more complex. The three categories merely provide convenient ways of describing clusters of attributes and do not imply that the attributes of any category are exclusive to it or that there exists some inevitable pattern of development which the political culture must follow.

The concept of cumulativeness, as used by Almond and Verba, whereby the diffuse, primary relationships of the more simple, traditional categories carry over into the more complex—for example from the parochial into the subject and from both of these into the participant culture—applies here, but so does a reverse process. When, as in Mexico, several interrelated political sub-cultures coexist in the same polity, the more simple may take on some of the attributes of the more complex. In pre-revolutionary Mexico some parochials not only recognized the existence of a national political system but were also willing and even anxious to operate in it once conditions provided the appropriate opportunity. Present-day subjects are influenced by participatory norms that affect their role as subjects but do not transform them automatically into fully aware and participating citizens.

In Mexico the relationship between the political sub-culture categories and the political structures is much more complex than the model suggests. It is not simply that three sub-cultures exist or that incomplete integration means that the members of a given sub-culture are apt to be inconsistent in their political sentiments, although this is true. The relationship is complicated further because historical events have combined with these factors to produce two overlapping but essentially incompatible patterns of national political structures based on distinct political norms. One set of structures, relating to subject-oriented values, includes many of the operational political structures such as the revolutionary party and the highly centralized authority-exercising mechanism known as the presidency. The other set of political structures consists of the formal agencies set up in 1857 and reaffirmed by the 1917 constitution, which are more suited to a participant political culture.

The relationships and political interactions between the members of each of the two nationally oriented subject and participant political sub-cultures and its appropriate set of political structures are neither fully consistent nor mutually exclusive. Substantial numbers of persons accept some of the norms appropriate to the other political culture without passing over to it. This works in both directions; some subjects relate to the participation norms or the input functions of the participant political culture but cannot operate within the formal, constitutional structures. Psychologically they reject the idea of voluntary submission to authority or their suspicious, uncompromising, and at times aggressive outlook precludes the kind of cooperative interpersonal relations that would make them responsible and effective participants. On the other hand, some participants who perceive clearly their individual role and responsibility in the input as well as the output functions of the national political process continue to accept and operate in harmony with the centralized authority structures, which obviously negate the effectiveness of the more responsible constitutional agencies. They do so because it is to their personal benefit. Participants are not automatically democrats. For that matter, democrats are not automatically philanthropists.

The basic question facing Mexico today is whether the increasingly frequent confrontation of the values and resulting action patterns of traditionalism by those of modernization will produce permanent and significant change in the political culture and in the operational political structures without also producing one of two results. The confrontation could result in either dissolution of the ongoing political system which evolved during the 1940's and 1950's or freezing and polarization of the three political sub-cultures (or at least the two nationally oriented ones) into a systemically mixed political system.

For reasons which by now must be apparent Mexico has developed during its period of political consolidation a political system which provides stability but is able to tolerate only a small degree of autonomy in institutional, organizational, local, and specialized groups and in the actions of individuals. If a certain number of shared norms are developing and if part of the political infrastructures accept the legitimacy of government participation in or control over their actions, the political authorities on their part have not felt able to allow much independence of action. Part of the cause of this situation is the heritage of Spanish authoritarianism, part is due to the revolutionary conditions under which the present political system evolved, and part is due to the attitudes toward political cooperation and acceptance of authority evinced by the majority of Mexicans.

The political structures have adjusted to the necessity of exercising a relatively high amount of control over the citizens, the local government units, and other agencies of the infrastructure such as functional interest associations. Therefore, although Mexico's society and economy have become more diversified and differentiated, with apparent expansion in the number of pluralistic organizations, these organizations are neither fully independent nor fully in accord with the restraints of the political system. As long as the government continues to hold on to them and to use them as protective associations rather than as independent bargaining mechanisms there will be little opportunity for the elites, much less the rank and file, to gain the kind of experience necessary for evolution of a democratic political culture.

To close this study, let us consider a paradox. As Mexico moved away from a predominantly parochial political culture the country needed some sort of nationalizing political structures to provide stability in the face of culture fragmentation, as differentiated patterns replaced the old diffuse ones. Given the divisive factors in Mexico's political culture, these political structures almost had to be those of authoritarian centralization, which in turn encouraged the norms most suitable for a subject political culture. In the beginning the authoritarian structures and the subject norms were consistent with and complementary to each other, providing the high degree of political stability that permitted substantial material progress. But this same political environment also contained the seeds of democratic, participant political values in the form of the high regard in which the norms of the constitution were held. Material development has allowed those democratic seeds to sprout and grow into the demands for abandonment of the less formal authoritarian political structures.

The hard question is how the political system can accommodate both sets of needs. Because sizable numbers of the populace are just moving from the parochial into the subject political sub-culture, and most of them reject authority, enforced legitimization continues to be necessary. But those who have become more modernized, imbued with new values or with new understandings of old values represented in the constitution, are bringing pressure upon the central government to ease its controls. The present political system is a compromise between these two sets of basically incompatible demands.

If the experience of Mexico had not already demonstrated that the political system is open and adaptive, that the older values of the political culture can adjust to new conditions, and that the political structures can change to meet the needs of a country in transition, one might despair of seeing these two sets of basically incompatible demands turn into one, with an effective political mechanism to service them. In fact if one takes into account all the factors we have considered in this study and expects only the possible within the life span of each generation, there is some reason to believe that a workable modern political system will evolve.

CHAPTER 10

Egypt: The Integrative Revolution[*]

LEONARD BINDER

Most explanations of the process of modernization in Middle Eastern countries are concerned with explaining the political pathology of these countries instead of attempting to understand the nature of their emerging societies.[1] Not only have such explanations tended to explain ideological and cultural change and political conflict in terms of a dichotomy of the modern and the traditional, the urban and the rural, but they have also insisted upon understanding the history of the last 150 years as a process of social breakdown and ideological confusion. There must be contrasted with this predilection of the orientalists and the Middle East specialists the emphasis upon integration and mobilization in the work of social scientists who are not area oriented. The concern many of us in the former tradition feel about the breakdown of traditional Islamic society and culture has led to a concentration upon the minutiae of the negative economic and social impact of the West upon the Middle East and an increasing concern with the role of charismatic leadership. But we have not yet learned enough about the creation of the new structures which have come to take the place of the old. Moreover, there is something very badly wrong with a theory which can postulate the disintegration of society in a one-way direction without looking at the same time for the emergence of new kinds of integrative structures and new organizations that are going to replace the previous ones. Few societies really fall apart. It is not only the role of charismatic leadership which has been overemphasized against the background of the breakdown thesis; there has been parallel overemphasis upon the modernizing role of the military, again without a careful examination of that group in order to see what its relationship may be to other elements of the society.

[*] The sub-title is taken from Clifford Geertz's fine essay, "The Integrative Revolution: Primordial Sentiments and Civil Politics in the New States," in Geertz, ed. *Old Societies and New States: The Quest for Modernity in Asia and Africa*, New York, The Free Press of Glencoe, 1963, pp. 105-157.
[1] H.A.R. Gibb, "Social Change in the Near East," in P. W. Ireland, ed. *Near East: Problems and Prospects*, Chicago, 1942.

LEONARD BINDER

Role of the Military

The Egyptian military forces, especially that part which has emerged to political dominance in recent years, cannot trace themselves back very far. Most recent observers agree that the part of the officer corps of the Egyptian army which has provided political leadership for Egypt in recent years can trace itself back only to the year 1936. And it has been pointed out that most of the members of the Revolutionary Command Council (which led the free officers in the revolution) were graduated from the military academy in 1938, having entered that school with the first group of "plebeian" cadets in 1936. Most of these officers can be identified with the class of middle-level agriculturalists rather than with the non-Egyptian Muslim minorities of Cairo and Alexandria which had been favored by the monarchy.[2]

The political transformation of Egypt is not the result of the very special skills or position of the Revolutionary Command Council within the armed forces of Egypt. The success of the Egyptian revolution must be explained with reference to the homogeneity of the population of Egypt and to the fact that most of the prerequisites of a unified and centrally rationalized political system had been provided by the reforms and changes of the preceding 150 years. It is doubtful that the 1952 *coup* was well planned or that the small group of leaders of the free officers were in control of an elaborate organization. A better suggestion might be that the group which eventually became the Revolutionary Command Council was one among many small groups of officers willing to take some risk to overturn the regime but who were working in isolation from one another. The distinction which goes to Nasser is that he was willing to act while the rest contented themselves with merely talking. For him the task of unifying the armed forces behind the revolution began after the coup and after the successful removal of King Farouk.

If the Egyptian military has been able to play an important role in the modernization of Egypt and if it will be able to play an even more important role in the future, it is because of its reorganization after the *coup d'état*. On the other hand, even if there was no organizational unity of an extensive sort which could be relied upon by the revolutionary officers, their instinct correctly told them that they had many fellow officers who felt as they did. That the leaders of

[2] P. J. Vatikiotis, *The Egyptian Army in Politics*, Bloomington, 1961, pp. 47-48 and 54-55.

the *coup* were members of the armed forces is not their most compelling characteristic for purposes of ideological analysis, although in an instrumental sense it was that membership which permitted them to carry out their plan successfully.

What is of greater importance from the point of view of our concern with political culture was their correct assessment of the attitudes of the groups with whom they were in relatively close contact. These groups were comprised of their fellow officers, of civil servants of roughly similar rank, of journalists, and of certain professionals all of whom could count their opposite numbers in parallel bureaucratized organizations. But the middle-ranking officers were also in contact and in deep sympathy with another class—the rural groups from which those members of the military were originally derived.

It might be well to emphasize that all these groups felt themselves the most politically deprived in prerevolutionary Egypt. Even if they argued that the peasants and the working classes in the cities were the most economically deprived, these middle-class people were particularly aware of the fact that non-Egyptians having no connection with the people were being favored above the broad mass of the indigenous population, and especially above the leading exponents of Egyptian provincial society. The weight of the word provincial is of course to separate such a society from that of Cairo and Alexandria. It is quite clear that in prerevolutionary times it was a lot better to be a member of a minority group, whether Muslim or not, than to be a member of the great majority of Muslim Egyptians of the Valley of the Nile. Those who have taken over under the new dispensation are those members of the massive majority who had managed to reach the highest levels of society without being co-opted into the very apex of the pyramid as it was before the revolution. These people, it now appears, were characterized by a substantial degree of unity of outlook and sympathy.

It was not easy to see the consequences of the revolution and the relative stability that would prevail thereafter because the cohesiveness of Egyptian society and culture was belied by the divergence in political culture between the politicians and the court on the one hand and the mass of Egyptians on the other. It does not belittle the political skill, leadership qualities, and undoubted charisma which are President Nasser's to point out that the political and administrative reforms which characterized the preceding century and a half and the defensive—at times even offensive—modernization which was pressed on by the government did in fact serve to integrate the social and economic structures, to shake the traditional basis of legitimacy, and to produce a counterelite among the indigenous population. One of the major sources of support for the present regime is the fact that it is considered to be Egyptian rather than a regime of foreigners. It might be argued that 150 years ago the people of Egypt would not have cared whether their regime was indigenous or not so long as it was Muslim. Today, however, its indigenous character is a matter of crucial importance at nearly all levels of society.

Although in prerevolutionary Egypt the central political problem seemed to be how fast and how far to modernize, it now appears, retrospectively, that the real problem was how to make modernization meaningful in terms of Egyptian society and in terms of the values of the new groups upon which modernization depended. At first the parliament, and particularly the Wafd, seemed to be able to supply this need, an impression which helped to explain the continued popularity of the Wafd as a symbol of the Egyptianization of government. But the King succeeded in wearing down the Wafd and eventually in bringing it to play the political game in his way. Even today the Wafd is not blamed so much for what it attempted to do as for its failure to be able to carry through its program. Much of the early program of the revolutionary regime was but the carrying out of the plans laid down under the Wafdist parliament. The Muslim Brethren aimed similarly at making modernization and nationalism more meaningful to the Egyptian people, but their religious orientation and their antagonism to the bureaucracy and the military prevented them from winning the support of the traditional ulama and of those two important classes.

The Free Officers, driven both by personal inclination and by the extremity of their circumstances at the time, took power and have since that time been attempting to do the same thing. They have been more successful both because of their dependence upon a broader base of support and because of the great similarity in their attitudes and those of their supporters. Their support came from the middle class, but now most importantly it rests upon the military, the bureaucracy, the rural bourgeoisie, and the ulama, from whom the present regime has won much useful cooperation. Those who might formerly be considered the most modern in political culture, that is, the privileged classes and the minorities, the business community, and the foreign residents, are now those who are most deprived. This victimization of the formerly privileged, or, from the point of view of the Egyptian, rectification of the gross lack of national consciousness and responsibility on the part of the previous rulers of Egypt, is doubtlessly one of the major bases of the popularity of the present regime.

The Middle Classes

For the middle classes, both urban and rural, the concept of government has become more integrated with their sense of self and their notion of their own identity. This is not to argue that their political lives have become integrated with their private lives. That they themselves are Egyptians and that their government is Egyptian is a matter of some relevance, but they cannot yet identify themselves wholly with every act of that government. For most of the educated the government remains the private affair of President Nasser's own inner circle. By and large this inner circle is trusted, but the fact is recognized that for an outsider to enter it is almost impossible. One does not seek to order one's life in accordance with some ideal which is similar to the ideal which might be postulated for the state. One attempts to order one's life, despite whatever the state might decide to do, with the full realization that numerous adjustments may have to be made. What the government decides to do is not always comfortable for the individual, but the individual has the feeling that it is probably good medicine and that the Egyptians need it. If members of the military appear to be more privileged than others, this is understandable. They have, after all, earned it by dismissing the King and by getting rid of the politicians.

On the other hand, the international achievements of the government are a source of pride to educated Egyptians. They are aware of the increased influence of Egypt in world affairs and particularly among the neutralist states. They are aware also of the interest shown in Egypt by the great powers. They are rather pleased at the discomfiture of Britain and France in the Middle East. But above all they are aware of the fear with which President Nasser is regarded by the rulers of neighboring Arab states.

The political culture of the educated Egyptian is largely determined by this framework. He cannot participate in government; he can only respond to it, and that response must be more or less favorable. This pattern makes more difficult the government's attempt to create a responsible and informed citizenry which will take the government's goals for its own. The concomitant of the general support the government does receive from the educated classes is the expectation that the government will care for the interests of these classes. Jobs must be supplied, housing must be provided, the cost of living must be kept down, and regular advancements to positions of prestige and good pay must be granted. Emphasis upon achievement is also somewhat limited by knowledge of the fact that no outsider can really get into the inner circle.

Achievement is rewarded, but all too often the achievement is a quantitative one rather than a qualitative one. Such emphasis can, however, be easily exaggerated, for the penalty for failure to achieve is imposed only upon the most important of those who have been taken into the ruling group. The possibility of dismissal for cabinet ministers and for ministerial secretaries is the one fact that distinguishes them from the inner circle and from those members of the military who have been brought close to the very highest levels of decision making. For the co-opted administrators and experts the pressure to produce ever-larger balance sheets and ever-increasing quantitative results is very strong. For those further down the line there are not many penalties to suffer. The most that can be expected is that the levels to which they may advance may be restricted.

Withal, it must be remembered that the major basis for political life in Egypt today may be characterized as being administrative or bureaucratic in nature. In place of the political news of yesteryear, the newspapers are now full of new directives, new reports, new announcements, new public relations presentations made by the various ministries, organizations, and economic agencies of the government. According to the press nothing really significant goes on in Egypt which is not the result of some government action. The only other kind of news carried may be an occasional human interest story or the report of a sensational crime or murder.

The only point of contact between the individual and the government whereby the individual can, in a manner of speaking, make demands is the elaborate system of receiving complaints and requests for the redress of grievance. This appears to have been an important secondary purpose of the National Union Organization and may become a purpose of the new Socialist Union. Every ministry has a special division for the receipt of such complaints. Newspapers may also function in this capacity, though not so often as in the past, and the presidency itself has a special bureau for this purpose.

For the average member of the educated classes this concept of the political as essentially administrative does not elicit participant reactions. Political support for the regime, while not deficient, is generally passive. The absence of opportunities for effective participation renders the government a relatively distant, cold object however much its leaders may appear psychologically familiar and warm. There can be no participation in political life as an individual with ideas of one's own or as a member of a group urging upon the society an alternative policy. There is only one policy, and everyone else must accommodate himself to that policy. It is in this light that the difficulties of the government in attempting to bring about voluntaristic support through mass-line organizations, such as the old National Union and its various branches, or such as the Congress of Popular Forces and the Socialist Union, are to be understood. Members of the educated classes dutifully play their part, when they are called upon, in these various organizations and their subordinate committees. They may take some limited action within the framework of such participation to see to it that the interests of their own occupational group are protected. Beyond this, and with very few exceptions, they tend to do and to say what is expected of them.

Opinions may be expressed with relative freedom, but in the end the wise citizen bows to the acknowledged sources of authority. Argument can proceed only to a certain limit and then must cease. If special interests are to be pursued, the organizations representative of such interests must somehow work their way into the administrative scheme. Worthy of note, even if only in passing, is that the administrative apparatus referred to is larger than the formal bureaucracy associated with the ministries; it extends even to the Socialist Union, to the press, and to all educational institutions. For interests which are not given to such formal organization there can be no political dimension. Traditional structures can no longer become the basis of political activity. The family is no longer to be thought of in political terms. The recent change from regional representation to occupational representation in the demise of the National Union and birth of the Socialist Union suggests that local interests will not in the future have major political significance. Nor can we expect that individual intellectuals or even schools of literary or humanistic or, for that matter, economic thought will apply any significant pressure upon the policies of the government. Insofar as people of this kind have any political weight in Egypt—and they have not much—they too are integrated into the general administrative scheme.

The tendency toward extreme administrative rationality is certainly present, but it must be remembered that even the highest leadership is comprised of what we might call first-generation moderns, and that the policies they are pursuing must ultimately be related to the mixture of traditional and Western values which comprises their own political culture. The aspiration of the political leaders of Egypt can best be understood in terms of their desire to modernize in order to preserve a maximum of the social and personal values associated with tradition. In this sense they share the attitudes of most of the educated classes. But such is the nature of the problems facing Egypt and of the international environment in which these policies are being pursued that this semitraditional leadership is compelled increasingly to destroy traditional values or to relegate them to a secondary position.

It is for this reason that the nature of traditional values is hardly a subject for public discussion. The problem of the adjustment of the individual in a transitional society and polity is reflected in short stories, a few novels, and in movies that touch but superficially upon the problem in taking up such themes as social climbing, romantic love, the conflict between the older and the younger generation, and in the humorous but nevertheless tender way in which traditional characters are treated.

For the educated classes therefore the expression of traditional sentiments in those areas of social life in which traditional values prevail are private affairs. They are to be carried on among friends and members of one's family on the increasingly rare occasions when one visits the village of one's origin, or are to be satisfied in an even more private fashion in reading stories and watching movies.

Adjustment of the educated individual to an administrative polity is a very real problem, but so great and so unmanageable are the economic and the demographic problems facing the government of Egypt that such personal matters cannot be considered as having any central importance. Individual adjustment is subordinated to the central task of achieving dignity for the nation, expressing the individuality of Egypt, and realizing the special contribution Egypt is to make to world culture. Furthermore tradition itself requires that the problems of the individual be considered private matters. The struggle of each educated individual to achieve dignity and to realize his individuality and somehow to express something of his own unique qualities is not a central concern of society or government.

There is little either in the policies of the present government or in tradition to encourage the individual to externalize his problems. In place of a concern with the problems of individual adjustment within the culture there is a fair degree of inept striving to diffuse the cultural atmosphere of smaller traditional structures to encompass the whole society. Sociologically the roots of this idealized pattern are in rural village life, and ideologically its roots are in the Islamic concept of the ummah, but these strivings receive a mixed response. On the one hand there are what appear to be the sentimentalists who applaud them, and on the other there are the rationalists and the hard-headed types who insist that what is needed is efficiency and not sentimentality. For both categories, however, it would appear that this atavistic *Gemeinschaft* is meaningful only in the general sense of expressing the emotional content of contemporary Egyptian nationalism for the educated classes. But it is probably quite irrelevant to their individual problems of adjustment within their families and within the larger urban society in which they find themselves.

This contrast between private tradition and public modernity exists within a political framework where the stated objective is an ideal democracy. In this ideal democracy perfect harmony is to be realized between the interest of the whole and the interest of the individual, between the educated classes and the uneducated classes, and between the people of the city and those of the countryside. But the transition to this ideal democracy is not to be entrusted to democratic means because of the fear that reactionary elements will take control of the process and divert it. Hence the polity is to be directed toward democracy by a leader with whom one may argue and to whom one may complain but from whom one may not ultimately differ.

It is not too difficult therefore even for the educated individual who is prone to use abstract political concepts to understand the real working of the political system in terms of his own family arrangement. The traditional family is still essentially an authoritarian institution, one in which much privacy is not permitted and in which minor deviations may be allowed, but wherein gross deviations are dealt with first by severe shaming and secondly by more severe deprivation. The adjustment of the individual is not a problem for the public as a whole; it is not one that can be made a subject of direct demands upon the government. Indeed such problems are not at all to be made public, and insofar as there is any open discussion of such matters the individuals concerned will doubtlessly feel greatly shamed. Egypt is not yet so modernized as to be able to suffer problems of a psycho-social nature to become matters of public concern.

The Lower Classes

Members of the rural lower classes and those more recently arrived in the city from rural areas can also identify themselves with the president and with the leadership of the United Arab Republic. Nasser is one of them. He can and often does speak to them in their own language. He frequently holds out the promise of direct benefits to this class of people, and insofar as the government's policies have borne heavily upon the educated classes—that is, those who have turned their backs on the culture of the people—this is a welcomed state of affairs. But whether or not such lower-class people have been among the direct beneficiaries of the reforms of the revolutionary government, they are not direct participants in political affairs nor, unlike the middle classes, do they desire to be such.

It does not appear that many of them read the press, nor would they be very much amused by what the press contains. Many of them do listen to the radio, primarily to local songs; and they no doubt appreciate the recent switch from didactic haranguing to dramatic sketches which point the same moral. Members of the government are heroes, and tales are told about their achievements in the coffee houses. These stories give great amusement to the listeners, and this is the manner in which most of the activities of the government are looked upon. It is much the same with public rallies and speeches and with demonstrations in which members of the lower classes are spectators or in fact participants.

It is somewhat different for factory labor and for semiskilled workers, as it is for retail and service employees who come into greater contact with the educated classes. These members of what we might call the upper-lower class have really been most disturbed by economic modernization and industrialization. For example, they realize well the value of education but know also that they cannot hope to provide their own children with more than a minimum of grammar school training. Their daily schedules require more punctuality and devotion to routine tasks than do those of the middle classes. Their housing is poor, even inadequate. It probably compares unfavorably with their recollection of the relative freedom of village life and village social relationships as compared to the narrowness of existence in one small room in a multi-storied apartment house in which one can hardly maintain that privacy about one's own affairs which is necessary to traditional dignity, and in which one can nevertheless not aspire to develop such familiar and understanding friendships with one's neighbors as characterize village life.

For the upper-lower classes, even more than for the middle classes, the problem of finding one's place in society, especially the problem of maintaining one's prestige as a householder, of keeping one's shameful acts from the eyes of outsiders, and of arranging for marriages is very difficult indeed. For these classes the political system promises much but delivers little. Improvements that can be made are small given the pressure upon the resources of the government. Furthermore the government's concern with these workers is not reflected in the attitudes of their employers even when they are government managers. One gains the impression that it is difficult for these people to identify themselves with the aspiration of the government and that they make no effort to understand the meaning of the socialist and democratic goals of President Nasser.

It is for these people, one feels, that the thesis of the social breakdown has had most relevance. They have not acquired even the external standards of modernization which characterize the middle classes, and they are so situated that they cannot realistically attempt to realize the traditional values they left behind them in the villages. To win these people over to even a minimum of civic political behavior appears to be a formidable task. This general characterization probably does not hold true for people who are employed in the larger factories (outside Cairo) which pursue a paternalistic policy.

For members of the middle classes who have not become major beneficiaries of the revolution the Egyptian political system is moderately oppressive in that (1) it makes more severe demands upon the performance of bureaucrats, teachers, managers, and the rest, in that (2) realistic estimates of how far one can progress are not optimistic enough to encourage individuals to hope for a sudden and complete transformation of their personal circumstances, and in that (3) nearly all political bargaining and hence fluidity have ceased and have been replaced by a much more fixed and bureaucratized arrangement. The system is more fair, but there is no chance to escape from the present and from the disenchantment of drab offices and schoolrooms and stifling family surroundings. The strong sense of a lack of freedom is not for the most part due to political controls, though these are much in evidence. The modernizing policies of the government are recognized as attempting to create greater freedom from tradition, poverty, and insecurity. But resources are so few, opportunities to be away from other people are so few, opportunities for careers are so set in advance, and family patterns so rigid, that an overwhelming conformity results for the great majority of the middle classes. It is with the induction of these classes into this conformity that we shall be primarily concerned when we now turn to examine some of the agencies of socialization in Egypt.

Agencies of Socialization

In concentrating upon the middle classes we are concerning ourselves with the "political" class in the special sense in which I have described Egyptian politics. Nevertheless it should be remembered that there are significant differences in the import of various socializing agencies for members of different classes and those engaged in diverse occupations. Nor should it be thought that an examination of socializing agencies can serve as a total explanation of why Egyptians think and act the way they do. The major means for political socialization in Egypt, as elsewhere, is actual experience with those in political authority; but this is merely to reiterate that political socialization is a continuous process akin to any form of learning and does not cease through the life of the individual. In the following we shall be more concerned with psychological preparation for the introduction of adult attitudes about politics rather than with the learning which comes from direct experience with political authorities. It is the former which is more closely related to the total cultural frame, while the latter is indistinguishable from the responsive behavioral consequences of the political process.

For the Egyptian middle classes the two most important institutions of socialization are the family and the school. These two represent opposite poles, for the home is the fortress of tradition and the school, more and more responsive to the contemporary political environment. These two agencies are also opposed to one another in that the home influences the attitudinal structure of the individual while the school influences his external behavior. In other words, but with some exaggeration, the home environment helps to explain the psychological basis of Egyptian political culture, and the school environment helps to explain its institutional basis.

In its impact on individuals the family varies from class to class. The most important distinction to be made between the lower and upper classes in this regard is that the lower and more traditional classes value the family more and accept its demands more willingly. The importance of the family also tends to vary with its material ability to benefit the individual; hence it tends to be more important in rural areas and among the higher urban classes, especially those with some land in the family. Contrariwise, the family is weakest among the urban lower-middle class and upper-lower class and somewhat stronger among the middle classes proper. It is somewhat expensive to keep up all one's family obligations; hence for some groups like the upper-lower class or urban proletariat the desire to maintain family ties and to uphold traditional virtue may be financially impossible of fulfillment but nevertheless a source of guilt. In the middle classes an opposite attitude, that is, one of resentment against traditional demands and restrictions, may result in a neglect of certain family obligations and a similar sense of guilt. It is, however, in the upper-lower and lower-middle classes that one more often meets with the semblance of deracination, with delinquency, and with gross social deviance.

The two most important characteristics of the Egyptian family are its extended character and the great disparity in the roles of the father and mother. Ideally a description of an extended family system should include some precise statement of the degrees of relationship and the character of the obligations of all the members. In Egypt, however, as opposed to primitive societies, there is no standard answer. By and large the traditional system is intact among the rural lower classes, where it is based on land ownership or rental rights to which the sons succeed upon the father's death. Until that time, when the family's holdings are divided, the families of the sons live together with the father in a single household. Increasingly among those who are better off some of the sons may be working in the city or in school. Among city families one meets much more frequently with the nuclear family household. Separate residence, especially in urban areas, makes upholding family obligations more difficult, but it certainly does not eliminate them.

Ideally the family is still the interest group par excellence, and the group to which the individual owes the greatest loyalty. The status of the family is the yardstick by which the status of the individual is judged except in cases where an individual has achieved prominence politically or by some other exceptional circumstance. Even for those employed in bureaucratized organizations, the family remains the most important basis of identification. It is, again ideally, a highly structured system of roles based upon an authority hierarchy, diffuse scope of interests, comprehensive mutual but asymmetrical obligations, and formalized patterns of relationships. It is a very powerful institution, and there can be little doubt that it molds the basic personality structure of the individual whether he accepts its strictures or tends to rebel. In facing the outside world the family is largely assimilated into the personality of its head and represents his prestige, his property, and his achievement. Nothing that will in any way affect the family's prestige may be done without first consulting both father and older brothers.

The cultural mechanism by which the family system works is the belief that there is a right way of doing all things, that is, a way appropriate to the status of the particular family in question. There is much preoccupation with matters of honor and shame, and the distinction between the two forms the basis of socializing the young. The traditional virtues of honor, honesty, sincerity, loyalty, duty, deference to age, submission to authority, and formal courtesies are all closely related to the family. Although there is some public emphasis on a few of these in the schools and in public speeches or novels, when the family is left behind, these virtues are weakened. It is further obvious that such virtues as applied in a family context comprise an important ingredient in the populistic nationalism which is implicit in the terms Arab socialism, the Arab society, and Arab culture as used by some members of the communications elite.

The roles of father and mother are central to an understanding of the family and, more important for our purposes, for understanding the orientations of individuals to those outside the family. The father dominates the household. He enjoys unlimited authority, commands the respect of all, distributes the rewards and dispenses punishment, and stays aloof from the children for the most part. His commands must be obeyed by wife or children equally. He is supposed to be a man of forceful personality, but his own success is measured in terms of maintaining the family's status rather than in economic or other forms of achievement. Of course this is an ideal picture, for in the cities men are often seen at the grocers doing the family shopping, and in middle-class households the acquisition of certain implements like a stove and refrigerator is a matter of such importance that the father must be involved.

The status of the mother not only is a reflection of the lower status of women in the society at large but also appears to have contributed to that lower social status. The mother is in nearly all things the opposite of the father. She is not a guardian of the family's prestige but its point of greatest vulnerability. She is not wise, forbearing, generous in friendship, and terrible in retribution. She is generally considered, at least in traditional circles, as concerned with trivia, a weak personality, permissive, somewhat dishonest, a dissimulator, and incapable of controlling her emotions. In traditional Muslim families the women are secluded, and, even if they are not veiled, the activity of middle-class Cairo women is quite closely restricted. As in the case of all other intimate family matters and especially those which might weaken or shame the family vis-à-vis outsiders, the women are matters for reticence at best and secrecy at worst.

The children grow up in a highly permissive atmosphere so long as they are in their mother's charge. At some time before adolescence the boys especially are increasingly subject to the father's discipline and his approving or disapproving judgements. Before this younger sons have gotten a taste of such strictness from their older brothers. They see their mothers as the source of indulgence, love, humour, and understanding but cannot fail to note that she is not a symbol of prestige but rather of shame. The father, on the other hand, is the symbol of authority and propriety. The mother represents the internal aspect of family relations, that which is never to be revealed to outsiders, and the father represents the outside aspect. The resultant ambivalence of attitudes is further enhanced by the fact that the mother is often genuinely self-effacing and self-sacrificing while the father is not only distant but self-indulgent as well. Moreover, despite the great pressure for family cooperation and mutual assistance and consultation, agreement is general that there is also immense sibling rivalry due in large part to the struggle to win greater attention and approval from the parents.

Even from this brief sketch we can derive a number of conclusions of great significance for the political culture of Egypt. In the first place, the kind of society which Egyptians want is one which reflects the virtues taught in the family and one which understands the essence of the national community in family terms. Second, all persons in positions of authority tend to be assimilated to the role and character of the father, or in rare cases to that of the mother. The individual who finds himself in a position of authority has already internalized the model of the father as the goal to which maturation and achievement of adult status will lead him, but he may find that the strategies of the mother are more helpful in subordinate roles. Third, equalitarian relations cannot be conceived of outside a framework of keen rivalry. Fourth, formalism and prestige are still rated more highly than achievement. Fifth, authority and power are thought to be aspects of personality and not attributes of certain roles. Sixth, matters of personal feelings, sentiments, social adjustment, and sex are all associated with the idea of shame. Seventh, sharing of confidences and especially lifting the veil of secrecy from any of the symbols of shame are grave and stupid mistakes which can only weaken the individual in his social dealings.

It is only in the villages that such family life exists within an integrative social environment. Elsewhere the secrecy which envelops family affairs is also the partition which compartmentalizes the public and private aspects of culture and personality. It is the educational system which inducts the individual into the public culture of the modernizing political system, and its work is reinforced by that of the other politically legitimized institutions such as bureaucratic agencies, interest groups, the Socialist Union, and the controlled communications media.

Unlike that of the family, the socializing function of the educational system affects only a selected group of Egyptians. It hardly need be added that this group, especially under the present regime, coincides roughly with the modernized classes: the greater the education, the higher the class. The basis of this selection is, generally speaking, by class, financial ability, urban versus rural residence, and the parents' level of education; but an important element of social mobility is built into this system since sons tend to do better than fathers except in the highest classes. The size of the educational system, and hence some measure of those who are exposed to diverse levels of modern culture, may be suggested by the figures below, showing number of students, by class of institution, for 1958-1959:

	Male	Female	Total
Primary	1,425,679	860,388	2,286,067
Preparatory			
General	182,449	65,343	247,792
Technical	23,320	6,428	29,753
Religious	19,574	——	19,574
Total Preparatory			297,119
Secondary			
General	94,902	20,706	115,608
Technical	40,031	9,981	50,012
Religious	12,181	——	12,181
Teachers Seminary	8,846	8,169	17,015
Total Secondary			194,816
Higher			
Institutes	8,158	3,160	11,318
Azhar	4,313	——	4,313
Universities	66,332	10,838	77,170
Total Higher			92,801

In 1957 it was estimated that 62 per cent of all children who came under the compulsory education law were in school, an increase from 35 per cent in 1949. A 1958 estimate puts the total number of these children in the 6 to 12 age bracket at 3,719,000. It is also interesting that in 1951-1952 the total number of university students (excluding the higher institutes) increased from 37,925 to 81,119.

From the foregoing it is possible to gain a general impression of the structure of the Egyptian educational system. There are fewer and poorer schools in the rural areas and better ones in the cities. The more advanced schools are also to be found in the cities, and the universities of Cairo, Ain Shams, and al-Azhar as well as most of the institutes are located in Gizeh and Cairo. There is also one university at Alexandria and one at Assiut. The system is complete, fairly standard Western in its conception, and after the primary grades is directed at university education. While the number of university students may not quite have kept pace, relative to the total population, with the number of primary students, it remains clear that this group is very large in comparison with the size of the educated classes it is destined to inflate. Nearly all university graduates aspire to government employment, and now that all large firms have been nationalized or brought under government control, this is the only employment open to them. In some cases, however, graduates have to wait two or three years or longer to be placed, and only so recently as 1961 an emergency decree forced the ministries to hire between 7,000 and 10,000 graduates to get them off the labor market.

If we recall that the essential nature of the Egyptian political system is administrative-bureaucratic and that its processes involve hierarchical and cooptative practices, we can grasp the critical socialization role played by the educational system. Educational practices emphasize the authority of the teacher, rote learning, formal curricula, uniformity, discipline, and routine. This is to be expected, although there are some reports of newer creative influences penetrating around the edges. In these respects the school resembles all nonfamily organizations and simply carries the general culture of social relations into the imported and adapted modern educational structure. Beyond this, however, and especially in the primary and preparatory schools strenuous efforts are made to develop a strong loyalty to the regime, to President Nasser, and to the religion of Islam. Textbooks are full of stories about medieval Islamic heroes and even about those who martyred themselves against Napoleon's troops or against the British more recently. Many pages are given over to Qur'anic passages or simplified excerpts from books on ethics. On relatively frequent occasions the first class each morning is given over to some political subject such as a discussion of the assassination of Lumumba, celebration of Port Said Day (the evacuation of the British and French troops therefrom in 1956), or Palestine Refugee Day. School children wear simple uniforms which emphasize their equality, though in some parts of Cairo only the children of the relatively poor go to the public school. Nevertheless the uniforms and the discipline add to the loss of individuality in the school and lend a further uncomfortableness when the youngsters line up in the schoolyard and sing the rousing "Nasser" anthem.

At the higher stages of schooling this kind of indoctrination is handled in other ways and usually outside the classroom. It is here that scouting, camping, and mass athletic or military demonstrations come in. Part of these activities are under the Ministry of Education and part under special bodies like the High Council on Youth Welfare. At the university level it is the latter and the controlled student groups or student commissions of the Socialist Union which are responsible for the indoctrination and for demonstrating the loyalty of the university. There are some ideologically oriented courses even at the university level. For example, all students have been required to take a course called "Arab Society." Similar influences are manifest in the curriculum of the new Faculty of Politics and Economics, in some courses given at the Military Academy, and in the curriculum of the Institute of Higher Arab Studies of the Arab League. On the other hand, whatever may be said about these courses, the intention behind them is not to propagandize but to train people for positions where such information will be needed, as in the Information Administration, in the Foreign Ministry, or in the corps of Military Attachés.

The more formal indoctrinating efforts of the school system present a picture of the Egyptian state and society as it would like to be or as it hopes to become. In this sense such efforts are part of a much wider effort of the broadcasting service, the Information Administration, the controlled ("reorganized") press, and the Socialist Union. The youngster is able to become familiar with the new political symbols and newer standards of loyalty and service to the nation which he will not be taught at home. He will begin to recognize the disparity between the two sets of standards to which he is exposed and will gradually adjust his external behavior in accordance with the demands of his school environment rather than solely in terms of his father's representational behavior. He will gradually learn to recognize the same national symbols when repeated on the radio, in the press, and in public speeches. He will become accustomed to participating in group demonstrations and generally become acquainted with the duties of an educated citizen in a modernizing oligarchy.

If the student manages to get into the university or into one of the higher institutes, his more specific socialization begins. Neither the overt picture of the regime nor the particular bits of knowledge he will gather in his classroom will be very helpful to him in his future career. His really practical training consists of understanding the way in which the university is organized, the career prospects and influence of each kind of specialization, and the relationship of extracurricular activities to his career advancement. Studying at the university is the student's first introduction into the bureaucratic atmosphere in which he will serve for the rest of his working life. It is at this time that his aspirations become more realistic and he develops a sense of common interest with his classmates.

The student will learn that the higher institutes with their more practical "how to do it" orientation enjoy a higher prestige and their graduates, better career prospects. They learn that graduates of the Faculty of Letters have been waiting three years to be placed. They find out that the military and political elite have not much respect for professors and academic types, that students themselves are somewhat suspect and subject at once to special control and special praise. They become aware of the role of the security officer assigned to the university by the Ministry of the Interior, and of the subordinate administrative authority of their teachers. The power of the Ministry of Education is evident after a time, and its control over student organizations and activities as well as its connections with the High Council on Youth Welfare are made manifest. Through the four years of his university education the student learns a great deal about the legalistic, formalistic, labyrinthic, administrative set-up in which he must find a place and work. He witnesses the manner in which those with real political power behave, how those with cultural prestige behave, and how those with petty administrative authority behave. If he is wise, he will come to understand where he will fit.

Imperfect a system though it may be, the university performs a very important socializing function for the administrative elite of the country. As they learned about the overt character of the political system and its ideal goals in grammar school, they learn about its internal workings, the flow of authority, prestige, and permitted deviations during their higher education. In a schematic way they will learn that the military come first, the economists second, the managers and technical experts third, the communications elite fourth, the general administrators fifth, and the professionals sixth.

All the other socializing institutions may be understood in terms of the educational system. At least insofar as the educated classes are concerned these institutions may be assimilated in their socializing roles to the symbolic goals of early education or the more practical goals of later education. Interest groups and bureaucratic organizations, regardless of their composition, tend to reinforce the university experience. The media of communication and political organizations are much more concerned with overt symbolic goals and tend to reinforce the experience of early education. Religious institutions, insofar as they are concerned with education, are becoming more and more integrated into the secular school system. Religious education remains an important means of social advancement for lower-class persons, but government control over the curriculum, over career placement, and over the financial resources of these institutions, when coupled with the requirement of government approval for the acquisition of high religious positions, is rendering the whole religious institution but an adjunct of state administration. The government is not hostile to religion by any means, and the number of religious students has greatly increased along with a doubling of the budget of al-Azhar since the revolution in 1952. The prestige of Islam has been raised by government support for the World Islamic Conference, by increased government concern about the pilgrimage, by the more frequent use of religion in international relations, and by the honorific political duties performed on all occasions by the Rector of al-Azhar. As a consequence of such favor the government can count on the substantial cooperation of the ulama. The smashing of the Muslim Brethren has left a fair number of the modernized religious in opposition to the government, but the neo-traditionalist Brethren maintained but an uneasy *modus vivendi* with the ulama. The cooperation of the ulama and the government extends even to the mosques and the content of Friday services, which tend generally to reinforce the public image of the regime in much the same way as does the press. All of this cooperation is carried on despite the fact that in many ways those studying in religious schools and those who call themselves ulama are predominantly traditional in their manner and dress, in values, and in social behavior. The education division of al-Azhar, in cooperation with voluntary groups, does maintain about 300 Quranic schools in the provinces. These are traditional preparatory schools for higher religious studies. Hence a fair number of religious students are not nearly so well prepared for what they will find in Cairo as the regular preparatory school students are.

The effect of urbanization and of economic reform and development on political culture is probably secondary for members of the educated middle class. The school system is far more important in making them aware of their political and social environment. The socialization of the lower classes is, however, more significantly affected by these trends since lower-class people are more likely to move about the country and to seek to change their employment as adults. For the new immigrant to the big city the impact of the change in his environment is likely to be somewhat mitigated by going to live among other immigrants from his own province, praying at the same mosque with them, and locating employment through them. With their assistance he will learn the wonders of the big city and about the strange customs of the more affluent classes. Despite this pressure-chamber function, the immigrant community does not provide the same environment found in the village nor are its prestige and social hierarchy the same. The man who can manage to make the most by doing least, who gets into petty trading or even into a small-time confidence racket, will tend to be more highly regarded than the village stalwart. The man who can get to the movies more often or who manages to take a divorcée as a second wife, or who has the most outlandish tales to tell in the coffee house is the most envied. It is for these people that the public activities and pronouncements of political leaders afford the greatest satisfaction and amusement. These really important men of personality and power, who defy the foreigner with impunity and yet speak a language the peasant can understand, these are good men. I doubt seriously that their understanding goes beyond this. They make no demands, no complaints of the government. Health, welfare, a job—all are matters of fate and not of politics.

A new immigrant to the city is not really a good prospect for an industrial job. It takes a more urbanized, perhaps even a highly educated person to succeed in getting one of those coveted positions and all the security that goes with it. Factory workers and the rest of the upper-lower class have a more practical notion of the benefits they derive from the government. Many of them are even aware of the elaborate arrangements of the government and the Socialist Union for the redress of grievances. A few will even know of some provisions of the Labor Law from which they benefit. They attribute these benefits to the good will of President Nasser and one or two of his close associates. Some at least are also aware of the new role of the police. The police are now more respectful in their treatment of ordinary citizens and will often favor them above members of the minorities. The police are also more in evidence—though in plain clothes—in searching out the activities of labor unions, craft unions, and associational groups as well as in checking hawkers' and porters' licenses, in controlling car parkers and garbage collectors, and even in finding out who is talking to whom in traditional (baladi) coffee houses. On balance, however—for there are few subversives among the lower classes—the changes are for the better. The ordinary Egyptian is now more important, and he can identify relatively easily with the great leader. His respect for power as an emanation of personality and charisma is relatively unmitigated by any desire for political liberty or any rivalry for sharing in its exercise. He does not find it strange that one man exceeds all others in power and authority but assumes, nevertheless, that the relationships among all the members of the Revolutionary Command Council are replete with love and mutual respect as behooves good friends.

In our discussion of the institutions of socialization into the political culture of contemporary Egypt we have stressed four aspects of cultural orientation each of which may be more or less prominent in particular individuals depending upon their degree of modernity and their class position. These four may be conveniently called the familistic-covert, the familistic-overt, the nationalistic-ideal, and the bureaucratic pragmatic as shown in the diagram below.

	Private	Public
Covert	1. family personality rivalry	3. bureaucratic pragmatic career
Overt	2. prestige power generosity	4. nationalism idealism cooperation

We have also indicated that there is no easy solution to integrating these four cultural tendencies or aspects despite the fact that the populistic and romantic elements in contemporary nationalism aspire in that direction. In any case, it is clear that with outsiders the Egyptians will discuss matters bearing on area 4, that is public-overt matters before 3, 2, and 1, in that order. Lower-class people will omit area 3 altogether, while many younger people and women will omit both areas 3 and 4, with some women being totally restricted in their cultural orientation to 1, that is, to the private-covert area.

In emphasizing the family and the educational system as the two most important agencies of primary political socialization for the Egyptian middle classes the impact of occupational differentiation later in life has been left aside. In the general sense of the term socialization we understand a process of preparation for participation in political life. The dividing line between preparation and participation must be somewhat arbitrary, and particularly so when student groups shade off into mass-line political organizations. Yet it seems important to distinguish at some point between general orientation and specialized learning. Besides, at some point in the gradual transition our interest shifts to the actual working of the political system.

The general orientation just described affects the attitudes and political behavior of persons who must perform in relatively specific roles. It is within this more structured type of situation that the tensions within the political culture are made more manifest. The form these tensions take are described in the following sections on the Egyptian elites. While primary emphasis is placed upon the relationship between political culture and elite structure, the relationship among elites should not be overlooked. When particular attention is paid to those relationships, it may be noted that even the diffuse political culture which is the product of tension-laden primary socialization processes tends to unite rather than divide the postrevolutionary elites of modern Egypt. The problems discussed are common to all. The divergences which beset Egyptian elites are the consequences of structural differentiation and the divergent impact of resource scarcities upon the elite structures.

The Military Elites

It is an inner core of the highest military elite which comprises the effective decision-making group in Egypt today. Most narrowly construed, this inner core is made up of but five men, the remaining members of the Revolutionary Command Council after the death of one, after the political exclusion of three and the possibly temporary retirement of two others. But in a broader sense it is the entire military officer corps which enjoys the position of the most influential and privileged political layer. Despite the fact that this situation is generally acknowledged and accepted, it would be incorrect to assume that the military have acceded to such a position as a consequence of a previously highly cooperative organization. In no sense did they comprise an integrated interest group in prerevolutionary times.[3]

---

[3] In recent years several attempts have been made to explicate the nature of the Egyptian military and the basis of their accession to power, but these have not enlightened us much. We must own to the fact that we have at present little solid information about the social composition of the Egyptian officer corps. Morroe Berger (*Military Elite and Social Change, Egypt since Napoleon*, Princeton, 1960) has given us some of the historical background of this group; P. J. Vatikiotis, *op.cit.* has added some details and expanded upon the background and experience of the most influential of the military; similar information was presented by Jean and Simonne La Couture (*Egypt in Transition*, London, 1958). Additional sources of bits of information are Nasser's *Philosophy of the Revolution*, Anwar-al-Sadat's *Revolt on the Nile*, and Rashid Barawy's *The Military Coup in Egypt*. The scope of the present essay does not permit a detailed review of the contributions of each

During the reign of Mohammed Ali (1806-1840) the Egyptian army was transformed from one based on Mameluke officers and their retainers to a more modern standing army based on the peasant soldier. The officer corps was changed somewhat as a result of more modern education and training, but it was still drawn largely from the Ottoman, Mameluke, Albanian, and Circassian military elite. Vatikiotis reports that under Ismail Pasha the sons of umdahs (village headmen) were given the privilege (or obligation) of serving as junior officers in the armed forces.[4] The 'Arabi revolt of 1879-1882 is connected with the decision of the Pasha (by that time already the Khedive) to dismiss from the armed forces some 2,000 of those officers. The officers were brought to Cairo for demobilization, where they were joined in their protest by a substantial part of the membership of the advisory National Assembly which had been established in 1866. Jacob Landau reports that nearly 80 per cent of the members were umdahs. Hence it is possible to trace the contemporary connections between the rural middle class and the modernized, professional, middle class (including the military) from 1879 right up to the present.

The accepted historical judgment of the 'Arabi revolt was that it was premature at best and (at worst) that 'Arabi himself was little qualified by temperament and wisdom to lead it. It is difficult, however, to be quite sure in what sense it was premature since the British occupation intervened to bring the movement to a close. The similarities between the 'Arabi revolt and the *coup d'état* of 1952 are so striking, especially with regard to the social backgrounds and cultural orientation of its leaders, as to suggest that the entire intervening period of the growth of liberal and parliamentary ideas under British influence was a meaningless diversion. This is of course an extreme statement which does not take account of the social, economic, and educational restructuring of Egypt in the intervening seventy years; but it is meant to stress the persistent cultural baseline to which all other developments must be related. If the 'Arabi revolt was premature, it was so in the sense that the class which was the exponent of "nativistic" or "populistic" nationalism was still small and, more importantly, that the ideas and cultural orientation of this group

---

of these works. The most that can be done is to present some general conclusions drawn from a reading of them and from a limited amount of personal observation. It need hardly be added that this is a subject about which it is not easy to acquire accurate information.

[4] Vatikiotis, *op.cit.*, pp. 8, 13.

had not yet become widespread among those who were politically aware in Egypt. While liberal constitutional ideas spread among a very thin class of the highly educated, the really integrative cultural change was occurring within the groups where nativist and anti-foreign ideas were spread. In 1882 the native military officer group was the only one directly blocked from advancement within a bureaucratized framework by a foreign element. By 1952 nearly all the educated middle class found itself in a similar situation as a consequence of the increasing bureaucratization of nearly all areas of public endeavor. In 1952 it was not only the alien Muslims who were holding the positions to which the new middle class aspired but both Middle Eastern and European non-Muslims as well: Copts, Armenians, Italians, Greeks, Lebanese, Jews, as well as British and French. An incomprehensible reversal of the usual allocation of benefits to majority and minority had occurred as a consequence of foreign rule and the emphasis upon alien values.

This growth of what might be called the " 'Arabi outlook" provided the ideological basis for the mass acceptance of the leadership of the Free Officers as the restructuring of Egyptian economy and society permitted them to take control in purely physical and administrative terms. The really complicated problem was that of determining an agreed policy and capturing secure control over the armed forces from which the only threat to the leadership of the Revolutionary Command Council could come. It is probably correct to say that there might have been a threat to the leadership of the RCC, but it may be seriously doubted that there was a real threat to the revolution itself.

In order to understand the vulnerability of the RCC we must bear in mind that their sole claim to authority was that they had taken the initiative. So weak was the legitimacy of their position that they repeatedly asserted their intention of returning to their barracks as soon as the revolution was completed, and too many politicians believed them. They were not senior officers and could not command the loyalty of the rest of the armed forces on the basis of rank and routine discipline, as was so in Pakistan or recently in Burma.

Furthermore, the essence of the culture of the military in Egypt, as in many other countries, is bureaucratic. Entrants into the military are not primarily seeking adventure or service of an ideal so much as a secure future in a career which gives them relatively high status, opportunity for advancement, and certain material benefits.

The officer group is much smaller and necessarily more cohesive than the civil service because most of its members pass through a single military academy and often a single staff school. In this regard it is worth recalling, as Vatikiotis has shown, that most of the members of the RCC were in attendance at the academy at the same time and they were in the first two classes after its reorganization in 1936.[5]

Despite the unity of the officer corps, especially among those who graduated after 1936 when the academy was opened to lower-middle-class candidates, we can discern evidence of divisiveness based on age groups, fields of specialization, staff and line differentia, old services versus new services such as the air corps and the paratroops, and educational differences resulting from the lateral entry of medical and engineering graduates. In the early postrevolutionary period, it appears that line officers were generally favored for advancement to high staff positions above lower staff officers. That is to say, it became more easily possible for line officers to reach general rank before the mandatory retirement age. More recently, however, the officer corps has expanded and the army has undertaken certain development tasks while at the same time increasing its emphasis on the more technical branches. As a consequence of these changes there has been a notable increase in the prestige of the engineering officers. Industrialization has increased the tendency toward early resignation to avoid retirement on a low pension and to get into one of the managerial or administrative jobs which, after nationalization, are the government's to hand out. Non-military estimates of the extent of such "job imperialism" are doubtlessly exaggerated, and many really able military men are denigrated in the process, but it is nevertheless true that there is a high ranking officer in the public relations bureau of the Chief of Staff who takes care of finding jobs for retiring officers.

At the present time it is widely felt that the military and police forces are solidly behind Nasser, and the denials that any substantial number were purged after the Syrian debacle carry conviction. The military officers do not now constitute a danger to the regime, but neither do they offer the possibility of breaking out of the development box in which Egypt finds itself through either taking command of the development effort or by changing the boundaries of Egypt. Their skills do not appear to be up to the requirements of such

[5] Vatikiotis, *op.cit.*, p. 45.

radical solutions. On the other hand, since the emphasis upon fighting skills as the basis for advancement has not yet completely given way to the emphasis upon technical skills, there can be little doubt of the improvement in morale of line officers and the improvement in fighting qualities of the Egyptian army since 1948 to complement their improved equipment.

For the rest, the military comprise but one more bureaucratized structure among many, exceeding the others only in the degree of favor they receive from the government and in their ability to move from one structure to another. The attitudes and political culture of the officer corps are not appreciably different from those in other professions, and it must be remembered that since there are few "military families" among the educated middle class most officers have close relatives who are university graduates working in the civilian ministries. Having a brother who is a civilian does not eradicate all cleavage between the two, however, for we have already seen that the Egyptian family is characterized by severe rivalry and competition among siblings. All that it determines is that underneath their diverse external bureaucratic and technocratic orientations there is the same native culture of the substantial village family. The implications of this mix for public policy have been such that rational, hierarchical techniques have been preferred, but the goals of such activity have not been to benefit the bureaucracy so much as to mitigate the conditions of the peasant and worker while supplying the government with investment funds. The tension between the civil service and the military results at least in part from the fact that the military officers have been excluded from the self-denying implications of this public policy framework.

The Bureaucratic Elites

The nature of the bureaucratic elites of Egypt has changed considerably since the Revolution of 1952. Before 1952, and in the early period of the Revolution, the bureaucracy was comprised of a relatively underprivileged educated middle-class group drawn largely from rural elements with medium-sized land holdings. This bureaucracy was subject to considerable political pressure from the political parties and from the court. It operated in a broader social context at once hostile to the activities of the bureaucracy and respectful of the intellectual attainments and the authority of its members. While the bureaucracy was rationally organized in the main, its operative process could be understood only in terms of traditional culture, authoritarianism, and status orientation. Hence, despite its rational organization, there could be little commitment to efficient policy implementation, to political neutrality, or to professional or technical values. As Morroe Berger has pointed out, the major commitment was to the attainment of security of employment, to regular career advancement, and to increasing income.[6] Success in attaining these goals turned on accommodative behavior and traditional bargaining rather than on carrying out assigned tasks efficiently or accepting responsibility.

The average civil servant is a man of university education, relatively young, and ill paid. He probably does not have the funds to marry and to establish an independent household. His outlook is only moderately optimistic, and his hopes are based on the regime's ability to fulfill some of its promises for achieving general prosperity. Most educated civil servants understand that the goal of the regime is to spread whatever benefits may be available as widely as possible, especially among the peasantry and industrial laboring groups, and that the government has no intention of devoting much of its resources to the civil service. Only a very few can hope to achieve positions of real importance within the civil service, but they all are assured of regular pay increases with seniority.

Aside from the very top bureaucratic elite it would appear that the highest-prestige positions are now held by professionals, technicians, and specialists of various sorts, as economic planners, accountants, and engineers of various kinds. If any position is more coveted than those described, it is that of managing director of one of the government-controlled companies. It is widely felt, however, that these plums are reserved for military officers who have transferred from the army into one of the great holding companies.

Egyptian managers have a largely pragmatic, efficiency-oriented point of view which puts little faith in the skill of Egyptian workers and perhaps too much faith in the productive capacity of modern machinery regardless of who tends that machinery.[7] But the managers must act within the framework provided by the persistent boards of directors, some members of which previously served those companies and some of whom have been added by the government from

[6] M. Berger, *Bureaucracy and Society in Modern Egypt*, Princeton, 1957, pp. 148-149.

[7] F. Harbison and I. A. Ibrahim, *Human Resources for Egyptian Enterprise*, New York, 1958.

among the politically aware. These in turn may be contrasted with the brash, self-assured group of graduates with degrees in economics and accounting who have become more highly favored than graduates of the Faculty of Law or Faculty of Letters, the former of which previously dominated all the important positions in the civil service. Of course the stronghold of the graduates of the Faculty of Economics is the Ministry of the Treasury, which employs many of these people as technical experts.

The scope of the graduates of the Faculty of Law is now more strictly limited to the Ministry of Justice and to the Council of State which, after having suffered a sharp decline following the failure of the lawyers to choose the right side in the Naguib-Nasser dispute, has lately risen to a more significant status. The Council of State appears to be the major channel for exertion of influence with the Presidency on behalf of the graduates of the Faculty of Law. Surprising as it may seem, the Council of State can count among its members many people who are committed to the ideal of the rule of law, and there have been some cases in which the government's attempts to ride roughshod over all legalistic opposition has been obstructed. Even in these cases the major emphasis has been on the prevention of administrative excesses and the protection of individual rights under very limited circumstances rather than the challenging of major policies such as nationalization of private firms and the expropriation of those who are considered to be enemies of the state.

All the members of the specialized services have received some distinctive orientation during the period of their higher university training, and each of these orientations tends to differ somewhat from the others. Despite the differences which arise from this training the major point of tension in the specialized services is still between those who have received higher university education and those who have entered from the military service. Even bearing this tension in mind, it is apparent that the sharpest cleavage in the civil service is between those in the specialized and favored services and those who carry out the more routine tasks of administration in the regular ministries. It is not only that those in the ranks of the ordinary civil service are less specialized, less modern in their outlook, and less professionalized in their orientation because of their employment; they are also far less optimistic about their own future and about the ability of the regime to really change things. This cleavage is the more significant for the reason that ultimately all the elaborate plans made at the upper levels of the bureaucracy and worked out by the technicians must be implemented by the ordinary civil servant at the grass-roots level.

In spite of this problem one can discern that a certain amount of the optimism and determination of the higher levels has been communicated to certain members at the lower levels. The regime still enjoys much good will which will carry it through the coming years, but eventually it will have to deliver if it is to maintain the support of the lower-ranking civil servants. Loss of their support will probably not be manifested in sabotage, much less in outright resistance to the regime; but to overcome the tremendous obstacles to development in Egypt, enthusiastic performance is required at all levels of the administrative system. Such performance is not now prevalent and it seems unlikely to be forthcoming in the near future.

Interest Group Elites

Unlike most underdeveloped countries Egypt is relatively well supplied with a wide variety of interest groups and associational groups of all kinds. Of course their situation is not that of interest groups and voluntary associations in open or competitive political systems. Some of the groups are quite old and can trace their history all the way back to the early part of this century. Others, like the Federation of Industries, go back at least forty years. But for the most part, interest groups and voluntary associations are far younger, the great bulk of them probably having been founded in the last two decades.

Knowledge of the different periods in which the various groups were formed contributes importantly to understanding their differential role in the Egyptian political system and their different emphases upon cooperation with or resistance to the various pressures of the government. Regardless of their original orientation, however, all interest groups and voluntary associations are presently subject to registration, and many of them operate under regulations laid down for them by the present government. All important groups have had regulations limiting and controlling their activities since their inception, but present-day control goes beyond laying down regulations and includes supervision of elections to all policy-making bodies and rather strict regulation of the conditions of employment of all subordinate office help. A further interesting and important development has been the decision to use certain interest groups as a basis of representation in the Congress of Popular Forces which met in 1962 to produce a new constitution and a new representational basis for the parliament elected in 1964.

In order to understand the growth of associational groups in Egypt within the context of the historical development of the Egyptian political system it is important to bear in mind that throughout the years in which the Egyptian polity was dominated by traditional elements, and during which the only effective opposition was made up of rather naïve liberals, the social and economic structural basis for a more modern type of political association and for a more highly rationalized administrative system was being laid down by means of the policy of defensive modernization. Most interest groups—unlike voluntary associations of a non-economic nature—had been granted a certain degree of administrative competence, a delegation of authority which was in fact a legitimization of their concern with relevant policy areas. While such an interest group pattern tended toward greater rationality than that of a feudal bureaucracy, it was nevertheless compatible with the traditional approach. Under such a system there was no great thought of regulating the activities of influential merchants, for example, in the interest of the society as a whole; there was rather an interest in the regulation of commercial activities in the interest of influential merchants who were regularly consulted by the government or by those standing in close political relationship with the political elite. Regulation was primarily in the interest of the influential members of the merchant community, who were members of the Chamber of Commerce, but certain additional functions which lightened the burden of government administration were also imposed upon such organizations. The same pattern held true for the Federation of Egyptian Industries until its recent reorganization. The Chamber of Commerce and the Federation of Industries looked upon themselves much as do similar interest groups in Western democratic countries. It was not so much a pluralistic emphasis they gave to the justification of their own political role, but rather their fulfilling a task that was considered in the public interest. This latter emphasis is to be understood as growing rather naturally out of the regulatory activities they performed for the government itself.

To be contrasted with this kind of interest group are the groups of the members of the free professions: the medical association, the bar association, the association of engineers, the association of accountants, and so on. These organizations represent graduates of the various faculties of the Universities of Cairo and Alexandria who have since become government employees, have established themselves in private business or, in some cases, have entered the military service as professionals. One of the main functions of such organizations has been to regulate entry into the relevant professions and to license members of those professions for practice within Egypt. Membership in the organizations is compulsory for anyone who wishes to practice. The membership of the policy-making councils of each of these professional associations has always been the matter of the highest political interest for those in power. During the period of the conflict and competition between the Wafd and the Royalist political parties leadership of the associations was generally held by one group or the other.

Because so many of their members were employed by the government or by the army, and because they were not of the most influential classes in Egypt at the time, the professionals were subject to some of the same disabilities and insecurities as were members of the civil service and even of the officer corps. Professional associations therefore had somewhat the character of high-class labor unions although in a closed-shop situation. The leadership could be divided between those who were of more or less aristocratic background and who were supported, after an adequate demonstration of their loyalty, by the King himself, and another group of less aristocratic background that was capable of demonstrating its political skill to the leadership of the Wafd. It is possible to argue that the professional associations saw their role as being properly carried out only within the framework of a competitive political system in which non-directive, pluralistic representation of interested views is legitimate within the broad framework of the public interest.

As already indicated, there has in recent years taken place a surprising rise in the number of associations. To those mentioned above could be added labor unions as well as associations for low professionals and those in municipal services. In addition to a considerable number of organizations active in fostering the interests of their own memberships there is a substantial number of charitable and quasi-civic organizations all registered with the Ministry of Social Affairs. A model constitution has been prepared by the ministry, and each association, whether backed by the ministry or not, must present its constitution and by-laws to the ministry for approval. Their budgets must also be approved and their accounts audited by the Ministry of Social Affairs.

If we exclude the charitable associations from our analysis, it appears that interest groups within Egypt fall into a relatively neat dichotomous pattern. On the one hand are associations of independently influential persons who conceive of their appropriate role as that of experts suggesting policy measures to the state and at the same time protecting the interests of their own memberships. Their outlook, however, is really not that of associational groups in constitutional democracies but rather that of associational concessionaires in essentially traditional political systems. The essence of the role of the traditional interest group is in their legitimization as specialized consultants of the government before policy is made.[8] On the other hand we find organizations of professionals of high and low prestige and of civil servants and industrial labor who conceive of their role as appropriate in a more or less rationalized and highly bureaucratized system of government. While they may feel they have something useful to contribute to policy making on occasion, their major concern is to protect the interests and raise the income of their membership. In return they willingly carry out the directives of the government, especially on regulation of their own profession. This difference is important to bear in mind in order to appreciate the differential experience of these groups with the government now that it has determined to rationalize and to control the bulk of interest groups and associational groups within Egypt.

As might be expected, groups dominated by a more or less traditional political outlook, and even professional groups that managed to achieve some degree of influence through cooperation with particular political parties in the prerevolutionary period, have had the most difficulty adjusting to the requirements of contemporary policy. Nearly all the other organizations have been sympathetic to the present rationalizing tendency of the Egyptian government and have cooperated fully with it. In all cases, the policy-making councils of interest groups have consisted of people the government could trust. With regard to the former group, however, there has been a strong tendency to see to it that the minister who is most closely concerned with the subject matter of the interest group be elected to the chairmanship of the policy-making council.

[8] For the use of this term see L. Binder, *Iran: Political Development in a Changing Society*, Berkeley, 1962, pp. 247ff.

The important point to bear in mind is that groups without great influence under the more traditional pattern of monarchical Egypt are more or less satisfied with the present close regulation by the government. They do not perceive such regulation as producing an uncomfortable limitation of their freedom but as an important legitimization of their existence and their contribution to the wealth and welfare of Egypt. They welcome this achievement of equal status with the previously influential groups consulted in the old days.

Consultation is relatively rare now, but an aspect of it was evident so long as the 1960 Parliament of the United Arab Republic was in session. In that Parliament, which was prorogued in 1961, members of various interest groups were represented and generally were placed by the speaker of the assembly on the subject-matter commissions of greatest interest to themselves. In those commissions they were capable of delaying passage of legislation and bringing their own views to bear upon decisions already made in the various ministries. While they had some moderate success, they were incapable of bringing about major changes in the areas of crucial policy decisions, particularly on economic matters.

With increasing government control over the economy, and with the increasingly large government share in all new investment, the older, more traditionally oriented interest groups are rapidly becoming like the newer more bureaucratically oriented groups. It is a matter of highest concern to the government that the leadership of the various interest groups should be cooperative with the various ministries and with the leadership of the Socialist Union. Insofar as the ministers themselves are not elected presidents of the various interest associations, individuals designated by ministers from the bureaucracy itself or the military are elected. Before its demise the National Union office charged with liaison with professional associations and the offices concerned with commerce and industry and even labor had not been given great authority for the control of secondary interest associations. So important have these activities been considered that it has been a matter for direct control by the closest associates of the President himself. Despite this extension of political control over interest groups in a rationalizing and hierarchical manner there is still ample scope for members of interest groups to represent grievances to the government. And, until very recently, there has been some opportunity for the leadership of interest groups to present to the government their views about the proper relationship between the administration and the interest groups.

Since pleas for the redress of grievances are one of the major legitimized techniques of the modernizing oligarchy, it is safe to expect that this channel for the articulation of specific interests will continue to remain open. On the other hand, it is quite clear that there will be less and less opportunity for the previous leadership of interest groups to assert views on the proper relationship of government and interest groups. In the representation of the people of Egypt in the Congress of Popular Forces interest groups were given more than their fair share. While there is little complaint on this score, efforts through the previous Parliament to revise government-imposed regulations for interest groups were clearly unsuccessful, and the cabinet was on the whole definitely unsympathetic to such efforts. It may very well be that the most important consequences of efforts about which the leadership of the Bar Association and the Chamber of Commerce were most optimistic will be the removal of the erstwhile leaders of those two organizations and their further subordination to the Ministry of Justice and the Ministry of Commerce.

Nevertheless one may expect that, if interest groups and the professionals in general are represented as importantly in the future Parliament as they were in the Congress of Popular Forces in 1962, they will retain some scope for expression of their views and a measure of freedom permitting their proper operation. One may further expect, insofar as such expressions do not run contrary to the direction of the socialist laws of July 1961, that they will be received and considered.

There is, however, some evidence that the government is growing less and less enthusiastic about the entire system of interest groups inherited from the previous regime. In most ministries and in most industrial, commercial, and financial enterprises of large size management committees or boards of directors have been instructed to include in their memberships representatives of employees, clerks, and ordinary workers. It is difficult, if not impossible, to say now whether or not this reform will result in opening a new and effective channel for interest articulation. Nor can we yet say whether or not one of the by-products of this reform will be the gradual elimination of secondary interest associations or will lead to their being soaked up into the various branches of the Socialist Union. Whatever specific solution is worked out, it is apparent that interest groups will be increasingly subordinated either to ministries concerned with their particular economic or service fields or by the Socialist Union or by the boards of directors or management committees of the major enterprises and bureaus of the government.

The Communications Elites

Since the Egyptian political system is dominated by the bureaucratic hierarchy which culminates in the President's immediate staff, all important political information is passed through official channels, though not always in accordance with the prescribed regulations. In addition the media of mass communications are entirely controlled by the government, either directly or indirectly, and are in very large part devoted to putting forward a desired public image.

It may be convenient to refer to our four cultural aspects in order to give some schematic notion of the types of political information and of the channels through which they move. The government-controlled media concentrate on area 4 (see diagram, p. 418), the public-overt type of information stressing the ideal goals of public policy, but also disseminate information regarding new regulations and the like which are included in the formal aspect of area 3. Political information which is of far greater significance to those employed by the government or to those who must deal with the government is passed through the channels described in area 3, i.e. primarily the informal channels of the administrative system itself, and usually by word of mouth. There is little significant information of a political nature that bears on area 2 except rumors or anecdotes about the relationships between the members of the top political elite: Nasser and his closest collaborators.

Of the mass media, only the radio and television programs are directly controlled by the government. Efforts to employ those media are supplemented by the work of the Information Administration. Egypt is known to have one of the most elaborate broadcasting facilities in the world. Its overseas broadcasts, many of which may be heard within the country, are more extensive than those of any country except the Soviet Union. Local programs are broadcast on several stations and include varied fare: music, news, commentary, dramatic sketches, prayers, speeches, lectures, and live sports reporting. Television broadcasts are limited to only a few hours a day and aside from prayers and patriotic materials rely on old movies and "canned" American programs such as "I Love Lucy" for entertaining their watchers. On the radio, lectures and quiz programs are directed at specific groups, while news broadcasts and commentaries, both highly slanted, are directed at the general public. These are not easily understood by the mass of the peasantry and the lower classes, but the same nationalist-oriented points are made to much greater effect in the dramatic sketches. They are often broadcast in the colloquial language and are sometimes humorous in intent, the virtues of the countryside being stressed, while familiar traditional, rural, and middle-class types are spoofed. In the heavier sketches there is nearly always some patriotic didacticism, as in one, "Keep silent, the enemy is listening," which I was privileged to watch. The villain was a British officer and the victim was a nice Egyptian girl. The scene was a cabaret where music was playing and glasses tinkled. When she told him what he wanted to learn, he abruptly ceased whispering sweet nothings in order to make his report to headquarters. The point was clear and was accompanied by a sufficiency of negative cultural symbols.

The Information Administration is a large institution and fairly efficient in serving the needs of its director and in routine tasks, but it has failed to make any substantial impact upon the domestic information market. Its major duties are to gather all news and comments relevant to Egypt from the world's press and radio and to digest them in a daily publication circulated to government offices. Its second task is to prepare sharp rebuttals to all unfriendly comment to be given to the director for appropriate use. The administration deals with foreign correspondents but cannot help them much when the Ministry of the Interior is cold to them. It prepares movies and literature for distribution by information officers attached to Egyptian diplomatic missions. It handles the translation of certain foreign books to be distributed by front firms without the benefit of copyright release. It encourages the writing of nationalist tracts by professors or journalists or its own staff of hack writers. It also aspires to set up information centers in all the major towns of Egypt, and it has managed to build a few booths and to install TV sets in them.

Newspapers and periodicals are largely managed by their own staffs, most of whom go back to prerevolutionary times. In 1960 the press was "reorganized" so that its ownership was vested in the National Union. All profits were to be distributed between management and employees. At that time the membership of the boards of directors of the major press houses was changed enough to give positions of dominance to the most trusted and cooperative of the government media elite. About three or four such people form the major links between the press and the government and are close enough to the regime not to require close control by it.

Before the reorganization press censorship prevailed and control was direct and for some editors oppressive. Now the problem in some cases is more one of losing control over the newspaper to the government's representative. On the government's side the change represents a growing tendency to go beyond regulation and to engage in outright operation of important enterprises—with the prize of management going to co-opted members of the political elite. The newspapers have not changed, but control over them has.

Most important periodicals are published by newspaper houses or by one or two special publishers also controlled by or only fronts for government agencies. The Ministry of Culture puts out its own series of general publications; most of the service ministries and economic ministries put out specialized publications. Nearly all important bureaus have their own public relations divisions. The Bureau for Cooperation, the Ministry of Agrarian Reform, and the High Council for Youth Welfare are probably the most prodigious publishers next to the Information Administration. There are a few religious journals, but casual perusal reveals that the lead article usually does not differ from the usual run-of-the-mill propaganda effort.

In contrast to what has gone before, the movies are not controlled and offer a welcome if not very artistic means of escape from the boredom of too oft-repeated political platitudes. The subjects of movies are most frequently in areas 1 and 2 of our cultural paradigm and are therefore popular with all classes and afford a particularly important psychological outlet.

The writers are of several types: top-drawer political commentators, professors, and academic products, literature graduates and others, who are generally young men who have filled the new bureaucratic information posts; older civil servants who do hack-writing or manage information offices; a few literary types interested in writing novels, plays, scenarios, and criticism; and many young reporters. All except the reporters are essentially civil servants and fit into a pattern already described. They do what they are supposed to do with greater or less enthusiasm (which varies inversely with age). Even the truly literary types are usually employed by the government since they could not otherwise make a living. Their way of life is different, however, from that of the others, and they appear to enjoy a richer social experience in a framework of informal associations with other artists. The professors write to supplement their incomes and to do what appears to be more socially useful work than teaching. The reporters are members of the journalists' syndicate, an interest group regulated by the government as all others are. The conditions of employment for reporters are all set down in the syndicate regulations, and dismissal is all but impossible. If reporters are not civil servants, they are the next best thing, but they are usually "outside men" and hence enjoy much greater freedom and may exercise more initiative than their bureaucratic counterparts. They might exercise more initiative had they greater skill or were there enough space left in the newspaper after all the official handouts, classified ads, and obituaries are printed. Few people make a good living at writing, but it is certainly more interesting than other work and enjoys somewhat higher prestige insofar as it is not mere reporting.

The character of the flow of political information and of public discussion of policy is controlled by the structure described. On rare occasions one gets a good discussion of a problem like the crisis of the Arab intellectual—good if one reads between the lines sufficiently well. But for the most part the content of communications is repetitive and narrow in its conception and poorly written. The ideal objectives of the government are continuously urged upon the reader, regardless of the subject at hand. By contrast really important policy changes are, in accordance with the administrative ethos of the system, kept secret until announced by the President in a major speech for which something of real impact is always reserved. Lesser leaders handle their own subordinate sensational information in the same way. In between the standard repetitions come at one from all sides and in great profusion.

The Educational Elite

Much of the relevant information about the Egyptian educational elite was set forth in our previous discussion of the educational system as a socializing institution. Teachers at all levels have been little studied, especially since the more rapid expansion of the educational system after the revolution of 1952. Nevertheless a few generalizations may help to round out the information already presented.

Despite the great importance placed on education by the new regime and the even greater regard for education among the population as a whole the status of teachers is low. It varies, as in other countries, according to the educational level, with the elementary teachers lowest and university professors highest. After the revolution the number of teachers at all levels expanded greatly as these figures show:

Year	Primary	Prep. Genl.	Prep. Tech.	Prep. Comm.	Prep. Agric.	2nd Agric. Genl.	Ind.	Comm.	Agric.	Teache
1949-50	46,688	—	184	—	41	4,405	1,191	400	245	260
1950-51	46,786	—	254	37	69	4,974	1,290	490	304	899
1951-52	51,323	—	279	35	63	6,960	1,408	594	382	1,184
1952-53	52,506	—	290	22	85	8,087	1,402	581	397	1,564
1953-54	45,869[a]	9,780	303	17	63	7,401	1,342	579	362	1,721
1954-55	43,461[b]	14,151	341	12	95	7,271	932	557	352	1,789
1955-56	48,173	16,018	424	18	122	8,238	1,203	605	311	2,157
1956-57	51,631	16,058	399	69	176	7,831	923	744	305	2,344
1957-58	54,766	15,754	627	192	301	7,981	1,068	1,158	458	2,264
1958-59	60,042	15,977	1,013	274	426	8,411	1,238	1,458	584	1,945

[a] Some schools changed to preparatory. [b] Old fashioned or traditional schools closed.

There have also been some shifts in the relative prestige positions of teachers at various levels. Without changing the elementary-to-university pecking order, it is apparent that the distances between the various statuses have been reduced. As noted previously, the prestige of university teachers in nearly all the traditional faculties outside of science and engineering has declined. In contrast the prestige of the high school teacher has increased as a result of the generally increased emphasis upon education and of the recognition that teachers perform a service to Egypt's foreign policy (the outstanding symbol of the regime's success) when they accept positions in neighboring Arab states. The number of such teachers increased from 458 in 1952 to 1,676 in 1957.

Possibly more important than these semi-ideological bases of increased prestige is the increased favor shown to teachers by the government since 1954, when teachers were permitted to form a syndicate similar to those of other professionals, some higher grades of the civil service were opened to them even if they did not switch to administrative work, and salaries were increased. Jobs as principals and inspectors multiplied as new schools were established. The special teacher training institutes were greatly increased in number and their graduates favored above those of the faculties of the university. Further evidence of increased prestige is to be found in the fact that around 10 per cent of those elected as executives of the National Union in 1959 were teachers (in the rural areas many came from "umdah families") whereas the number of professors was negligible.[9]

It is apparent that the previous policy was at least in part the result of the events of 1954, when university students and professors were on Naguib's side. At that time Kemal al Din Hussain took over the university and punished, by administrative means, all suspects. In addition the High Council for Youth Welfare was established to turn the students to more productive activity. There is little doubt that the present regime is suspicious of all nontechnical and nonscientific intellectuals. Nevertheless, their low political status is in glaring contrast to their high cultural status. It appears that in the general shift away from rural and geographical representation in the Congress of Popular Forces, the latent prestige of the university asserted itself. Perhaps there was even more, for there was relatively strong university representation in the 250 member Preparatory Council which determined the representative formula of the Congress in December 1961. That is, it could be that in the reaction to the separation of Syria and the apprehension lest the former privileged class move for power, the government *sought* to mobilize all middle-class forces and particularly the professors and students at the universities who might provide support for the "reactionaries" if not quickly mollified.

It is still too early to predict how important will be these straws in the wind. There is a sharp conflict at the cultural rather than at the ideological level, of which the prestige ranking of the intellectuals is but one manifestation. We have already referred to the conflict between the integrative, nativist, nationalist spirit, and the rational-technocratic spirit which is imposed on Egypt's leaders by the problems of development. In the educational system there is another but stranger aspect of the same thing. *Intellectuals*, as opposed to technicians, are not only politically suspect, but they do not appear to contribute directly to development. On the other hand, there remains a strong traditional respect for learned men, especially those learned in the humanistic branches, which is further sustained, almost

---

[9] The same balance held true for the prorogued Parliament but changes appeared to be in the making, for in the Congress of Popular Forces of 1962 there were 117 teachers and 105 professors and instructors from the higher institutes. That change certainly overstates the importance of university teachers, but it is long overdue.

paradoxically, by the former immense prestige of these people as the gatekeepers of the garden of Western education, modernity, self-respect, and social mobility for the traditional middle class. In contrast to this powerful attraction, the school teacher is another lower-grade government employee, and the attention he has been shown is directly related to such nonglamorous ends as the desire to expand primary education, to redirect secondary students to technical education, and to attempt in new ways to mobilize the support of the lower classes through getting the teacher to work with his pupils after hours, to work with their parents in parent-teachers associations and to bear the brunt of the dirty work of the Socialist Union at the grass-roots level.

While it is certainly an exaggeration of the importance of the university people to relate their political status to the possible democratization of the regime, it is nevertheless true that most professors in the older and non-technical faculties preferred the party and open parliamentary system of the pre-1952 period even though they did not support the King. Most of them still think in the liberal constitutional terms of Lutfi al-Sayyid and Khalid Muhammad Khalid. On the other hand, stronger men than these have succumbed to political favor and have sacrificed political ideals.

Since the intellectuals are weak and small in number, and since they are partly traditionalists at least in their family lives, the real question of democratization appears to turn first on the resolution of the conflict between the nativist-nationalist culture and the rational-technocratic culture which is abuilding. Thereafter it will be important to consider the way in which the liberal political culture of the humanist intellectuals articulates sociologically and ideologically with nativist-nationalism. The teachers, lower-grade civil servants, and members of other lower-prestige professional associations do not appear to be either sufficiently convinced in their liberalism or sufficiently powerful politically to do more than sustain whatever trend emerges.

The Socioeconomic Elites

The Egyptian socioeconomic elites break down into five relatively small groups: the rural middle class of notables owning more than 15 or so feddan of land; the traditional merchant families; the somewhat more modernized members of the Chamber of Commerce; the old group of industrialist landowners and industrialist financiers; and the new group of government-appointed managers of economic enterprises.

While of quite limited importance in socioeconomic terms, and of little more than local importance in political influence, the rural middle class is the most important of these groups within the more specific terms of an analysis of elite socialization in Egypt. This is so because the rural middle-class family has been the social link among members of the bureaucratized elites, as previously noted, and the origin of a great many, perhaps even the majority, of those elites. The rural middle-class family was, therefore, a concrete structural link as well as a common socializing agency.

If the family remains the major group to which the individual owes loyalty, and if the family still means for most Egyptians the extended family, then the interpenetration of both modernist and traditional elements within a single family is a matter of particular interest. This interpenetration is particularly important when we find it among families who have some degree of political influence and some political status and access under the present system such as may be found among members of the Socialist Union. The struggle between traditionalism and modernity in political culture, as in other fields, is a struggle going on within individuals as well as between them. Perhaps even more importantly, it is one that goes on within families, and the solution of the struggle will no doubt have a radical effect on the place of the family in Egyptian society.

In trying to get at the Egyptian's picture of himself and his nation and at the kind of political and economic reform he would like to bring into being most written tracts are of little use. Most authors resort to a vague terminology which appears romantic and nostalgic, an appropriate understanding of which cannot be gained without a closer examination of some of the characteristics of the families of the middle-class elites of Egypt. These families are composed of traditional and modern elements. The agricultural family base, the root of the inner elements of the family, which remains in the villages, may still provide some financial support for members of the family who have moved to the cities. With these points in mind, we can begin to understand in more concrete sociological terms the inner meaning of such phrases as "Arab Socialism" and "the goodness of Arab society." Contemporary Egyptian nationalism, or at least the spirit behind it, has an intrinsic connection with the culture of middle-class agrarian families. This is not to argue, however, that this cultural confluence and the families associated with it will continue to dominate the development of the Egyptian political system, or even the political culture of that country.

It appears that continuing to favor this very small rural group is a luxury Egypt probably will not be able to afford. Furthermore, the obstacles in the way of development and resource mobilization are so great, and the tendency toward rational technocratic solutions so strong, and finally the rural groups so narrow in terms of their broad relationship with a much larger middle class, that it seems unlikely that this rural class will continue to receive special benefits (especially in exclusion from land reform laws) from the present regime. If the allocation of benefits does shift from the countryside to the city, and if the burden of maintaining family connections with the city becomes too great for this small rural middle class, it would appear that the presently deep feelings about where the root of the family exists may change. When these feelings change, and the family is considered legitimately based in the city, concomitant cultural changes may be expected as well.

Those changes we expect to come about are already implicit in the composition of the Congress of Popular Forces in which agricultural elements have been reduced from nearly one-half in the National Union to about one-sixth. Even more significant, however, is the fact that the composition of the Congress was devised on an occupational rather than a regional basis. If the same pattern is followed in the new parliament, we can safely expect that the representation of the rural middle class will be far smaller and far less important than it was in the National Union and in the previous parliament. Such a shift does not represent a cultural change or a change in the sentiments of the influential people in the present regime, but it certainly indicates a decline in the benefits that will be allocated to the rural middle-class elements.

Nevertheless with regard to the performance of the recruitment functions within the political system we must note that co-optation through the educational system and through the higher institutes does not constitute a total explanation. It must take its place beside political recruitment, through what we have recognized as the operative manifestation of the meaning of the term "good and loyal Egyptian." If our investigations have any validity, it would appear that the meaning of this term is closely related to a class of families rooted in the countryside and branching out into the cities in professional and technical occupations. Co-optation is based not only on academic achievement or academic experience but also upon the family background of the individual. To put the matter in other terms, those who will be chosen will be the ones for whom an affirmative answer can be given to the question of whether he is one of *us* or not.

The traditional merchant families, which overlap with the members of the Chamber of Commerce, do not appear to have strong connections with agriculture. They are, however, traditionals and tend to be religious and urban, though they are more frequently found in the provincial centers. At least they appear to be more influential in the provincial centers, where they need not compete with a more modernized commercial class. This is not to argue that they have any substantial political influence, but they were represented in the National Union, they place ads praising Nasser in the newspapers, and they are considered pillars of the community. On the other hand, this class cannot be associated with the culture of the rural middle class for, as is well known, the traditional merchant and the agriculturist are at odds with one another. The village umdah's social circle of influence extends to the whole village while the traditional merchant's is far narrower. In addition, the generosity and other traits we have associated with the overt aspect of familistic culture are less evidenced by and less demanded and expected from the traditional merchant. The latter tends to be turned inward upon himself and his family, seeking to achieve that dignity associated with the generosity of the umdah by piety and religious works. His sphere is only marginally touched by the activities of the Ministry of Supply and, until the administrative resources of Egypt are greatly increased, he will have little to fear. But he will also contribute little to cultural and political change in Egypt.

The members of the Chamber of Commerce—those who have the more important businesses in the major cities—have been hard hit by the July 1961 Socialist laws. All of the larger enterprises have had to accept the government as a partner in the business. They have also had to set up boards of directors which include civil servants as well as employee representatives. Long before the July laws foreign trade and currency restrictions had reduced their business and their profits. It was also apparent from a relatively early stage that the military elite was out of sympathy with these people. Nevertheless they were not greatly penalized until economic events overtook both them and the government. It appears that the government had no thought either of moving into the commercial sphere of these people or of giving up the hope that they could contribute to the development of Egypt through private investment until the government had nationalized British and French enterprises in 1956-1957 and until serious planning after that date revealed that the task of investment was far beyond the capacity of the business class. The lack of sympathy for the business class facilitated the solution to the problem of mobilizing their limited economic potentiality by bureaucratic means. The business class has simply had to accommodate itself to increasing regulation and control as the government has sought ever more desperately to glean any available capital surplus.

The business class is certainly the most varied in culture of all the socioeconomic elites. There are among them those who have moved up from traditional merchant status; there are also the minority entrepreneurs; and there are engineers and truck drivers turned contractors, lawyers turned bankers, and economists turned distributors. The traditionals may be included among the traditional merchant group. The university graduates appear to have a generally liberal and parliamentary attitude toward politics. The minority entrepreneurs are out of sympathy with Egyptian nationalization and might be characterized culturally by a strong in-group feeling toward their own community. Many indeed are the equivalent of the traditional merchant with appropriate adjustments made for religious differences of course. Their unsympathetic attitude toward Egyptian aspirations is matched by severe hostility from the other side. With the passage of the July laws and the separation of Syria, all pretence ended, and the minority middle class was no longer capable of inducing the government to make a show of non-discrimination to gain prestige with the West.

The older industrialists, especially the landowning industrialists like Serag al Din, the entrepreneurs like Abboud, and the managers and directors of the Misr group, have all been pushed aside after receiving initial support by the government. Much more so than on the business elite, the government at first banked on the small but vigorous class of industrialists to help in modernizing the country. Moreover, despite their individualism and self-confidence, their pragmatic approach was congenial both to the pragmatism of the non-ideological RCC and the rational-technocratic attitudes of the top military and bureaucratic elites. But as the new investment capital failed to materialize and as the government gained managerial experience—especially through the Economic Development Organization, which took over the British and French enterprises and the Nasr Organization which ran the military factories established in Farouk's time—it was felt that this group could be dispensed with. At the same time, jobs as managing directors were looked upon as the prime plums next to those of ministry directors and secretaries. These positions were taken over by civil servants from the Ministry of Industries, the Ministry of the Treasury, and by army engineers, along with some of the earlier managerial employees.

The cultural outlook of both the majority of the old managers and of the new managers is essentially similar, except that the former group legitimized their privilege through their financial and social manipulative acuity as well as by managerial skill, while the latter have depended upon managerial skill alone. They believe this skill gives them the right to succeed to the position of the former owners in every way, including the determination of business policy as well as management.

Culturally the new managers are pragmatic, rationalist, technocratic, secularist, Westernized, and generally unsympathetic to romantic nativist ideas. The ever-growing efforts to industrialize and raise standards of living suggest that their influence will rise. Nevertheless the apparently insurmountable obstacles to real development pose a serious problem. If the present hopes are persistently disappointed, will the government try to lull the awakened masses while satisfying itself with keeping the loyalty of the administrative and managerial classes by increased rewards, or will it continue to seek mass support to the point where the "classes" are eliminated?

Conclusion

In Egypt we have seen that a new political elite emerged from the revolution of 1952 and quickly acquired political stability because of its kinship with and cultural roots in a traditional rural middle class. These roots permitted the new elite to express its modernizing aspirations in terms acceptable to traditional influentials. It was helped in gaining stable control by the fact that many socioeconomic adjustments had already been made through the defensive modernization of the previous regime. In Mosca's terms, we might say that the appearance of the contemporary Egyptian political elite signifies the emergence of a new social type.[10]

[10] G. Mosca, *The Ruling Class*, New York, 1939, pp. 103ff.

Political change in Egypt has occurred as the result of two efforts of the new elite, first, the effort to preserve itself from the competition of the party elites of the monarchical period, and second, to devise an institutional framework to accord somewhat more with its own instrumental predilections. As to the first it would be incorrect to assert that there is a great cultural cleavage between the old politicians and the military-political elite. There are important differences, however, in the closeness of the connection of the latter with rural Egypt and in its greater bureaucratic experience and consequent acceptance of achievement norms. These differences are sufficient to explain the greater trust in which the military elite is held, but they are not enough to refute the claims of some Wafdists that if the King alone had been removed they could have done the job just as well.

The desire to find an institutional pattern that would accord with its own orientation led the military elite to reject orthodox parliamentarism and multi-partism and to prefer a mobilizational system instead. This preference did not manifest itself in 1952 but was, rather, the result of particular situational developments. The military elite feared that the return of a multi-party parliament would mean the return of political practices in which its members were relatively unskilled. Hence the particulars of how the contemporary Egyptian politico-military elite came to devise new political methods or draw selectively from the old cannot be explained by reference to any comprehensive theory but depends upon an understanding of some of the features peculiar to Egypt itself.

The sound structural prerequisites for the change in the Egyptian polity from a predominantly traditional-conventional system to a predominantly rational-hierarchical one already existed before the revolution. The cultural prerequisites existed in more- or less-latent form among the middle ranks of the officer corps before 1952. The process by which this potential change was manifested in the transformation of the political processes of the Egyptian system was itself political; that is, political change occurred as a consequence of the resolution of a series of specific issues as they arose. It may further be argued that each discrete resolution was remarkably free of ideological constraint because, as pointed out elsewhere, no coherent ideological statement of the goals of the present regime has been made.[11]

---

[11] L. Binder, "Nasserism: The Protest Movement in the Middle East," in M. Kaplan, ed. *The Revolution in World Politics*, New York, 1962, p. 154.

But since contributions to an ideology are currently being made, it will become increasingly difficult to resolve new issues without regard for the way in which things have been done up to now. The really complex problem arises from the impact of certain material factors which have strengthened the rationalizing tendencies beyond the immediate purposes of the revolution and have led to ideological orientations which are in conflict with underlying political cultural tendencies. The whole process may be summed up as the transformation of the culture of the rural middle-class extended family into the ideology of Arab Socialism.

Let us attempt to restate some of the special characteristics of the Egyptian political situation which have led to the results described. We start with a factor which is not so special—the relatively unimportant place of formal ideology in Egyptian politics. It is not so special in that the same tendency is shared by most of the political elites of the emerging nations. We are not losing sight of Pan-Arabism, Arab Socialism, Negritude, African Socialism, Pyadawtha, Pantja Sila, the basic democracies, and Ram Raj. The point is that all of these represent some effort at expressing the unique selfhood or primordialism of some one or another traditional social class. What they are really concerned with is the problem of becoming modern without losing all selfhood. In more psychological terms we might say these symbols are being used as walls to prevent modernity from penetrating into and revealing in all their nakedness the shame elements of traditional culture. In those cultural areas that are public and overt—that is, the areas served by ideology—there is, at least in Egypt, a refreshing attitude of pragmatism.

The pace of events in Egypt has been so rapid that the normal sequence is: things happen; then the government devises some short-term response; in the application and implementation of its response a broader policy is formulated; and finally people are commissioned to restate the policy and justify it in ideological terms. This is not a general rule, but it is the way in which things have happened in Egypt since 1952, and the pattern has no doubt been repeated in many other underdeveloped areas. For Egypt especially this tendency has been strong because: (1) the politico-military elite is culturally non-ideologically inclined and anti-intellectual; (2) intellectuals themselves have a low political standing besides having little conception of their "proper" role or little courage; (3) intellectuals in Egypt are not concerned with development and modernization, but often with a formalized, humanistically conceived body of knowledge; (4) the problems involved in transforming a society are not well understood by any group; (5) the problems of development, at any rate, are all but insoluble and hence do not encourage realistic ideological efforts; (6) the kernel of any suitable ideological solution must deal with the issue of personal identity which remains a private matter concealed by overt acceptance of Arabism.

Egypt's cultural-ideological problem is therefore not dissimilar from that of many underdeveloped areas; but Egypt, it appears, has made notably greater progress than others in this regard. Without having devised a formal ideology to be taught in the schools, the Egyptian elite has been able to capitalize on the prevalence of an inchoate, unarticulated, political culture shared by both urban and rural elites, to create a relatively efficient and culturally integrated polity.

The reasons for this past success are: (1) the predominant homogeneity of the population; (2) the relatively efficient system of communications and transportation; (3) the relatively large Westernized and industrial sector (in absolute terms more than as a percentage of the total population); (4) the relatively more efficient administration system; and (5) the relatively more easily manageable social and economic structure.

Egypt's success may also be attributed to the special character of its political elite. This elite has no formidable cultural enemy in a legitimate aristocracy however one may choose to define the term. When Nasser began to talk about the "reactionaries," nobody knew what to do with this addition to the political lexicon. That there were bad men like the Badrawis and the Serag al-Dins was admitted, but who were the reactionaries?

The present elite is essentially a bureaucratic, middle-class elite, and the cultural implications of that fact may become increasingly important. But, at least until very recently, a more significant fact was its close connection with the traditional rural middle class. Apparently this connection is stronger than in other countries. Examples are: Iran, where the connections and contributions of the ulama to the urban middle class are very significant and where landownership has a more important aristocratic connotation in some parts of the country; Lebanon, where there has occurred an even greater social mobility allowing peasant families to achieve important positions in the very influential economic and business elite; and Turkey, where the previous Ottoman bureaucracy has contributed greatly to the ranks of the contemporary political elite.

Despite the stress here on this favorable aspect of the Egyptian elite we must bear in mind that there is nevertheless a wide gap in culture between the urban bureaucratic elite and the rural and urban lower classes. However, the government is making strenuous efforts to bridge that gap at the expense of the interests and influence of both the rural and urban middle classes. In other words, it tends to ignore or ride roughshod over articulate political demands emanating from those who are politically aware, while attempting to win the enthusiastic but obedient loyalty of the masses.

These considerations lead us to the weaknesses and less attractive aspects of the present regime. It is apparent to anyone who has stayed in Cairo even a few days that the government has set its goals too high. These goals are not the product of articulate demands but are derived from attempts to make Egypt compare with Western industrialized countries. Despite strenuous efforts by the government to mobilize support for these goals through its use of the media and through its mass-line organizations no real attempt has been made to share responsibility for determining and achieving goals. Development is desired for the people but not by the people. The bureaucratic-hierarchical emphasis has led to political rationalization without realism. Side by side with the administrative system, the hierarchy of first the National Union and now the Socialist Union have been created and various groups have discussed and rediscussed the development plan with the sole result that unrealistic goals have been imposed upon the technicians in the Planning Commission. Thus far the various attempts to provide a mass organizational base for the government have not succeeded. In reality, however, these have been half-hearted attempts which were not meant to succeed. No mass party base exists; the regime is based on a naïve populism in doctrine and a peculiar social stratum in practice. As a consequence of the near-unconscious preference for people connected with the privileged stratum a degree of inconsistency enters into the recruitment process. Ostensibly based upon education and achievement, the intuitive recognition of members of the rural-urban middle-class stratum as being like minded and politically loyal limits the rationality of recruitment.

The important political processes of the Egyptian system may be briefly summarized here in elaborating the preceding.[12] The Egyptian political system is a modernizing autocracy dominated by a bureaucratically oriented elite.[13] Its processes are in essence administrative, but the central process of recruitment into the political elite is co-optative first and rational, "universal-achievement" based second. The system maintenance process, engaged in almost wholly by governmental structures is in the main mobilizational and propagandistic. The only legitimate way in which demands may be articulated is through an elaborate upward-reaching arrangement which we may call the process of redress of individual grievance. Negative system challenging, that is, political activity stemming from alienation from and active opposition to the regime, is little engaged in, but whenever manifested it is swiftly suppressed. The major group of political prisoners are Communists. Positive system challenging, or opposition to the regime in order to win greater benefits from it, highly prevalent before 1952, is now no longer permitted.

When one examines the rather important success Egypt has achieved along the cultural-ideological dimension and then the great obstacles to the achievement of the material goals which the government has set for itself, the paradoxical nature of political change and political-cultural change in Egypt (and elsewhere, too) becomes manifest. With the stabilization of the revolutionary regime, one might argue that the Egyptian nation had begun to find itself. Presumably a cultural and political formula was being produced that would result in real integration and mutual understanding from which stable government might ensue. Moreover stable government would be but a by-product of the creation of a culturally integrated system in which political demands might be freely expressed because, in the end, failure to win full gratification would not lead to alienation but to accommodative and understanding acceptance.

We are not proposing a formula for "how to be happy though poor," but the fact remains that for the foreseeable future there will continue to be wide discrepancies in per capita income in diverse countries. Except for the difficulties caused by the "demonstration effect," there is no reason to believe that democratic government, or at least a mature and realistic political life, cannot be achieved by

[12] See L. Binder, *Iran*, Chapter I, for an elaboration of the framework for the analytical summary which follows (see especially p. 35).

[13] For the use of the term "modernizing autocracy," see E. Shils, *Political Development in the New States*, 's-Gravenhage, 1962, p. 67. Shils' term is modernizing oligarchy.

a low-income country. The first requirement is undoubtedly enough pride in oneself so that the superficialities of national glory can be looked at in a cold and practical manner. Perhaps this is not the first requirement. Perhaps what is needed first is open and informed discussion of what national glory requires, so that if steel mills are really more desired than increased per capital income, the implications of the decision will be understood. But this too is a digression, for what we have learned is that Egypt now stands at a crossroads. If the top political elite cultivates the social elements which have ridden to power and prestige with it, if it permits the Socialist Union and the new parliament to become efficient as well as ornamental institutions, there is some chance for the transformation of the presently dominant political culture into one that will sustain a democratic welfare state. Not only is the present political culture integrative; its exponents are not negligible in either skills or numbers. The combination of the intellectual elite, the business groups (excluding the minorities), and the rural notables, if admitted to real influence by the military-bureaucratic political elite, would be a formidable coalition of liberal, competitive, mutually respectful, and no doubt nationalistic elements. If these strata are permitted to form the base of the political pyramid, to be gradually extended to other groups as conditions permit, that will be no less a revolution for Egypt than was that of 1952, and there will be little doubt that Egypt will be more truly Egyptian and probably no less wealthy than the product of the alternative administrative state will be.

CHAPTER 11

Soviet Russia: Orthodoxy and Adaptiveness

FREDERICK C. BARGHOORN

Soviet political culture, judged by the criteria of the modern "civic culture" of certain Western countries including the United States, is at once advanced and backward. The totalitarian system built by Stalin on foundations laid down by Lenin and maintained, although with certain modifications, by Stalin's successors possesses mobilizing and integrative capabilities made possible by advanced communications technology. In thoroughness and intensity of political socialization, especially of elite cadres, and in systematic use of mass media for political purposes the Union of Soviet Socialist Republics indeed far surpasses the Western democracies except perhaps in periods of all-out war. However, as Edward Shils pointed out in an article in *Encounter* for October 1961, the "modernity" of the Soviet Union is a "tyrannically deformed manifestation of potentialities which are inherent in the process of modernization," since its pressures for "mobilization of the masses" produce "a coerced conformity" rather than a freely given consent.

Most Western intellectuals today probably share the repugnance expressed by Shils toward the systematic attitude manipulation practiced by a Soviet regime which has largely substituted for Stalin's awe-inspiring terror an increasingly sophisticated program of mass and specialized elite political indoctrination and of social pressures at all levels. However, the Soviet system, both Stalinist and post-Stalin, possesses strengths which we who are committed to the civic political culture can easily overlook. These consist, very briefly, of a high sense of relevancy about matters of significance for the survival and power of the nation, clarity in the relating of public policy to centrally determined community goals, and the sense of purpose and confidence in ultimate success conferred by dedication to an ideology of worldwide revolutionary social transformation. At least a considerable proportion of the population derive from these practices and perspectives sufficient satisfaction to generate enthusiastic support for the total Soviet system.

In spite of the development of a high degree of specialization of skills in the political, as well as in the economic and other spheres, legitimate, openly functioning associational interest groups of the kind that play such a conspicuous role in many Western polities and even in the political systems of some of the emerging nations are absent from the Soviet political scene. The political system, although it is far less "monolithic" than it appears to be on superficial examination, is not pluralistic either, if by pluralism one means a society in which parties, pressure groups, and individuals vie with one another in offering different solutions for problems of community concern and have access to audiences the shifting preferences of which can influence the shaping of public policy. Policy struggles are confined to the upper levels of the political elite, with a tendency toward wider participation, however, during succession crises, as reflected, for example, in the cultural "thaw" after Stalin's death, and in the restoration of collective leadership after Khrushchev's fall, but without the latter's practice of expanding the numbers of persons attending party plenums.

Moreover in this system all political—as well as economic and cultural—decisions are presented in terms of the official creed of "Marxism-Leninism." The interpretation of this ideology is entrusted ultimately to the supreme political leadership, although its dissemination is the responsibility of communicators trained in party institutions as theoreticians, propagandists, and journalists. Despite the pretensions of Soviet Communists to possession of a "scientific," "materialistic" world outlook, theirs is in fact a kind of mystique, a sacred, allegedly infallible doctrine of the "laws of social development," the operation of which leads inevitably to world communism. The manipulation of this official doctrine by the Soviet elite serves not only to legitimize its power but also to inhibit the development at all levels of critical intellectual inquiry and of individual esthetic and even emotional expression. The established practice—less crudely applied since the death of Stalin but still central to Soviet communism—of denouncing those who "deviate" from party policies and interpretations on the ground that unauthorized opinions damage the interests of the "people,"—if indeed they do not represent sinister machinations of the international bourgeoisie against the Soviet Union—often imparts to Soviet political communication a strident tone. This emotionalism has been balanced since Stalin's death by the demand that all propaganda be linked with "life." Soviet ideology today represents an interesting blend of dogmatism and a common sense, production-oriented practicalism.

Certainly in such an atmosphere uninhibited discussion of issues does not flourish. On the contrary the normal situation is one in which citizens are encouraged to demonstrate to the authorities that they support official policy enthusiastically and are exerting their full efforts to assist in its implementation. Indeed even to remain silent—as rebellious Soviet writers did for an impressively long period in the face of the Kremlin's demand that they recant in 1956-1957 and again, in some instances, in 1963—requires considerable courage. This is a pattern of "crypto-politics," to borrow a phrase from T. H. Rigby, in which political bargaining and competition assume to a far greater degree than is the case even in the transitional societies of Southeast Asia, for example, the forms of secretive intrigues and conspiracies among highly placed members of a tightly organized political elite, reflected, albeit only partially and obscurely, in more or less esoteric political communications.[1] One of the crucial questions for the future is whether the circle of participants in decision making will widen significantly and perhaps even bring about a modification of the present centralized pattern.

A partisan, mobilized subject political culture continues to prevail in the Soviet Union. Not only the 11.5 million members and candidate members of the Communist Party of the Soviet Union—according to figures published in the journal *Party Life* in November 1964—or the nearly 20 million members of the All-Union Lenin-Communist League of Youth (*Komsomol*), as well as the 60 million Soviet citizens enrolled in the party-directed Soviet trade unions, but indeed, all Soviet citizens are expected by the party leadership to participate as actively and consciously as their energies and abilities permit in effectuating the "full-scale construction of communism"— the over-all goal for Soviet society proclaimed at the Twenty-first Extraordinary Congress of the CPSU in 1959 and spelled out in detail at the Twenty-second Party Congress. The latter Congress set forth a twenty-year program of goals for Soviet society. Thus, while the decision-making and policy-executing members of the political elite—which is virtually synonymous with the seasoned cadres,

---

[1] On the nature of political competition in the Soviet system, and the kinds of political communication in which it is reflected, see, for example, Robert Conquest, *Power and Policy in the U.S.S.R.*, New York, 1961, and Myron Rush, *The Rise of Khrushchev*, Washington, D.C., 1958.

or "apparatus," of CPSU—are regarded as conscious activists, the mass of the population and indeed also the rank-and-file members of the ruling party are assigned the role of what one might describe as participatory subjects.

However, among some strata of Soviet society, such as the literary, artistic, and scientific intelligentsia, as well as students, especially in the humanities, there are aspirations toward a civic political culture. Such aspirations, flowing partly from the never-extinguished liberal traditions of the pre-Soviet Russian intelligentsia, partly from the libertarian aspects of Marxism, and partly from knowledge of Western doctrines and institutions, have always existed in the Soviet Union. Increased freedom of personal and also of published expression since the death of Stalin contributed both to their intensification and to knowledge concerning them in the outside world. Stalin repressed by violence and terror aspirations incompatible with the interests of party, state, and society as he perceived them. Khrushchev, assuming leadership at a more advanced age than Stalin did and, by personal inclination and the favorable circumstances of increased Soviet wealth and security, less impelled than his predecessor to rule by terror, played down the use of fear as an instrument of control and made greater use of such incentives as pride in Soviet industrial technological achievements and in the Soviet Union's growing international status. More particularly, he stressed welfare measures and material rewards designed to spur the effort of industrial workers and especially of collective farmers, who benefited by improvements in pensions, raising of wages in the lowest categories, and higher prices for crops delivered to the state. Khrushchev's successors are pledged to similar policies.

The post-Stalin regime has sought to turn to its own purposes the diffuse aspirations of the Soviet population for improvement in what by West European, American, or even Japanese standards is still a discouragingly drab, monotonous pattern of material culture, as well as for personal security, for a measure of privacy, and for a modicum of access to "bourgeois" material and cultural output. At the same time the party leadership has made plain that changes and reforms must be contained within and be compatible with maintenance of CPSU leadership and its interpretation of Marxist-Leninist doctrine. In particular, even the faintest expression of aspirations toward political pluralism has been sternly rebuffed.

During the period of ferment in eastern Europe, especially in

Poland and Hungary, but before the dramatic political events in those countries in October and November 1956, the Soviet press published statements which implied that there were, indeed, some elements in Soviet society which entertained pluralistic aspirations. For example, *Pravda* for July 6, 1956 in an article entitled, "The Communist Party Is the Inspirer and Leader of the Soviet People," accused "some people abroad" of wishing to see non-Communist parties, financed by foreign capital and serving foreign interests, "created" in the Soviet Union. While the editorial declared that the Soviet people did not need such parties and reiterated the standard Soviet argument that a multiplicity of political parties was characteristic of a society with antagonistic classes and clashing interests, and therefore would be out of place in the Soviet Union, it also implicitly admitted that not all Soviet citizens fully shared this view. The editorial stated that of course it was necessary to observe the principles of collective leadership and of party and Soviet democracy in order to overcome shortcomings in Soviet life; but it also stated that "in persistently fulfilling these principles, it is necessary to struggle vigorously against any attempts at petty bourgeois anarchistic denial of the role of leaders in state, party, and economic work. . . ."

The post-Stalin combination of continuity with the totalitarian past and of quasi-democratic reforms was reflected in the program of the CPSU published in draft form in *Pravda* for July 30, 1961 and in final form in the same and other newspapers for November 2, 1961.[2] In addition to spelling out in some detail the goal, set forth by Khrushchev at the Twenty-first Party Congress in 1959, of developing Soviet democracy by gradually turning over to "public organizations," such as sports societies, the trade unions, and the *Komsomol*, functions previously performed by state agencies, the 1961 program also proclaimed the principle that "the dictatorship of the working class will cease to be necessary before the state withers away."[3] Thus the new program set in motion a process, democratic in its implications, of replacement of the "dictatorship of the proletariat" by a state "expressing the interests and will of the people as a whole."

The program also contained provisions for regular "renewal" of

---

[2] The most useful of the several English translations available of the 1961 program is in *Soviet Communism: Programs and Rules*, ed. Jan F. Triska, San Francisco, 1962. Besides the 1961 program and party rules, this volume also contains the 1919 program and the 1952 rules.

[3] Triska, *op.cit.*, p. 98.

the membership of directing bodies, both of the CPSU and the Soviet state. Even though rapid "renewal" is no novelty in the Soviet Union, where, especially during Stalin's great purges in 1936-1938, it was applied on a vast and brutal scale and perhaps was included in the program merely to legitimize future purges, it could, if appropriately implemented, serve to confer upon rank and file members of the party and other political organizations some influence over their leaders. The 1961 program at the same time in every section and almost on every page emphasized, as did subsequent official comment, that in the future as in the past the party would continue to be the supreme organ of Soviet society for the articulation and aggregation of interests, and for social and political mobilization. Indeed, subsequent political writing has emphasized dialectically, perhaps, that just because more scope is to be given for "democracy" and for "public initiative," it is necessary to further strengthen the one force which can unify all of those energies and channel them in accordance with the interests of the society as a whole.

Along similar lines, it is pointed out that the party is not to be allowed to become a mere "cultural-enlightenment" organization. Part Two, Section I, of the program, for example, declares that "the main economic task of the Party and the Soviet people is to create the material and technical basis of communism within two decades."[4] The same section also states that "the Party will do everything to enhance the role of science in the building of communist society...." In the portion of the program dealing with military matters it is stated that while the CPSU defends "the gains of socialism and the cause of world peace," the party also "maintains that as long as imperialism exists the threat of aggressive wars will remain." Consequently the CPSU, as in Stalin's day, "considers it necessary to maintain the defensive power of the Soviet state and the combat preparedness of its armed forces at a level ensuring the decisive and complete defeat of any enemy who dares to encroach upon the Soviet Union."[5] Besides thus reasserting the traditional principle of party control of the Soviet armed forces, this section of the program, providing as it does for the continued existence of the Soviet state, and its organs of force and compulsion, so long as "imperialism" exists, can be invoked to justify a wide range of foreign policy actions.

In the section on nationality questions it is stated that "the Party neither ignores nor overaccentuates national characteristics," and then

[4] *ibid.*, p. 71.   [5] *ibid.*, p. 105.

follow a series of "tasks" which the party "sets" in the sphere of nationality relations.[6] In the spheres of ideology, education, instruction, science, and culture also a long list of party "tasks" is set forth. For example, the party "calls for the education of the population as a whole in the spirit of scientific communism and strives to ensure that all working people master the ideas of Marxism-Leninism, that they fully understand the course and perspectives of world development, take a correct view of international and domestic events and consciously build their life on communist lines."[7] The section on science asserts that "The Party will adopt measures to extend and improve the material facilities of science" and adds that it is a "point of honor" for Soviet scientists to take a leading place in world science in all key fields.[8] The section on "cultural development, literature and art" assures workers in these fields that the party will do everything to assist them and at the same time stipulates that "the art of socialist realism" is "based on the principles of partisanship and kinship with the people," and that its development "goes hand in hand with the cultivation" of the "progressive traditions of world culture."[9] The final section of the program, entitled "The Party in the Period of Full-scale Communist Construction," contains among others, the following highly significant statement: "The unshakable ideological and organizational unity of the Party is the most important source of its invincibility, a guarantee for the successful solution of the great tasks of communist construction."[10]

Emphasis upon "unity" within the party was also a feature of many speeches delivered at the Twenty-first and Twenty-second Congresses and was particularly conspicuous in the address to the Twenty-second Congress by Frol R. Kozlov, at the time at least regarded by most experts as the man most likely to succeed Khrushchev as head of the CPSU. In discussing the party rules Kozlov made it clear that no agitation by "factions" against the "general line" of the party would be tolerated. Molotov, Kaganovich, Malenkov, and the others who were castigated at or since the June 1957 party plenum as the "anti-party group" were not arrested, and were indeed not expelled from the party until 1964 despite recommendations of expulsion by some leaders and denunciation at the Twenty-first and Twenty-second Congresses, and subsequently, as "splitters," "factionalists," or even "criminals." However, they lost all influence and their reputations

---

[6] *ibid.*, pp. 107-109.   [7] *ibid.*, p. 111.   [8] *ibid.*, p. 120.
[9] *ibid.*, pp. 121-122.   [10] *ibid.*, p. 128.

were thoroughly besmirched. Purges which, unlike those of the Stalin era, do not appear to involve exile, imprisonment, or execution of their targets, have continued to be an instrument of Soviet high politics but they are now probably subordinate to a more or less gradual personnel recruitment and training process.

Nowhere in the long list of tasks and prescriptions contained in the 1961 party program is there any indication that the party will ever "wither away." Indeed, the promised democratization of and gradual dismantling of the formal machinery of the state is to be achieved by improving and strengthening the CPSU, the real, essential, and inner machinery of political authority. The long-range goal is to be "social self-administration" but the effort to improve society is never to cease.

The bulk of this paper will be devoted to the functions and structures of the CPSU, to interrelationships and interactions between the CPSU and the occupational, social, and ethnic groups in Soviet society which the CPSU continues to guide and control, and to the processes of political socialization and elite recruitment by which the party strives to maintain and strengthen its position vis-à-vis the various groups and sub-cultures of the Soviet polity and to mobilize them behind its policies. Also we shall be concerned with problems and difficulties encountered by the party in performing its functions and maintaining the morale of its cadres, such as the prevention and control of discontent, deviations, and disaffection among intellectuals, the student youth, and other groups. Before we tackle these formidable problems, however, it will be useful to identify some major variables and stages in the development of Soviet political culture.

Perhaps the most significant single condition of the collapse of the tsarist regime, and also probably one of the most important elements in the shaping of Soviet society was the economic and cultural backwardness of Russia. For decades before its breakdown in 1917, and particularly during the last thirty or forty years of its existence, the Russian empire supported a great power status in the international arena on an inadequate economic, technological, and cultural base. Russian economic growth was rapid, especially in the two or three decades before 1914, but the total pattern of Russian political and economic development remained conspicuously inferior to that of the Western states which Russia sought to emulate. To say this of course in no way implies lack of respect for the brilliant achievements of Russians in such fields as literature, music, mathematics, and the natural sciences. Perhaps partly because these achievements fostered among Russian intellectuals a sense of the potentialities of their people, an acute consciousness of the disadvantages, dangers, and shame of backwardness and a determination to close the economic and cultural gap between Russia and the advanced Western countries were major strands in the thinking of the Russian intelligentsia, especially of its radical wing.

Of course Western influences were strongest among the elite elements of Russian society, ranging from the court and ruling bureaucracy down through the politically weak but economically vigorous middle classes to the radical intelligentsia. One important effect on Russia of gradual Westernization was increasing differentiation between the culture of the European-oriented elite and that of the tradition-bound, ritualistically religious, subservient but increasingly restive Russian villager, who even in 1917 constituted the overwhelming majority of the population. Differences between the styles of life of town and country folk, of the traditionalist majority and the modernized minority of Russian society, together with economic, technical, and administrative backwardness and inefficiency and, finally, the shock of the military defeats of 1905 and 1914-1917 to which all of these defects and stresses contributed, helped pave the way for the triumph in Russia of an ideology whose adherents restored the unity of society by coercion. Western influence, and particularly comparison between Russian backwardness and Western progress, stimulated the growth of both liberal and socialist doctrines and political parties. It is not without interest and a certain irony that N. Valentinov, who knew Lenin in the early years of the nineteenth century in Switzerland, has written: "What attracted us in Marxism was . . . its Europeanism. It came from Europe and it smacked not of domestic rusticity but of something new and fresh and attractive. Marxism was a messenger promising that we would not remain a semi-Asiatic country, but from an eastern country would be turned into a western one, with western culture and western institutions and attributes, representing a free political system."[11]

Lenin and his colleagues in the regime which came to power in November 1917 were sufficiently consistent Marxists, at least in terms of formal doctrines, to profess to hope that the Russian revolution would be the spark which would ignite the socialist revolution in the

[11] N. Valentinov, *Vstrechi s Leninym*, New York, 1953, p. 50.

advanced industrial countries of central and western Europe. The bolshevik Left, including such figures as Bukharin, and to a considerable degree Trotski, were convinced that socialism could not strike real roots in a country as backward as Russia.[12] Lenin, however, and particularly the brutally pragmatic Stalin, tended strongly and increasingly to identify the survival and the interests of the bolshevik-ruled Soviet Russian state with the cause of the Communist world revolution, of which, at least until the establishment of Communist regimes in eastern Europe and eastern Asia following World War II, the Soviet Union was held to be the base and ruling center.

Stalin's policy of "socialism in one country"—which never repudiated the objective of ultimate extension of the Soviet system throughout the world—left the Soviet Union face-to-face with the old problem of relative backwardness vis-à-vis the advanced industrial countries of the world and, if anything, in an even more acute form than that which confronted tsarist Russia. Realization of the dangers and embarrassments of backwardness helped shape a Soviet image of Western capitalism as a mortal threat to the survival of the Soviet regime. Other factors conducive to Soviet anxiety and hostility included the weakness and poverty resulting from years of international and civil war; the continued hostility of Japan, of France, Britain, the United States, and other Western powers, already manifested during the formative years of the Soviet regime by military intervention and aid to the enemies of the bolshevik regime, irresolute though these policies were; the bolshevik doctrine, a central tenet of which was an irreconcilable struggle between the forces of "socialism" and those of "imperialism"; the need of the bolshevik regime, forced to impose severe sacrifices on a population to which it had held out glowing promises of future benefits, for external targets against which to turn aggressive impulses generated by internal frustrations.

Generalizing on the differences between advanced Western countries and "have-not" powers, such as Russia, Theodore H. von Laue has written: "The 'have' powers are those which, in addition to enjoying the willing cooperation of their citizens in providing the necessary means of power, could also develop (or have hitherto de-

[12] A perceptive analysis of the development of Soviet political practice and doctrine under conditions of the failure of the socialist revolution to expand beyond the borders of Soviet Russia, is contained in Robert V. Daniels, *The Conscience of the Revolution*, Cambridge, Mass., 1960.

veloped) their strength out of their own resources, spontaneously, autochthonously. They have preserved their full sovereignty, in other words, changing predominantly or almost exclusively as a result of domestic pressures and at their own sovereign rate of speed. The 'have-nots,' on the other hand, have had to adopt the alien institutions of the West often at breakneck speed and frightful sacrifice, a tempo largely dictated by the Western rate of growth."[13]

Von Laue's formulation tends perhaps to obscure the component of aggressiveness in bolshevism by calling attention to only one of its roots, but it makes a contribution to our understanding of important aspects of Soviet political behavior, particularly in the field of political socialization. The persistent Russian cultural inferiority complex toward the West has helped to engender fears of the subversive potential of freedom of communication and has reinforced the effects of anxiety regarding what, until relatively recently, was a genuine Soviet inferiority not merely in economic development but also in military power. These worries heavily influenced Soviet educational and cultural policies, and were reflected in the most authoritative ideological pronouncements of the political leadership. Stalin's famous warning, in a speech to Soviet industrial managers in 1931, that unless the Soviet Union caught up with the advanced capitalist countries in ten years, she would be crushed, and his doctrine of "capitalist encirclement," finally repudiated by Khrushchev in March 1958, reflected a realistic appreciation of the dangers and disadvantages of material backwardness in a hostile world. It was more difficult for the Communists to admit cultural backwardness than to confess that there was still a technological gap between the Soviet Union and its "capitalist" rivals, since almost from the beginning Moscow had proclaimed the moral superiority of "socialism" to the surviving "bourgeois" order in the West.[14]

Industrialization, with all that it implied in terms of deprivational changes and drastic pressures upon a largely illiterate, unskilled, and uneducated population with a very small industrial working class and a great shortage of competent administrators and professionals, and the stimulus which it furnished to the creation, under party leadership, of cadres for the political, economic, and other skill

[13] Theodore H. von Laue, "Problems of Modernization," in Ivo J. Lederer, ed. *Russian Foreign Policy*, New Haven and London, 1962, pp. 69-108 (quotation on p. 71).

[14] On Khrushchev's repudiation of the "encirclement" thesis, see Boris Meissner, *Russland unter Chruschtschow*, Munich, 1960, p. 260.

groups necessary to staff an industrial society, was perhaps as important a factor in the development of the Soviet quasi-modern polity as the rivalry between Soviet Russia and the capitalist world was. The military, diplomatic, and propaganda struggle with capitalism went hand in hand with forced-draft industrialization. The imposition of these policies upon the Soviet population, and in particular upon the peasantry, after the collectivization of agriculture in 1928-1931 forced not only to furnish surplus labor for the factories and recruits for the armed forces but also to live close to a subsistence level, and at times below that, required the development of a police system of unparalleled dimensions. The Stalinist totalitarian revolution which in the late 1920's and early 1930's fastened upon the Soviet Union an unprecedentedly severe and comprehensive system of political and ideological controls met with opposition not only among the peasants, particularly in the Ukraine and other non-Russian areas, as well as among the nomadic peoples of central Asia, who suffered frightfully in the process of forced conversion to the status of collective farmers, but also among intellectuals, including some of the more idealistic and humanitarian Communists. Stalin's main response to opposition and resistance, real or fancied, was the building of a powerful police network which he always kept firmly under his control, and which he used to conduct successive purges; those of 1936-1938 were so terrifying that their memory still affects the political attitudes and behavior even of many Soviet youths.

By the late 1930's, although the Soviet standard of living was still lower than it had been before the beginning of the first Five Year Plan in 1928, it was beginning to rise slowly. Also the mass of the Soviet population was beginning to benefit from the results of the administrative, educational, and social welfare policies which accompanied the industrial development of the Soviet Union. On the other hand the consolidation of Stalinist totalitarianism had suppressed the impulses toward intellectual freedom and cultural and national pluralism which survived the relatively mild era of the NEP, from 1921 to 1928. World War II, while it imposed incalculable sacrifices upon the peoples of the Soviet Union, also brought some relaxation of ideological regimentation and police terror. Since the energies of the regime were concentrated upon survival in the struggle against the Nazis and their allies, it was necessary, for example, to make certain concessions to the traditional national sentiments of the Soviet peoples, particularly the Great Russians, constituting about 50 per cent of the total population. The war was followed by re-consolidation of internal political and ideological controls and by renewal of the political struggle against the West, directed at first mainly against the British, and then especially against the United States, which began in 1949 to be described as even more aggressive and imperialistic than Nazi Germany or imperial Japan had been. The period from roughly the end of 1947 until Stalin's death on March 5, 1953 was among the grimmest in Soviet history. To be sure, by 1948 the economy had in the main recovered from the effects of war and the foundations had been laid for the spectacular Soviet scientific achievements which were to redound to the credit of the Khrushchev regime. Although Russia was not shaken by major convulsions such as the mass purges of 1936-1938, coercion of Western-oriented Soviet intellectuals was intensified. Intellectuals of Jewish extraction in particular were terrorized by Stalin's campaign, begun by Zhdanov, in the criticism of certain writers in 1946, against "cosmopolitanism" which was designed to turn to hatred traditionally friendly sentiments toward the United States, which had been reinforced by the joint struggle against the Nazis, and directed with special force against Jews suspected of links with either the newly founded state of Israel or with the United States.

The death of Stalin, while it spurred anxiety about the future, especially in the little band of at first badly frightened men to whom power now passed, also stimulated hope. Soviet intellectuals for the first time in years could breathe almost freely. Stalin's death spurred speculation among Western scholars regarding possible lines of development of Soviet domestic and foreign policy. Two books published in 1953 and a third, in 1954 indicated the main lines of American speculation about the future of the Soviet political system. Merle Fainsod, to judge by the conclusion of the first edition of his major study, *How Russia Is Ruled*, seemed to feel that significant changes in the Soviet system were unlikely. Fainsod wrote in the last sentence of that work: "The totalitarian regime does not shed its police-state characteristics; it dies when power is wrenched from its hands." W. W. Rostow in *The Dynamics of Soviet Society* envisaged the possibility of a struggle for power among Stalin's heirs which might "bring politically into play the dissatisfactions and positive aspirations of various groups." Barrington Moore, Jr., in a study which remains a classic work of socio-political analysis, expressed the view that the range of alternatives posed by Rostow and Fainsod did not "encompass adequately all the possibilities, or even all those that can be considered rather probable." In addition to the possibilities of the maintenance virtually unchanged of the Stalin style of totalitarianism or its early and castastrophic breakdown, Moore in his *Terror and Progress USSR* (1954) foresaw the possibility of the development in the Soviet Union of either "a rationalist technocracy or a limited and traditionalist despotism." In the body of his book, and particularly in its brilliant concluding chapter, Moore leaned toward the view, confirmed by developments since he wrote, that for the foreseeable future the Soviet system would evolve in a somewhat more rationalist and technocratic direction than had been the case in the late Stalin era. None of these studies foresaw all the major lines of development of the last ten years, although Moore's analysis in particular proved to be of exceptional predictive value. The development of Soviet society since Moore wrote has been in the direction of technical rationality envisaged by him, with a considerable reduction of the role of naked and punitive power. However, the Communist Party leadership, particularly as exercised by Khrushchev, displayed an unpredicted and surprising capacity for incorporating into its organizational structure and increasingly flexible official doctrine a wide range of apparently contradictory aspirations and attitudes. Still, as Meissner has pointed out, the Khrushchev regime represented a transitional period in Soviet development, characterized by a number of contradictions, reflected in the effort "to renew the spirit of the Soviet system without substantially altering its totalitarian substance."[15] It remains to be seen whether his colorless but perhaps more efficient successors can achieve better results than the ebullient Nikita.

Let us now analyze the political culture, the broad outlines and history of which we have sketched. We can deal briefly with the hierarchical, bureaucratic structure of the CPSU and its continued, in some ways enhanced, exercise of supremacy with respect to all major political and administrative functions, which have, however, since 1953 been performed in a more sophisticated, rational, and even gentle fashion than under Stalin. These matters have been extensively treated in a number of excellent studies.[16] Of course we

---

[15] Meissner, *op.cit.*, p. 266.
[16] Besides the already mentioned works of Fainsod, Moore, and Rostow, two first-rate studies by the Australian political scientist T. H. Rigby should be mentioned. The first of these, "The Selection of Leading Personnel in the Soviet State and Communist Party," was a thesis submitted for the degree of Doctor of Philosophy

should not exaggerate the extent of our knowledge even about relatively well-known aspects of the Soviet political system. As Alfred Meyer observes, "we have only the foggiest notions" about the making of the most important kinds of decisions in the Soviet Union, such as those concerned in the balancing of the requirements of rapid economic growth with matters of military preparedness, consumer satisfaction, the rational allocation of resources, and so forth. We have very little knowledge also about the ups and downs of the political careers of top Soviet leaders, and in many cases we do not even know the names of important middle-rank decision makers. A good illustration of the obscurity which surrounds matters of high political import in the Soviet Union was the perplexing transfer of I. V. Spiridonov from his vital position as first secretary of the Leningrad *oblast* committee of the CPSU to the honorific position of chairman of the Soviet of the Union of the Supreme Soviet of the Soviet Union, which may perhaps have reflected a change in the status of Frol R. Kozlov, who formerly headed the Leningrad party organization. Leading experts of Western governments were apparently unable to find a satisfactory explanation of the background and significance of this event, which occurred in connection with participation by Khrushchev in a meeting of the bureau of the Leningrad *obkom*.[17]

The CPSU is identified both in its own statutes and in article 126 of the Soviet constitution as "the leading and guiding force of Soviet society." As Rigby notes, every one of its members and candidate members is invested to some degree with "leading and guiding" functions. Rigby divides the party membership into three main categories, each of which plays a distinctive role in the system of party leadership. The first is that of full-time party functionaries, including secretaries, department and section chiefs, and instructors of party

---

to the University of London in 1954. Hereafter cited as Rigby, *Selection*. Rigby also contributed to the valuable pamphlet published by the Australian Political Studies Association entitled *Policy-making in the U.S.S.R.*, Melbourne, 1962, pp. 1-26; L. G. Churchward also contributed a paper to this pamphlet, and each author commented on the interpretations of the other. This pamphlet will be cited hereafter as Rigby, *Policy-making*. See also the contributions of Zbigniew Brzezinski, Alfred G. Meyer, and Robert C. Tucker to the discussion in *Slavic Review*, Vol. XX, No. 3, October 1961, pp. 351-388; Herbert McClosky and John E. Turner, *The Soviet Dictatorship*, New York, 1960; John N. Hazard, *The Soviet System of Government*, Chicago, 1957; and Frederick C. Barghoorn, "The USSR: Monolithic Controls at Home and Abroad," in Sigmund Neumann, ed. *Modern Political Parties*, Chicago, 1956, pp. 219-283.

[17] *Pravda*, May 4, 1962.

committees, who play an important role in linking the committees with, for example, collective farms or enterprises in their area of jurisdiction. Rigby estimated that this category in 1954 amounted to about 250,000 full-time functionaries and some 300,000 secretaries of primary party organizations, mostly part-time workers, who performed the party's "central tasks" of "giving guiding directions, verifying their fulfillment, and selecting personnel."

The second category identified by Rigby was "all those Party members who are distributed as leaders through the various levels of the administrative, productive, 'cultural,' and 'voluntary' organizations of Soviet society." Unlike the *apparatchiki*, who are oriented toward the over-all leadership of the party, the members of this second group are "concerned with completing planned assignments in a limited field of activity with its own logic and sectional interests." Rigby's characterization of this second category helps us to locate the latent and increasingly vigorous but still rather amorphous pluralistic tendencies of the Soviet polity. To some degree at least these party members, who are under pressure to give their primary loyalty to the party but who are also by training and occupation functional specialists in industrial management or military science for example, develop perspectives which diverge from those of the full-time party functionaries and may lead to friction or even to policy disputes between them and the former. On the other hand, to the extent that the party apparatus functions successfully as a "ministry of coordination," aggregating the interests of various functional agencies and occupational groups, it may appear to government bureaucrats—whose ranks at the upper levels at least are more or less interchangeable with those of the apparatus—as well as to other skill-group leaders to perform functions beneficial to the society as a whole.[18]

Finally, there are the rank-and-file party members. They do not serve in positions of authority either in the party apparatus itself or in state or "public" organizations.[19] However, these "privates" in the Soviet political army constitute the foundation of the Soviet power pyramid. They furnish recruits for the upper echelons, disseminate party-approved attitudes, communicate the party's policies

---

[18] On the role of the party apparatus, especially its middle-rank officials, for example at the *obkom* secretarial level, as a coordinating body, see Jerry F. Hough, "The Role of the Local Party Organs in Soviet Industrial Decision-making," Ph.D. dissertation, Harvard University, Cambridge, Mass., 1961.

[19] Rigby, *Selection*, p. 52.

to non-party people, supply information to their party organizations—thus acting as an auxiliary political intelligence network—and are expected to set an example to the non-party "masses" of superior work performance and dedicated citizenship.

The structure of the party, which is the model for all kinds of political and social organizations in the Soviet Union, combines mobilizational and penetrative capacities with a high degree of compartmentalization. Units and agencies are sealed off both vertically and horizontally from relationships and information the party command considers unnecessary for the effective performance of their functions. This results in a situation in which the political experience of 95 per cent of the party membership is limited to what goes on in local primary organization, at the bottom of the political ladder.[20] To be sure, from time to time, particularly in periods when the central party authorities are seeking to stimulate rank-and-file enthusiasm, or when they are preoccupied with matters distracting their attention from internal party administration, a measure of spontaneity is permitted in, for example, elections of secretaries of primary party organizations. In 1955-1957 spontaneity apparently reached a high point unknown since the 1920's. By January 1957 revolt against official candidates was even being advocated at conferences of *raion* party organizations.

Demands by rank-and-file members of local party organizations for at least some freedom of choice in electing their executive committees may have coincided with Khrushchev's desire to replace aging, "conservative" party cadres with younger, more vigorous and efficient men and women. Khrushchev also pushed, in the party as well as in the other Soviet bureaucracies, for a reduction of administrative staffs and red tape—in Russia as in America a perennial demand voiced by reformers.[21] The drive to economize on paper-shuffling personnel is part of a general Kremlin pressure for efficiency. In particular it is related to the tendency of the post-Stalin leadership to seek increased industrial and agricultural productivity through improvements in the selection, training, and deployment of party and government personnel.

A measure of vast importance to Khrushchev's program for streamlining the party's organization was adopted at the November 1962

---

[20] Rigby, *Policy-making*, p. 18; Barghoorn, *op.cit.*, pp. 232-33.

[21] For perceptive comment on these trends, see the article by Paul Wohl, "Changing of the Guard," *The New Leader*, April 17, 1961, pp. 11-13.

CPSU plenum. It was decided that the hierarchy of party organizations, from the fifteen republic party central committees down through the primary party organizations at the lowest level, should be restructured on a dual basis, with a parallel chain of republic and *oblast* bureaus responsible for industrial and agricultural affairs respectively. The old rural *raion* party organizations were abolished. Thus a greater degree of specialization of function was introduced into the system of party direction of the national economy. Party functionaries engaged in guiding the economy would, so Khrushchev argued, now have more clearly defined responsibilities than in the past and hence could be expected to exercise firmer, more efficient leadership.[22] The 1962 reforms represented a logical continuation of the consolidation which got fully underway in March 1958, when Khrushchev, already First Secretary of the CPSU, also became chairman of the Council of Ministers of the Soviet Union. The Khrushchevian consolidation was followed by a tightening of Kremlin control both over the internal operations of the party and over economic and other functions of state and "public" organizations. For example, the Central Committee of the CPSU under date of June 26, 1959 published a decree entitled, "Concerning the Formation in Primary Party Organizations of Production and Commercial Enterprises of Commissions for the Carrying Out by the Party Organizations of the Right of Control of the Activity of the Administrations of Enterprises."[23] Articles appeared frequently demanding improvement of "party, state, and social control," and emphasizing that "the struggle for timely and precise fulfillment of party decisions is the basis of all the activity of party organizations and their leading organs."[24] Such statements, it is now clear, reflected severe difficulties.

At the November 1964 CPSU plenum the post-Khrushchev regime repealed Khrushchev's reorganization of two years before. It now appears that they had good reason to do so, as it—together with the many other reorganizations of which Khrushchev was so fond—had created considerable confusion. The degree of decentralization and especially the duplication and overlapping inherent in the Khru-

---

[22] For details of the reorganization of the structure of the party, see the revised edition of Fainsod, *How Russia is Ruled*, Cambridge, Mass., 1963, especially pp. 226-227, 411, 513, 515, and 519.
[23] Text in *Zapisnaya knizhka partiinogo aktivista*, Moscow, 1960, pp. 149-165.
[24] "Sovershenstvovat partiiny, gosudarstvenny i obshchestvenny kontrol," *Partiinaya zhizn*, No. 4, May 1962, p. 4 (full text of article on pp. 3-7).

shchev organizational pattern were probably incompatible with effective functioning of a centrally planned economy still suffering from shortages. Khrushchev by his numerous reorganizations created irritation in the ranks of the party apparatus. But he failed to employ the repressive measures against those whom he had antagonized which alone might have enabled him to guarantee his power position against a conspiracy such as the one by which he was overthrown in October 1964.

The struggle for monolithism, so central to Stalin's regime was continued by Khrushchev. Another feature of Stalin's contribution to the shaping of the quasi-modern Soviet polity which was continued by his successors was the attempt to equip party members, particularly members of the full-time party apparatus who are occupied in liaison work with military, managerial, scientific, and other trained professionals, with adequate training in the fields of work of those whose functions the party *apparatchiki* are assigned to supervise. This professional, often highly technical training is a supplement to specifically political-ideological education, discussed later. This dual-purpose professionalization is greatly facilitated by the rapid rise in the general level of education of party leaders, and indeed of party members generally, especially since the end of World War II. As early as 1949 about 85 per cent of the delegates to the congress of the Communist Party of the Ukraine, for example, had completed secondary education.[25] As Armstrong notes, "The party has placed enormous emphasis on increased education, not only because it directly improves the official's job performance but because it prepares him to cope with the problems of an increasingly complex society and to deal with the growing number of well-educated persons in the general population."[26] In this connection it is interesting that as of July 1, 1961 the CPSU had within its ranks more than 55,000 persons holding degrees of either doctor or candidate of sciences—the two Soviet graduate degrees roughly equivalent to the Ph.D. and the M.A. in the United States. Rapid progress in increasing the educational qualifications of party functionaries is indicated by the statement in an article by Frol R. Kozlov that, while in 1956, 25.7 per cent of *raion* and city committee party secretaries had a higher education, this percentage was "now"—no date was

---

[25] John A. Armstrong, *The Soviet Bureaucratic Elite*, New York, 1959, pp. 31-32.
[26] *ibid.*, p. 33.

given—76.9.[27] Also Kozlov reported at the Twenty-Second Congress of the CPSU that more than nine-tenths of the party secretaries at the *oblast* level had a higher education.

A very high proportion of the leadership cadres of the CPSU have an engineering education. Biographical data published in the Soviet Union in 1960 indicated that the majority of members and candidate members of the presidium of the CPSU as of that year had been graduated from engineering or technical institutes or from party political training institutions.[28] Apparently not only the party apparatus but also the Soviet bureaucracy generally are heavily staffed with engineers and other technically trained personnel. According to a National Science Foundation release early in 1962, "nearly one-third of all Soviet engineers, scientists, and agricultural specialists are engaged in administrative tasks and in running the government, reflecting the Soviet belief that they can perform these tasks better than non-technically trained professionals."[29] Massive and rapidly continuing improvement in general and specialist educational levels of the Soviet elite, particularly within the party apparatus, probably has contributed greatly to the capability of the party in facilitating the technical modernization of the Soviet Union and at the same time in preventing the skill groups developed by this process from seriously challenging the party's claim that it and it alone represents and articulates the interests of all the functioning groups of Soviet society.

The party seeks to enjoy the advantages of division of labor but to avoid the perils of pluralism. Within the ranks of its own apparatus it has encouraged a considerable measure of specialization. The apparatus includes "line" and "staff" officers, the latter being broken down into such categories as cadres and indoctrination specialists.[30] In its top-to-bottom direction of the Soviet educational system the party has often encouraged exceedingly narrow specialization.[31] However, the party has thus far been successful in keeping the specialists under control by a combination of differential material and

[27] Reported by Harry Schwartz in the *New York Times*, February 18, 1962, on the basis of data published in the CPSU organizational magazine, *Partiinaya zhizn*. For the data on educational level of party secretaries, see Frol R. Kozlov, *KPSS-partiya vsego naroda*, Kommunist, No. 8, May, 1962, pp. 10-21 (data cited on p. 15). See also Kozlov's speech, "On Changes in the Statutes of the CPSU," in *Pravda* for October 29, 1961.
[28] *Zapisnaya knizhka*, pp. 101-107.
[29] NSF-62-102, January 15, 1962, p. 3.
[30] Armstrong, *op.cit.*, Chaps. IV, V, VI, VII.
[31] See, for example, Nicholas DeWitt, *Education and Professional Employment in the U.S.S.R.*, U.S. Government Printing Office, 1961.

psychological rewards for achievement; by the already-mentioned principles of penetration and compartmentalization, one significant feature of which is control by party committees at all levels of the "nomenclature" of officials in all fields of work, including science, the arts and education; and also through an elaborate, comprehensive, and differentiated political socialization mechanism. Finally, it should be noted that although the use of violence and police terror has substantially diminished since the death of Stalin—evidence of this is furnished by such measures as the amnesties of the early post-Stalin years, the return of many political prisoners to their residences and places of work, etc.—the Committee of State Security, with its formidable apparatus of trained cadres and secret informers is available if needed to deal with any threats that may arise to the authority of the party leadership. The development of a genuinely pluralistic society or polity would appear to be impossible until or unless the present system of party controls becomes far more seriously eroded than at present by new forces and attitudes.

However, both the Soviet social structure and political structure do have certain pluralistic aspects. The party subjects pluralistic structures and aspirations to the organizational and communications pressures for homogenization, standardization, and centralization, of which it disposes such a formidable array. The problem of pluralism confronted by the party has two main aspects. It must cope with the survivals of attitudes and customs associated with the largely pre-scientific, and pre-industrial, traditional society upon which the CPSU since it seized power in 1917 has been straining to impose its harsh but dynamic ethos of "progress." Nationalism, religion, and other "survivals of capitalism"—to borrow a favorite term of the official interpreters of Soviet Marxism—are among the elements of traditionalist pluralism with which the party must even today still deal. While the party has been gradually overcoming these forces, at least to the point of reducing to manageable proportions their capability of openly challenging its authority, it has also been confronted by new challenges and problems posed by the aspirations of social strata basically loyal to the "socialist" system to which they owe their status but irritated by particular policies or organizational arrangements. One might characterize these new challenges as unintended consequences of the regime's own achievements. On the basis of the aspiration of certain segments of the Soviet intelligentsia, particularly some of the critically minded writers, at least the rudiments or the foreshadowing of a kind of Soviet "loyal opposition" has at times appeared to be visible. Further development of these within-system aspirations could in time profoundly alter the temper and even the structure of the Soviet polity. We must exercise extreme care in evaluating the prospects for what George F. Kennan in his famous "X" article published in *Foreign Affairs* in 1947 envisaged as a "mellowing" of the Soviet system. Not only is the society integrated tightly by a tough and ruthless political apparatus, but even the more discontented elements of the elite still tend to suffer from an aggression-generating inferiority complex about Russia's international prestige, and are suspicious of Western, especially American and German, "imperialists" and also are probably fearful of the threat to their privileged status which a substantial loosening of state controls over the worker and peasant masses might entail. However, profound changes could result from pressures generated by a combination of the leaders' needs for efficiency and the interests of various functional groups.

The Soviet system has always made provision for a limited degree of legitimate social and administrative pluralism. Thus the formal, constitutional structure of the Soviet government is a federal one. The Soviet Union is divided into fifteen union republics, nineteen autonomous republics, five autonomous *oblasts*, and ten national *okrugs*, or territories. Each of these classes of units has, respectively, twenty-five, ten, five, and one vote in the Soviet of Nationalities, one of the two chambers of the bicameral Soviet parliament. In addition to these and other constitutional provisions there has existed since the first RSFSR constitution (1919) and the first USSR constitution (ratified January, 1924) a complex pattern of legal, administrative, educational, and cultural arrangements designed to facilitate and guarantee such expressions of national and ethnic values as the CPSU leadership regarded as expedient and considered compatible with its over-all objectives. National and ethnic pluralism has always been regarded by the Soviet rulers as in the nature of a necessary evil, and the ultimate ideal was, and remains, as the recent party program points out, "a single worldwide culture of Communist society."[32]

Limited decentralization of public administration, particularly in the area of industrial management, in the post-Stalin period has somewhat increased the administrative functions of the constituent republics, although decentralization was clearly intended as a measure to

[32] Triska, *op.cit.*, p. 109.

increase the efficiency of the national economy rather than as a concession to the political aspirations of the non-Russian nationalities. Of course the significance of Soviet federalism in terms of the political rights of the non-Russian nationalities of the Soviet Union is and always has been severely limited because the ruling Communist Party is described as and functions primarily as an "international" organization, directed from Moscow and shifting personnel from one part of the country to another at Moscow's command. Similarly, the economy of the Soviet Union is and always has been administered on the basis of national rather than federal principles. In addition, particularly since the early 1930's, a centralist, assimilationist cultural policy with heavy emphasis upon the Russian language and selected aspects of Russian culture has tended to reduce Stalin's famous formula according to which Soviet nationality policy was "national in form, socialist in content" to granting non-Russians the right to say, in their native languages if they wished, the same things and to think the same thoughts as the members of the Russian nation, described by Stalin in his famous toast to the Red Army marshals in May 1945 as the "leading nation" of the Soviet Union. To be sure, the doctrine of Russian leadership was expressed after the death of Stalin in a less strident and irritating manner than previously, and the assimilationist practices associated with it were applied more tactfully and skillfully than before. Partial restitution was made for some of the worst excesses committed by Stalin in the sphere of national relations. With the exception of the Volga Germans and the Crimean Tatars, the seven peoples deported entire by Stalin during World War II for alleged collaboration with the Germans were partly restored to their former status.[33]

Current nationality policy appears to be a judicious blend of concessions to national sentiments and continuation of the Stalin policy of assimilation. As Khrushchev stated in a speech on October 18, 1961 to the Twenty-second Party Congress, two tendencies are operating in the national question: each nation of the Soviet Union is undergoing further development with the expansion of the rights of the Union and Autonomous Republics, and at the same time the nations are drawing closer to one another with increasing mutual influence and enrichment of one another's cultures. The post-Stalin

[33] On Soviet nationality policy, see R. Conquest, *The Soviet Deportation of Nationalities*, London and New York, 1960; Frederick C. Barghoorn, *Soviet Russian Nationalism*, New York, 1956; and Alex Inkeles and Raymond A. Bauer, *The Soviet Citizen*, Cambridge, Mass., 1959, Chap. XV.

policy toward the non-Russian nationalities emphasizes aspects of national development that tend to bring the nations closer together in their economic and cultural characteristics. Recent Soviet writing on internal nationality problems stresses the value, for example, of exchange of labor force among the republics, such as occurred in connection with building of the hydroelectric stations at Kuibyshev, Volgograd (until October 1961 Stalingrad), Irkutsk, and Bratsk, or the settling of the virgin lands of northern Kazakhstan by Russians, Ukrainians, and others.[34] It is significant that in his important speech of November 19, 1962 to the CPSU plenum Khrushchev expressed satisfaction regarding "the constant exchange of qualified cadres among the nations" of the Soviet Union.

The unifying doctrine of "Soviet patriotism," designed to tie all Soviet citizens regardless of national origin into a single political community emotionally identified with the party-state authority, and pressure to learn the Russian language continue to be powerful homogenization instruments of the party in its effort to eliminate vestiges of "nationalism" and "chauvinism." The definition of these terms of course is a prerogative of the Kremlin. Russian is taught as a supplementary language in all Soviet elementary schools in the non-Russian political units, and in many schools located in non-Russian political administrative units Russian is the primary language of instruction, with the local, native languages being taught as a supplementary subject. Soviet data indicate that in 1955-1956 about two-thirds of all primary and secondary school pupils attended Russian language schools where all subjects were taught in Russian exclusively.[35]

Since, according to the most recent Soviet Census of January 1959, Russians constituted 114,114,000 of the total Soviet population of 208,827,000, the above data on language instruction may be regarded as among many indications that Russification, within the framework of course of over-all party policy, remains a central feature of Soviet nationality policy.[36]

[34] See, for example, articles by A. Azizyan, in *Kommunist*, No. 15, October 1961, and N. Gadzhiev, *Kommunist*, No. 1, January 1962. It may be indicative of embarrassment or concern over the "nationality problem" that Kozlov in the article cited earlier gives no data on the national composition of the CPSU, although he furnishes considerable statistical material on other elements of the party's social structure.

[35] DeWitt, *op.cit.*, p. 112. See also Yaroslav Bilinsky, "The Soviet Education Laws of 1958-9 and Soviet Nationality Policy," in *Soviet Studies*, Vol. XIV, No. 2, October 1962, pp. 138-157.

[36] For above population figures, see *SSSR v tsifrakh v 1960 godu*, Moscow, 1961, p. 70.

A measure of the underdevelopment of Soviet society, at least in terms of the social structures of advanced industrial nations, including Japan, is afforded by the fact that not much less than half the total Soviet population still consists of collective farm peasants and their families, of workers on the state farms (*sovkhozy*) who, unlike the collective farmers, are paid regular wages, and of other residents of the countryside. According to official Soviet figures 38.8 per cent of the population as of 1959 were engaged in agriculture, but the same source included in the category of "workers and employees of town and village," an unspecified percentage of the non-peasant population, so that we can conclude that from some points of view probably considerably more than 38.8 per cent of the population are "rural."[37]

The peasants, besides clinging most firmly to national sentiments and prejudices, are also the stratum of the Soviet population in which traditional religious sentiments are strongest. The status of religion in the Soviet Union may be regarded as an interesting aspect of relations between the Kremlin and the peasantry, although of course the problem of religion is not entirely a peasant problem. The regime during the war provided a measure of legitimacy for organized religion by setting up two control and liaison bodies, namely the Council for the Affairs of the Russian Orthodox Church and the Council for the Affairs of Religious Cults. After the war, although these bodies remained in existence and indeed are still functioning, the traditional anti-religious propaganda of the Soviet press and other communications media, suspended to foster unity in the struggle against the Nazi, was resumed. Some indication of the concern caused to the party leadership by the continued influence of religion, and in particular by the influence of various sects, is afforded by a decree of the central committee of the CPSU dated July 7, 1954 and entitled, "Concerning Serious Errors in the Scientific-Atheistic Propaganda and Measures for Its Improvement."[38] Among other things this decree stated that many party organizations had neglected their duty of energetically conducting atheistic propaganda, and that as a result "the church and various religious sects have significantly increased their activity, have strengthened their cadres and, flexibly adapting themselves to contemporary circumstances, are energetically disseminating religious ideology among the backward strata of the

---

[37] *ibid.*, pp. 27-35.
[38] *Voprosy ideologicheskoi raboty*, Moscow, 1961, pp. 61-65.

population." The decree went on to charge that churches were devoting particular attention to women and the youth and that they were utilizing choruses and orchestras in order to increase their attractiveness. They were at the same time engaging in the dissemination of religious literature and conducting missionary activities. This decree and similar evidence in official Soviet publications indicate the continued existence of groups, drawn largely from the peasantry, both Russian and non-Russian, and in particular the Turkic-speaking peasantry of central Asia, with its Moslem religion and cultural heritage, which have not assimilated the official Marxist-Leninist ideology and which to some degree at least are capable of resisting the party's pressures toward cultural assimilation, as manifested, in the case especially of the Kazakhs, Turkmen, Uzbeks, and others, by "survivals of feudalism," in attitudes toward women, refusal to intermarry with Slavs, and the like.

Legitimate party-organized and party-controlled organizations exist in the Soviet Union to guide the activities of various occupational and professional groups. The highest-ranking and best paid scientists and scholars belong to the Academy of Sciences of the USSR, familiarly called the "big academy" to distinguish it from such lesser though important bodies as the Academy of Pedagogical Sciences, the Agricultural Academy, and others. Through the Union of Soviet Writers, writers are brought within the framework of the party's system of social mobilization. But at the same time, and particularly since the death of Stalin, this organization to some degree at least furnishes the writers with a channel for the defense of their group aspirations and interests. Similarly there are organizations of painters, composers, journalists, and practitioners of other occupations. The most numerous and powerful skill groups, such as industrial managers or military officers, are not organized in professional unions. However, cognizance is taken of the functional roles and sense of identity of such groups in a number of ways. The Central Committee of the CPSU has normally had special sections for science, for schools, and for military affairs, for example, and there is a special system of party organizations for the armed forces separate from the regular system of territorial party organizations. Then too the managerial elite, the military, the scientists and other skill groups are in a sense represented in the CPSU Central Committee, along with officials of the party apparatus, who have always been the most numerous element in the membership of the Central Committee. It should also be kept in mind that since the early 1930's managers, professionals, and other members of the intelligentsia have been represented in the Communist Party as a whole to a degree far out of proportion to their percentage of the total Soviet population. Conquest estimates that about a third of the total party membership consists of "members of the Party who have directed the main branches of Soviet industry, the planning centers and that large section of the State apparatus devoted to economic matters (in effect practically the whole State apparatus except for the administrative machinery, foreign affairs, and the armed forces."[39] Allowing for representation within the party of other intelligentsia elements, it is clear that the CPSU is far from being a "proletarian" party, although Khrushchev, in an effort to reduce intelligentsia domination, pushed a vigorous policy of including an increasing percentage of factory workers and collective farm peasants among new recruits to the party. In 1960, 43.1 per cent of new members were manual workers and 21.7 per cent were collective farmers, compared with 30.4 per cent workers and 21.3 per cent farmers in 1955. However, as Harry Schwartz noted in an already-cited report in the *New York Times* for February 2, 1961, 48 per cent of party members as of 1960 were "white-collar employees."

In completing this brief inventory of occupational and social groups which receive various forms of recognition of their identity and interests in the Soviet polity, we should mention the fact that both wage-earning workers and salaried employees are organized in the All-Union Central Council of Trade Unions (VTSPS), a mammoth system of industrial unions. However, there are different provisions for vacations and so forth for various social groups. As is well known, neither the VTSPS nor its affiliates are permitted to engage in what in the West would be regarded as free collective bargaining. The Soviet doctrine that in the Soviet Union there are no class conflicts implies that labor strikes are unnecessary. In any case, with the exception of sporadic, *ad hoc* manifestations of labor unrest, whatever representation is granted in the Soviet system to the interests of labor is channeled through the party-controlled VTSPS, headed in 1964 by V. Grishin, a member of the CPSU presidium. Unions—as well as the already mentioned organizations for the elite professions, such as artists—seek to organize the leisure-time activities of their members in clubs, "palaces of culture," et cetera. The spirit in which the di-

[39] Conquest, *Power and Policy*, pp. 46-47.

rectors of these facilities are expected to approach this task is suggested in an article on a VTSPS conference on workers' clubs. It pointed out that the mere "killing of time" had nothing in common with "the Communist way of life," in which leisure was "not a passive but an active factor in the upbringing of the new man."[40] The preface to a book on the functions of clubs for navy personnel, to mention another example, pertaining to an almost unexplored aspect of Soviet life, states that organized leisure contributes to success in military and political training.[41]

In official mythology the industrial worker is the leading class of Soviet society. Obviously there is a wide gulf between myth and reality as perceived by non-Communist foreigners at least. Does this gulf exist also in the mind of the Soviet worker? Much in Soviet policies, including secrecy practices designed to shield Soviet workers from subversive influences, indicates that it does. However, it would probably be a serious error to imagine that the Soviet factory, railroad, or construction worker is seething with discontent. The Soviet factory and trade union have achieved some success in their prescribed function as "schools of communism." Certainly the worker in the Soviet Union feels a sense of superiority to the farmer and perhaps derives satisfaction from it. Also, particularly in the case of the highest-paid, skilled categories—Soviet wages, based on a complicated piece-rate system, are highly differentiated—he is better off materially than lower-level members of the intelligentsia, not to mention clerical workers. In many respects indeed the pattern of distribution of relative material values resembles that in other industrial countries, and it is perhaps not idle speculation to assume a certain similarity also of attitude patterns, stratum by stratum.

However, many burdens and frustrations, unknown since the early, deprivational stages of industrialization in the West, have long beset the Soviet worker. He is not, for example, allowed to strike. When this writer raised the question of the rights of labor in a conversation with a *Pravda* editor in 1956, the latter angrily shouted, "Are you advocating that workers strike against the state?" The worker's housing, now being rather rapidly improved, is and long has been of wretched quality. His general standard of living, unless he belongs to the minority of the highly skilled, remains so low that Maurice Hindus writing in 1961 reported that the average Soviet

---

[40] *Komsomolskaya Pravda*, December 2, 1960, p. 2.
[41] *Klub voinskoi chasti*, Moscow, 1961, p. 5.

worker could not support his family without the assistance of a working wife. To some degree, this situation reflects the growing Soviet aspiration for a living standard of comfort and gadgetry. Despite the myth of the proletariat, his social status is far lower than that of the "educated" class, as Soviet workers themselves often call members of the bureaucratic and professional categories. It is striking that relatively few factory bench workers are included in the membership of Soviet "delegations" sent abroad or among the parties of Soviet tourists who travel now in Africa, Europe, Asia, and even in the United States. This illustration perhaps symbolizes the relatively modest status of the worker in the workers' state. Khrushchev, however, instituted measures to elevate the status and improve the material situation of Soviet workers, and on the whole it appears that they have had the effect of reducing discontent and arousing hope. The latter may in the future present the problem of how far to go in devoting scarce resources to satisfying what the Soviet leadership and press frequently admit, and even boast, are the increasing demands of the Soviet working class.

The Soviet system makes no formal provision for workers or other elements of the population in their capacity as consumers to articulate their interests or to lobby in support of such interests. However, it is not unreasonable to suppose that to some degree the party, even in the Stalin era, was guided in its economic policy by realization that if consumption levels were pushed too low the health and the morale of consumers would suffer and discontent might become troublesome. Most foreign observers who have written reports on Soviet attitudes appear to agree that there is, despite post-Stalin reforms, considerable discontent regarding living standards. It is interesting in this connection that when in June 1962 prices charged in government stores for meat and butter—the latter, incidentally, often unobtainable—were raised 30 per cent and 25 per cent, respectively, the official announcement of this unwelcome news, by implication at least, blamed the increases on the necessity for the Soviet Union to hold its own in the international arms race.[42] The above decree, besides thus seeking to deflect discontent outward, revealed, in its disclosure that prices paid to collective farmers for meat were to be substantially increased, concern about peasant attitudes.

---

[42] Perceptive comment on this action was contained in an article by Victor Zorza, in *Manchester Guardian Weekly*, June 7, 1962. For the decree announcing it, see *Kommunist*, No. 8, May 1962, pp. 3-9.

Lest the impression be created that Soviet post-Stalin "consumerism" represents a step toward early development of the mature mass-consumption economy, it should be noted that heavy emphasis is placed in Soviet policy statements on communal or collective rather than individual use of major appliances, for example, and even in the areas of clothing and footwear frills are frowned upon. Unlike in Japan, where the automobile industry is beginning to boom, Soviet policy thus far excludes production of passenger cars for mass consumption. As Ralph Nader indicated perceptively in the *Christian Science Monitor* for July 19, 1962, the Soviet government is acutely aware of the potentially unsettling consequences for the present still rather austere Soviet style of life. Nevertheless even the modest Khrushchevian moves toward a more consumer-oriented economy may have consequences of ultimate political significance.

An increased supply of consumer goods permits a certain freedom of choice to purchasers. It whets appetites. It makes more difficult rule by coercion, for the idea develops that superior effort is to be rewarded materially, whereas under Stalin emphasis was more upon punishment for failure than reward for success. Moreover increasing the supplies of consumer goods creates problems of marketing which put an increasing premium upon managerial administrative skills and perhaps reinforce a bit the general tendency in Soviet society toward elevation of the functional autonomy of economic administrators.

The largest single segment of the population, the farmers, is also the most disadvantaged with respect to representation in the party and government and with respect to channels by which its grievances and aspirations may be brought to the attention of the party leaders. Collective farmers do not belong to unions and of course have no equivalent of the kinds of organizations through which farmers in the United States, for example, can bring pressure to bear upon legislators. However, there is little doubt that the moods of the collective farmers are kept under close observation through the rural party organizations, the Ministry of Agriculture, and the network of informers of the secret police. In spite of its exceptional poverty of organizational resources—exceptional even by Soviet standards—the collective farm peasantry has proved to be one of the most difficult social forces for the party to control. Indeed it could be argued that the peasants and the creative writers are the two social groups which have offered the most effective resistance to the party's efforts at coordination and control.[43]

Soviet industrialization, and the penetration of the village by motion pictures, radio, television—and of course the role of the schoolteacher as link between the industrializing city and the changing village—have already wrought a substantial transformation of peasant ways of life and thought. In his recent book, *House Without a Roof*, published in 1961, that seasoned observer of Russian peasant society Maurice Hindus quotes a peasant girl asking, "Why should we workers on the land be different from girls who work in factories?" But Hindus also points out that what Khrushchev in a 1959 speech referred to as "kulak psychology," namely the desire for individual enrichment, remains a source of worry to the Kremlin.

Hindus and, more emphatically, Nicholas Vakar in the perceptive study *The Taproot of Soviet Society* (1962), point to the surviving element of rusticity in Russian peasant culture, the heritage which in Vakar's opinion exercised a preponderant influence on the development of Soviet culture as a whole, which is even today being only gradually overcome. Despite the powerful impact of industrialization, peasants in the Soviet Union clearly differ culturally from city workers and in particular from city bureaucrats, administrators, and professionals, to a far greater degree than American farmers differ from the urban population of the United States. Rural-urban differences are compounded by ethnic factors. The Uzbek or Kazakh peasant—the latter not remote in time from a pastoral economy—or even the peasant of Armenia or Georgia probably speak limited Russian with a strong accent. Their urban compatriots, however, apparently strive for assimilation into the dominant Russian Soviet culture, although, it should be noted, there are authorities, such as Richard Pipes, who have expressed the view that the assimilation of the Central Asian intelligentsia, for example, into the Russian Soviet pattern is superficial, and that in fact separate and in some ways anti-Russian national consciousness has actually increased among the Central Asian Turkic peoples as a result of Sovietization. This point is mentioned here in part to draw attention to the fragmentation—ethnic, status-wise, and in other ways—of the various groups in Soviet society which in one way or another offer resistance to the mobilizational and control program of the CPSU.

[43] On this point, see Conquest, *Power and Policy*, pp. 18, 22-24, 82-83 and Chap. VI.

Soviet writers, in their interactions with the party leadership, have probably come closer than any professional, occupational, or other group to operating as a conscious interest group. For this reason, and because such a relative abundance of materials is available on the writers, it should be useful to survey party-literary relationships in the post-Stalin period.[44] There are considerable differences of emphasis and opinion among Western students of the situation and significance of the writers in post-Stalin Soviet society. There seems, however, to be general agreement that the degree of freedom enjoyed by Soviet writers today, even though it is contained within controls exercised by the Kremlin, is heartening. Indeed even the limited freedom and the level of personal security enjoyed by Soviet writers and by other categories of intellectuals today would have been unthinkable under Stalin. In his effort to rejuvenate Soviet society and to restore true "Leninism" Khrushchev needed the assistance of writers in exposing such weaknesses and abuses in Soviet life as the routinism and passivity of party and government bureaucrats, suppression by the bureaucracy of creative initiative on the part of younger cadres and, in general, those aspects of Stalinism which Khrushchev chose to attack in his famous "secret speech" of February 1956.

Some of the bolder spirits among Soviet intellectuals were natural allies of Khrushchev as a reformer. On the other hand, although the available evidence indicates that the vast majority of even the most critical Soviet intellectuals desire improvement within the existing Soviet system—with particular reference of course to those aspects of the system that affect them most directly—rather than its transformation into capitalist democracy, or socialism of the type advocated, for example, by the British Labor Party, their demands exceed those considered legitimate by the party leadership. For one thing, at least some of the Soviet writers have demanded full professional autonomy. But if writers were to be granted the right to produce as they saw fit, the concept of the "leading role" of the party would of

---

[44] On this subject, see, for example, Max Hayward, "The Thaw and the Writers," pp. 111-121 of Richard Pipes, ed. *The Russian Intelligentsia*, New York, 1961; Ronald Hingley, "Hards and Softs in Soviet Literature," *The New Leader*, May 14, 1962, pp. 24-26; Priscilla Johnson, "New Heretics in Soviet Writing," *Saturday Review*, May 5, 1962, pp. 8-11; Hugh McLean and Walter N. Vickery, *The Year of Protest 1956*, New York, 1961. This last is an anthology of Soviet "protest" writing, with an introduction and notes by McLean and Vickery. The most comprehensive and systematic study of the political significance of literature in the Soviet Union is Harold Swayze's important study, *Political Control of Literature in the USSR*, Cambridge, Mass., 1962.

course be challenged. Perhaps even more fundamental has been the tendency of some writers, such as Vladimir Dudintsev in his *Not by Bread Alone*, to criticize the morality of Communist rule, at least as it prevailed under Stalin, with the implication that reforms far more fundamental than any that Khrushchev has apparently considered either desirable or possible were necessary. As McLean and Vickery point out, Dudintsev's novel created a sensation, and public interest in the discussion of it at a meeting of the Moscow Writers Union in October 1956 was enormous. In a courageous speech, only partly reported in the Soviet Union, the respected Soviet writer and critic Konstantin Paustovski attacked the new Soviet "bourgeoisie," as Paustovski called the bureaucrats, symbolized by Dudintsev's character, Drozdov, who, he declared, "dare to claim the right to represent the people—without the people's consent." Incidentally, Paustovski also ridiculed the provincialism and chauvinism of many of the Soviet officials selected as members of Soviet delegations sent abroad.[45] In late 1956 and 1957 the party leadership curbed the rebellious writers. Fundamental criticism of the kind presented by Dudintsev and a number of other writers, particularly in the two issues of the collection *Literary Moscow*, disappeared for a time from the Soviet printed page. However, such events as the publication in 1961 of Evgeni Evtushenko's poem, "Babyi Yar," attacking Soviet anti-Semitism, called the attention of the world to the fact that the literary ferment in Soviet Russia was continuing. Evtushenko had been expelled from the *Komsomol* in 1957 following the appearance of one of his poems in *Literary Moscow*, but in spite of this fact he was permitted to continue publication.[46] Later he was readmitted to the *Komsomol*.

Also Evtushenko was permitted to travel widely in Western Europe and the United States. This fact of course raised the suspicion that the Kremlin was exploiting, for foreign propaganda purposes, the modicum of freedom that it had granted to Soviet writers. However there was more to the matter than that, as the cancellation of Evtushenko's projected trip to America in 1963, together with other events, was to demonstrate. Aleksandr Tvardovski, editor of *Novy Mir*, one of the organs of the Union of Soviet writers and an alternate member of the CPSU Central Committee, delivered a speech

---

[45] McLean and Vickery, *op.cit.*, p. 159. Full text of Paustovski's speech on pp. 155-159.
[46] Conquest, *Power and Policy*, p. 81.

to the Twenty-second Party Congress in which he proclaimed that the duty of a writer was not to "uplift" his readers but to tell them "the full truth about life." This was one of a number of indications that the party leadership was still disposed to allow the writers considerable latitude and to permit the continued existence of what Ronald Hingley has described as "a state of officially tolerated feud" between the more liberal and the more orthodox Soviet writers.[47] Interestingly, Kozlov, in his 1962 article in *Kommunist*, declared that the party recognized the right of artists to exercise "individuality" (*individualnost*).

By late 1962 unorthodox tendencies had manifested themselves in Soviet literature, and other arts also, to such a degree that the Kremlin once again felt it necessary to sound a retreat. Following such events as publication of Alexander Solzhenitsyn's *One Day in the Life of Ivan Denisovich*, in *Novy Mir*, many Soviet creative intellectuals experienced what soon proved to be a premature sense of release from the fetters of rigid ideological controls. *One Day*, for the first time in the pages of the Soviet press, told at least part of the truth about Stalin's labor camps. Its appearance signaled receipt by Soviet publishing houses of a flood of similarly accusatory manuscripts.

A few months later, in February and March 1963, Evtushenko published his controversial "Autobiography" in the French weekly *L'Express*. Although Evtushenko was to claim that his views had been distorted by the editors of *L'Express*, the violent attacks on him in the Soviet press and by Khrushchev personally probably resulted not so much from what he said as from the time and source of their publication. Evtushenko had once too often perhaps assumed the role of spokesman for Khrushchev's "liberal" interpretation of Soviet communism, forgetting that an essential aspect of Khrushchev's policy consisted in a judicious balance between the "progress" extolled by Evtushenko and the "neo-Stalinism" which he had so frequently denounced.

Khrushchev's portentous speech of March 8, 1963 reiterated the CPSU's firm intention of forcing Soviet writers and artists to conform to the canons of socialist realism as interpreted by the party. However, as of midsummer of 1963 the firm line laid down in this speech had been only partially implemented in terms of administrative measures. The situation of Soviet writers had clearly deteriorated,

---

[47] Hingley, *op.cit.*, p. 24.

but it was uncertain whether the party was prepared to proceed ruthlessly to enforce conformity upon non-conformists, by terror if necessary. The fall of Khrushchev was not followed by any early or significant change in the situation of Soviet writers. As in other fields the new leadership pursued a cautious, groping policy, combining somewhat disturbing demands for orthodoxy—as in the *Pravda* editorial of November 22, 1964, criticizing the persistence of "group attitudes" among some writers—with renewal of permission to Evtushenko and other popular poets to give public readings of their verses.

In all probability the Soviet leaders are confident that the already somewhat aging "angry young men" of Soviet literature—the Evtushenkos, Voznesenskis, Aksenovs, and others—could be tamed or if necessary silenced without arousing dangerous discontent or doing irreparable harm to the morale of the Soviet creative *intelligentsiya*. As for the future, the regime apparently plans to rely upon improved training and screening devices to produce writers imbued both with ideological zeal and professional skill. There is much talk of the necessity of work experience and of a knowledge of "life" for the oncoming generation of writers. Only time will tell whether the products of such supervision will be capable of producing works of creative imagination and not mere fictionalized propaganda, and whether their output will satisfy Soviet readers.

Soviet writers, especially since the death of Stalin, have presented a very broad spectrum of findings, judgments, and demands. It seems almost presumptuous to attempt to summarize them here. However, there is value perhaps in identifying three literary tendencies which, judging partly by official criticism of them, have political significance. These might be characterized as the subjective, the objective, and the expressly political—though in the case of the last named we have in mind literary works in which political criticism is far more indirect than direct or overt.

For a long time some Soviet writers such as the poetess Anna Akhmatova, condemned by Andrei Zhdanov in 1946 for boudoir "decadence" and "eroticism," have sought to express in their art their own personal emotions and their individual vision of the meaning of life. This tendency has normally been opposed, even repressed, apparently because the party has considered that "lyricism," romanticism, and other "subjective" attitudes tended to distract attention from official objectives and to weaken morale by encouraging escapism of various kinds.

On the other hand realism, other than the officially approved "socialist realism," which is actually a form of didacticism, has also been frowned upon. The chief target of the savage official criticism of the Leningrad writers in 1946 was the satirist Zoshchenko, partly because he dared openly to present the seamy side of Soviet reality. This was also one of the main factors in the criticism leveled by Khrushchev himself against some Soviet writers in 1957 and later.

What we call political criticism consists largely in presenting in an unfavorable light party officials, factory directors, and other characters symbolizing the Soviet elite, or even the total Soviet political and social order. Even the boldest Soviet writers such as Dudintsev have made clear that they were not attacking what they conceived to be the essential values of Marxism-Leninism. Only Boris Pasternak, in his *Dr. Zhivago*, went so far as to openly reject the bolshevik revolution and its works, and that undoubtedly was the reason for the fury in the Kremlin when Pasternak was awarded the Nobel prize for literature in 1958.

However, in some ways a professedly loyal believer such as Dudintsev presents more troublesome problems than a Pasternak. In a sense what Dudintsev did was to take at face value the promises made by Khrushchev that the Leninist gospel was to be realized in practice. The utopianism inherent in this sort of approach to life appeals to the more idealistic Soviet readers, including some party members. Dudintsev of course was not permitted to continue to exercise what he conceived to be the writer's prerogative of interpreting on his own the relationship between Marxist doctrine and Soviet reality. The fate of Pasternak and of the far more representative writer Dudintsev —according to some reports he is today a thoroughly dejected man—indicates the limits beyond which social or philosophical criticism cannot be carried. Complete rejection of official aesthetic doctrine, as in the case of the young Jewish poet Brodski, can still be punished by imprisonment or exile.

Repression of both the subjective and objective tendencies referred to earlier has been less severe. The fact that such tendencies, and others not here discussed, have continued to manifest themselves attests to the existence of intellectual and emotional vitality in Soviet society. It may also point to a kind of alliance between some relatively flexible, tolerant elements in the CPSU and those writers who, though patriotic in the Soviet sense of the term, seek to reconcile official norms with the demands of artistic integrity. From the point of view of the most orthodox elements in the party, even innocuous realism or subjectivism are potentially dangerous, for the variety of perceptions they present challenges, as Swayze has noted, the validity of a unified, allegedly consistent, official ideology.

The writer and artist in Communist society have potential political significance far greater than those brought up in the American tradition might imagine. Khrushchev himself took cognizance of this fact after events in Hungary and Poland had called it forcefully to his attention. In Russia, as in other underdeveloped countries, literature was traditionally almost the only vehicle of free moral-political judgment. This tradition, though attenuated, survives in the Soviet Union. One may well ask why, if the role of the writer is potentially so dangerous, writers have been so favored as they have been by a regime under which successful writers enjoy the highest available standard of living—even Pasternak after his condemnation lived until his death in considerable luxury in the literary "colony" of Peredelkino, near Moscow. One reason appears to be that the Soviet leaders have always understood that only the arts could breathe into the political socialization and communication effort the emotional element necessary for effective impact. But if artists were to perform these functions, reasoned Khrushchev and his lieutenants, they must be rewarded not only materially but also with as much freedom as compatible with the ideological security of the community.

Some Soviet writers and artists have, whenever the Kremlin's mood and situation allowed, pressed to widen the corral in which they are confined. The post-Stalin literary ferment has probably been politically significant in helping to articulate the interests not only of writers but also of various segments of the Soviet intelligentsia as a whole. Unorthodox writing has tended somewhat to mitigate the fragmenting and isolative effects of Stalinist organizational and communications compartmentalization. It has perhaps been one of a number of forces tending to foster self-awareness of various social groups. Certainly the public or semi-public literary debates in Moscow, especially but not only in 1956, may have served as a kind of bridge linking together students, writers, critics, and others. Although not directly related to all this, other developments tending to "shake up" society and to stimulate critical thinking might also be appropriately mentioned in connection with literary trends. Among these developments might be Khrushchev's denunciation of aspects of Stalinism, increased contact with "bourgeois" foreigners, and perhaps contact and interaction between secondary school graduates of intelligentsia background, and genuine "proletarians" in the factories, as a perhaps unintended consequence of the post-Stalin educational reforms.

While much of Soviet literature continues to perform a propaganda function, the considerable degree of solidarity displayed by writers in the face of pressure exerted even by Khrushchev himself and the at least partial restoration of the traditional role of literature in Russia as the custodian of the conscience of society may have considerable significance for the future.[48] During trips to the Soviet Union in November 1958 and August 1959 I heard from two young and apparently patriotic Soviet citizens expressions of admiration for Paustovski and Dudintsev. It is not impossible that the post-Stalin dialogue between Soviet writers and the party may have initiated a process which, whatever its future vicissitudes may be, will contribute in the long run to a degree of liberalization of Soviet society which in comparison with contemporary conditions may be as surprising as the present situation is in comparison with the terroristic conformity which prevailed under Stalin.

We have less information on the situation and attitudes of Soviet painters, sculptors, architects, and composers than is available about writers. In general, creative artists, except for a minority of often politically powerful individuals such as the portraitist Gerasimov, who specialized in heroic canvases of the leader, or Alexander Fadeev, boss of Soviet literature from late 1946 until October 1953, suffered severe frustrations under Stalin, especially during those years, but have been able to function somewhat more freely since the dictator's death. Obviously the details are intricately complex and the distribution of frustrations uneven. For example, the regime's continued disapproval of "abstract art"—a term apparently applied to anything even faintly non-representational—renders the position of painters rather difficult. One hears of bold spirits who hang their unorthodox works behind curtains or even carpets while eking out a living by

---

[48] Khrushchev's interventions were recorded, for example, in the article under his name entitled "For a Close Tie of Literature and Art with the Life of the People," which brought together—presumably edited—statements he had made to various groups of writers, artists, and other creative intellectuals in *Kommunist*, No. 12, August 1957, and his other major article in *Kommunist*, No. 7, May 1961.

doing posters, and such. Architects, on the other hand, seem to have been granted greatly increased freedom in recent years.

Stresses and strains appear to be at a relatively low level between the party and physicists, chemists, mathematicians, and members of other disciplines least affected by the impact of Marxist-Leninist doctrine. However, there is evidence that some, perhaps many, leading Soviet natural scientists opposed basic features of changes in Soviet educational policy introduced in recent years, especially in the educational reforms of 1958. Those scientists apparently felt that requiring graduates of secondary schools to work for two years before entering higher educational institutions lessened dependence upon entrance examinations and other academic criteria, increased emphasis upon political criteria, and would lead to a lowering of the quality of Soviet scientific training.[49] To some degree scientists and educators were able to soften the impact of the reforms, partly by persuading Khrushchev to make them somewhat less drastic than he had originally intended, partly by finding loopholes in the regulations actually put into effect. Even social scientists—historians, legal scholars, biologists, and psychologists—have been allowed more freedom, including greatly increased access to foreign publications, than the bare minimum necessary for performing their functions which the Stalin regime grudgingly accorded them. However, the practitioners of intellectual crafts have been perhaps under even greater pressure than during the Stalin era to produce results deemed by the practical-minded Khrushchev to be of value in strengthening the Soviet economy. It is interesting in this connection that Khrushchev in 1957 complained that among Soviet economists and philosophers there were "people removed from life, from the practice of communist construction."[50] In his address to the Twenty-first Extraordinary Party Congress Khrushchev said among other things that it was "the duty of our economists, philosophers, and historians to study deeply the laws governing the transition from socialism to communism, to study the experience of economic and cultural development, to help train the working people in a communist spirit." Scholars in the social sciences, he continued, "face the task of creatively generalizing and giving bold theoretical solutions of new problems raised by life...." However, true to the tradition of Soviet Marxism,

---

[49] Some indication, in veiled form, of such sentiments is given, for example, in the article by a high-level Soviet educational administrator, V. Stoletov, in *Kommunist*, No. 16, November 1958.

[50] *Kommunist*, No. 12, 1957, p. 17.

with its mixture of pragmatism and ritualistic orthodoxy, Khrushchev added that it was necessary to "expose bourgeois ideology, to fight for the purity of Marxist-Leninist theory."[51]

As David Burg has pointed out, the Soviet intelligentsia, despite some improvement in its situation since the death of Stalin, continues to face the fundamental problem posed by Soviet totalitarianism.[52] Emphasizing the continued supremacy in the Soviet system of the party bureaucracy, Burg notes that "The other members of the Soviet elite have neither political nor personal rights. They do not participate in decisions affecting their country's fate and, further, they do not even have command over their own lives."[53] To be sure, high-ranking natural scientists, rewarded for their efforts with comfortable standards of living and a social status far above that enjoyed by their American counterparts, allowed considerable freedom of contact —albeit of a rather stiff and formal character, both in the Soviet Union and at scientific and professional meetings abroad with foreign colleagues—and provided with a relative abundance of equipment and the best working conditions the regime can arrange, have probably on the whole achieved a reasonably satisfactory *modus vivendi* with the regime. Indeed some competent foreign observers have expressed the view that the improved conditions of the post-Stalin period have created a mood of optimism and self-confidence among Soviet natural scientists.[54] Eugene Rabinowitch, in an article entitled "Soviet Science—A Survey" in *Problems of Communism* for March-April 1958, expressed the view that natural science was the freest sector of Soviet society. Compared to historians, economists, sociologists, and writers, natural scientists, in the opinion of Rabinowitch, were to a much greater degree "their own masters." Science, for this reason among others, had great attractiveness as a career for bright young people.

Rabinowitch, in this writer's opinion, was correct in his finding that Soviet natural scientists enjoy important advantages over other segments of the creative intelligentsia. However, that superior freedom is enjoyed to a lesser degree by biologists, for example, than by

---

[51] *Vneocherednoi XXI sezd Kommunisticheskoi partii sovetskogo soyuza*, Vol. I, Moscow, 1951, p. 61.
[52] David Burg, "Observations on Soviet University Students," in Pipes, *The Russian Intelligentsia*, pp. 80-100.
[53] *ibid.*, p. 84.
[54] Such is the conclusion of R. F. Marshak, in his article "Nature of the Soviet Scientific Challenge," in the *Bulletin of the Atomic Scientists*, January 1958.

physicists. In biology the baneful influence of the demagogic Russian "Burbank," Trofim D. Lysenko, which appeared to be terminated by Stalin's death, had been to a disturbing degree restored by Khrushchev. But fortunately his successors have apparently repudiated Lysenko and Soviet geneticists have been given the green light for full-scale development of their science.

Soviet scientists belong to what Soviet people sometimes refer to as the "learned world" (*ucheny mir*). As this term implies, theirs is indeed a highly esteemed world not only apart from that of the workers and peasants but also remote from the more sensual world of the arts and from other segments of the intelligentsia sub-society. So far as this writer has been able to learn, the style of life of Soviet scientists—this is probably true also of historians and social scientists—is, one might perhaps say, genteel, dedicated to their own work, but respectful also of "higher culture" in general, and somewhat ascetic. In a way it is "Victorian" and also somewhat escapist, at least so far as politics is concerned. Nevertheless one cannot help speculating as to whether or not scientists, particularly "military scientists," may not in the future indirectly exercise increasing influence on Soviet politics simply because of the vital nature of the functions they perform. The pinnacle of the Soviet "learned world" is of course the party-controlled but immensely respected membership of the Academy of Sciences of the USSR.

Foreign observers of the Soviet political scene who have at times expressed the view that either the industrial managers or the military commanders might wrest control of Soviet society from the party apparatus have thus far been proved in error. To be sure, during the period of Malenkov's ascendancy, roughly from the death of Stalin until the summer of 1954, and again for a few months in late 1956 and early 1957, it appeared that the "technocrats" were gaining in power relative to the more ideologically oriented members of the top party elite. Also the presence in the party presidium from February 1956 until his sudden dismissal in October 1957 of Marshal G. K. Zhukov represented a high-water mark thus far of professional military influence on Soviet high politics. However, the party apparatus, headed by Khrushchev, has successfully demonstrated its ability, at least for the present, to combine a degree of satisfaction of the professional interests of the managerial and military elites with maintenance of party control over these groups and the coordination of their activities with goals and policies formulated by the party leadership.

The communications media, as previously indicated, reasserted the doctrine of party supremacy, which was a major theme of the party program adopted in 1961. Persons whose careers had been made primarily in the party apparatus elbowed out of the presidium, the central committee, and other decision-making bodies of the CPSU at least some of the members of these organs whose lives had been spent mainly in the ministerial bureaucracy, particularly in its economic chains of command. Concurrently, in the party organizations of the constituent republics, party secretaries were moved into state posts, such as chairmen of the republic councils of ministers.[55]

Abolition in 1957 of most of the economic ministries and the setting up of the councils of national economy may well have pleased Soviet factory managers by relieving them of the necessity of clearing many decisions with superiors in Moscow. On the other hand this reform can be regarded as a blow directed by Khrushchev against powerful technocrats such as Pervukhin and Saburov, who apparently were associated with the Malenkov faction. In its elevation of the professional coordinators at the expense of a particular interest group the economic reform may have had consequences somewhat similar to those brought about in the field of literature by the downfall of Dmitri Shepilov, who, in Khrushchev's language—which became ritualistic by repetition—"joined" the anti-party group. Shepilov, apparently popular among liberal Soviet intellectuals during the period 1956-1957 when he was the party leader charged with supervision of the "ideological front," had received the nickname of "Dmitri *progressivny*" (Dmitri the progressive).[56] In his literary as in his economic and other policies Khrushchev made it clear that, while he desired reform and rejuvenation, he desired also that the agent of "democratization" should be the CPSU. This was the paradox of "Khrushchevism," this attempt to achieve decentralization *via* central control, to foster "legality" without limiting the powers of an essentially autocratic agency, to elicit initiative by exhortation?

The economic reform apparently had mixed consequences—as well as mixed motives, including not only the promotion of efficiency but also the strengthening of Khrushchev's power—but on balance

---
[55] See, for example, Radio Free Europe, "Background Information USSR," April 13, 1959.
[56] Meissner, *op.cit.*, p. 39.

it was probably welcomed by most members of the managerial elite. Certainly it was a step in the direction of increased autonomy for factory managers, for example, and toward efficiency of management. However, it had the potential disadvantage of encouraging economic regionalism, which the Kremlin was clearly not prepared to tolerate. Under date of April 24, 1958 the presidium of the Supreme Soviet of the Soviet Union issued a decree "Concerning Responsibility for the Non-fulfillment of Plans and Tasks in the Supplying of Products," the first paragraph of which reads as follows: "It is established that the non-fulfillment by directors and other leading personnel of enterprises, economic organizations, councils of national economy, ministries and departments, of plans and tasks in the supplying of products to other economic-administrative regions, or union republics, and also for the needs of the country as a whole, is a crude violation of state discipline and entails disciplinary, material, or criminal responsibility."[57] The Soviet economic press was at pains to emphasize that the new economic regions were to be regarded as arrangements to facilitate achievement of party objectives. Whatever measure of increased autonomy for Soviet industrial administrators resulted from the 1957 reform was at least partly curtailed by a later tightening of controls.

In 1961 and 1962, by a series of what Fainsod has characterized as "recentralizing" measures, the powers and functions of the councils of national economy were considerably reduced and the responsibilities of party organizations in the guidance of the national economy were correspondingly enhanced. The tendency toward recentralization received impetus particularly at the November 1962 plenum, which decreed that the number of councils of national economy was to be reduced from about 100 to some 40 and also set up a new Central Asian Bureau of the CPSU to control the new, expanded Central Asian National Economic Council. Most important in terms of reasserting party control over the economy and the managerial elite was the establishment at this plenum of the powerful new Party-State Control Committee, headed by Aleksandr N. Shelepin, one of the vigorous young men elevated to power by Khrushchev. Khrushchev in a speech reported in *Pravda* and other major Soviet newspapers for November 20, 1962 assigned to the new agency such functions as verifying the actual execution of the directives of the party and the government, assuring the utilization of "reserves" of economic re-

[57] *Vedomosti verkhovnogo soveta*, May 28, 1958, p. 499.

sources, and exposing inefficiency, malfeasance, and embezzlement on the part of administrators. Two years later, as indicated by his elevation to full presidium membership, Shelepin apparently played a substantial role in the conspiracy to oust Khrushchev.

Obviously the continued ability of the CPSU to perform its functions of coordination and mobilization, and indeed to maintain its very existence, depends upon the loyalty and enthusiasm of at least a considerable segment of Soviet youth. As with regard to almost every problem of interpreting the situation of the Soviet Union, the opinions of foreign observers, including participants in the U.S.-Soviet exchange of graduate students and young scholars which began in the fall of 1958, differ concerning the attitudes of Soviet students and other youths toward the regime. Some observers stress the patriotism of Soviet youth and its at least passive acceptance of official doctrine. Others, such as David Burg, himself a former Soviet student, perceive a considerable degree of resentment and conscious opposition to the Soviet system among at least the student youth (see note 52). There is certainly evidence of considerable concern regarding the mood of Soviet youth, particularly student youth, in the mind of Khrushchev and other ranking party leaders, although it is difficult to estimate the intensity of that concern. Numerous statements have been made by the leaders of the *Komsomol* regarding, for example, the dangers to Soviet youth inherent in excessively free contacts with foreign students and other young people. Among Khrushchev's own statements on this subject one of the most striking was his indication, at the Twenty-first Extraordinary Congress in 1959, of the belief that Soviet youths were more susceptible than their elders to corruption by alien influences just because they had never lived under a "capitalist" system. Khrushchev said that "we cannot overlook the possibility of bourgeois influence, and we are obligated to conduct a struggle against it" and in particular, he added, against the penetration of "alien views and customs" among the youth.[58] Khrushchev indicated that because of this situation it was important that the youth knew well the "heroic history of the communist party," and the "revolutionary traditions" of the working class.

A number of important policy decisions of the Khrushchev regime, including the educational reform and the intensification of internal party propaganda following the Central Committee's decree of Jan-

[58] *Vneocherednoi XXI sezd*, Vol. I, p. 58.

uary 9, 1960, were probably motivated at least in part by concern regarding the state of mind of Soviet youth.

As I have pointed out, the Soviet system makes at least some limited provision for open, legitimate representation of interest groups. It also, willy-nilly, permits a certain amount of covert bargaining and collusion, denounced infrequently and usually in extremely guarded language in the party press as "familialness" (*semeistvennost*, or *semeistvo*). As Rigby puts it, "it is true that the leadership does not wholly prevent parts of the machine 'deviating' to further ends generated of themselves: managers or workers individually or in collusion divert resources to enrich themselves or otherwise render their lives more comfortable; writers and artists depart from the prescribed subjects and methods to satisfy their own artistic impulses; party leaders engineer mediocre appointments to enhance their patronage opportunities, and so on." Rigby expresses the opinion that such deviations are "kept down to levels not seriously prejudicial to the achievement of at least the short-term goals set by the leaders."[59] A search of *Partiinaya zhizn* for the year 1960 turned up four fairly detailed criticisms of "familialness." The already cited article in the same publication for May 1962, demanding the perfection of "party, state, and social control," also contained examples of collusion regarded as detrimental to the carrying out of party policies. As Swayze notes, mutual-protection groups plague the regime in literature as well as in other spheres.

Let us now survey the processes of political socialization and elite recruitment employed by the CPSU to inculcate in the Soviet population beliefs and attitudes it considers necessary and desirable. Leninism might with considerable accuracy be described as a doctrine of the use of political communication and political socialization for the overthrow of capitalism and the transformation of societies in which the levers of power have been seized by Communists into "socialist," and eventually "communist," societies. To say this not to accept the pretensions of Leninists that they are really achieving the objectives and values associated by Marx and Engels with socialism. Indeed it is an assumption of this paper that the Soviet type of social revolution produces only a quasi-modern polity in which the citizen tends to become a participatory subject, an "eager robot."[60]

---

[59] Rigby, *Policy-making*, p. 3.
[60] The phrase "eager robot" was used by Ralph T. Fisher, Jr. in his article "The Soviet Model of the Ideal Youth," in Cyril E. Black, ed. *The Transformation of Russian Society*, Cambridge, Mass., 1961.

Soviet political socialization appears to seek the development of planned free will. The Soviet citizen must be obedient to the commands of his superiors, disciplined, efficient, and skilled, and at the same time highly "conscious" and responsible. His inspiration comes from Big Brother, but he alone must assume the responsibility and pay the penalty for moral transgressions or practical failures.[61]

"Communist morality," the inculcation of which is a major concern of the Soviet educational system and the mass media of communication, is both relativistic and absolutist. It is relativistic in that it rests upon Lenin's dictum that morality is determined by the interests of the party in leading the class struggle of the working people for the overthrow of capitalism and the building of socialism. It is absolutist in its insistence that until this struggle is successfully concluded every citizen, whether or not he is a member of the party or one of its affiliated mass organizations, is expected to dedicate himself whole-heartedly to the welfare of the community as defined by the party leadership. Soviet morality and the Soviet world outlook are also, both exceptionally rigid and exceptionally flexible. The party's goals can and do change, sometimes suddenly and without warning, but at any given time they are sacred and binding upon the citizenry. Soviet propaganda and agitation, Soviet education and cultural life are still guided by principles embodied in a frequently republished resolution adopted by the Tenth Party Congress in 1921, according to which: "The party of revolutionary Marxism radically rejects the search for forms of party organization or methods of work absolutely correct and suitable for all stages of the revolutionary process. On the contrary, the forms of organization and the methods of work are entirely determined by the peculiarities of the given, concrete historical situation and by the tasks that flow directly from this situation."[62]

To the non-Communist the attempt by means of overt propaganda as well as manipulation of the life situation of the individual to create the "new Soviet man" may appear to be a futile exercise, doomed to fail because it is contrary to "human nature," with its seemingly infinite capacity for resistance to and evasion of discipline and controls and for deviant behavior, ranging from escapist passivity to

---

[61] The development of the assumptions underlying the demands made upon the Soviet citizen in the Stalinist ethos, which has not been fundamentally altered since his death, was analyzed in the excellent study by Raymond A. Bauer, *The New Man in Soviet Psychology*, Cambridge, Mass., 1952.

[62] *KPSS v resolyutsiyakh i resheniyakh, 1898-1925*, 2 vols., Moscow, 1953.

anomic explosiveness. The Soviet leadership, by implication and to some extent explicitly, admits the tremendously difficult nature of the tasks it sets for itself in the fields of political socialization and communication. However, in spite of its willingness to resort to what it probably regards as tactical retreats, evidenced for example in granting to Soviet intellectuals somewhat greater artistic expression and scientific inquiry, and in increased access of Soviet citizens to "bourgeois" cultural products, the post-Stalin regime, particularly since 1959, has sought to expand and render more effective the system of communications built up by Stalin. While, more than ever, some official statements on the functions of political communication and socialization stress the link between propaganda and agitation on the one hand and efficiency, love of labor, and the industrial virtues generally on the other, the party also keeps alive—indeed has re-emphasized—the utopian goals inherent in "communism." It now proclaims that at least the "material-technical" prerequisites of communism can be attained in some twenty years.

Thus an unremitting effort is made to imbue the everyday life of the citizenry with a lofty sense of purpose. At the same time the party demands that propaganda and agitation be brought "closer to life," be specific, action oriented, and adapted to the predispositions of various age groups, nationalities, educational levels, and other segments of the audience to which it is directed.

Also the party demands that propaganda and agitation be increasingly "massive" and reach all segments of the population. The 10,000-word Central Committee decree of January 9, 1960 "On the Tasks of Party Propaganda in Present-Day Conditions" complained that "some groups of the population are in general" not reached by it.[63]

The January 9, 1960 decree was followed by a series of organizational measures designed to maximize both the intensity and the scope of "ideological work," which in recent years has often been characterized as "the central task of party and public organizations."[64]

[63] Text in Soviet newspapers for January 10, 1960, and in *Voprosy ideologicheskoi raboty*, pp. 144-163. Extensive comment on this decree is contained in Abraham Brumberg's article, "New Formula for Soviet Propaganda," *The New Leader*, August 15-22, 1960, pp. 16-20. See also recent Soviet statements, such as Khrushchev's assertion, at the Twenty-second Congress, quoted in *Pravda* editorial of December 30, 1961, entitled "For High Efficacy of Ideological Work," that ideological work is not an end in itself but an important means for the resolution of the basic tasks of the building of Communism. This editorial, among other things, hailed the establishment of "ideological commissions," in primary party organizations in Leningrad and Moscow, and urged further extension of that practice.

[64] *Voprosy ideologicheskoi raboty*, p. 4.

At a central committee conference held in September 1960 Leonid F. Ilichev, then head of the central committee agitation and propaganda sector for the non-Russian republics, and now a secretary of the central committee, declared that the need to step up ideological work derived "from the present-day domestic and international situation."[65]

Ilichev's guarded indications, at the above conference, of the motives for the redoubled Soviet political communication effort of the last two or three years should probably be viewed in the context of the Khrushchevian foreign policy of "peaceful co-existence," to which Ilichev enthusiastically referred. The partial reopening of Russia necessitated by such features of this policy as expansion of "cultural relations" with, for example, the United States heightened the risks of subversion of Soviet citizens by "bourgeois" ideas. The Kremlin prescribed intensified propaganda as the main antidote.

Moreover "peaceful competition" with capitalism, accompanied by and, one may hypothesize, requiring abandonment of Stalin's excessive use of terror as an instrument of social control inside the Soviet Union, spurred efforts to strengthen consensus in Soviet society as constraint receded in significance.

Also it was necessary to repair the damage done to the legitimacy of the Soviet system by widespread knowledge of Khrushchev's "secret speech" in 1956, with its revelations of Stalin's crimes, and by ferment among Soviet students and intellectuals concomitant with and partly caused by intellectual stirrings and political unrest in Poland and Hungary. Finally—among other possible factors—Khrushchev's belief that Soviet communism could be revitalized by a return to "Leninism," meaning to him "inner-party democracy," and priority of a mixture of material incentives and ideological appeals over naked violence, undoubtedly played a part in causing him, once his power had been effectively consolidated, to launch a new "saturation" propaganda campaign.

The term "saturation" is used advisedly. Reports by perceptive travelers to the Soviet Union in recent years indicate that a determined effort is being made to bring the word of Moscow to the most remote hamlet; one even hears of the establishment of "agitation points" near the feet of peaks of mountains in the Caucasus. Moreover such art forms as the drama, motion pictures, and even classical music are employed, with greater subtlety than in Stalin's era but

[65] *Pravda*, September 14, 1960.

also with a relentless simultaneity of presentation in the far reaches of the vast Soviet land.

Communications controls in the Soviet Union are of course associated with and reinforced by administrative, economic, legal, and police measures. The success of an individual in working his way through the Soviet bureaucratic maze and getting ahead in the Soviet world depends in large part upon his ability to satisfy his colleagues and superiors that he enthusiastically shares, or at least is capable of effectively disseminating, officially approved values. Far more than in the "capitalist" world, pessimism in this kind of society becomes, one might say, a socially punishable offense.

Soviet political communication is dedicated not merely to establishing positive identifications between the CPSU and the Soviet citizenry but also to excluding from the consciousness of its audience messages and stimuli, "facts" and attitudes, which might interfere with the achievement of the party's objectives. The protection of society against dangerous external influences—and against the "survivals of capitalism" within—requires among other things maintenance of a massive system of censorship.

Censorship in the Soviet Union is exercised partly through formal, institutional controls and partly through the impact of the over-all totalitarian polity on intellectual, cultural, and spiritual activity. While the direct controls are more formidable than those available, for example, to the tsarist regime, they are not as important as the more indirect ones. The latter, especially the constant pressure of the all-penetrating party and secret police networks, tend to create a climate of fear in which the individual learns to police his own communications behavior, to conform to what he believes are politically acceptable norms.

Formal censorship is exercised by Glavlit (Chief Administration for the Affairs of Literature and Publishing Houses) established in 1922. Its duties include, besides protection of military and economic secrets and prevention of pornography, prohibition of publication of materials which "agitate" against the Soviet authority. However, it does not exercise authority over some of the most important types of publication, including newspapers published by the CPSU. Editors of many publishing houses are deputized to act as representatives of Glavlit in determining the publishability of works submitted to them.[66]

[66] Alex Inkeles, *Public Opinion in Soviet Russia*, Cambridge, Mass., 1951, pp. 184-188.

Indirect censorship and supervision are effected by the party in its day-to-day operations by such devices as selection and training of editors and journalists and the issue of directives governing the content of newspapers and the work of agencies of communication and organizations of communicators.[67] Interesting in this connection is the "promise," in a message to the CPSU from the First All-Union Congress of Journalists in 1959, to "struggle against hostile ideology."[68] Suffice it to mention here a few striking illustrations. The Soviet Union is the only major power where Khrushchev's "secret speech" of 1956 has not been published. Although Boris Pasternak's novel *Dr. Zhivago* was awarded the Nobel Prize for literature in 1958, it was never published in the Soviet Union. A good many copies published abroad in Russian and in translations into other languages did, however, come into the hands of Soviet citizens. Khrushchev's talks to writers in 1957 and 1958 were published, presumably in bowdlerized form, only after long delay.

Despite some relaxation of controls over communication, access by Soviet citizens to information continues to be hampered by total or partial suppression, distortion, and delay. This whole pattern reinforces the effectiveness of Soviet political socialization but at the same time reveals its failure to achieve its objective of shaping citizens immune to subversive influence.

As sophisticated students of propaganda and other forms of attitude formation emphasize, the most difficult task confronting the analyst of these phenomena is appraisal of their impact. The authors of the most comprehensive study ever made of Soviet attitudes came to the conclusion that the Soviet system, at least after the death of Stalin, seemed "to enjoy the support of popular consensus."[69] The extensive Soviet literature on "ideological work" takes the position that although this effort has by no means fully achieved its objectives, it can achieve them in the future if it is effectively organized and energetically pursued. The rise of Khrushchev was, as indicated above, accompanied by increasing emphasis upon the value of propaganda and agitation not merely in the formation and dissemination of appropriate attitudes but also for the solution of immediate prac-

---

[67] *ibid.*, Chaps. 13 and 14. See also numerous items in *Voprosy ideologicheskoi raboty*, and such party handbooks as *Spravochnik partiinogo rabotnika*; see also *Programma po kursu zhurnalistiki*, published by Higher Party School, Moscow, 1958.
[68] *Izvestiya*, November 15, 1959, front page.
[69] Inkeles and Bauer, *The Soviet Citizen*, p. 397 (see also Chaps. X, XI and XII).

tical problems of administration and production. Incidentally, Khrushchev, in the section of his report to the Twentieth Congress of the CPSU in 1956 on "Problems of Ideological Work," used the word propaganda almost in the sense in which Soviet writers have traditionally used the term agitation. This blurring of the distinction between principles and "theory" on the one hand and everyday political communication on the other is perhaps characteristic of Khrushchev's pragmatism, but it also reflects the diminution of the significance of Marxism as a tool of critical analysis in the Soviet Union, and its transformation into something approaching a ritualistic vocabulary. This process has its roots in the revision of Marxism by Stalin and also by Lenin, which transformed it from a tool of analysis into an official ideology. One of the weaknesses of the Soviet political socialization process in all probability is the ever-increasing gulf between the Marxist-Leninist formulas used to describe reality, both inside the Soviet Union and in the "capitalist" world, and the perception of these realities which at least some Soviet citizens derive from personal experience and to a certain extent also from communications emanating from the non-Soviet world. Against these weaknesses, however, must be set the strengths derived from the association of Soviet political socialization and communication with rapid economic growth, scientific and technical achievement, the provision of welfare services, particularly in such fields as education and public health and, finally, pride in the commanding role played by the Soviet Union in world affairs.

The development of a massive, monopolistic, comprehensive, and penetrating mechanism of overt manifest political socialization and communication is perhaps the most conspicuous and most easily studied aspects of Soviet "ideological work." This machinery includes not merely the press, radio, television, and so on, but also what Inkeles calls "personal oral agitation."[70] Participation in an "agitation collective" is perhaps the most common type of activity by means of which rank-and-file party members perform the obligatory, unpaid, "voluntary" service required of all members of the CPSU. Although agitational activity, for example in factories during the lunch hour, is a constant, persistent everyday feature of Soviet life, it assumes especially massive proportions during campaigns for elections to the Supreme Soviet. At those times as many as three or four million party agitators, assisted by hundreds of thousands of "non-party bolsheviks,"

[70] Inkeles, *Public Opinion in Soviet Russia*, p. 123.

extol the virtues of nominees in these curious one-party elections. At the same time they take the occasion offered by these massive spectacles to once again assure Soviet citizens that their lives are incomparably happier and nobler and their political system vastly more democratic than that under which the victims of "capitalism" are for the present still forced to live. This type of political communication "is especially important in the Soviet Union, where the party has been attempting to introduce great numbers of new values on a large scale in a very short space of time."[71]

Another interesting feature of the coordinated Soviet political communications system is its massive employment of lectures. According to *Pravda* for October 22, 1961, members of the All-Union Society for the Dissemination of Political and Scientific Knowledge delivered about five million lectures in the first half of that year. For members of the Soviet intelligentsia, whether or not they belong to the party, the delivery of lectures in accordance with a centrally determined plan represents a community service roughly comparable at their social-status level to the agitational work performed by party members who are factory workers and office workers and by some non-party "activists" who presumably aspire to party membership. According to the *Pravda* item referred to above, the All-Union Society assists the party organizations "in the Communist upbringing of the working people." In a decree dated August 27, 1959 the Central Committee of the CPSU stated, *inter alia*, that although the majority of members of the All-Union Society—learned men, party and Soviet workers, representatives of the "village intelligentsia," and the like—were guided by patriotic motives, too many of them were still being paid for giving lectures, and in many of the Society's organizations, there were "narrow groups of lecturers, who have turned the giving of lectures into a source of regular income."[72]

The over-all structure and scope of the Soviet mass media are well enough known not to require description here.[73] However, a few quotations illustrating the spirit in which the Soviet communications elite approaches, or is supposed to approach, its tasks may be useful. N. G. Palgunov, in a pamphlet published when he was head of TASS (Telegraphic Agency of the Soviet Union), which supplies most of the foreign news available to Soviet citizens—in addition to its cables

[71] Inkeles, *loc.cit.*
[72] *Voprosy ideologicheskoi raboty*, pp. 138-139.
[73] In addition to Inkeles, *Public Opinion in Soviet Russia*, see, for example, Wilbur Schramm, *One Day in the World's Press*, Stanford, 1959.

there are the dispatches of a few special correspondents maintained by *Pravda, Izvestiya,* and a few other major press organs—defined news as "agitation by means of facts." Palgunov went on to say that of course not all events needed to be reported in the newspapers and that in any event the purpose of news was to "contribute to the solution by the Soviet people of the tasks of construction of communism confronting it."[74] Palgunov's statement is in the spirit of Lenin, who defined the press as "a collective organizer."

In 1959 the Central Committee criticized the foreign news coverage of *Izvestiya,* stating among other things that "in the exposition of international life and foreign policy the newspaper must constantly conduct propaganda for the foreign policy actions of the Soviet government, the struggle of the Soviet Union for peace and the relaxation of international tension, and must expose and uncover the imperialistic character of the foreign policy of the capitalist states and in particular of the United States of America." While not surprising, this directive from the top executive organ of the ruling Communist Party of the Soviet Union to the second most important newspaper in the country to do everything in its power to create a negative image of the United States is interesting and disturbing.[75] The collection of decrees from which the above quotation was taken also included severe criticism, dated April 5, 1958, of the Ministry of Culture of the Soviet Union and the publishing houses under its control for publishing too many translations of such foreign works as the Sherlock Holmes stories of Sir Arthur Conan Doyle. Along the same lines, another decree published in that volume expressed concern about the ideological perils to which Soviet seamen were subjected while voyaging abroad.

The inner workings, and particularly the effectiveness of the Soviet agencies for indirect or analogous political socialization, are exceedingly difficult to study. We know that after a brief period of somewhat eccentric but idealistic radicalism in the early 1920's, when some members of the party thought that not only the state and law but also the family and the school would begin immediately to "wither away," the regime turned with increasing effectiveness to a program of utilizing all of these major social institutions for purposes of control and mobilization. To supplement the socialization

[74] N. G. Palgunov, *Osnovy informatsii v gazete,* Moscow University Press, 1955, p. 35.
[75] *Voprosy ideologicheskoi raboty,* p. 277.

function of educational institutions and the family and, particularly during the period when much of the work of dismantling and transforming the old society into the new was still in its earlier stages, to take over some of the functions traditionally performed by school and family, the party established the *Komsomol*, the young pioneers, and the young Octobrists. The latter two organizations, which reach down into the age groups below fifteen, feed into the *Komsomol*, which in turn acts as a recruiting and screening device for the CPSU itself.

The findings available in scholarly studies indicate that all these institutions and organizations have performed the tasks assigned to them more or less satisfactorily from the point of view of the Kremlin. While in many subtle ways the family influenced the training of children in directions not fully congruent with the party's desires, Kent Geiger concluded his thorough investigation of the relationship between regime pressures and family resistance with the statement that "The family has on the whole not been a significant force in resisting the ideological indoctrination of Soviet young persons. While there is some evidence that politically tinged parent-youth conflict was a prominent feature in the prewar Soviet family, of equal or greater importance is the fact that Soviet parents so frequently minimized such conflict by their adaptive-conforming responses to the regime's ideology."[76]

Despite the shattering impact of the bolshevik revolution and forced-draft industrialization, the Soviet family, or rather its intelligentsia stratum, seems to have retained the capability of passing on to its children status advantages. Granick points to the big advantage of Soviet "white-collar children" over their working-class and peasant competitors in gaining access to the managerial elite.[77] Burg characterizes the Soviet elite as "hereditary" and states that "it is the children of the intelligentsia who virtually monopolize the better known universities and such distinguished institutions as the Aviation Institute and the Institute of Foreign Relations in Moscow."[78] In this connection it may be of interest to recall a conversation I had with a very high Soviet official in 1956. He, obviously a cultivated person, said that his wife and he both belonged to the same scientific profession and that their son was also being trained in that field. When I

---

[76] Inkeles and Geiger, *Soviet Society*, p. 557. See also Chaps. VIII and IX of Inkeles and Bauer, *The Soviet Citizen*.
[77] David Granick, *The Red Executive*, New York, 1960, Chap. 3.
[78] Burg, in *The Russian Intelligentsia*, pp. 80-81.

asked the Soviet official how children chose their professions in the Soviet Union, he replied with a smile, "Father decides." While much more work needs to be done on problems suggested by the foregoing, it seems clear that there still exists in the Soviet Union an "intelligentsia sub-culture" which apparently is not likely to lose its relative advantages in the foreseeable future. The continued existence of this social formation, its tendencies toward development of particularistic interests, and its proclivity for entertaining sentiments not congruent with bolshevik militancy present worrisome problems to the party leadership. Like the problem of student youth, discussed earlier, which in large measure is a product of the existence of this partly hereditary intellectual elite, this problem is causing concern regarding its attitudes and potential future divisive impact on Soviet society which can well be a motivating force behind some of Khrushchev's radical reforms. Those reforms are designed ultimately to curb, but are probably incapable—unless better financed than the Soviet Union can now afford—of seriously affecting the status advantages enjoyed by members of the intelligentsia and their children. When at the Twenty-first Extraordinary CPSU Congress in 1959 Khrushchev referred to one of his favorite educational projects, namely the establishment of boarding schools, he used language suggesting in the long run such a design. He said:

"We have to heighten the role of the state and society in the upbringing of children, intensify assistance to the family by the state and society. For this purpose it is planned to undertake extensive construction of boarding schools, nurseries and kindergartens. In 1965 boarding school enrollment will be not less than 2,500,000. The number of children in kindergartens will increase from 2,280,000 to 4,200,000 in the seven years. In the future it is planned to provide the possibility of raising all children in boarding schools, which will facilitate solution of the tasks of communist upbringing of the growing generation and of drawing fresh millions of women into the ranks of active builders of communist society."[79] Failure to achieve planned—and relatively modest—goals in this as in other Khrushchevian reforms indicates the difficulty of reversing the tendencies toward elitism in Soviet society.[80] It should be pointed out, however, that on the present scale at least the boarding school movement is

[79] *Vneocherednoi XXI sezd*, Vol. I, p. 60.
[80] On some aspects of this difficulty, insofar as it is manifested in educational problems, especially those connected with the boarding schools, see DeWitt, *Educational and Professional Employment*, pp. 97-103.

not so much a weapon to curb the elite as a device to prevent the spread of such evils as delinquency resulting from inadequate home care.

Of course another great purge of the Stalin type is not inconceivable as the regime's ultimate weapon for shaking up Soviet society, but it would so seriously damage the human resources upon which the success of the Soviet Union in the current international competition depends, and might also perhaps encounter such dangerous resistance, that it seems unlikely. It should be remembered that the present-day Soviet elite younger generation are in large part the children of workers, and to a certain extent even of peasants, whose social status was created by the regime itself in the industrialization process of the 1930's and 1940's. To a considerable degree indeed the current Soviet elite consists of former proletarians and their children. This and related facts may for some time prevent the development of acutely dangerous class antagonisms in the still highly mobile Soviet society.

Political indoctrination in the Soviet Union begins in the kindergarten and continues through the educational system and indeed throughout life. Although the Soviet school system is formally decentralized, integration of curriculum and teaching methods, and of course political training are achieved through government agencies and the party and its auxiliaries as well as through the activities of the Academy of Pedagogical Sciences, which dominates all Soviet research in such fields as educational psychology. By means of their often impressive work in the organization of hobby and study groups in dozens of fields, ranging from astronomy and geology, for example, through language studies, to chess, the young pioneers and the *Komsomol* perform, in addition to their strictly political socialization activities, vocational guidance and recreational functions which probably contribute greatly to the attachment of the growing generation to the Soviet social system.

There is in the Soviet Union an elaborate and differentiated system of institutions for the training of members of the Communist Party. The highest level of this system is represented by the Higher Party School in Moscow, which offers a four-year course, and by the Academy of Social Sciences, also in Moscow and also directly administered by the CPSU Central Committee. Below this level there are republic, *oblast*, inter-*oblast* and *raion* party schools. At the base of this pyramid is the *politshkola*, for training rank-and-file Communists with a limited educational background. When an ordinary party member of worker or peasant status completes the two-year program of the *politshkola* he then enters a *kruzhok*, or study circle, and after that is expected to continue to raise his level of political "consciousness" by "independent" study of prescribed "classics" of Marxism-Leninism. In addition there are "evening universities" of Marxism-Leninism designed to serve the needs primarily of party members who do not aspire to careers as members of the apparatus and who have a higher or at least a secondary education. For the political guidance of very high-ranking members of the intelligentsia, both party and non-party, there are also other institutions, including some very impressive ones, such as the House of Savants in Leningrad, which I visited in 1956.

A Central Committee decree of June 26, 1956, stated that during the preceding ten years more than 55,000 persons had been graduated from "local party schools" and that the Higher Party School had graduated 2,843. In addition more than 6,000 persons had been graduated by the correspondence section of the Higher Party School. The vast majority of these graduates, according to the decree, were occupied in "party and Soviet work." The above decree published the model study plans of the four-year inter-*oblast* party schools. These study plans were of two types. The one for "line" officials included, besides political subjects such as the history of the CPSU, dialectical and historical materialism, political economy, and the history of "the international labor and national liberation movement," a long list of technical subjects, including bookkeeping, as well as statistics and mathematics. The other study plan, for journalists, included the political subjects referred to above as well as journalism, "stylistics," and a few other professional specialties.[81] In keeping with the Khrushchevian emphasis on things pragmatic, the above decree denounced "dogmatism" in political training institutions and demanded that in the future greater attention be paid to concrete economic problems and to the organization of industry and agriculture. However, the decree also stipulated that students in both the "line" and journalistic faculties of the four-year party school would be required to pass "state examinations" in the history of the CPSU, dialectical and historical materialism, and political economy.

Anything like a full description, not to say analysis, of the Soviet system of specialized political training for party and government functionaries would require book-length treatment. Moreover in order to provide more than the most superficial impression of the

[81] *Spravochnik partiinogo rabotnika*, Moscow, 1957, pp. 410-415.

magnitude of the total Soviet program of political education it would be necessary to deal with many subjects scarcely touched upon in this paper, such as the system of examinations in political subjects required for entry into and for graduation from higher educational institutions and graduate schools. Elite recruitment procedure not only for members of the party apparatus but also for achievement of the higher education necessary for entry into the upper ranks of Soviet professional life includes examinations in political subjects. For example, all persons entering upon programs of graduate study must take competitive examinations in the history of the CPSU.[82] Thus one feature of the complicated maze through which the ambitious Soviet citizen must thread his way in seeking to raise his political or professional status is an upwardly graduated set of political training requirements.

It may be appropriate to conclude this essay with some speculation regarding the future development of Soviet political culture. The development of this system was shaped by the use of a revolutionary instrument, namely the CPSU, as the agency of over-all economic and political development. Has the party become an anachronism? Has it performed its functions, and fulfilled its purposes? Does it survive today as a kind of supercivil service, a "new class" of the powerful and privileged, or even a monolith in name only, concealing the reality of an increasingly differentiated pluralism?

Party leaders answer such questions with an indignant negative. It is, however, significant that they consider it necessary to discuss them at all. Frol R. Kozlov, for example, notes that "it is asked" if the "guiding role of the party must gradually become weaker."[83] Kozlov replies that "only a party, commanding a knowledge of the laws of social development, uniting in its rank the most advanced representatives of the people," etc., can lead the development of Communist society. This is of course a conventional answer. Perhaps more convincing is Kozlov's contention that the party's role must be maintained and even magnified to guide and coordinate the rapid economic growth still necessary in industry and agriculture and to provide the "centralized, planned leadership" which will prevent local initiative "from being transformed into sectionalism."[84] In any case, Kozlov

---

[82] *Aspirantura, spravochnik dlya postupayushchikh v aspiranturu i soiskatelei uchenykh stepenei*, Moscow, 1960, p. 15.

[83] Kozlov, *op.cit.*, p. 18.

[84] *ibid.*, p. 20.

underlines the Kremlin's determination that the role of the party as a "social organization of the higher type" will grow.

For the participatory subject culture to be transformed into a civic culture at least two changes would have to occur. First, the political monopoly of a self-selecting political elite would have to be replaced by a conception of citizenship in which, at least potentially and to a degree in practice, political influence would be available to all citizens, who would be free to choose and even to create channels of access to government. Second, the economic, professional, and other functional elites would have to achieve far more autonomy than they at present enjoy. How can all of this come to pass? It probably cannot at all in the foreseeable future, but significant progress toward greater diversity and freedom seems likely.

Three main lines of speculation are suggested. We can dispose very briefly of the possibility that the peasants, disaffected members of non-Russian nationalities, or other strata relatively unassimilated to the dominant political culture might sabotage or even overthrow the Soviet regime. Given the vested interest of the present elite in averting a socio-political cataclysm, continued urbanization and industrialization, widespread consensus regarding at least the defense of the country against external interference and, last but not least, the sheer power and determination of the CPSU cadres, the collapse, by violence or stagnation, of the present Soviet polity seems so unlikely as to be unworthy of serious consideration. If it did occur, it would in all probability lead not to the establishment of a more liberal regime but to a new form of totalitarianism.

What seems infinitely more likely than violent collapse is gradual evolution—with zigs and zags of course—toward a system in which functional, specialized elites, such as industrial managers, writers and other communicators, scientists, and others, will achieve a level of autonomy sufficient to substantially modify, if not the structure, at least the modes of operation of Soviet political institutions.

An area of limited functional autonomy existed even during the Stalin era, as indicated for example by the abolition of military commissars during the Soviet-Finnish war of 1939-1940 and again, after their re-institution, in 1942—balanced, to be sure, by partial continuation of their function in the party-control role exercised by the *zampolit*, or deputy commander for political affairs. This example illustrates the zig-zag pattern of what may be or may become a gradual evolution toward a measure of autonomous function for segments of an increasingly differentiated elite. Somewhat similarly, many of the demands voiced after Stalin's death by novelists, poets, dramatists, and critics for increased freedom of expression, interpretation, and technique had been manifested earlier, particularly during World War II, only to be suppressed, apparently permanently—at least to outward appearances—by the ideological reconversion of 1946-1953. One can draw both pessimistic and optimistic conclusions from such episodes. If they illustrate the persistence of demands for change in the direction of freedom and diversity, they also indicate continuity in the CPSU's ability to contain and control such demands though not to eliminate them.

On balance a cautiously positive perspective for the continued trend toward rationality and permissiveness and reduction of terror and crude violence in the Soviet polity seems warranted. Willy-nilly, the regime must permit managers, bureaucrats, scientists, and communicators to obtain the training and enjoy the conditions necessary for the efficient performance of their functions. These functions in turn are necessary for the achievement of the regime's domestic and foreign policy objectives. It seems almost certain that as the numbers, both absolute and relative to the total society, and concomitantly, the prestige of the Soviet skill groups grow, their influence will also increase. Important features of the contemporary international configuration tend to support the credibility of such a speculation. Current nuclear power competition puts a premium upon development of skills which foster the scientific ethos. At the same time, the imperatives of survival in the nuclear age foster caution regarding the use of violence.

Such trends as we perceive probably tend to strengthen the hand of the Soviet managerial, scientific, and artistic elites as against the power of the party functionaries, particularly the professional theoreticians, propagandists, and agitators. Insofar as the official ideology derives its strength from fear of an "imperialist threat," its influence may diminish with continued preservation of even the uneasy contemporary international "peace." But at the same time the probability, both in Moscow and in Washington, that a high level of military-scientific preparedness will be maintained seems to assure growth of the influence of scientists and others whose effective efforts are required in the process.

Other trends less closely related than those to which attention has, however casually, been directed seem to strengthen the supposition that the locus of power will continue to swing toward the managerial, technical, and artistic intelligentsia. Paradoxically, the success of the party in defeating the "class enemy" may in the very long run render superfluous or at least modify some of the functions of the party. In 1956 the dramatist Pogodin has one of his characters say that "we no longer have hostile classes," and, logically enough, ask, "Who is there to hate?"[85] If some day the full logical consequences of the line of reasoning suggested in Pogodin's ruminations are drawn, the bargaining position of Soviet writers vis-à-vis the party will be strengthened. Party control over the arts has rested in considerable measure on the conviction that art, like other forms of communication, is a weapon in the life and death struggle against the political enemy.

Closely related to the foregoing line of speculation is a third, concerned with changes in the norms and attitudes of the ruling CPSU which seem already to have begun and are likely to continue. To maintain control over the increasingly educated and culturally sophisticated society which it has in large measure created, the party finds it necessary, as indicated earlier, to equip its own cadres with both general and specialized education and training. These processes, extremely complicated in detail, perhaps have certain broad consequences which can be clearly perceived. An increasingly educated party, as part of an increasingly educated society, will be also an increasingly sophisticated and critical party. An increasingly differentiated party membership—reflecting interaction with the skill group it controls, but by which it is also influenced—will be more relativistic, perhaps more pluralistic than the present-day party.

The fall of Khrushchev occurred so recently that it is perhaps premature to evaluate its significance. Thus far it does not appear to involve a major change in policy lines, but rather to have reflected intense concern in the presidium and central committee regarding the harmful effects of Khrushchev's style of leadership. The new leadership seems to be even more pragmatic and production-oriented than was Khrushchev, and just as anxious to raise the Soviet levels of material life. It differs, however, in being more sober, realistic and conscious of the immensity of the economic and administrative difficulties confronting the party as it grapples with the problems of an increasingly complex society. This spirit of sobriety is reflected in criticism of Khrushchev for his alleged "hare-brained schemes" and

---

[85] Swayze, *Political Control of Literature*, p. 176.

his failure to heed either the lessons of experience or the advice of men of science, as, for example, in his insistence upon planting corn on the best Ukrainian winter wheat land.

The treatment of Khrushchev by his colleagues offers a few crumbs of comfort to those outside observers who hope for the development in Russia of a polity responsive to domestic and foreign opinions and capable of making public policy by discussion and analysis rather than on the basis of prejudice, caprice and coercion. Failure to accord to Khrushchev even the courtesy of mentioning his name in the spate of criticisms which followed his ouster was shabby. However, there are constructive developments. The transition was smooth and non-violent. Above all it marked the first occasion, apparently, in Russian history when a new political leadership was chosen by a consensual and relatively rational process—albeit a tiny oligarchy. And the content and tone of the criticism directed against Khrushchev by his successors are relatively mild in the Soviet context. In light of past experiences it seems unlikely that this latest Soviet collective leadership will long endure, and in particular that its present composition will remain unchanged for many months—indeed, within less than three months after the October *coup d'etat* four of the two dozen members of the top ruling bodies had been ousted.

However, the fact of greatest potential positive significance for the prospects of a "constructive" Soviet political development was the doctrine that even the highest party and state leaders must justify their eminence by deeds and must consult with and heed the opinions of their colleagues. This view, set forth in *Party Life*, No. 20, for October 1964, represented a logical development of Khrushchev's attempt, in the crisis of 1957, to base his regime on a consensus in the central committee and the presidium. It is true that he violated this principle and created around himself a new "cult of personality." However, he paved the way for his own defeat in the ongoing political struggle by failing to buttress his very unStalin-like "cult" with a personal terror machine. He may also have paved the way for a period of rather drab, painful, but in the end, constructive rule by technocratic Communists concerned with the efficient administration Russia so badly needs. Given good luck at home and abroad, such a period might lay the foundations for a gradual broadening of political participation, and for sounder, more orderly and more rational policy than the pseudo-Leninism of Khrushchev, now implicitly rejected as demagogic and potentially dangerous.

CHAPTER 12

COMPARATIVE POLITICAL CULTURE*

SIDNEY VERBA

THIS century has seen rapid changes in both the real world of politics and the study of politics. In the political world new nations appear suddenly at every turn and old ones change or disappear as fast. The new and changing nations face problems that challenge the imaginations of statesmen and the capacities of institutions. The needs and aspirations are many, and the tools available to meet them are barely adequate. And in the study of politics one can sense a parallel. New approaches, new methods, new theories proliferate on all sides, in many cases inspired by the rapid changes in the political world. The new politics—politics in new areas, politics of a new type—appear to require a new political science to understand them. And just as the demands of a changing political world strain the tools of the statesman, so do the intellectual problems of comprehension of these changes strain the tools of the scholar.

But though the world of politics and political science are both in periods of rapid change, in both there is continuity with the past. The problems of the new states are in some sense problems other states have faced in the past: how to create a stable political system; how to make such a system effective in meeting demands placed upon it; how to adapt to changing environments or to internal changes within a society. The problems may come faster and with more urgency, but they are not completely new ones. Nor, on the other hand, have they ceased to be problems in the older nations. They have been the abiding concern of the students of politics—both the "new" political scientists dealing with the new states and the older

---

*NOTE: This paper draws on some discussions by a group assembled at the Center for Advanced Study in the Behavioral Sciences by the Social Science Research Council's Committee on Comparative Politics during the summer of 1962. I am grateful to the members of the group: Gabriel Almond, Frederick Barghoorn, Leonard Binder, James Coleman, Alex Inkeles, Joseph LaPalombara, Daniel Lerner, Lucian Pye, Dankwart Rustow, Robert Scott, and Robert Ward. I am also grateful to Harry Eckstein for suggestions as to how to approach political culture. The author is grateful to the Center of International Studies of Princeton University and to the Center for Advanced Study in the Behavioral Sciences for providing the opportunity to prepare this paper.

students and philosophers of politics. Why do some states survive and others fail? How do nations change? From what kind of polity to what other kind? What crucial tasks face the statesman, and how should he be trained to meet them? How is democracy established, and what makes it survive? And what are the role and obligations of the ordinary citizen? Though the way in which the contemporary political scientist may attempt to answer these questions differs from the approach of earlier students of politics, the substantive concerns are abiding ones.

I. *The Political Culture Approach*

The authors of the papers in this volume have been concerned with these abiding problems. The approach used to these problems stresses the element of "political culture."[1] The political culture of a society consists of the system of empirical beliefs, expressive symbols, and values which defines the situation in which political action takes place. It provides the subjective orientation to politics. The political culture is of course but one aspect of politics. If one wanted a full picture of the process of politics in a nation one would have to consider many other aspects as well. We have focused on the cultural aspect for several reasons. For one thing, though political systems represent complex intertwinings of political culture with other aspects of the political system both formal and informal, it is difficult with the tools currently at hand to deal with the totality of political systems all at once. One is almost forced to look at one aspect or another. Second, we believe that the political culture of a society is a highly significant aspect of the political system.

There are many other aspects of the political system that could have been selected for close analysis. For a long time students of politics dealt with formal political institutions. If one wanted to explain why a political system survived or failed, why it was successful or unsuccessful, one looked at its constitution. How were laws passed? Was

---

[1] The term "political culture" is beginning to find currency in the political science literature. The first use of the term in roughly the way it is used in this volume (at least that I am aware of) is in Gabriel Almond, "Comparative Political Systems," *Journal of Politics*, Vol. 18, 1956. Another early use of the term is in Samuel Beer and Adam Ulam, eds. *Patterns of Government*, New York, Random House, 1958.

The use of the word "culture" is perhaps a bit unfortunate in this context. Surely few other words in the social sciences have a greater variety of uses. It is used here because it has some currency in the literature, and any substitute word would just introduce more confusion. Furthermore, as used in this essay, the term refers to a rather general approach to politics and some imprecision in its definition is probably not too crucial. This point will be discussed further below.

the system a presidential or a parliamentary one? Was there an independent judiciary? Of particular interest to those studying democratic systems were the structures of electoral systems. Did a nation have a single-member district electoral system or some form of proportional representation? Political scientists have since turned to other questions as well, particularly questions about what has been called the "infrastructure" of politics—those institutions not directly within the government that play a major role in political decisions. In particular political parties and interest groups have come under close scrutiny. Our interest in this volume was to look beyond the structures of politics to the beliefs that affect the ways in which people act within these political institutions.

This concentration upon political culture should not be taken to imply that other aspects of the political system are not important for the functioning of that system. They are both important and intimately related to the political culture. The political culture of a nation, for instance, derives from, among other things, the experiences that individuals have with the political process. One way to learn about political beliefs is to observe the ways in which political structures operate. These beliefs affect and are affected by the way in which the structures operate and there is a close circle of relationships between culture and structure. The justification for separating out the cultural aspect for attention is that it may facilitate the analysis of these relationships.

The study of political culture is not new. It would be both presumptuous and historically inaccurate to argue that the essays contained in this book or the works of other political scientists concerned with what we have called political culture deal with aspects of the political system that have previously been ignored. Writers on politics, particularly those who have tried to explain why the political system of a nation operated the way it did, have been aware of and commented upon the belief systems of the members of the nations about which they have written. Surely the works of Montesquieu, Tocqueville, and Bagehot represent contributions to the study of political culture, and one finds concern with such problems at least as far back as the Greeks. Nor is the interest in political culture a subject that we can claim to rediscover for contemporary political science. Many recent students of politics have focused upon the factors we consider to be important aspects of political culture.

These disclaimers about the political culture approach are needed because of an unfortunate tendency in the social sciences to oversell new concepts and to assume that the mere labeling of an old phenomenon with a new term represents a breakthrough in our understanding. The term "political culture" refers—as the essays in this book clearly suggest—to a very general phenomenon which can be approached from many points of view. The concept of political culture serves to focus our attention on an aspect of political life, and such a focus of attention is useful. The concept makes it easier for us to separate the cultural aspect of politics from other aspects (as well as the political culture from other forms of culture) and to subject it to more detailed and systematic analysis. The process of separating out the cultural aspects of politics puts us in a position to see more clearly the place they have within the political system. The term "political culture" ties our study of political beliefs to sociological and anthropological works on culture and focuses our attention on basic values, cognitions, and emotional commitments. It also focuses our attention on a subject that has been of major concern to the students of culture —the process by which such values, cognitions, and emotional commitments are learned. The study of political culture leads invariably to the study of political socialization, to the learning experiences by which a political culture is passed on from generation to generation and to the situations under which political cultures change. The study of political culture may also lead to a new perspective on the political history of a nation (discussed more fully below) by which one focuses on the ways in which basic political beliefs are affected by the memories of political events.

To focus one's attention on a significant aspect of political life is useful, but it is only the beginning of the analysis and explanation of political phenomena. What really is important is not that one deals with political culture, but how one deals with it and how it is used to further our understanding of politics. To say that political culture is important is not very informative; to say what aspects of political culture are determinants of what phenomena—what the significant political beliefs are, and how they are related to other aspects of politics—may be very important. The several essays in this book do not represent contributions to political science because they show that political culture is a helpful concept in understanding and explaining political change and modernization; rather they are contributions insofar as they isolate those aspects of political culture that are most relevant for problems of political change and show how they are relevant to those problems. In this concluding essay I shall try to do the same task on a more general level and without reference to any particular nation.

But before turning to the specific dimensions of political culture that appear to be of most use in understanding problems of political change, we shall consider the question of why this particular focus is important. What exactly is it that we focus upon when we use the term "political culture"? Political culture does not refer to the formal or informal structures of political interaction: to governments, political parties, pressure groups, or cliques. Nor does it refer to the pattern of interaction among political actors—who speaks to whom, who influences whom, who votes for whom. As we use the term "political culture" it refers to the system of beliefs about patterns of political interaction and political institutions. It refers not to what is happening in the world of politics, but what people believe about those happenings. And these beliefs can be of several kinds: they can be empirical beliefs about what the actual state of political life is; they can be beliefs as to the goals or values that ought to be pursued in political life; and these beliefs may have an important expressive or emotional dimension.[2]

Political culture forms an important link between the events of politics and the behavior of individuals in reaction to those events; for, although the political behavior of individuals and groups is of course affected by acts of government officials, wars, election campaigns, and the like, it is even more affected by the meanings that are assigned those events by observers. This is to say no more than that people respond to what they perceive of politics and how they interpret what they see.[3] From the cultural point of view, for

[2] The term "belief" is one that can cause almost as much trouble as "culture." It is used in this essay to refer not only to the cognitive aspects of thought—which will be referred to as "empirical beliefs"—but to the evaluative and expressive aspects as well. The specific thoughts that people have about politics involve no clear differentiation into their cognitive, evaluative, and expressive components, but usually involve a combination of all three. Furthermore, I use the term "belief" rather than "attitude" or "opinion" because I am interested in patterns of thought more deeply rooted and more general than the latter two terms imply.

[3] Though politics is often defined in terms of its relationship to violence and coercion (the state defined as the possessor of the monopoly of legitimate coercion, for instance), it is interesting how little of political importance involves the direct application of violence. One can of course affect a person's political behavior through the direct use of violence or coercion, in which case the beliefs about or interpretations of the violent act by the victim may be irrelevant. But violence plays a larger political role as a threat. Or, if violence is actually applied, what is of political

instance, we would look at political history not so much as a series of objective events but as a series of events that may be interpreted quite differently by different people and whose effects on future events depend upon this interpretation. The terms "meaning" and "interpretation," it should be stressed, are relational terms. They do not refer to what exists in the mind of the individual or to what happens in the outside world, but to the interaction between the two. And in this interaction it would be wrong to assume that either the previously held beliefs or the external events necessarily are dominant. An event will be interpreted in terms of previously held beliefs; but preconceptions can only go so far in affecting interpretation. (How far, indeed, may be a very important question and a very important source of differentiation among political cultures.)

Of course basic patterns of political belief affect not merely how individuals respond to external events. Since these basic belief systems consist of existential beliefs, general values that set the goals of behavior, norms that regulate the means used to achieve goals, as well as emotional attachments, these belief systems also affect when and in what ways individuals become involved in political life. Looked at this way, it can be seen that political culture represents a system of control vis-à-vis the system of political interactions.[4] Political culture regulates who talks to whom and who influences whom. It also regulates what is said in political contacts and the effects of these contacts. It regulates the ways in which formal institutions operate as well. A new constitution, for instance, will be perceived and evaluated in terms of the political culture of a people. When put into practice in one society it may look quite different from the same constitution instituted in another nation with another political culture. Similarly, political ideologies are affected by the cultural environment into which they are introduced. History is full of examples of constitutions that did not "take" as the constitution writers had hoped because their application was mediated through a particular political culture, and history is full of examples of the ways in which political ideologies have been adapted to fit the pre-existing culture of the nation into which they were introduced.

---

relevance is more often the effect of the violent act on those who learn of it. And the two latter uses of violence involve interpretations and beliefs.

[4] On the role of cultural systems as controllers of social systems see Talcott Parsons, "General Introduction" in Parsons *et al.*, *Theories of Society*, New York, The Free Press of Glencoe, 1961, Vol. I, p. 35.

CONCLUSION

POLITICAL BELIEFS

Political culture is very broadly defined in this essay. The term refers to all politically relevant orientations whether of a cognitive, evaluative, or expressive sort. It refers to the orientations of all the members of a political system; and it refers to orientations to all aspects of politics. This broad and rather loose definition is useful for this essay, one purpose of which is to direct attention to a general area of concern. And it is useful so long as political culture in the general sense is not used as an explanatory term in propositions about political systems. If political culture is so generally defined, it is of little use to say that the political culture of nation X explains why it has political structures of the form Y. Rather one must specify what aspects of political culture—what beliefs about what subjects—are the important elements for explaining the operation of political systems. In a later section of this essay I suggest some dimensions of political culture that seem particularly relevant for explanatory purposes, dimensions which will emphasize political beliefs of the most general sort. Thus the political-culture focus of this paper differs from that of many of the attitude studies that deal with rather specific political attitudes such as partisan affiliation, attitudes on international issues, and beliefs on specific issues of domestic policy. In contrast, in this paper I shall try to specify some of the more general aspects of political beliefs that seem particularly relevant for comparisons among nations that may differ radically in the specificities of their political situation. This is not to argue that specific political attitudes are not important; indeed they are much more reliable guides to political action than beliefs about politics in general. But the more general beliefs are important in giving over-all direction to political tendencies and in providing grounds for the justification of the attitudes on more specific political topics.

Thus the empirical beliefs we are interested in in this approach to political culture are the fundamental beliefs about the nature of political systems and about the nature of *other* political actors. In particular it is quite important to discover what political beliefs are—to borrow a term from Milton Rokeach—primitive beliefs. Primitive political beliefs are those so implicit and generally taken for granted that each individual holds them and believes all other individuals hold them. They are the fundamental and usually unstated assumptions or postulates about politics. In this sense they are unchallengeable since no opportunity exists to call them into question.[5] It may be, for instance, that one of the major characteristics of the transitional political cultures within developing nations and one of the major sources of their instability is the fact that there are few such unchallenged primitive political beliefs.

Similarly, in terms of the evaluative mode of orientation, we shall be concerned with the most general level of values—the guiding principles that set the general goals of a political system—rather than with the preferences for specific kinds of policies. And in terms of expressive commitment we shall try to deal with the fundamental symbols of political integration and with fundamental patterns of loyalty rather than with the specific satisfactions and dissatisfactions concerning politics. The selection of such a set of political orientations involves the risk that they may be so general as to be of little use in explaining behavior. But in the perspective of cross-national comparisons of political cultures this is not so, for one can find rather sharp differences among different political cultures in terms of these most general beliefs, a fact that makes them a useful explanatory tool.

Fundamental political beliefs are, furthermore, particularly relevant to the study of change. They play a major role in guiding the ways in which institutions develop and change. To a large extent these beliefs may represent stabilizing elements in a system; they may motivate the actors in a political system to resist change in the

[5] See Milton Rokeach, *The Open and the Closed Mind*, New York, Basic Books, 1960, pp. 40-42. I am using the concept of primitive beliefs in connection with political beliefs somewhat differently from the way Rokeach uses the term but in a way that is not, I believe, inconsistent with his meaning. By primitive beliefs he refers to such basic beliefs as that in one's own identity and in the nature of physical reality. These are so taken for granted that one assumes all others agree with one. Therefore the question is never opened. The primitive political beliefs I refer to are not quite as primitive as the ones Rokeach cites, for the political beliefs held in one society are not necessarily shared by those in other political systems. Or indeed the assumptions of one sub-group of a society may not be shared by the other members of that society. (It is perhaps only when one has a sub-group of society whose fundamental assumptions about politics differ from the assumptions predominant in that society that one can properly talk of a political "sub-culture.") Thus, political beliefs may be primitive and unquestioned only for the group within which the individual lives. He may, for instance, be aware that there are other patterns of political belief but not consider them as relevant. And of course the political beliefs of the ordinary man are not structured according to the logic of comparative political analysis. The fact that the universality of the belief would be called into question if he considered political systems other than his own may offer no challenge to the depth of his belief in them. Furthermore one basic political belief—that in one's political identity—is the sort Rokeach has in mind and, as we shall see, one of the most crucial of political beliefs.

name of traditional beliefs or they may lead to fundamental modifications of innovative institutions so that they fit the traditional culture. The essays in this volume are replete with examples of the ways in which traditional belief systems have served to control and modify patterns of change. But though fundamental political beliefs may be closely connected with the maintenance of existing patterns of politics, this is not necessarily the case. In a number of ways the cultural patterns in a society may generate change. Not all political cultures are well integrated and consistent. There may be many sources of strain within such cultures: sets of beliefs that are incompatible with other beliefs, sets of beliefs held by one segment of society and not another, or unmanageable incongruities between belief and reality. Under such circumstances the culture may accelerate change as part of a search for a new and more integrative set of beliefs. Furthermore it is possible for a culture to incorporate change as part of its fundamental belief system. One of the hallmarks of modernity within the realm of culture may be the acceptance and indeed the positive value of continuing change and innovation—to put it somewhat paradoxically—the institutionalization of innovation. And lastly, it must be pointed out that the fundamental general beliefs we have been talking about are themselves not immutable. The basic political values of a group may not be easily changed, yet under certain types of pressure and over time they can change rather drastically.[6] The essays on political cultures in this volume illustrate that point. The political cultures in the nations studied impinge upon attempted changes in patterns of political interaction—in many cases to impede these changes, in some cases to facilitate them. But the political cultures in these nations are themselves in flux.

The changeability of basic political beliefs is indeed a crucial question to the elites of the developing nations. It is customary to think that cultural dimensions are unchanging factors that form the setting within which politics is carried on; that culture conditions politics, but not vice versa. Certainly this was the main argument of much of the national character literature. But the situation is sharply different today. Basic beliefs have now become the object of direct concern and attempted manipulation by the political elites in many nations. This is especially true in the new nations, but it

[6] On the stability but changeability of basic values see Florence R. Kluckhohn and Fred R. Strodtbeck, *Variations in Value Orientation*, Evanston, Row, Peterson, 1961, pp. 9-10.

may also be true in more established nations when a political elite is trying to found a new type of political system. Thus in Germany as well as in Egypt or India basic political beliefs have become the object of direct governmental concern.[7] With a great deal of sophistication and with a great deal of self-consciousness, elites in those countries have taken upon themselves the task of remaking the basic belief systems in their nations as part of their over-all task of nation building. Basic political attitudes have of course always been in part the objects of conscious manipulation—as when adults teach children what are considered to be the basic virtues—but the new cultural policies involve attempts to create new patterns of beliefs, not merely to transmit established patterns to new generations. And these attempts are being made at a time when technological changes in the realm of communications and symbol manipulation may make such policies particularly effective. In any case, the student of political culture would be wise to accept the fact that what seem today to be fundamental sets of political beliefs may be quickly cast aside.

Before dealing with the more specific dimensions of belief which seem particularly important for the understanding of political change, two more general points about political culture must be considered. One has to do with the relationship between political culture and the general cultural system of a society, and the other, with the problem of the distribution of political beliefs and the extent to which political culture refers to political meanings shared by the members of a political system.

CULTURE AND POLITICAL CULTURE

The distinction between political culture and the more general cultural system of a society is an analytical one. Political culture is an integral aspect of more general culture, the set of political beliefs an individual holds, being of course part of the totality of beliefs he holds. Furthermore the basic belief and value patterns of a culture—those general values that have no reference to specific political objects—usually play a major role in the structuring of political culture. Such basic belief dimensions as the view of man's relation

[7] References in this essay to cultural patterns of the nations covered in this book are, unless otherwise specified, to the respective essays in this volume. See also on this point McKim Marriott, "Cultural Policies in the New States," in Clifford Geertz, ed. *Old Societies and New States; The Quest for Modernity in Asia and Africa*, New York, The Free Press of Glencoe, 1963, pp. 27-56.

to nature, as time perspective, as the view of human nature and of the proper way to orient toward one's fellow man, as well as orientation toward activity and activism in general would be clearly interdependent with specifically political attitudes.[8] In a culture in which men's orientation toward nature is essentially one of fatalism and resignation their orientation toward government is likely to be much the same. Political cultures in which the activities of the government are considered in the same class with such natural calamities as earthquakes and storms—to be suffered but outside of the individual's control—are by no means rare, and one would assume that such an attitude would be closely related to a fatalistic attitude toward man's role in relation to nature. The beliefs described in southern Italy and prerevolutionary Mexico are examples of that orientation, and suggest that such a combination of fatalism toward nature and toward government may be general in peasant societies. On the other hand, if the basic cultural orientation toward the environment is one of mastery over nature rather than passivity, this too would have an effect on political orientations. It might take place in two ways. Insofar as the cultural system committed a society to attempt to master and manipulate its physical environment, it is likely that the government will be expected to be an active agent in the process. Furthermore individuals might generalize to politics from their other beliefs. A belief in one's personal ineffectiveness might be generalized to a belief in one's inability to master the political environment, as Scott suggests is the case in Mexico. Similarly one's view of human nature probably has a close connection with one's view of political actors. In Italy and Ethiopia a deeply felt sense of distrust in people in general is reflected in a striking sense of distrust within the realm of politics. Conversely, the individual who believes that man is by nature trustworthy and cooperative is more likely to trust political leaders as well as political opponents, and more likely to be willing to cooperate with them.[9]

The focus on the relationship between basic belief structure and

[8] This set of basic values is taken from Kluckhohn and Strodtbeck, *op.cit.*, pp. 11-20.

[9] That individuals who are high in "faith in people" are more likely to trust political leaders and think that they act for the people's benefit is supported by the work of Morris Rosenberg, "Misanthropy and Political Ideology," *American Sociological Review*, Vol. 21, 1956, pp. 690-695. A cross-cultural study which illustrates the same connection between general attitudes toward other people and political attitudes is Gabriel A. Almond and Sidney Verba, *The Civic Culture*, Princeton, Princeton University Press, 1963; cf. especially Chap. 10.

political beliefs is of great use in determining what political attitudes are important to consider in describing a political culture. Too often, as Robert Lane has pointed out forcefully,[10] students of politics have asked questions about those political attitudes which political scientists consider important—about attitudes toward political issues or toward partisan affiliation. When the individual does not respond in ways that fit the researcher's view as to what a consistent political ideology is (for instance, he does not take consistent and well-reasoned liberal or conservative positions), he is considered to have no political ideology. But by focusing on basic value orientations—often implicit assumptions about the nature of man and the nature of physical reality—we may find a set of political attitudes that, though not structured as the political philosopher might structure them, nevertheless have a definite and significant structure. Since an individual's involvement in society is likely to be only peripherally political—since he is likely to invest more concern and affect in his personal relations or economic relations than in his political ones—it is quite likely that he will structure his political attitudes in ways that derive from his structuring of attitudes toward these more salient areas of activity rather than in terms of the ways in which political scientists or political theorists structure the political world.[11]

Though political culture is closely connected with other aspects of the cultural system, the analytical separation from general culture of those values, cognitions, and expressive states with political objects is useful. It is useful because it allows us to concentrate on those areas of attitudes

[10] Robert Lane, *Political Ideology*, New York, The Free Press of Glencoe, 1962, Chap. 26.
[11] On this general point see Almond and Verba, *op.cit.*, Chaps. 6 and 10. The mode of structuring political beliefs by the students of the subject suggests in turn that much of what, in the absence of direct evidence on political attitudes, we have assumed to be the political culture of a society may in fact be the political ideology of political elites or the political theory of political scientists. The attitudes of the ordinary man may not be structured around those aspects of politics that concern political elites or political scientists. Some recent work by Philip Converse and Georges Dupeux ("Politicization of the Electorate in France and the United States," *Public Opinion Quarterly*, Vol. 26, 1962, pp. 1-23) suggests that the familiar characterization of French political culture as involving a number of highly ideological and principled political subcultures may be more a characterization of political elites than of the political mass. The French electorate appears to be quite a bit less ideologically oriented than one would expect from a consideration of the nature of political debates in the National Assembly of the Fourth Republic.

Of course the political culture of the elites may be more important than that of the mass, but the example suggests that one might have to be careful in describing the elite culture also. The categories of belief of the analyst may be different from those of the elites studied.

that are most relevant for politics. It is useful also because the connection between general culture and political culture is not one of complete identity. Under some circumstances, for instance, there may be discontinuities between the values associated with political interactions and those associated with interactions of other sorts—personal or economic interactions, for instance. By separating political beliefs from other beliefs one can explore the nature of their interrelationship.

The relationship among the various beliefs that individuals have—both political and non-political—represents one of the most important topics of discussion for the student of political culture. Though in dealing with culture we tend to think of patterned relationships among beliefs, this ought not to imply that all sets of beliefs are perfectly integrated. It may be that political beliefs are sharply discontinuous from or in some way inconsistent with other beliefs. One can conceive of a society in which cynicism is reserved for politics but does not pervade other social interactions. A more usual situation would be one in which the formal values stressed in the political realm were not consistent with those stressed in other areas of social life. One of the predominant features of the cultural patterns in most of the transitional nations discussed in this volume is that belief systems stressing modernity in politics are sharply different from the more traditional beliefs associated with other aspects of life, and this may cause severe strain for those who are forced to act within the political culture and the more general culture at the same time.[12] Similarly, the relationship between basic political beliefs and political behavior is not unambiguous. The same belief can be converted into action in a number of ways, just as the same action can have its roots in many alternate beliefs. But though the relationship between political beliefs and general beliefs on the one hand and political behavior on the other may vary, it is clear that they are never irrelevant to each other. Inconsistencies between belief and belief or between

[12] In this connection see Almond and Verba, *op.cit.*, Chaps. 10 and 15. We argue there that the extent to which the political value system interpenetrates with the system of general social values is a major dimension of political culture with significant implications for the operation of the political system. See also the discussion below of discontinuities in the socialization process when the values in one sphere of life are not congruent with those in some other.

Harry Eckstein's discussion of Weimar Germany, where authority patterns in non-political relationships were sharply different from those formally institutionalized in politics, is relevant here. The attendant strains from such discontinuity resemble those in new nations where new political norms are laid upon a traditional base (see Eckstein's *A Theory of Stable Democracy*, Princeton, Center of International Studies, 1961).

belief and action have significant implications for a political system.[13]

Furthermore, when a relationship is found between political beliefs and general social beliefs, one cannot assume that general social beliefs affect political beliefs with no reciprocal effects. Though it is probably true that individuals are more likely to generalize from basic social values to political values, political values may very well have effects on values in other spheres of life. In democratic political systems the belief that one ought to participate in political decisions is often used as a justification for participation in non-political decisions. In Germany and the United States, for instance, "democracy" in the home or in the school have been justified in terms of their appropriateness for a democratic political system.

THE HOMOGENEITY OF CULTURE

Lastly a word must be said about the problem of cultural homogeneity in a political system. The focus on political *culture* rather than political *attitudes* implies a concentration upon the attitudes held by all the members of a political system rather than upon the attitudes held by individuals or particular categories of individuals. As anthropologists have used the term "culture," it has frequently referred to those aspects of belief systems that are shared by members of a society and that are distinctive to that group.[14] Our approach is somewhat different. To concentrate only on shared beliefs might lead one to overlook situations where significant political beliefs were held only by certain groups, and where the very fact that these attitudes were not shared by most members of the system was of crucial importance. This is particularly a problem as one begins to deal with societies as large and complicated as the nation-state. Our approach is to begin with a set of belief dimensions that seem particularly crucial for the understanding of the operation—in particular the development and adaptability—of a political system, and then ask whether or not members of a political system share attitudes on these dimensions.

[13] Not all such inconsistencies are destabilizing. See the discussion of the role of inconsistencies between behavior and belief within democratic political systems in Almond and Verba, *op.cit.*, Chap. 15, which gives examples of the way in which inconsistencies play a positive role in democratic stability.

[14] "By 'culture' we mean that historically created definition of the situation which individuals acquire by virtue of participation in or contact with groups that tend to share ways of life that are in particular respects and in their total configuration distinctive." (Clyde Kluckhohn, "The Concept of Culture," in *Culture and Behavior*, Richard Kluckhohn ed., New York, The Free Press of Glencoe, 1962.)

CONCLUSION

The degree to which basic political attitudes are shared within a political system becomes thus a crucial but open question. A major pole of differentiation among political cultures is the number of basic political attitudes that are widely shared and the patterning of the differences in political belief among the various groups in society. To a greater or lesser extent, all the essays in this volume deal with important differences between the political culture of various elite groups and mass political culture; and, as the essays on Italy and Ethiopia remind us, differences among regions or among ethnic communities may be as large as differences among nations. Of course for the purposes of predicting the political future of a nation the beliefs of certain groups are more crucial than others—those in actual political power, members of organized groups, those living near the centers of communications, and the like. But in an era of rapid political change when the mobilization of mass support is so eagerly pursued, few political sub-cultures can be ignored.

The degree to which political beliefs are shared may be a good indicator of the cohesiveness of a society. But this is probably more true of certain types of beliefs than of others, as discussed below. Some basic political values may indeed lead to conflict if shared on the level of generality we are discussing. Thus all members of a system—to use an example discussed more fully later—may share a belief that output of the political system ought to benefit a fairly parochially defined group—their own family or perhaps their local region. But though this implies a sharing of political values on one level—a shared set of criteria for evaluating governmental output—the fact that on a different level the specific group used as a criterion differs among the members of the system could lead to conflict. Similarly, the existence of an "ideological" political style through a shared cultural norm may institutionalize divisiveness. Though the commitment to ideology is shared throughout the system, the ideologies to which individuals are committed vary from group to group.

II. *Dimensions of Political Culture*

The discussion so far has dealt largely with the justification and usefulness of the political culture approach. It now becomes necessary to look more closely at *how* one might approach the study of political culture. The following sections will not present an integrated theory of political culture but rather, in the light of the previous chapters, try to set forth some significant dimensions within which the subject could be viewed as well as some propositions as to the relationship among dimensions. The dimensions are selected with a view to their relevance to the study of political change or modernization.

In dealing with the dimensions of political culture we shall concentrate, for the reasons suggested above, on general political beliefs. Such beliefs are usually mixtures of cognitions about politics as well as standards of evaluation. But our discussion will focus somewhat more on evaluation, in particular on those basic political values that represent the most general beliefs about the ends of political activity, about the nature of the political process, and about the place of the individual within it. Our first task will be to describe these basic values and the ways in which they can vary.

Political systems are complicated. There are a number of institutions deeply involved in politics, many political actors, and many political issues. About what aspects of a political system would it be useful to know the basic orientations of the members of that system? Ought we to care about their attitudes toward specific candidates and political parties as they affect election results? Ought we to care about their attitudes on specific issues? As anyone who has ever designed a survey interview on political affairs knows, the number of subjects to ask questions about is almost unlimited. There are, however, several criteria that can serve as useful guides for the selection of the significant aspects of cultural orientation. In the first place, we would look for aspects that are relevant cross-nationally. It would be of little use in a volume of this sort which deals with the political cultures in a number of societies to specify dimensions of political culture that are meaningful in one system alone and that are of little or no use to political analysis in general. And the search for generally applicable dimensions is useful since it leads one to focus on the fundamental aspects of a political system. Second, we should seek aspects of politics about which most people in a political system would be expected to have orientations (that is, to have beliefs, values, and expressive feelings about) or aspects of politics about which it would be significant if individuals had no orientations—were unaware of, did not care about, were uninvolved in. And third, since one of the chief concerns in this volume—and in the entire series of which it is a part—is political modernization, the set of objects of political value orientation selected should be relevant to this problem.

CONCLUSION

The beliefs dealt with below focus around the nation-state. Thus we deal with patterns of identification with the nation-state rather than patterns of identification in general; with expectations of performance by the national political elites rather than with expectations of performance in general. To some extent this is arbitrary. Politically relevant beliefs can be found in connection with many other institutions. Beliefs about family relations may be relevant to "family politics" (they may be beliefs about patterns of parental authority or power, for instance) or they may be relevant to politics on the level of the state (they may be, for instance, beliefs as to the legitimacy of nepotistic standards in national political decision making). But the focus on beliefs about politics on the national level is useful for several reasons. For one thing, it gives some limitation to an otherwise limitless subject. Furthermore, for most political problems, and especially for the problems associated with change and modernization in the contemporary world, the nation-state is the key unit. It tends to be the major unit within which the allocation of resources for change takes place as well as the most significant integrating force in the society. Or (and this hedges the point in the previous sentence without, I believe, reducing its significance) if the nation-state is not the central focus for resource allocation and the mobilization of commitment, it is in competition for that role with some other institution.[15] Thus the focus on the nation-state will lead us to the important political beliefs that are relevant for the problem of political development. Furthermore other beliefs—say, about authority in the family or about the role of nepotism—can be dealt with insofar as they impinge upon the national political belief systems.

---

[15] There are several reasons why the nation-state, and in particular the national government, is in this key role. For one thing, the structure of international politics is such that the decision as to what is the national government and what is the appropriate definition of the scope of the nation-state is often made internationally before it has been made domestically. Recognition as a nation often comes from the United Nations long before it comes from the inhabitants of the nation. But once this is done, the national government becomes immediately relevant for problems of change and development, if only because it will have a large amount of control over international developmental resources. Furthermore the tasks of social change in the twentieth century, one can argue, require a high degree of central coordination. This in turn implies a single coordinating agency (for the simple reason that if one has two coordinating agencies, there is a need for a coordinator to coordinate the coordinators). It is therefore possible for one to conceive of the central government performing this role or of the central government conflicting with some other institution for the performance of this role; but because of the central position the government holds, it is hard to conceive of some other institution's performing this role without generating competition with the government.

NATIONAL IDENTITY

Perhaps the most crucial political belief involves that of political identity. Of what political unit or units does the individual consider himself a member, and how deep and unambiguous is the sense of identification? By national identity I refer to the beliefs of individuals and the extent to which they consider themselves members of their nation-state. The importance of this belief cannot be overstressed. It is not merely a question of the physical location an individual assigns to himself, as he might identify himself by saying "I live on such and such a street." Rather the identification with the nation may be and often is one of the basic beliefs that serve to define an individual for himself. It is for him a serious problem and one that is in many ways similar to that of religious identification. In this sense it becomes relevant that the question of national identity is often phrased in somewhat mystical terms—that one searches for it, that nations need it, that people fear the loss of it.

The question of national identity is the political culture version of the basic personal problem of self-identity. Erik Erikson has argued that the "crisis of identity" must be resolved if a mature and stable personality is to develop, and Lucian Pye has shown how such a crisis of identity affects elites in a rapidly changing society.[16] Similarly one can argue that the first and most crucial problem that must be solved in the formation of a political culture, if it is to be capable of supporting a stable yet adaptable political system, is that of national identity.

Unless those individuals who are physically and legally members of a political system (that is, who live within its boundaries and are subject to its laws) are also psychologically members of that system (that is, feel themselves to be members) orderly patterns of change are unlikely. It is the sense of identity with the nation that legitimizes the activities of national elites and makes it possible for them to mobilize the commitment and support of their followers. The most potent kind of commitment that political elites can arouse is to the political system per se—that is, a commitment to it over and above its actual performance. It is only such a rain-or-shine commitment that will allow a system to survive the many kinds of crises

---

[16] Erik H. Erikson, *Childhood and Society*, New York, Norton, 1950; and Lucian Pye, *Politics, Personality, and Nation Building*, New Haven, Yale University Press, 1962.

CONCLUSION

that are likely to arise during processes of rapid social change.[17] And unless most members of a system identify themselves as members of that system, such generalized loyalty will be hard to generate.

From the point of view also of political elites the problem of national identity may be the first one that must be faced. Unless they are sure of their identity the many other problems of change will have to wait. As Pye has pointed out in his study of Burmese elites, the absence of a well-defined sense of identity creates a host of tensions and frustrations among the Burmese elites that makes the process of change more difficult. For whatever reasons, it seems clear that the problem of identity for the members of a nation is one that cannot be postponed.

The development of a clear and unambiguous sense of identity is more than a facilitating factor in the creation of a nation; it may be in some sense the major constituting factor of a new nation. Thus nation building—the creation of a set of political structures called a nation-state—proceeds very often by the institutionalization of commitment to common political symbols. It is not merely that the symbol represents the nation, but that the creation of the symbol is coterminous with the creation of the nation.

The creation of a national identity among the members of a nation is the cultural equivalent of the drawing of the boundaries of the nation. And just as nations may have unsettled or ambiguous boundaries, so may the sense of identity of the members of that system be unsettled and ambiguous. In some societies communications are at a low level, the aspirations of the elites to penetrate and transform the society are low, and in the interest of the masses in taking some participatory role in their nation's life is nonexistent. Under these circumstances, the absence of national identity may not be a problem; it may be possible for a nation to survive quite well despite the fact that many or most of those who live within its boundaries identify with some more parochial group such as family or tribe or region. But this description fits few of the nations of the modern world. Though there are many people still involved solely in private relations and parochial concerns, the tendency in most societies, for a variety of reasons, is for more and more people to become concerned with the central units of political integration. As Binder points out in his essay here, 150 years ago few Egyptians probably cared whether

[17] On this point see Seymour M. Lipset, *Political Man*, New York, Doubleday, 1960, Chap. 3.

the central regime was indigenous or not. Today this is a matter of crucial importance at almost every level of society. And it places greater burdens on the nation-state to satisfy the needs of its citizens to be affiliated.[18]

Political change and development add a new dimension to the issue of identity. Whether or not the members of a political system have a strong and positive identification with their nation becomes important, whereas earlier the crucial question was whether they were positively opposed to the nation. Italy is an example. As LaPalombara points out in this volume, there are some Italians who positively reject their nation, but the number is relatively small. Rather, the bulk of the population is indifferent and unconcerned. Their national identification is neither salient nor a source of pride. The strong sense of regional affiliation does not imply separatist tendencies (with the special exception of South Tyrol), but it does involve an absence of commitment to Italy. And where development and change become the order of the day, and where there are some groups positively challenging the system, the indifference of the bulk of the population becomes a severe problem.

The set of political beliefs about national identity can take many forms. At one extreme one can think of societies in which the shared sense of identity is what we have called an assumption or primitive belief. Membership in the nation is so taken for granted—and the boundaries that separate members from non-members, so clear—that the subject comes in for little discussion or consideration. Of the nations discussed in this volume, Britain certainly and probably Japan and Ethiopia have had long histories of relatively well-established and secure national identities. And the identification has centered around important and generally accepted national symbols. It is perhaps no coincidence that of the nations dealt with in this volume it is in the three monarchies that the sense of national identity appears most firmly rooted in tradition. But these nations provide a further lesson. Problems of identity are never solved once and for all for a nation. In each of these three nations new problems have aroused new concern with national identity, and in each case the central symbols, including the monarch, have been called into question.

In other societies the question, "Who am I?", in the political sense

[18] See on this point Edward A. Shils, "The Macrosociological Problem: Consensus and Dissensus in the Larger Society," in Donald Ray, ed. *Trends in Social Science*, New York, Philosophical Library, 1961, pp. 60-83.

is a much more burning one. For many of the new nations of the world, where central political symbols vie with tribal and other local affiliations, the problem is particularly acute. The loyalty to some subnational unit—the loyalty that makes some people consider themselves as Balubas, or Venetians, or Alabamans before they consider themselves Congolese, or Italians, or Americans—is the major source of cultural conflict within nations. But the competition between more parochial political units and the nation-state is not the only kind of conflict that can produce an uncertainty in political identity. Even though all members of a political system identify with the same political unit, identity problems can arise if there is some ambiguity in the definition of that unit. This is likely to be the case when various types of boundaries—legal, linguistic, cultural, religious, ethnic—are not coterminous. Compare Germany with Japan or Britain. The lack of coordination between cultural, linguistic, and political boundaries has caused serious identity problems throughout German history, problems that have been relatively absent in the other two nations where political boundaries have been clearly defined and coordinate with linguistic and cultural boundaries. Identity problems can also arise for groups who consider themselves members of the nation within which they are living but who are not so accepted by the dominant culture bearers of that nation. Perhaps one generalization that can be made about the "participation explosion" going on in the world is that the elites who will survive are those most capable of giving the symbols of full citizenship to the new groups who are asking for them.

Perhaps the most interesting type of uncertainty in political identity occurs when there is some lack of self-confidence or self-esteem associated with people's political identity. Lack of self-confidence in their identity might be accentuated by the kinds of problems cited above—say, an uncertainty in national boundaries—but that is different. All the residents in a nation may agree on the scope of the nation with which they identify, but the meaning of that identity may be uncertain to them. Here we have the opposite of a primitive belief; we have a belief that is constantly open to question. Compare the American literary tradition of asking, "What does it mean to be an American?" with the relative absence of such questioning in British literature.[19] The historical reasons for this kind of question-

[19] Consider the song in Gilbert and Sullivan's *H.M.S. Pinafore*: "Oh he might have been a Russian/ Or French or Turk or Prussian/ Or perhaps Ital-i-an/ But

ing—whether those deriving from the need to assimilate immigrant groups into a new continent as in the United States, or from the long history of disunity as in Germany—are beyond the scope of this paper. But whatever the reasons, such an uncertainty in identity may be one of the major defining characteristics of a political culture.

Whether or not a nation has a well-defined and ego-satisfying identity has important consequences for its politics. Other problems are likely to be pushed aside until the central problem is met; "What is my nation?" must be answered before "What kind of a nation?" The histories of divided nations such as Italy and Germany as well as the histories of the former colonies suggest the power of the identity problem, for almost invariably the problems of unity and independence—problems basic to identity—push other problems such as democracy or social reform aside. Furthermore in the absence of an established identity one is likely to engage in identity-creating acts—be these aggressions against other nations or other expressions of nationalism. And indeed wars and revolutions—if against the proper enemy and for the right cause—can be a major way of suddenly switching loyalties from parochial groups to the nation-state and of building political commitment in a hurry.[20]

Once the issue of national identity becomes salient and loyalty to sub-national units alone is no longer satisfactory for either mass or elite, there are several ways in which the problem can be resolved. On the one hand, loyalty and commitment to the nation-state may be developed as a replacement and substitute for other loyalties; loyalty to the state is conceived of as in conflict with loyalties to tribe, region, ethnic community, or, in extreme cases, the family itself. In this solution—which is close to what Apter has referred to as a "political religion" system[21]—the central political symbols become the primary focus of individual commitment. At the other extreme is what one might call an "incorporative" solution to the conflict between parochial commitment and identification with the nation-state. In this case the commitment to the nation is added to

---

in spite of all temptation/ To belong to other Nation/ He remains an Englishman." The reason this is funny is that the possibility it raises is so ludicrous—that an Englishman might be anything else but an Englishman. Would the joke be as funny if one praised a man for choosing to be an American?

[20] On this point see Sidney Verba and Gabriel A. Almond, "National Revolutions and Political Commitment," in Harry Eckstein, ed. *Essays on Internal War*, New York, The Free Press of Glencoe, 1964.

[21] David Apter, "Political Religion in the New Nations," in Geertz, ed. *Old Societies and New States*, pp. 57-104.

CONCLUSION

but does not replace the more traditional, parochial commitments. Individuals develop a multiple set of loyalties when loyalties on various levels are believed not to be in conflict. The latter kind of solution, one can argue, is most conducive to the creation of a political culture supportive of democracy—a political culture in which political commitment is tempered by multiple commitments to other social units.[22]

But the latter kind of solution, in which a stable pattern of national identity develops that does not challenge the other identifications of the individual, may be difficult of achievement especially within the new nations of the world. In these societies the demands for rapid change, the fact that these changes involve challenges to the authority of the parochial units with which the individual was previously identified, and the fact that these parochial units are on the same level of integration as the nation-state—that is, the local tribe or community vie with the nation-state for the role of the largest unit of political integration to which the individual is committed—make it likely that traditional parochial loyalties and national loyalty will be considered as alternatives between which one must choose.[23] If a modern nation-state, with its high level of centralized decision making, is to encompass a variety of loyalties to more parochial subnational units without these local loyalties leading to fragmentation and divisive tensions, both national elites and local masses must believe that multiple loyalties are possible. Where members of local communities consider demands for national loyalty to be threats to the survival of their communities or where national elites consider traditional local commitments to endanger national integration—Weiner suggests both conditions exist in India—the choice may be between the acceptance of fragmentation or an attempt to destroy local commitments through an enforced political religion.

But the choice may not be an all-or-nothing one. Even if one were to choose a political-religion type of solution, the destruction of parochial loyalties does not come about so easily. As Barghoorn points out in his essay on the Soviet Union, the regime has had to deal with the continuing nationality problem as well as with the new subnational loyalties to professional and occupational groups. In Mexico and Egypt compromise solutions are being attempted. Mexico ex-

---

[22] For an elaboration of this point see Almond and Verba, *The Civic Culture*, Chap. 15.
[23] See Clifford Geertz, "The Integrative Revolution," in Geertz, *op.cit.*, pp. 105-157.

hibits many of the characteristics of the political-religion solution—a political system united around the symbols of a great national revolution, a single party, a certain revolutionary *élan*—but it lacks a single enforced ideology and incorporates a great plurality of competing groups within its single-party structure. Egypt has a revolutionary and modernizing elite oriented to significant social change; but their cultural and kinship roots in a traditional, rural middle class have tended to ameliorate the conflict between the nation and the local community. And some sort of compromise between the two political cultures in India is a likely solution in that nation.

IDENTIFICATION WITH ONE'S FELLOW CITIZENS

The sense of national identity deals with a vertical form of identification—the sense of attachment that individuals have to some superordinate political unit and to the symbols of that political unit. A second significant dimension of identification is the horizontal identification with one's fellow citizens—the sense of integration individuals have with the other people who inhabit the political system. Just as a political culture may be characterized by the extent to which the members share a well-defined sense of national identity, so it can be characterized by the extent to which individuals identify with each other as members of the same system. In particular the extent to which members of a political system have trust and confidence in their fellow political actors is a crucial aspect of the horizontal integration of a political culture. It is likely to be closely related to one's general view of human nature: some cultures incorporate much more favorable views of one's fellow men than others do. As Levine points out, the Amhara culture stresses the untrustworthiness of all those outside the family and often of those within that narrow circle as well; and this has also been a major theme in Italian political culture.[24] The limits of trust and cooperativeness that are set in the family affect the range of people with whom one can have confident political relationships. Just as those outside the family are considered antagonistic, so political opponents or those with different economic interests are seen as antagonists. As LaPalombara points out, hostility to those outside the family is paralleled by a belief that election campaigns, relations among secondary associations, and labor-management relations involve conflict and hostility.

[24] See the essays by Levine and LaPalombara in this volume. Pye makes a similar point in his study of Burmese politics (see Pye, *Politics, Personality*, pp. 205-206).

CONCLUSION

But it is also possible that one might have beliefs about individuals as political actors that are somewhat independent of beliefs about people in general. Where politics involves a high level of antagonistic conflict among groups with opposing interests and ideologies, it is possible one would have a lower impression of the trustworthiness of individuals when they are considered in political terms—say in terms of a partisan affiliation—than when they are considered in general.[25] Or, where politics and political activities are considered somewhat disreputable, one may reserve a separate set of less-trusting beliefs and values for individuals who enter politics.

This sense of confidence in other political actors is a particularly crucial aspect of a democratic political culture. Unless individuals trust their political opponents they are going to be rather unwilling to turn over government power to those opponents. Individuals will engage in peaceful competition with those of opposing political views and allow the alternation of power among competing elites— a requisite of a democratic political system—only if the danger of such competition and alternation of power is not too great. And one characteristic that would limit the felt danger of such an alternation would be a belief in the fundamental trustworthiness of those involved in politics and the feeling that they are members of the "same community."[26] As Rose points out, British politics depends heavily on patterns of interpersonal trust, a trust that is especially important in a political system such as that in Britain where so much of politics involves customary and not very explicitly defined (but usually rigidly observed) norms of political interaction. The shock of the Profumo scandal from the political point of view was caused not so much by the lascivious details of the affair but by the fact that the pattern of interpersonal trust had been challenged.

Political trust has relevance as well for non-democratic systems. In all political systems the general sense of trust individuals have in those who hold political power is a resource that the latter may use in wielding that power. If non-elites do not in some way identify with and have confidence in political elites, the elites will have to exact obedience by more forceful and perhaps more destabilizing means.

The sense of identification with some superordinate political

[25] On this point see Almond and Verba, *op.cit.*, Chap. 10.
[26] See on this point Harold Lasswell, "Democratic Character," in *The Political Writings of Harold D. Lasswell*, Glencoe, Ill., The Free Press, 1951; Robert Lane, *op.cit.*, pp. 400-406; and Almond and Verba, *op.cit.*

symbol and the sense of identification with one's fellow political actors are likely to be quite closely related. Where members of a political system do not share a common superordinate identification but rather identify with a variety of sub- (or perhaps supra-) national political units such as tribe or region, it will be obviously impossible to develop the sense of common membership upon which much of their trust and confidence in their fellow political actors must rest. Conversely, if individuals share a sense of national identity, they will be bound together by one of the most fundamental of political beliefs. As Eckstein has put it, once the question of English national identity was settled in the twelfth century, "there was always some sort of cement to bind the English, even in the worst times of political strife, and always something to make disagreement seem less absolute."[27] Yet though attitudes toward the nation as symbol and those toward one's fellow participants in the political system are closely related, they may vary independently. If there is any meaning to the old quip that "every Frenchman loves France and hates every other Frenchman," it suggests that even where there is a generally shared sense of membership in a nation, the horizontal lines of integration among individuals and groups in the political system may be quite a bit weaker.

GOVERNMENTAL OUTPUT

The beliefs discussed so far deal with the definition of the polity. Beliefs about national identity define the polity in terms of its central symbols; beliefs about one's fellow citizens define the polity in terms of its members. But beyond these general beliefs are important political beliefs about how the polity operates—not what it *is*, but what it *does*. In particular it is the expectations the members of a system have as to the output of the government—what they believe it will and ought to do for and to them—that are relevant here.

In dealing with political culture on a very general level it becomes impossible to consider the variety of expectations individuals can have about governmental output. The range of governmental activities is almost limitless, and beliefs as to what these activities ought to be are certainly as wide. It may be useful therefore to consider the simpler question of whether or not the members of a political system expect *any* output from their government. One can conceive, at

[27] Eckstein, "The British Political System," in Beer and Ulam, eds. *Patterns of Government*, p. 82.

one extreme, of a parochial political culture in which individuals expect no output from the central institutions of the political system. As the term is used in *The Civic Culture*, a parochial is an individual involved in his family or perhaps his community but little concerned with government. Whatever wants he has he expects to be satisfied elsewhere—by an institution such as the family perhaps or by his own efforts. At the other extreme would be a society in which the political belief structure involved expectations of governmental performance and activity in most spheres of human activity.

The transition from a political culture in which individuals have little or no expectation that the government will act to affect their lives, or where they are perhaps even unaware of the existence of any specialized set of political structures, to a political culture in which beliefs about governmental performance are prominent may represent one of the most significant stages in the development of a political culture. Of equal importance would be the transition from a situation in which the dominant beliefs about governmental output stress the role of the government in maintaining the existing patterns of value-allocation to a situation in which basic political beliefs involve expectations that the activities of the government will produce changes in society or in the lives of its members. The cultural component of the difference between a traditional and a modernizing political system may be the extent to which expectations exist that the activities of the political system will produce some transition in society. But changes of this sort are not irreversible. In many of the more industrialized and affluent societies of the West there has been a clear tendency toward a "depoliticization" or "privatization" of life; a tendency to limit the range of issues for which political solutions are sought.

Beliefs about the desirability of governmental activity are an aspect of the political culture with significant implications for the effectiveness and stability of a political system. These beliefs set the goals of the political system and define the load (or overload) that the culture places on that system. The extent to which the political values of a society involve expectations that governmental activity will improve or change society depends in part on the general beliefs as to the possibility and desirability of changing and improving one's environment. Societies in which the culture emphasizes activist and achievement orientations are more likely to generate political beliefs that load a heavy weight of demands on the political process. But general beliefs in the possibility of changing one's environment and more specific beliefs that improvement comes through the activity of government may vary independently. There may be high expectations of change but little expectation that the activities of the government will be the major generator of that change. The initiation of change in the social system or in one's position in it will be expected from, say, the economic system, but not from the political system. Nineteenth century America is probably an example. In the modern world, however, the extent to which expectations of social improvement involve expectations that this will be accomplished through the activities of the government is striking. Not only is the belief spreading that the world can be changed, but in almost all cases where this belief arises, it is the government that is expected to fulfill it.

The rise in expectations among the masses as to governmental output places pressures upon the elites to satisfy them. But these pressures for change and the belief that the government ought to take the responsibility for generating such change do not necessarily or even usually originate within the political mass. Rather the belief may have its origin in attempts by the elites to crack traditional patterns in order to mobilize the society for social change. In Mexico or Turkey, for instance, governmental intervention to improve life on the village level has been motivated by the central political elites and has often faced the resistance of local communities. And in Egypt the attempts to change the society are motivated less by pressures from below than by the image the Egyptian elites have of more industrialized societies. Or, such pressures can be generated by a counter elite. But such elite-originated pressures can destroy the parochialism of the masses and lead the masses to expect change. In a sense, the elites are then called upon to deliver what they themselves led the masses to expect.

We have been considering beliefs about governmental output on a very general level; not with specific policies that are desired, but with the question of whether any policies are desired and whether these policies are expected to produce change in society. There is one other important aspect of the value orientation toward governmental output on this level of generalization: the criteria used to judge governmental policies, in particular the groups that individuals take into account. Individuals are simultaneously members of many social systems, from the family up to and indeed beyond the nation. The basic political values of a particular political culture may stress more or less narrow group interests as criteria of evaluation. If Banfield's discussion of southern Italy is correct, all governmental activity is judged in terms of one value: its impact on the nuclear family.[28] At the other extreme one can conceive of a political culture which stresses a form of ideological nationalism whereby the only legitimate criteria for evaluating governmental performance are national, and in which sub-national criteria—be they personal, familistic, or organizational—are considered illegitimate. Some modernizing movements stress such commitments. Clearly the beliefs held about national identity and in particular the way in which these beliefs relate to beliefs about identification with more parochial groups will have a major effect on the criteria used to evaluate governmental performance.

It is unlikely that a political culture would stress only one criterion. Banfield's characterization of the "amoral familists" of southern Italy suggests such a single-value political culture, but it is likely that this picture represents an exaggeration. For any political culture one would want to know the mixture of criteria. Of particular importance would be the number of criteria operative at the same time. The greater the variety of criteria of evaluation, the more would the culture represent a "pluralistic" political culture. A mass political culture, in Kornhauser's use of the term, would be one in which criteria of evaluation were polarized around considerations of personal values and considerations of national values.[29] Aside from the number of membership criteria that are likely to be invoked in evaluating governmental output, the stability of the criteria is important. On the one hand one can conceive of a culture in which the same criterion or set of criteria is invoked for all governmental activities. On the other, it is possible to conceive of a more flexible culture under which various situations trigger off various criteria. Some governmental activities might be evaluated in terms of individual gain or loss, others in terms of religious affiliation, others in terms of some conception of an overriding national interest.[30]

[28] Edward Banfield, *The Moral Basis of a Backward Society*, New York, The Free Press of Glencoe, 1959.

[29] William Kornhauser, *The Politics of Mass Society*, New York, The Free Press of Glencoe, 1961.

[30] Studies of American voting behavior suggest a flexible pattern of this sort. Under certain circumstances different group affiliations are brought to the fore as criteria of evaluation. Thus before 1960 the degree of religious commitment was not a relevant criterion for Protestant Americans in deciding their vote. In the 1960 election this aspect of religious affiliation was raised to a salient criterion. Compare the discussions of the relationships between church attendance and voting behavior of Protestants in Bernard Berleson, Paul Lazarsfeld, and William McPhee, *Voting*,

One other aspect of the cultural attitudes toward governmental output is of crucial significance. Not all governmental output consists of goods and services that benefit members of the society. Much of what the government does consists of regulation of individual behavior or of extraction of goods and services from the members of a society. Just as it makes a significant difference in a political system what expectations the members have as to what the government ought to do *for* them, so it makes a crucial difference what they believe the government ought to do *to* them. At issue here is the extent to which the government is considered a legitimate authoritative decision-making body; that is, it is considered proper that the individual member of the political system suspend his own evaluation of the governmental regulation and obey it simply because it is made by authorities who are supposed to make such regulations.

On the most general level one could think of this as involving an attitude of respect for the political system, or more specifically as a set of values supporting obedience to law. At the opposite pole would be a belief that the political system is a hostile and exploitative force, a belief manifested more specifically as incivism toward law. The latter set of political values will clearly be closely related to the criteria used for evaluating governmental output; the more narrow these criteria, the more likely is the attitude toward governmental regulation to be one of disrespect. The extent to which the political value structure consists of values that further respect for the political system and obedience to specific laws represents a major aspect of a political culture. The generalized support for the activities of the political system that such beliefs would generate may be the most important kind of support that members of a political system can give.

THE PROCESS OF MAKING DECISIONS

Beliefs about the way in which the government makes decisions or the way in which it ought to make decisions are the last general aspect of political beliefs to be discussed. Just as the first question one could ask about governmental output was whether or not there were some expectations about the government's performance, so the first question one can ask about the way in which decisions are made

---

Chicago, University of Chicago Press, 1954, pp. 67-68; and Philip Converse *et al.*, "Stability and Change in 1960: A Reinstating Election," *American Political Science Review*, Vol. LV, 1961, pp. 269-280.

is whether or not there are salient beliefs about this subject. Are there beliefs about the way in which the government processes the input of demands from society? In some societies there are in fact few such beliefs, or such beliefs as there are on this subject are not important. People know little and care little about how decisions are made; they care merely whether the output of the government is beneficial or not. This would be so in a society in which most people considered themselves subjects of the government rather than participants with a legitimate voice in deciding what the government does.[31] The political culture in Tokugawa Japan would be an example. As Ward describes it, it was "characterized by attitudes of habitual obedience and subjugation to duly constituted authority compounded with the sentiment that government is something that is done to the common people and largely at their expense by their socio-political superiors."

Once it is determined whether or not the rules by which decisions are made are considered important, the next question one can ask is whether there is agreement on these rules—whatever they may be. Perhaps even more important than the question of consensus on the output of the political process is the question of consensus on the rules for determining that output. Of particular relevance are the beliefs about the proper role of the individual member of society in the political process. How does the individual view his own role in the political process? Beliefs about the proper behavior of non-elites may vary from a belief that one can and should actively intervene in the political process to stress on the futility and illegitimacy of such intervention. No political culture will stress either polar type completely. Even in democratic political systems one that stresses participation in decisions is likely at the same time to value deference to government authority; and the values within an authoritarian political system are likely to involve some participatory role for the individual.

The question of identity, as suggested above, is closely related to the problem of the mobilization of the commitment of the members of a political system to that system—their emotional attachment to the polity and their willingness to commit resources to it. Governmental performance is also intimately related to the problem of the mobilization of commitment. Where expectations of performance have been established, failure to perform can prevent the development of

---

[31] See on this point Almond and Verba, *op.cit.*, Chaps. 1 and 8.

such general commitment to the system. Conversely, it is possible that experience with successful performance in terms of the citizenry's expectations of governmental output can create a deeper sense of commitment to the political system that does not depend upon specific performance of governmental tasks. But the most interesting relationship of political commitment with other beliefs is that with orientations to political participation. At an earlier stage in political history satisfactory performance by the government in the realm of output might have insured that the members of that system were willing to commit their efforts and resources to the support of the system. But in the twentieth century the service state that administers output—no matter how successfully—may not be able to produce a deep and affective commitment to the system. Thus Binder writes about Egypt that "the absence of opportunities for effective participation renders the government a relatively distant and cold object" despite the fact that elites have succeeded in creating a rather effective administrative relationship with their citizens. And in Germany as well, as I suggest in my essay on German political culture, the administrative orientation to government may be intimately related to the rather cool attitude Germans have to their political system.

III. The Relations Among Political Beliefs

The specification of the important dimensions of political belief is not as important for improving our understanding of the operation of political systems as is the specification of the relationships among these dimensions. In the previous section numerous such relationships have been suggested. In this section I would like to focus on the way in which political beliefs can be incorporated into each other and on the importance of that incorporation.

As an individual becomes more and more involved in politics, as the content of this political belief system becomes both richer and of greater significance to him, what happens to the earlier political beliefs he had? Are they replaced by the new beliefs or do the new beliefs merge with them? This distinction may be of great significance in understanding the development of political cultures. Thus, as suggested in the discussion of national identity, the development of identification with the nation-state can be at the expense of identifications with the more parochial units with which the individual previously identified, or national identification can coexist side by side with the local. Similarly the belief that he can participate meaningfully in the governmental decision-making process can replace the belief that he is essentially the subject of the government's law making, or the participant orientation to government can develop on top of, without replacing, the subject orientation to the government. Where the citizen's belief in his right to participate replaces his subject orientation, the result is likely to be a challenge to the independent authority of the political elites. The ultimate result of such a stress upon popular participation at the expense of elite independence might be a populistic regime where governmental effectiveness would suffer. But where the belief that he can participate is merged with a belief that he still is the subject of laws, the independent authority of government will be protected and a better balance between citizen participation and governmental effectiveness will be maintained.[32]

In general the problem here is the extent to which change and modernization in political culture involve rejection of earlier, more traditional patterns or incorporation of the new beliefs into the pre-existing ones. If one can build new political beliefs upon a firm base of traditional ones—as Rose suggests has generally been the case in Britain, where new beliefs appear while old ones rarely disappear—it may be possible to achieve change without severe social disruption. The traditional symbols and primordial affiliations can help to bind the members of the system together in face of the disruptions that rapid social change brings. And the more passive political beliefs serve to temper the demands for political participation. But such incorporation is never easy and it is always at a price. If traditional beliefs can help preserve stability while change takes place, they can also serve to impede change. It is interesting that in the three nations dealt with in this book that have entered the modern world with their traditional institutions and symbols most fully intact—Britain, Japan, and Ethiopia—these traditional institutions and symbols have begun to appear to be impediments to needed political change.

IV. Political Style

Political beliefs play a major role in determining the operation of the political process since they set the culturally defined goals for that process; but, though the over-all goals of the system are set by

[32] On this general point see Almond and Verba, *op.cit.*, Chap. 15; and Eckstein in Beer and Ulam, *op.cit.*

the structure of beliefs, particularly evaluative beliefs, much of the activity directed toward the achievement of these goals is regulated by "political style."[33] By political style I refer to two aspects of political belief systems. The first, which is strictly cultural, involves the structure or formal properties of political belief systems, that is, not the substance of beliefs but the way in which beliefs are held. The second aspect lies on the border between the system of political culture and the system of political interaction, and involves those informal norms of political interaction that regulate the way in which fundamental political beliefs are applied in politics.

Students of politics—particularly those who have worked on comparisons between British and Continental politics—have long written of two political styles, the ideological and the pragmatic. The former, the style of the *Weltanschauungsparteien* of the Continent, involves a deeply affective commitment to a comprehensive and explicit set of political values which covers not merely political affairs but all of life, a set of values which is hierarchical in form and often deduced from a more general set of "first principles." A pragmatic political style on the other hand consists of an evaluation of problems in terms of their individual merits rather than in terms of some preexisting comprehensive view of reality. One deals with the issue at hand, perhaps in terms of some guiding principles, but not as an instance of some over-all scheme.

It is likely that this distinction between ideological and pragmatic politics involves several different dimensions. One can distinguish between open and closed belief systems; between explicit and implicit belief systems; and between belief systems that stress expressive behavior and those that stress instrumental political behavior. Thus a set of beliefs may be more or less open. The more open they are, the more likely is the individual who holds them to compromise with those who hold other beliefs, to change his beliefs if they are challenged by new information, or to modify them to fit a situation. The more closed the beliefs are, the less likely are they to be changed or compromised when challenged. The individual with a closed belief structure is unlikely either to change a belief if he receives new information to challenge that belief or to adjust his goals to accord with the available means.

Closely related to the degree of openness of a belief system is its

[33] The term is from Herbert Spiro (*Government by Constitution*, New York, Random House, 1959), whose discussion of the subject was found to be very helpful.

degree of explicitness. Some value systems are highly articulated, carefully thought out, and comprehensive. In other systems the cultural goals are more implicit. And this difference is related to the degree of openness of the beliefs. Though not all implicit belief structures are flexible or all explicit ones rigid and closed, there is a sense in which the explication of a belief structure introduces a measure of rigidity. Once one's ultimate goals are made explicit it becomes more difficult to compromise them in a specific case. An implicit goal system allows more flexibility since the goals of the culture are not present as overt criteria for judging any policy, and so it is possible to justify a policy in terms of the expediencies of the situation without explicitly violating the cultural goals. An implicit set of political goals is more flexible and less fragile. Because the goals can be modified more easily—if, for instance, the available means make goal attainment impossible—they are less likely to be abandoned completely as one might abandon an explicit ideology if one recognized flaws in it. Furthermore the very implicitness of the value system suggests that it represents a set of primitive beliefs so taken for granted that it needs no explicit codification. In fact explicit political ideologies arise when one wants to create a political system that is not supported by the implicit primitive beliefs of the population. If one has appropriate beliefs, one does not need the ideology. Where democratic beliefs are deeply ingrained, for instance, a democratic ideology needs less explicit emphasis.

The implicit-explicit distinction in relation to political beliefs suggests a problem for the development of "modern" political systems. One of the hallmarks of "modernity" is the substitution of rational calculation for traditional criteria in the making of decisions. Rational calculation—essentially a means-ends calculation—implies the explication of one's goals. But the explication of all goals—if indeed that were possible—would introduce a rigidity into the policy-making process that would certainly be destabilizing in the long run. The adjustment of goals and the development of flexible policy would be difficult. Furthermore, by making all goals explicit, all goals are in a sense opened to question; nothing is kept "sacred." Thus stability in "modernized" systems may depend upon the maintenance of a residue of non-rationality—of the traditional, implicit, and unquestioned values discussed in the previous section—that keeps certain aspects of the political system out of the realm of rational means-ends calculations.

The third distinction involved in the ideological-pragmatic polarity is that between the stress on the expressive side of politics and the stress on the instrumental side. This is perhaps the most significant general distinction that can be made about political beliefs. It is essentially a distinction between, on the one hand, beliefs that stress political activity carried on for its own sake or political institutions that are valued for their own sake and, on the other, beliefs that focus on political activity or political institutions in terms of their usefulness for producing other satisfactions. The various dimensions of political belief discussed above can all be viewed in the light of this distinction. Beliefs relevant to national identity, for instance, may have a heavy expressive loading in which the major satisfactions derive from the identification itself. On the other hand, one's commitment to and identification with one's nation might be much more in terms of the instrumental performance of the system and in terms of the specific benefits that are perceived as deriving from being a member of that nation.[34] Similarly, one can think of beliefs relevant to the role of the individual as participant in politics that stress participation for its own sake and others that stress the instrumental payoffs of such participation. In the former case primary satisfaction derives from the very act of participation; in the latter case satisfaction derives from the achievement of other goals through political participation.

The role of words and the role of ritual in politics are intimately related to the expressive-instrumental distinction. A highly expressive political style would lay heavy stress on the use of appropriate words to describe political acts, and the words might become more important than the acts to which they refer. Such heavy commitment to the specific words by which it describes politics can result in great political inflexibility since it is possible to discredit policies by labeling them with discreditable political symbols—as one can discredit a social policy in the United States by labeling it "socialism." On the other hand, when used cleverly, the proper-sounding label can legitimize acts that would otherwise be rejected on their merits. The same can be said of ritual. On the one hand, great stress can be laid upon the use of proper ritual in carrying on political interaction

[34] See in this connection, Almond and Verba, *op.cit.*, Chap. 9. The expressive-instrumental distinction is discussed and developed in Ulf Himmelstrand, *Social Pressures, Attitudes and Democratic Processes*, Stockholm, 1960.

and little on the results of that interaction. On the other, the ritual may not be as important as the outcome.

The importance of expressive political behavior should not be underrated. One has only to watch middle-class liberals in a move to reform a local political machine, or participants in a civil rights rally (pro or anti), to know that much of the excitement, the emotional satisfaction and, indeed, the fun of politics comes from the pursuit of the goal, not its accomplishment. This suggests further that the two forms of involvement are not mutually exclusive. Quite the contrary. Perhaps the strongest political movements have been those that have managed to provide both satisfaction from the political involvement per se as well as deep commitment to the attainment of instrumental goals.

There is a tendency, especially among Anglo-Saxon commentators on politics, to connect political stability with a pragmatic political style that stresses open, implicit, and instrumental political beliefs. And the connection makes sense. Such a political style facilitates compromise and bargaining and prevents political opposition from being generalized beyond the specific situation at hand. One can more easily reject a political opponent on a particular issue without rejecting him as a total human being than one could if one's belief system were more consistent and closed. However, as the discussion of the usefulness of implicit traditional criteria of politics suggested, a political style of pure pragmatism may not be the best road to stability. Too much may be left open to compromise for any stable value base to remain. It is perhaps only when *some* basic beliefs remain implicit and "primitive" and when the commitment to them is heavily expressive that one can have the underlying stability that allows a more pragmatic approach in relation to other beliefs. This is why we have stressed the role of a firmly established "primitive" national identity in one area of political controversy so that other problems can be dealt with on their merits.

It is not necessary that all aspects of politics be handled with the same political style. In many political systems certain topics are dealt with in an open and instrumental manner, while other topics are the subject of a more closed and expressive approach. British politics, for instance, combines a rigidity and expressive concern with proper ritual (though perhaps not much explicitness) with regard to the ways in which political decisions are made with a flexibility and substance orientation with regard to the substance of policy. In contrast,

French politics suggests a somewhat greater openness in connection with the way in which political decisions are made (electoral systems and constitutions have been manipulated for partisan advantage) combined with somewhat more rigidity in terms of the content of governmental policy.

Another major distinction in the style with which politics is carried on involves the extent to which a differentiation is made between the political and other spheres of life. This distinction has much to do with the ways in which political beliefs are applied to political activity; in particular, with the range of interactions for which the political belief system is applicable. One can ask about the extent to which private relations are politicized; the extent, for instance, to which personal relations are dominated by political criteria. In Britain, for example, friendship across party lines is quite legitimate and quite common within Parliament. And the same is found on the mass level. When asked if they believed that partisan affiliation would make any difference for entry into close personal ties, an overwhelming proportion of a sample in Britain replied that personal relationships ought not to be judged in terms of partisan political criteria. In Italy, on the other hand, partisan criteria were considered quite legitimate as criteria for entry into close personal relationships.[35] And just as political criteria can intrude into personal situations, so can personal relations intrude into politics—to exacerbate or make more mild political conflict. As Ward points out in his essay on Japanese political culture, personal ties that cut across party lines—ties usually dating back to school days—often serve to ameliorate political antagonism. In a society in which political criteria are used in all spheres of life politics knows no limits. It will certainly be a less mild politics than that in a society where some kinds of human relationship are kept non-political.

The degree of politicization of private life is likely to be closely related to the way in which the identity problems have been resolved. One would expect that political criteria would permeate all aspects of life where either one has a national identity that involves the enforced rejection of all other identifications—in the "political religion" solution, referred to above—or a fragmented identity where commitment is to a set of competing sub-national units. It is only where national identity is developed without the destruction of more parochial loyalties or without robbing them of their legitimacy that

[35] For data on this subject see Almond and Verba, *op.cit.*, Chap. 5.

political commitment can be combined with a set of norms that limits the range of applicability of political criteria.

Closely related to this aspect of political style is that of the rules of civility of political interactions. In some political systems there may be highly elaborate forms of political intercourse which govern political interactions. These norms may prescribe special forms of courtesy to be used in political debate, may set limits upon the nature of political attacks, may prescribe ceremonies of reconciliation among political opponents. On the other hand, politics may be a no-holds-barred form of interaction. Norms limiting the degree of politicization of personal relations and enforcing civility in political controversies play a major role in regulating the nature of political interactions. They limit the intensity of political conflict and maintain channels of communication and accommodation among political opponents.

POLITICAL BELIEFS AND POLITICAL STYLE

The discussion of basic political beliefs and of political style should not suggest that these aspects of political culture are independent—that any set of basic beliefs or values is likely to be associated with any set of norms of political interaction. The most important characteristic of a political culture is that it is a patterned set of orientations toward politics in which specific norms and general values are mutually related. Certain patterns of political style are more likely to develop within particular kinds of belief structures. In general, a non-ideological political style with a high degree of civility in political intercourse and a low degree of politicization of personal life is likely to develop where there is a strong sense of national identity and where the horizontal ties of political integration are strong. The sense of common membership in a political community facilitates the maintenance of such norms of political interaction as pragmatic bargaining and civility. And, without denying the probable primacy of the political value structure in determining the political style of a nation, one can certainly argue that a political style of this sort is likely to reinforce the integration of a political system.

V. *The Origins of Political Culture*

Political cultures are learned. There are broadly two possible sources for such learning: (1) One is experience in non-political situations that have an impact on attitudes toward political objects.

These experiences in turn consist of either pre-adult experiences with family, school, or peer group; or adult extra-political experiences with family or peers or at the work place or in non-political associations. (2) The other is experience with the operation of the political process—contact with political or governmental figures, exposure to communications about politics—or reports of the experiences of others.[36] The latter form of influence on political culture is what one might call "political memory." This derives from the individual's own personal experiences with the political system from which he draws inferences about the nature of that process. These inferences then become part of the individual's political belief system and lead to evaluations applied to new situations. More important in the formation of political memory may be the inferences drawn from political events that antedate or go beyond the individual's personal experience. In this latter case socialization experiences in school, family, and elsewhere play a major role in transmitting the inferences from political history from generation to generation. However, it is useful to consider separately the process by which the political memories of a political culture are formed and the process of transmission of these memories.

(1) THE IMPACT OF NON-POLITICAL EXPERIENCES ON POLITICAL CULTURE

As with the general basic value structure of a culture, basic political values are quite probably set fairly firmly early in life. They are set in the family, in the school, and in contacts with the peer group. Part of these socialization experiences consist of explicit teachings of political values—explicit teachings by parents or teachers as to the respect one owes authority, for instance, or as to the nature of politics and the political system. It is probable, however, that the lessons the individual draws about the political process from his experiences come less from direct and explicit teaching than from in-

[36] A third important source of political culture needs further exploration, the foreign models that nations attempt to follow. There is little doubt that any attempt to consider political culture from the perspective of individual nations isolated from external influences is a mistake. The elites of contemporary nations look to other nations as do the masses. What they seek to borrow and how they mold what they borrow may be determined in large part by the culture they had before they turned their eyes outward; but the foreign models may be potent nevertheless. And this is true not only of the new developing nations. Certainly tsarist Russia was influenced by foreign models, and one cannot understand contemporary politics in Japan or Germany without considering the impact of the occupations and the foreign models presented by them.

CONCLUSION

direct inferences drawn from experiences not intended to have an effect on political attitudes. Thus the individual may "overhear" conversations about politics which give a different view of the political process than the explicit teaching at home or in the school gives.

The most important early experiences with implications for basic political values, however, may have no explicit political content at all. In early social situations the child will learn certain basic lessons about the nature of authority, the trustworthiness and supportiveness of other people, the manipulability of the environment, and the desirability of such manipulation. Such basic values are learned early, and it is quite likely that individuals will generalize from these values to values applicable to politics.[37] Furthermore individuals will in the schools also learn lessons as to the basic stratification patterns in society—what the criteria are for success, what their own place in the system is. Where the explicit values taught to children and the implicit lessons they learn from experience coincide, one has powerful socialization indeed. Thus all lessons and experiences of the Amhara child in Ethiopia stress authority and create a strong sense of the importance of deference to authority. Furthermore what one learns to expect from politics as a child can in part involve self-fulfilling prophecies. In Italy children learn to distrust others. When they are older they act on the assumption that all others are hostile and antagonistic—and of course thereby create the situation they expect to find.

The pattern of socialization in relation to authority and interpersonal trust is probably most important in forming later political beliefs, particularly, beliefs relevant to democratic politics. Democratic politics implies a set of relationships among political actors that is both relatively equalitarian in terms of power and relatively non-conflictual. Unless there can be some equality of power—systems of bargaining or mutual checks and balances, for instance—it is hard to describe the system as democratic. Yet unless these equalitarian power relations can be kept below a certain level of conflict, peaceful political change—the alternation of rival elites, for instance—will be impossible. But the belief that equalitarian power relationships can be non-conflictual may be difficult to develop in cultures such as in Egypt, Amhara, or Italy, where the socialization process stresses

[37] See Robert Le Vine, "Political Socialization and Culture Change," in Geertz, ed. *op.cit.*, pp. 280-303; and Almond and Verba, *op.cit.*, Chap. 12.

both hierarchical authority patterns and distrust of those outside the primary group. There is under these circumstances no exposure to relationships that combine trust and equality. The choice becomes one between hierarchy and conflict.

(2) EXPERIENCE WITH THE POLITICAL PROCESS AS A FORMATIVE INFLUENCE ON POLITICAL CULTURE

The study of political socialization has concentrated so heavily on pre-political experiences that it is often forgotten that much of what an individual believes about the political process is learned from observations of that process. One's attitudes toward governmental output—the expectations one has, the satisfactions derived from the output—will obviously be affected by what output the government produces. Similarly one's beliefs about one's fellow political actors depend heavily on how in fact they behave. This is not to deny that the set of predispositions with which an individual enters politics—predispositions formed in pre-adult years—affect the inferences he draws from observing the process. Yet what he sees of the political process interacts with his predispositions to affect his political beliefs. In fact one of the major determinants of a political culture may be the way in which pre-political experiences relate to the inferences one would draw from politics itself. Insofar as these are sharply different—for instance, authority patterns in non-political situations differ substantially from those patterns within politics—the possibility of developing a stable political culture in which the cultural expectations of governmental performances are congruent with actual governmental performance may be slight. Gaps in the socialization process, whereby what one is prepared for in pre-adult socialization experiences in the family and the school do not match what one learns from participation in politics, may be a major source of political disorientation and strain. The contrast is perhaps sharpest between Britain, where, as Rose points out, there is little gap between the socialization process and the political process, and many of the new nations where the gap between the traditional values political actors have learned in the home are in sharp contrast with the standards now applied in the political system.[38]

[38] The argument about the relationship between political stability and the authority patterns experienced within politics and outside politics is developed in Eckstein, *Theory of Stable Democracy*. For a discussion of a striking case where discontinuities between socialization and current politics are particularly large, see Pye, *Politics*,

CONCLUSION

The problem is quite general and quite important. In all modern societies and in all societies in transition toward modernity there will be inevitable gaps between the more affective and particularistic standards of the family and the standards applied in politics and economics. In traditional societies where "familistic" criteria permeate the political realm this may be less true. What may be crucial in modern and transitional societies is the size of the gap. And indeed the gap may be narrowed by the family itself losing, for good or ill, some of its traditional characteristics and coming to resemble in some respects more secondary institutions.[39]

But in seeking the roots of political culture one must look beyond the direct political experiences of the individual. The political memories passed from generation to generation and the ways these memories are formed are crucial. One is forced to consider the historical experiences of a nation from the point of view of their impact on political beliefs. One cannot deal with French political attitudes without referring to the great crises of French history—the French Revolution and the various revolutions and upheavals of the nineteenth century—and the way in which these crises live in the political memories of Frenchmen. In Germany or Italy one cannot deal with political culture without considering the impact of Naziism or Fascism. One thinks for instance of the pre-Hitler and the post-Hitler generations. In the new nations the colonial experiences and the processes of attaining independence play similar formative roles. It is not merely those who actually experienced totalitarianism or colonialism or revolution whose political attitudes are affected by the experience, though it makes a difference whether or not one in fact had such experiences. The impact of the Nazi experience, for instance, will continue to be felt in German political culture long after those who actually experienced it have died, just as the French Revolution or the American Civil War or the Mexican Revolution continue to play major roles in the political cultures of those nations.

Personality, and Nation Building. Among the Burmese elites he studied the gap has created severe frustrations and anxieties.

[39] On this general question see Eckstein, *op.cit.*, and Pye, *op.cit.*, as well as S. N. Eisenstadt, *From Generation to Generation*, Glencoe, Ill., The Free Press, 1956; Helmut Schelsky, *Die Skeptische Generation*, Dusseldorf-Koln, 1957; and Almond and Verba, *op.cit.*, Chap. 12. See also the discussion of comparative studies of German and American child-rearing in my essay on German political culture in this volume.

VI. *Political Crises*

The political histories of nations are long and complicated, and there are many types of events that could have an effect on a political culture. What in the political histories of nations ought one to look at in order to see the impact of historical events on political culture? The above discussion of the impact of events on beliefs suggests where one might look. One would want to consider the way in which the political system has dealt with the significant problems it has faced in the past. The discussion of the major dimensions of political belief also suggests what these significant problems are. In dealing with political beliefs we looked at beliefs relevant to the sense of national identity, to the sense of identity with one's fellow citizens, to the performance of the government, and to the governmental decision processes. Each of these sets of political beliefs suggests a set of political problems that political systems are likely to face. What is important is the way in which problems involving these subjects arise and how they are resolved. From the point of view of the formation of political beliefs, what may be most significant is whether these problems resulted in salient political crises. On the one hand, problems may be solved incrementally, by small and quiet steps. On the other, they may lead to crises—salient events like wars, revolutions, overt challenges to governmental legitimacy—in which passions are aroused and the very survival of the system is often at stake. And while incremental problem solving has an important effect on political beliefs, it is the salient crises that are most likely to form a people's political memory.

(1) NATIONAL IDENTITY AND POLITICAL HISTORY

The major determinants of the sense of national identity of the members of a political system may be the set of historical events by which the nation was formed. The process by which the legal and physical boundaries of a nation are set is crucial. The sense of national identity may be created by this very process. Anti-colonial wars that create new states also create an identification with the nation that did not exist before. On the other hand, a national unity created by conquest of reluctant peoples or by the intrusion of some outside power may leave lasting divisive scars on the political culture.

The setting of the physical and legal boundaries of a political system is one way in which national identity is formed, but it is possible for other salient crises to play major roles in the creation of a sense of nationhood. A major revolution or a war with a foreign nation may be crucial in creating identification with a nation and the symbols of the nation. The expressive symbols of many nations revolve around such violent events. These crises set the psychological boundaries of the nation; they may shift identifications from some other political unit—perhaps a sub-national political unit such as a tribe or village—to the nation.[40]

(2) THE INDIVIDUAL'S IDENTIFICATION WITH HIS FELLOW CITIZENS AND POLITICAL HISTORY

Just as there are political crises that play a major role in the attitudes individuals have toward the nation of which they are members, so are there crises that form basic political attitudes toward their fellow citizens. One can look at the salient crises of a nation's history in terms of the inferences individuals draw from them about their fellow citizens. Do the crises of a nation's history lead the members of that nation to share a common sense of community, or are the crises divisive so that various groups in society learn to distrust each other? LaPalombara in his essay on Italy points out that all the critical events in Italian history have been divisive. The Renaissance and *Risorgimento* were middle-class Northern Italian movements which divided Italy culturally rather than uniting it. And the memories of Fascism and of the resistance to it are also quite divisive in quality.

Such divisive political events which teach groups to distrust each other are probably a prime source of a political culture low in a sense of political integration. The society in which the political history is a history of group conflict is hardly likely to be one in which the horizontal ties among the citizens of the political system are strong.

(3) THE DECISIONAL PROCESS AND POLITICAL HISTORY

The political crises most relevant to the set of beliefs about the decisional process are those connected with the demands of new groups to participate in that process. There are few societies in which crises of this sort have not taken place; and such crises form much of the political history of modern states. The history of the expansion

---

[40] See on this subject Verba and Almond, "National Revolutions and Political Commitment," in Eckstein, ed. *Essays on Internal War*, for a discussion of the role of the Mexican Revolution of 1910-1920 in the formation of a sense of identity with the Mexican political system.

of the franchise or of the demand for some voice in politics by the middle and working classes for instance is an essential part of the history of democracy.

The way in which demands for participation are met plays a major role in the development of attitudes toward political participation and integration. If the new groups demanding a voice in politics are welcomed by those who hold political power, the integration of the political system is likely to be maintained. The nature of the response of the incumbent political elites to the demands of new groups for participation in the political process will affect the way in which these groups view their role as actors in the political system. If the participatory demands of new groups are accepted as legitimate by incumbent elites, the new groups are more likely to conceive of their participant role as compatible with the maintenance of a position of independent authority by the political elites. The political value structure will under these circumstances stress a combination of values supporting influence over the political decision-making process and deference to political authority. On the other hand, if the incumbent elites do not accept the new participatory demands as legitimate, those who demand this participation are likely to conceive of such participation as requiring the overthrow of the older authority structure in order to be effective. Participation will be thought of as involving a conflict with other authority structures. Rather than there being belief structure that facilitates the sharing of political power and that incorporates older more deferential political beliefs with the beliefs supporting political participation, there will be a sharp break in the development of the political culture. The new values of political participation will replace and destroy older attitudes supporting political deference.[41]

The way in which crises of participation are resolved also affects the political style of those brought into participation. Participation tends to produce responsibility. The individual or group that believes it can participate meaningfully in political decisions is more likely

---

[41] As Lipset puts it, "Whenever new groups become politically active . . . easy access to the *legitimate* political institutions tends to win the loyalty of the new groups to the system, and they in turn can allow the old dominating strata to maintain their old status. In nations like Germany where access was denied for prolonged periods, first to the *bourgeoisie* and later to the workers, and where force was used to restrict access, the lower strata were alienated from the system and adopted extremist ideologies which, in turn, kept the more established groups from accepting the worker's political movement as a legitimate alternative" (*Political Man*, pp. 79-80).

CONCLUSION

to focus upon the attainment of relatively limited and practical political goals. If barred from participation, the habit of compromise in the name of the achievement of the possible will not develop and, as Spiro has suggested, an ideological approach to politics is more likely.[42] One will focus on distant, more milennial goals which even if unattainable will be more psychologically rewarding than smaller more practical goals which, since they too are unattainable due to the lack of influence over the government, will appear petty and trivial.

(4) PERFORMANCE AND POLITICAL HISTORY

The participation crises and the way they are resolved have major effects on the values associated with governmental performance. The scope, nature, and attainability of the output are affected by opportunities to participate. But attitudes toward governmental output also are affected by the way in which two other crises connected with that output are resolved. One crisis is what one might call the crisis of penetration, the other, the crisis of distribution. The former refers to the process by which the bureaucratic arms of governmental control penetrate the society. At an early stage this may involve

[42] See Spiro, *Government by Constitution*, Chap. 14. He gives several examples of the way in which an ideological political style develops by exclusion from political participation. On the other hand, involvement in actual political decisions almost invariably leads to the development of a more pragmatic approach owing to the exigencies of such decisions. There is much evidence for this proposition, and it merits underlining as a very useful generalization about political attitude formation.

A. J. Whyte, for instance, writing about the effect of the suppression of self-determination in Italy in the nineteenth century, notes two habits of mind created by exclusion from political participation:

"The first was political inexperience; the second, the now ingrained habit of conspiracy. These two failings were the legacy left by Metternicht. In his determination to suppress every manifestation of self government, throughout a period of over thirty years, he had not only robbed Italy of all political experience but had forced her into a mentality of chronic conspiracy. The quick Italian mind was full of political ideas but with no practical experience of the difficulties of realizing them. Carried away by their own line of rhetoric, conceiving the ends without considering the means, they made the "business of government" a vocal panorama of unattainable ideals. The effect of the spirit of conspiracy on the other hand was to create the belief that in order to get things done it was necessary to work against the government rather than with it." (*The Evolution of Modern Italy*, Oxford, Blackwell, 1950, p. 85).

Tocqueville made a similar point in contrasting British and French writings on politics: "While in England those who wrote about politics and those who engaged in it shared the same life ... in France the political world was sharply divided into two non-communicating provinces. ... In one [the politicians] administered, in the other [the writers] formulated abstract principles. Above the real society, little by little an imaginary society took shape in which everything seemed simple and coordinated, uniform, just, and rational" (*L'ancien Regime et le Revolution*, quoted in Giovanni Sartori, *Democratic Theory*, Detroit, Wayne State University Press, 1962, pp. 44-45).

merely the ability to establish law and order in an area or the ability to extract taxes or services. If this penetration involves violence, if it is viewed largely as an exploitative penetration or if it is an ineffectual and incomplete penetration, the values associated with governmental output will be affected. If the penetration by the government is very limited—if, for instance, it cannot even maintain a minimum of law and order—the cultural values associated with such penetration are likely to involve no expectations of governmental performance or, if there are such expectations, to involve at the same time a sense of alienation and frustration. Similarly, the way in which the governmental penetration of the society is effected will affect whether the governmental system is viewed as a system that can produce beneficial outputs for the populace or as an exploitative force.

The crisis of distribution is the second crisis relevant to governmental output. This involves the way in which the political system solves demands for it to take an active role in the distribution of goods and services in a society—either to deliver such goods and services directly through the performance of welfare functions, or to play a major role in the redistribution of private wealth in a society through an equitable tax structure.

The crucial aspects of this crisis involve the questions whether or not the political system can respond to demands for distributive output, in what manner it responds, and under whose auspices it responds. Whether or not the system responds will affect the values associated with governmental performance as well, perhaps, as the over-all sense of identification with the political system. Furthermore the way in which the system responds and the auspices under which it responds will have a significant effect on the integrative political values of the system. The way in which demands for distribution are met may lead members of the political system to consider the elites as hostile elements because they refuse the demands or to consider other demanding groups in the system as enemies because their demands are competing.

Just as the various dimensions of political belief are related one to another, so are the various historical problems we have been discussing. In general one can ask of all these problems whether they are once and for all resolved or whether they persist as continuing problems in a system. And does their solution or attempted solution involve a crisis? Related to this question is that of the phasing of the problems—do they all come at the same time, or are they resolved in some serial order? Lastly, it may well be that there are orders of resolution that have important effects on the political culture. To go deeply into these questions would be beyond the scope of this essay,[43] but one can suggest a few tentative generalizations. The more problems that arise simultaneously, the greater is the difficulty of solving any one of them in a way that makes for a stable and integrated political culture. It is not merely that one problem is added to the other, but rather that one exacerbates the other. Thus if those who desire some new participatory role in decision making also desire some radical change in the distribution of goods and services in the society, the incumbent elites are less likely to grant them the right to participate. And the consequences for the political culture are likely to be that beliefs about both governmental performance and the decisional process come to involve more distant and unattainable goals. Similarly, whether or not any particular crisis has an integrative or disintegrative effect on the political culture may depend upon the sequence in which crises arise. The above discussion of national identity suggests that, unless this problem is solved first, other problems that arise will be difficult of solution. Similarly, unless lessons of political trust have been learned before demands for participation arise, such demands are likely to produce tension and fragmentation.

In the new nations of the world the overwhelming burden is that they must create new political cultures before any of these problems are solved and, indeed, while they are attempting to solve all of them at once. And the very question of identity—the first and most basic issue—is often unanswered.

[43] A relevant discussion is found in Dankwart Rustow, "Political Leadership in the Emerging Countries," Washington, The Brookings Institution, 1963 (mimeographed).

CONTRIBUTORS

FREDERICK C. BARGHOORN, born July 4, 1911, in New York City, received his B.A. at Amherst in 1934 and Ph.D. at Harvard in 1941. He served in the Department of State from 1941 to 1947, during which time he was assigned to the U.S. Embassy in Moscow from November 1942 to March 1947. Since 1947 he has been a member of the Department of Political Science at Yale University. He is author of *The Soviet Image of the United States; Soviet Russian Nationalism; The Soviet Cultural Offensive; Soviet Foreign Propaganda*, 1964.

LEONARD BINDER, born in Boston, Massachusetts, 1927, is Associate Professor and Chairman of the Department of Political Science at the University of Chicago. He has held fellowships from the Ford Foundation, the Rockefeller Foundation, the Social Science Research Council, and the Woodrow Wilson Foundation. He has conducted research in Pakistan, Iran, and Egypt. His work has appeared in journals concerned with political science and with Middle East studies. He is author of *Religion and Politics in Pakistan; Iran: Political Development in a Changing Society*; and *The Ideological Revolution in the Middle East.*

DONALD N. LEVINE, born in New Castle, Pennsylvania, 1931, is Assistant Professor of Sociology and Social Sciences at the University of Chicago. He has published articles in the fields of sociological theory and Ethiopian studies. His book *Wax and Gold: Tradition and Innovation in Ethiopian Culture* is being published by the University of Chicago Press.

JOSEPH LAPALOMBARA, born in Chicago, 1925, is Professor of Political Science at Yale University. He was Chairman of the Department of Political Science at Michigan State University from 1958 to 1963. In 1957-1958 he was a visiting professor at the University of Florence and in 1963-1964 he spent a research year in Italy on a Rockefeller Foundation award. In 1961-1962 he was a fellow at the Center for Advanced Study in the Behavioral Sciences. His main research interest is the field of comparative political institutions and behavior. He is editor of *Bureaucracy and Political Development*; co-editor of *Elezioni e Comportamento Politico in Italia*; and author of *Interest Groups in Italian Politics, The Italian Labor Movement: Problems and Prospects*, and other works. He has also published in the professional journals of the United States, Italy, Germany, and Spain.

LUCIAN W. PYE, born in China, 1921, is Professor of Political Science at the Massachusetts Institute of Technology, and a Senior Staff member of the Center for International Studies. He is Chairman of the Social Science

CONTRIBUTORS

Research Council's Committee on Comparative Politics. He has done field work in Southeast Asia and Hong Kong and has served in various capacities in the organization of scholarly associations and governmental agencies. He is author of *Politics, Personality, and Nation-Building*; *Guerrilla Communism in Malaya*; and co-author of *The Politics of the Developing Areas* and *The Emerging Nations*.

RICHARD ROSE, born in St. Louis, Missouri, 1933, is Lecturer in Government at Manchester University, England. Since 1951 he has moved back and forth between American and English universities. From 1958 to 1960 he was a student of Nuffield College, Oxford. Primarily his research interests are in comparative political behavior and in political parties. This work is summed up in *Politics in England*. He is co-author of *The British General Election of 1959* and *Must Labour Lose?*; and co-editor of "Comparative Political Finance," a special issue of the *Journal of Politics*.

DANKWART A. RUSTOW was born in Berlin, 1924. He is Professor of International Social Forces at Columbia University, a consultant to the U.S. Department of State, and a member of the Board of Governors of the Middle East Institute. He received his early education in Germany and Turkey, his Ph.D. from Yale University, and taught at Princeton University from 1952 to 1959. He is author of *The Politics of Compromise*; *Politics and Westernization in the Near East*; co-editor of *Political Modernization in Japan and Turkey*; co-author of *The Politics of the Developing Areas*, and of *Modern Political Systems: Asia*; a contributor to the *Encyclopaedia of Islam* (2d ed.); and a contributor to many scholarly journals and publications in the United States and abroad.

ROBERT E. SCOTT, born in Chicago, 1923, is Professor of Political Science at the University of Illinois. He has done field work and acted as consultant for private organizations in Latin America—particularly in Mexico, Central America, and Peru—and in Spain. He is author of *Mexican Government in Transition*; co-author of *Latin American Politics and Government, Nation-Building*; and author of numerous articles on aspects of Latin American politics.

SIDNEY VERBA, born in New York City, 1932, is Professor of Political Science at Stanford University. In 1963-1964 he was a Fellow at the Center for Advanced Study in the Behavioral Sciences. His major field of interest is in comparative political behavior. He is author of *Small Groups and Political Behavior*; co-author of *The Civic Culture*; and co-editor and co-author of *The International System: Theoretical Essays*.

ROBERT E. WARD, born in San Francisco, 1916, is Professor of Political Science at the University of Michigan and a senior staff member of its Center for Japanese Studies. He has lived and worked in Japan on a num-

CONTRIBUTORS

ber of occasions. He is co-author of *Village Japan*; editor and co-author of *Modern Political Systems: Europe*; *Modern Political Systems: Asia*; and *Political Modernization in Japan and Turkey*. His writings include numerous articles in the fields of Far Eastern and comparative politics.

MYRON WEINER, born in New York City, 1931, is Professor of Political Science at the Massachusetts Institute of Technology and a Senior Research Associate at its Center for International Studies. He has done extensive field work in India since 1953. During his career he has held fellowships from the Ford Foundation, the Rockefeller Foundation, the Social Science Research Council, and the John Simon Guggenheim Foundation. In the past he has been a consultant to the Ford Foundation and is now serving as a consultant to the Department of State. He is author of *The Politics of Scarcity*; *Party Politics in India*; *Political Change in South Asia*; and co-author of *The Politics of the Developing Areas*.

INDEX

Der Spiegel, 153-54, 170
Dette Publique, 179
Deutsch, Karl, 138n, 169n
Dewey, John, 193
De Witt, Nicholas, 469n, 473n
Dey, S. K., 236n
Díaz, Porfirio, 335, 338
Dicey, A. V., 125n
Dicks, Henry V., 132n
Di Renzo, Gordon, 295, 295n
Disraeli, 91
distrust, in Italian politics, 290-93
Dogan, Mattei, 287n, 320
Dönmes, 176
Dore, Ronald P., 29, 31, 46n
Doyle, Sir Arthur Conan, 502
Drekmeier, Charles, 238, 238n
Dudintsev, Vladimir, 482, 485, 487
Dupeux, Georges, 523n

Eberlein, Klaus D., 148n, 153
Eckstein, Harry, 84n, 163n, 533n, 537n, 553n, 554n, 556n
economic change, in Italy, 323-24
economic development, in India, 233
economic planning, in India, 202-4
eddel, 261
Edelman, Murray, 378
Edelstein, Alex S., 166n
Edinger, Lewis, 138n, 169n
Edo, 36
Education, and British civil service, 115-17; and English political culture, 107-10; in Egypt, 411-19, 435-38; German schools, 160-62; in India, 240; in Italy, 313-14; in Japan, 29-30, 44-50; in Mexico, 340-41, 374-77; Turkish, 181-82, 193-94
Egypt, 15, 17, 83, 245
Egyptian political culture, army in, 397-98; bureaucratic elite in, 423-26; communications elite of, 423-35; family, 407-11; integration of, 443-49; interest elite, 426-32; middle class, 400-405; military elite of, 419-23; socioeconomic elite of, 432-43
Eichmann trial, 170
Eisenstadt, S. N., 163n, 554n
Eldersveld, Samuel, 7n
Elite political culture, in India, 200-202, 227-37, conflict and tension in Indian, 235-37; in Mexico, 382-84; in Turkey, 185-200
Elizabeth, Queen, 100
Ellwein, Thomas, 161n, 165n
England, 16, 17, 19, 23-25; degree modernized, 86-92; go[vernment ma]chinery, 91-92; indust[rial], literacy, 86; mass med[ia], 87n; model of stab[le] party system, 90-9[...]come, 88; politi[cal]; 91; political recr[uitment]; sure groups, 90[...]
English political [culture], gins of, 83-[...] 105-12; sy[...] *values* [...] governme[nt] ence, 94[...] ership, [...] collectiv[...] benefits, 9[...] static society[...] similation, 99[...]
Enver, 180, 185
Epstein, Leon, 102[n]
Erastian principles, 8[...]
Erikson, Erik H., 330n,
Eser, Wolfgang, 154n
Etatism, in Turkey, 183
Ethiopia, 15, 17, 26
Ethiopian political culture, comm[unal] spirit, 262-66; distinctive features [...] 246-50; human nature in, 256-61[...] modernization of, 269-73; orientation toward authority, 250-56; rationalization of, 273-80
ethnic loyalties, in India, 229-31
Eulau, Heinz, 7n
European Common Market, 124, 128, 324
Evan, William M., 159n
Evtushenko, Eugeni, 482-83

Fadeev, Alexander, 487
Fainsod, Merle, 462, 467n, 492
family, in Egypt, 407-11; in English political culture, 106-7; in Ethiopia, 250-51; in Germany, 154-60; in Italy, 317-18; in Mexico, 350-52
Fanfani, 328
Fascism, *see* Fascists
Fascists, 293, 295, 318
Faul, Erwin, 148n
Fayerweather, John, 349n
Ferrarotti, Franco, 311n
feudalism, in Japan, 28-35
Fiat, 311
Fisher, Ralph T., Jr., 494n
Fofi, Goffredo, 325n
Form, W. H., 370n, 373n

567

..hn N., 464n
D., 120n
84n

...niel, 292n
Hough, Jerry F., 465n
House of Commons, 95
Hughes, Edward, 114n, 115n
human nature, in Ethiopian political culture, 256-61
Hurewitz, J. C., 182n

Ibrahim, I. A., 424n
identification with fellow citizens, 535-37
ideologies, 5
Ieyasu, 30
income, per capita in England, 88
India, 16-18, 26, 83
Indian political culture, communalism in, 209-13; conflict resolution in, 213-18; democratization in, 207-8; dispersion of power in, 204-7
 elite culture: 227-37, socialization into, 238-41; spirit of sacrifice in, 231-33
 ethnic loyalty in, 229-31; mass culture, 208-27; planning in, 202-4; status politics in, 208-9
Industrial Revolution, 103
industrialization, in England, 88
Inönü, Ismet, 186
Integration, imperfect in Italian political culture, 298-303
intelligentsia, in India, 199
interest group elites, Egyptian, 426-32
Ilichev, Leonid F., 497
Inkeles, Alex, 498n, 499n, 500n, 501n, 503n, 512n
Iran, 245
Ireland, 127
Ireland, P. W., 396n
Irish Nationalists, 91
Irish problem, 101
Islamic law, 174

34n, 552n

..ture, change in, 168-
 view of, 138-46; and
 160-62; family role, 154-
 ..rticipation in by sex, 157-59;
 ..lization in, 154-68
 , H.A.R., 176n, 396n
 ..litti, Giovanni, 309
 ..ade, William, 333n, 349n
Gladstone, William, 91, 115
Glass, D. C., 106n, 109n
Goldthorpe, J. M., 107n
Gonzalez, Francisco, 354n
Gopal, Ram, 227n
government, forms of, 4
government machinery in England, 91-92
governmental outputs, 537-41
Granick, David, 503n
Greaves, H.R.G., 115n
Grove, J. W., 114n, 121n
Guerrero, Rogelio Díaz, 354n, 355n, 365n
Gujarat, 211
Guttsman, W. L., 90n

Habermas, 162n, 165, 165n
Hagen, Everett, 84n
Haile Selassie, 266, 267, 274, 280
..all, John W., 29, 31
..., 31-32
..ison, F., 424n
..n, 211
.., Selig S., 213n
 R. M., 88n
 Max, 481n

568